Principles of

Operations Management

Second Edition

Barry Render

Charles Harwood Professor of Operations Management
Roy E. Crummer Graduate School of Business, Rollins College

Jay Heizer

Jesse H. Jones Professor of Business Administration
Texas Lutheran University

PRENTICE HALL, Upper Saddle River, New Jersey 07458

Library of Congress Cataloging-in-Publication Data

Render, Barry
Principles of operations management / Barry Render, Jay Heizer.
p. cm.
Includes bibliographical references and index.
ISBN 0-13-256736-9
1. Production management. I. Heizer, Jay H. II. Title.
TS155.R382 1996
658.5—dc21 96-46593
CIP

Director of Production and Manufacturing: Joanne Jay
Managing Editor: Katherine Evancie
Project Manager: Susan Rifkin
Editor-in-Chief: Richard Wohl
Acquisitions Editor: Tom Tucker
Marketing Manager: Nancy Evans
Manufacturing Manager: Vincent Scelta
Senior Manufacturing Supervisor: Paul Smolenski
Design Director: Patricia Wosczyk
Cover Art: Kenny Beck
Interior Design: Kristen Weber/Kenny Beck
Cover Design: Lorraine Castellano
Composition: York Production Services
Production Coordinator: David Cotugno

A Simon & Schuster Company
Upper Saddle River, New Jersey 07458

Photo credits begin on page viii, which constitutes an extension of the copyright page.

Printed in the United States of America
10 9 8 7 6 5 4 3 2 1

ISBN: 0-13-256736-9

Prentice-Hall International (UK) Limited, *London*
Prentice-Hall of Australia Pty. Limited, *Sydney*
Prentice-Hall Canada, Inc., *Toronto*
Prentice-Hall Hispanoamericana, S.A., *Mexico*
Prentice-Hall of India Private Limited, *New Delhi*
Prentice-Hall of Japan, Inc., *Tokyo*
Simon & Schuster Asia Pte. Ltd., *Singapore*
Editora Prentice-Hall do Brasil, Ltda., *Rio de Janeiro*

PRENTICE HALL SERIES in DECISION SCIENCES

Barry Render, CONSULTING EDITOR
Roy E. Crummer Graduate School of Business, Rollins College

Applied Statistics

Basic Business Statistics, 6th Edition, '96
Berenson, Levine

Statistics for Managers Using Microsoft Excel, '97
Levine, Berenson, Pellissier

Data Analysis Using Regression Models, '96
Frees

Business Statistics for Quality and Productivity, '95
Levine, Ramsey, Berenson

Statistics for Management, 7th Edition, '97
Levin, Rubin

Short Course in Business Statistics, Levin, Rubin

Cases in Business Statistics,
Klimberg, Arnold, Berger

Applied Statistics, 4th Edition, '93
Neter, Wasserman, Whitmore

Statistics for Business and Economics, 4th Edition, '95
Newbold

Business Cases in Statistical Decision Making,
Peters, Gray

Brief Business Statistics, '88
Watson, Billingsley, Croft, Huntsberger

Statistics for Management and Economics, 5th Edition, '94, Watson, Billingsley, Croft, Huntsberger

Production and Operations Management

Readings in Production and Operations,
Ahmadian, Afifi, Chandler

Business Logistics Management, 3rd Edition, Ballou

Operations Strategy, Garvin

Business Forecasting, 5th Edition, Hanke, Reitsch

Games and Exercises for Operations Management,
Heineke, Meile

Production and Operations Management, 4th Edition, '96, Heizer, Render

Cases and Readings in Production and Operations Management, Latona, Nathan

Cases in Manufacturing and Service System Management, Mabert

Operations Management, 3rd Edition
McClain, Thomas, Mazzola

Service Operations Management,
Murdick, Render, Russell

Production Planning and Inventory Control, 2nd Edition, Narasimhan, McLeavy, Billington

Managing Business and Engineering Projects,
Nicholas

Principles of Operations Management, 2nd Edition, '97
Render, Heizer

Principles of Operations Management with Tutorials, 2nd Edition, '97, Render, Heizer

Production and Operations Management,
Russell/Taylor

Plant and Service Tours in Operations Management, 4th Edition, Schmenner

Production Operations Management, 5th Edition
Schmenner

Service Operations Management, Schmenner

Topics in Just-In-Time Management, Schneiderjans

Operations Strategy, Stonebraker, Leong

Management Science/Quantitative Methods

Quantitative Concepts, 2nd Edition,
Eppen, Gould, Schmidt

Management Science, Mathur, Solow

Management Science, 4th Edition, Moore, Lee, Taylor

Quantitative Analysis for Management,
6th Edition, '97, Render, Stair

Introduction to Management Science,
5th Edition, Cook, Russell

Introductory Management Science,
4th Edition, Eppen, Gould, Schmidt

Cases and Readings in Management Science,
2nd Edition, Render, Stair, Greenberg

Introduction to Management Science,
5th Edition, '96, Taylor

Software

QS Version 2.1, Chang

QSB+ Version 2.1, Chang

Personal STORM Version 3.0, STORM Software Inc.

Lee, *AB:QM Version 4.0*

Weiss, *AB:POM Version 4.0*

Weiss, *QM for Windows 1.0*

Weiss, *POM for Windows 1.0*

To Donna and Charlie

To Kay, Donna, Kira, and Janée

Photo Credits

CHAPTER 1: p. 2: Peter Blakely/SABA, p. 3: Corbis-Bettmann, p. 4 L&R: Corbis-Bettmann.
CHAPTER 2: p. 28: Kevin Horan Photography, p. 36 Top: Corbis-Bettmann, p. 36 Bottom: Ralph Hestoft/SABA.
SUPPLEMENT 2: p. 47: Ted Horowitz/Bristol Meyers-Squibb, p. 53: Jeff Greenburg/The Picture Cube, p. 57: Bob Daemmrich/The Image Works, p. 62: Courtesy of ICI Paints.
CHAPTER 3: p. 94: Scott Adams/© 1995 United Features Syndicate, p. 97 L: Courtesy of Barry Render, p. 97 C: Courtesy of J. M. Juran, p. 97 R: Courtesy of Philip B. Crosby, p. 106 L&R: Michael L. Abramson, p. 107: Barry Bonzer/Tony Stone Images.
SUPPLEMENT 3: p. 122: Courtesy of AVX Corp., p. 124: Courtesy of the Harley-Davidson Juneau Avenue Archives; all rights reserved, p. 126: Ted Horowitz/The Stock Market.
CHAPTER 4: p. 143: Courtesy of Shouldice Hospital, p. 144 clockwise from L: Rick Etkin/Tony Stone Images; Al Messerschmidt/Folio, Inc.; Ben Blankenburg/Leo De Wys, Inc.; Simon Feldman/Envision; Robert Rathe/Folio, Inc.; p. 148: Courtesy of Maytag Corporation, p. 149: Courtesy of NCR Corporation, p. 151: J. R. Simplot photo, p. 153 L&R: Control Data Systems, Inc., p. 159: Springer/Gamma Liaison.
CHAPTER 5: p. 170: Courtesy of The Nucor Corporation, p. 171: Robert Frerck/Woodfin Camp & Associates, p. 172: Jim Schafer, Pittsburgh, PA, p. 175: L&R: Mark M. Lawrence, p. 176: L&R: Steve Woit, p. 177: Watmough Holdings PLC, p. 178: Andrew Sachs/Tony Stone Images, p. 180 L&R: Louis Psihoyos, p. 182: Courtesy of Sterling Software, p. 185: Charlie Gupton Photography, p. 193: John Madere for International Paper.
CHAPTER 6: p. 203: A. Tannenbaum/Sygma Photo News, p. 205 Top: Jay Heizer, p. 205 Bottom: Cartoon Features Syndicate, p. 209: Jay Heizer, p. 212: Courtesy of Federal Express, p. 213: Bruce Thomas/The Stock Market.
CHAPTER 7: p. 231: Toby Sanford/General Electric Company, p. 233: Choice Hotels International, p. 235 L: Courtesy of Flight Dynamics, Inc., p. 235 R: Chris Sorenson, p. 235 Bottom: Andy Freeberg, p. 236: Philip Saltonstall, p. 237 L: Courtesy of Apple Computer Incorporated, p. 237 C: Courtesy of Kinesis Corporation, p. 237 R: Courtesy of Data Hand Systems, Inc., p. 238: Courtesy of 3M Health Care, p. 241 Bottom: Martin Venegas/Allsport USA, p. 241 Top: Don Grossman, p. 242: Lincoln Electric Co., p. 251: David A. Zickl.
CHAPTER 8: p. 267: Pittsburgh International Airport, p. 269: Michael Grecco/Stock Boston, p. 270: Auto Simulations, p. 278: Mares-Manton Photography, p. 279: Chris Usher Photography, p. 282: Dan Lamont/Matrix International, p. 285: The Tyson Corporation.
CHAPTER 9: p. 310: John Coletti/Uniphoto, p. 311: Courtesy of Levi Strauss Assoc., Inc., p. 318: Courtesy of Western Atlas, Inc.
CHAPTER 10: p. 346: Courtesy of Wheeled Coach Industries.
CHAPTER 11: p. 380: Malcolm S. Kirk/Peter Arnold, Inc., p. 381: Courtesy of Toyota Motor Manufacturing, Kentucky, p. 387 and 388: Courtesy of the Harley-Davidson Juneau Avenue Archives; all rights reserved, p. 389: Courtesy of New United Motor Manufacturing Co., Inc., p. 390: W. B. Spunberg/The Picture Cube, p. 391: Courtesy of The McDonald's Corporation.
SUPPLEMENT 11: p. 402: Courtesy of Boeing Commercial Airplane Group, p. 404: Michael L. Abramson, p. 405: Wilkinson Spooner/Gamma Liaison, p. 407: Louis Grimes.
CHAPTER 12: p. 419: Chris Sorenson, p. 421: Courtesy of Deere & Company, p. 422 L&R: Anheuser-Busch, Inc.
CHAPTER 13: p. 447: Courtesy of Northrop-Grumman, p. 452: David Madison/Duomo, p. 458: Jack Van Antwerp/The Stock Market, p. 459: CMCS News, p. 465: Jeff Aronson.
CHAPTER 14: p. 483: Courtesy of Primavera Systems Inc.; Primavera Project Planner ® and (P3®) are registered trademarks of Primavera Systems Inc., p. 484: Courtesy of SAS Institute, p. 489: Philip Jones Griffiths/Bechtel, p. 491: Photri, p. 496: British Airways, p. 498: Courtesy of Orlando Utilities Commission.
SUPPLEMENT 14: p. 519: Courtesy of Orlando Utilities Commission.

About the Authors

Barry Render is the Charles Harwood Distinguished Professor of Operations Management at the Crummer Graduate School of Business at Rollins College, in Winter Park, Florida. He received his M.S. in Operations Research and his Ph.D. in Quantitative Analysis at the University of Cincinnati (1975). He previously taught at George Washington University, University of New Orleans, Boston University, and George Mason University, where he held the GM Foundation Professorship in Decision Sciences. Dr. Render has also worked in the aerospace industry for General Electric, McDonnell Douglas, and NASA.

Professor Render has co-authored nine textbooks with Prentice-Hall, including *Quantitative Analysis for Management, Service Operations Management, Introduction to Management Science, Production and Operations Management,* and *Cases and Readings in Management Science.* His more than one hundred articles on a variety of management topics have appeared in *Decision Sciences, Interfaces, Information and Management, Journal of Management Information Systems, Socio-Economic Planning Sciences,* and *Operations Management Review,* among others.

Dr. Render has also been honored as an AACSB Fellow and named as a Senior Fulbright Scholar in 1982 and again in 1993. He was twice vice president of the Decision Science Institute Southeast Region and was Software Review Editor for *Decision Line* from 1989 to 1995. He is Prentice-Hall's series editor for Decision Sciences textbooks. Professor Render has been actively involved in consulting for government agencies and for many corporations, including NASA, FBI, U.S. Navy, Fairfax County, Virginia, and C&P Telephone. He teaches production and operations management courses in Rollins College's MBA and Executive MBA programs. In 1995 he was named as that school's Professor of the Year, and in 1996 was selected by Roosevelt University to receive the St. Claire Drake Award for Outstanding Scholarship.

Jay Heizer holds the Jesse H. Jones Chair of Business Administration at Texas Lutheran University in Seguin, Texas. He received his B.B.A. and M.B.A. from the University of North Texas and his Ph.D. in Management and Statistics from Arizona State University (1969). He was previously a member of the faculty at Memphis State University, the University of Oklahoma, Virginia Commonwealth University, and the University of Richmond. He has also held visiting positions at Boston University, George Mason University, and Czech Management Center.

Dr. Heizer's industrial experience is extensive. He learned the practical side of production/operations management as a machinist apprentice at Foringer and Company, production planner for Westinghouse Airbrake, and at General Dynamics, where he worked in engineering administration. Additionally, he has been actively involved in consulting in the operations management and MIS areas for a variety of organizations including Philip Morris, Firestone, Dixie Container Corporation, Columbia Industries, and Tenneco. He holds the CPIM certification from the American Production and Inventory Control Society.

Professor Heizer has co-authored five books and has published two dozen articles on a variety of management topics. His papers have appeared in the *Academy of Management Journal, Journal of Purchasing, Personnel Psychology,* and *Engineering Management,* among others. He has taught production and operations management courses in undergraduate, graduate, and executive programs.

Brief Contents

Part I
Introduction to Operations Management

1 *Operations and Productivity* 1

2 *Operations Strategy for Goods and Services* 27

Supplement: Forecasting 45

Part II
Building World-Class Operations

3 *Total Quality Management* 89

Supplement: Quality via Statistical Process Control 115

4 *Design of Goods and Services* 141

5 *Process and Capacity Design* 169

6 *Selecting the Location* 201

7 *People and Work Systems* 227

8 *Layout Designs* 265

Part III
Managing World-Class Operations

9 *Inventory for Independent Demand* 305

10 *Inventory for Dependent Demand* 343

11 *Just-in-Time Systems* 375

Supplement: Supply-Chain Management 397

12 *Aggregate Scheduling* 415

13 *Short-Term Scheduling* 445

14 *Project Scheduling* 479

Supplement: Maintenance Management 517

Appendices

A Normal Curve Areas and How to Use the Normal Distribution A2

B Using POM for Windows A5

C Answers to Self-Tests A12

D Answers to Even-Numbered Problems A16

Glossary A25

Index I1

Contents

Preface xxiii

PART I

INTRODUCTION TO OPERATIONS MANAGEMENT 1

1 OPERATIONS AND PRODUCTIVITY 1

What Is Operations Management? 3
Heritage of Operations Management 3
Organizing for the Creation of Goods and Services 5
Why Study OM? 6
What Operations Managers Do 7
Where Are the Jobs in OM? 10
Operations in the Service Sector 11
Differences Between Goods and Services 11
Growth of Services 12
Service Pay 12
The Productivity Challenge 15
Productivity Measurement 15
Productivity Variables 16
Productivity and the Service Sector 18
Summary 20
Key Terms 20
Solved Problem 21
Discussion Questions 21
Self-Test Chapter 1 22
Operations in Practice Exercises 23
Problems 23
Case Study: National Air Express 24
Bibliography 25

2 OPERATIONS STRATEGY FOR GOODS AND SERVICES 27

Identifying Missions and Strategies 28
Mission 28
Strategy 28
Decisions of OM 32
Operations Strategy Issues 34
Research 34
Preconditions 34
Dynamics 35
Strategy Implementation 37
Identify Key Tasks 38
Build and Staff the Organization 38
Summary 39
Key Terms 39
Solved Problem 39
Discussion Questions 40
Operations in Practice Exercise 40
Problems 40
Self-Test Chapter 2 41
Case Studies: Johannsen Steel Company 42
Michelin, Inc. 43
Bibliography 43

SUPPLEMENT TO CHAPTER 2: FORECASTING 45

What Is Forecasting? 46
Forecasting Time Horizons 46
The Influence of Product Life Cycle 47

Types of Forecasts 48
The Strategic Importance of Forecasting 48
Human Resources 48
Capacity 48
Supply-Chain Management 48
Forecasting Approaches 49
Overview of Qualitative Methods 49
Overview of Quantitative Methods 50
Eight Steps to a Forecasting System 50
Time Series Forecasting 50
Decomposition of a Time Series 50
Moving Averages 52
Weighted Moving Averages 52
Exponential Smoothing 54
Exponential Smoothing with Trend 58
Trend Projections 58
Seasonal Variations in Data 61
Causal Forecasting Methods: Regression Analysis 62
Using Linear Regression Analysis to Forecast 63
Standard Error of the Estimate 65
Correlation Coefficients for Regression Lines 66
Multiple Regression Analysis 68
Monitoring and Controlling Forecasts 68
Adaptive Smoothing 70
Forecasting the Service Sector 70
The Computer's Role in Forecasting 71
Summary 72
Key Terms 72
Using POM for Windows in Forecasting 73
Using Excel Spreadsheets in Forecasting 74
Solved Problems 76
Discussion Questions 78
Operations in Practice Exercise 78
Self-Test Supplement 2 79
Problems 80
Case Study: The North-South Airline 87
Bibliography 88

PART II

BUILDING WORLD-CLASS OPERATIONS 89

3 TOTAL QUALITY MANAGEMENT 89

Defining Quality 90
Why Quality Is Important 91
International Quality Standards 93
Japan's Industrial Standard 94
Europe's ISO 9000 Standard 94
U.S. Standards 94
ISO 14000 94
Total Quality Management 95
Continuous Improvement 96
Employee Empowerment 96
Benchmarking 96
Just-in-Time (JIT) 98
Knowledge of TQM Tools 98
Tools for TQM 98
Quality Function Deployment 98
Taguchi Technique 100
Pareto Charts 102
Process Charts 103
Cause-and-Effect Diagrams 104
Statistical Process Control (SPC) 104
The Role of Inspection 105
When and Where to Inspect 106
Source Inspection 107
Service Industry Inspection 107
Total Quality Management in Services 107
Summary 109
Key Terms 109
Self-Test Chapter 3 110
Discussion Questions 111
Operations in Practice Exercise 111
Problems 111
Case Study: Milt and Michael's Cleaning 112
Bibliography 113

SUPPLEMENT TO CHAPTER 3: QUALITY VIA STATISTICAL PROCESS CONTROL 115

Statistical Process Control (SPC) 116
Control Charts for Variables 118
The Central Limit Theorem 119
Setting Mean Chart Limits ($\overline{x}$-Charts) 120
Setting Range Chart Limits (R-Charts) 122
Control Charts for Attributes 124
Acceptance Sampling 127
Operating Characteristic Curve 127
Average Outgoing Quality 129
Summary 129
Key Terms 130
Using POM for Windows 130
Using Excel Spreadsheets for Statistical Process Control 131
Solved Problems 132

Discussion Questions 133
Self-Test Supplement 3 134
Operations in Practice Exercise 135
Problems 135
Case Study: SPC at the Gazette 139
Bibliography 140

4 DESIGN OF GOODS AND SERVICES 141

Goods and Services Selection 142
Product Options 142
Generation of New Product Opportunities 143
Product Life 144
Time-Based Competition 145
Product Development 147
Product-by-Value 148
Defining and Documenting the Product 149
Make or Buy 149
Group Technology 150
Computer-Aided Design and Computer-Aided Manufacture 152
Documents for Production 154
Service Design 155
Documents for Services 157
Product Reliability 158
Improving Individual Components 158
Providing Redundancy 159
Transition to Production 160
Summary 161
Key Terms 161
Using POM for Windows for Reliability Analysis 162
Solved Problems 162
Discussion Questions 163
Operations in Practice Exercise 163
Self-Test Chapter 4 164
Problems 165
Case Study: GE's Rotary Compressor 167
Bibliography 168

5 PROCESS AND CAPACITY DESIGN 169

Three Process Strategies 170
Process Focus 171
Product Focus 171
Repetitive Focus 172
Moving Toward Lean Production 172
Comparison of Process Choices 174
Machinery, Equipment, and Technology 175
Numerical Control 175
Process Control 176
Robots 176
Automated Guided Vehicles (AGVs) 177
Flexible Manufacturing System (FMS) 177
Computer-Integrated Manufacture (CIM) 178
Process Reengineering 178
Time-Function Mapping 180
Work-Flow Analysis 181
Choosing a Service Process Strategy 182
Service-Sector Considerations 182
Customer Interaction and Process Strategy 183
Other Service Process Opportunities 185
Capacity 186
Capacity Management 186
Forecasting Capacity Requirements 187
Demand Management 188
Break-Even Analysis 189
Making the Investment 193
Strategy-Driven Investments 194
Investment, Variable Cost, and Cash Flow 194
Summary 194
Key Terms 195
Solved Problems 195
Discussion Questions 196
Self-Test Chapter 5 197
Operations in Practice Exercise 198
Problems 198
Case Study: Service at Minit-Lube, Inc. 200
Bibliography 200

6 SELECTING THE LOCATION 201

The Strategic Importance of Location 202
Factors That Affect Location Decisions 203
Labor Productivity 203
Exchange Rates 203
Costs 205
Attitudes 205
Methods of Evaluating Location Alternatives 206
The Factor-Rating Method 206
Locational Break-Even Analysis 206
Center-of-Gravity Method 209
The Transportation Model 211
Service Location Strategy 212
How Hotel Chains Select Sites 213
The Telemarketing Industry 214
Summary 215
Key Terms 215
Using POM for Windows 216

Using Excel Spreadsheets to Solve a Factor-Rating Problem 217
Solved Problems 217
Discussion Questions 219
Self-Test Chapter 6 220
Operations in Practice Exercise 221
Problems 221
Case Study: Southern Recreational Vehicle Company 224
Bibliography 225

7 PEOPLE AND WORK SYSTEMS 227

People and Work Systems 228
Constraints on People and Work Systems 228
Job Classifications and Work Rules 229
Job Design *229*
Labor Specialization 230
Job Expansion 230
Psychological Components of Job Design 231
Self-Directed Teams 232
Motivation and Incentive Systems 234
Ergonomics and Work Methods 234
Labor Standards and Work Measurement 240
Historical Experience 241
Time Studies 242
Predetermined Time Standards 247
Work Sampling 249
Summary 252
Key Terms 252
Using Excel Spreadsheets for Time Study 253
Solved Problems 253
Self-Test Chapter 7 256
Discussion Questions 257
Operations in Practice Exercise 257
Problems 258
Case Studies: The Fleet That Wanders; Lincoln Electric's Incentive Pay Systems 262
Bibliography 264

8 LAYOUT DESIGNS 265

Strategic Importance of Layout Decisions 266
Matching Layouts to Strategies—Some Examples 266
Types of Layouts 267
Fixed-Position Layout 268
Process-Oriented Layout 269
Cellular Layout 274
Focused Work Center and Focused Factory 276
Office Layout 277
Retail Store Layout 278
Warehousing and Storage Layouts 279
Crossdocking 279
Product-Oriented Layout 280
Assembly Line Balancing 280
Summary 286
Key Terms 286
Using POM for Windows for Layout Design 287
Solved Problems 289
Self-Test Chapter 8 293
Discussion Questions 294
Operations in Practice Exercise 294
Problems 294
Case Studies: State Automobile License Renewals 300
Des Moines National Bank 301
Bibliography 303

PART III

MANAGING WORLD-CLASS OPERATIONS 305

9 INVENTORY FOR INDEPENDENT DEMAND 305

Functions of Inventory 306
Types of Inventory 306
Inventory Management 307
ABC Analysis 307
Record Accuracy 308
Cycle Counting 309
Control of Services Inventories 309
Inventory Models 309
Independent versus Dependent Demand 309
Holding, Ordering, and Setup Costs 310
Inventory Models for Independent Demand 311
The Basic Economic Order Quantity (EOQ) Model 312
Minimize Costs 312
Reorder Points 316
Production Order Quantity Model 317
Quantity Discount Models 320
Probabilistic Models with Constant Lead Time 323
Fixed-Period Systems 326
Summary 327
Key Terms 328
Using POM for Windows 329
Using Excel Spreadsheets to Solve Inventory Problems 330

Solved Problems 332
Discussion Questions 334
Operations in Practice Exercise 334
Problems 334
Self-Test Chapter 9 335
Case Studies: Sturdivant Sound Systems; Martin-Pullin Bicycle Corporation 340
Bibliography 341

10 INVENTORY FOR DEPENDENT DEMAND 343

Dependent Inventory Model Requirements 344
Master Production Schedule 344
Specifications or Bills-of-Material 346
Accurate Inventory Records 348
Purchase Orders Outstanding 349
Lead Times for Each Component 349
Benefits of MRP 350
MRP Structure 350
MRP Management 354
MRP Dynamics 354
MRP and JIT 355
Lot-Sizing Techniques 355
Extensions of MRP 358
MRP in Services 359
Restaurant Example 359
Distribution Example 361
Summary 361
Key Terms 361
Using POM for Windows to Solve MRP Problems 362
Discussion Questions 363
Solved Problem 364
Self-Test Chapter 10 365
Operations in Practice Exercise 366
Problems 366
Case Study: Service, Inc. 372
Bibliography 373

11 JUST-IN-TIME SYSTEMS 375

Just-in-Time Attacks Waste and Variability 376
Waste Reduction 376
Variability Reduction 376
Pull versus Push 378
Suppliers 378
Goals of JIT Partnerships 378
Concerns of Suppliers 380
JIT Layout 381
Distance Reduction 382
Increased Flexibility 382
Impact on Employees 382
Reduced Space and Inventory 382
Inventory 383
Hidden Variability 383
Inventory Reduction 383
Small Lots Essential 383
Setup Costs Driven Down 384
Scheduling 385
Level-Material-Use Schedules 386
Kanban 387
Quality 389
Employee Empowerment 389
JIT in Services 390
Summary 391
Key Terms 391
Discussion Questions 392
Self-Test Chapter 11 393
Operations in Practice Exercise 394
Case Study: Electronic Systems, Inc. 394
Bibliography 395

SUPPLEMENT TO CHAPTER 11: SUPPLY-CHAIN MANAGEMENT 397

Strategic Importance of Supply-Chain Management 398
Purchasing 399
Operations Environment 400
Service Environments 400
Make or Buy 400
Purchasing Strategies 401
Many Suppliers 401
Few Suppliers 402
Vertical Integration 403
Keiretsu Networks 404
Virtual Companies 405
Purchasing Management 405
Vendor Relations 405
Purchasing Techniques 407
Materials Management 408
Distribution Systems 409
Benchmarking Supply-Chain Management 410
Summary 410
Key Terms 410
Self-Test Supplement 11 411
Discussion Questions 412
Operations in Practice Exercise 412

Problems 412
Case Studies: Factory Enterprises, Inc.; Thomas Manufacturing Company 413
Bibliography 414

12 AGGREGATE SCHEDULING 415

The Strategic Importance of Aggregate Scheduling 416
The Planning Process 416
The Nature of Aggregate Scheduling 417
Aggregate Planning Strategies 419
Capacity Options 419
Demand Options 420
Mixing Options to Develop a Plan 420
Level Scheduling 421
Methods for Aggregate Scheduling 421
Graphical and Charting Methods 422
Mathematical Approaches for Planning 426
Comparison of Aggregate Planning Methods 429
Disaggregation 429
Aggregate Scheduling in Services 430
Restaurants 430
Miscellaneous Services 431
National Chains of Small Service Firms 431
Airline Industry 431
Hospitals 431
A Case Study of Aggregate Scheduling in a Law Firm 431
Summary 432
Key Terms 433
Using POM for Windows for Aggregate Planning 433
Solved Problems 434
Discussion Questions 436
Self-Test Chapter 12 437
Operations in Practice Exercise 438
Problems 438
Case Study: Southwestern State College 443
Bibliography 444

13 SHORT-TERM SCHEDULING 445

Strategic Importance of Short-Term Scheduling 446
Scheduling Issues 446
Forward and Backward Scheduling 447
Scheduling Criteria 448
Scheduling Process-Focused Work Centers 448
Loading Jobs in Work Centers 449
Gantt Charts 449
Assignment Method 451
Sequencing Jobs in Work Centers 454
Priority Rules for Dispatching Jobs 454
Critical Ratio 458
Sequencing N Jobs on Two Machines: Johnson's Rule 459
Limitations of Rule-Based Systems 460
Finite Scheduling 461
Theory of Constraints 461
Bottleneck Work Centers 462
Repetitive Manufacturing 462
Scheduling for Services 464
Scheduling Nurses with Cyclical Scheduling 465
Summary 466
Key Terms 466
Using POM for Windows to Solve Scheduling Problems 466
Solved Problems 467
Discussion Questions 471
Operations in Practice Exercise 471
Self-Test Chapter 13 472
Problems 473
Case Study: The NASA Space Shuttle 478
Bibliography 478

14 PROJECT SCHEDULING 479

The Strategic Importance of Project Management 480
Project Planning 480
Project Scheduling 481
Project Controlling 482
Project Management Techniques: PERT and CPM 483
The Framework of PERT and CPM 483
Activities, Events, and Networks 484
Dummy Activities and Events 486
PERT and Activity Time Estimates 488
Critical Path Analysis 489
The Probability of Project Completion 493
Cost-Time Trade-Offs and Project Crashing 495
Applying Project Scheduling to Service Firms 498
Installing a New Computer System 498
Relocating St. Vincent's Hospital 498
A Critique of PERT and CPM 500
Summary 500
Key Terms 500
Using POM for Windows 501
Using Excel Spreadsheets for Project Scheduling 501

Solved Problems 503
Self-Test Chapter 14 507
Discussion Questions 508
Operations in Practice Exercise 508
Problems 508
Case Study: The Family Planning Research Center of Nigeria 514
Bibliography 516

SUPPLEMENT TO CHAPTER 14: MAINTENANCE MANAGEMENT 517

The Strategic Importance of Maintenance 518
Maintenance Categories 519
Implementing Preventive Maintenance 519
Simulation Models for a Maintenance Policy 522
Key Terms 522
Discussion Questions 522
Self-Test Supplement 14 523
Problems 523
Case Study: Worldwide Chemical Company 524
Bibliography 525

APPENDICES A1

A Normal Curve Areas and How to Use the Normal Distribution A2
B Using POM for Windows A5
C Answers to Self-Tests A12
D Answers to Even-Numbered Problems A16

GLOSSARY A25

INDEX I1

Preface

Welcome to *Principles of Operations Management*, second edition, written as a concise introduction to the field of operations management. In this book we present a state-of-the-art view of the primary activities of the operations function in organizations. The operations function is an exciting area of management that has a profound effect on both production and productivity. Few activities have as much impact on the quality of our lives. We present discussion and examples for both manufacturing and services, placing special emphasis on the service sector since three-quarters of all jobs fall in this category. The goal of this text is to present the field of operations as realistic, practical activities that can improve the quality of our lives.

Operations management includes a blend of topics from accounting, industrial engineering, management, management science, and statistics. Operations management jobs can be challenging, important, and rewarding, and can lead to successful careers. The inside front cover of the book illustrates the wide variety of career opportunities available. And even if you are not employed in the operations area, the techniques can often be applied to other disciplines, and can help you understand how the discipline functions and impacts your life.

Organization of the Text

Part One of *Principles of Operations Management* sets the stage for the subject with two chapters that provide an introduction to operations management, productivity, services, and operations strategy. In addition, Part One includes a supplement addressing the important topic of forecasting. Part Two and Part Three are written with two concepts in mind: *building* operations and *managing* operations. In Part Two, we *build* operations by addressing issues related to quality, product and service design, processes, location, people and work systems, and layout. In Part Three, we *manage* operations by scheduling (aggregate, short-term, and project), supply-chain management/purchasing, inventory control and just-in-time systems, and maintenance. Part Four contains six tutorials describing analytical techniques that are used in making a series of operations decisions. The techniques are decision trees and tables, linear programming, the transportation model, learning curves, waiting line models, and simulation.

Two Versions of the Text. This text is available to professors and students in two versions: *Principles of Operations Management,* a paperback, and *Principles of Operations Management with Tutorials,* which is hardbound. Parts One, Two, and Three of both books are identical. However, Part Four is available only in *Principles of Operations Management with Tutorials.*

The combination of chapters, supplements, and tutorials, quantitative and qualitative material, discussion questions and cases, problems of various difficulty, and software flexibility (POM for Windows or Excel spreadsheets) allow substantial course flexibility. We believe that the result is two versions of a text that lends itself to various levels of presentation as well as to individual styles of instruction. *Principles of Operations Management* is designed to be used as either an undergraduate or graduate text.

FOCUS OF THE SECOND EDITION

The second edition of *Principles of Operations Management* represents a major revision in our treatment of this exciting and dynamic topic. Our new thrust is to take a much more strategic and managerial approach to operations and to use strategy as a unifying link in every chapter. This approach stresses operations management as a powerful tool for reaching the organization's objectives. This new direction is seen throughout the book. The second edition also includes new chapters on "Operations Strategy for Goods and Services," "Supply-Chain Management," and "Just-in-time Systems."

In addition, we placed a much greater emphasis on the role of service operations. This involved major revisions in almost every chapter to reflect the growing service economy in the United States and the world. However, we have not neglected the importance of analytical tools in tackling operations problems. We present these in an integrated fashion to help achieve the firm's overall strategy and fulfill its operations mission.

Here are some details about our changes in content:

Strategic Focus. We not only added a new chapter (chapter 2), "Operations Strategy for Goods and Services," but have integrated a discussion of strategy into every topic and chapter. Chapter 2 sets the stage for the importance of operations strategy as a competitive weapon in every organization.

This new chapter provides sample mission statements from Circle K, American Airlines, and the American Red Cross, and then ties company missions to operations missions. We also introduce Michael Porter's classic work on achieving missions by: (1) differentiation, (2) cost leadership, and (3) quick response. Research from the Strategic Planning Institute and information on how strategies change are also topics covered in Chapter 2.

Service Operations. The treatment of service operations has changed substantially in this edition, with the integration of service coverage throughout. The tone is set in Chapter 1, with a major section titled "Operations in the Service Sector." Each chapter then follows up with further discussion. In Chapter 4, "Design of Goods and Services," for example, we now deal with service selection, service design, and documents for services as major topics. Five new service cases have been added to the six service-oriented cases from the first edition.

State-of-the-Art Developments. We have added to or expanded our coverage of total quality management (TQM) tools, house of quality, benchmarking, time-based competition, keiretsu, virtual organizations, process reengineering, learning organizations, just-in-time, supply-chain management, finite scheduling, and the theory of constraints.

International Examples. A **global perspective** of both world-class manufacturing and world-class services is used to present the best theory and practice wherever it is found. We provide scores of new international examples.

POM for Windows Computer Analysis. Replacing our DOS software (AB:POM), this excellent windows-based software is a major upgrade, with graphic and sensitivity analysis. Sample printouts are provided at the end of most chapters. Twenty modules (topics) are covered in POM for Windows, with detailed documentation in Appendix B. The following printout provides an illustration of how POM for Windows is used to solve a statistical process control problem. (This screen also appears in Supplement 3. For a listing of all modules, see Program B.2 in Appendix B.)

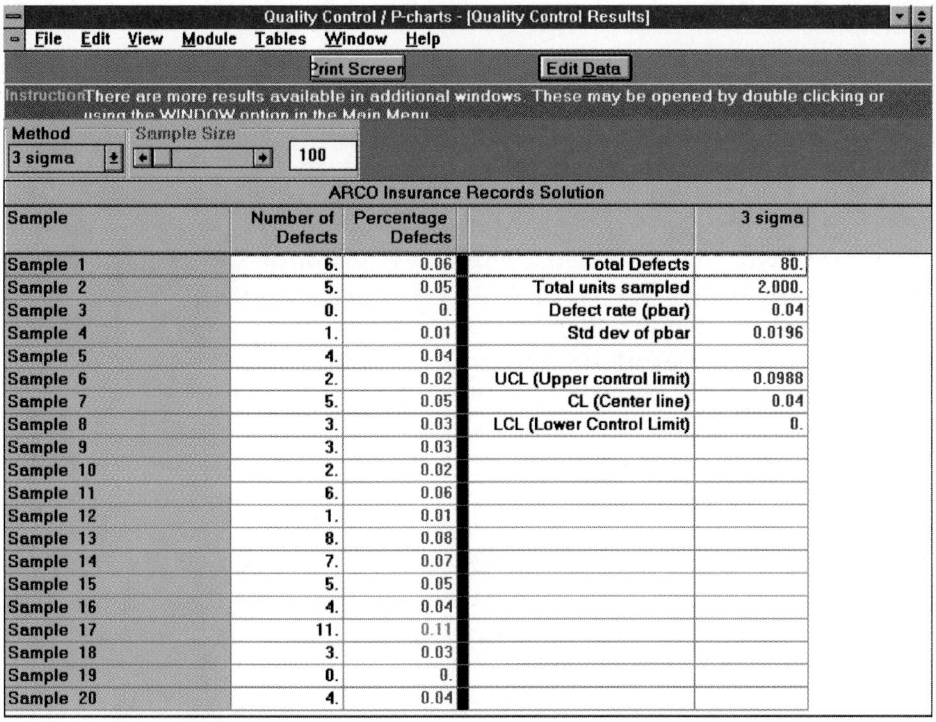

Quality Control / P-charts - [Quality Control Results]

File Edit View Module Tables Window Help

Print Screen | Edit Data

Instruction There are more results available in additional windows. These may be opened by double clicking or using the WINDOW option in the Main Menu

Method: 3 sigma | Sample Size: 100

ARCO Insurance Records Solution

Sample	Number of Defects	Percentage Defects		3 sigma
Sample 1	6.	0.06	Total Defects	80.
Sample 2	5.	0.05	Total units sampled	2,000.
Sample 3	0.	0.	Defect rate (pbar)	0.04
Sample 4	1.	0.01	Std dev of pbar	0.0196
Sample 5	4.	0.04		
Sample 6	2.	0.02	UCL (Upper control limit)	0.0988
Sample 7	5.	0.05	CL (Center line)	0.04
Sample 8	3.	0.03	LCL (Lower Control Limit)	0.
Sample 9	3.	0.03		
Sample 10	2.	0.02		
Sample 11	6.	0.06		
Sample 12	1.	0.01		
Sample 13	8.	0.08		
Sample 14	7.	0.07		
Sample 15	5.	0.05		
Sample 16	4.	0.04		
Sample 17	11.	0.11		
Sample 18	3.	0.03		
Sample 19	0.	0.		
Sample 20	4.	0.04		

Excel Spreadsheets. This new feature details an Excel spreadsheet approach to problem-solving in the following chapters/supplements: Supplement 2 (forecasting), Supplement 3 (statistical quality control), Chapter 6 (location), Chapter 7 (time and motion), Chapter 9 (inventory), Chapter 14 (project management),

Tutorial 1 (decision tables/trees), Tutorial 2 (linear programming), Tutorial 4 (learning curves), Tutorial 5 (queuing), and Tutorial 6 (simulation). A sample Excel screen for a small time-and-motion study appears below.

Enter the observed job elements, performance ratings, and observations in columns A through G.

Calculate the Average time for each element using the sum and count functions as shown in column H.

Calculate the Normal Times using the Performance ratings, then sum these and use the result and the Allowance factor to determine the standard time.

Remember that the allowance factor is used by multiplying together the reciprocal of one minus the allowance factor and the total normal time. This is NOT the same as multiplying the normal time by one plus the allowance factor.

Microsoft Excel - PAGED.XLS

	A	B	C	D	E	F	G	H	I
1	Using EXCEL Spreadsheets to Solve Time-Study Problems								
2									
3				Cycle Observed					
4				(in Minutes)					
5	Job Element	Performance Rating	1	2	3	4	5	Average Time	Normal Time
6	Type Letter	1.20	8	10	9		11	=SUM(C6:G6)/COUNT(C6:G6)	=B6*H6
7	Type Envelope	1.05	2	3	2	1	3	=SUM(C7:G7)/COUNT(C7:G7)	=B7*H7
8	Stuff, Stamp Seal	1.10	2	1		2	1	=SUM(C8:G8)/COUNT(C8:G8)	=B8*H8
9									
10							Total Normal Time		=SUM(I6:I9)
11	Allowance Factor	0.15					Standard Time		=I10/(1-B11)

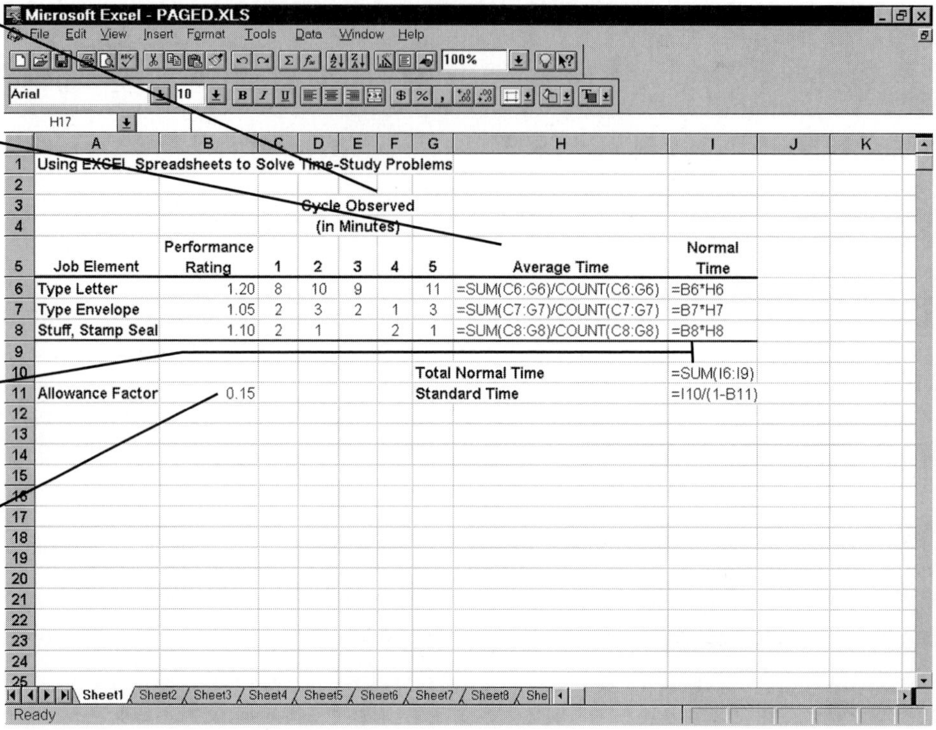

Treatment of Quantitative Materials. As the operations course evolves into a more managerially oriented subject, many professors have chosen to provide more coverage of strategy, services, quality, JIT, and other non-quantitative topics. Our second edition has placed the topics of decision trees and tables, linear programming, the transportation method, learning curves, queuing theory, and simulation in the version of the book called *Principles of Operations Management with Tutorials.* This provides greater flexibility for instructors teaching both longer and shorter academic courses.

Expanded Treatment of Just-in-Time (Chapter 11) and Supply Chain Management (Supplement to Chapter 11). This new chapter and supplement cover these critical topics in detail, with the latest research and ideas included. In the JIT chapter, for example, we introduce the relations between JIT and suppliers, JIT layout, and issues of JIT involving inventory, scheduling, quality, employee involvement and services. In our unique supplement on supply chain management, we deal with the strategic implications of this topic and introduce such concepts as vertical integration, keiretsu networks, virtual firms, materials management, and benchmarking.

CHAPTER BY CHAPTER CHANGES

To highlight the extent of the revision of our earlier edition, here are a few of the changes on a chapter-by-chapter basis.

Chapter 1. Operations and Productivity. An extensive revision of this chapter sets the tone for goods *and* services throughout. It includes a new service case study.

Chapter 2. Operations Strategy for Goods and Services. This is a new chapter that features mission statements, Michael Porter's material on strategy, ten decisions that are made in operations, and a new case study.

Supplement to Chapter 2. Forecasting. This technical supplement contains new material on strategy and on the service sector. It includes new POM for Windows and Excel sections and a new service case study.

Chapter 3. Total Quality Management. This chapter is a major revision of TQM, with new treatments of ISO 9000 and ISO 14000, house of quality material, and a new service case study.

Supplement to Chapter 3. Quality Via Statistical Process Control. This supplement has been shortened to include less material on sampling plans. It contains new POM for Windows and Excel sections.

Chapter 4. Design of Goods and Services. This chapter is a major rewrite with more material on service design. It includes a new case study (General Electric) and new POM for Windows software for reliability analysis.

Chapter 5. Process and Capacity Design. This chapter is also a major revision, with new sections on process reengineering (with time function mapping and work-flow analysis). There is more emphasis in the second edition on choosing a service process, as well as a new case study.

Chapter 6. Selecting the Location. This chapter now emphasizes the strategic implications of location decisions and contains a new section on service location. There are also new POM for Windows and Excel sections.

Chapter 7. People and Work Systems. We reorganized this chapter extensively, with new figures, art, and tables. We now provide coverage of lean production and learning organizations. The chapter contains a section on Excel spreadsheets for use in time and motion studies and includes a new case study on incentive pay systems at Lincoln Electric.

Chapter 8. Layout Designs. This chapter now emphasizes strategic implications of layout, has a new treatment of "crossdocking," a new POM for Windows section, and a new case study.

Chapter 9. Inventory for Independent Demand. We added a new section on services inventory and deleted the topic of marginal analysis. The chapter includes new POM for Windows and Excel sections and a new case study.

Chapter 10. Inventory for Dependent Demand (MRP). Our revision includes new sections on MRP in Services, and on linking MRP and JIT, including "buckets" and "backflushing." There is also a POM for Windows section.

Chapter 11. Just-In-Time Systems. This all new chapter emphasizes suppliers and relationships. It contains sections on JIT layout, inventory, scheduling, quality, empowerment, and JIT in services. There is also a new case study.

Supplement to Chapter 11. Supply Chain Management. This new supplement expands our first edition's treatment of purchasing management with an emphasis on strategic implications of supply chain management. It includes sections on keiretsu, virtual companies, material management, and benchmarking. The supplement also discusses "drop shipping" and "postponement". It includes two new case studies.

Chapter 12. Aggregate Scheduling. This is the first of three resequenced chapters on scheduling. Chapter 12 has a new emphasis on strategic issues and on scheduling in services, including an analysis of aggregate scheduling in a law firm. There is also a section on POM for Windows.

Chapter 13. Short-Term Scheduling. We include new material on strategic issues, and new sections on forward and backward scheduling, on finite scheduling, on the Theory of Constraints, and on bottleneck work centers. The chapter also has greater emphasis on services, with an example of how to schedule nurses in a hospital. There is also a section on POM for Windows.

Chapter 14. Project Scheduling. This revised chapter has a greater emphasis on strategy and services, with new examples from a computer firm and hospital. It includes a discussion of "work breakdown structure" and has sections on POM for Windows and Excel. There is a new service-oriented case study.

Supplement to Chapter 14. Maintenance Management. This supplement contains a new section on strategic issues and a new case study.

Tutorials 1–6, available only in *Principles of Operations Management with Tutorials,* were Supplements 1, 4, 5, 7, 8, and 11 in our first edition.

Tutorial 1. Decision Tools. The focus on this tutorial is now just on decision trees and decision tables, with less material on mathematical models than the first edition. There is a new section on POM for Windows and Excel.

Tutorial 2. Linear Programming. This tutorial has been shortened by deleting material on the simplex method and focusing on the graphical approach and sensitivity analysis. There are sections on POM for Windows and Excel spreadsheets with Solver.

Tutorial 3. Transportation Modeling. This tutorial has also been shortened with a deletion of the MODI method. This is a new section on POM for Windows and a new case study.

Tutorial 4. Learning Curves. This major revision now includes an arithmetic approach, logarithmic approach, and coefficient approach (tables). There is additional material on learning curves in services, numerous new problems, and new sections on POM for Windows and Excel.

Tutorial 5. Waiting Line Models. This tutorial has new sections on POM for Windows and Excel.

Tutorial 6. Simulation. There are new sections on POM for Windows and Excel, and a new service case study.

OUR INTERNET CONNECTION AND HOME PAGE

Principles of Operations Management has its own home page on the Internet, with exciting new exercises and challenging assignments. This link to the Internet uses the benefits of this world-wide network to provide you with additional up-to-the-minute illustrations from real world companies. It also includes numerous additional case studies and homework problems. We encourage you to use the Internet for research and operations problem-solving, and we want to encourage professors to integrate the Internet in the operations management course.

The Internet connection icon in the text directs the reader to additional materials and resources on the World Wide Web of the Internet dealing with topics and organizations discussed in each chapter. You can link to this home page inside Prentice-Hall's World Wide Web site via either a university or home Internet service. The address is http://www.prenhall.com/renderpom.

The home page for your book is organized both chapter-by-chapter and by topic. For example, most chapters include additional cases, data base homework problems, and assignments for touring and investigating an operations topic at real companies that are linked to our home page. There is also a *New York Times* "POM Themes of the Times" section on the home page. This relates the *New York Times* articles that are available free to your class to a series of discussion and homework questions that appear only on the home page. And with our virtual tours section, you can visit ten exciting companies, ranging from an auto manufacturer to a hospital, directly through the home page. These tours also contain discussion questions that can be used as class assignments. We think the home page will be both easy to use and a student motivator, and we look forward to your feedback.

PEDAGOGICAL FOCUS AND FEATURES

Our goal in this revision is to provide the finest pedagogical package available to students and instructors in the operations discipline. We think we have succeeded. Here are some of the features to help enhance learning and teaching.

Marginal Notes to Students. This new feature provides interesting and motivational sidebars to students. There are more than a half a dozen per chapter, including quotes from famous people, tips for learning, and highlights of major points.

Operations in Practice Exercises. This edition provides a new feature at the end of each chapter that challenges the student to face cultural, ethical, or controversial issues of business today. These paragraph-long thinking exercises are ideal for class breakout and discussion. They involve thought-provoking topics that can spice up a class or allow for small group discussion analysis.

Case Studies. We have introduced 13 new case studies into the second edition. Most of these have been developed by leading operations management academics throughout the United States. The cases are generally one to two pages in length, making them short enough to cover in weekly assignments. But they also deal with situations in a realistic, detailed manner that adds depth to each chapter. Almost all cases are based on real world companies.

Solved Problems. Once again, solved problems are included in this edition. They are provided as models for students as they work unsolved problems on their own.

Solutions to Even Numbered Problems. Brief answers to all of the even numbered problems in this book appear in Appendix D.

Three Levels of Homework Problems. The number of end-of-chapter problems has increased and each is identified as one of three levels: introductory (one dot), moderate (two dots), and challenging (three dots).

Self-Tests. Each chapter, supplement, and tutorial contains a one page self-test, consisting of true-false, multiple choice, and fill-in the blank questions. Answers to these are found in Appendix C. Students can check their level of comprehension after reading the chapter's material.

Photos. In this edition, over 100 full-color photos appear, along with detailed captions tying them to the contents of their chapters and to specific components. These photos and captions are intended to increase student interest and add depth to each topic.

Student Lecture Notes. Our study guide, called "Student Lecture Notes," is a printed version of the Powerpoint slides and is also available for purchase. Prepared by Professor John McGill, this guide contains over 1,250 slides, displayed three per page with lines next to each slide to facilitate note taking during the lecture.

Also Available for Instructors

POM Interactive CD-ROM. State of the art presentations are available with this 14 lecture, full-color CD-ROM, which includes videos, photos, animations, and slides.

Powerpoint Presentation Graphics. *Principles of Operations Management,* second edition, has the finest package of Powerpoint slides available. Created and class-tested by Professor John McGill, there are on average, over 130 slides per chapter, 3,200 in all, with extensive graphics, including animations. The Powerpoint slides include class exercises as well as comprehensive lecture materials. All of these materials can be customized.

***New York Times* Supplement, Themes of POM.** Free to adapters, this 12 page newspaper, edited by Professor Render, provides exciting current articles dealing with operations, from *The New York Times.*

Other Instructor Resources. Also available to instructors is our author-prepared solutions manual, a Test Bank (prepared by Professor Corrine M. Karuppan), a data disk for all homework problems solvable with POM for Windows (or AB:POM), and a wide variety of videos.

Acknowledgments

We thank the many individuals who were kind enough to assist us in this endeavor. The following professors provided insights that guided us in this revision:

Ronald K. Satterfield
University of South Florida

Larry A. Flick
Norwalk Community Technical College

Michael Pesch
St. Cloud State University

Donald Hammond
University of South Florida

Andy Litteral
University of Richmond

Shane J. Schvaneveldt
Webber State College

B. P. Lingeraj
Indiana University

Ranga V. Ramasesh
Texas Christian University

We also wish to acknowledge the help of the reviewers of the first edition of this text and the reviewers of our other book, *Production and Operations Management*, fourth edition. Without the help of these fellow professors, we would never have received the feedback needed to put together a teachable text. The reviewers are listed in alphabetical order:

.Sema Alptekin
University of Missouri–Rolla

Jean-Pierre Amor
University of San Diego

Moshen Attaran
California State University–Bakersfield

John H. Blackstone
University of Georgia

Theodore Boreki
Hofstra University

Mark Coffin
Eastern California University

Henry Crouch
Pittsburgh State University

Barbara Flynn
Iowa State University

Damodar Golhar
Western Michigan University

Jim Goodwin
University of Richmond

James R. Gross
University of Wisconsin–Oshkosh

Marilyn K. Hart
University of Wisconsin–Oshkosh

James S. Hawkes
University of Charleston

George Heinrich
Wichita State University

Zialu Huq
University of Nebraska–Omaha

Paul Jordan
University of Alaska

Larry LaForge
Clemson University

Hugh Leach
Washburn University

Laurie E. MacDonald
Bryant College

Mike Maggard
Northeastern University

Arthur C. Meiners, Jr.
Marymount University

Joao Neves
Trenton State College

Niranjan Pati
University of Wisconsin–LaCrosse

David W. Pentico
Duquesne University

Leonard Presby
William Patterson State College of New Jersey

M. J. Riley
Kansas State University

Narendrea K. Rustagi
Howard University

Teresita S. Salinas
Washburn University

Robert J. Schlesinger
San Diego State University

Avanti P. Sethi
Wichita State University

Girish Shambu
Canisius College

Susan Sherer
Lehigh University

Vicki L. Smith-Daniels
Arizona State University

Stan Stockton
Indiana University

John Swearingen
Bryant College

Kambiz Tabibzadeh
Eastern Kentucky University

Rao J. Tatikonda
University of Wisconsin–Oshkosh

Bruce M. Woodworth
University of Texas–El Paso

In addition, we appreciate the fine people at Prentice-Hall who provided both help and encouragement: Rich Wohl, our editor-in-chief, Tom Tucker, our editor, and Susan Rifkin, our wonderful production editor. Linda Calvert Jacobson aggressively edited a number of chapters, improving their readability. Reva Shader developed the superb index for this text and Kay Heizer provided the glossary and proofing. Donna Render, Jessie Render, Sue Crabill, and Heather Bowers provided the accurate typing and proofing so critical in a rigorous textbook.

We also appreciate the efforts of colleagues who have helped to shape the entire learning package that accompanies this text: Professor Howard Weiss (Temple University) developed POM for Windows microcomputer software; Professor John McGill (Trenton State University) developed the excellent Powerpoint graphics; Vijay Gupta (Temple University) proofed our solutions manual and provided the data disk solutions; and Professor Corrine M. Karuppan (Southeast Missouri State University) created our Test Bank. We have been fortunate to have been able to work with all of these people.

We wish you a pleasant and productive introduction to operations management.

Barry Render
Roy E. Crummer Graduate School of Business
Rollins College
Winter Park, FL 32789
Phone: (407) 646-2657
FAX: (407) 646-1550
Email: BRENDER@ROLLINS.EDU

Jay Heizer
Texas Lutheran University
1000 W. Court Street
Seguin, TX 78155
Phone: (210) 372-6056
FAX: (210) 372-8096
Email: HEIZER_J@TXLUTHERAN.EDU

Principles of
Operations Management

Operations and Productivity

1

CHAPTER OUTLINE

What Is Operations Management?
Heritage of Operations Management
Organizing for the Creation of Goods and Services
Why Study OM?
What Operations Managers Do
Where Are the Jobs in OM?
Operations in the Service Sector
Differences Between Goods and Services ■ Growth of Services ■ Service Pay
The Productivity Challenge
Productivity Measurement ■ Productivity Variables ■ Productivity and the Service Sector
Summary ■ Key Terms ■ Solved Problem ■ Discussion Questions ■ Self-Test Chapter 1 ■ Operations in Practice Exercises ■ Problems ■ Case Study: National Air Express ■ Bibliography

LEARNING OBJECTIVES

When you complete this chapter you should be able to:

IDENTIFY OR DEFINE:

Production and productivity
Operations management (OM)
What operations managers do
The three major functions of a business
Services

DESCRIBE OR EXPLAIN:

A brief history of operations management
Career opportunities in operations management
The future of the discipline
The difficulty of measuring productivity

The global business system is changing the way everyone communicates, lives, and works. It is accelerating as the economies of the former Soviet block and China develop and open. The pace of technological change is quickening as computers and communication networks make it possible for firms to react faster to innovations and shifts in demand. The new global information links connect customers, retailers, and manufacturers with the stroke of a key, the click of a mouse button, or a touch on a screen. Ideas, innovations, money transfers, and designs now move in seconds.

The use of technology in this new information age has all but collapsed traditional barriers that once existed. Companies now make worldwide products. Ford makes a world car. Gillette makes a world razor. Microsoft makes Internet programs used around the world. McDonald's hamburgers taste the same in Moscow, Tel Aviv, Bangkok, and Chicago. These firms are just a few examples of the integrated international production system. Not only is movement of electrons cheap and fast, but huge ships and airplanes make the movement of goods less expensive and increasingly rapid.

These changes have a tremendous impact on the operations of firms. Companies that at one time were local became national, then regional, and now global. The technology that manifests itself in computers, communication, and lower transportation costs are terrific drivers toward globalization. As Western nations release their defense budgets for more productive uses, curtail their government sectors, privatize their industries, and open global markets, we will see a great era of economic growth accelerate. This globalization explosion means we are living in an exciting and challenging decade, with new jobs, new opportunities for success, and wonderful new options for operations managers.

As we progress through this text, we will discover how to manage operations in this global economy. An array of informative examples, charts, text, and pic-

From the new gas station near your campus to the new Lukoil service station in Siberia, the world economy is expanding as are the opportunities for operations managers.

tures illustrate concepts and provide information. Examples of operations management range from Minit-Lube and McDonald's to General Motors and Disney World. We will see how operations managers create the goods and services that enrich our lives.

In this chapter we first define operations management, explaining its heritage and the exciting role operations managers play in this discipline. Then we discuss production and productivity in both goods and service producing firms. This is followed by a discussion of operations in the service sector and the challenge of managing an effective production system.

What Is Operations Management?

Production is the creation of goods and services. **Operations management (OM)** is the set of activities that creates goods and services through the transformation of inputs into outputs. Activities creating goods and services take place in all organizations. In manufacturing firms, the production activities that create goods are usually quite obvious. In them, we can see the creation of a tangible product such as a Sony TV or a Ford Bronco.

production

operations management (OM)

In other organizations that do not create physical products, the production function may be less obvious. It may be "hidden" from the public and even from the customer. An example is the transformation that takes place at a bank, airline office, or college.

Often when services are performed, no tangible goods are produced. Instead, the product may take such forms as the transfer of funds from a savings account to a checking account, the filling of an empty seat on an airline, or the education of a student. Regardless of whether the end product is a good or service, the production activities that go on in the organization are often referred to as operations or *operations management*.

Heritage of Operations Management

The field of OM is relatively young, but its history is rich and interesting. Our lives and the OM discipline have been enhanced by the innovations and contributions of numerous individuals. We introduce a few of these people in this section.

Frederick W. Taylor's *Principles of Scientific Management* revolutionized manufacturing. A scientific approach to the analysis of daily work and the tools of industry frequently increased productivity 400%. For instance, by 1913, Model T Fords were being assembled with less than two hours of labor.

Eli Whitney (1800) is credited for the early popularization of interchangeable parts, which was achieved through standardization and quality control in manufacturing. Through a contract he signed with the U.S. government for 10,000 muskets, he was able to command a premium price because of their interchangeable parts.

Frederick W. Taylor (1881), known as the father of scientific management, contributed to personnel selection, planning and scheduling, motion study, and the now popular field of human factors. One of his major contributions was his belief that management should be much more resourceful and aggressive in the improvement of work methods. Taylor and his colleagues, Henry L. Gantt and Frank and Lillian Gilbreth, were among the first to seek systematically the best way to

Frank and Lillian Gilbreth were interested in finding the one best way to accomplish work tasks. In pursuit of this effort, they invented a wide variety of techniques and devices. One technique was to use cameras to record movement by attaching lights to an individual's arms and legs. In that way they could track the movement of individuals while performing various jobs.

produce. Another of Taylor's contributions was the belief that management should assume more responsibility for:

1. Matching employees to the right job.
2. Providing the proper training.
3. Providing proper work methods and tools.
4. Establishing legitimate incentives for work to be accomplished.

NOTE
Charles Sorensen was the man who towed an automobile chassis on a rope over his shoulders through the Ford plant while others added parts.

By 1913, Henry Ford and Charles Sorensen combined what they knew about standardized parts with the quasi-assembly lines of the meat-packing and mail-order industries and added the concept of the assembly line where men stood still and material moved.

Quality control is another historically significant contribution to the field of OM. Walter Shewhart (1924) combined his knowledge of statistics with the need for quality control and provided the foundations for statistical sampling and quality control. W. Edwards Deming (1950) believed, as did Frederick Taylor, that management must do more to improve the work environment and processes so that quality can be improved. A summary of significant events in operations management is shown in Figure 1.1.

industrial engineering

management science

physical sciences

Operations management will continue to progress with contributions from other disciplines, including **industrial engineering** and **management science.** These disciplines, along with statistics, management, and economics, have contributed substantially to greater productivity.

Innovations from the **physical sciences** (biology, anatomy, chemistry, physics) also have contributed to advances in OM. These advances include new adhesives, chemical processes for printed circuit boards, gamma rays to sanitize food products, and molten tin tables on which to float a higher-quality molten glass as it cools. The design of products and processes often depend on the biological and physical sciences.

information sciences

An especially important contribution to OM has come from the **information sciences,** which we define as the systematic processing of data to yield information. The information sciences are contributing in a major way toward improved productivity while at the same time providing society with a greater diversity of goods and services.

Decisions in operations management require individuals who are well versed in *management science*, in *information science*, and often in one of the *biological or*

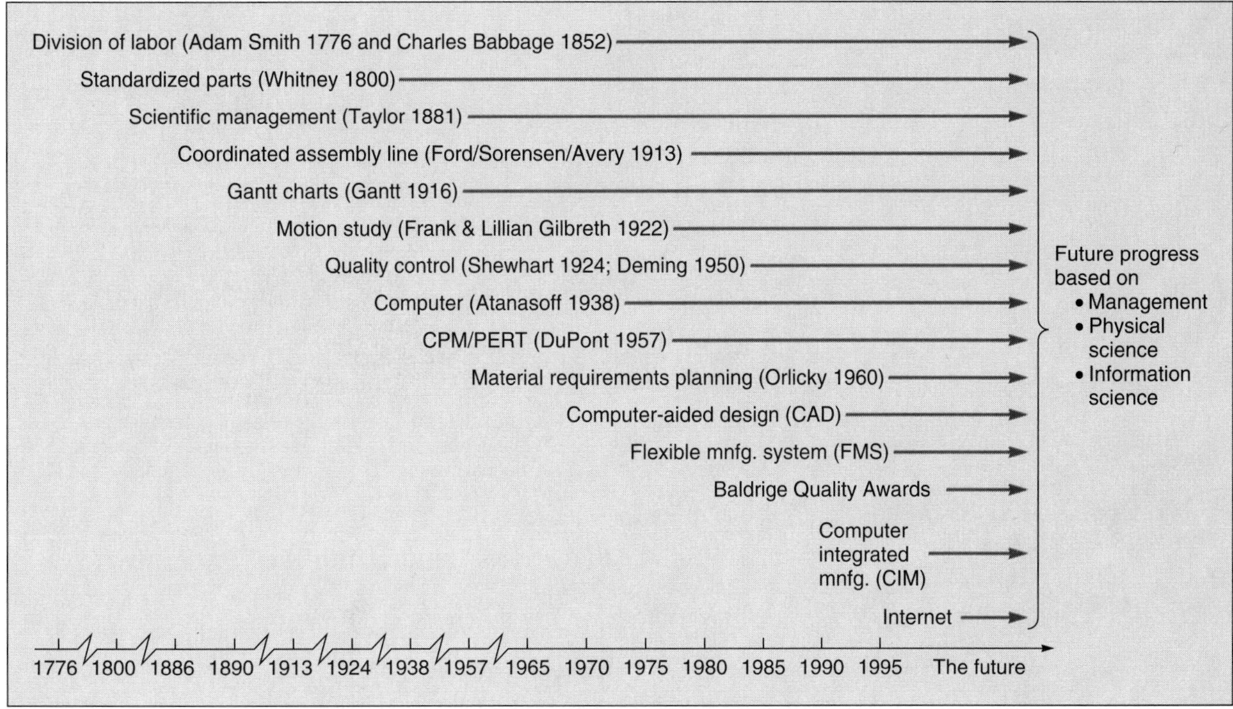

FIGURE 1.1 Significant Events in Operations Management

physical sciences. In this chapter we will take a look at the diverse ways a student can prepare for careers in operations management. Let us first look, though, at how we organize firms to create goods and services.

NOTE
The concepts of computing, described in a paper presented by Prof. Atanasoff at the U. of Iowa in 1938, helped John Mauchly and J. Presper Eckert develop the ENIAC, an electron-tube computer, at the U. of Pennsylvania.

Organizing for the Creation of Goods and Services

To create goods and services, all organizations perform three functions (see Figure 1.2). These functions are the necessary ingredients not only for production but also for an organization's survival.

1. *Marketing*, which generates the demand or at least takes the order for a product or service (nothing happens until there is a sale).
2. *Production/operations*, which creates the product.
3. *Finance/accounting*, which tracks how well the organization is doing, pays the bills, and collects the money.

Universities, churches or synagogues, and businesses all perform these functions.

Any institution, even a volunteer group such as the Boy Scouts of America, is organized to perform these three basic functions. Figure 1.3 shows how an airline, a bank, and a manufacturing firm organize themselves to perform these functions. The blue shaded areas of Figure 1.3 show the operations functions in these firms.

Goods/Service	Organization	Marketing	Operations	Finance/Accounting
Food	Burger King	Advertise on TV Give away promotional materials Sponsor kids' leagues	Make hamburgers/fries Maintain equipment Design new facilities	Pay suppliers Collect cash Pay employees Pay bank loans
Education, research	University of New Orleans	Mail catalogs Call on high schools	Research for truth Disseminate truth	Pay faculty/staff Collect tuition
Cars, trucks	Ford Motor Company	Advertise on TV, in newspapers, etc. Support auto racing Offer rebates	Design automobiles Manufacture parts Assemble automobiles Develop suppliers	Pay suppliers, employees Prepare budgets Pay dividends Sell stock
Celebrations of life	First Presbyterian Church	Call on newcomers	Conduct weddings Conduct funerals Conduct services	Count contributions Keep track of pledges Pay the mortgage, other bills

FIGURE 1.2 THREE FUNCTIONS REQUIRED OF ALL ORGANIZATIONS

WHY STUDY OM?

We study OM for four reasons. First, OM is one of the three major functions of any organization (as is shown in Figures 1.2 and 1.3), and it is integrally related to all the other business functions. All organizations market (sell), finance (account), and produce (operate), and it is important to know how the OM segment of organizations functions. Therefore we study *how people organize themselves for productive enterprise.*

Second, we study OM because we want to know *how goods and services are produced.* The production function is the segment of our society that creates the products we use.

Third, we study OM *because it is such a costly part of an organization.* A large percentage of revenue of most firms is spent in the OM function. Indeed, OM provides a major opportunity for an organization to improve its profitability and enhance its service to society. Example 1 considers how a firm might increase its profitability via the production function.

EXAMPLE 1

Rifkin Technologies is a small firm that must double its dollar contribution to overhead in order to be profitable enough to purchase the next generation of production equipment. The management has determined that, if the firm fails to increase contribution, its bank will not make the loan and the equipment cannot be purchased. If the firm cannot purchase the equipment, the limitations of the old equipment will force Rifkin Technologies to go out of business and, in doing so, put its employees out of work and discontinue producing goods and services for its customers. Table 1.1 shows a simple profit-and-loss statement and three strategic options for the firm. The first strategic option is a *marketing option* where good management may increase sales by 50%. By increasing sales by 50%, contribution

TABLE 1.1 OPTIONS FOR INCREASING CONTRIBUTION

		MARKETING OPTION[a]	FINANCE/ ACCOUNTING OPTION[b]	OM OPTION[c]
	Current	*Increase Sales Revenue 50%*	*Reduce Finance Costs 50%*	*Reduce Production Costs 20%*
Sales	$100,000	$150,000	$100,000	$100,000
Costs of goods	−80,000	−120,000	−80,000	−64,000
Gross margin	20,000	30,000	20,000	36,000
Finance costs	−6,000	−6,000	−3,000	−6,000
	14,000	24,000	17,000	30,000
Taxes at 25%	−3,500	−6,000	−4,250	−7,500
Contribution[d]	$ 10,500	$ 18,000	$ 12,750	$ 22,500

[a]Increasing sales 50% increases contribution by $7,500 or 71.0% (7,500/10,500).
[b]Reducing finance costs 50% increases contribution by $2,250 or 21.0% (2,250/10,500).
[c]Reducing production costs 20% increases contribution by $12,000 or 114.0% (12,000/10,500).
[d]Contribution to fixed cost (excluding finance costs) and profit.

will in turn increase 71%, but increasing sales 50% may be more than difficult; it may even be impossible.

The second strategic option is a *finance/accounting option* where finance costs are cut in half through good financial management. But even a reduction of 50% is still inadequate for generating the necessary increase in contribution. Contribution is increased by only 21%.

The third strategic option is an *OM option* where management reduces production costs by 20% and increases contribution by 114%. Given the conditions of our brief example, we now have a bank willing to lend additional funds to Rifkin Technology.

Example 1 underscores the important role of developing an effective strategy for the operations activity of a firm. It is also the approach taken by many companies as they face growing global competition.

The fourth reason for studying OM is to understand what operations managers do. By understanding what these managers do, you can develop the skills necessary to be such a manager. This will help you explore the numerous and lucrative career opportunities in OM.

WHAT OPERATIONS MANAGERS DO

All good managers perform the basic functions of the management process. The **management process** consists of *planning, organizing, staffing, leading,* and *controlling*. Operations managers apply this management process to the decisions they make in the OM function. Managers contribute to production and operations

management process

FIGURE 1.3

ORGANIZATION CHARTS FOR TWO SERVICES AND A MANUFACTURING ORGANIZATION

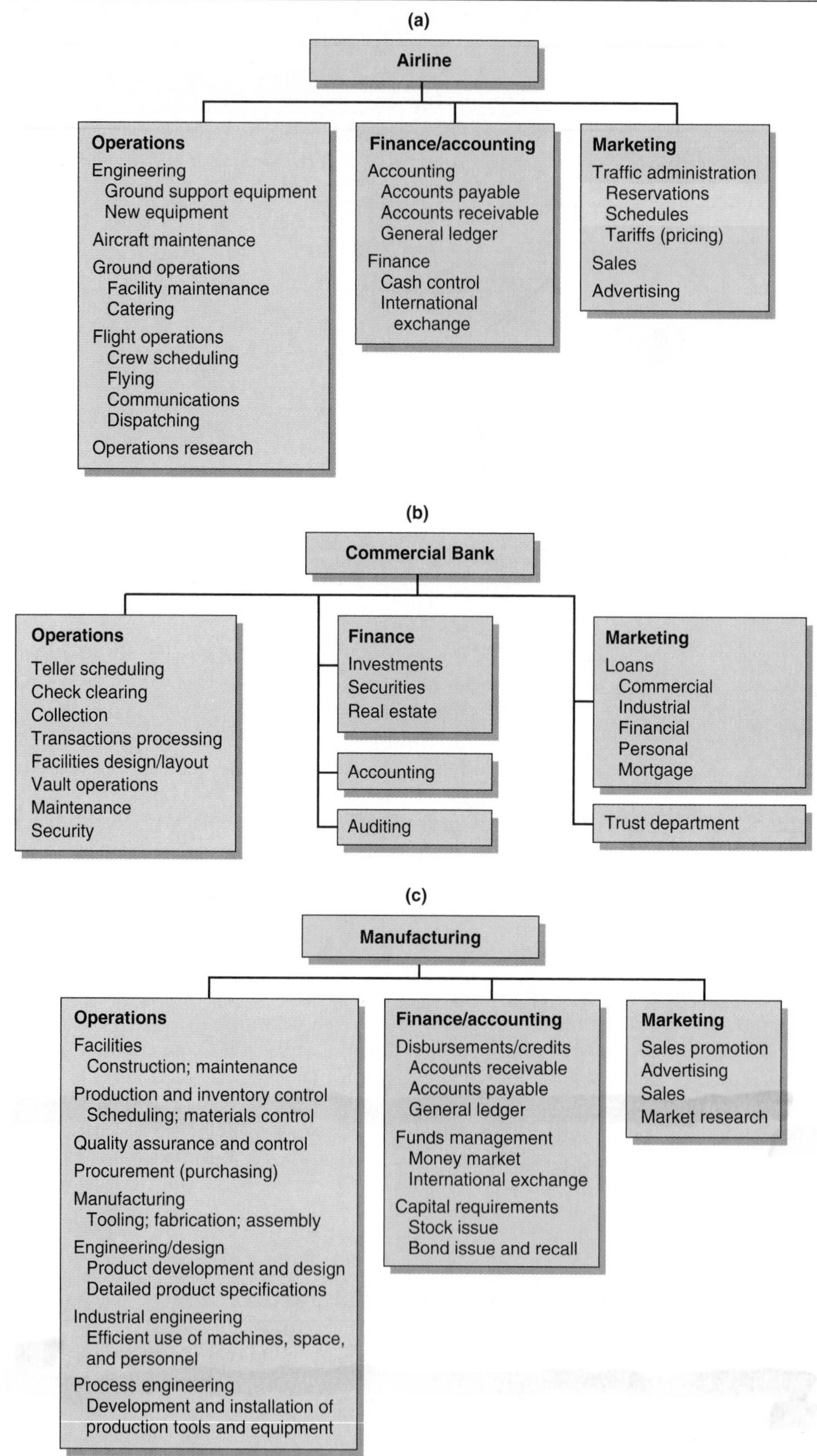

(a) An Airline and (b) a Bank, and (c) a Manufacturing Organization. The blue areas are OM activities.

through the activities shown in Table 1.2. Each of these activities requires planning, organizing, staffing, leading, and controlling.

The activities shown in Table 1.2 require that operations managers make numerous decisions. These decisions allocate resources that affect the strategy and operating efficiency of the firm. In this text we provide an introduction to the proper way to make these decisions. We also note the impact that these decisions may have on the firm's strategy and productivity.

TABLE 1.2 Decisions That OM Managers Make

SOME OPERATIONS QUESTIONS	DECISION AREA	CHAPTER
How can the OM function contribute to organizational objectives?	Strategy	2
What are our criteria for planning? How many units would we expect to sell?	Forecasting	2 Supplement
Who is responsible for quality? How do we define the quality we want in our service or product?	Quality management	3, 3 Supplement
What product or service should we offer? How should we design these products and services?	Service and product design	4
What process will these products require and in what order? What equipment is necessary for these processes?	Process and capacity design	5
Where should we put the facility? On what criteria should we base the location decision?	Location	6
How do we provide a reasonable work environment? How much can we expect our employees to produce?	People and work systems	7
How should we arrange the facility? How large must the facility be to meet our plan?	Layout design	8
How much inventory of each item should we have? When do we reorder?	Inventory, Material Requirements Planning	9, 10
Should we make or buy this component? Who are our good suppliers and how many should we have?	JIT ("just-in-time") and supply-chain management	11, 11 Supplement
Is subcontracting production a good idea? Are we better off keeping people on the payroll during slowdowns?	Intermediate, short-term, and project scheduling	12, 13, 14
Who is responsible for maintenance?	Maintenance	14 Supplement

WHERE ARE THE JOBS IN OM?

How does one get started on a career in operations? The decisions identified in Table 1.2 are made by individuals who work in the disciplines shown in the blue areas of Figure 1.3. Competent business students who know their accounting, statistics, finance, and OM have an opportunity to enter the entry-level positions in all of these areas. As you read the text, look at the disciplines that can assist you in making these decisions. Then take courses in those areas. The more background an OM student has in accounting, statistics, information systems, and mathematics, the more job opportunities that will be available. About 40% of *all* jobs are in OM. The following are just a few of the areas where opportunities exist for OM graduates in the late 1990s:[1]

1. *Technology/methods*: The greatest opportunities today are in the fields that make use of technology and the techniques of continuous improvement. These include computer applications, maintenance, warehousing, order tracking, work flow, and ergonomics.
2. *Facilities/space utilization:* The development of work cells, facility consolidation, layout improvements for storage of raw materials, warehousing, work-in-progress, and finished goods all provide tremendous opportunities.
3. *Strategic issues:* Identifying new opportunities, providing vision, organizational development, measurement and reporting systems, benchmarking, and creating and sustaining peak performance are ranked as major opportunities.
4. *Response time:* Speed and reaction time by an organization and its suppliers, reduction of setup times, and product design times are viewed as critical in today's fast-paced environment.
5. *People/team development:* Throughout the production and distribution system the topics of employee involvement and empowerment, leadership, communication, and team development are all crucial for maximizing productivity opportunities.
6. *Customer service:* As customers demand more customized products, as services become more important, and as technology becomes a larger ingredient in many products, order fulfillment, after-sale service, and equipment uptime all are key for operational success.
7. *Quality:* Product quality and information quality remain crucial to operations success.
8. *Cost reduction:* As always, operations managers must focus on doing more with less through simplification, streamlining, and focusing on resources to get the job done at minimal costs.
9. *Inventory reduction:* Reduction and faster movement of inventory throughout the supply chain, cutting damage and shrinkage, and just-in-time arrival of inventory all help release assets for more productive purposes.
10. *Productivity:* Productivity enhancements are the only way we can improve our standard of living. It is the operations manager's continuing task to see that this is done.

[1]Adapted from Tompkins Associates, Inc., Raleigh, NC, as reported in *OR/MS Today* (December 1995): 17–18.

Operations in the Service Sector

The service sector is defined differently by different people. Even the U.S. government has trouble generating a consistent definition for services. Because definitions vary, much of the data and statistics generated about the service sector are inconsistent. However, we will define **services** as including repair and maintenance, government, food and lodging, transportation, insurance, trade, financial, real estate, education, legal, medical, entertainment, and other professional occupations.[2]

services

Differences Between Goods and Services

Let's examine some of the differences between goods and services. First, a service is *usually intangible* (for example, your purchase of a ride in an empty airline seat between two cities) as opposed to a tangible good.

Second, services are often *produced and consumed simultaneously;* there is no stored inventory. For instance, the beauty salon produces a haircut that is consumed simultaneously, or the doctor produces an operation that is "consumed" as it is produced. We have not yet figured out how to inventory haircuts or appendectomies.

Third, *many services are unique.* Your mix of financial coverage, such as investments and insurance policies, may not be the same as anyone else's, just as the medical procedure or a haircut produced for you is not exactly like anyone else's.

Fourth, a service has *high customer interaction.* Services are often difficult to standardize, automate, and be as efficient as we would like because customer interaction demands uniqueness. This uniqueness in many cases is what the customer is paying for; therefore, the operations manager must ensure that the product is designed so that it can be delivered in the required unique manner.

Fifth, services have *inconsistent product definition.* Product definition may be rigorous, as in the case of an insurance policy, or casual, as in the case of a haircut. Moreover, the haircut definition not only varies with each customer, but often with each haircut, even for the same customer. Similarly, the insurance policy, although rigorously defined, varies with regard to customer, type of coverage, and amount of coverage.

In spite of these differences between goods and services, there is still an operations function to be performed. This occurs when the insurance company defines the product (say an insurance policy), processes the purchase transaction, issues premium statements, and processes those premiums. The same would be the case for a stock or bank transaction where the "back room," which is the operations center, handles the transaction. So, although service products are often unique, the operations function continues to perform a transformation function (as was shown earlier in the organization charts in Figure 1.3).

Table 1.3 also indicates some of the differences that exist between goods and services. The distinction between goods and services is, however, seldom clear cut. In reality, almost all services are a mixture of service and a tangible product; similarly, the sale of many goods includes or requires a service. For instance, many products have the service components of financing and transportation. Many also require after-sale training and maintenance. When a tangible product is *not* included in the service, we may call the industry a **pure service** industry. While there are not very many pure service industries, one example is counseling.

pure service

[2]This definition is similar to the categories used by the U.S. Bureau of Labor Statistics.

TABLE 1.3 DIFFERENCES BETWEEN GOODS AND SERVICES

ATTRIBUTES OF GOODS	ATTRIBUTES OF SERVICES
Tangible product	Intangible product
Product can be resold	Difficult to resell service
Product can be inventoried	Many services cannot be inventoried
Production is usually separate from consumption	Production and consumption may take place simultaneously
Some aspects of quality are measurable	Many aspects of quality are difficult to measure
Selling is distinct from production	Selling is often a part of the service
Customer interaction is often low	Customer interaction is often high
Product is transportable	Provider, not product, is often transportable
Site of facility is important for cost	Site of facility is important for customer contact
Often easy to automate	Often difficult to automate
Revenue is generated primarily from the product	Revenue is often generated from a bundle of services

Figure 1.4 shows the range of *services* in a product. The range is extensive and shows the pervasiveness of service activities.

FIGURE 1.4

MOST GOODS CONTAIN A SERVICE AND MOST SERVICES CONTAIN A GOOD

SOURCE: For similar presentations see Earl W. Sasser, R. P. Olsen, and D. Daryl Wyckoff, *Management of Service Operations* (New York: Allyn and Bacon), p. 11; and G. Lynn Shostack, "Breaking Free from Product Marketing," *Journal of Marketing* (April 1987).

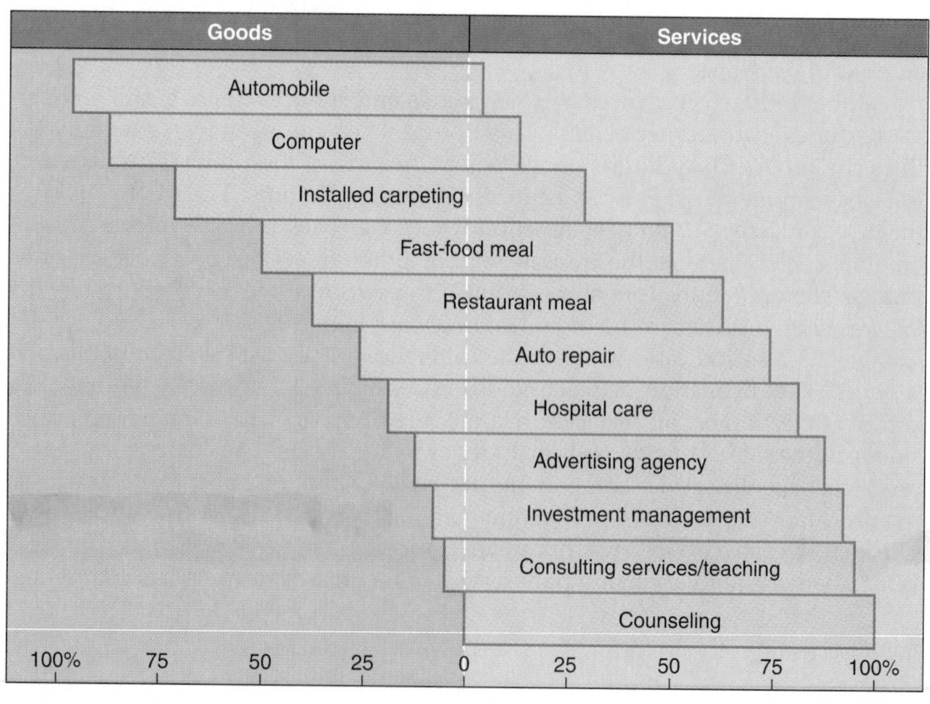

Growth of Services

Services now constitute the largest economic sector in advanced societies. Service-sector employment in the United States is shown in Figure 1.5(a). Historically, until about 1900 most Americans were employed in agriculture. Increased agricultural productivity allowed people to leave the farm and seek employment in the city. The manufacturing and service sectors began to grow, with services becoming the dominant employer in the early 1920s and manufacturing employment peaking at about 32% in 1950. Similarly, productivity increases in manufacturing have allowed more of our economic resources to be devoted to services, as Figures 1.5(a) and (b) show. Consequently, much of the world can therefore now enjoy the pleasure of education, health services, entertainment, and the myriad of other things we call services. Figure 1.5(c) indicates the explosive growth of U.S. export of services, and Figure 1.5(d) shows the growth of employment in U.S. services. Examples of firms and percentage of employment in the **service sector** are shown in Table 1.4.

service sector

Service Pay

While there is a common perception that service industries are low paying, in fact, many service jobs pay very well. Operations managers in the maintenance facility of an airline are very well paid, as are the operations managers who supervise computer services to the financial community. About 42% of all service workers have wages that exceed the national average. However, the average is driven

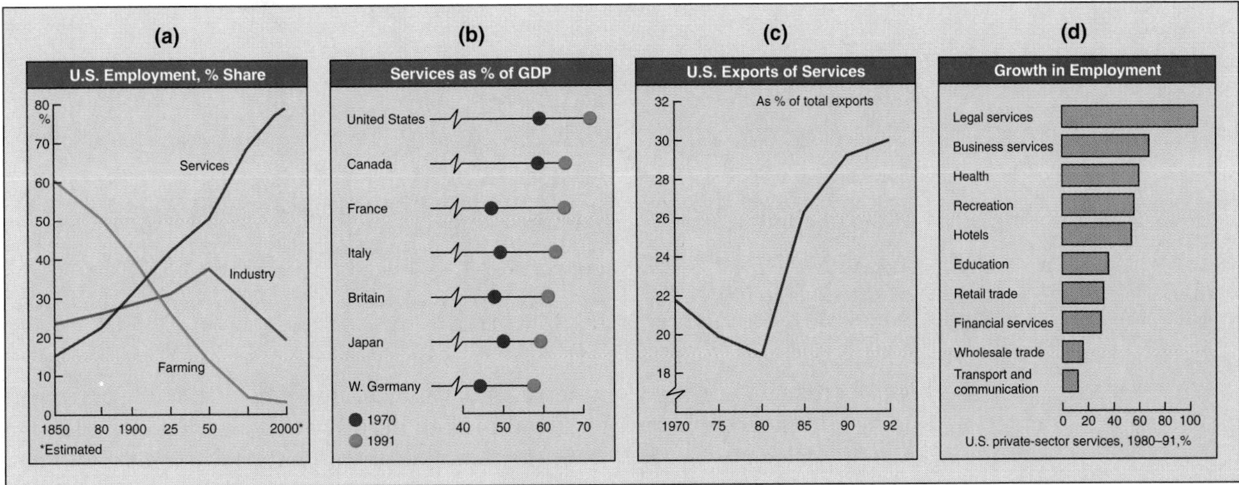

FIGURE 1.5 DEVELOPMENT OF THE SERVICE ECONOMY

SOURCE: Adapted from U.S. Labor Statistics Bureau; OECD; National statistics; U.S. Commerce Department; "The Final Frontier," *The Economist*, February 20, 1993, p. 63.

TABLE 1.4 EXAMPLES OF ORGANIZATIONS IN EACH SECTOR

SECTOR	EXAMPLE	PERCENTAGE OF JOBS
Service Sector		
Government	U.S., State of Alabama, Cook County	16.8%
Education	New York City PS 108, Notre Dame University	1.4%
Food, Lodging	McDonald's, Luby's Cafeteria, Motel 6, Hilton Hotels	7.2%
Entertainment	Walt Disney, Paramount Pictures	1.0%
Trade (retail, wholesale)	Walgreen's, Wal-Mart, Nordstrom's	21.9%
Transportation, Utilities	Pacific Gas & Electric, American Airlines, Santa Fe R.R., Roadway Express	5.0%
Finance, Insurance, Real Estate	Citicorp, American Express, Prudential, Aetna, Trammell Crow	5.7%
Legal	Hunton & Williams, Local law offices	0.6%
Medical	Mayo Clinic, Humana Hospitals	7.7%
Social Services and Other	San Diego Zoo, Smithsonian Museum	2.5%
Repair and Maintenance	IBM maintenance, Xerox maintenance, Pitney-Bowes	0.6%
Business Services	Snelling and Snelling, Waste Management, Inc.	6.1%
Manufacturing Sector	General Electric, Ford, U.S. Steel, Intel	16.2%
Construction Sector	Bechtel, McDermott	4.0%
Mining Sector	Homestake Mining	0.6%
Agriculture	King Ranch	2.7%

SOURCE: *Statistical Abstract of the United States*, 1994, Table 642.

down because 14 of the Commerce Department categories of the 33 service industries do indeed pay below the all-private industry average. Retail trade, one of these, which pays only 61% of the national private industry average, is large. But even considering the retail sector, the average wage of all service workers in 1993 was about 96% of the average of all private industries.[3]

[3]Stein, Herbert, and Murray Foss. *The New Illustrated Guide to the American Economy* (Washington, DC: The AIE Press, 1995), p. 30.

THE PRODUCTIVITY CHALLENGE

The creation of goods and services requires the transformation of resources into goods and services. **Productivity** implies the enhancement of this transformation. Enhancement means favorable comparison of the quantity of resources employed (inputs) to the quantity of goods and services produced (outputs) (see Figure 1.6). A reduction in inputs while output remains constant, or an increase in output while inputs remain constant, represents an improvement in productivity. In an economic sense, inputs are land, labor, capital, and management, which are combined into a production system. Management creates this production system, which provides the conversion of inputs to outputs. Outputs are goods and services, including such diverse items as guns, butter, education, improved judicial systems, and ski resorts.

productivity

Measurement of productivity is an excellent way to evaluate a country's ability to provide an improving standard of living for its people. *Only through increases in productivity can the standard of living improve.* Moreover, only through increases in productivity can labor, capital, and management receive additional payments. If returns to labor, capital, or management are increased without increased productivity, prices rise. On the other hand, downward pressure is placed on prices as productivity increases, because more is being produced with the same resources.

Since 1889 the United States has been able to increase productivity at an average rate of nearly 2.5% per year. Such growth doubles our wealth every 30 years. However, we have been unable in recent years to sustain that productivity increase. If U.S. productivity continues to lag, inferiority in the quality of life will soon be upon us. In this text we examine how to improve productivity by building and managing the operations function.

Productivity Measurement

The measurement of productivity is, in some cases, quite direct. Such is the case when productivity can be measured as labor-hours per ton of a specific type of

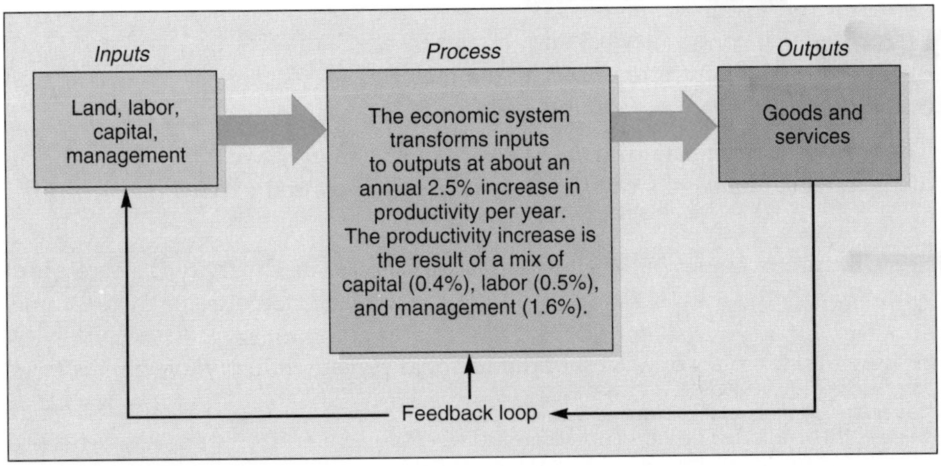

FIGURE 1.6

THE ECONOMIC SYSTEM TRANSFORMS INPUTS TO OUTPUTS

Inputs
Land, labor, capital, management
Process
The economic system transforms inputs to outputs at about an annual 2.5% increase in productivity per year. The productivity increase is the result of a mix of capital (0.4%), labor (0.5%), and management (1.6%).
Outputs
Goods and services
Feedback loop

An effective feedback loop evaluates process performance against a plan. In this case, it also evaluates customer satisfaction and sends signals to those controlling the inputs and process.

steel or as the energy necessary to generate a kilowatt of electricity.[4] An example of this is

$$\text{Productivity} = \frac{\text{Units produced}}{\text{Input used}}$$

$$= \frac{\text{Units produced}}{\text{Labor-hours used}} = \frac{1000}{250} = 4$$

In many instances, however, substantial measurement problems do exist.[5] Some of these measurement problems are:

1. *Quality* may change while the quantity of inputs and outputs remains constant. Compare a radio of this decade with one of the 1940s. Both are radios, but few people would deny that the quality has improved. The unit of measure—a radio—is the same, but the quality has changed.
2. *External elements*[6] may cause an increase or decrease in productivity for which the system under study may not be directly responsible. A more reliable electric power service may greatly improve production, thereby improving the firm's productivity because of this support system rather than because of managerial decisions made within the firm.
3. *Precise units of measures* may be lacking. Not all automobiles require the same inputs—some cars are subcompacts; others are 911 Turbo Porsches.

Productivity measurement is particularly difficult in the service sector where the end product can be hard to define. For example, the quality of your haircut, the outcome of a court case, or service at a retail store are all ignored in the economic data. In some cases adjustments are made for the quality of the product sold, but *not* the quality of the sales performance or a broader product selection, each of which allow for a more intelligent purchase by the consumer. Note the quality measurement problems in a law office, where each case is different, altering the accuracy of the measure "cases per labor-hour" or "cases per employee."

Productivity Variables

productivity variables

The 2.5% average annual productivity increase in the United States is dependent upon three **productivity variables:**

1. *Labor,* which contributes 0.5% to the increase.
2. *Capital,* which contributes 0.4% to the increase.
3. *Management,* which contributes 1.6%.

These three factors are critical to improved productivity. They represent the broad areas in which managers can take action to improve productivity.

LABOR. Improvement in the contribution of labor to productivity is the result of a healthier, better educated, and better nourished labor force. Some increase may

---

[4]The quality and time period are assumed to remain constant.

[5]See John W. Henrici, "How Deadly Is the Productivity Disease?" *Harvard Business Review* **59** (November-December 1981): 123–129, for discussion of measurement problems at the national level; and David J. Sumanth, *Productivity Engineering and Management* (New York: McGraw-Hill, 1984), for an excellent discussion at the company level.

[6]These are exogenous variables, that is, variables outside of the system under study that influence it.

also be attributed to a shorter workweek. Historically, about 20% of the annual improvement in productivity is attributed to improvement in the quality of labor. Three key variables for improved labor productivity are:

1. Basic education appropriate for an effective labor force.
2. Diet of the labor force.
3. Social overhead that makes labor available, such as transportation and sanitation.

In developed nations, a fourth challenge to management is *maintaining and enhancing the skills of labor* in the midst of rapidly expanding technology and knowledge. Recent data suggest that the average American 17-year-old knows half of the mathematics that the average Japanese at the same age knows. More generally, elementary and secondary students in the United States fall near the bottom of any comparative international test,[7] and about half cannot answer the questions in Figure 1.7.

NOTE
Many American high schools have nearly a 50% drop-out rate in spite of having a wide variety of programs available.

Overcoming shortcomings in the quality of labor while other countries have a better labor force is a major challenge. Perhaps improvements can be found not only through increasing competence of labor, but also via a fifth item, *better utilized labor with a stronger commitment.* Management-by-objectives, motivation, flex time, and the human resource strategies discussed in Chapter 7, as well as improved education, may be among the many techniques that will contribute to increased labor productivity. Improvements in labor productivity are possible; however, they can be expected to be increasingly difficult and expensive.

NOTE
Between 20% and 30% of United States workers lack the basic skills they need for their current jobs. (*Source:* Nan Stone, *Harvard Business Review*)

CAPITAL. Human beings are tool-using animals. Capital investment provides those tools. Capital investment has increased in the United States every year except during a few very severe recession periods. Annual capital investment in the United States has increased until recent years at the rate of 1.5% of the base investment. This means that the amount of capital invested after allowances for depreciation has grown by 1.5% per year.

Inflation and taxes increase the cost of capital, making capital investment increasingly expensive. When the capital invested per employee drops, as it has in

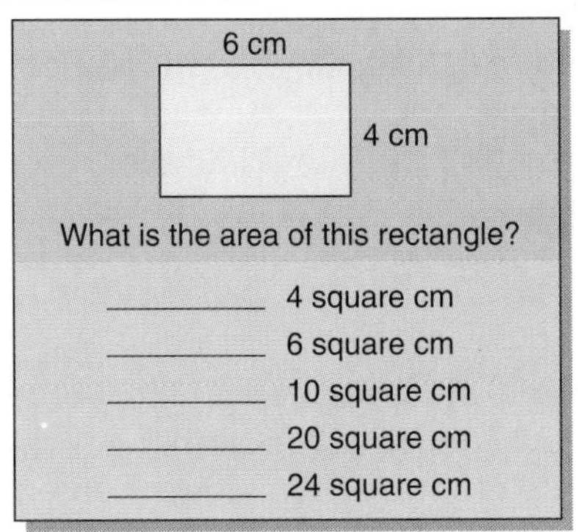

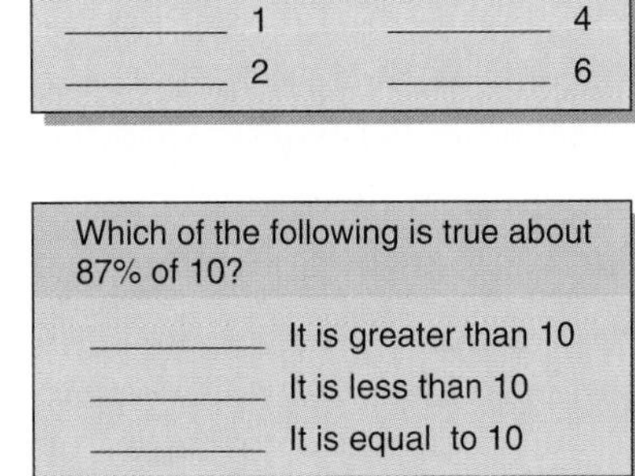

FIGURE 1.7

ABOUT HALF (48.9%) OF THE 17-YEAR-OLDS IN THE UNITED STATES CANNOT CORRECTLY ANSWER QUESTIONS OF THIS TYPE

SOURCE: Education Testing Service.

[7]Michael L. Dertouzos, Richard K. Lester, and Robert M. Solow, *Made in America: Regaining the Productive Edge* (Cambridge, MA: MIT Commission on Industrial Productivity, MIT Press, 1989); also see "U.S. Science Students Near Root of Class," *Science* **239** (March 1988): 1237; also see Richard M. Wolf, "The NAEP and International Comparisons," *Phi Delta Kappan* (April 1988): 580–581.

NOTE
A National Academy of Sciences panel of academics and business executives called for lightening the taxation of corporate profits and broadening tax breaks for capital gains to reduce the cost of capital, spur corporate investment and improve American living standards. *(Source:* David Wessel, *Wall Street Journal)*

recent years, we can expect a drop in productivity. Using labor rather than capital may reduce unemployment in the short run, but it also makes economies less productive and therefore lowers wages in the long run. The trade-off between capital and labor is continually in flux. Additionally, the higher the interest rate, the more projects requiring capital are "squeezed out," that is, are not pursued because the potential return on investment for a given risk has been reduced. Managers adjust their investment plans to changes in capital cost.

MANAGEMENT. Management is a factor of production and an economic resource. Management is responsible for ensuring that labor and capital are effectively used to increase productivity. Management accounts for almost two-thirds of the annual 2.5% increase in productivity (about 1.6% of 2.5% annual increase). It includes improvements made through the application of technology and the utilization of knowledge.

knowledge society

This application of technology and utilization of new knowledge requires training and education. Education will remain an important high-cost item in postindustrial societies. Most Western societies are knowledge societies. A **knowledge society** is one in which much of the labor force has migrated from manual work to work based on knowledge. The effective operations manager will *ensure that available knowledge and technology are utilized.*

The *more effective utilization of capital,* as opposed to additional capital, is also important. The manager, as a productivity catalyst, is charged with the task of making improvements in capital productivity within existing constraints. Productivity gains in knowledge societies require managers who are comfortable with technology and management science.

Operations managers must also successfully address the ever changing trade-off between labor and capital. Recent data suggest that an increase in education (about one year of education) produces an 11% increase in productivity, while a 10% capital investment yields a 3.4% increase in manufacturing and a 3.9% increase in nonmanufacturing industries.[8]

The productivity challenge is difficult. A country cannot be a world-class competitor with second-class inputs. Poorly educated labor inputs, inadequate capital inputs, and dated technology are second-class inputs. High productivity and high-quality outputs require high-quality inputs.

Although U.S. productivity rates are now lower than many other industrialized countries (see Figure 1.8a), the United States still leads in gross domestic product (GDP) per capita (see Figure 1.8b). The American worker remains the most productive in the world, producing on average $49,600 in goods and services—$5,000 to $10,000 more per worker than their Japanese and German counterparts.

Productivity and the Service Sector

The service sector provides a challenge to the accurate measurement of productivity and productivity improvement. The traditional analytical framework of economic theory is based primarily on goods-producing activities. Consequently, most published economic data relate to goods production. But the data do indicate that in recent years, as our contemporary service economy has increased in

[8]"More Education Increases Productivity," *IIE Solutions* (October 1995).

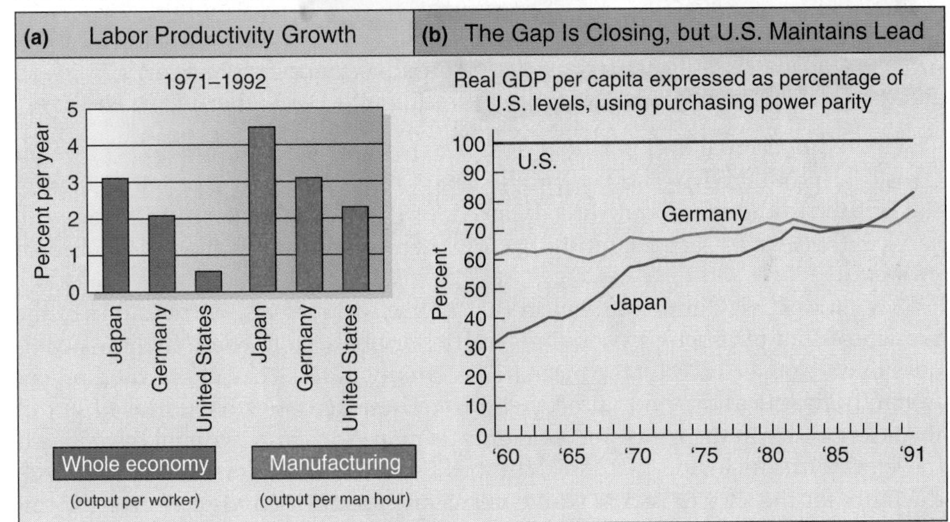

FIGURE 1.8

A COMPARISON OF PRODUCTIVITY IN THE UNITED STATES, JAPAN, AND GERMANY

SOURCES: (a) Adapted from *The Economist*, February 13, 1993, p. 67; (b) Bureau of Labor Statistics, based on OECD price calculation, as reported in *Forbes*, September 14, 1992, 43.

size, we have had slower growth in productivity. As Figure 1.8(a) shows, the recent overall U.S. productivity rate is well below the historical 2.5% and below current productivity levels in both Japan and Germany. In Figure 1.8(a), where manufacturing productivity is shown separately, productivity is over 2%, but with services included, productivity drops to less than 1%.

The productivity issue is evident in Table 1.5 where the service sector absorbs 76% of employment but provides only 64% of the GDP. On the other hand, manufacturing generates 25% of the GDP with only 16% of employment. While we must conclude that the service sector is less efficient measured in this way, we should not be surprised.

Productivity of the service sector has proven difficult to improve because service sector work is

1. Typically labor-intensive (for example, counseling, teaching).
2. Frequently individually processed (for example, investment counseling).

TABLE 1.5 **PERCENTAGE OF GROSS DOMESTIC PRODUCT (GDP) AND EMPLOYMENT**

	% OF GDP[a]	% OF EMPLOYEES[b]
Services	64	76
Manufacturing	25	16
Agriculture	3	3
Construction/Mining	8	5
	100	100

SOURCES: (a) *Statistical Abstract of the United States*, 1991.
(b) *Statistical Abstract of the United States*, 1994.

3. Often an intellectual task performed by professionals (for example, medical diagnosis).
4. Often difficult to mechanize and automate (for example, a haircut).
5. Often difficult to evaluate for quality (for example, performance of a law firm).

NOTE
Playing a Mozart string quartet still takes four musicians the same length of time.

The more intellectual and personal the task, the more difficult it is to achieve increases in productivity. The low productivity of the service sector is reflected in the fact that although about three-quarters of the U.S. labor force is engaged in service, the service sector contributes less than two-thirds of the gross national product.

Low productivity improvement in the service sector is also attributable to the growth of low productivity activities in the service sector. These include activities not previously a part of the measured economy, such as child care, food preparation, house cleaning, and laundry service. These activities have moved out of the home and into the measured economy as more and more women have joined the workforce. Inclusion of these activities has probably resulted in lower productivity for the service sector, while, in fact, actual productivity has probably increased as these activities are now more efficiently produced than previously.[9]

All industrialized countries, however, have these same problems and the United States remains the world leader in overall productivity *and* service productivity. Retailing is twice as productive in the United States as in Japan, where laws protect shopkeepers from discount chains. The U.S. telephone industry is at least twice as productive as Germany's government monopoly. And the U.S. banking system is 33% more efficient than Germany's banking oligopolies. But, because productivity is central to the operations manager's job and because the service sector is so large, we take special note in this text of how to improve productivity in the service sector.

SUMMARY

Operations, marketing, and finance/accounting are the three functions basic to all organizations. The operations function creates goods and services. Much of the progress of operations management has been made in the twentieth century, but since the beginning of time, humankind has been attempting to improve its material well-being.

As societies have become increasingly affluent, more of their resources are devoted to services. In the United States, nearly three-quarters of the workforce is employed in the service sector. And while productivity improvements are difficult to achieve in the service sector, operations management is the primary vehicle for making that improvement.

KEY TERMS

Production *(p. 3)*
Operations management (OM) *(p. 3)*
Industrial engineering *(p. 4)*
Management science *(p. 4)*
Physical sciences *(p. 4)*
Information sciences *(p. 4)*
Management process *(p. 7)*
Services *(p. 11)*
Pure service *(p. 11)*
Service sector *(p. 13)*
Productivity *(p. 15)*
Productivity variables *(p. 16)*
Knowledge society *(p. 18)*

[9]Allen Sinai and Zaharo Sofianou. "The Service Economy—Productivity Growth Issues" (CSI Washington, DC) *The Service Economy* (January 1992): 11–16.

SOLVED PROBLEM 1.1

Productivity can be measured in a variety of ways, such as labor, capital, energy, material usage, and so on. At Modern Lumber, Inc., Art Binley, president and producer of apple crates sold to growers, has been able, with his current equipment, to produce 240 crates per 100 logs. He currently purchases 100 logs per day, and each log requires three labor-hours to process. He believes that he can hire a professional buyer who can buy a better-quality log at the same cost. If this is the case, he can increase his production to 260 crates per 100 logs. His labor-hours will increase by eight hours per day.

What will be the impact on productivity (measured in crates per labor-hour) if the buyer is hired?

SOLUTION

$$\text{Current labor productivity} = \frac{240 \text{ crates}}{100 \text{ logs} \times 3 \text{ hours}} = \frac{240}{300} = .8 \text{ crates per labor-hour}$$

$$\text{Labor productivity with buyer} = \frac{260 \text{ crates}}{(100 \text{ logs} \times 3 \text{ hours}) + 8 \text{ hours}} = \frac{260}{308} = .844 \text{ crates per labor-hour}$$

Using current productivity (.80) as a base, the increase will be 5.5%: .844/.8 = 1.055 or a 5.5% increase.

DISCUSSION QUESTIONS

1. Define operations management in your own words. Will your definition accommodate both manufacturing and service operations?
2. Consider the potential contribution of information sciences to OM. Why is the management of information of such great importance in the management of "production"?
3. Figure 1.3 outlines the marketing, operations, and finance/accounting function of three organizations. Prepare a chart similar to Figure 1.3 outlining the same functions for
   - **a.** a large metropolitan newspaper
   - **b.** a local drugstore
   - **c.** a college library
   - **d.** a local service organization (such as Boy Scouts, Girl Scouts, Rotary International, Lions, Grange)
   - **e.** a doctor's or dentist's office
   - **f.** a jewelry factory
4. Do the preceding assignment for some other enterprise of your choosing, perhaps an organization where you have worked.
5. What is the difference between production and operations?
6. Identify three disciplines that will contribute in a major way to the future development of OM.
7. Can you identify the operation function(s) of a past or current employer? Draw an organization chart for the operations function of that firm.
8. What are the three classic functions of a firm?
9. What departments might you find in the OM function of a home appliance manufacturer?
10. Describe the registration system at your university. What are its inputs, transformations, and outputs?
11. What are the similarities and differences in the transformation process between a fast-food restaurant and a computer manufacturer?
12. Identify the transformation that takes place in your automobile repair garage.

SELF-TEST ■ CHAPTER 1

- *Before taking the self-test* refer back to the learning objectives listed at the beginning of the chapter and the key terms listed at the end of the chapter.
- Use the key at the back of the text to *correct* your answers.
- *Restudy* pages that correspond to any questions you answered incorrectly or material you feel uncertain about.

1. The "father" of scientific management is
   a. Henry Ford
   b. Eli Whitney
   c. Frederick W. Taylor
   d. Nelson Piquet

2. The three major business functions necessary to all organizations are
   a. marketing, finance, operations
   b. accounting, personnel, operations
   c. marketing, accounting, personnel
   d. marketing, accounting, operations

3. OM jobs constitute what percentage of all jobs?
   a. 20% c. 18%
   b. 35% d. 40%

4. The systematic processing of data to yield information is a part of
   a. scientific management
   b. information sciences
   c. industrial engineering
   d. management science

5. Productivity increases when
   a. inputs increase while outputs remain the same
   b. inputs decrease while outputs remain the same
   c. outputs decrease while inputs remain the same
   d. inputs and outputs increase proportionately

6. The capital investment each year in the United States usually
   a. decreases
   b. remains constant
   c. increases
   d. decreases unless favorably taxed
   e. is very cyclical

7. Productivity increases each year in the United States are the result of three factors:
   a. labor, capital, management
   b. engineering, labor, capital
   c. engineering, capital, quality control
   d. engineering, labor, data processing
   e. engineering, capital, data processing

8. Which appears to provide the best opportunity for increases in productivity?
   a. labor
   b. capital
   c. management
   d. none of the above

9. When returns to labor, capital, or management are increased without increased productivity, prices
   a. rise
   b. fall
   c. stay the same
   d. unable to determine

10. Problems in the measurement of productivity include
    a. the unknown effect of external elements
    b. the absence of precise units of measure
    c. the effects of quality over time
    d. all of the above
    e. none of the above

11. The person who introduced standardized, interchangeable parts was
    a. Eli Whitney
    b. Henry Ford
    c. Adam Smith
    d. W. Edwards Deming
    e. Frederick W. Taylor

12. Organizations that produce something other than physical products are called
    a. transformation organizations
    b. data transfer groups
    c. service organizations
    d. cultural goods transformers
    e. all of the above

13. The person who developed plantwide quality control systems was
    a. Eli Whitney
    b. Henry Ford
    c. Adam Smith
    d. W. Edwards Deming
    e. Frederick W. Taylor

14. The service sector constitutes what percentage of employment in the United States?
    a. 6.6 c. 16.2
    b. 2.7 d. 76.3

15. Production is ____________________.

16. The three fundamental functions of any business are __________, __________, __________.

17. Operations management directs and controls ____________________.

OPERATIONS IN PRACTICE EXERCISES

1. As the administrative manager in a law office you have been asked to develop a system for evaluating productivity of the 15 lawyers in the office. What difficulties are you going to have in doing this and how are you going to overcome them?
2. As Figure 1.7 and the discussion in this chapter suggest, the United States educational system is far from the best in the world. Other nations, such as Japan and Israel, excel in academic education, and Germany is the leader in technical training through apprenticeship programs. What are the strengths and weaknesses of the U.S. educational system? What features would we want to emulate from Japan, Germany, or other nations? What is the role of business and the production/operations manager when the education system fails to provide world-class inputs, but consumers expect world-class outputs?

PROBLEMS

- **1.1.** Art and Sandy Binley make apple crates for resale to local growers. They and their three employees invest 50 hours per day making 150 crates.
  - **a.** What is their productivity?
  - **b.** They have discussed reassigning work so the flow through the shop is smoother. If they are correct and they can do the necessary training, they think they can increase crate production to 155 per day. What is their new productivity?
  - **c.** What is their increase in productivity?
- **1.2.** Joanna produces Christmas tree ornaments for resale at local craft fairs and Christmas bazaars. She is currently working a total of 15 hours per day to produce 300 ornaments.
  - **a.** What is Joanna's productivity?
  - **b.** Joanna thinks that by redesigning the ornaments and switching from use of a contact cement to a hot-glue gun she can increase her total production to 400 ornaments per day. What is her new productivity?
  - **c.** What is the increase in productivity?
- **1.3.** Carl Sawyer makes billiard balls in his Dallas plant. With the recent increase in taxes, his costs have gone up and he has a new-found interest in efficiency. Carl is interested in determining the productivity of his organization. He has last year's records and good current data. He would like to know if his organization is maintaining the national average of 2.5% annual increase in productivity. He has the following data:

	LAST YEAR	NOW
Production	1,000	1,000
Labor (hours)	300	275
Resin	50	45
Capital invested ($)	10,000	11,000
Energy (Btu)	3,000	2,850

Show the productivity change for each category and then determine the annual improvement for labor-hours, the typical standard for comparison.

- **1.4.** The approximate figures for service jobs in certain countries are shown in the following table. Overall productivity increases are highest in Japan, Germany, and the United States (in that order). What conclusions might you draw about productivity and the percentage of services in the economy?

PERCENTAGE OF JOBS THAT ARE SERVICE JOBS	
United States	78
Germany	62
Japan	57

1.5. Lackey's, a local bakery, is worried about increased costs—particularly energy. Last year's records can provide a fairly good estimate of the parameters for this year. Charles Lackey, the owner, does not believe things have changed much, but he did invest an additional $3,000 for modifications to the bakery's ovens to make them more energy efficient. The modifications were supposed to make the ovens at least 15% more efficient, but extra labor-hours were required to become familiar with the process changes. Charles has asked you to check the energy savings of the new ovens and also to look over other measures of the bakery's productivity to see if the modifications were beneficial. You have the following data to work with:

	LAST YEAR	NOW
Production (dozen)	1,500	1,500
Labor	350	325
Capital	15,000	18,000
Energy	3,000	2,750

1.6. As a library assignment, find the U.S. productivity rate for the (a) latest quarter and (b) latest year.

1.7. As a library assignment, find the U.S. productivity rate (increase) last year for the (a) national economy, (b) manufacturing sector, and (c) service sector.

CASE STUDY

National Air Express

National Air is a competitive air express firm with offices around the country. Frank Smith, the Chattanooga, Tennessee, station manager, is preparing his quarterly budget report, which will be presented at the Southeast regional meeting next week. He is very concerned about adding capital expense to the operation when business has not increased appreciably. This has been the worst first quarter he can remember: snowstorms, earthquakes, and bitter cold. He has asked Martha Lewis, field services supervisor, to help him review the available data and offer possible solutions.

SERVICE METHODS

National Air offers door-to-door overnight air express delivery within the United States. Smith and Lewis manage a fleet of 24 trucks to handle freight in the Chattanooga area. Routes are assigned by area, usually delineated by zip code boundaries, major streets, or key geographical features, such as the Tennessee River. Pickups are generally handled between 3:00 P.M. and 6:00 P.M., Monday through Friday. Driver routes are a combination of regularly scheduled daily stops and pickups that the customer calls in as needed. These call-in pickups are dispatched by radio to the driver. Commitments are made in advance with regular pickup stops concerning the time the package will be ready, but most call-in customers want as late a pickup as possible, but before they close (usually at 5:00 P.M.).

When the driver arrives at each pickup location, he or she provides supplies as necessary (an envelope or box if requested) and must receive a completed air waybill for each package. Because the industry is extremely competitive, a professional, courteous driver is essential to retaining customers. Therefore, Smith has always been concerned about drivers not rushing a customer to complete his or her package and paperwork.

BUDGET CONSIDERATIONS

Smith and Lewis have found that they have been unable to meet their customers' requests for a scheduled pickup on many occasions in the past quarter. While on average, drivers are not handling any more business, some days they are unable to arrive at each location on time. Smith does not think he can justify increasing costs by $1,200 per week for additional trucks and drivers while productivity (measured in shipments per truck/day) has remained flat. The company has established itself as the low-cost operator in the industry but at the same time has committed itself to offering quality service and value for its customers.

DISCUSSION QUESTIONS

1. Is the productivity measure of shipments per day per truck still useful? Are there alternatives that might be effective?
2. What, if anything, can be done to reduce the daily variability in pickup call-ins? Can the driver be expected to be at several locations at once at 5:00 P.M.?
3. How should we measure package pickup performance? Are standards useful in an environment that is affected by the weather, traffic, and other random variables? Are other companies having similar problems?

SOURCE: Adapted from a case by Phil Pugliese under the supervision of Professor Marilyn M. Helms, University of Tennessee at Chattanooga.

BIBLIOGRAPHY

Babbage, C. *On the Economy of Machinery and Manufacturers,* 4th ed. London: Charles Knight, 1835.

Drucker, P. F. *The Concept of the Corporation.* New York: Mentor, 1946.

Drucker, P. F. "The New Productivity Challenge." *Harvard Business Review,* 69, no. 6 (November/December 1991): 69.

Fabricant, S. *A Primer on Productivity.* New York: Random House, 1969.

Harbison, F., and C. A. Myers. *Management in the Industrial World.* New York: McGraw-Hill, 1959.

Hounshell, D. A. *From the American System to Mass Production 1800–1932: The Development of Manufacturing.* Baltimore: Johns Hopkins University Press, 1985.

Smith, A. *An Inquiry into the Nature and Causes of the Wealth of Nations.* London: Strahan and Cadell, 1776.

Taylor, F. W. *The Principles of Scientific Management.* New York: Harper & Brothers, 1911.

Wrege, C. D. *Frederick W. Taylor, the Father of Scientific Management: Myth and Reality.* Homewood, IL: Business One Irwin, 1991.

Wren, D. A. *The Evolution of Management Thought.* New York: Ronald Press, 1994.

Operations Strategy for Goods and Services

2

CHAPTER OUTLINE

Identifying Missions and Strategies

Mission ■ Strategy

Decisions of OM

Operations Strategy Issues

Research ■ Preconditions ■ Dynamics

Strategy Implementation

Identify Key Tasks ■ Build and Staff the Organization

Summary ■ Key Terms ■ Solved Problem ■ Discussion Questions ■ Operations in Practice Exercise ■ Problems ■ Self-Test Chapter 2 ■ Case Studies: Johannsen Steel Company; Michelin, Inc. ■ Bibliography

LEARNING OBJECTIVES

When you complete this chapter you should be able to:

IDENTIFY OR DEFINE:

Mission
Strategy
Ten decisions of OM

DESCRIBE OR EXPLAIN:

Specific approaches used by OM to achieve strategic concepts

How can we satisfy our customers? This is, perhaps, the most important question that a firm can ask itself and its people. Customer needs and wants run the full gamut, from tangible products (a defect-free, safe tire), to the aesthetic (the color scheme and art work in a doctor's waiting room that put patients at ease), to the psychological (friendly reception from a sales clerk when asked for assistance). A company can satisfy these needs and wants by developing and fulfilling missions and strategies, which can be as diverse as the customers they serve.

For instance, Hunter Fan has established itself as a premier maker of quality ceiling fans that lower heating and cooling costs for its customers. 3M maintains its outstanding performance through innovation. Nucor Steel satisfies customers by being the lowest cost steel producer in the world.

Clearly strategies differ. Each of these strategies was established in the light of the threats and opportunities in the environment, and the strengths and weaknesses of the organization. Ultimately, every strategy is an attempt to answer that all-important question for every firm: "How do we satisfy a customer?"

The U.S. home-appliance market is growing annually at 2% or less, about half of that projected for Europe. Therefore, Whirlpool chairman David Whitwam's strategy is to take Whirlpool global. Whirlpool recently acquired major interest in Ingils Limited of Canada, Vitromatic of Mexico, and a 53% stake in N. V. Philips in the Netherlands. Whirlpool has also moved toward global procurement of 35 strategic materials and components. Appliance giants Maytag, Electrolux, and GE have similarly developed and implemented global strategies to enable them to compete internationally and to be a part of the new European Community.

IDENTIFYING MISSIONS AND STRATEGIES

An effective operations management effort must have a *mission so it knows where it is going* and a *strategy so it knows how to get there.*

Mission

Economic success, indeed survival, is the result of identifying missions to satisfy a customer's needs and wants. We define the organization's **mission** as its purpose—what it will contribute to society. Mission statements provide boundaries and focus for organizations and the concept around which the firm can rally. The mission states the rationale for the organization's existence. Developing a good strategy is difficult, but it is much easier if the mission has been well defined. The mission can also be thought of as the intent of the strategy—what the strategy is to achieve. Figure 2.1 provides three examples of mission statements.

Once an organization's mission has been decided, each functional area within the firm determines its supporting mission. By "functional area" we mean the major disciplines required by the firm, such as marketing, finance/accounting, and production/operations. Missions for each function are developed to support the firm's overall mission. Figure 2.2 provides a hierarchy of sample missions.

Strategy

With the mission established, strategy and its implementation can begin. **Strategy** is an organization's action plan to achieve the mission. Each functional area has a strategy for achieving its mission and for helping the organization reach the overall mission. In the following sections we will describe how strategies are developed and implemented.

Michael Porter has suggested that firms achieve missions in three conceptual ways: (1) differentiation, (2) cost leadership, and (3) quick response.[1] These can

[1]Michael E. Porter, *Competitive Strategy: Techniques for Analyzing Industries & Competitors* (New York: The Free Press, 1980).

FIGURE 2.1

Mission Statements for Three Organizations

SOURCE: Alex Miller and Gregory G. Dess, *Strategic Management* (New York: McGraw Hill, 1996), p. 9; and annual reports.

Circle K

We believe our primary business is not so much retail as it is service oriented.

Certainly, our customers buy merchandise in our stores. But they can buy similar items elsewhere, and perhaps pay lower prices.

But they're willing to buy from Circle K because we give them added value for their money.

That added value is service and convenience.

As a service company, our mission is to:
Satisfy our customers' immediate needs and wants by providing them with a wide variety of goods and services at multiple locations.

American Airlines

We will be the global market leader in air transportation and related information services. That leadership will be attained by:

Setting the industry standard for safety and security.

Providing world-class customer service.

Creating an open and participative work environment that seeks positive changes; rewards innovation; and provides growth, security, and opportunity to all employees.

Providing consistently superior financial returns for shareholders.

American Red Cross

The mission of the American Red Cross is to improve the quality of human life; to enhance self-reliance and concern for others; and to help people avoid, prepare for, and cope with emergencies.

be summarized as saying customers want goods and services that are (1) better, or at least different, (2) cheaper, and (3) faster. Operations managers translate these *strategic concepts* into tangible tasks to be accomplished. Any one or combination of these three strategic concepts can generate a system that has a unique advantage over competitors. Let us now look at each of these approaches.

COMPETING ON DIFFERENTIATION. Texas Instruments (TI) is the leading manufacturer of "commodity" semiconductor chips. But the company wanted to differentiate itself and respond to market demand for *customized* chips. Geographically dispersed factories in the United States, Europe, and Asia were tied together through the creative use of information technology. TI has created a worldwide "virtual factory" that successfully integrates manufacturing across continents. The new virtual factory has slashed the time it takes to fill custom chip orders by 50%.

FIGURE 2.2

SAMPLE MISSIONS FOR A COMPANY, THE OPERATIONS FUNCTION, AND MAJOR DEPARTMENTS IN AN OPERATIONS FUNCTION

Sample Company Mission

To pursue a diversified, growing, and profitable worldwide manufacturing business in electronic components, apparatus, and systems; and to service these products for industry, commerce, agriculture, government, and home.

Sample Operations Management Mission

To produce products consistent with the company's mission as the worldwide low-cost manufacturer.

Sample OM Department Missions

Quality management	To attain the exceptional quality that is consistent with our company mission and marketing objectives by close attention to design, procurement, production, and field service opportunities for enhancing design.
Product design	To lead in research and engineering competencies in all areas of our primary business, designing and producing products and services with outstanding quality and inherent customer value.
Process design	To determine and design or produce the production process and equipment that will be compatible with low-cost product, high quality, and a good quality-of-work life at economical cost.
Layout design	To achieve, through skill, imagination, and resourcefulness in layout and work methods, production effectiveness, and efficiency while supporting a high quality-of-work life.
Location selection	To locate, design, and build efficient and economical facilities that will yield high value to the company, its employees, and the community.
Human resources	To provide a good quality-to-work life, with well-designed, safe, rewarding jobs, stable employment, and equitable pay, in exchange for outstanding individual contribution from employees at all levels.
Supply-chain management	To cooperate with suppliers and subcontractors to develop innovative products and stable, effective, and efficient sources of supply.
Scheduling	To achieve high levels of throughput and timely customer delivery through effective scheduling.
Inventory	To achieve low investment in inventory consistent with high customer service levels and high facility utilization.
Maintenance	To achieve high utilization of facilities and equipment by effective preventive maintenance and prompt repair of facilities and equipment.

COMPETING ON COST LEADERSHIP. Southwest Airlines has been a consistent money-maker while other U.S. airlines have lost billions. Southwest has done this by fulfilling a need for low-cost and short-hop flights. Their operations strategy has included use of secondary airports and terminals, first-come-first-served seating, few fare options, smaller crews flying more hours, snacks-only or no meals, and no downtown ticket offices.

Wal-Mart has also been grabbing market share for 20 years with a *low-cost strategy*. It has driven down store overhead costs, shrinkage, and distribution costs. Its rapid transportation of goods, reduced warehousing costs, and direct shipment from manufacturers has resulted in high inventory turnover and made it a low-cost leader.

NOTE
Free trade may move us to an era where we have a floating factory. A six-person crew takes a factory from port to port where the best market, material, labor, and tax advantages can be obtained.

COMPETING ON QUICK RESPONSE. Pizza Hut serves its lunchtime pizza within 5 minutes or you get it for free. Similarly, Bennigan's will serve any item on the lunch menu in 15 minutes or lunch is free. And while you aren't given a free computer, Intel, the manufacturer of the 386, 486, Pentium, and P6 computer processors competes on speed to market to win orders.

In practice these three concepts of differentiation, cost leadership, and quick response are often translated into the six specific strategies shown in Figure 2.3. Through these six specific strategies a well-directed operations function can increase productivity and generate a competitive advantage. **Competitive advantage** implies the creation of a system that has a unique advantage over competitors. The operations function is most likely to be successful when the operations

competitive advantage

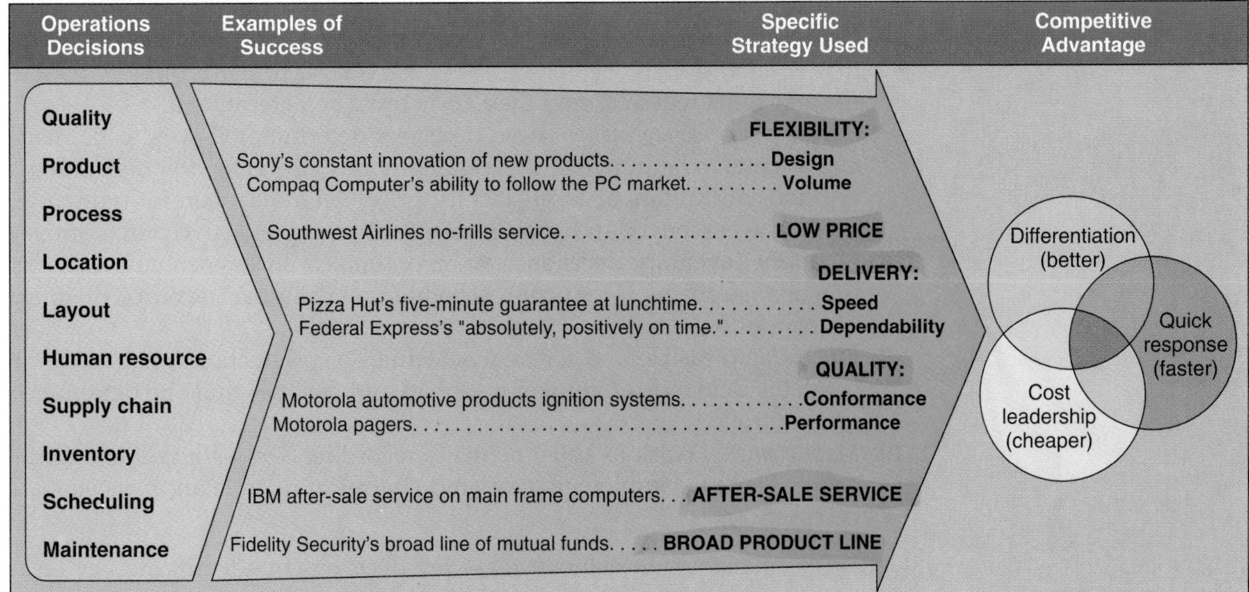

FIGURE 2.3 OPERATIONS MANAGEMENT'S CONTRIBUTION TO STRATEGY

SOURCE: For related presentation, see Jeffrey G. Miller and Aleda Roth, "A Taxonomy of Manufacturing Strategies," *Management Science* 40, no. 3 (March 1994): 285–304.

NOTE
"In the future, there will be just two kinds of firms: those who disrupt their markets and those who don't survive the assault." Professor Richard D'Aveni, author of *Hypercompetition*

strategy is integrated with other functional areas of the firm and supports the overall company objectives.[2] Proper execution of the following ten decisions by operations managers will allow these strategies to be achieved.

DECISIONS OF OM

operations decisions

Differentiation, cost leadership, and quick response are best achieved when the operations manager makes effective decisions based on ten areas of influence. These are collectively known as **operations decisions.** The ten decisions of OM that support missions and implement strategies are:

1. *Quality.* The customer's quality expectations must be determined and policies and procedures established to identify and achieve that quality.
2. *Goods and service design.* Designing goods and services defines much of the transformation process. Costs, quality, and human resource decisions interact strongly with the design. Designs often set the lower limits of cost and the upper limits of quality.
3. *Process and capacity design.* Process options are available for products and services. Process decisions commit management to specific technology, quality, human resource use, and maintenance. These expenses and capital commitments will determine much of the firm's basic cost structure.
4. *Location selection.* Facility location decisions for both manufacturing and service organizations may determine the firm's ultimate success. Errors made at this juncture may overwhelm other efficiencies.
5. *Layout design.* Capacity needs, personnel levels, purchasing decisions, and inventory requirements influence layout. Additionally, the processes and materials must be sensibly located in relation to each other.
6. *People and work systems.* People are an integral and expensive part of the total system design. Therefore, the quality-of-work life provided, the talent and skills required, and their costs must be determined.
7. *Supply-chain management.* These decisions determine what is to be made and what is to be purchased. Consideration is also given to quality, delivery, and innovation, at a satisfactory price. An atmosphere of mutual respect between buyer and supplier is necessary for effective purchasing.
8. *Inventory.* Inventory decisions can be optimized only when customer satisfaction, suppliers, production schedules, and human resource planning are considered.
9. *Scheduling.* Feasible and efficient schedules of production must be developed; the demands on human resources and facilities must be determined and controlled.
10. *Maintenance.* Decisions must be made regarding desired levels of maintenance. Plans for implementation and control of maintenance systems are necessary.

Operations managers implement these ten decisions by identifying key tasks and the staffing to achieve them. But the implementation of the decisions is in-

[2]Michael E. Porter, *Competitive Advantage: Creating and Sustaining Superior Performance* (New York: The Free Press, 1995).

fluenced by a variety of issues including a product's mix of goods and services (see Table 2.1). Few products are either all goods or all services. While the ten decisions remain the same for both goods and services, their importance and method of implementation depend upon this mix of goods and services. Throughout this text we discuss how strategy is accomplished in both goods and services through these ten operations management decisions.

TABLE 2.1 The Ten Operations Management Decisions Used to Meet the Demands of Both Goods and Services

OPERATIONS DECISIONS	GOODS	SERVICES
Quality	Many objective quality standards.	Many subjective quality standards.
Goods and service design	Product is usually tangible.	Product is not tangible. A new range of product attributes—a smile.
Process and capacity design	Customer is not involved in most of the process.	Customer may be directly involved in the process—a haircut. Capacity must match demand to avoid lost sales—customers often avoid waiting.
Location selection	May need to be near raw materials or labor force.	May need to be near customer—car rental.
Layout design	Layout can enhance production efficiency.	Can enhance product as well as production—layout of a fine-dining restaurant.
People and work systems	Workforce focused on technical skills. Labor standards can be consistent. Output-based wage system possible.	Direct workforce usually needs to be able to interact well with customer—bank teller. Labor standards vary depending on customer requirements—legal cases.
Supply-chain management	Supply-chain relationships critical to final product.	Supply-chain relationships important but may not be critical.
Inventory	Raw materials, work-in-process, and finished goods may be inventoried.	Most services cannot be stored so other ways must be found to accommodate changes in demand.
Scheduling	Ability to inventory may allow leveling of output rates.	Customers primarily concerned with meeting the customer's immediate schedule.
Maintenance	Maintenance is often preventive and takes place at the production site.	Maintenance is often "repair" and takes place at the customer's site.

OPERATIONS STRATEGY ISSUES

Once a firm has formed a mission, developing and implementing a specific strategy requires that the operations manager consider a number of issues. We will examine these issues in three ways. First, we look at what *research* tells us about effective operations management strategies. Second, we identify some of the *preconditions* to developing effective OM strategy. Third, we look at the *dynamics* of OM strategy development.

Research

PIMS

Strategic insight has been provided by the findings of the Strategic Planning Institute.[3] Its **PIMS** program (profit impact of market strategy) was established in cooperation with the General Electric Corporation. PIMS has collected nearly 100 data items from about 3,000 cooperating organizations. Using the data collected and high *return on investment* (ROI)[4] as a measure of success, PIMS has been able to identify some characteristics of high ROI firms. Among those characteristics that impact strategic OM decisions are:

1. High product quality (relative to the competition).
2. High capacity utilization.
3. High operating effectiveness (the ratio of expected to actual employee productivity).
4. Low investment intensity (the amount of capital required to produce a dollar of sales).
5. Low direct cost per unit (relative to the competition).

These five PIMS findings are pervasive measures that support a high return on investment and should therefore be considered as an organization develops a strategy. In the analysis of a firm's relative strengths and weaknesses, these characteristics can be measured and evaluated. The specific strategic approaches suggested earlier in Figure 2.2 indicate where an operations manager may want to go, but without achieving the five characteristics of high return on investment firms suggested by the PIMS analysis, that journey may not be successful.

Preconditions

Operations managers need to understand the following preconditions to an effective OM strategy:

1. *Present and changing environment*, that is, the economic and technological conditions in which the company is attempting to execute its strategy.
2. *Competitive demands*, which require that the operations manager identify both the competitors and their own strengths and weaknesses. Competing with a "me too" strategy is usually foolish. Therefore, understanding exactly what competitors are trying to do is a requirement of a successful strategy.
3. *Knowing the company's strategy*, so the operations function can be designed and implemented to support that strategy.

---

[3]R. D. Buzzel and B. T. Gale, *The PIMS Principles* (New York: The Free Press, 1987).

[4]Like other performance measures, *return on investment* (ROI) has limitations, including sensitivity to the business cycle, depreciation policies and schedules, book value (goodwill), and transfer pricing.

4. *Product life cycle,* which dictates the limitations of what the operations strategy can be. The operations manager must identify where each product currently resides in its product life cycle.

Dynamics

Strategies change. They change for two reasons. First, strategy is dynamic because of *changes within the organization.* All areas of the firm are subject to change. Changes may be in a variety of areas including purchasing, finance, technology, and product life. All may make a difference in an organization's strengths and weaknesses and therefore its strategy. Figure 2.4 shows possible change in both overall strategy and OM strategy during the product's life.

Second, strategy is dynamic because of *changes in the environment.* Komatsu, an international manufacturer of large earth-moving equipment, provides an exam-

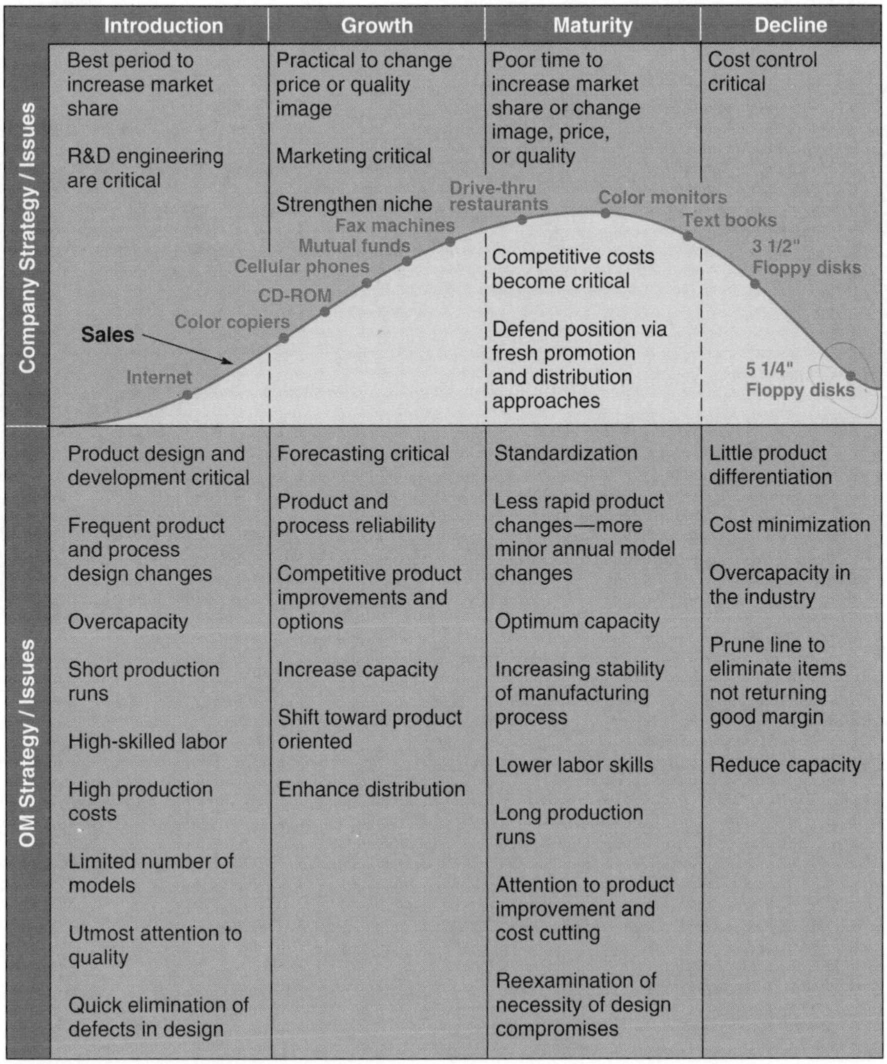

	Introduction	Growth	Maturity	Decline
Company Strategy / Issues	Best period to increase market share R&D engineering are critical	Practical to change price or quality image Marketing critical Strengthen niche	Poor time to increase market share or change image, price, or quality Competitive costs become critical Defend position via fresh promotion and distribution approaches	Cost control critical
OM Strategy / Issues	Product design and development critical Frequent product and process design changes Overcapacity Short production runs High-skilled labor High production costs Limited number of models Utmost attention to quality Quick elimination of defects in design	Forecasting critical Product and process reliability Competitive product improvements and options Increase capacity Shift toward product oriented Enhance distribution	Standardization Less rapid product changes—more minor annual model changes Optimum capacity Increasing stability of manufacturing process Lower labor skills Long production runs Attention to product improvement and cost cutting Reexamination of necessity of design compromises	Little product differentiation Cost minimization Overcapacity in the industry Prune line to eliminate items not returning good margin Reduce capacity

Sales curve: Internet, Color copiers, CD-ROM, Cellular phones, Mutual funds, Fax machines, Drive-thru restaurants, Color monitors, Text books, 3 1/2" Floppy disks, 5 1/4" Floppy disks

FIGURE 2.4

STRATEGY AND ISSUES DURING A PRODUCT'S LIFE

SOURCE: Various; see, for instance, Michael E. Porter, *Techniques for Analyzing Industries and Competitors* (New York, The Free Press, 1980).

The strategy for the retail sector has changed dramatically. Instead of just being resellers of goods (top photo), retailers are now leaders in innovation and management of the distribution chain (bottom photo).

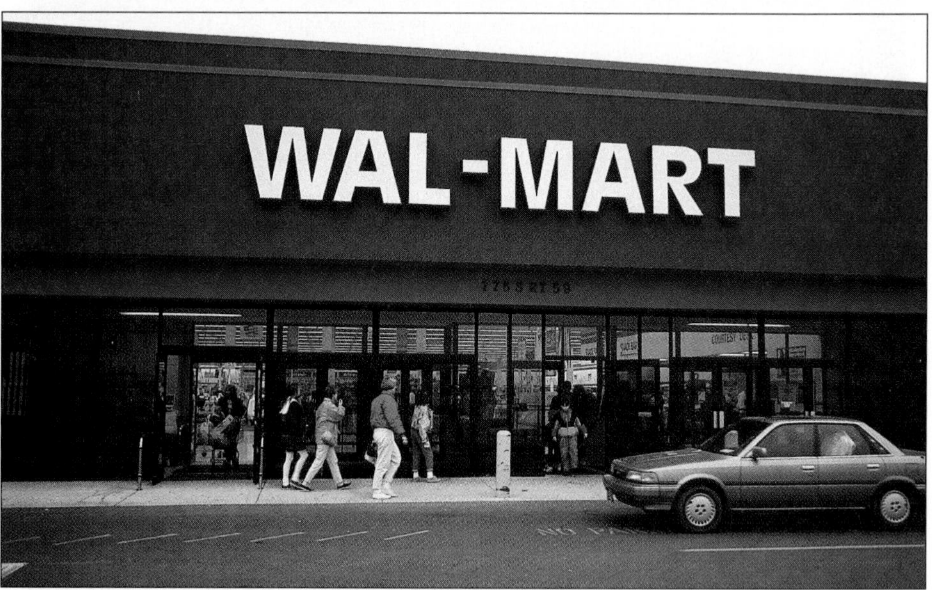

ple of how strategy must change as the environment changes. In its worldwide competition with Caterpillar, Komatsu has had to adopt strategies of quality enhancement and product-line growth. To fight the ever higher value of the yen, Komatsu's strategy moved to cost reduction and finally to off-shore manufacturing to reduce cost further. Its strategies, like many OM strategies, are increasingly global. Microsoft also had to quickly adapt to a changing environment. Microsoft's shift in strategy was caused by the Internet. Microsoft moved to distributing some software products over the Internet to provide both fast and economic delivery of products to its customers.

STRATEGY IMPLEMENTATION

Firms evaluate their strengths and weaknesses as well as the opportunities and threats of the environment. Then they position themselves through their decisions to have a competitive advantage. The idea is to maximize opportunities and minimize threats. The strategy is continually evaluated against the value provided to the customer and competitive realities. Figure 2.5 shows this procedure.

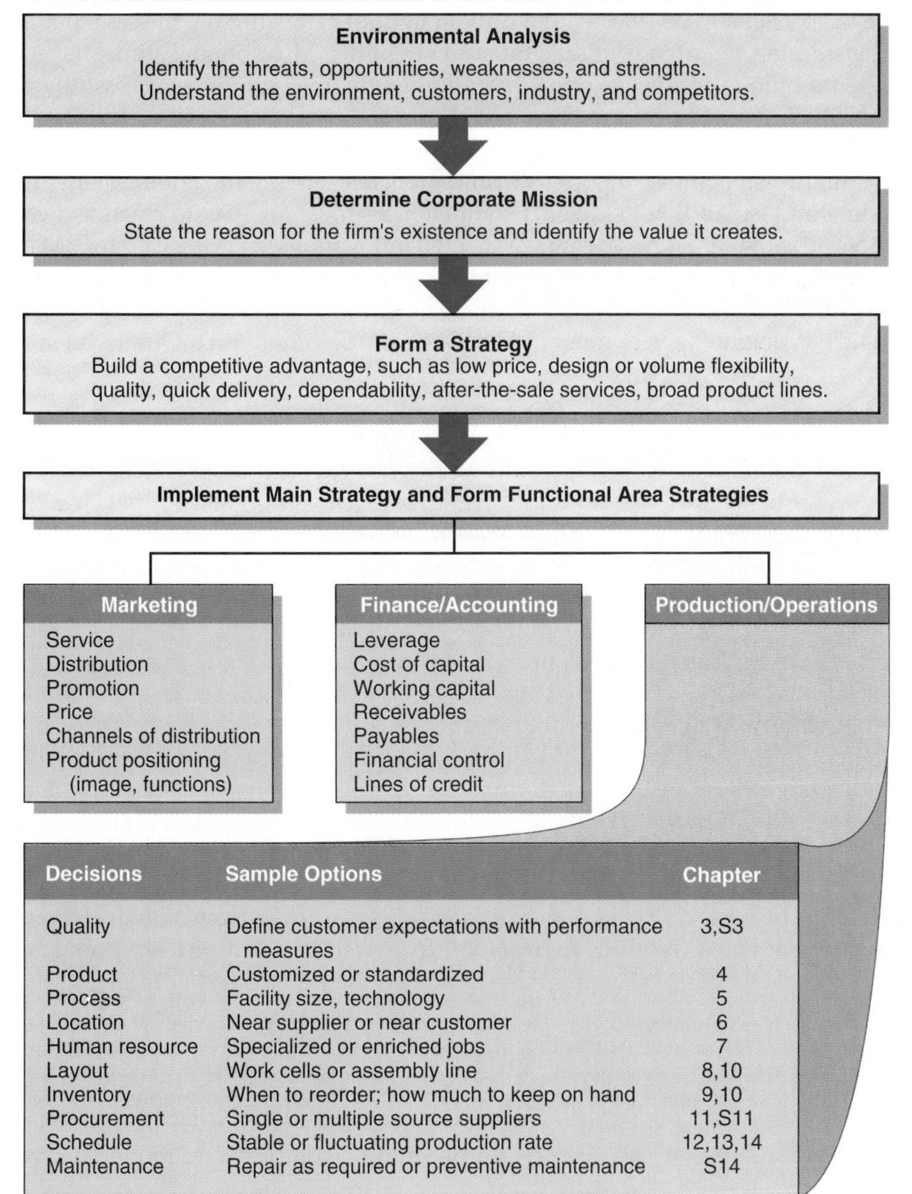

Environmental Analysis
Identify the threats, opportunities, weaknesses, and strengths.
Understand the environment, customers, industry, and competitors.
Determine Corporate Mission
State the reason for the firm's existence and identify the value it creates.
Form a Strategy
Build a competitive advantage, such as low price, design or volume flexibility, quality, quick delivery, dependability, after-the-sale services, broad product lines.
Implement Main Strategy and Form Functional Area Strategies
Marketing
Service
Distribution
Promotion
Price
Channels of distribution
Product positioning (image, functions)
Finance/Accounting
Leverage
Cost of capital
Working capital
Receivables
Payables
Financial control
Lines of credit
Production/Operations
Decisions | Sample Options | Chapter
Quality | Define customer expectations with performance measures | 3,S3
Product | Customized or standardized | 4
Process | Facility size, technology | 5
Location | Near supplier or near customer | 6
Human resource | Specialized or enriched jobs | 7
Layout | Work cells or assembly line | 8,10
Inventory | When to reorder; how much to keep on hand | 9,10
Procurement | Single or multiple source suppliers | 11,S11
Schedule | Stable or fluctuating production rate | 12,13,14
Maintenance | Repair as required or preventive maintenance | S14

FIGURE 2.5

AN OPERATIONS STRATEGY PROCEDURE

NOTE
"The enemy must not know where I intend to give battle. For if he does not know where I intend to give battle, he must prepare in a great many places. And when he prepares in a great many places, those I have to fight in any one place will be few." Sun Tzu

Identify Key Tasks

Since no firm does everything particularly well, a successful strategy implementation requires identifying those tasks that are key to success. The operations manager asks, "What tasks must be done particularly well for a given operations strategy to succeed? Which elements contain the highest likelihood of failure, and which will require additional commitment of managerial, monetary, technological, and human resources? Which activities will help the OM function provide a competitive advantage?" For example, in a manufacturing firm, the most important ingredient in the OM mission may be on-time shipment to customers (scheduling tactics) or product design (heart valves). In an emergency care center, however, the focus may be on having the proper personnel present (human resource strategy) and pharmaceuticals available (inventory tactics).

Key tasks need to be selected not only in light of achieving the mission, but also by considering the organization's internal strengths. Most organizations have developed a unique competence that has allowed them to compete successfully and achieve their present position. Even new firms are usually started because they believe that they can provide a unique capability to the organization. Porter called these unique capabilities, **distinctive competencies.**[5] An organization usually finds building and expanding its distinct competencies to be an asset to creating a competitive advantage. Those advantages can be innovations, as is the case for 3M and Rubbermaid, or low-cost manufacturing capability at Emerson Electric, or quality at Motorola and McDonald's. Distinctive competencies can also exist in other areas such as engine development at Honda or site selection at La Quinta Inns.

distinctive competencies

Build and Staff the Organization

The operations manager's job is a three-step process. Once a strategy has been developed, the second step is to group activities into an organizational structure. The third step is to staff it with personnel who will get the job done. The manager works with subordinate managers to build plans, budgets, and programs that will successfully implement strategies that achieve missions. Firms tackle this organization of the operations function in a variety of ways. The organization charts shown in Chapter 1 (Figure 1.3) indicate the way some firms have organized to perform the required activities.

The organization of the operations function and its relationship to other parts of the organization varies with the OM mission. For example, short-term scheduling in the airline industry is dominated by volatile customer travel patterns. Day-of-week preference, holidays, seasonality, college schedules, and so on, all play a role in changing flight schedules. Consequently, airline scheduling, although an OM activity, can be a part of marketing. Effective scheduling in the trucking industry is reflected in the amount of time trucks travel loaded. However, scheduling of trucks requires information from delivery and pick-up points, drivers, and other parts of the organization. When the organization of the OM function results in effective scheduling in the air passenger and commercial trucking industries, a competitive advantage can exist.

NOTE
"The manufacturing business of tomorrow will not be run by financial executives, marketers, or lawyers inexperienced in manufacturing, as so many United States companies are today." Peter Drucker

The operations manager provides a means of transforming inputs into outputs. The transformations may be in terms of storage, transportation, manufacturing,

[5]Michael E. Porter, "The Competitive Advantage of Nations," *Harvard Business Review* 90, no. 2 (March-April 1990): 73–93.

dissemination of information, and utility of the product or service. *The operations manager's job is to implement an OM strategy that will increase the productivity of the transformation system and provide competitive advantage.*

To assure maximum OM contribution to the organization, the operations department needs to focus on those key tasks that are identified as crucial to its success. The operations manager asks, "What activities must be done particularly well for a given operations strategy to be especially successful? Which elements contain the highest likelihood of failure, and which will require additional commitment of managerial, monetary, technological, and human resources?"

SUMMARY

Though it is a challenging task, operations managers can improve productivity in a competitive, dynamic world economy. They can build and manage OM functions that contribute in a significant way to the competitiveness of an organization. Organizations identify their strengths and weaknesses. They then develop effective missions and strategies that account for these strengths and weaknesses and complement the opportunities and threats of the environment. If this is done well, the organization can have competitive advantage and be a world-class performer. Such performance is the responsibility of the professional manager, and professional managers are among the few in our society who *can* achieve this performance. The challenge is great, and the rewards to the manager and to society substantial.

KEY TERMS

Mission *(p. 28)*
Strategy *(p. 28)*
Competitive advantage *(p. 31)*
Operations decisions *(p. 32)*
PIMS program *(p. 34)*
Distinctive competencies *(p. 38)*

SOLVED PROBLEM 2.1

How does a company in the very mature and established meatpacking industry gain a competitive advantage?[6] Iowa Beef Packers (IBP) was able to win a strong competitive advantage by restructuring traditional beef-processing operations. In beef packing, traditional operations involved raising cattle on scattered farms and ranches, shipping them live to labor-intensive, unionized slaughtering plants, and then transporting whole sides of beef to grocery retailers whose butcher departments cut them into smaller pieces and packaged them for sale to grocery shoppers.

SOLUTION

IBP revamped traditional operations with a radically different strategy. Large automated plants employing nonunion labor were built near economically transportable supplies of cattle. Then the meat was partially butchered at the processing plant into smaller, high-yield cuts (sometimes sealed in plastic ready for purchase), boxed, and shipped to retailers. IBP's inbound cattle transportation ex-

continued on next page

penses, traditionally a major cost item, were cut significantly by avoiding major losses that occurred when live animals were shipped long distances. Additionally, major outbound shipping-cost savings were achieved by not having to ship whole sides of beef with their high waste factor. IBP's strategy was so successful that it was, by 1985, the largest U.S. meatpacker, surpassing the former industry leaders, Swift, Wilson, and Armour.

[6]Adapted from information in Michael E. Porter, *Competitive Advantage* (New York: Free Press, 1985), p. 109; Arthur A. Thompson, Jr., and A. J. Strickland III, *Strategy Formulation and Implementation* (Homewood, IL: BPI/Irwin, 1989).

DISCUSSION QUESTIONS

1. Identify the ten decisions of operations management.
2. Identify the mission and strategy of your automobile repair garage. What are the manifestations of the ten OM decisions at the garage? That is, how is each of the ten decisions accomplished?
3. Answer Question 2 for some other enterprise of your choosing.
4. Based on what you know of the automobile industry, how has the OM strategy of General Motors or Ford changed in the last ten years?
5. As a library assignment, identify the mission of a firm and the strategy that supports that mission.
6. How does an OM strategy change during a product's life cycle?

OPERATIONS IN PRACTICE EXERCISE

IBM at one time had a 70% market share in the computer business. Most of that business was in large computers, known as mainframe computers. Throughout the 1980s and 1990s, technology and markets favored computer networks, then personal computers (PCs), and now computer networks and PCs. IBM has had a difficult time adjusting. IBM's sales, employment, and percentage of installed computers have dropped. From an OM perspective, how might IBM have matched its strengths and weaknesses with the opportunities and threats of the environment?

PROBLEMS

2.1. Find an article in the business literature (such as *Business Week, The Wall Street Journal, Forbes,* or *Fortune*) that (1) documents an organization's current OM strategy and (2) documents a *change* in an organization's OM strategy.

2.2. Identify how changes in the external environment affect the OM strategy for a company. For instance, discuss what impact the following external factors might have on OM strategy:
- **a.** Major increases in oil prices.
- **b.** Water- and air-quality legislation.
- **c.** Fewer young prospective employees entering the labor market in 1985 through 1995.
- **d.** Inflation versus stable prices.
- **e.** Legislation moving health insurance from a benefit to taxable income.

2.3. Identify how changes in the internal environment affect the OM strategy for a company. For instance, discuss what impact the following internal factors might have on OM strategy:
- **a.** Maturing of a product.
- **b.** Technology innovation in the manufacturing process.
- **c.** Changes in product design that move Compaq's disk drives from $3\frac{1}{2}$-inch floppy drives to CD-ROM drives.

2.4. Determine from library research the mission of the following—AT&T, United Way, Microsoft, Southwest Airlines, and another organization of your choosing.

2.5. For the organization chosen in Problem 2.4, determine the strategy of the operations function.

SELF-TEST ■ CHAPTER 2

- *Before taking the self-test*, refer back to the learning objectives listed at the beginning of the chapter and the key terms listed at the end of the chapter.
- Use the key at the back of the text to correct your answers.
- *Restudy* pages that correspond to any questions you answered incorrectly or material you feel uncertain about.

1. Which of the following are not characteristics of high return-on-investment firms?
   - a. high variety of product options
   - b. high product quality relative to the competition
   - c. high capacity utilization
   - d. low investment intensity
   - e. all are characteristic of high ROI firms

2. Among the ways for a firm to use effectively its OM function to yield competitive advantage are
   - a. rapid design changes
   - b. speed of delivery
   - c. maintain a variety of product options
   - d. all of the above
   - e. none of the above

3. A mission statement is beneficial to an organization because it
   - a. is a statement of the organization's economic purpose
   - b. provides a basis for the organization's culture
   - c. identifies important constituencies
   - d. establishes a basis for strategy formulation
   - e. none of the above

4. A mission statement is
   - a. an action plan
   - b. a set of goals
   - c. the decisions that must be made to achieve goals
   - d. the purpose of an organization
   - e. none of the above

5. A strategy is
   - a. a functional area of the firm
   - b. the purpose for which an organization is established
   - c. the goal that is to be achieved
   - d. an action plan to achieve a mission
   - e. none of the above

6. Michael Porter suggested that firms achieve missions by
   - a. the ten decisions around which this text is organized
   - b. through flexibility, quality, delivery, low price, after-sale service, and breadth of product line
   - c. differentiation, cost leadership, and quick response
   - d. all of the above

7. The PIMS program developed a number of criteria that were based on evaluating firms who did well at:
   - a. profitability
   - b. sustained sales growth
   - c. achieving their mission
   - d. high return on investments

8. During the introductory stage of a product's life cycle, the operations manager is likely to find that he or she must focus on issues that deal with
   - a. elimination of defects in design, frequent product changes, product design, and development criteria
   - b. comparative product improvements, increasing capacity, and enhanced distribution
   - c. standardization determining optimum capacity and longer production runs
   - d. reduced product differentiation, cost minimization, and over capacity in the industry

9. During the growth phase of a product's life cycle, the operations manager is likely to have issues that focus on:
   - a. elimination of defects in design, frequent product changes, product design, and development criteria
   - b. comparative product improvements, increasing capacity, and enhanced distribution
   - c. standardization determining optimum capacity and longer production runs
   - d. reduced product differentiation, cost minimization, and over capacity in the industry

10. During the maturity phase of a product's life cycle, the operations manager is likely to have issues that focus on:
    - a. elimination of defects in design, frequent product changes, product design, and development criteria
    - b. comparative product improvements, increasing capacity, and enhanced distribution
    - c. standardization determining optimum capacity and longer production runs
    - d. reduced product differentiation, cost minimization, and over capacity in the industry

11. During the decline phase of a product's life cycle, the operations manager is likely to have issues that deal with:
    - a. elimination of defects in design, frequent product changes, product design, and development criteria
    - b. comparative product improvements, increasing capacity, and enhanced distribution
    - c. standardization determining optimum capacity and longer production runs
    - d. reduced product differentiation, cost minimization, and over capacity in the industry

12. The purpose or rationale for an organization's existence is its ____________.

13. A plan designed to achieve a mission is a ________.

14. The ten decisions of operations management are: ________, ________, ________, ________, ________, ________, ________, ________, ________, and ________.

CASE STUDY

Johannsen Steel Company

Johannsen Steel Company (JSC) was established by three Johannsen brothers in 1928 in Pittsfield, Rhode Island. The brothers began JSC by concentrating on high-quality, high-carbon, high-margin steel wire. Products included "music wire" for instruments such as pianos and violins; copper, tin, and other coated wires; and high-tensile wire for the newly emerging aircraft industry. JSC even pioneered new types of wire.

Throughout the 1930s and 1940s, JSC prospered while maintaining its reputation for high-quality products and in-house design and construction of its own equipment. In 1946, the last remaining Johannsen brother sold the company to West Virginia Steel for $4 million. For its investment, West Virginia Steel (WVS) obtained three Johannsen steel mills located in Pittsfield, Rhode Island (500 employees), Akron, Ohio (100 employees), and Los Angeles (16 employees), and two steel wire warehouses—one in Chicago (8 employees) and one in Los Angeles (4 employees). WVS kept Johannsen completely intact as a wholly owned subsidiary.

The 1940s and 1950s witnessed increasing JSC sales to the U.S. military and to U.S. automakers and tire makers. JSC also sold wire for use in staples, nails, cables, cookie cutters, steel brushes/wire wheels, and electrical products, leading to a continued healthy upward climb in sales and profits.

1960 was a climactic year for the U.S. steel industry. A prolonged steel strike of 14 weeks caught steel customers off guard. With stocks nearly exhausted, steel customers throughout the United States looked for alternative sources. Up to this point, competition from Japanese steel plants had been minimal. However, with few options, steel customers turned to the Japanese. They found the quality, price, and even delivery of steel to be very acceptable. No longer was competition from offshore steel makers to be insignificant.

The combination of offshore steel competition and a productivity-minded economy drove steel prices down to very competitive levels throughout the 1960s and 1970s. Attention in the industry and in JSC turned toward cost cutting and sales expansion as means to maintain profit levels.

The selection of Joe Thomas, formerly the sales manager of JSC, as its president in 1978 resulted in a further emphasis on sales expansion. And, indeed, sales grew by nearly 2 million pounds per year through the 1970s and 1980s. The growth in sales revenue paralleled the tonnage sold. However, after-tax profits on sales throughout the late 1980s were never above 2%.

Because profits had been meager since the mid-1970s for both JSC and WVS, the "mother corporation" was spending little on capital investment unless a 40% return on investment (ROI) before taxes could be demonstrated. WVS had other restrictions on its JSC subsidiary. Sixty percent of JSC's total purchase of steel rod (the raw material for steel wire) had to be purchased from WVS, even though it was well acknowledged throughout the industry that WVS's steel rod was the lowest in quality. Also the smaller size of WVS rod coils (300 lb), compared to the newest industry sizes from Bethlehem Steel (1,500 and 3,000 lb), increased the number of machine setups and production cost.

To use up their quota of WVS steel rods and spread overhead costs over more tonnage (thus reducing allocated overhead per ton), Joe Thomas ordered his sales people to increase sales at least 10% per year. And they did. Orders and revenue for the more common grades of steel wire products such as staple wire, stitching wire, tire bead wire, and brush wire continued to increase. The prices of these steel wire products slowly continued to fall as the Japanese, in particular, manufactured these products with greater efficiency.

Johannsen Steel nonetheless maintained its reputation for high quality throughout the 1970s and 1980s. It won prestigious NASA and computer industry contracts and still produced "music wire" and other high-carbon grades. The percentage of these high-quality/high-margin sales to total sales continued to decrease, however.

Wire-drawing machinery now was so sophisticated that JSC no longer designed or produced its own machines. In fact, by the 1980s JSC often purchased used equipment.

Although several new JSC product innovations had appeared every few years, these were highly irregular and not significant. To control costs, the research and development (R&D) lab staff had not increased in size or funding for many years. JSC had much of its original equipment (some over 50 years old), which was in good working order. However, equipment and building maintenance costs continued to rise.

The sales salaries were low, with 6% commissions paid on all sales generated. To cut costs, sales staff travel was considerably reduced.

In conversation with John Green, JSC's operations manager, Joe Thomas was overheard to say, "I can't understand why our profits are now at zero. Sales are up again. Scrap rates are reasonable (5%), even our raw material costs per ton shipped are lower. John, if we can just lower our labor cost and maintenance costs per shipped ton and spread our fixed overhead costs over more tonnage, I am sure we can pull ourselves out of this."

DISCUSSION QUESTIONS

1. What would be a good mission statement for (a) Johannsen Steel and (b) for the production function of Johannsen Steel?
2. What does an analysis of external threats, opportunities, and internal strengths and weaknesses suggest?
3. Review the ten OM decisions discussed in this chapter and determine the reasons (both strategic and tactical) behind JSC's problems. What are JSC's options, and what strategic or tactical decisions should it make?
4. What tools and techniques would help you in your analysis of JSC or in explaining your recommendations to top management?

SOURCE: Professor Roger J. Gagnon (University of North Carolina-Charlotte). Names of the firm and principals have been changed, but the situation and issues described are actual.

CASE STUDY

Michelin, Inc.

After World War II, the Michelin family forged into the development of its controversial new product, the radial tire. Although it experienced great success with that tire, Michelin was still only seventh in the worldwide tire industry by the late 1960s. At that point, the company decided on an international growth strategy.

Michelin ran up heavy debts and losses as it proceeded to build new factories at the rate of two a year in the late 1970s. A few years later, the oil shock deflated the tire market, but, the company survived. Michelin's secret is that it is continuously willing to sacrifice short-term concerns for its two long-term objectives: quality and market share.

Hoping to avoid unions, Michelin prefers to build plants in the southern United States. Eighty percent of production is in numerous countries outside France, and the French represent only a small minority of employees.

Michelin consistently spends 5% of sales on research, which is the same percentage as Japan's Bridgestone. (Goodyear attributes *its* heavy research spending as the reason that it alone of the U.S. majors has avoided a takeover.)

Although Michelin concentrates on tires and tire components, it does make maps and restaurant guides for motorists. Goodyear and Bridgestone produce more than 25% of revenue from nontire products, but tires represent more than 90% of Michelin's sales. Almost all materials, including steel belting and synthetic rubber used in its tires, are produced by Michelin.

Michelin is mainly concerned about its long-term position as exemplified by its purchase of Uniroyal Goodrich. This transaction clearly will push up debt and hold down profits. But for Michelin the acquisition is strategic; its costs are secondary.

DISCUSSION QUESTIONS

1. What strategies of Michelin have been implemented by the production function?
2. What is Michelin's competitive advantage?

BIBLIOGRAPHY

Barney, Jay B. "Looking Inside for Competitive Advantage." *Academy of Management Executive* IX, 4 (November 1995): 49–61.

Drucker, P. F. "The Emerging Theory of Manufacturing." *Harvard Business Review* (May-June 1990): 94.

Edmondson, H. E., and S. C. Wheelwright. "Outstanding Manufacturing in the Coming Decade." *California Management Review* 31 (Summer 1989): 70–90.

Gale, B. T. "Can More Capital Buy Higher Productivity." *Harvard Business Review* 58, no. 4 (July-August 1980): 78–86.

Kaplan, Robert S., and David P. Norton. "Using the Balanced Scorecard as a Strategic Management System." *Harvard Business Review* (January-February 1996): 75–85.

Malhotra, M. K., D. C. Steele, and V. Grover. "Important

Strategic and Tactical Manufacturing Issues in the 1990s." *Decision Sciences* 25, no. 2 (March-April 1994): 189–214.

Ohmae, K. "The Borderless World." *Sloan Management Review* 32 (Winter 1991): 117.

Ohmae, K. "Getting Back to Strategy." *Harvard Business Review* 66 (November-December 1988): 149–156.

Porter, M. E. *The Competitive Advantage of Nations*. New York: The Free Press, 1990.

Skinner, W. *Manufacturing: The Formidable Competitive Weapon*. New York: John Wiley, 1985.

Stalk, George, Jr. "Time—The Next Source of Competitive Advantage." *Harvard Business Review* 66 (July-August 1988): 41–51.

Womack, J. P., D. T. Jones, and D. Roos. *The Machine That Changed the World*. New York: Rawson Associates, 1990.

Supplement 2

Forecasting

SUPPLEMENT OUTLINE

What Is Forecasting? Forecasting Time Horizons ■ The Influence of Product Life Cycle

Types of Forecasts

The Strategic Importance of Forecasting Human Resources ■ Capacity ■ Supply-Chain Management

Forecasting Approaches Overview of Qualitative Methods ■ Overview of Quantitative Methods ■ Eight Steps to a Forecasting System

Time Series Forecasting Decomposition of a Time Series ■ Moving Averages ■ Weighted Moving Averages ■ Exponential Smoothing ■ Exponential Smoothing with Trend ■ Trend Projections

Seasonal Variations in Data

Causal Forecasting Methods: Regression Analysis Using Linear Regression Analysis to Forecast ■ Standard Error of the Estimate ■ Correlation Coefficients for Regression Lines ■ Multiple Regression Analysis

Monitoring and Controlling Forecasts Adaptive Smoothing

Forecasting in the Service Sector

The Computer's Role in Forecasting

Summary ■ Key Terms ■ Using POM for Windows in Forecasting ■ Using Excel Spreadsheets in Forecasting ■ Solved Problems ■ Discussion Questions ■ Operations in Practice Exercise ■ Self-Test Supplement 2 ■ Problems ■ Case Study: The North-South Airline ■ Bibliography

LEARNING OBJECTIVES

When you complete this supplement you should be able to:

IDENTIFY OR DEFINE:

Forecasting
Types of forecasts
Time horizons
Approaches to forecasts

EXPLAIN:

Moving averages
Exponential smoothing
Trend projections
Regression analysis

Every day managers make decisions without knowing what will happen in the future. Inventory is ordered without certainty as to what sales will be; new equipment is purchased despite uncertainty about demand for products; and investments are made without knowing what profits will be. In the face of uncertainty, managers are always trying to make better estimates of what will happen in the future. Making good estimates is the main purpose of forecasting.

In this supplement we examine different types of forecasts, and we present a variety of forecasting models such as moving averages, exponential smoothing, and linear regression. Our purpose is to show that there are many ways for managers to predict the future. We also provide an overview of the subject of business sales forecasting and describe how to prepare, monitor, and judge the accuracy of a forecast. Good forecasts are an *essential* part of efficient service and manufacturing operations; they are also an important modeling tool for decision making.

WHAT IS FORECASTING?

forecasting

NOTE
An interesting quote: "Those who can predict the future have never been appreciated in their own times." Quality control expert, Philip Crosby

Forecasting is the art and science of predicting future events. It may involve taking historical data and projecting them into the future with some sort of mathematical model. It may be a subjective or intuitive prediction of the future. Or forecasting may involve a combination of these, that is, a mathematical model adjusted by a manager's good judgment.

As we introduce different forecasting techniques in this chapter, you will realize that there is seldom one single superior method. What works best in one firm under one set of conditions may be a complete disaster in another organization, or even in a different department of the same firm. In addition, you will realize that there are limits as to what can be expected from forecasts. They are seldom, if ever, perfect; they are also costly and time-consuming to prepare and monitor.

Few businesses, however, can afford to avoid the process of forecasting by just waiting to see what happens and then taking their chances. Effective planning depends on a forecast of demand for the company's products.

Forecasting Time Horizons

Forecasts are usually classified by the future time horizon that they describe. The three categories, all of which are useful to operations managers, are:

1. *Short-range forecasting.* This has a time span of up to one year but is generally less than three months. It is used for planning purchasing, job scheduling, workforce levels, job assignments, and production levels.
2. *Medium-range forecasting.* A medium-range, or intermediate, forecast generally spans from three months up to three years. It is useful in sales planning, production planning and budgeting, cash budgeting, and analyzing various operating plans.
3. *Long-range forecasting.* Generally three years or more in time span, long-range forecasts are used in planning for new products, capital expenditures, facility location or expansion, and research and development.

NOTE
Our forecasting ability has improved, but it has been outpaced by an increasingly complex world economy.

Medium- and long-range forecasts have three features that differentiate them from short-range forecasts. First, intermediate and long-range forecasts deal with

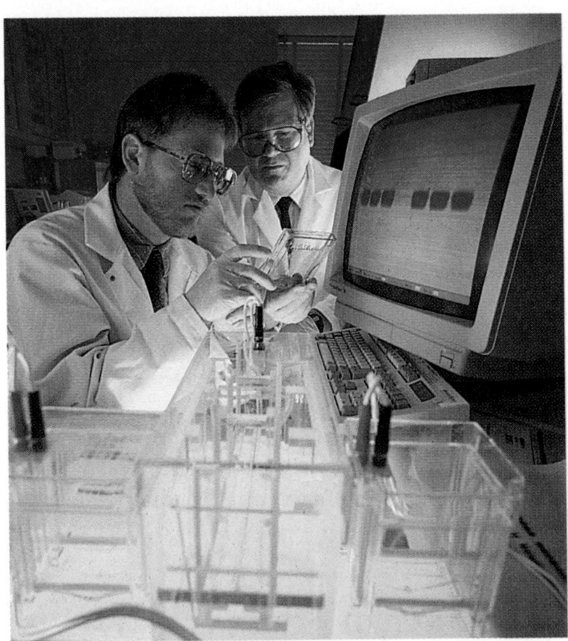

To get a grasp on future trends in the world of medical research, Bristol-Myers Squibb Company questioned 220 well-known research scientists. These leaders made a *jury of executive opinion* suggesting that the treatment of disease will concentrate on the disease's cause. In other words, rather than treat diseases like cancer through symptom elimination, medical treatment will focus on attacking individual cells of the disease itself. As a result of this qualitative forecasting, Bristol-Myers created the fluorescence-activated cell sorter, which targets antibodies of tumor cells through the use of lasers and computers.

more comprehensive issues and support management decisions regarding planning and products, plants, and processes. Implementing some facility decisions, such as opening a new Saturn auto manufacturing plant, can take five to eight years from inception to completion. Second, short-range forecasting usually employs different methodologies than do longer-term ones. Mathematical techniques such as moving averages, exponential smoothing, and trend extrapolation (all of which we shall examine shortly) are common to short-range projections. Broader, *less* quantitative methods are useful in predicting such issues as whether a new product, like the optical disk recorder, should be introduced in a company's product line. And third, as you would expect, short-range forecasts tend to be more accurate than longer-range forecasts. Factors that influence demand change every day; so as the time horizon lengthens, it is likely that one's forecast accuracy will diminish. It almost goes without saying, then, that sales forecasts need to be updated regularly in order to maintain their value. After each sales period, the forecast should be reviewed and revised.

The Influence of Product Life Cycle

Another factor to consider when developing sales forecasts, especially longer ones, is the product's life cycle. Products, and even services, do not sell at a constant level throughout their lives. Most successful products pass through four stages: (1) introduction, (2) growth, (3) maturity, and (4) decline.

Products and services in the first two stages of their life cycle need longer forecasts than those in the maturity and decline stages. Forecasts are useful in projecting different staffing levels, inventory levels, and factory capacity as the product passes from the first to the last stage. The subject of introducing new services and products, and their life cycles, is treated in more detail in Chapter 4.

TYPES OF FORECASTS

Organizations use three major types of forecasts when planning the future of their operations. The first two, economic and technological forecasting, are specialized techniques that may be outside the role of the operations manager; they are described briefly here. The emphasis in this book will be on the third, demand forecasts.

economic forecasts

1. ***Economic forecasts*** address the business cycle by predicting inflation rates, money supplies, housing starts, and other planning indicators.

technological forecasts

2. ***Technological forecasts*** are concerned with rates of technological progress, which can result in the birth of exciting new products, requiring new plants and equipment.

demand forecasts

3. ***Demand forecasts*** are projections of demand for a company's products or services. These forecasts, also called sales forecasts, drive a company's production, capacity, and scheduling systems and serve as inputs to financial, marketing, and personnel planning.

THE STRATEGIC IMPORTANCE OF FORECASTING

Good forecasts are of critical importance in all aspects of a business; the forecast is the only estimate of product demand until actual demand becomes known. Forecast demand drives decisions in many areas. Let us look at the impact of product forecast on three functions: (1) human resources, (2) capacity, and (3) supply-chain management.

Human Resources

Hiring, training and laying-off workers all depend on anticipated demand. If the human resources department has to hire additional workers without warning, the amount of training declines and the quality of the workforce suffers. A large Louisiana chemical firm almost lost its biggest customer when a quick expansion to round-the-clock shifts led to a total breakdown in quality control on the second and third shifts.

Capacity

When capacity is inadequate, the resulting shortages can mean undependable delivery, loss of customers, and loss of market share. This is exactly what happened to Nabisco, in 1993, when it underestimated the huge demand for its new low-fat Snackwell Devil's Food Cookies. With their production lines on overtime, Nabisco still could not keep up with demand, and it lost customers.[1] When excess capacity is built, on the other hand, costs can skyrocket.

Supply-Chain Management

Good supplier relations and the ensuing price advantages for materials and parts depend on accurate forecasts. Auto manufacturers who want TRW Corporation

[1] "Man Walked on the Moon, but Man Can't Make Enough Devil's Food Cookie Cakes," *The Wall Street Journal*, September 28, 1993, pp. 1–2.

to guarantee sufficient airbag capacity need to provide accurate forecasts to TRW so TRW knows that its plant expansions are justified. In the global commodity marketplace, where components for Boeing 777 jets, for example, are manufactured in dozens of countries, coordination driven by forecasted schedules is critical. To predict for transportation to Seattle for final assembly at the lowest possible cost means no last-minute surprises that can harm already low profit margins.

FORECASTING APPROACHES

Two general approaches are used in forecasting: quantitative forecasting and qualitative forecasting. **Quantitative forecasts** employ a variety of mathematical models that use historical data and/or causal variables to forecast demand. Subjective or **qualitative forecasts** incorporate important factors such as the decision maker's intuition, emotions, personal experiences, and value system in reaching a forecast. Some firms use one approach; some use the other; but in practice a combination or blending of the two styles is usually most effective.

quantitative forecasts

qualitative forecasts

NOTE
During stable times, forecasting is easy; it is just this year's performance plus or minus a few percentage points.

Overview of Qualitative Methods

In this section we consider five different *qualitative* forecasting techniques:

1. ***Jury of executive opinion.*** This method takes the opinions of a small group of high-level managers, often in combination with statistical models, and results in a group estimate of demand.
2. ***Sales force composite.*** In this approach, each salesperson estimates what sales will be in his or her region; these forecasts are then reviewed to ensure they are realistic, then combined at the district and national levels to reach an overall forecast.
3. ***Delphi method.*** This iterative group process allows experts, who may be located in different places, to make forecasts. There are three different types of participants in the Delphi process: decision makers, staff personnel, and respondents. The decision makers usually consist of a group of five to ten experts who will be making the actual forecast. The staff personnel assist the decision makers by preparing, distributing, collecting, and summarizing a series of questionnaires and survey results. The respondents are a group of people whose judgments are valued and are being sought. This group provides inputs to the decision makers before the forecast is made.
4. ***Consumer market survey.*** This method solicits input from customers or potential customers regarding their future purchasing plans. It can help not only in preparing a forecast but also in improving product design and planning for new products.
5. ***Naive approach.*** This simple way to forecast assumes that demand in the next period is the same as demand in the most recent period. In other words, if sales of a product, say, Motorola cellular phones, were 68 units in January, we can forecast that February's sales will also be 68 phones. Does this make any sense? It turns out that for some product lines, selecting this **naive approach** is a cost-effective and efficient forecasting model.

jury of executive opinion

sales force composite

Delphi method

consumer market survey

naive approach

Overview of Quantitative Methods

We address four quantitative forecasting methods in this supplement. They are:

1. **Moving averages** } Time series models
2. **Exponential smoothing** } Time series models
3. **Trend projection** } Time series models
4. **Linear regression** } Causal model

time series

NOTE
Here are two famous quotes: "You can never plan the future from the past." Sir Edmund Burke; "I know of no way of judging the future but the past." Patrick Henry

TIME SERIES MODELS. The **time series** models of forecasting predict on the basis of the assumption that the future is a function of the past. In other words, they look at what has happened over a period of time and use a series of past data to make a forecast. If we are predicting weekly sales of lawn mowers, we use the past weekly sales for lawn mowers in making the forecast.

CAUSAL MODELS. Linear regression, a causal model, incorporates into the model the variables or relationships that might influence the quantity being forecast. A causal model for lawn mower sales might include relationships such as new housing starts, advertising budget, and competitors' prices.

Eight Steps to a Forecasting System

Regardless of the method used to forecast, the same eight steps are followed:

1. Determine the use of the forecast—what objectives are we trying to obtain?
2. Select the items that are to be forecasted.
3. Determine the time horizon of the forecast—is it short-, medium-, or long-range?
4. Select the forecasting model(s).
5. Gather the data needed to make the forecast.
6. Validate the forecasting model.
7. Make the forecast.
8. Implement the results.

These steps present a systematic way of initiating, designing, and implementing a forecasting system. When the system is to be used to generate forecasts regularly over time, data must be routinely collected, and the actual computations used to make the forecast can be done automatically, usually by computer.

TIME SERIES FORECASTING

NOTE
Using data that are 20 years old (e.g., from housing prices or tuition rates) may not be so useful that it is needed to forecast next year's values. It is not always necessary to use *all* data.

A time series is based on a sequence of evenly spaced (weekly, monthly, quarterly, and so on) data points. Examples include weekly sales of IBM PCs, quarterly earnings reports of AT&T stock, daily shipments of Eveready batteries, and annual U.S. consumer price indices. Forecasting time series data implies that future values are predicted *only* from past values and that other variables, no matter how potentially valuable, are ignored.

Decomposition of a Time Series

Analyzing time series means breaking down past data into components and then projecting them forward. A time series typically has four components: trend, seasonality, cycles, and random variation.

1. *Trend (T)* is the gradual upward or downward movement of the data over time.
2. *Seasonality (S)* is a data pattern that repeats itself after a period of days, weeks, months, or quarters (the latter being from where the term *seasonality* arose, that is, the seasons: fall, winter, spring, and summer). There are six common seasonality patterns:

PERIOD OF PATTERN	LENGTH	NUMBER OF SEASONS IN PATTERN
Week	Day	7
Month	Week	$4–4\frac{1}{2}$
Month	Day	28–31
Year	Quarter	4
Year	Month	12
Year	Week	52

3. *Cycles (C)* are patterns in the data that occur every several years. They are usually tied into the business cycle and are of major importance in short-term business analysis and planning.
4. *Random variations (R)* are "blips" in the data caused by chance and unusual situations; they follow no discernible pattern. Random variations are often deleted by dropping out time periods (such as, weeks, months) that are obviously aberrations, or by dropping the high and low values when the series has at least a dozen entries.

Figure S2.1 shows a time series and its components.

Two general forms of time series models are used in statistics. The most widely used is a multiplicative model, which assumes that demand is the product of the four components:

$$\text{Demand} = T \times S \times C \times R$$

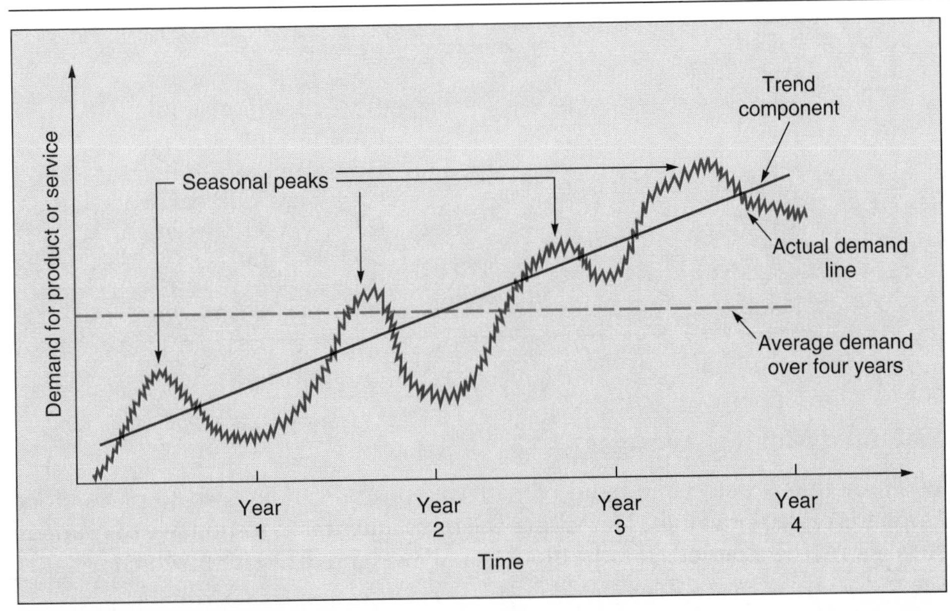

FIGURE S2.1

Product Demand Charted over Four Years with Trend and Seasonality Indicated

An additive model provides an estimate by adding the components together. It is stated as:

$$\text{Demand} = T + S + C + R$$

In most real-world models, forecasters assume that the random variations are averaged out over time. They then concentrate on only the seasonal component and a component that is a combination of trend and cyclical factors.

Moving Averages

moving averages

Moving averages are useful if we can assume that market demands will stay fairly steady over time. A four-month moving average is found by simply summing the demand during the past four months and dividing by 4. With each passing month, the most recent month's data are added to the sum of the previous three months' data, and the earliest month is dropped. This tends to smooth out short-term irregularities in the data series.

Mathematically, the simple moving average (which serves as an estimate of the next period's demand) is expressed as:

$$\text{Moving average} = \frac{\Sigma\text{Demand in previous } n \text{ periods}}{n} \tag{S2.1}$$

where n is the number of periods in the moving average—for example, four, five, or six months, respectively, for a four-, five-, or six-period moving average.

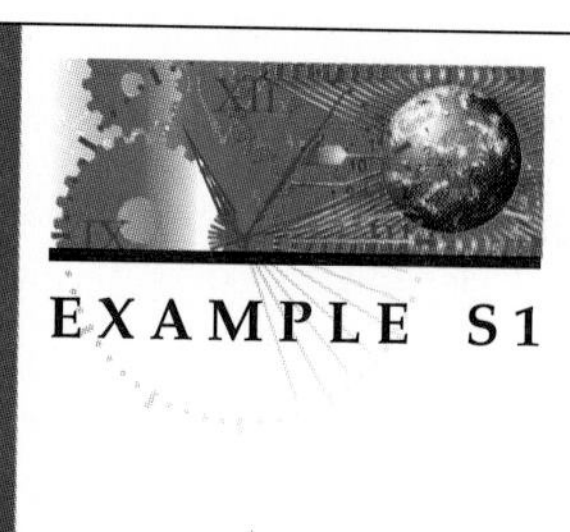

EXAMPLE S1

Lawn mower sales at Bob's Hardware Store are shown in the middle column of the following table. A three-month moving average appears on the right.

MONTH	ACTUAL MOWER SALES	THREE-MONTH MOVING AVERAGE
Jan.	10	
Feb.	12	
Mar.	13	
Apr.	16	$(10 + 12 + 13)/3 = 11\frac{2}{3}$
May	19	$(12 + 13 + 16)/3 = 13\frac{2}{3}$
June	23	$(13 + 16 + 19)/3 = 16$
July	26	$(16 + 19 + 23)/3 = 19\frac{1}{3}$
Aug.	30	$(19 + 23 + 26)/3 = 22\frac{2}{3}$
Sept.	28	$(23 + 26 + 30)/3 = 26\frac{1}{3}$
Oct.	18	$(26 + 30 + 28)/3 = 28$
Nov.	16	$(30 + 28 + 18)/3 = 25\frac{1}{3}$
Dec.	14	$(28 + 18 + 16)/3 = 20\frac{2}{3}$

Weighted Moving Averages

When there is a detectable trend or pattern, weights can be used to place more emphasis on recent values. This makes the techniques more responsive to changes since more recent periods may be more heavily weighted. Deciding which weights

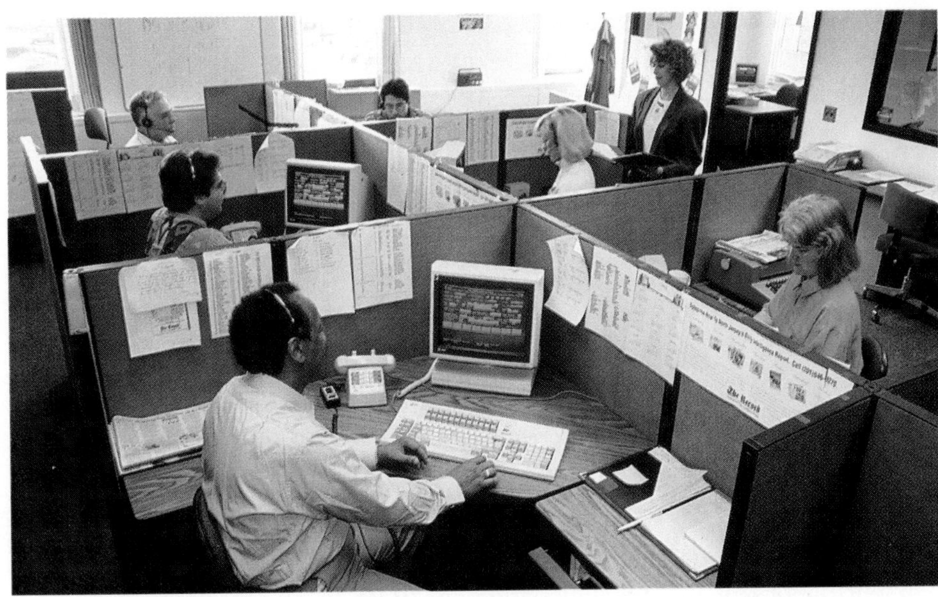

L. L. Bean, Inc., uses two time series models to forecast incoming calls at its Freeport, Maine, order center. Modeling call volumes allows for efficient scheduling of staff and saves \$300,000 annually that might have been lost to unanswered calls or overscheduling of operators.

to use requires some experience and a bit of luck. Choice of weights is somewhat arbitrary since there is no set formula to determine them. If the latest month or period is weighted too heavily, the forecast might reflect a large unusual change in the demand or sales pattern too quickly.

A weighted moving average may be expressed mathematically as:

$$\text{Moving average} = \frac{\Sigma(\text{Weight for period } n)(\text{Demand in period } n)}{\Sigma\text{Weights}} \quad \text{(S2.2)}$$

EXAMPLE S2

Bob's Hardware Store (See Example S1) decides to forecast lawn mower sales by weighting the past three months as follows:

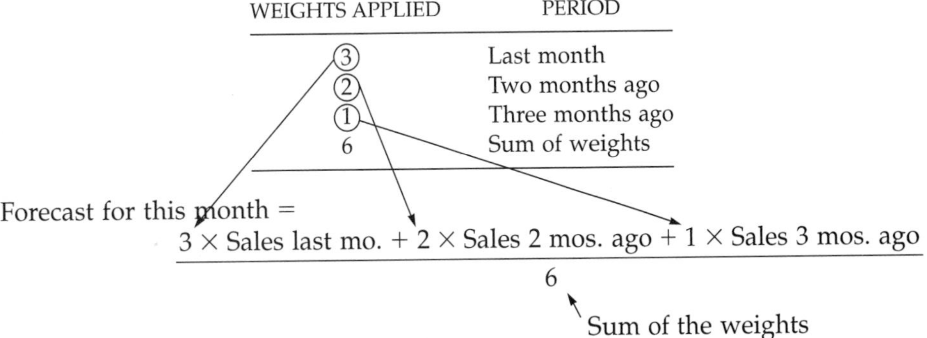

WEIGHTS APPLIED	PERIOD
3	Last month
2	Two months ago
1	Three months ago
6	Sum of weights

Forecast for this month =

$$\frac{3 \times \text{Sales last mo.} + 2 \times \text{Sales 2 mos. ago} + 1 \times \text{Sales 3 mos. ago}}{6}$$

Sum of the weights

The results of this weighted average forecast are shown in the following table.

MONTH	ACTUAL MOWER SALES	THREE-MONTH WEIGHTED MOVING AVERAGE
Jan.	10	
Feb.	12	
Mar.	13	
Apr.	16	$[(3 \times 13) + (2 \times 12) + (10)]/6 = 12\frac{1}{6}$
May	19	$[(3 \times 16) + (2 \times 13) + (12)]/6 = 14\frac{1}{3}$
June	23	$[(3 \times 19) + (2 \times 16) + (13)]/6 = 17$
July	26	$[(3 \times 23) + (2 \times 19) + (16)]/6 = 20\frac{1}{2}$
Aug.	30	$[(3 \times 26) + (2 \times 23) + (19)]/6 = 23\frac{5}{6}$
Sept.	28	$[(3 \times 30) + (2 \times 26) + (23)]/6 = 27\frac{1}{2}$
Oct.	18	$[(3 \times 28) + (2 \times 30) + (26)]/6 = 28\frac{1}{3}$
Nov.	16	$[(3 \times 18) + (2 \times 28) + (30)]/6 = 23\frac{1}{3}$
Dec.	14	$[(3 \times 16) + (2 \times 18) + (28)]/6 = 18\frac{2}{3}$

In this particular forecasting situation, you can see that weighting the latest month more heavily provides a much more accurate projection.

Both simple and weighted moving averages are effective in smoothing out sudden fluctuations in the demand pattern in order to provide stable estimates. Moving averages do, however, have three problems. First, increasing the size of n (the number of periods averaged) does smooth out fluctuations better, but it makes the method less sensitive to *real* changes in the data. Second, moving averages cannot pick up trends very well. Since they are averages, they will always stay within past levels and will not predict a change to either a higher or lower level. Finally, moving averages require extensive records of past data.

Figure S2.2, a plot of the data in Examples S1 and S2, illustrates the lag effect of the moving average models.

Exponential Smoothing

exponential smoothing

Exponential smoothing is a forecasting method that is easy to use and efficiently handled by computers. Although it is a type of moving average technique, it involves very *little* record keeping of past data. The basic exponential smoothing formula can be shown as follows:

$$\text{New forecast} = \text{Last period's forecast} + \alpha\,(\text{Last period's actual demand} - \text{last period's forecast}) \qquad \text{(S2.3)}$$

smoothing constant

where α is a weight, or **smoothing constant,** that has a value between 0 and 1, inclusive. Equation S2.3 can also be written mathematically as:

$$F_t = F_{t-1} + \alpha(A_{t-1} - F_{t-1}) \qquad \text{(S2.4)}$$

where

F_t = New forecast

F_{t-1} = Previous forecast

α = Smoothing constant ($0 \leq \alpha \leq 1$)

A_{t-1} = Previous period's actual demand

NOTE
Exponential smoothing may have an obscure-sounding name, but it is actually widely used in business and an important part of many computerized inventory control systems.

The concept is not complex. The latest estimate of demand is equal to our old estimate adjusted by a fraction of the difference between the last period's actual demand and the old estimate.

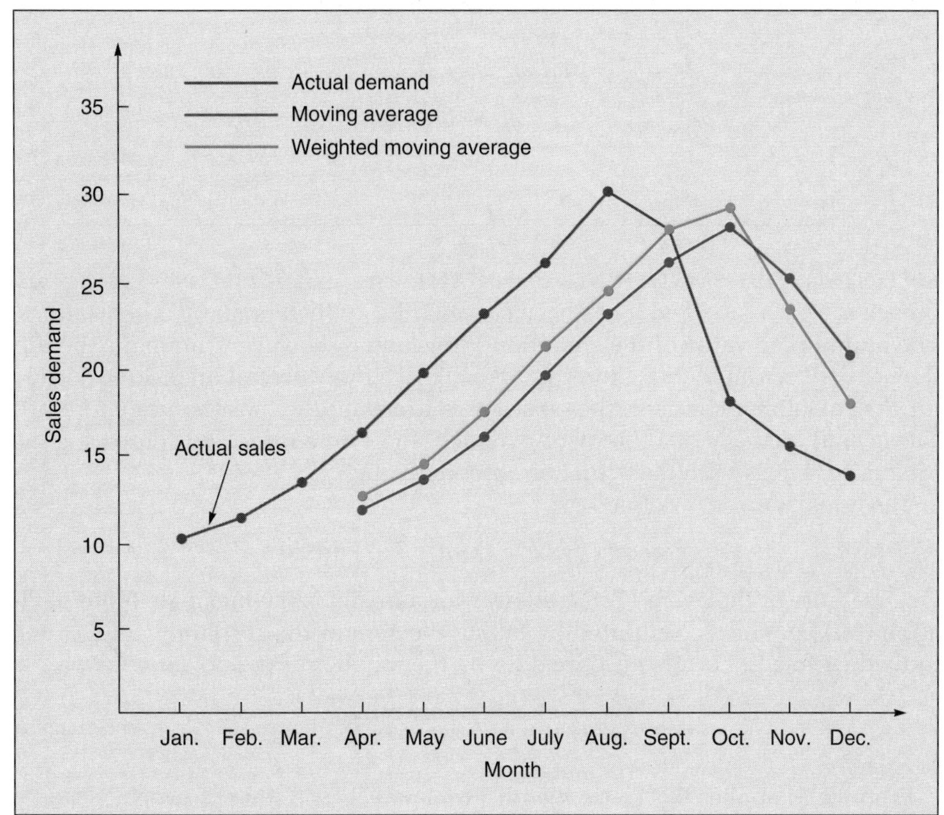

FIGURE S2.2

ACTUAL DEMAND VERSUS MOVING AVERAGE AND WEIGHTED MOVING AVERAGE METHODS FOR BOB'S HARDWARE STORE

EXAMPLE S3

In January, a travel agent who specializes in cruises predicted a February demand for 142 one-week cruises. Actual February demand was 153 cruises. Using a smoothing constant of $\alpha = .20$, we can forecast the March demand using the exponential smoothing model. Substituting into the formula, we obtain:

$$\text{New forecast}_{(\text{for March demand})} = 142 + .2(153 - 142) = 144.2$$

Thus the demand forecast for one-week cruises in March is rounded to 144.

The *smoothing constant*, α, is generally in the range from .05 to .50 for business applications. It can be changed to give more weight to recent data (when α is high) or more weight to past data (when α is low). The importance of older past periods declines quickly as α is increased. When α reaches the extreme of 1.0, then in Equation S2.4, $F_t = 1.0A_{t-1}$. All the older values drop out, and the forecast becomes identical to the naive model mentioned earlier in this chapter. That is, the forecast for the next period is just the same as this period's demand.

The following table helps illustrate this concept. For example, when $\alpha = .5$, we can see that the new forecast is based almost entirely on demand in the last three or four periods. When $\alpha = .1$, the forecast places little weight on recent demand and takes *many* periods (about 19) of historic values into account.

	WEIGHT ASSIGNED TO				
Smoothing Constant	*Most Recent Period* (α)	*2nd Most Recent Period* $\alpha(1-\alpha)$	*3rd Most Recent Period* $\alpha(1-\alpha)^2$	*4th Most Recent Period* $\alpha(1-\alpha)^3$	*5th Most Recent Period* $\alpha(1-\alpha)^4$
$\alpha = .1$	.1	.09	.081	.073	.066
$\alpha = .5$	.5	.25	.125	.063	.031

SELECTING THE SMOOTHING CONSTANT. The exponential smoothing approach is easy to use, and it has been successfully applied in many organizations. The appropriate value of the smoothing constant, α, however, can make the difference between an accurate forecast and an inaccurate forecast. In picking a value for the smoothing constant, the objective is to obtain the most accurate forecast. The overall accuracy of a forecasting model can be determined by comparing the forecasted values with the actual or observed values.

The forecast error is defined as:

$$\text{Forecast error} = \text{Demand} - \text{Forecast}$$

mean absolute deviation (MAD)

One measure of the overall forecast error for a model is the **mean absolute deviation (MAD).** This is computed by taking the sum of the absolute values of the individual forecast errors and dividing by the number of periods of data (n):

$$MAD = \frac{\Sigma|\text{Forecast errors}|}{n} \qquad \text{(S2.5)}$$

Example S4 applies this concept with a trial-and-error testing of two values of α.

EXAMPLE S4

The Port of New Orleans has unloaded large quantities of beef from South American ships during the past eight quarters. The port's operations manager wants to test the use of exponential smoothing to see how well the technique works in predicting tonnage unloaded. He assumes that the forecast of grain unloaded in the first quarter was 175 tons. Two values of α are examined, $\alpha = .10$ and $\alpha = .50$. The following table shows the *detailed* calculations for $\alpha = .10$ only:

QUARTER	ACTUAL TONNAGE UNLOADED	ROUNDED FORECAST USING $\alpha = .10$[a]	ROUNDED FORECAST USING $\alpha = .50$[a]
1	180	175	175
2	168	176 = 175.00 + .10(180 − 175)	178
3	159	175 = 175.50 + .10(168 − 175.50)	173
4	175	173 = 174.75 + .10(159 − 174.75)	166
5	190	173 = 173.18 + .10(175 − 173.18)	170
6	205	175 = 173.36 + .10(190 − 173.36)	180
7	180	178 = 175.02 + .10(205 − 175.02)	193
8	182	178 = 178.02 + .10(180 − 178.02)	186
9	?	179 = 178.22 + .10(182 − 178.22)	184

[a]Forecasts rounded to the nearest ton.

To evaluate the accuracy of each smoothing constant we can compute the absolute deviations and MADs.

QUARTER	ACTUAL TONNAGE UNLOADED	ROUNDED FORECAST WITH $\alpha = .10$	ABSOLUTE DEVIATION FOR $\alpha = .10$	ROUNDED FORECAST WITH $\alpha = .50$	ABSOLUTE DEVIATION FOR $\alpha = .50$
1	180	175	5	175	5
2	168	176	8	178	10
3	159	175	16	173	14
4	175	173	2	166	9
5	190	173	17	170	20
6	205	175	30	180	25
7	180	178	2	193	13
8	182	178	4	186	4
Sum of absolute deviations			84		100
$\text{MAD} = \dfrac{\Sigma\lvert\text{Deviations}\rvert}{n}$			10.50		12.50

On the basis of this analysis, a smoothing constant of $\alpha = .10$ is preferred to $\alpha = .50$ because its MAD is smaller.

Most computerized forecasting software includes a feature that automatically finds the smoothing constant with the lowest forecast error. Some software modifies the alpha value if errors become larger than acceptable.

MEAN SQUARED ERROR. The **mean squared error (MSE)** is another way of measuring overall forecast error. MSE is the average of the squared differences be-

mean squared error (MSE)

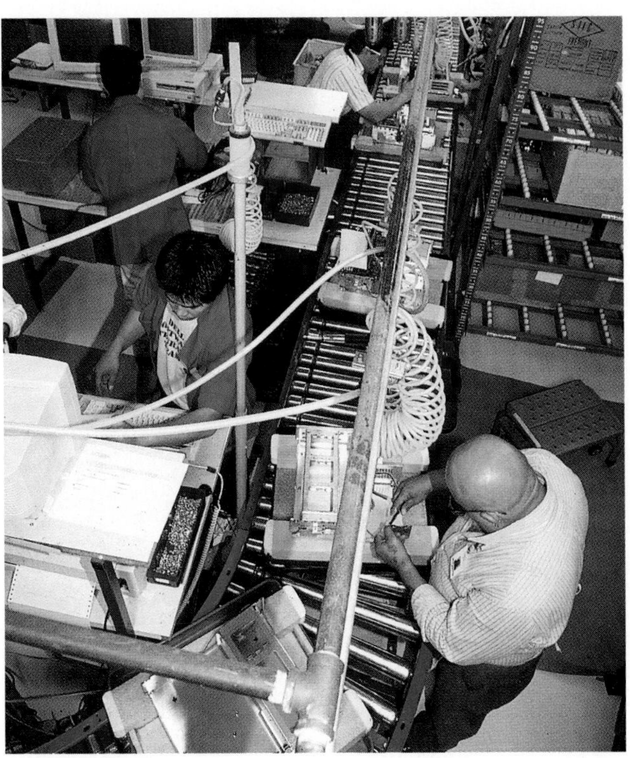

Just three weeks after IBM announced its new home computer line in September 1994, the firm sold out its supply through year end and was unable to fill holiday orders. Why? IBM attributes the shortage to conservative forecasting—a chronic problem of miscalculating demand for PCs. This potential revenue loss of $100 million follows similar forecasting problems for IBM's popular Think Pad portable PC two years earlier.

tween the forecasted and observed values. Its formula is

$$MSE = \frac{\Sigma \text{Forecast errors}^2}{n} \tag{S2.6}$$

Exponential Smoothing with Trend

As with any moving average technique, simple exponential smoothing fails to respond to trends. To smooth out trend corrections, we can compute a simple exponential smoothing forecast as above, and then adjust for positive or negative lags. Simple exponential smoothing is often referred to as first-order smoothing, and trend-adjusted smoothing is called second-order, or double, smoothing. Other advanced exponential smoothing models are also in use, including seasonal-adjusted and triple smoothing, but these are also beyond the scope of this book.[2]

Trend Projections

trend projection

The last time series forecasting method we will discuss is **trend projection.** This technique fits a trend line to a series of historical data points and then projects the line into the future for medium- to long-range forecasts. Several mathematical trend equations can be developed (for example, exponential and quadratic), but in this section we will look at *linear* (straight-line) trends only.

If we decide to develop a linear trend line by a precise statistical method, we can apply the *least squares method.* This approach results in a straight line that minimizes the sum of the squares of the vertical differences from the line to each of the actual observations. Figure S2.3 illustrates the least squares approach.

FIGURE S2.3

THE LEAST SQUARES METHOD FOR FINDING THE BEST-FITTING STRAIGHT LINE, WHERE THE ASTERISKS ARE THE LOCATIONS OF THE SEVEN ACTUAL OBSERVATIONS OR DATA POINTS

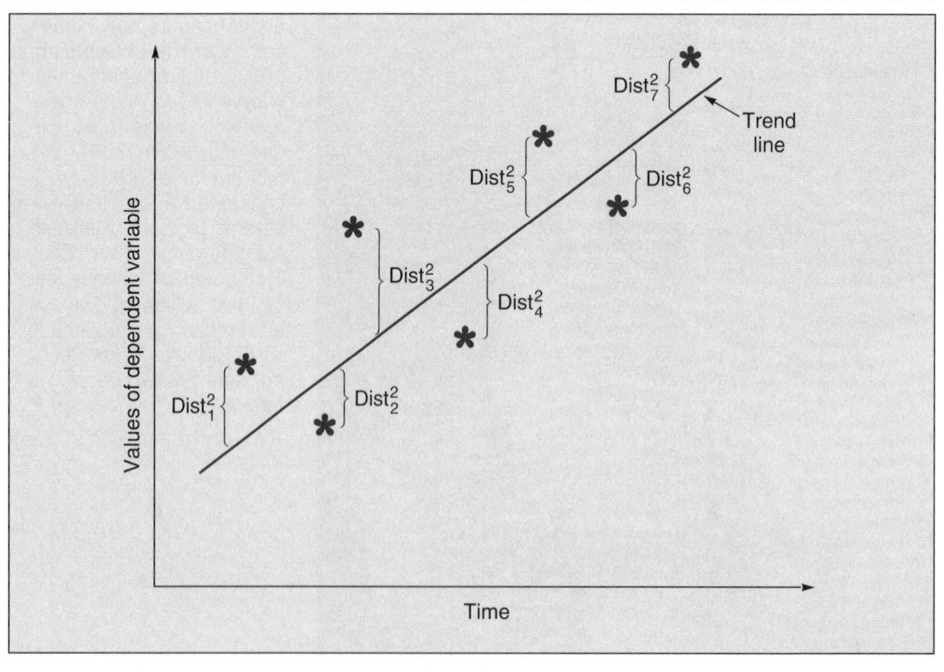

[2]For more details, see E. S. Gardner, "Exponential Smoothing: The State of the Art," *Journal of Forecasting* 4, 1 (March 1985); R. Brown, *Smoothing, Forecasting, and Prediction* (Englewood Cliffs, NJ: Prentice-Hall, 1973).

A least squares line is described in terms of its y-intercept (the height at which it intercepts the y-axis) and its slope (the angle of the line). If we can compute the y-intercept and slope, we can express the line with the following equation:

$$\hat{y} = a + bx \tag{S2.7}$$

where

$\hat{y}$ (called "y hat") = Computed value of the variable to be predicted (called the dependent variable)

a = y-axis intercept,

b = Slope of the regression line (or the rate of change in y for given changes in x),

x = Independent variable (which is *time* in this case)

Statisticians have developed equations that we can use to find the values of a and b for any regression line. The slope b is found by

$$b = \frac{\Sigma xy - n\overline{x}\overline{y}}{\Sigma x^2 - n\overline{x}^2} \tag{S2.8}$$

where

b = Slope of the regression line

Σ = Summation sign

x = Values of the independent variable

y = Values of the dependent variable

$\overline{x}$ = Average of the value of the x's

$\overline{y}$ = Average of the values of the y's

n = Number of data points or observations

We can compute the y-intercept a as follows:

$$a = \overline{y} - b\overline{x} \tag{S2.9}$$

Example S5 shows how to apply these concepts.

EXAMPLE S5

The demand for electrical power at N.Y. Edison over the period 1990–1996 is shown below, in megawatts. Let us fit a straight-line trend to these data and forecast 1997 demand.

YEAR	ELECTRICAL POWER DEMANDED	YEAR	ELECTRICAL POWER DEMANDED
1990	74	1994	105
1991	79	1995	142
1992	80	1996	122
1993	90		

With a series of data over time, we can minimize the computations by transforming the values of x (time) to simpler numbers. Thus, in this case, we can designate 1990 as year 1, 1991 as year 2, and so on.

YEAR	TIME PERIOD	ELECTRICAL POWER DEMAND	x^2	xy
1990	1	74	1	74
1991	2	79	4	158
1992	3	80	9	240
1993	4	90	16	360
1994	5	105	25	525
1995	6	142	36	852
1996	7	122	49	854
	$\Sigma x = 28$	$\Sigma y = 692$	$\Sigma x^2 = 140$	$\Sigma xy = 3{,}063$

$$\overline{x} = \frac{\Sigma x}{n} = \frac{28}{7} = 4 \qquad \overline{y} = \frac{\Sigma y}{n} = \frac{692}{7} = 98.86$$

$$b = \frac{\Sigma xy - n\overline{x}\overline{y}}{\Sigma x^2 - n\overline{x}^2} = \frac{3{,}063 - (7)(4)(98.86)}{140 - (7)(4^2)} = \frac{295}{28} = 10.54$$

$$a = \overline{y} - b\overline{x} = 98.86 - 10.54(4) = 56.70$$

Hence, the least squares trend equation is $\hat{y} = 56.70 + 10.54x$. To project demand in 1997, we first denote the year 1997 in our new coding system as $x = 8$:

$$\begin{aligned}(\text{Demand in 1997}) &= 56.70 + 10.54(8)\\ &= 141.02, \text{ or } 141 \text{ megawatts}\end{aligned}$$

We can estimate demand for 1998 by inserting $x = 9$ in the same equation:

$$\begin{aligned}(\text{Demand in 1998}) &= 56.70 + 10.54(9)\\ &= 151.56, \text{ or } 152 \text{ megawatts}\end{aligned}$$

To check the validity of the model, we plot historical demand and the trend line in Figure S2.4. In this case, we may wish to be cautious and try to understand the 1995–1996 swings in demand.

FIGURE S2.4

ELECTRICAL POWER AND THE COMPUTED TREND LINE

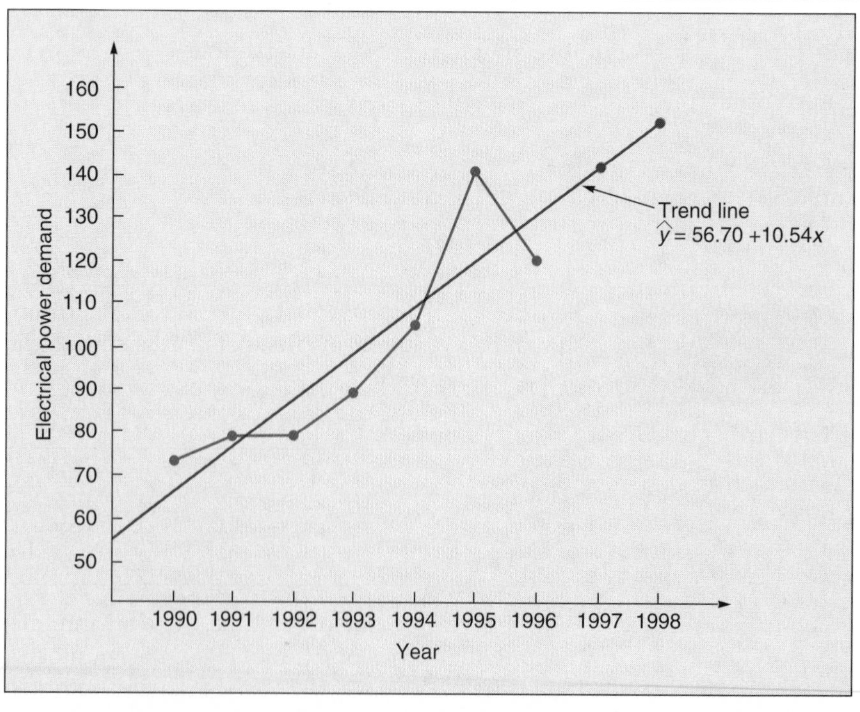

SEASONAL VARIATIONS IN DATA

Time series forecasting such as that in Example S5 involves looking at the *trend* of data over a series of time observations. Sometimes, however, recurring variations at certain seasons of the year make a *seasonal* adjustment in the trend line forecast necessary. Demand for coal and fuel oil, for example, usually peaks during cold winter months. Demand for golf clubs or suntan lotion may be highest in summer. Analyzing data in monthly or quarterly terms usually makes it easy for a statistician to spot seasonal patterns. Seasonal indices can then be developed by several common methods. Example S6 illustrates one way to compute seasonal factors from historical data.

NOTE
Because John Deere understands seasonal variations, it has been able to obtain 70% of its orders in advance of seasonal use (through price reductions and incentives such as free interest) so it can smooth production.

EXAMPLE S6

Monthly sales of IBM notebook computers at Hardwareland are shown below for 1995–1996.

MONTH	SALES DEMAND *1995*	SALES DEMAND *1996*	AVERAGE 1995–1996 DEMAND	AVERAGE MONTHLY DEMAND[a]	AVERAGE SEASONAL INDEX[b]
Jan.	80	100	90	94	.957
Feb.	75	85	80	94	.851
Mar.	80	90	85	94	.904
Apr.	90	110	100	94	1.064
May	115	131	123	94	1.309
June	110	120	115	94	1.223
July	100	110	105	94	1.117
Aug.	90	110	100	94	1.064
Sept.	85	95	90	94	.957
Oct.	75	85	80	94	.851
Nov.	75	85	80	94	.851
Dec.	80	80	80	94	.851
			Total average demand =	1,128	

[a]Average monthly demand $= \frac{1{,}128}{12 \text{ months}} = 94$

[b]Seasonal index $= \frac{\text{Average 1995–1996 demand}}{\text{Average monthly demand}}$

Using these seasonal indices, if we expected the 1997 annual demand for computers to be 1,200 units, we would forecast the monthly demand as follows:

MONTH	DEMAND	MONTH	DEMAND
Jan.	$\frac{1{,}200}{12} \times .957 = 96$	July	$\frac{1{,}200}{12} \times 1.117 = 112$
Feb.	$\frac{1{,}200}{12} \times .851 = 85$	Aug.	$\frac{1{,}200}{12} \times 1.064 = 106$
Mar.	$\frac{1{,}200}{12} \times .904 = 90$	Sept.	$\frac{1{,}200}{12} \times .957 = 96$
Apr.	$\frac{1{,}200}{12} \times 1.064 = 106$	Oct.	$\frac{1{,}200}{12} \times .851 = 85$
May	$\frac{1{,}200}{12} \times 1.309 = 131$	Nov.	$\frac{1{,}200}{12} \times .851 = 85$
June	$\frac{1{,}200}{12} \times 1.223 = 122$	Dec.	$\frac{1{,}200}{12} \times .851 = 85$

For simplicity, trend calculations were ignored and only two periods were used for each monthly index in the above example. Example S7 illustrates how indices that have already been prepared can be applied to adjust trend line forecasts.

EXAMPLE S7

The president of Marc Smith's Chocolate Shop has used time series regression to forecast retail sales for the next four quarters. The sales estimates are \$100,000, \$120,000, \$140,000, and \$160,000 for the respective quarters. Seasonal indices for the four quarters have been found to be 1.30, .90, .70, and 1.15, respectively.

To compute a seasonalized or adjusted sales forecast, we just multiply each seasonal index by the appropriate trend forecast:

$$\hat{y}_{\text{seasonal}} = \text{Index} \times \hat{y}_{\text{trend forecast}}$$

Hence for

$$\begin{aligned}
&\text{Quarter I:} && \hat{y}_{\text{I}} = (1.30)(\$100{,}000) = \$130{,}000 \\
&\text{Quarter II:} && \hat{y}_{\text{II}} = (.90)(\$120{,}000) = \$108{,}000 \\
&\text{Quarter III:} && \hat{y}_{\text{III}} = (.70)(\$140{,}000) = \$98{,}000 \\
&\text{Quarter IV:} && \hat{y}_{\text{IV}} = (1.15)(\$160{,}000) = \$184{,}000
\end{aligned}$$

CAUSAL FORECASTING METHODS: REGRESSION ANALYSIS

Causal forecasting models usually consider several variables that are related to the variable being predicted. Once these related variables have been found, a statistical model is built and used to forecast the variable of interest. This approach is more powerful than the time series methods that use only the historic values for the forecasted variable.

Glidden Paints' assembly lines fill thousands of cans per hour. To predict demand for its products, the firm uses causal forecasting methods such as linear regression, with independent variables such as disposable personal income and GNP. Although housing starts would be a natural variable, Glidden found it correlated poorly with past sales. It turns out that most Glidden paint is sold through retailers to customers who already own homes or businesses.

Many factors can be considered in a causal analysis. For example, the sales of a product might be related to the firm's advertising budget, the price charged, competitors' prices, and promotional strategies, or even the economy and unemployment rates. In this case, sales would be called the *dependent variable*, and the other variables would be called *independent variables*. The manager's job is to develop the best statistical relationship between sales and the independent variables. The most common quantitative causal forecasting model is **linear regression analysis.**

linear regression analysis

Using Linear Regression Analysis to Forecast

We can use the same mathematical model we employed in the least squares method of trend projection to perform a linear regression analysis. The dependent variables that we want to forecast will still be $\hat{y}$. But now the independent variable, x, need no longer be time.

NOTE
Regression is commonly used as a tool in economic and legal cases: It is the technique of choice in race, age, and sex discrimination lawsuits.

$$\hat{y} = a + bx$$

where

$\hat{y}$ = Value of the dependent variable, sales here

a = y-axis intercept

b = Slope of the regression line

x = Independent variable

EXAMPLE S8

Richard Nodel owns a construction company that builds offices in Detroit. Over time, the company has found that its dollar volume of renovation work is dependent on the Detroit area payroll. The following table lists Nodel's revenues and the amount of money earned by wage earners in Detroit during the years 1991–1996.

NODEL'S SALES ($ hundreds of thousands), y	LOCAL PAYROLL ($ hundreds of millions), x
2.0	1
3.0	3
2.5	4
2.0	2
2.0	1
3.5	7

Nodel's management wants to establish a mathematical relationship that will help it predict sales. First, they need to determine whether there is a straight-line (linear) relationship between area payroll and sales, so they plot the known data on a scatter diagram (see page 64).

It appears from the six data points that a slight positive relationship exists between the independent variable, payroll, and the dependent variable, sales. As payroll increases, Nodel's sales tend to be higher.

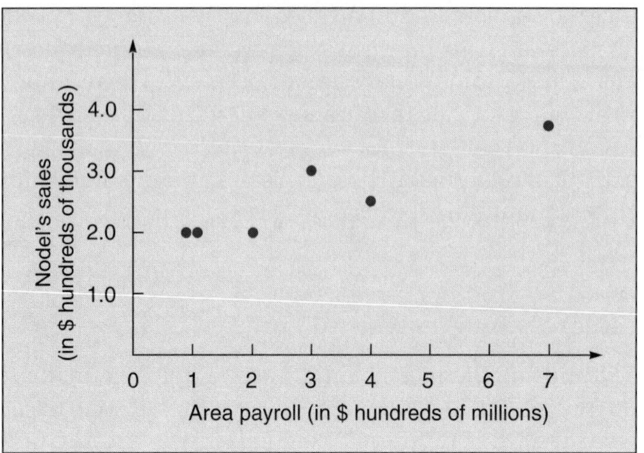

We can find a mathematical equation by using the least squares regression approach.

SALES, y	PAYROLL, x	x^2	xy
2.0	1	1	2.0
3.0	3	9	9.0
2.5	4	16	10.0
2.0	2	4	4.0
2.0	1	1	2.0
3.5	7	49	24.5
$\Sigma y = 15.0$	$\Sigma x = 18$	$\Sigma x^2 = 80$	$\Sigma xy = 51.5$

$$\bar{x} = \frac{\Sigma x}{6} = \frac{18}{6} = 3$$

$$\bar{y} = \frac{\Sigma y}{6} = \frac{15}{6} = 2.5$$

$$b = \frac{\Sigma xy - n\bar{x}\bar{y}}{\Sigma x^2 - n\bar{x}^2} = \frac{51.5 - (6)(3)(2.5)}{80 - (6)(3^2)} = .25$$

$$a = \bar{y} - b\bar{x} = 2.5 - (.25)(3) = 1.75$$

The estimated regression equation, therefore, is:

$$\hat{y} = 1.75 + .25x$$

or

$$\text{Sales} = 1.75 + .25 \text{ payroll}$$

If the local chamber of commerce predicts that the Detroit area payroll will be $600 million next year, we can estimate sales for Nodel with the regression equation:

$$\text{Sales (in hundred thousands)} = 1.75 + .25(6)$$
$$= 1.75 + 1.50 = 3.25$$

or

$$\text{Sales} = \$325{,}000$$

The final part of Example S8 illustrates a central weakness of causal forecasting methods like regression. Even when we have computed a regression equation, it is necessary to provide a forecast of the independent variable x—in this case, payroll—before estimating the dependent variable y for the next time period. Although this is not a problem for all forecasts, you can imagine the difficulty of determining future values of *some* common independent variables (such as unemployment rates, gross national product, price indices, and so on).

Standard Error of the Estimate

The forecast of $325,000 for Nodel's sales in Example S8 is called a *point estimate* of y. The point estimate is really the mean, or expected value, of a distribution of possible values of sales. Figure S2.5 illustrates this concept.

To measure the accuracy of the regression estimates we need to compute the **standard error of the estimate,** $S_{y,x}$. This is called the *standard deviation of the regression.* Equation S2.10 is a similar expression to that found in most statistics books for computing the standard deviation of an arithmetic mean:

standard error of the estimate

$$S_{y,x} = \sqrt{\frac{\Sigma(y - y_c)^2}{n - 2}} \qquad \text{(S2.10)}$$

where

y = y-value of each data point

y_c = the computed value of the dependent variable, from the regression equation

n = the number of data points

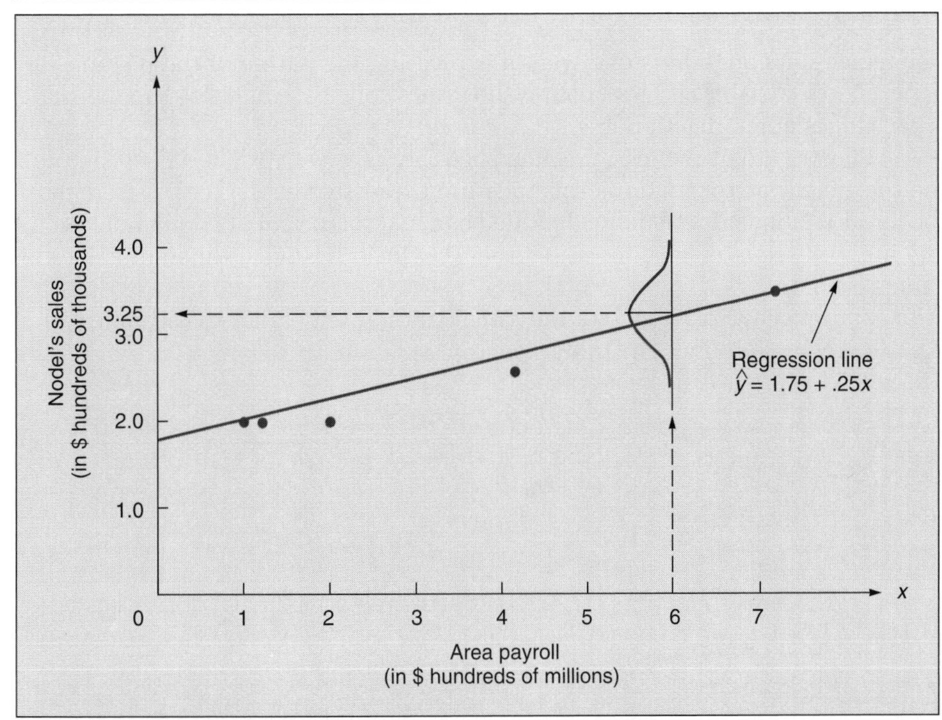

FIGURE S2.5

DISTRIBUTION ABOUT THE POINT ESTIMATE OF $600 MILLION PAYROLL

Equation S2.11 may look more complex, but it is actually an easier-to-use version of Equation S2.10. Either formula provides the same answer and can be used in setting up prediction intervals around the point estimate.[3]

$$S_{y,x} = \sqrt{\frac{\Sigma y^2 - a\,\Sigma y - b\,\Sigma xy}{n-2}} \tag{S2.11}$$

EXAMPLE S9

Let us compute the standard error of the estimate for Nodel's data in Example S8. The only number we will need that is not available to solve for $S_{y,x}$ is Σy^2. Some quick addition reveals $\Sigma y^2 = 39.5$. Therefore,

$$S_{y,x} = \sqrt{\frac{\Sigma y^2 - a\,\Sigma y - b\,\Sigma xy}{n-2}}$$

$$= \sqrt{\frac{39.5 - 1.75(15.0) - .25(51.5)}{6-2}}$$

$$= \sqrt{.09375} = .306 \text{ (in \$ hundred thousands)}$$

The standard error of the estimate is then $30,600 in sales.

Correlation Coefficients for Regression Lines

The regression equation is one way of expressing the nature of the relationship between two variables.[4] The equation shows how one variable relates to the value and changes in another variable.

coefficient of correlation

Another way to evaluate the relationship between two variables is to compute the **coefficient of correlation.** This measure expresses the degree or strength of the linear relationship. Usually identified as r, the coefficient of correlation can be any number between $+1$ and -1. Figure S2.6 illustrates what different values of r might look like.

To compute r we use much of the same data needed earlier to calculate a and b for the regression line. The rather lengthy equation for r is:

$$r = \frac{n\,\Sigma xy - \Sigma x\,\Sigma y}{\sqrt{[n\,\Sigma x^2 - (\Sigma x)^2][n\,\Sigma y^2 - (\Sigma y)^2]}} \tag{S2.12}$$

[3]When the sample size is large ($n > 30$), the prediction interval for an individual value of y can be computed using normal tables. When the number of observations is small, the t-distribution is appropriate. See Neter, Wasserman, and Whitmore, *Applied Statistics*, 4th ed. (Newton, MA: Allyn & Bacon, 1994).

[4]Regression lines are not "cause-and-effect" relationships. They describe only the relationship between variables.

EXAMPLE S10

In Example S8 we looked at the relationship between Nodel Construction Company's office building sales and payroll in Detroit. To compute the coefficient of correlation for the data shown, we need only add one more column of calculations (for y^2) and then apply the equation for r.

y	x	x^2	xy	y^2 ← New column
2.0	1	1	2.0	4.0
3.0	3	9	9.0	9.0
2.5	4	16	10.0	6.25
2.0	2	4	4.0	4.00
2.0	1	1	2.0	4.00
3.5	7	49	24.5	12.25
$\Sigma y = 15.0$	$\Sigma x = 18$	$\Sigma x^2 = 80$	$\Sigma xy = 51.5$	$\Sigma y^2 = 39.5$

$$r = \frac{(6)(51.5) - (18)(15.0)}{\sqrt{[(6)(80) - (18)^2][(6)(39.5) - (15.0)^2]}}$$

$$= \frac{309 - 270}{\sqrt{(156)(12)}} = \frac{39}{\sqrt{1872}}$$

$$= \frac{39}{43.3} = .901$$

This r of .901 appears to be a significant correlation and helps to confirm the closeness of the relationship between the two variables.

Although the coefficient of correlation is the measure most commonly used to describe the relationship between two variables, another measure does exist. It is called the *coefficient of determination*. This is simply the square of the coefficient of

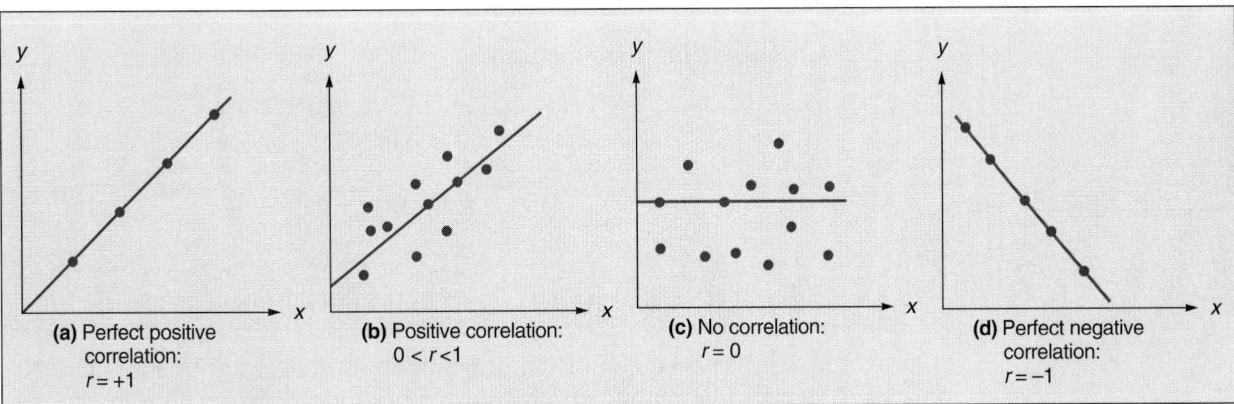

FIGURE S2.6 FOUR VALUES OF THE CORRELATION COEFFICIENT

NOTE
A high r^2 doesn't always mean one variable will be a good predictor of the other. Skirt lengths and stock market prices may be correlated, but raising one doesn't mean the other will go up or down.

correlation, namely, r^2. The value of r^2 will always be a positive number in the range of $0 \leq r^2 \leq 1$. The coefficient of determination is the percentage of variation in the dependent variable (y) that is explained by the regression equation. In Nodel's case, the value of r^2 is .81 ($.901^2 = .811$), indicating that 81% of the total variation is explained by the regression equation.

Multiple Regression Analysis

multiple regression

Multiple regression is a practical extension of the model we just observed. It allows us to build a model with several independent variables. For example, if Nodel Construction wanted to include average annual interest rates in its model to forecast renovation sales, the proper equation would be:

$$\hat{y} = a + b_1x_1 + b_2x_2 \tag{S2.13}$$

where

$\hat{y}$ = the dependent variable, sales

a = y-intercept

b_1 and b_2 = slopes of the regression line

x_1 and x_2 = values of the two independent variables, area payroll and interest rates, respectively

The mathematics of multiple regression becomes quite complex (and are usually tackled by computer), so we leave the formulas for a, b_1, and b_2 to statistics textbooks.

EXAMPLE S11

The new multiple regression line for Nodel Construction, calculated by computer software, is:

$$\hat{y} = 1.80 + .30x_1 - 5.0x_2$$

We also find that the new coefficient of correlation is .96, implying the inclusion of the variable x_2, interest rates, adds even more strength to the linear relationship.

We can now estimate Nodel's sales if we substitute values for next year's payroll and interest rate. If Detroit's payroll will be $600 million and the interest rate will be .12 (12%), sales will be forecast as:

$$\begin{aligned} \text{Sales (\$ hundred thousands)} &= 1.80 + .30(6) - 5.0\,(.12) \\ &= 1.8 + 1.8 - .6 \\ &= 3.00 \end{aligned}$$

or

$$\text{Sales} = \$300{,}000$$

MONITORING AND CONTROLLING FORECASTS

Once a forecast has been completed, it is important that it not be forgotten. No manager wants to be reminded when his or her forecast is horribly inaccurate, but a firm needs to determine why the actual demand (or whatever variable is being examined) differed significantly from that projected.

One way to monitor forecasts to ensure they are performing well is to employ a tracking signal. A **tracking signal** is a measurement of how well the forecast is predicting actual values. As forecasts are updated every week, month, or quarter, the newly available demand data are compared to the forecast values.

tracking signal

The tracking signal is computed as the *running sum of the forecast errors* (RSFE) divided by the *mean absolute deviation* (MAD):

$$\text{Tracking signal} = \frac{\text{RSFE}}{\text{MAD}} = \frac{\Sigma(\text{Actual demand in period} - \text{Forecast demand in period } i)}{\text{MAD}} \tag{S2.14}$$

where

$$\text{MAD} = \frac{\Sigma|\text{Forecast errors}|}{n}$$

as seen earlier in Equation S2.5.

Positive tracking signals indicate that demand is greater than forecast. Negative signals mean that demand is less than forecast. A good tracking signal, that is, one with a low RSFE, has about as much positive bias as it has negative bias. In other words, small biases are okay, but the positive and negative ones should balance one another so the tracking signal centers closely around zero bias.

Once tracking signals are calculated, they are compared to predetermined control limits. When a tracking signal exceeds an upper or lower limit, a flag is tripped. This indicates a problem with the forecasting method, and management may want to reevaluate the way it forecasts demand. Figure S2.7 shows the graph of a tracking signal that is exceeding the range of acceptable variation. If the model being used is exponential smoothing, perhaps the smoothing constant needs to be readjusted.

How do firms decide what the upper and lower tracking limits should be? There is no single answer, but they try to find reasonable values—in other words, limits not so low as to be triggered with every small forecast error, and not so high as to allow bad forecasts to be regularly overlooked. George Plossl and Oliver

NOTE
A few famous forecasts somewhat lacking in accuracy: "I think there is a world market for maybe five computers." Thomas Watson, chairman of IBM, 1943; "I have traveled the length and breadth of this country and talked with the best people, and I can assure you that data processing is a fad that won't last out the year." The editor in charge of business books for Prentice Hall, 1957; "There is no reason anyone would want a computer in their home." Ken Olson, president, chairman and founder of Digital Equipment Corp., 1977.

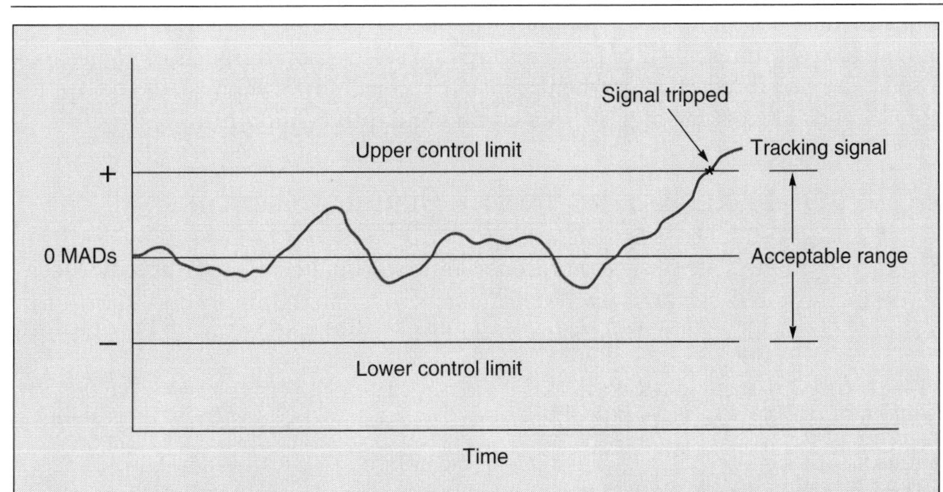

FIGURE S2.7

A PLOT OF TRACKING SIGNALS

Wight, two inventory control experts, suggested using maximums of ±4 MADs (for high-volume stock items) and ±8 MADs (for lower-volume items).[5] Other forecasters suggest slightly lower ranges. One MAD is equivalent to approximately .8 standard deviations, so that ±2 MADs = ±1.6 standard deviations, ± 3 MADs = ±2.4 standard deviations, and ±4 MADs = ±3.2 standard deviations. This suggests that for a forecast to be "in control," 89% of the errors are expected to fall within ±2 MADs, 98% within ±3 MADs, or 99.9% within ±4 MADs.[6]

Example S12 shows how the tracking signal and RSFE can be computed.

EXAMPLE S12

Spot-Less Dry Cleaners' quarterly sales (in thousands), as well as forecast sales and error computations, are shown below. The objective is to compute the tracking signal and determine whether forecasts are performing adequately.

QUARTER	FORECAST SALES	ACTUAL SALES	ERROR	RSFE	|FORECAST| ERROR	CUMULATIVE ERROR	MAD	TRACKING SIGNAL
1	100	90	−10	−10	10	10	10.0	−1
2	100	95	− 5	−15	5	15	7.5	−2
3	100	115	+15	0	15	30	10.0	0
4	110	100	−10	−10	10	40	10.0	−1
5	110	125	+15	+ 5	5	55	11.0	+ .5
6	110	140	+30	+35	30	85	14.2	+2.5

$$\text{MAD} = \frac{\Sigma|\text{Forecast errors}|}{n} = \frac{85}{6} = 14.2$$

$$\text{Tracking signal} = \frac{\text{RSFE}}{\text{MAD}} = \frac{35}{14.2} = 2.5 \text{ MADs}$$

This tracking signal is within acceptable limits. We see that it drifted from −2.0 MADs to +2.5 MADs.

Adaptive Smoothing

adaptive smoothing

Adaptive forecasting refers to computer monitoring of tracking signals and self-adjustment if a signal passes its preset limit. For example, when applied to exponential smoothing, the α coefficients are first selected on the basis of values that minimize error forecasts, and then adjusted accordingly whenever the computer notes an errant tracking signal. This is called **adaptive smoothing.**

FORECASTING IN THE SERVICE SECTOR

Forecasting in the service sector presents some unusual challenges. A major technique in the retail sector is to track demand by maintaining good short-term records. For instance, a barber shop catering to men needs to expect peak flows

[5]See G. W. Plossl and O. W. Wight, *Production and Inventory Control* (Englewood Cliffs, NJ: Prentice-Hall, 1967).

[6]To prove these three percentages to yourself, just set up a normal curve for ±1.6 standard deviations (z values). Using the normal table in Appendix A you find that the area under the curve is .89. This represents ±2 MADs. Likewise, ±3 MADs = ±2.4 standard deviations encompasses 98% of the area, and so on for ±4 MADs.

on Fridays and Saturdays. Indeed most barber shops will be closed Sunday and Monday and many call in extra help Friday and Saturday. A downtown restaurant on the other hand may need to track conventions and holidays for effective short-term forecasting.

Specialty retail facilities, such as a flower shop, may have other unusual demand patterns and the patterns differ depending on the holiday. When Valentine's Day falls on a weekend, flowers can't be delivered to an office and those romantically inclined are likely to celebrate with an outing rather than flowers. If a holiday falls on a Monday, some of the celebration may also take place on the weekend, reducing flower sales. However, when Valentine's Day falls in midweek, flowers are often the optimal way to celebrate because of busy midweek schedules. Flowers for Mother's Day are to be delivered Saturday or Sunday regardless so this forecast varies less. Because of these special demand patterns, many service firms maintain records of sales, noting not only the day of the week, but also unusual events, including the weather, so patterns and correlations which influence demand can be developed.

Fast-food restaurants are well aware of not only weekly and daily, but even hourly demands that influence sales. Therefore, detailed forecasts of demand are needed. Rather than maintain a manual log, many firms now use point-of-sale computers that track sales by time period, perhaps every 15 minutes. Figure S2.8 shows the hourly forecast for a typical fast-food restaurant.

THE COMPUTER'S ROLE IN FORECASTING

Forecast calculations are seldom performed by hand in this day of computers. Many academic and commercially packaged programs are readily available to handle time series and causal projections.

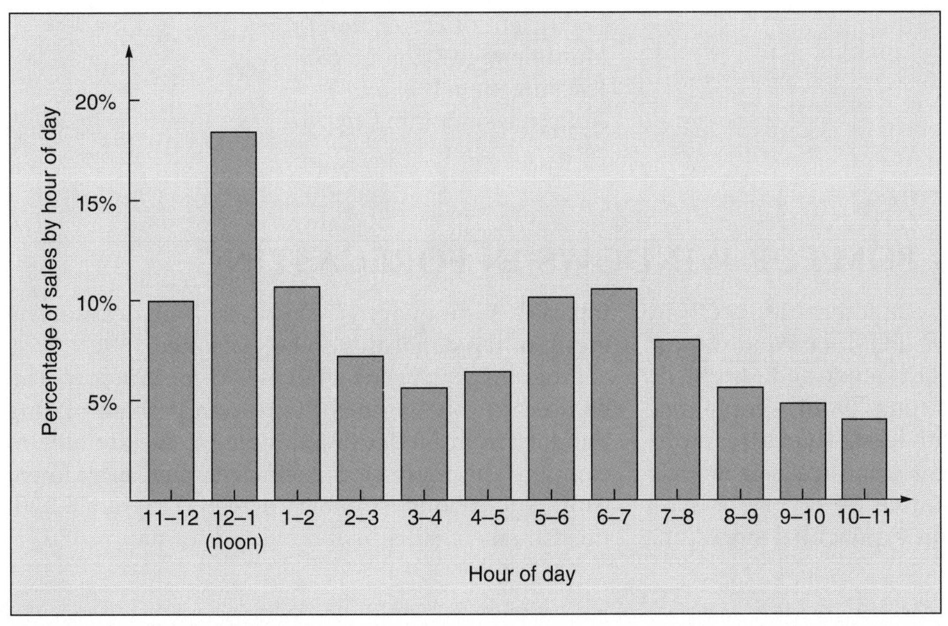

FIGURE S2.8

FORECAST OF SALES BY HOUR FOR A FAST-FOOD RESTAURANT

Popular mainframe-oriented packages include General Electric's *Time Series Forecasting*, and IBM's IMPACT (Inventory Management Program and Control Technique). Popular packages for PCs are SAS, SPSS, BIOMED, SYSTAB, POM for Windows, and Minitab. POM for Windows and Excel spreadsheets are both illustrated shortly.

SUMMARY

Forecasts are a critical part of the operations manager's function. Demand forecasts drive the production, capacity, and scheduling systems in a firm and affect the financial marketing, and personnel planning functions.

In this supplement we introduced a variety of qualitative and quantitative forecasting techniques. Qualitative approaches employ judgment, experience, intuition, and a host of other factors that are difficult to quantify. Quantitative forecasting uses historical data and causal relations to project future demands.

No forecasting method is perfect under all conditions. And even once management has found a satisfactory approach, it must still monitor and control its forecasts to make sure errors do not get out of hand. Forecasting can often be a very challenging, but rewarding, part of managing.

KEY TERMS

Forecasting *(p. 46)*
Economic forecasts *(p. 48)*
Technological forecasts *(p. 48)*
Demand forecasts *(p. 48)*
Quantitative forecasts *(p. 49)*
Qualitative forecasts *(p. 49)*
Jury of executive opinion *(p. 49)*
Sales force composite *(p. 49)*
Delphi method *(p. 49)*
Consumer market survey *(p. 49)*
Naive approach *(p. 49)*
Time series *(p. 50)*
Moving averages *(p. 52)*
Exponential smoothing *(p. 54)*
Smoothing constant *(p. 54)*
Mean absolute deviation (MAD) *(p. 56)*
Mean squared error (MSE) *(p. 57)*
Trend projection *(p. 58)*
Linear regression analysis *(p. 63)*
Standard error of the estimate *(p. 65)*
Coefficient of correlation *(p. 66)*
Multiple regression *(p. 68)*
Tracking signal *(p. 69)*
Adaptive smoothing *(p. 70)*

USING POM FOR WINDOWS IN FORECASTING

In this section, we look at our forecasting software package, POM for Windows. POM for Windows can project moving averages (both simple and weighted), handle exponential smoothing (both simple and trend-adjusted), forecast with least squares trend projection, and solve linear regression (causal) models.

Program S2.1 uses Example S4's Port of New Orleans data to illustrate an exponential smoothing forecast. A summary screen of error analysis and a graph of the data can also be generated.

Program S2.2A shows how POM for Windows can be used to solve a linear regression problem. Using the data from Nodel in Example S8, we are able to compute the regression coefficients and error measures. An optional summary screen (Program S2.2B) presents the results in abbreviated format.

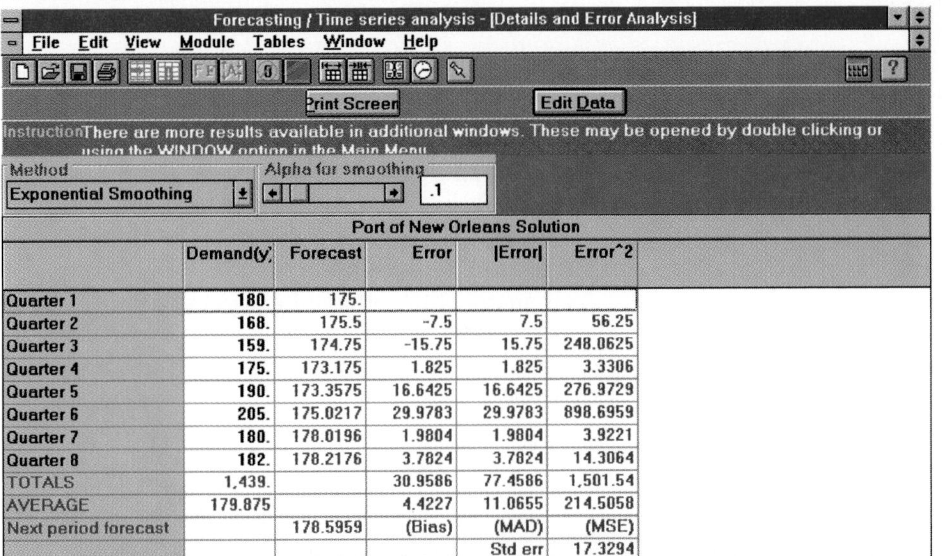

Forecasting / Time series analysis - [Details and Error Analysis]

File Edit View Module Tables Window Help

Print Screen Edit Data

Instruction There are more results available in additional windows. These may be opened by double clicking or using the WINDOW option in the Main Menu

Method: Exponential Smoothing

Alpha for smoothing: .1

Port of New Orleans Solution

	Demand(y)	Forecast	Error	|Error|	Error^2
Quarter 1	180.	175.			
Quarter 2	168.	175.5	-7.5	7.5	56.25
Quarter 3	159.	174.75	-15.75	15.75	248.0625
Quarter 4	175.	173.175	1.825	1.825	3.3306
Quarter 5	190.	173.3575	16.6425	16.6425	276.9729
Quarter 6	205.	175.0217	29.9783	29.9783	898.6959
Quarter 7	180.	178.0196	1.9804	1.9804	3.9221
Quarter 8	182.	178.2176	3.7824	3.7824	14.3064
TOTALS	1,439.		30.9586	77.4586	1,501.54
AVERAGE	179.875		4.4227	11.0655	214.5058
Next period forecast		178.5959	(Bias)	(MAD)	(MSE)
				Std err	17.3294

PROGRAM S2.1

POM FOR WINDOWS EXPONENTIAL SMOOTHING EXAMPLE, USING PORT OF NEW ORLEANS' DATA

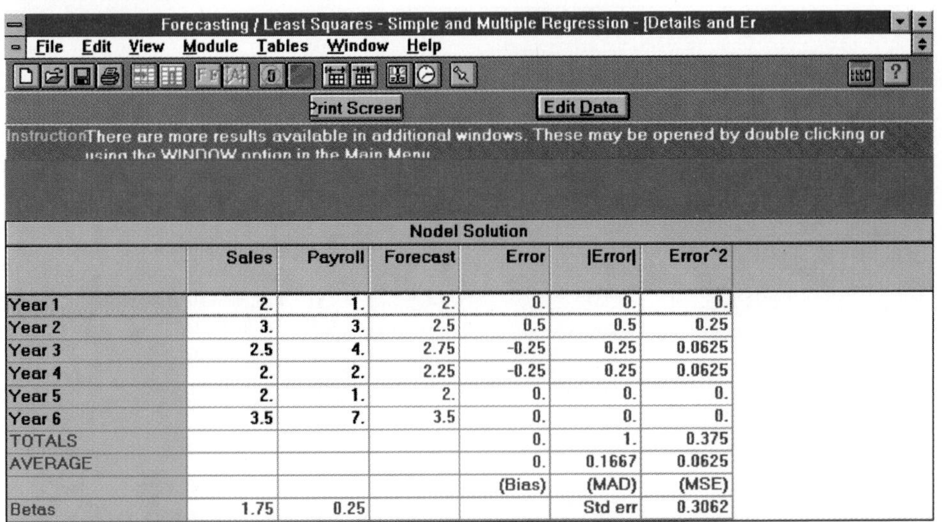

Forecasting / Least Squares - Simple and Multiple Regression - [Details and Er

File Edit View Module Tables Window Help

Print Screen Edit Data

Instruction There are more results available in additional windows. These may be opened by double clicking or using the WINDOW option in the Main Menu

Nodel Solution

	Sales	Payroll	Forecast	Error	|Error|	Error^2
Year 1	2.	1.	2.	0.	0.	0.
Year 2	3.	3.	2.5	0.5	0.5	0.25
Year 3	2.5	4.	2.75	-0.25	0.25	0.0625
Year 4	2.	2.	2.25	-0.25	0.25	0.0625
Year 5	2.	1.	2.	0.	0.	0.
Year 6	3.5	7.	3.5	0.	0.	0.
TOTALS				0.	1.	0.375
AVERAGE				0.	0.1667	0.0625
				(Bias)	(MAD)	(MSE)
Betas	1.75	0.25			Std err	0.3062

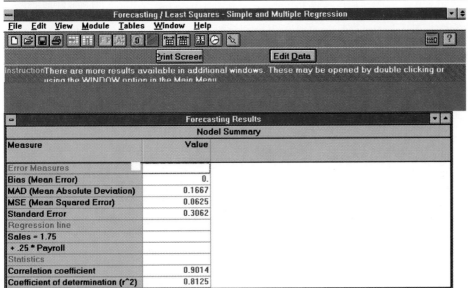

PROGRAM S2.2A

POM FOR WINDOWS LINEAR REGRESSION PROGRAM USING EXAMPLE S8 DATA. THIS IS THE OVERVIEW SCREEN.

Forecasting / Least Squares - Simple and Multiple Regression

File Edit View Module Tables Window Help

Print Screen Edit Data

Instruction There are more results available in additional windows. These may be opened by double clicking or using the WINDOW option in the Main Menu

Forecasting Results

Nodel Summary

Measure	Value
Error Measures	
Bias (Mean Error)	0.
MAD (Mean Absolute Deviation)	0.1667
MSE (Mean Squared Error)	0.0625
Standard Error	0.3062
Regression line	
Sales = 1.75	
+ .25 * Payroll	
Statistics	
Correlation coefficient	0.9014
Coefficient of determination (r^2)	0.8125

PROGRAM S2.2B

POM FOR WINDOWS LINEAR REGRESSION PROGRAM USING EXAMPLE S8 DATA. THIS IS THE SUMMARY SCREEN FOR OUTPUT THAT APPEARS IN PROGRAM S2.2A.

USING EXCEL SPREADSHEETS IN FORECASTING

Excel and other spreadsheets are frequently used for forecasting. Both exponential smoothing and regression analysis are supported by built-in Excel functions.

Program S2.3 illustrates the use of Excel in solving the Port of New Orleans' exponential smoothing problem (see Example S4).

Since regression analysis is a common task performed with spreadsheets, spreadsheet makers have gone to great lengths to integrate sophisticated procedures for performing regression. Excel offers several plots and tables to those interested in more rigorous analysis of regression problems.

Programs S2.4 and S2.5 illustrate the input and output of an Excel regression on data from Example S8. As in many of the other add-in packages to Excel, regression offers a variety of analyses. Try checking the different boxes to see what other outputs are offered by Excel.

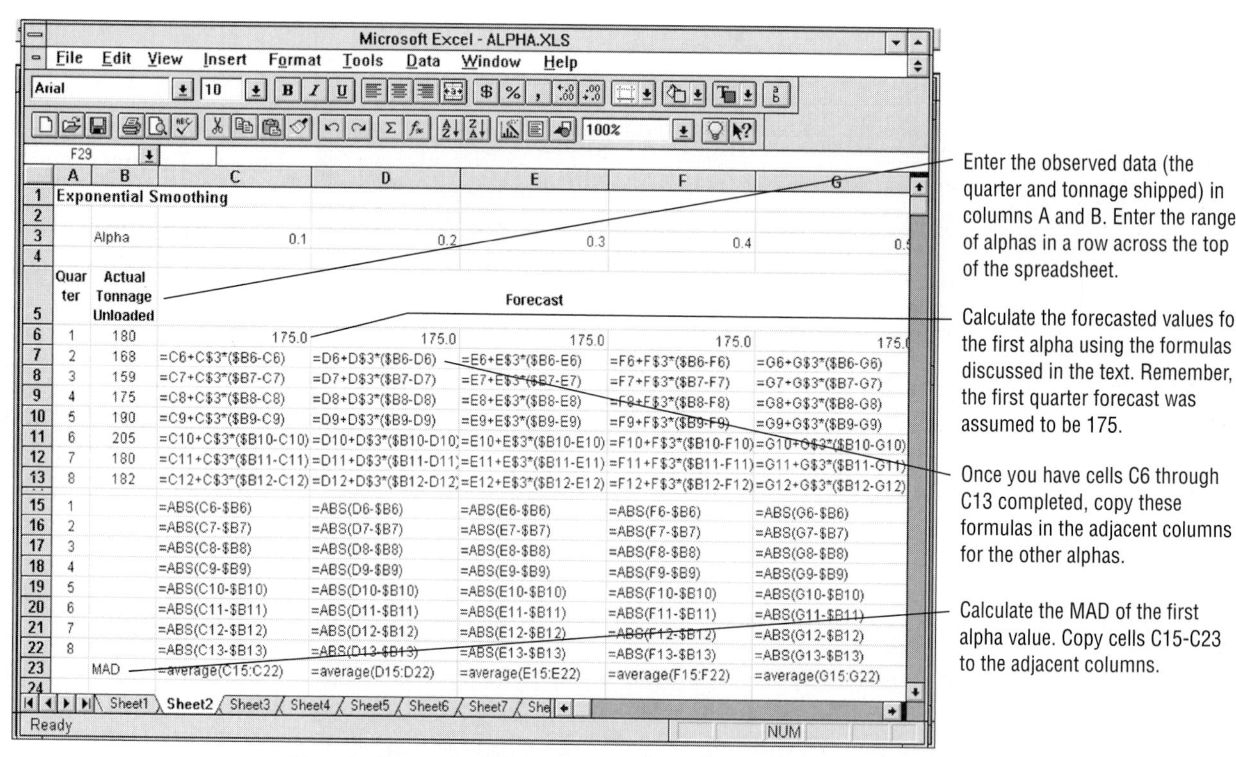

	A	B	C	D	E	F	G
1	Exponential Smoothing						
2							
3		Alpha	0.1	0.2	0.3	0.4	0.
4							
5	Quarter	Actual Tonnage Unloaded			Forecast		
6	1	180	175.0	175.0	175.0	175.0	175.
7	2	168	=C6+C$3*($B6-C6)	=D6+D$3*($B6-D6)	=E6+E$3*($B6-E6)	=F6+F$3*($B6-F6)	=G6+G$3*($B6-G6)
8	3	159	=C7+C$3*($B7-C7)	=D7+D$3*($B7-D7)	=E7+E$3*($B7-E7)	=F7+F$3*($B7-F7)	=G7+G$3*($B7-G7)
9	4	175	=C8+C$3*($B8-C8)	=D8+D$3*($B8-D8)	=E8+E$3*($B8-E8)	=F8+F$3*($B8-F8)	=G8+G$3*($B8-G8)
10	5	190	=C9+C$3*($B9-C9)	=D9+D$3*($B9-D9)	=E9+E$3*($B9-E9)	=F9+F$3*($B9-F9)	=G9+G$3*($B9-G9)
11	6	205	=C10+C$3*($B10-C10)	=D10+D$3*($B10-D10)	=E10+E$3*($B10-E10)	=F10+F$3*($B10-F10)	=G10+G$3*($B10-G10)
12	7	180	=C11+C$3*($B11-C11)	=D11+D$3*($B11-D11)	=E11+E$3*($B11-E11)	=F11+F$3*($B11-F11)	=G11+G$3*($B11-G11)
13	8	182	=C12+C$3*($B12-C12)	=D12+D$3*($B12-D12)	=E12+E$3*($B12-E12)	=F12+F$3*($B12-F12)	=G12+G$3*($B12-G12)
15	1		=ABS(C6-$B6)	=ABS(D6-$B6)	=ABS(E6-$B6)	=ABS(F6-$B6)	=ABS(G6-$B6)
16	2		=ABS(C7-$B7)	=ABS(D7-$B7)	=ABS(E7-$B7)	=ABS(F7-$B7)	=ABS(G7-$B7)
17	3		=ABS(C8-$B8)	=ABS(D8-$B8)	=ABS(E8-$B8)	=ABS(F8-$B8)	=ABS(G8-$B8)
18	4		=ABS(C9-$B9)	=ABS(D9-$B9)	=ABS(E9-$B9)	=ABS(F9-$B9)	=ABS(G9-$B9)
19	5		=ABS(C10-$B10)	=ABS(D10-$B10)	=ABS(E10-$B10)	=ABS(F10-$B10)	=ABS(G10-$B10)
20	6		=ABS(C11-$B11)	=ABS(D11-$B11)	=ABS(E11-$B11)	=ABS(F11-$B11)	=ABS(G11-$B11)
21	7		=ABS(C12-$B12)	=ABS(D12-$B12)	=ABS(E12-$B12)	=ABS(F12-$B12)	=ABS(G12-$B12)
22	8		=ABS(C13-$B13)	=ABS(D13-$B13)	=ABS(E13-$B13)	=ABS(F13-$B13)	=ABS(G13-$B13)
23		MAD	=average(C15:C22)	=average(D15:D22)	=average(E15:E22)	=average(F15:F22)	=average(G15:G22)

PROGRAM S2.3 EXCEL SPREADSHEET FOR EXPONENTIAL SMOOTHING

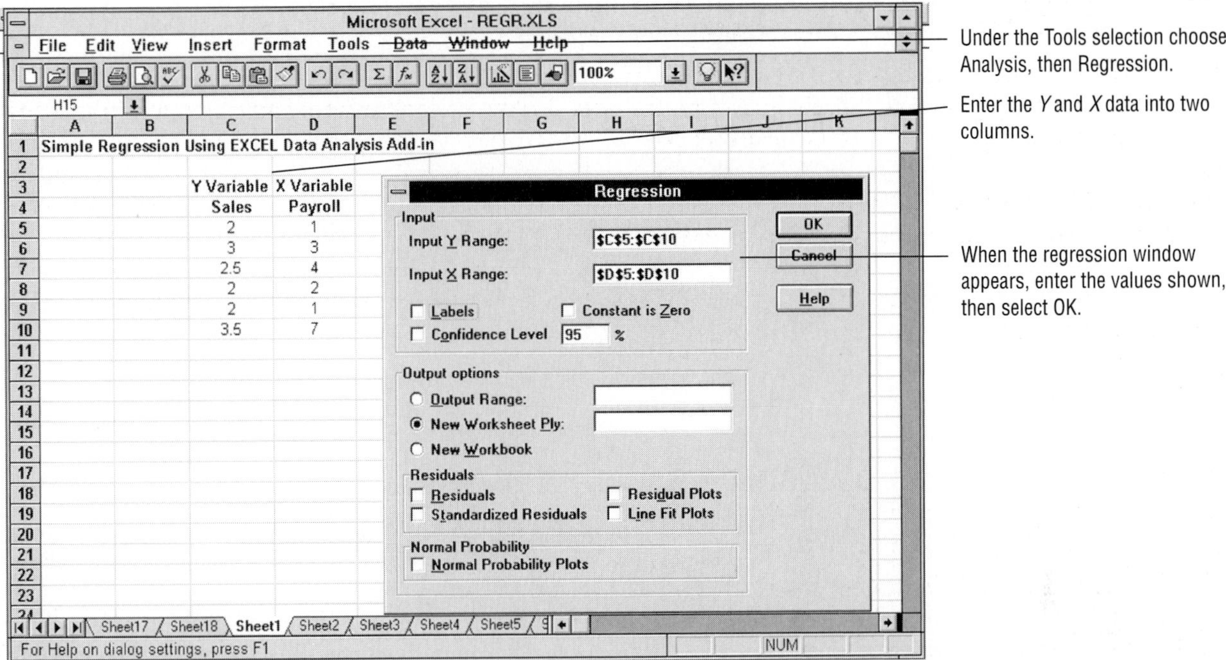

PROGRAM S2.4 USING EXCEL TO SOLVE THE NODEL CONSTRUCTION REGRESSION PROBLEM

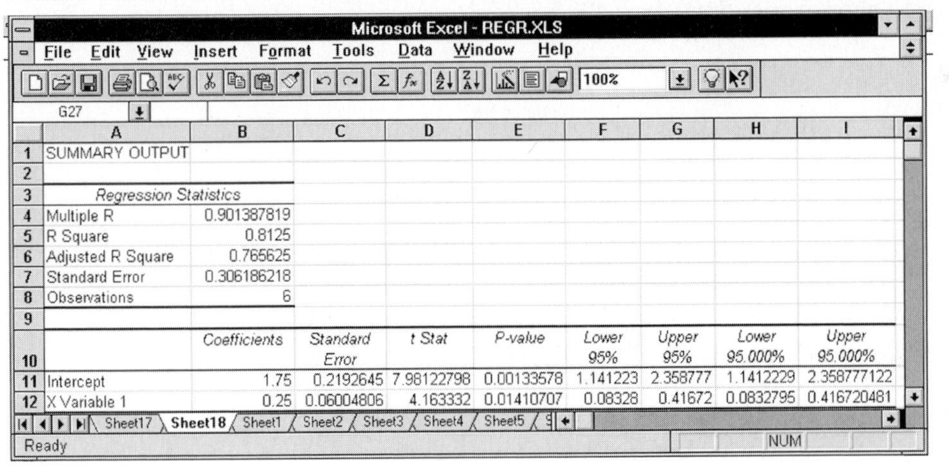

SUMMARY OUTPUT

Regression Statistics	
Multiple R	0.901387819
R Square	0.8125
Adjusted R Square	0.765625
Standard Error	0.306186218
Observations	6

	Coefficients	Standard Error	t Stat	P-value	Lower 95%	Upper 95%	Lower 95.000%	Upper 95.000%
Intercept	1.75	0.2192645	7.98122798	0.00133578	1.141223	2.358777	1.1412229	2.358777122
X Variable 1	0.25	0.06004806	4.163332	0.01410707	0.08328	0.41672	0.0832795	0.416720481

PROGRAM S2.5

OUTPUT FROM EXCEL'S REGRESSION ANALYSIS IN PROGRAM S2.4

SOLVED PROBLEM S2.1

Sales of Green Line Jet Skis have grown steadily during the past five years (see table). Gary Heldman, the sales manager had predicted in 1991 that 1992 sales would be 410 jet skis. Using exponential smoothing with a weight of $\alpha = .30$, develop forecasts for 1993 through 1997.

YEAR	SALES	FORECAST
1992	450	410
1993	495	
1994	518	
1995	563	
1996	584	
1997	?	

SOLUTION

YEAR	FORECAST
1992	410.0
1993	422.0 = 410 + .3 (450 − 410)
1994	443.9 = 422 + .3 (495 − 422)
1995	466.1 = 443.9 + .3 (518 − 443.9)
1996	495.2 = 466.1 + .3 (563 − 466.1)
1997	521.8 = 495.2 + .3 (584 − 495.2)

SOLVED PROBLEM S2.2

Memberships in the Body-Builder Health Club, Chicago's largest, have been recorded for the past nine years. Management would like to determine the mathematical trend of memberships in order to project future space needs. This estimate would help the club determine whether a future expansion will be needed. Given the following time series data, develop a regression equation relating memberships to time. Then forecast 1998 memberships. Memberships are in the thousands:

YEAR	1988	1989	1990	1991	1992	1993	1994	1995	1996
MEMBERSHIP	17	16	16	21	20	20	23	25	24

SOLUTION

YEAR	TRANSFORMED YEAR, x	MEMBERSHIPS, y (in thousands)	x^2	xy
1988	1	17	1	17
1989	2	16	4	32
1990	3	16	9	48
1991	4	21	16	84
1992	5	20	25	100
1993	6	20	36	120
1994	7	23	49	161
1995	8	25	64	200
1996	9	24	81	216
1996	$\Sigma x = 45$	$\Sigma y = 182$	$\Sigma x^2 = 285$	$\Sigma xy = 978$

$$\bar{x} = \frac{45}{9} = 5, \qquad \bar{y} = \frac{182}{9} = 20.22$$

$$b = \frac{\Sigma xy - n\bar{x}\bar{y}}{\Sigma x^2 - n\bar{x}^2} = \frac{978 - (9)(5)(20.22)}{285 - (9)(25)}$$

$$= \frac{978 - 909.9}{285 - 225} = \frac{68.1}{60} = 1.135$$

$$a = \bar{y} - b\bar{x} = 20.22 - (1.135)(5) = 20.22 - 5.675$$

$$= 14.545$$

$$\hat{y} \text{ (memberships)} = 14.545 + 1.135x$$

The projection of memberships in 1998 (which is $x = 11$ in the coding system used) is:

$$\hat{y} = 14.545 + (1.135)(11) = 27.03$$

or 27,030 members in 1998.

SOLVED PROBLEM S2.3

Quarterly demand for rhinoplasty surgeries (commonly called "nose jobs") at a Beverly Hills clinic is forecast with the equation:

$$\hat{y} = 10 + 3x$$

where x = quarters, and

Quarter I of 1995 = 0
Quarter II of 1995 = 1
Quarter III of 1995 = 2
Quarter IV of 1995 = 3
Quarter I of 1996 = 4
and so on

and

$$\hat{y} = \text{Quarterly demand}$$

The demand for this particular surgery is seasonal (due to summer and winter holidays), and the indices for Quarters I, II, III, and IV are .80, 1.00, 1.30, and .90, respectively. Forecast demand for each quarter of 1997. Then seasonalize each forecast to adjust for quarterly variations.

SOLUTION

Quarter II of 1996 is coded $x = 5$; Quarter III of 1996, $x = 6$; and Quarter IV of 1996, $x = 7$. Hence, Quarter I of 1997 is coded $x = 8$; Quarter II, $x = 9$; and so on.

$\hat{y}$ (1997 Quarter I) = 10 + 3(8) = 34
Adjusted forecast = (.80)(34) = 27.2

$\hat{y}$ (1997 Quarter II) = 10 + 3(9) = 37
Adjusted forecast = (1.00)(37) = 37

$\hat{y}$ (1997 Quarter III) = 10 + 3(10) = 40
Adjusted forecast = (1.30)(40) = 52

$\hat{y}$ (1997 Quarter IV) = 10 + 3(11) = 43
Adjusted forecast = (.90)(43) = 38.7

DISCUSSION QUESTIONS

1. Briefly describe the steps that are used to develop a forecasting system.
2. What is a time series forecasting model?
3. What is the difference between a causal model and a time series model?
4. What is a judgmental forecasting model, and when is it appropriate?
5. What is the meaning of least squares in a regression model?
6. What are some of the problems and drawbacks of the moving average forecasting model?
7. What effect does the value of the smoothing constant have on the weight given to the past forecast and the past observed value?
8. Briefly describe the Delphi method.
9. What is MAD, and why is it important in the selection and use of forecasting models?

OPERATIONS IN PRACTICE EXERCISE

In 1996, the Board of Regents, responsible for all public higher education funding in a large midwestern state, hired a consultant to develop a series of enrollment forecasting models, one for each college. These models used historical data and exponential smoothing to forecast next year's enrollments. Based on the model, which included a smoothing constant (α) for each school, each college's budget was set by the Board. The head of the Board personally selected each smoothing constant, based on what she called her "gut reactions and political acumen."

What do you think the advantages and disadvantages of this system are? Answer from the perspective of (a) the Board of Regents and (b) the president of each college. How can this model be abused, and what could be done to remove any biases? How can a *regression model* be used to produce results that favor one forecast over another?

SELF-TEST ■ SUPPLEMENT 2

- *Before taking the self-test* refer back to the learning objectives listed at the beginning of the supplement and the key terms listed at the end of the supplement.
- Use the key at the back of the text to *correct* your answers.
- *Restudy* pages that correspond to any questions you answered incorrectly or material you feel uncertain about.

1. Forecasting time horizons include
   a. long range
   b. medium range
   c. short range
   d. all of the above

2. A forecast that projects company's sales is a(n)
   a. economic forecast
   b. technological forecast
   c. demand forecast

3. Quantitative methods of forecasting include
   a. sales force composite
   b. jury of executive opinion
   c. consumer market survey
   d. exponential smoothing
   e. all are quantitative methods

4. The method that considers several variables that are related to the variable being predicted is
   a. exponential smoothing
   b. multiple regression
   c. weighted moving average
   d. all of the above

5. Exponential smoothing is an example of a causal model.
   a. True b. False

6. A time series model incorporates the various factors that might influence the quantity being forecast.
   a. True b. False

7. Decomposing a time series refers to breaking down past data into the components of
   a. constants and variations
   b. trends, cycles, and random variations
   c. strategic, tactical, and operational variations
   d. long-term, short-term, and medium-term variations

8. In exponential smoothing, when the smoothing constant is high, more weight is placed on the more recent data.
   a. True b. False

9. Two popular measures of forecast accuracy are
   a. total error and average error
   b. average error and median error
   c. median error and minimum error
   d. mean absolute error and mean squared error

10. Trend-adjusted exponential smoothing is also referred to as seasonal order smoothing.
    a. True b. False

11. Unfortunately, regression analysis can only be used to develop a forecast based upon a single independent variable.
    a. True b. False

12. A fundamental weakness of causal forecasting methods is that we must first forecast the value of the independent variable, *then* apply that value in the forecast of the dependent variable.
    a. True b. False

13. With regard to a regression-based forecast, the *standard error of the estimate* gives a measure of
    a. the overall accuracy of the forecast
    b. the time period for which the forecast is valid
    c. the time required to derive the forecast equation
    d. the maximum error of the forecast

14. One method of choosing among various smoothing constants when using exponential smoothing is to evaluate the mean absolute deviation (MAD) for each smoothing constant, and choose the smoothing constant that provides the minimum MAD.
    a. True b. False

15. No single forecast methodology is appropriate under all conditions.
    a. True b. False

16. The difference between a dependent and an independent variable is that ________.

17. Quantitative forecasting methods include:
    a. ____ b. ____ c. ____ d. ____

18. A time series variable typically has the four components:
    a. ____ b. ____ c. ____ d. ____

19. Qualitative forecast methods include:
    a. ____ b. ____ c. ____ d. ____
    e. ____

20. The purpose of a *tracking signal* is to: ________

21. The difference between a *moving average* model and an *exponential smoothing* model is that: ________

PROBLEMS

S2.1. Daily high temperatures in the city of Houston for the last week have been as follows: 93, 94, 93, 95, 96, 88, 90 (yesterday).

a. Forecast the high temperature today, using a three-day moving average.
b. Forecast the high temperature today, using a two-day moving average.
c. Calculate the mean absolute deviation based on a two-day moving average.

S2.2. For the following data, develop a three-month moving average forecast.

MONTH	Jan.	Feb.	Mar.	Apr.	May	June	July	Aug.	Sept.	Oct.	Nov.	Dec.
AUTO BATTERY SALES	20	21	15	14	13	16	17	18	20	20	21	23

S2.3. Given the following data, develop a three-year moving average forecast of demand

YEAR	1	2	3	4	5	6	7	8	9	10	11
DEMAND	7	9	5	9	13	8	12	13	9	11	7

S2.4. Susan Goodman has developed the following forecasting model:

$$\hat{y} = 36 + 4.3x$$

where

$\hat{y}$ = demand for Aztec air conditioners

x = the outside temperature (°F)

a. Forecast demand for the Aztec when the temperature is 70°F.
b. What is demand for a temperature of 80°F?
c. What is demand for a temperature of 90°F?

S2.5. Data collected on the yearly demand for 50-lb bags of grass seed at Bob's Hardware Store are shown in the following table. Develop a three-year moving average to forecast sales. Then estimate demand again with a weighted moving average in which sales in the most recent year are given a weight of 2 and sales in the other two years are each given a weight of 1. Which method do you think is best?

YEAR	1	2	3	4	5	6	7	8	9	10	11
DEMAND FOR GRASS SEED (thousands of bags)	4	6	4	5	10	8	7	9	12	14	15

S2.6. Develop a two- and a four-year moving average for the demand for bags of grass seed in Problem S2.5.

S2.7. In Problems S2.5 and S2.6, four different forecasts were developed for the demand for grass seed. These four forecasts are a two-year moving average, a three-year moving average, a weighted moving average, and a four-year moving average. Which one would you use? Explain your answer.

S2.8. Use exponential smoothing with a smoothing constant of .3 to forecast the demand for grass seed given in Problem S2.5. Assume that last period's forecast for year 1 is 5,000 bags to begin the procedure. Would you prefer to use the exponential smoothing model or the weighted average model developed in Problem S2.5? Explain your answer.

S2.9. Using smoothing constants of .6 and .9, develop forecasts for the sales of Green Line Jet Skis. See Solved Problem S2.1 at the end of this supplement.

• **S2.10.** What effect did the smoothing constant have on the forecast for Green Line Jet Skis? See Solved Problem S2.1 and Problem S2.9. Which smoothing constant gives the most accurate forecast?

• **S2.11.** Use a three-year moving average forecasting model to forecast the sales of Green Line Jet Skis. See Solved Problem S2.1 at the end of this supplement.

• **S2.12.** Using the trend projection method, develop a forecasting model for the sales of Green Line Jet Skis. See Solved Problem S2.1 at the end of this supplement.

: **S2.13.** Would you use exponential smoothing with a smoothing constant of .3, a three-year moving average, or trend to predict the sales of Green Line Jet Skis? Refer to Solved Problem S2.1 and Problems S2.11 and S2.12.

⋮ **S2.14.** Demand for heart transplant surgery at Washington General Hospital has increased steadily in the past few years, as seen in the following table:

YEAR	1	2	3	4	5	6
HEART TRANSPLANT SURGERIES PERFORMED	45	50	52	56	58	?

The director of medical services predicted six years ago that demand in year 1 would be for 41 surgeries.

a. Use exponential smoothing, first with a smoothing constant of .6 and then with one of .9, to develop forecasts for years 2 through 6.

b. Use a three-year moving average to forecast demand in years 4, 5, and 6.

c. Use the trend projection method to forecast demand in years 1 through 6.

d. With MAD as the criterion, which of the above four forecasting approaches is best?

• **S2.15.** A careful analysis of the cost of operating an automobile was conducted by a firm. The following model was developed:

$$Y = 4{,}000 + 0.20X$$

where

$$Y = \text{Annual cost}$$

$$X = \text{Miles driven}$$

a. If a car is driven 15,000 miles this year, what is the forecasted cost of operating this automobile?

b. If a car is driven 25,000 miles this year, what is the forecasted cost of operating this automobile?

c. Suppose that one car was driven 15,000 miles and the actual cost of operating this was $6,000, while a second car was driven 25,000 miles and the actual operating cost was $10,000. Calculate the mean absolute deviation for this.

• **S2.16.** Given the following data, use exponential smoothing ($\alpha = 0.2$) to develop a demand forecast. Assume the forecast for the initial period is 5.

PERIOD	1	2	3	4	5	6
DEMAND	7	9	5	9	13	8

: **S2.17.** Calculate (a) MAD and (b) MSE for the following forecast versus actual sales figures:

FORECAST	100	110	120	130
ACTUAL	95	108	123	130

: **S2.18.** Given the following data, use the least squares regression to derive a forecasting equation. What is your estimate of the demand in period 7?

PERIOD	1	2	3	4	5	6
DEMAND	7	9	5	11	10	13

: **S2.19.** Given the following data, use least squares regression to develop a relationship between the number of rainy summer days and the number of games lost by the Boca Raton Cardinal baseball team.

YEAR	RAINY SUMMER DAYS	GAMES LOST BY THE CARDINALS
1	15	25
2	25	20
3	10	10
4	10	15
5	30	20
6	20	15
7	20	20
8	15	10
9	10	5
10	25	20

: **S2.20.** Sales of industrial vacuum cleaners at Richard D. Reis Supply Co. over the past 13 months are shown below:

MONTH	Jan.	Feb.	Mar.	Apr.	May	June	July	Aug.	Sept.	Oct.	Nov.	Dec.	Jan.
SALES (in thousands)	11	14	16	10	15	17	11	14	17	12	14	16	11

a. Using a moving average with three periods, determine the demand for vacuum cleaners for next February.

b. Using a weighted moving average with three periods, determine the demand for vacuum cleaners for February. Use 3, 2, and 1 for the weights of the most recent, second most recent, and third most recent periods, respectively. For example, if you were forecasting the demand for February, November would have a weight of 1, December would have a weight of 2, and January would have a weight of 3.

c. Evaluate the accuracy of each of these methods.

d. What other factors might Reis consider in forecasting sales?

: **S2.21.** The operations manager of a musical instrument distributor feels that demand for bass drums may be related to the number of television appearances by the popular rock group Green Shades during the previous month. The manager has collected the data shown in the following table:

DEMAND FOR BASS DRUMS	3	6	7	5	10	8
GREEN SHADES TV APPEARANCES	3	4	7	6	8	5

a. Graph these data to see whether a linear equation might describe the relationship between the group's television shows and bass drum sales.

b. Use the least squares regression method to derive a forecasting equation.

c. What is your estimate for bass drum sales if the Green Shades performed on TV nine times last month?

S2.22. A study to determine the correlation between bank deposits and consumer price indices in Birmingham, Alabama, revealed the following (which was based on $n = 5$ years of data):

$\Sigma x = 15 \quad \Sigma x^2 = 55 \quad \Sigma xy = 70 \quad \Sigma y = 20 \quad \Sigma y^2 = 130$

a. Find the coefficient of correlation. What does it suggest to you?
b. What is the standard error of the estimate?

S2.23. The accountant at Leslie Wardrop Coal Distributors, Inc., notes that the demand for coal seems to be tied to an index of weather severity developed by the U.S. Weather Bureau. That is, when weather was extremely cold in the United States over the past five years (and hence the index was high), coal sales were high. The accountant proposes that one good forecast of next year's coal demand could be made by developing a regression equation and then consulting the *Farmer's Almanac* to see how severe next year's winter will be. For the data in the following table, derive a least squares regression and compute the coefficient of correlation of the data. Also compute the standard error of the estimate.

COAL SALES, y (in millions of tons)	4	1	4	6	5
WEATHER INDEX, x	2	1	4	5	3

S2.24. Thirteen students entered the OM program at Rollins College two years ago. The following table indicates what their grade-point averages (GPAs) were after being in the program for two years and what each student scored on the SAT exam when he or she was in high school. Is there a meaningful relationship between grades and SAT scores? If a student scores a 350 on the SAT, what do you think his or her GPA will be? What about a student who scores 800?

STUDENT	A	B	C	D	E	F	G	H	I	J	K	L	M
SAT SCORE	421	377	585	690	608	390	415	481	729	501	613	709	366
GPA	2.90	2.93	3.00	3.45	3.66	2.88	2.15	2.53	3.22	1.99	2.75	3.90	1.60

S2.25. Dr. Jerilyn Ross, a New York City psychologist, specializes in treating patients who are phobic and afraid to leave their homes. The following table indicates how many patients Dr. Ross has seen each year for the past ten years. It also indicates what the robbery rate was in New York City during the same year.

YEAR	NUMBER OF PATIENTS	CRIME RATE (robberies) PER 1,000 POPULATION
1	36	58.3
2	33	61.1
3	40	73.4
4	41	75.7
5	40	81.1
6	55	89.0
7	60	101.1
8	54	94.8
9	58	103.3
10	61	116.2

Using trend analysis, how many patients do you think Dr. Ross will see in years 11, 12, and 13? How well does the model fit the data?

S2.26. Using the data in Problem S2.25, apply linear regression to study the relationship between the crime rate and Dr. Ross's patient load. If the robbery rate increases to 131.2 in year 11, how many phobic patients will Dr. Ross treat? If the crime rate drops to 90.6, what is the patient projection?

• **S2.27.** Accountants at the firm Gets and Farnsworth believed that several traveling executives submit unusually high travel vouchers when they return from business trips. The accountants took a sample of 200 vouchers submitted from the past year; they then developed the following multiple regression equation relating expected travel cost ($\hat{y}$) to number of days on the road (x_1) and distance traveled (x_2) in miles:

$$\hat{y} = \$90.00 + \$48.50x_1 + 40x_2$$

The coefficient of correlation computed was .68.

a. If Bill Tomlinson returns from a 300-mile trip that took him out of town for five days, what is the expected amount he should claim as expenses?

b. Tomlinson submitted a reimbursement request for $685. What should the accountant do?

c. Should any other variables be included? Which ones? Why?

• **S2.28.** In the past, Laura Gustafson's tire dealership sold an average of 1,000 radials each year. In the past two years, 200 and 250, respectively, were sold in the fall, 300 and 350 in the winter, 150 and 165 in the spring, and 300 and 285 in the summer. With a major expansion planned, Mrs. Gustafson projects sales next year to increase to 1,200 radials. What will the demand be each season?

• **S2.29.** Suppose the number of auto accidents in a certain region is related to the regional number of registered automobiles in thousand (b_1), alcoholic beverage sales in $10,000s ($b_2$), and decrease in the price of gasoline in cents (b_3). Furthermore, imagine that the regression formula has been calculated as:

$$Y = a + b_1X_1 + b_2X_2 + b_3X_3$$

where

$$Y = \text{Number of automobile accidents},$$

$$a = 7.5,\ b_1 = 3.5,\ b_2 = 4.5,\ \text{and}\ b_3 = 2.5$$

Calculate the expected number of automobile accidents under the following conditions:

	X_1	X_2	X_3
(a)	2	3	0
(b)	3	5	1
(c)	4	7	2

• **S2.30.** The following multiple regression model was developed to predict job performance as measured by a company job-performance evaluation index based on a pre-employment test score and college grade-point average (GPA).

$$Y = 35 + 20X_1 + 50X_2$$

where

$$Y = \text{Job-performance evaluation index}$$

$$X_1 = \text{Pre-employment test score}$$

$$X_2 = \text{College GPA}$$

a. Forecast the job-performance index for an applicant who had a 3.0 GPA and scored 80 on the pre-employment score.

b. Forecast the job performance index for an applicant who had a 2.5 GPA and scored 70 on the pre-employment score.

S2.31. City government has collected the following data on annual sales-tax collections and new car registrations:

ANNUAL SALES-TAX COLLECTIONS (millions)	1	1.4	1.9	2	1.8	2.1	2.3
NEW CAR REGISTRATIONS (thousands)	10	12	15	16	14	17	20

Determine the following:

a. The least squares regression equation.

b. The estimated sales-tax collections if new car registrations total 22.

c. The coefficients of correlation and determination.

S2.32. Passenger miles flown on Northeast Airlines, a commuter firm serving the Boston hub, are shown below for the past 12 weeks:

WEEK	1	2	3	4	5	6	7	8	9	10	11	12
ACTUAL PASSENGER MILES (in thousands)	17	21	19	23	18	16	20	18	22	20	15	22

a. Assuming an initial forecast for week 1 of 17,000 miles, use exponential smoothing to compute miles for weeks 2 through 12. Use $\alpha = .2$.

b. What is the MAD for this model?

c. Compute the RSFE and tracking signals. Are they within acceptable limits?

S2.33. Bus and subway ridership in Washington, D.C., during the summer months is believed to be heavily tied to the number of tourists visiting that city. During the past 12 years, the following data have been obtained:

YEAR	NUMBER OF TOURISTS (millions)	RIDERSHIP (millions)	YEAR	NUMBER OF TOURISTS (millions)	RIDERSHIP (millions)
1	7	1.5	7	16	2.4
2	2	1.0	8	12	2.0
3	6	1.3	9	14	2.7
4	4	1.5	10	20	4.4
5	14	2.5	11	15	3.4
6	15	2.7	12	7	1.7

a. Plot these data and decide if a linear model is reasonable.

b. Develop a regression relationship.

c. What is expected ridership if 10 million tourists visit the city in a year?

d. Explain the predicted ridership if there are no tourists at all.

e. What is the standard error of the estimate?

f. What is the model's correlation coefficient and coefficient of determination?

S2.34. Emergency calls to the 911 system of Winter Park, Florida, for the past 24 weeks are shown below.

WEEK	CALLS	WEEK	CALLS	WEEK	CALLS
1	50	9	35	17	55
2	35	10	20	18	40
3	25	11	15	19	35
4	40	12	40	20	60
5	45	13	55	21	75
6	35	14	35	22	50
7	20	15	25	23	40
8	30	16	55	24	65

a. Compute the exponentially smoothed forecast of calls for each week. Assume an initial forecast of 50 calls in the first week, and use $\alpha = .1$. What is the forecast for the 25th week?

b. Reforecast each period using $\alpha = .6$.

c. Actual calls during the 25th week were 85. Which smoothing constant provides a superior forecast? Explain and justify the measure of error used.

S2.35. Boston Power and Light has been collecting data on demand for electric power in its BC subregion for only the past two years. Those data are shown below:

	DEMAND IN MEGAWATTS			DEMAND IN MEGAWATTS	
MONTH	*Last Year*	*This Year*	MONTH	*Last Year*	*This Year*
Jan.	5	17	July	23	44
Feb.	6	14	Aug.	26	41
Mar.	10	20	Sept.	21	33
Apr.	13	23	Oct.	15	23
May	18	30	Nov.	12	26
June	15	38	Dec.	14	17

The utility needs to be able to forecast demand for each month next year in order to plan for expansion and to arrange to borrow power from neighboring utilities during peak periods. Yet the standard forecasting models discussed in this supplement will not fit the data observed for the two years.

a. What are the weaknesses of the standard forecasting techniques as applied to this set of data?

b. Since known models are not really appropriate here, propose your own approach to forecasting. Although there is no perfect solution to tackling data such as these (in other words, there are no 100% right or wrong answers), justify your model.

c. Forecast demand for each month next year, using the model you propose.

S2.36. Attendance at Orlando's newest Disney-like attraction, Vacation World, has been as follows:

YEAR	QUARTER	GUESTS (in thousands)
1994	Winter	73
	Spring	104
	Summer	168
	Fall	74
1995	Winter	65
	Spring	82
	Summer	124
	Fall	52
1996	Winter	89
	Spring	146
	Summer	205
	Fall	98

Compute seasonal indices, using all of the above data.

S2.37. Samantha Shader, manager of Shader's Department Store, has used time series extrapolation to forecast retail sales for the next four quarters. The sales estimates are \$120,000, \$140,000, \$160,000, and \$180,000 for the respective quarters. Seasonal indices for the four quarters have been found to be 1.25, .90, .75, and 1.15, respectively. Compute a seasonalized or adjusted sales forecast.

Internet Data Base Application See our website at http://www.prenhall.com/renderpom for a challenging, computer-based problem.

CASE STUDY

The North-South Airline

In 1996, Northern Airlines* merged with Southeast Airlines to create the fourth largest U.S. carrier. The new North-South Airline inherited both an aging fleet of Boeing 727-200 aircraft and Stephen Ruth. Ruth was a tough former Secretary of the Navy who stepped in as new president and chairman of the board.

Ruth's first concern in creating a financially solid company was maintenance costs. It was commonly surmised in the airline industry that maintenance costs rose with the age of the aircraft. He quickly noticed that historically there has been a significant difference in the reported B727-200 maintenance costs (from ATA Form 41s) both in the airframe and engine areas between Northern Airlines and Southeast Airlines, with Southeast having the newer fleet.

On November 12, 1996, Peg Young, vice president for operations and maintenance, was called into Ruth's office and asked to study the issue. Specifically, Ruth wanted to know (1) whether the average fleet age was correlated to direct airframe maintenance costs, and (2) whether there was a relationship between average fleet age and direct engine maintenance costs. Young was to report back with the answer, along with quantitative and graphical descriptions of the relationship, by November 26.

Young's first step was to have her staff construct the average age of Northern and Southeast B727-200 fleets, by quarter, since the introduction of that aircraft to service by each airline in late 1989 and early 1990. The average age of each fleet was calculated by first multiplying the total number of calendar days each aircraft had been in service at the pertinent point in time by the average daily utilization of the respective fleet to total fleet hours flown. The total fleet hours flown was then divided by the number of aircraft in service at that time, giving the age of the "average" aircraft in the fleet.

The average utilization was found by taking the actual total fleet hours flown at September 30, 1996, from Northern and Southeast data, and dividing by total days in service for all aircraft at that time. The average utilization for Southeast was 8.3 hours per day, and the average utilization for Northern was 8.7 hours per day. Because the available cost data were calculated for each yearly period ending at the end of the first quarter, average fleet age was calculated at the same points in time.

The Fleet data are shown in Table 1. Airframe cost data and engine cost data are both shown paired with fleet average age.

DISCUSSION QUESTION

Prepare Peg Young's response to Stephen Ruth.

*Dates and names of airlines and individuals have been changed in this case to maintain confidentiality. The data and issues described here are actual.

TABLE 1 NORTH-SOUTH AIRLINE DATA FOR BOEING 727-200 JETS

	NORTHERN AIRLINE DATA			SOUTHEAST AIRLINE DATA		
Year	*Airframe Cost per Aircraft*	*Engine Cost per Aircraft*	*Average Age (hours)*	*Airframe Cost per Aircraft*	*Engine Cost per Aircraft*	*Average Age (hours)*
1990	$51.80	$43.49	6,512	$13.29	$18.86	5,107
1991	54.92	38.58	8,404	25.15	31.55	8,145
1992	69.70	51.48	11,077	32.18	40.43	7,360
1993	68.90	58.72	11,717	31.78	22.10	5,773
1994	63.72	45.47	13,275	25.34	19.69	7,150
1995	84.73	50.26	15,215	32.78	32.58	9,364
1996	78.74	79.60	18,390	35.56	38.07	8,259

Internet Case Study See our Internet home page at http://www.prenhall.com/renderpom for this additional case study: Akron Zoological Park.

BIBLIOGRAPHY

Box, G. E. P., and G. Jenkins. *Time Series Analysis: Forecasting and Control.* San Francisco: Holden Day, 1970.

Brown, R. G. *Statistical Forecasting for Inventory Control.* New York: McGraw-Hill, 1959.

Chambers, J. C., C. Satinder, S. K. Mullick, and D. D. Smith. "How to Choose the Right Forecasting Techniques." *Harvard Business Review* 49 (July-August 1971): 45–74.

Gardner, E. S. "Exponential Smoothing: The State of the Art." *Journal of Forecasting* 4 (March 1985).

Georgoff, D. M., and R. G. Murdick. "Managers Guide to Forecasting." *Harvard Business Review* 64 (January-February 1986): 110–120.

Mahmoud, E. "Accuracy in Forecasting: A Summary." *Journal of Forecasting* (April-June 1984).

Makridakis, S., S. C. Wheelright, and V. E. McGee. *Forecasting: Methods and Applications,* 2nd ed. New York: John Wiley and Sons, 1983.

Murdick, R., and D. M. Georgoff. "Forecasting: A Systems Approach." *Technological Forecasting and Social Change,* 44 (1993): 1–16.

Murdick, R., B. Render, and R. Russell. *Service Operations Management.* Boston: Allyn & Bacon, 1990.

Parker, G. C., and E. L. Segura. "How to Get a Better Forecast." *Harvard Business Review* 49 (March-April 1971): 99–109.

Render, B., and R. M. Stair. *Introduction to Management Science.* Boston: Allyn & Bacon, 1992.

Render, B., and R. M. Stair. *Quantitative Analysis for Management,* 6th ed. Upper Saddle River, NJ: Prentice-Hall, 1997.

Total Quality Management

3

CHAPTER OUTLINE

Defining Quality

Why Quality Is Important

International Quality Standards

Japan's Industrial Standard ■ Europe's ISO 9000 Standard ■ U.S. Standards ■ ISO 14000

Total Quality Management

Continuous Improvement ■ Employee Empowerment ■ Benchmarking ■ Just-in-Time (JIT) ■ Knowledge of TQM Tools

Tools for TQM

Quality Function Development ■ Taguchi Technique ■ Pareto Charts ■ Process Charts ■ Cause-and-Effect Diagrams ■ Statistical Process Control (SPC)

The Role of Inspection

When and Where to Inspect ■ Source Inspection ■ Service Industry Inspection

Total Quality Management in Services

Summary ■ *Key Terms* ■ *Self-Test Chapter 3* ■ *Discussion Questions* ■ *Operations in Practice Exercise* ■ *Problems* ■ *Case Study: Milt and Michael's Cleaning* ■ *Bibliography*

LEARNING OBJECTIVES

When you complete this chapter you should be able to:

IDENTIFY OR DEFINE:

Quality
Malcolm Baldrige Awards
Deming, Juran, and Crosby
Taguchi technique

DESCRIBE OR EXPLAIN:

Why quality is important
Total Quality Management (TQM)
House of quality
Pareto charts
Process charts
Quality robust products
Inspection
Cause-and-effect diagrams

The dominant issue for many firms is quality. Along with *rapid product development times, flexibility in meeting customer demands* (customized products), and *low selling prices, quality* is a key, strategic option. However, the wonderful thing about total quality management is that it can help with all operations strategies. Quality through empowerment and quality control reduces product development times. This allows companies to focus on their customers and become more adept at meeting their needs. Additionally, reduction in scrap and rework reinforces efforts to reduce costs and achieve low selling prices. For instance, Motorola's quality effort has allowed it to move from 6,000 rejects per million just five years ago to only 40 defects per million now. Motorola believes that it has saved $700 million in manufacturing costs over that period.[1] Determining quality expectations is critical to building and managing the operations function.

Quality impacts the *entire organization* from supplier to customer and from product design to maintenance. Figure 3.1 lays out the strategy for an organization, be it manufacturing or service, to use to achieve Total Quality Management. The ultimate goal is to become an effective organization with a competitive advantage.

In this chapter we first define and discuss the importance of *quality*. We then present the concept of total quality management (TQM) and its tools. In the supplement to this chapter, we explore the subject of statistical quality control.

DEFINING QUALITY

NOTE
Quality may be in the eyes of the beholder but to build a product, operations managers must define what the beholder expects.

True total quality management systems are driven by identifying and satisfying customer needs. Total quality management takes care of the customer. Consequently, we accept the definition of *quality* as adopted by the American Society for Quality Control: "The totality of features and characteristics of a product or service that bear on its ability to satisfy stated or implied needs."[2]

However, others believe that definitions of *quality* fall into several categories.[3] Some definitions are *user-based*. They propose that quality "lies in the eyes of the beholder." Marketing people like this approach, and so do customers. To them, higher quality means better performance, nicer features, and other (sometimes costly) improvements. To production managers, quality is *manufacturing-based*. They believe that quality means conforming to standards and "making it right the first time." Yet a third approach is *product-based*, which views quality as a precise and measurable variable. For example, really good ice cream has high butterfat levels.

NOTE
Other perspectives of quality include: 1) serviceability, 2) appearance, 3) reliability, 4) perceived quality.

This text develops approaches and techniques to address all three categories of quality. The characteristics that connote quality must first be identified through research (a user-based approach to quality). These characteristics are then translated into specific product attributes (a product-based approach to quality). Then the manufacturing process is organized to ensure that the products are made precisely to the specifications (a manufacturing-based approach to quality). A process that ignores any one of these steps will not result in a quality product.[4]

---

[1] *The Economist*, January 4, 1992, p. 61.

[2] Ross Johnson and William O. Winchell, *Production and Quality* (Milwaukee, WI: American Society for Quality Control, 1989), p. 2.

[3] David A. Garvin, "What Does 'Product Quality' Really Mean?" *Sloan Management Review* 26, 1 (Fall 1984): 25–43.

[4] See Garvin (Fall 1984): 29.

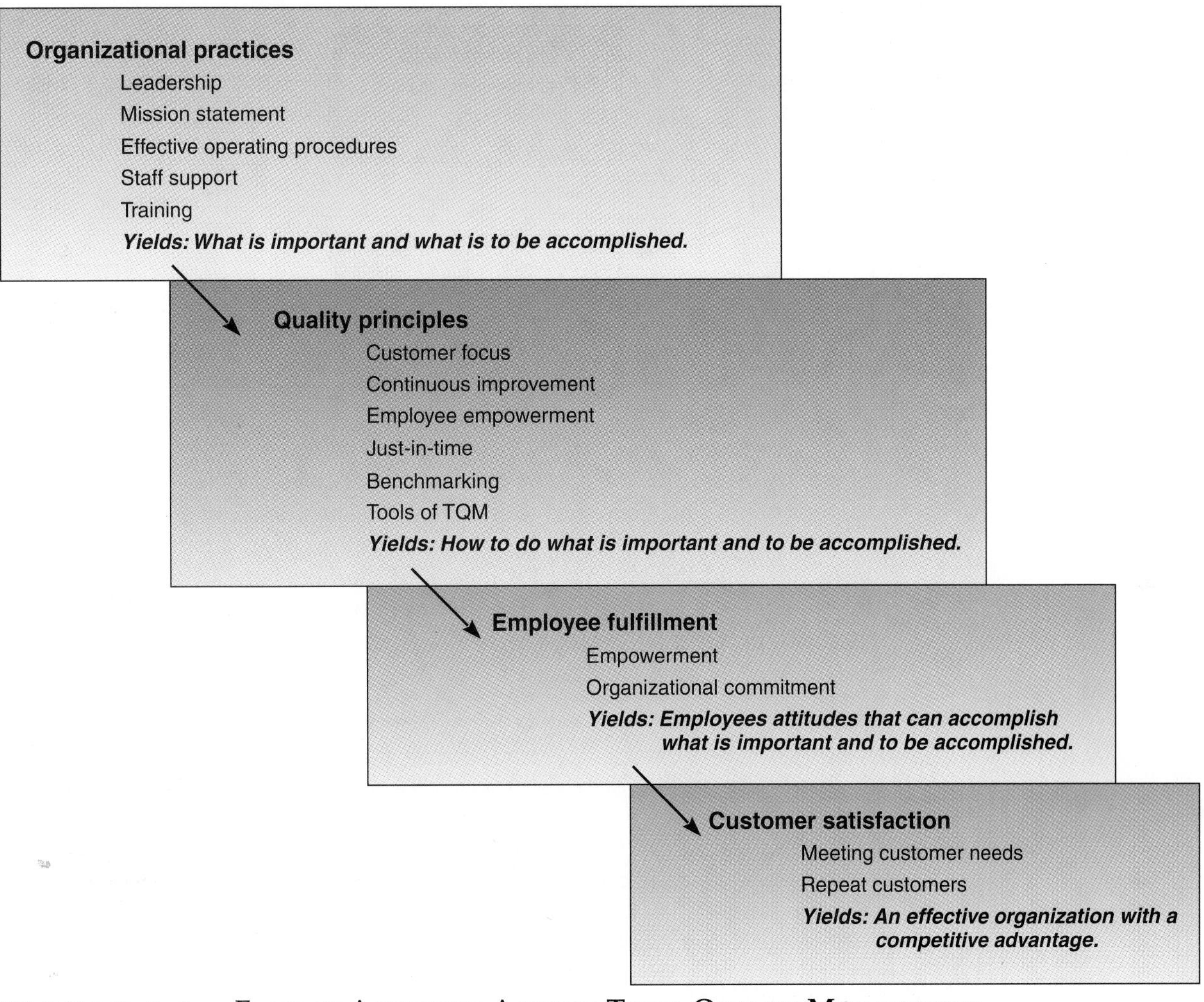

Organizational practices
Leadership
Mission statement
Effective operating procedures
Staff support
Training
Yields: What is important and what is to be accomplished.
Quality principles
Customer focus
Continuous improvement
Employee empowerment
Just-in-time
Benchmarking
Tools of TQM
Yields: How to do what is important and to be accomplished.
Employee fulfillment
Empowerment
Organizational commitment
Yields: Employees attitudes that can accomplish what is important and to be accomplished.
Customer satisfaction
Meeting customer needs
Repeat customers
Yields: An effective organization with a competitive advantage.

FIGURE 3.1 FLOW OF ACTIVITIES ACHIEVE TOTAL QUALITY MANAGEMENT

WHY QUALITY IS IMPORTANT

Quality goods and services are strategically important to the company and to the country it represents. The quality of a firm's products, the prices it charges, and the supply it makes available are all factors that determine demand. In particular, quality affects a firm in four ways:

1. *Costs and market share.* Figure 3.2 shows that improved quality can lead to increased market share and cost savings. Both can affect profitability as well. Likewise, improving reliability and conformance means fewer defects and lower service costs. One study of air-conditioner manufacturers even showed that quality and productivity were positively related. In the United States, companies with the highest quality were five times as productive (as measured by units produced per labor-hour) as companies with the poorest quality.[5] The traditional perspective has been to minimize the total cost

[5]Garvin (Fall 1984): 36.

FIGURE 3.2

TWO WAYS QUALITY CAN IMPROVE PROFITABILITY

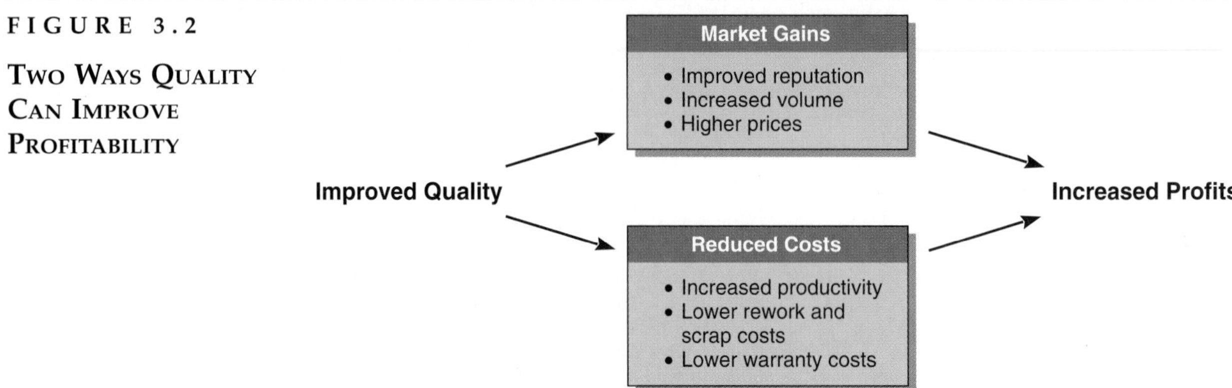

of quality effort plus the cost of poor quality. However, determining the cost of poor quality has focused too much on the short term, and cost is usually underestimated. Therefore, when the implications of an organization's long-term costs and the potential for increased market share are considered, total quality costs may well be at a minimum when 100% of the goods or services are perfect and defect free.

TABLE 3.1 RECENT WINNERS OF THE MALCOLM BALDRIGE NATIONAL QUALITY AWARD

Winner
1995
Armstrong World Industries, Inc. Lancaster, PA (manufacturing)
Corning Inc. Wilmington, NC (manufacturing)
1994
GTE Directories Corp. Dallas/Ft. Worth, TX (service)
Wainwright Industries St. Peters, MO (small business, manufacturing)
AT&T Power Systems Dallas, TX (service)
1993
Eastman Chemical Kingsport, TN (manufacturing)
Ames Rubber Hamburg, NJ (small business)
1992
AT&T Morristown, NJ (manufacturing)
Texas Instruments Dallas, TX (manufacturing)
AT&T Universal Card Services Jacksonville, FL (service)
Ritz-Carlton Hotels Atlanta, GA (service)
Granite Rock Watsonville, CA (small business)

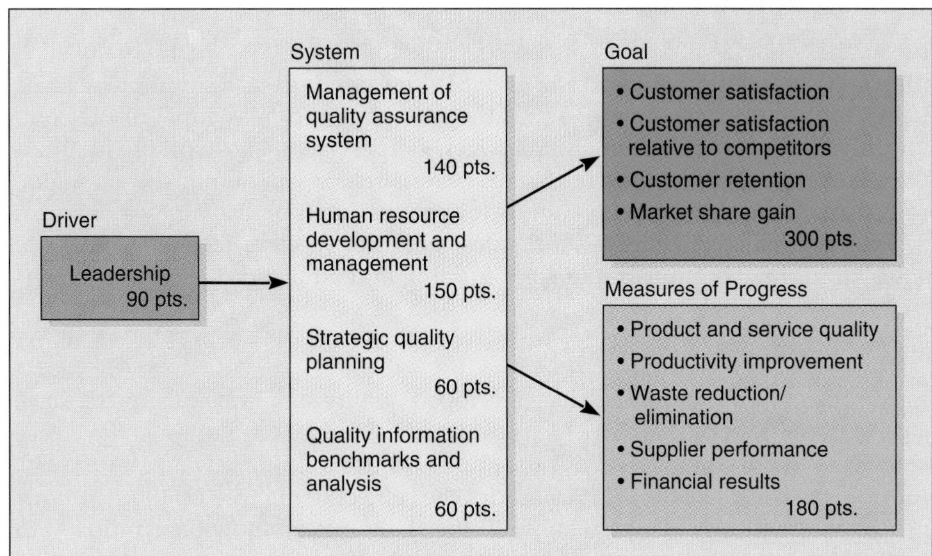

FIGURE 3.3

Malcolm Baldrige National Quality Award Criteria

2. *Company's reputation*. An organization can expect its reputation for quality—be it good or bad—to follow it. Quality will show up in perceptions about the firm's new products, employment practices, and supplier relations. Self-promotion is not a substitute for quality products.
3. *Product liability*. The courts increasingly hold everyone in the distribution chain responsible for the product. Additionally, organizations that design and produce faulty products or services can be held liable for damages or injuries resulting from their use. The Consumer Product Safety Act of 1972 sets and enforces product standards by banning products that do not reach those standards. Drugs that accidentally cause birth defects, insulation that leads to cancer, or auto fuel tanks that may explode upon impact can all lead to huge legal expenses, large settlements or losses, and terrible publicity.
4. *International implications*. In this technological age quality is an international, as well as an operations, concern. For both a company and a country to compete effectively in the global economy, its products must meet quality and price expectations. Inferior products harm both firms and nations and can have severe implications for balance of payments.

NOTE
"The cost of quality is the expense of doing things wrong." Quality control expert, Philip Crosby

The international implications of quality are so important that in 1988 the United States established the *Malcolm Baldrige National Quality Award* for quality achievement. The award is named for former Secretary of Commerce Malcolm Baldrige. Recent winners are shown in Table 3.1. Figure 3.3 presents the critera for the awards.

International Quality Standards

The international implications have also fostered a number of international standards. Japan, the European Community, and the United States have each developed their own quality standards.

Japan's Industrial Standard

The Japanese have even developed a specification for TQM, which is published in Japan as Industrial Standard Z8101-1981. The standard states, "Implementing quality control effectively necessitates the cooperation of all people in the company, involving top management, managers, supervisors, and workers in all areas of corporate activities such as market research, research and development, product planning design, preparations for production, purchasing, vendor management, manufacturing, inspection, sales, and after-services, as well as financial control, personnel administration, and training and education."

Europe's ISO 9000 Standard

ISO 9000

The European Community (EC) has developed quality standards called **ISO 9000, 9001, 9002, 9003,** and **9004.** The focus of the EC standards are to force the establishment of quality management procedures on firms doing business in the EC.

Several factors make the ISO 9000 series the subject of interest: (1) the standards are achieving worldwide acceptance, (2) the standards are now being applied to some products made or imported by the EC, and (3) adherence to the standards may be necessary for product certification.

Even small U.S. firms, such as New York's Rice Aircraft, are recognizing the value of ISO 9000 certification. This family-owned parts distributor saw the strategic implications of undergoing the rigorous ISO 9000 rules. For instance, Rice recently won a $3 million contract with American Airlines, which confirms that it was impressed that a firm as small as Rice was meeting international quality standards. ISO 9000 is not without critics, however, as the popular comic strip "Dilbert" implies.

U.S. Standards

The United States has long had military specifications for defense contracts and in recent years the American Quality Control Society has developed specifications equivalent to the EC's. They are Q90, Q91, Q92, Q93, and Q94.

ISO 14000

ISO 14000

The continuing internationalization of quality is evident with the E.C.'s development of **ISO 14000.** ISO 14000 is a new EC environmental management stan-

By Scott Adams

dard that contains five core elements. Those five core elements are: (1) environmental management, (2) auditing, (3) performance evaluation, (4) labeling, and (5) life-cycle assessment. The new standard could have several advantages:

- Positive public image and reduced exposure to liability.
- Good systematic approach to pollution prevention through the minimization of ecological impact of products and activities.
- Compliance with regulatory requirements and opportunities for competitive advantage.
- Reduction in need for multiple audits.

This standard, or some variation of it, will probably soon be accepted worldwide.

Total Quality Management

Total quality management (TQM) refers to a quality emphasis that encompasses the entire organization, from supplier to customer. TQM stresses a commitment by management to have a continuing company-wide drive toward excellence in all aspects of products and services that are important to the customer.

total quality management (TQM)

Building a total quality management environment is important because quality decisions influence each phase of building and managing world-class operations. Every chapter that follows deals with some aspect of building or managing a world-class organization. Without an emphasis on TQM, none of the other decisions that leaders make can result in a firm that can compete as a leader in world markets.

NOTE
"If quality isn't ingrained in the organization, it will never happen." Quality control expert, Philip Crosby

Quality expert W. Edwards Deming used 14 points (see Table 3.2) to indicate how he would implement quality improvement. We develop these into five concepts. The five concepts for an effective TQM program are: (1) continuous improvement, (2) employee empowerment, (3) benchmarking, (4) just-in-time (JIT), and (5) knowledge of tools.

TABLE 3.2 Deming's 14 Points for Implementing Quality Improvement

1. Create consistency of purpose.
2. Lead to promote change.
3. Build quality into the product; stop depending on inspections to catch problems.
4. Build long-term relationships based on performance instead of awarding business on the basis of price.
5. Continuously improve product, quality, and service.
6. Start training.
7. Emphasize leadership.
8. Drive out fear.
9. Break down barriers between departments.
10. Stop haranguing workers.
11. Support, help, and improve.
12. Remove barriers to pride in work.
13. Institute a vigorous program of education and self-improvement.
14. Put everybody in the company to work on the transformation.

Source: Deming revised his 14 points a number of times over the years. See W. Edwards Deming, "Philosophy Continues to Flourish," *APICS—The Performance Advantage* 1, 4 (October 1991): 20.

Continuous Improvement

TQM requires a never-ending process that we call continuous improvement, where perfection is never achieved but always sought.

Kaizen

The Japanese use the word **Kaizen** to describe this on-going process of incremental but continuous improvement. Americans use *TQM*, *zero-defects*, and *six sigma* to describe its continuing improvement efforts. Whatever word or phrase is used, operations managers are key players in building a work culture that endorses continuous improvement. Quality is a never-ending quest.

NOTE
"There is absolutely no reason for having errors of defects in any product or service." Quality control expert Philip Crosby

Employee Empowerment

employee empowerment

Employee empowerment means involving employees in every step of the production process. Consistently, the literature suggests that some 85% of quality problems have to do with materials and processes, not with employee performance. Therefore, the task is to design equipment and processes that produce the desired quality. This is best done with a high degree of involvement by those who understand the shortcomings of the system. Those dealing with the system on a daily basis understand it better than anyone else. When nonconformance occurs, the worker is seldom wrong. Either the product was designed wrong, the system that makes the product was designed wrong, or the employee was improperly trained.[6] Although the employee may be able to help solve the problem, the employee rarely causes it.

Techniques for building employee empowerment include: (1) building communication networks that include employees, (2) encouraging open, supportive supervisors, (3) moving both managerial and staff responsibilities to production employees, (4) building high-morale organizations, and (5) using formal techniques such as team building and quality circles.

quality circle

Teams can be built to address a variety of issues. One popular approach to team building is quality circles. Quality circles have proven to be a cost-effective way to increase productivity as well as quality. A **quality circle** is a group of between 6 and 12 employees who volunteer to meet regularly to solve work-related problems. The members, all from the same work area, receive training in group planning, problem solving, and statistical quality control. They generally meet about four hours per month (usually after work, but sometimes on company time). Although the circle members are not rewarded financially, they do receive recognition from the firm. A specially trained manager, called the facilitator, usually helps train the circle members and keeps the meetings running smoothly.

Benchmarking

benchmarking

Benchmarking is another ingredient in a company's TQM program. **Benchmarking** involves selecting a demonstrated standard of performance that represents the very best performance for processes or activities very similar to yours. The idea is to develop a target at which to shoot, then to develop a standard or benchmark against which to compare your performance. A model for developing benchmarks is:[7]

---

[6]See a related discussion in Asher Israeli and Bradley Fisher, "The Worker Is Never Wrong," *Quality Progress* (October 1989): 95.

[7]Adapted from Michael J. Spendolini, *The Benchmarking Book* (New York: Amcom, 1992).

Leaders in the Fight for Quality:
W. Edwards Deming (left). The awarding of the Deming Prize for quality control on Japanese TV is a national event. After World War II, Dr. Deming went to Japan to teach quality. And the Japanese learned. In his quality crusade, Deming insisted that management accept responsibility for building good systems. The employee, he believed, cannot produce products that on the average exceed the quality of what the process is capable of producing. Dr. Deming died in 1993.
J. M. Juran (middle). A pioneer in teaching the Japanese how to improve quality, Juran believes strongly in top management commitment, support, and involvement in the quality effort. He is also a believer in teams that continually seek to raise quality standards. Juran varies from Deming somewhat in focusing on the customer and defining quality as fitness for use, not necessarily the written specifications.
Philip B. Crosby (right). *Quality Is Free* was Crosby's attention-getting book published in 1979. Crosby's traditional view has been that "with management and employee commitment great strides can be made in improving quality." He also believes that in the traditional trade-off between the cost of improving quality and the cost of poor quality, the cost of poor quality is understated. The cost of poor quality should include all of the things that are involved in *not* doing the job right the first time.

- Determine what to benchmark.
- Form a benchmarking team.
- Identify benchmarking partners.
- Collect and analyze benchmarking information.
- Take action to match or exceed the benchmark.

In the ideal situation, you find one or more organizations with operations similar to yours who are demonstrated leaders in the particular areas that you want to study. Then you compare yourself (benchmark yourself) against them. The company need not be in your industry; indeed, to establish world-class standards, it may be best to look outside of your industry. This involves finding an industry that excels in the area that you want to benchmark. If one industry has learned how to compete via rapid product development, but your industry has not, it does no good to study your industry.

This is exactly what Xerox and Chrysler did when they went to L.L. Bean for order-filling benchmarks. What did copier parts and cars have in common with Beans' outdoor paraphernalia? Nothing. But Bean showed Xerox how to "pick" orders three times faster and showed Chrysler how to use flowcharts to spot wasted movements.[8]

[8]*Business Week,* November 30, 1992, p. 74–75.

Benchmarks can and should be established in a variety of areas. Total quality management requires measurable benchmarks.

Just-in-Time (JIT)

The philosophy behind just-in-time (JIT) is one of continuous improvement and enforced problem solving. JIT forces quality from suppliers and from each step of the manufacturing or service process because no inventory is available to absorb the variations. Consequently, the system must produce at high quality levels. Because JIT drives out variability, there is no scrap, rework, inventory investment, and wasted effort in the production/service process.

Knowledge of TQM Tools

Because we want to empower employees to implement TQM, and because TQM is a continuing effort, everyone in the organization must be trained in the techniques of TQM. The tools of TQM are diverse and expanding. In the following section we focus on some of the tools and techniques that are helpful in the TQM crusade.

TOOLS FOR TQM

Six tools/techniques that aid the TQM effort are: (1) quality function deployment (house of quality), (2) Taguchi techniques, (3) Pareto charts, (4) process charts, (5) cause-and-effect diagrams (fish-bone charts), and (6) statistical process control.

Quality Function Deployment

quality function deployment (QFD)

An effective total quality management program translates customer desires into specific, designable characteristics. **Quality function deployment (QFD)** is the term we use to: (1) determine the functional design that will satisfy the customer and (2) translate customer desires into target designs. We use QFD early in the production process to help us determine where to deploy quality efforts.

house of quality

The **house of quality** is a technique for defining the relationship between customer desires and product (or service) attributes. Only by defining this relationship in a rigorous way can operations managers build products and process with features desired by customers. Defining this relationship is the first step in building a world-class production system. To build the house of quality, we perform six basic steps:

1. Identify customer *wants.*
2. Identify product/service attributes. (Think of attributes as *how* the product/service will meet the *wants.*)
3. Relate the customer *wants* to the product/service *hows.*
4. Conduct an evaluation of competing products.
5. Develop performance specifications for product/service *hows.*
6. Assign (deploy) *hows* to the appropriate place in the transformation process.

NOTE
The earlier a potential loss can be identified, the better the potential loss can be addressed by design or process change.

Example 1 shows how to construct a house of quality.

EXAMPLE 1

Through extensive market research, Great Cameras, Inc., determined customer *wants.* Those *wants* are shown on the left of the house of quality below and are: lightweight, easy to hold steady, no double exposures, easy to use, and reliable. Then the product development team determined *how* the organization is going to translate those customer *wants* into product design and process attribute targets. The product development team then translated those customer *wants* into specific attributes or *hows* across the top portion of the house of quality. These attributes are low electricity requirements, aluminum components, auto focus, auto exposure, auto rewind, and ergonomic design.

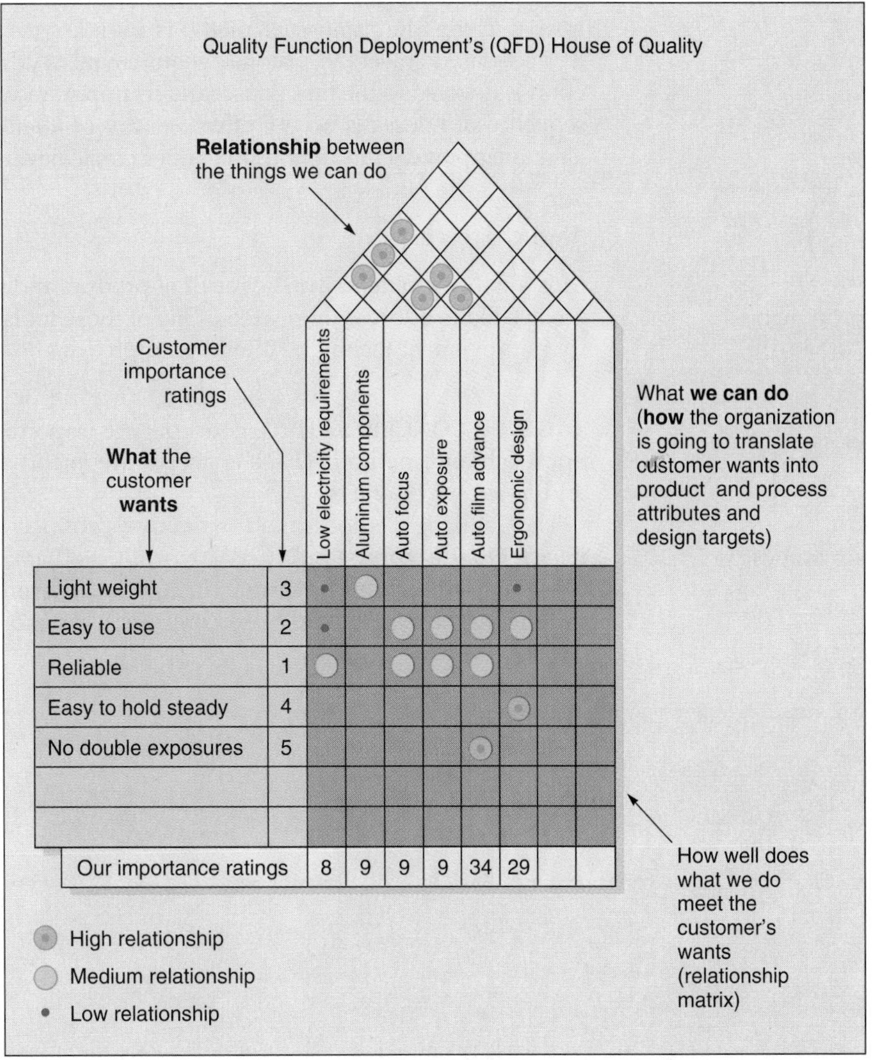

The product team then evaluated each of the customer *wants* against the *hows*. In the matrix of the house, the team evaluated how well their design will meet customer needs. Similarly, in the "roof" of the house, the product development team developed the relationship between the attributes. Finally, the team developed importance ratings for their design attributes and a ranking of how to proceed with product and process design.

A variety of modifications can be made to the house of quality. For instance, it can be used in much the same way as shown in Example 1 to evaluate how a competitor meets customer demands.

While the house of quality is a very formal way of identifying customer requirements and matching those wants to the product and service design characteristics, its power allows us to do more. This concept can be applied throughout operations management. As Figure 3.4 indicates, the firm's design characteristics become the input to House 2, which are satisfied by *specific components.* Similarly, the concept is carried over to House 3, where the specific components are to be satisfied through *particular production processes.* Once those production processes are defined, they become the inputs to a quality plan that will ensure conformance of those processes in House 4. The fourth house includes the *quality plan,* methods, sample sizes, and so forth to achieve the quality necessary to meet the customer requirements. Although much of the literature and effort is devoted to the first house, and its importance is not to be underestimated, the sequence of houses is a very effective way of identifying, communicating, and engaging employees throughout the system in achieving customer satisfaction.

Taguchi Technique

Taguchi method

Most quality problems are the result of product and process design. Therefore, tools are needed to address these areas. One of those tools is the **Taguchi method,** a quality improvement technique aimed at improving both product and process design.[9]

TAGUCHI CONCEPTS. Three concepts are important to understanding Taguchi's approach and method. These concepts are *quality robustness, quality loss function,* and *target specifications.*

quality robust

The Taguchi method calls for making products and processes that are *quality robust.* **Quality robust** products are products that can be produced uniformly and consistently in adverse manufacturing and environmental conditions. The idea is to remove the *effects* of adverse conditions instead of removing the causes.

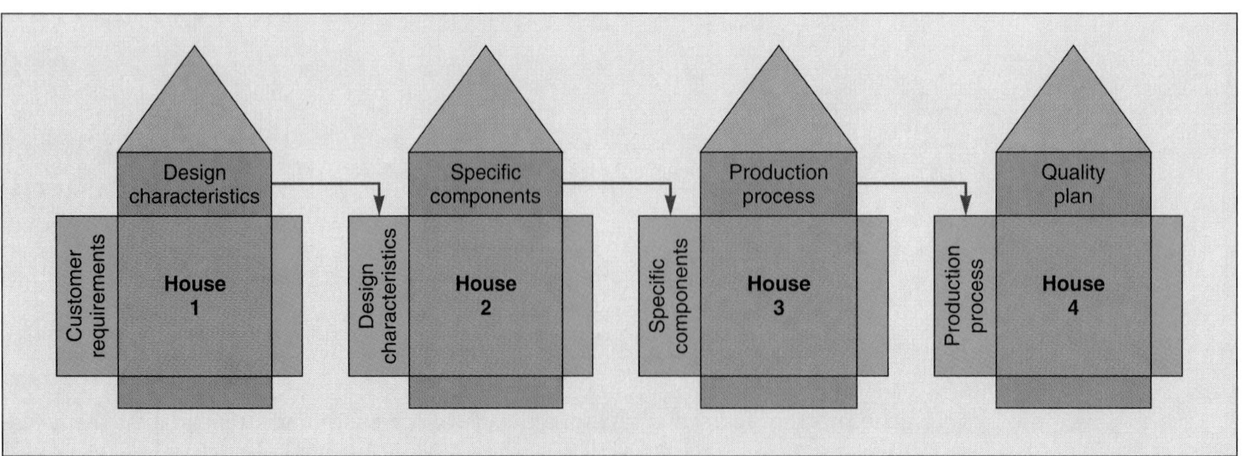

FIGURE 3.4 HOUSE OF QUALITY SEQUENCE

[9]R. N. Kackar, "Taguchi's Quality Control, Parameter Design, and the Taguchi Method," *Journal of Quality Technology* (October 1985): 176–188; and Lance Ealey, "Taguchi Basics," *Quality* (November 1988): 30–32.

Taguchi suggests that removing the effects is often cheaper than removing the causes and more effective in producing a robust product. In this way small variations in materials and process do not destroy product quality.

Taguchi has also defined what he calls a quality loss function. A **quality loss function (QLF)** identifies all costs connected with poor quality and shows how these costs increase as the product moves away from being exactly what the customer wants. These costs include not just customer dissatisfaction but also warranty and service costs; internal inspection, repair, and scrap costs; and costs that can best be described as costs to society. Notice that Figure 3.5 (a) shows the quality loss function as a curve that increases at an increasing rate; it takes the general form of a simple quadratic formula:

quality loss function

NOTE
"It is much less expensive to prevent errors than to rework, scrap, or service them." Quality control expert Philip Crosby

$$L = D^2C$$

where

L = Loss

D^2 = Square of the deviation from the target value

C = Cost of avoiding the deviation

All the losses to society due to poor performance are included in the loss function. The smaller the loss, the more desirable the product. The farther the product is from the target value, the more severe the loss.

Taguchi observed that the traditional way of looking at specifications (that is, the product is good until it fails to fall within the tolerance limits) is too simplistic. As shown in Figure 3.5 (b), conformance-oriented quality produces more units

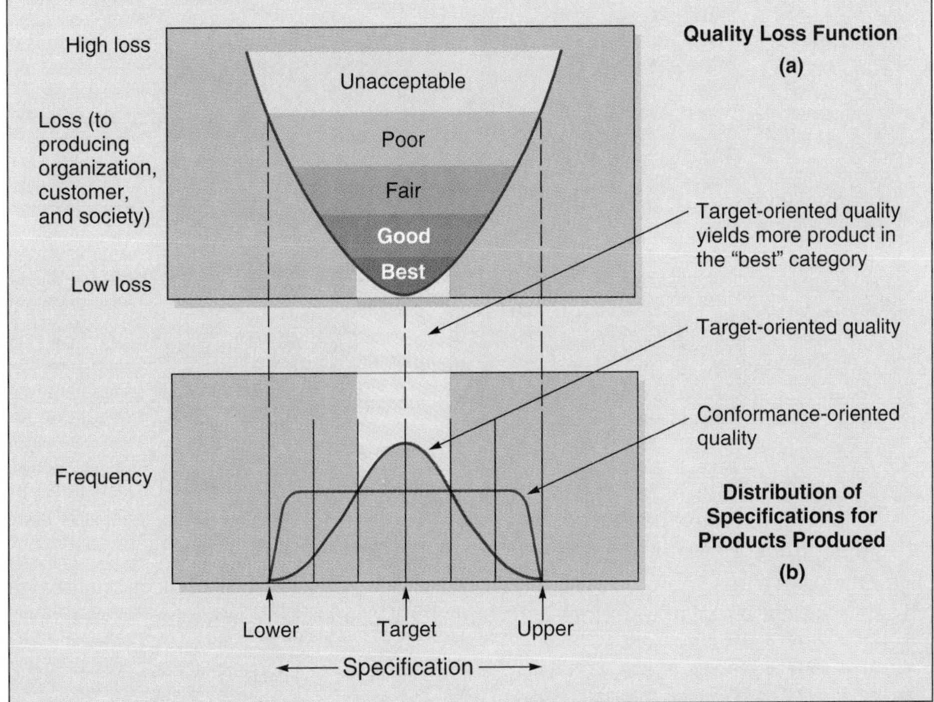

FIGURE 3.5

(a) QUALITY LOSS FUNCTION; (b) DISTRIBUTION OF PRODUCT PRODUCED

Taguchi aims for the target, because products produced near the upper and lower acceptable specifications result in higher quality loss function.

farther from the target; therefore, the loss (cost) is higher in terms of customer satisfaction and benefits to society.

target value

Target value is a philosophy of continuous improvement to bring the product exactly on target.

Pareto Charts

Pareto charts

Pareto charts are a method of organizing errors, problems, or defects to help focus on problem-solving efforts. They are based on the work of Alfredo Pareto, a nineteenth-century economist. Joseph M. Juran popularized Pareto's work when he suggested that 80% of a firm's problems are a result of only 20% of the causes.

Example 2 indicates that of the five types of defects identified, the vast majority were of one type, scratches.

EXAMPLE 2

Custom Wine Glasses of Leadville, Colorado, has just collected the data from 75 defects from the day's production. The boss decides to prepare a Pareto analysis of the defects. The data provided are scratches, 54; porosity, 12; nicks, 4; contamination, 3; and miscellaneous, 2.

The Pareto chart shown indicates that 72% of the defects were the result of one cause, scratches. The majority of defects will be eliminated when this one cause is corrected.

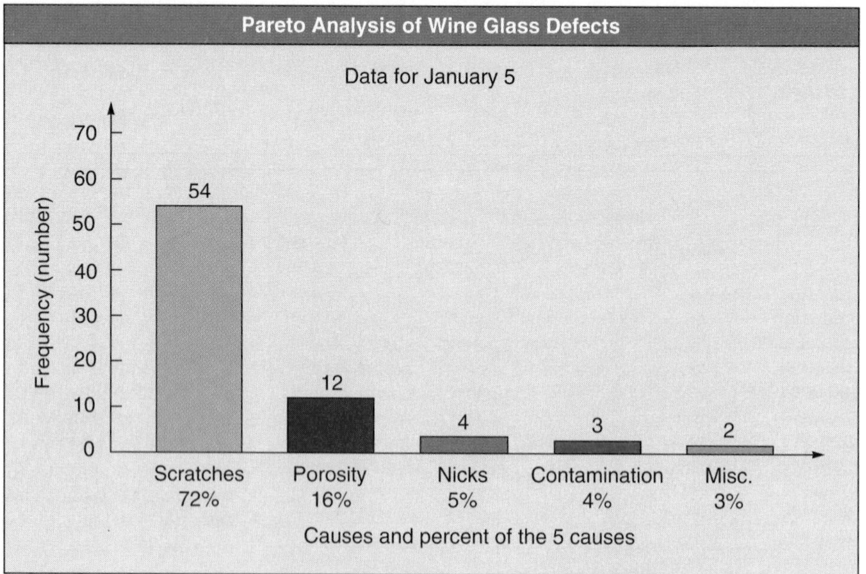

Pareto analysis indicates which problems may yield the greatest payoff. This is what Pacific Bell discovered when it tried to find a way to reduce damage to buried phone cable, the number one cause of phone outages. Pareto analysis showed that 41% of cable damage was caused by construction work. Armed with this information, Pacific Bell was able to devise a plan to reduce cable cuts by 24% in one year, saving $6 million.[10]

[10] *The Wall Street Journal*, February 24, 1994, p. A-1.

Process Charts

Process charts are designed to help us understand a sequence of events (that is, the process) through which a product travels. The process chart graphs the steps of the process and their relationship. This type of analysis can:

process charts

1. Help identify the best data collection points.
2. Isolate and track the origin of problems.
3. Identify the best place for process checks.
4. Identify opportunities for travel distance reduction.

As shown in Example 3, a process chart organizes information about a process in a graphical matter, using five standard symbols and distance.

EXAMPLE 3

The I. Tamarkin Chicken Processing Plant in Little Rock, Arkansas, would like to understand more about its packing and shipping process. After observation of the packing and shipping line and discussion with the operators, you prepare the following process chart. This type of analysis should help you determine (1) where inspection and data collection could take place (perhaps after automatic weighing and labeling and after automatic sealing and after quick freeze), (2) the opportunities for reducing distance traveled, (3) where to look should certain types of problems arise.

Present Method [X] PROCESS CHART
Proposed Method [X]
SUBJECT CHARTED *Packing and Shipping Process* DATE *1/1/97*
CHART BY *HRC*
CHART NO. *1*
DEPARTMENT *Packing and Shipping* SHEET NO. *1* OF *1*

DIST. IN FEET	TIME IN MINS.	CHART SYMBOLS	PROCESS DESCRIPTION
10'		○ ⇨ □ D ▽	To Packing Station
—		○ ⇨ □ D ▽	Pack
2'		○ ⇨ □ D ▽	To Weigh Station
—		○ ⇨ □ D ▽	Weigh
2'		○ ⇨ □ D ▽	To Airtight Sealing, Weighing and Labeling
—		○ ⇨ □ D ▽	Automatic Sealing, Weighing and Labeling
50'		○ ⇨ □ D ▽	To Quick Freeze Storage
—		○ ⇨ □ D ▽	Quick Freeze Storage
25'		○ ⇨ □ D ▽	To Bulk Packing
—		○ ⇨ □ D ▽	Bulk Packing
40'		○ ⇨ □ D ▽	To Shipping Dock
		○ ⇨ □ D ▽	Load on Shipping Truck
		○ ⇨ □ D ▽	
		○ ⇨ □ D ▽	
		○ ⇨ □ D ▽	
		○ ⇨ □ D ▽	
			TOTAL

The standard American Society of Mechanical Engineers (ASME) process symbols are ○ = operation; ⇨ = transportation; □ = inspection; D = delay; ▽ = storage

As you will see in our discussion of people and work systems in Chapter 7, process charts can be useful analytical tools in a wide variety of other applications.

Cause-and-Effect Diagrams

cause-and-effect diagram

Ishikawa diagram

fish-bone chart

One of many available tools helpful in identifying possible locations of quality problems and inspection points is the **cause-and-effect diagram,** also known as an **Ishikawa diagram** or a **fish-bone chart.** Figure 3.6 illustrates a simple chart (note the shape resembling the bones of a fish) for an everyday quality control error—a dissatisfied airline customer. Each bone represents a possible source of error.

The way to get started on any cause-and-effect diagram is to have four categories: material, machinery/equipment, manpower, and methods. These four "M's" are the "causes." They provide a good checklist for initial analysis. When such a chart is systematically developed, possible quality problems and inspection points are highlighted.

Statistical Process Control (SPC)

Statistical process control is concerned with monitoring standards, making measurements, and taking corrective action as a product or service is being produced.

FIGURE 3.6

FISH-BONE CHART (OR CAUSE-AND-EFFECT DIAGRAM) FOR PROBLEMS IN AIRLINE CUSTOMER SERVICE

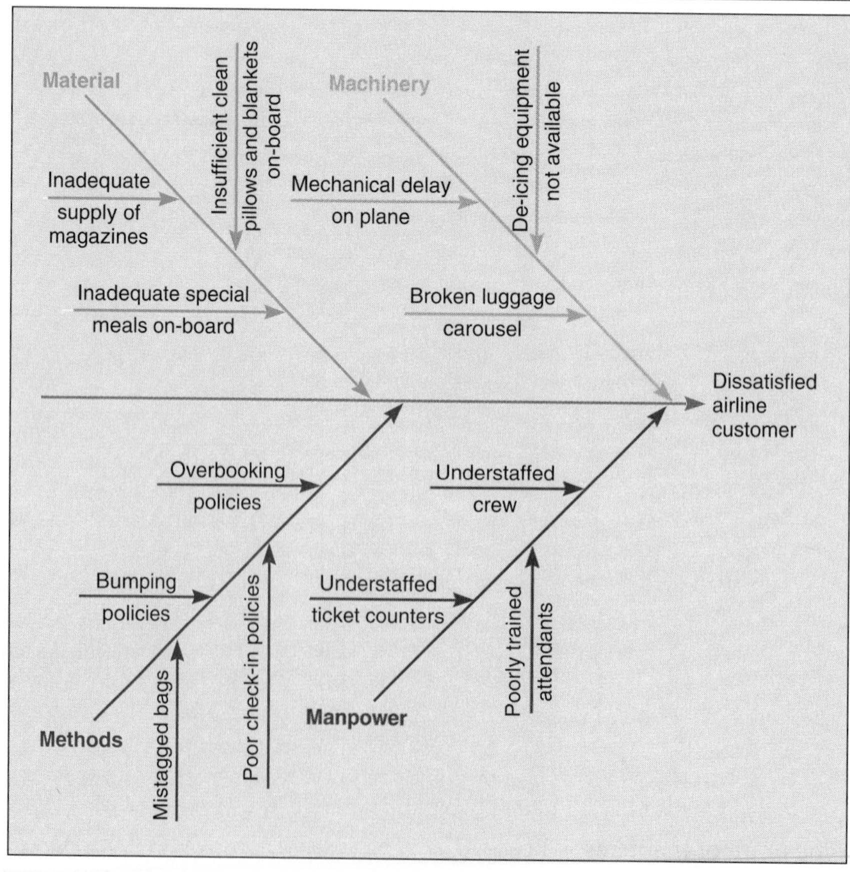

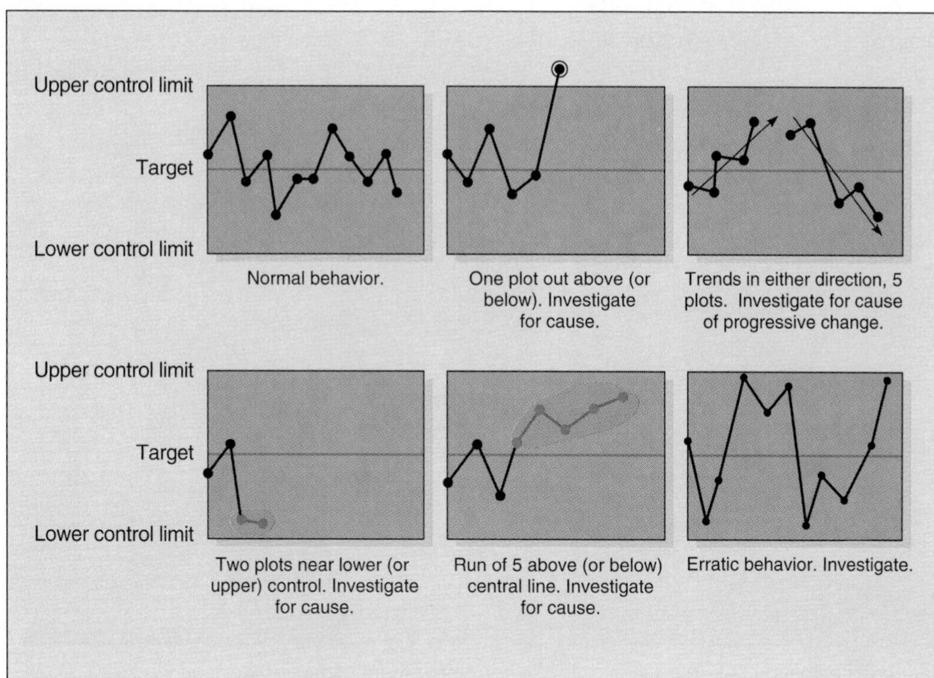

FIGURE 3.7

PATTERNS TO LOOK FOR ON CONTROL CHARTS

Adapted from Bertrand L. Hansen and Prabhakar Ghare, *Quality Control and Application*, © 1987, p. 92. Reprinted by permission of Prentice-Hall, Inc., Upper Saddle River, NJ.

Samples of process outputs are examined; if they are within acceptable limits, the process is permitted to continue. If they fall outside certain specific ranges, the process is stopped and, typically, the assignable cause is located and removed.

Control charts are graphs that show upper and lower limits for the process we want to control. A **control chart** is a graphic presentation of data over time. Control charts are constructed in such a way that new data can be quickly compared to past performance. Upper and lower limits in a control chart can be in units of temperature, pressure, weight, length, and so on. We take samples of the process output and plot the average of these samples on a chart that has the limits on it.

control chart

Figure 3.7 graphically reveals the useful information that can be portrayed in control charts. When the average of the samples falls within the upper and lower control limits and no discernible pattern is present, the process is said to be in control; otherwise, the process is out of control or out of adjustment.

The supplement to this chapter details how control charts of different types are developed. It also deals with the statistical foundation underlying the use of this important tool.

THE ROLE OF INSPECTION

To make sure an operation is producing at the quality level expected, inspection of some or all of the items is needed. This **inspection** can involve measurement, tasting, touching, weighing, or testing of the product (sometimes even destroy-

inspection

Motorola's Accelerated Life Testing (ALT) facility tests extreme conditions of temperature shock, dust, water, and vibrations. Here cellular phones are undergoing a water test.

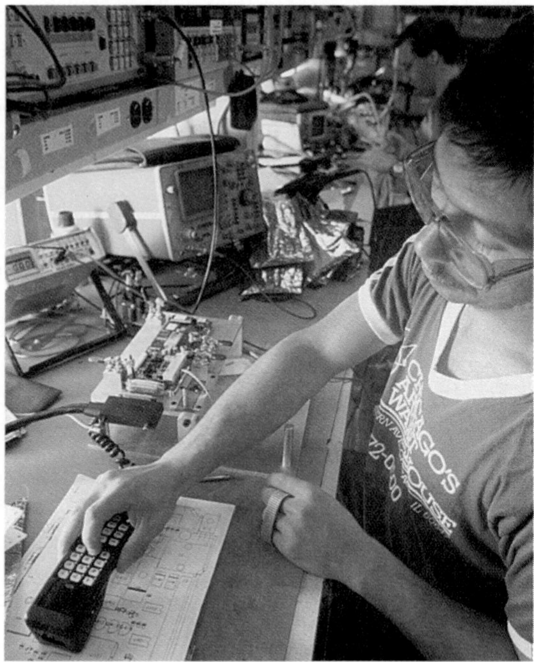
When automated inspection devices work at Motorola they are used. However, when manual intervention in the testing process is appropriate, as is shown here, it is used.

ing it when doing so). The goal of inspection is to detect a bad product immediately. Inspection does not correct deficiencies in the system or defects in the products; nor does it change a product or increase its value.

There are two basic issues relating to inspection:

1. When to inspect.
2. Where to inspect.

When and Where to Inspect

Deciding when and where to inspect depends on the type of process and the value added at each stage. Inspection in manufacturing firms can take place at any of the following six points if the cost of inspection is less than the likely loss from not inspecting:

NOTE
One of the themes of our treatment of quality is that "quality cannot be inspected into a product."

1. Inspect at your supplier's plant while the supplier is producing.
2. Inspect at your plant upon receipt of goods from your supplier.
3. Inspect before costly or irreversible processes.
4. Inspect during the step-by-step production process.
5. Inspect when production is complete.
6. Inspect before shipment from your plant.

Pareto charts, process charts, and cause-and-effect diagrams, discussed in the previous section, are TQM tools to aid in this "when and where" to inspect decision. However, inspection is not a substitute for a robust product produced by a good process. Inspectors are only human: They become bored; they become tired; and the inspection equipment itself has variability. Even with 100% inspection, inspectors cannot guarantee perfection. Therefore, employee empowerment is usually a better solution.

For example, at Velcro Industries, as in many organizations, quality was viewed by machine operators as the job of "those QC people." Inspections were based on random sampling, and if a part showed up bad, it was thrown out. The company decided to pay more attention to operators, to machine repair and design, to measurement methods, communications, and responsibilities, and to invest more money in training. Over time, Velcro was able to pull half its quality control people out of the process, as defects continued to decline.

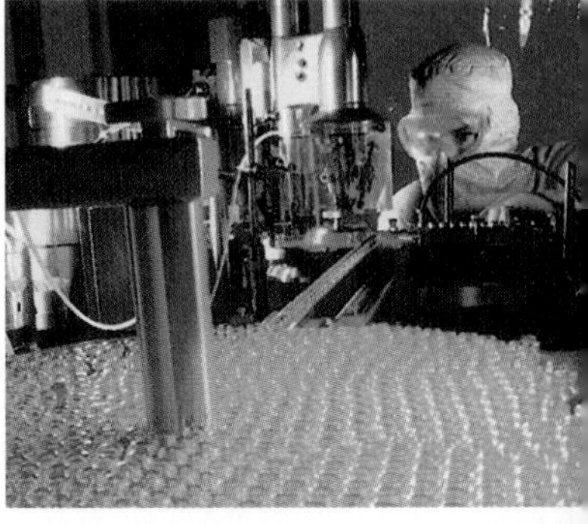

Designing a high-quality process that fills these pharmaceutical bottles in sterile conditions is much more fruitful than having an inspector evaluate the bacteria count on bottles filled in a poor system. Good quality systems focus on quality processes instead of after-the-fact inspections.

Source Inspection

Consistent with the concept of employee empowerment, individual employees self-check their work and that of the employee preceding them. This type of "source" inspection may be assisted by the use of controls such as a fail-safe device called a *poka-yoke*. A **poka-yoke** is a foolproof device or technique that ensures production of good units every time. It uses checklists or special devices to avoid errors, and provides quick feedback of problems. The idea is to *treat the next step in the process as the customer,* ensuring delivery of a good product to the next "customer" in the production process.

poka-yoke

Service Industry Inspection

In *service*-oriented organizations, inspection points can take on a wide range of locations, as illustrated in Table 3.3. Again, the operations manager must decide where inspections are justified. Pareto charts and process charts may prove useful when making these judgments.

Total Quality Management in Services

Quality of services is more difficult to measure than quality of manufactured goods.[11] Generally though, a user of a service has a few characteristics and attributes in mind that he or she uses as a basis for comparison among alternatives. Lack of one attribute may eliminate a specific service firm from consideration. Quality also may be perceived as a whole bundle of attributes where many lesser characteristics are superior to those of competitors.

Extensive interviews with consumer focus groups identified ten general attributes or determinants of service quality (see Table 3.4). The same study also drew the following conclusions:[12]

1. *Consumers' perceptions of service quality result from a comparison of their expectations before they receive their actual experience with the service.* In other words, service quality is judged on the basis of whether it meets expectations.

[11]This section is adapted from Robert Murdick, Barry Render, and Roberta Russell, *Service Operations Management* (Boston: Allyn & Bacon, 1990), pp. 421–422.

[12]L. Berry, V. Zeithaml, and A. Parasuraman, "Quality Counts in Services, Too," *Business Horizons* (May-June 1985): 45–46.

TABLE 3.3 INSPECTION POINTS IN THREE SERVICE ORGANIZATIONS

TYPE OF ORGANIZATION	SOME POINTS OF INSPECTION	ISSUES TO CONSIDER
Bank America	Teller stations	Shortages, courtesy, speed, accuracy
	Loan accounts	Collateral, proper credit checks, rates, terms of loans, default rates, loan ratios
	Checking accounts	Accuracy, speed of entry, rate of overdraws
Macy's Department Store	Stockrooms	Clean, uncluttered, organized, level of stockouts, ample supply, rotation of goods
	Display areas	Attractive, well-organized and stocked, visible goods, good lighting
	Sales counters	Neat, courteous, knowledgeable personnel; waiting time; accuracy in credit checking and sales entry
Chili's Restaurant	Kitchen	Clean, proper storage, unadulterated food, health regulations observed, well-organized
	Cashier station	Speed, accuracy, appearance
	Dining areas	Clean, comfortable, regular monitoring by personnel

2. *Quality perceptions are derived from the service process as well as from the service outcome.* The way the service is performed can be a crucial component of the service from the consumer's point of view.
3. *Service quality is of two types, normal and exceptional.* First, there is the quality level at which the regular service is delivered, such as the bank teller's handling of a transaction. Second, there is the quality level at which "exceptions" or "problems" are handled. This implies that a quality control system must recognize and have prepared a set of "plan Bs" for less-than-optimal operating conditions. In addition, when a problem occurs, the low-contact firm may suddenly become a high-contact firm. Thus good customer relations are important in maintaining quality, regardless of the type of service.

Follow-up interviews with service managers suggest that service quality can be measured by how effectively a service can close the gaps between expectations and the service provided. As the vice president of Savin, a copier service company in Stamford, Connecticut, states, "A company's fortunes ride on the quality of its service."[13]

[13]*The Wall Street Journal*, November 4, 1991, p. A18.

TABLE 3.4 DETERMINANTS OF SERVICE QUALITY

Reliability involves consistency of performance and dependability. It means that the firm performs the service right the first time and also means that the firm honors its promises.

Responsiveness concerns the willingness or readiness of employees to provide service. It involves timeliness of service.

Competence means possession of the required skills and knowledge to perform the service.

Access involves approachability and ease of contact.

Courtesy involves politeness, respect, consideration, and friendliness of contact personnel (including receptionists, telephone operators, and so on).

Communication means keeping customers informed in language they can understand and listening to them. It may mean that the company has to adjust its language for different consumers—increasing the level of sophistication with a well-educated customer and speaking simply and plainly with a novice.

Credibility involves trustworthiness, believability, honesty. It involves having the customer's best interests at heart.

Security is the freedom from danger, risk, or doubt.

Understanding/knowing the customer involves making the effort to understand the customer's needs.

Tangibles include the physical evidence of the service.

SOURCE: Excerpted from A Parasuraman, Valerie A. Zeithaml, and Leonard L. Berry, "A Conceptual Model of Service Quality and Its Implications for Future Research" *Journal of Marketing* (Fall 1985): 44.

SUMMARY

Quality is a term that means different things to different people. But it is defined in this chapter as the totality of features and characteristics of a product or service that bear on its ability to satisfy stated or implied needs. Defining quality expectations is critical to satisfying customers and winning orders.

Quality requires building a total quality management (TQM) environment because quality cannot be inspected into a product. The chapter also addresses five TQM concepts: continuous improvement, employee empowerment, benchmarking, just-in-time, and knowledge of TQM tools. The six TQM tools introduced in this chapter are house of quality, Taguchi method, Pareto charts, process charts, cause-and-effect diagrams, and statistical process control.

KEY TERMS

ISO 9000 *(p. 94)*
ISO 14000 *(p. 94)*
Total quality management (TQM) *(p. 95)*
Kaizen *(p. 96)*
Employee empowerment *(p. 96)*
Quality circle *(p. 96)*
Benchmarking *(p. 96)*
Quality function deployment (QFD) *(p. 98)*
House of quality *(p. 98)*
Taguchi method *(p. 100)*
Quality robust *(p. 100)*
Quality loss function *(p. 101)*
Target value *(p. 102)*
Pareto charts *(p. 102)*
Process charts *(p. 103)*
Cause-and-effect diagram *(p. 104)*
Ishikawa diagram *(p. 104)*
Fish-bone chart *(p. 104)*
Control chart *(p. 105)*
Inspection *(p. 105)*
Poka-yoke *(p. 107)*

SELF-TEST ■ CHAPTER 3

- *Before taking the self-test* refer back to the learning objectives listed at the beginning of the chapter and the key terms listed at the end of the chapter.
- Use the key at the back of the text to *correct* your answers.
- *Restudy* pages that correspond to any questions you answered incorrectly or material you feel uncertain about.

1. The U.S. National Quality Award is named after
   a. Taguchi
   b. Deming
   c. Juran
   d. Crosby
   e. Baldrige

2. Taguchi's quality loss function is a
   a. linear formula
   b. negative exponential
   c. hyper exponential
   d. quadratic
   e. all of the above

3. The Taguchi method includes three major concepts. These concepts are all of the following except
   a. employee involvement
   b. remove the effects of adverse conditions
   c. quality loss function
   d. target specifications

4. Cause-and-effect diagrams are also known as
   a. quality loss charts
   b. target specification graphs
   c. fish-bone charts
   d. Ishikawa diagrams
   e. a and b
   f. c and d

5. Attribute inspection measures:
   a. if the product falls within a specific range
   b. if product responsiveness is adequate
   c. if cause and effect are present
   d. if the product is good or bad

6. In this chapter, *quality* is defined as:
   a. the degree of excellence at an acceptable price and the control of variability at an acceptable cost
   b. how well a product fits patterns of consumer preferences
   c. the totality or features and characteristics of a product or service that bears on its ability to satisfy stated or implied needs
   d. even though it cannot be defined, you know what it is

7. 100% inspection
   a. will always catch all of the defective parts
   b. means that only good parts will be shipped to a customer
   c. is always practical and generally a good idea
   d. means that every part is checked to see whether or not it is defective

8. Quality function deployment's house of quality is designed to address
   a. customer "wants"
   b. the organization's "hows"
   c. the relationship between customer "wants" and the organization's "hows"
   d. the ranking of customer "wants"
   e. all of the above

9. The six tools of total quality management are ________, ________, ________, ________, ________, and ________.

10. In addition to the product per se, quality has major implications for a company. Among these additional implications are ________, ________, ________, ________, and ________.

11. The work of Genichi Taguchi is primarily concerned with the development of ________.

12. Quality cannot be ________ into a product.

13. The five basic concepts of TQM are: ________, ________, ________, ________, and ________.

14. ISO 14000 is an EC standard to address ________.

DISCUSSION QUESTIONS

1. Provide your own definition of quality.
2. Name several goods or services that do not require high quality. Why?
3. Do you think the establishment of the *Malcolm Baldrige National Quality Award* had much effect on the quality of products actually produced in the United States?
4. How can a university control the quality of its output (that is, its graduates)?
5. What are the major concepts of TQM?
6. Find a recent article on quality circles and summarize its major points. Do you think quality circles will be commonplace in all U.S. firms? Why?
7. How can a firm build a climate of continuous improvement?
8. What are the three basic concepts of the Taguchi method?
9. What are six tools of TQM?
10. What is the "house of quality"?
11. Why is the target-oriented performance better than conformance-oriented performance?
12. What are ten determinants of service quality?
13. What is the quality loss function (QLF)?
14. What does the formula $L = D^2C$ mean?
15. How would you change the Baldrige Award criteria?
16. What are the four "M's" of a cause-and-effect diagram?

OPERATIONS IN PRACTICE EXERCISE

The Oklahoma City plant of Tursine Electronics assembles printed circuit boards with a quality rating that is both deplorable and dropping. Indeed, it is worse than any of the company's other plants. To complicate matters, labor relations are difficult and morale low, resulting in high turnover and absenteeism. The new plant manager, who had been sent in to straighten things out, believes that the facility will be closed unless dramatic productivity and quality improvements are made. Quality has become too important a factor in the industry.

How can the manager turn this plant around, build a quality product, and instill quality into the workforce?

PROBLEMS

: **3.1.** Use the quality function deployment's house of quality technique to construct a relationship matrix between customer "wants" and "how" you as a production manager would address them. Consider the *wants* and *hows* of the following:
   a. ice cream
   b. a soft drink

. **3.2.** Conduct an interview with a prospective purchaser of a new bicycle and translate the customer's "*wants*" into the specific "*hows*" of the firm.

. **3.3.** Use Pareto analysis to investigate the following data collected on a printer circuit board assembly line.
   a. Prepare a graph of the data.
   b. What conclusions do you reach?

DEFECT	NUMBER OF DEFECT OCCURRENCES
Wrong component	217
Components not adhering	146
Excess adhesive	64
Misplaced transistors	600
Defective board dimension	143
Mounting holes improperly positioned	14
Circuitry problems on final test	92

3.4. Develop a process chart for one of the following:
  a. changing an automobile tire
  b. paying a bill in a restaurant
  c. making a deposit at your bank

3.5. Prepare a process chart for one of the following:
  a. a fast-food drive-thru window (single window)
  b. a two-station drive-thru window (pay at one, pick up at second)
  c. the registration process at your college

3.6. Draw a fish-bone chart detailing reasons why a bolt might not be correctly matched to a nut on an assembly line.

3.7. Draw a fish-bone chart showing why a typist you paid to prepare a term paper produced a document with numerous errors.

CASE STUDY

Milt and Michael's Cleaning

The owner of Milt and Michael's Cleaning has decided that a quality improvement program must be implemented in its dry cleaning service. Customers bring clothes to one of five stores or pickup stations. Orders are then delivered to the cleaning plant twice (morning and afternoon) each day, with deliveries of orders being made to the stores at the same time, allowing for same-day service by customer request.

The stores are opened at 7:00 A.M. by a full-time employee. This person is relieved at 3:00 P.M. by a part-time employee, who closes the store at 6:00 P.M.

When the clothes are received from the customer, a five-ply ticket showing the customer name, phone number, due date, and special requests is prepared. One ply is given to the customer as a claim check, and the store keeps one ply (to show what they have in process). The clothes and the remaining plies of the ticket are put in a nylon laundry bag for delivery to the plant.

The cleaning plant has the following departments:

Mark-in. Each order is removed from the bag; items are tagged for identification later and sorted into large buggies according to due date, type of garment, and cleaning requirements. The buggies are moved to the cleaning department as they become full. Also at mark-in, garments are checked for spots, stains, tears, or other special handling. The problem is written on a strip-tag (a $\frac{1}{2}$-inch wide paper tape) and attached to the garment with the identification tag.

Cleaning. The buggies are emptied into the cleaning machine one item at a time to allow for inspection. The primary items checked for are foreign objects and spots and stains requiring special attention. For example, an ink pen left in a pocket could ruin the whole load. As items are removed from the cleaning machine, they are placed on hangers and moved by conveyor to the pressing department.

Pressing. There are four presses: one for silks, one for pants, and two general-purpose. On an ordinary day, three of the presses will be operating, but which three of the four are operating will depend upon the total demand and product mix that particular day. As items are pressed, they are placed on a conveyor that delivers them to the assembly department.

Assembly. Cleaned items are grouped into customer orders, bagged, and put in the appropriate queue for delivery to the respective store. At this time, two plies (of the remaining three) of the ticket are attached to the order, and one ply stays at the plant to show this order was completed. When the customer picks up the order, one ply will stay on the order.

The store will retain the last ply and pull the corresponding ply from its work-in-process file to show that this order is complete.

At present, a majority of the employees are cross-trained to allow for flexibility. The table indicates the production employees and the positions for which they are trained. A P indicates this is the primary duty or the one the employee performs most often. A check indicates that the employee is also trained in that function.

		PRESSES		
Employee	*Cleaning*	*General Purpose*	*Silks*	*Pants*
David	P	√		√
Tasha	√	√		P
Len	√	P	√	
Mary		√	P	√
Betty (part-time)	√	√		√
Mike (part-time)	√	√		√

For example, one day David may only clean; the next day he cleans a while and then presses pants. This presents a problem in determining who put a double crease in Mrs. Jones's slacks, but the owner believes this flexibility in scheduling is valuable and must be maintained.

Although Milt and Michael's Cleaning is a larger-than-average cleaning operation, total annual revenues are approximately $500,000. Therefore, any suggestions must be relatively inexpensive.

DISCUSSION QUESTIONS

1. Design the quality program. Consider the following issues:
   a. Where should inspection(s) occur?
   b. How will accountability be achieved?
   c. What factors (variables, attributes, other considerations) should be checked?
   d. Is statistical process control (SPC) appropriate? At what point?
2. What are the cost items for implementing your plan? Give a budget, including equipment, supplies, and labor-hours (divided into types of labor).
3. What records should be kept to measure the success of the program in terms of cost, quality performance, and service to the customer?

SOURCE: Professor Marilyn S. Jones, Winthrop University.

Internet Case Study See our Internet home page at http://www.prenhall.com/renderpom for this additional case study: Westover Electrical.

BIBLIOGRAPHY

Akao, Y., ed. *Quality Function Deployment: Integrating Customer Requirements into Product Design.* Cambridge, MA: Productivity Press, 1990.

Berry, L. L., A. Parasuraman, and V. A. Zeithaml. "Improving Service Quality in America: Lessons Learned." *The Academy of Management Executive* 8, no. 2 (May 1994): 32–52.

Besterfield, D. H. *Quality Control*, 4th ed. Englewood Cliffs, NJ: Prentice Hall, 1994.

Carr, L. P. "Applying Cost of Quality to a Service Business." *Sloan Management Review* 33, no. 4 (Summer 1992): 72.

Costin, H. *Readings in Total Quality Management.* New York: Dryden Press, 1994.

Crosby, P. B. *Let's Talk Quality.* New York: McGraw-Hill, 1989.

______. *Quality Is Free.* New York: McGraw-Hill, 1979.

Denton, D. K. "Lessons on Competitiveness: Motorola's Approach." *Production and Inventory Management Journal* 32, no. 3 (Third Quarter 1991): 22.

DeVor, R. E., T. Chang, and J. W. Sutherland. *Statistical Quality Design and Control: Contemporary Concepts and Methods.* New York: Macmillan, 1992.

Dobyns, L., and C. Crawford-Mason. *Quality or Else: The Revolution in World Business.* New York: Houghton Mifflin. 1991.

Evans, J. R., and W. M. Lindsay. *The Management and Control of Quality*, 2d ed. New York: West, 1993.

Feigenbaum, A. V. *Total Quality Control*, 3d ed. New York: McGraw-Hill, 1991.

Forker, L. B. "Quality: American, Japanese, and Soviet Perspectives." *The Academy of Management Executive* 5, no. 4 (November 1991): 63–73.

Foster, S. T., Jr. "Designing and Initiating a Taguchi Experiment in a Services Setting." OM *Review* 9, no. 3: 37–50.

Hart, M. K. "Quality Tools for Decreasing Variation and Defining Process Capability." *Production and Inventory Management Journal* 33, no. 2 (Second Quarter 1992): 6.

Hauser, J. R. "How Puritan-Bennett Used the House of Quality." *Sloan Management Review* 34, no. 3 (Spring 1993): 61–70.

Juran, J. M. "Made in the U.S.A.: A Renaissance in Quality." *Harvard Business Review* 14, no. 4 (July-August 1993): 35–38.

Miller, J. G. *Benchmarking.* Homewood, IL: Business One Irwin, 1992.

Peace, G. S. *Taguchi Methods: A Hands-On Approach.* Reading, MA: Addison-Wesley, 1993.

Price, F. *Right Every Time: Using the Deming Approach.* New York: Marcel Dekker, 1990.

Ryan, T. P. *Statistical Methods for Quality Improvement.* New York: John Wiley, 1989.

Schonberger, R. J. "Is Strategy Strategic? Impact of Total Quality Management on Strategy." *The Executive* 6, no. 3 (August 1992): 80.

Vaziri, H. K. "Using Competitive Benchmarking to Set Goals." *Quality Progress* 25, no. 10 (October 1992): 81.

Quality via Statistical Process Control

Supplement 3

SUPPLEMENT OUTLINE

Statistical Process Control (SPC)

Control Charts for Variables ■ The Central Limit Theorem ■ Setting Mean Chart Limits ($\bar{x}$-Charts) ■ Setting Range Chart Limits (*R*-Charts) ■ Control Charts for Attributes

Acceptance Sampling

Operating Characteristic Curve ■ Average Outgoing Quality

Summary ■ Key Terms ■ Using POM for Windows ■ Using Excel Spreadsheets for Statistical Process Control ■ Solved Problems ■ Discussion Questions ■ Self-Test Supplement 3 ■ Operations in Practice Exercise ■ Problems ■ Case Study: SPC at the Gazette ■ Bibliography

LEARNING OBJECTIVES

When you complete this supplement you should be able to:

IDENTIFY OR DEFINE:

Assignable and natural causes of variations
Attribute and variable inspection
Acceptance sampling
Process control
$\bar{x}$-charts
R-charts
LCL and UCL
Central limit theorem
OC curve
Producer's risk
Consumer's risk

EXPLAIN:

The role of statistical process control in operations

In the mid-1980s, Motorola was in trouble. Japanese companies such as NEC, Toshiba, and Hitachi were gobbling up the company's markets in pagers, cellular phones, and semiconductor chips. Something had to be done. Motorola's management responded with a bold plan that included rapid product development, sharply upgraded quality, and a determination to reduce manufacturing costs. A key element in this plan was a statistical way of measuring quality called *six sigma.* In an era when many organizations viewed *three sigma* as acceptable, *six sigma* was radical. For example, *three sigma* is equivalent to 15,000 out of every million newborn babies being dropped by doctors and nurses each year, while *six sigma* means not having more than 3.4 errors per million. By 1988 Motorola won a Baldrige National Quality Award and was well on its way to performing at this exceptional world-class level.

In this supplement, we address statistical process control—the same techniques used at Motorola to achieve six sigma. We also introduce acceptance sampling. *Statistical process control* is the application of statistical techniques to the control of processes. Acceptance sampling is used to determine acceptance or rejection of a lot of material evaluated by inspection or test of a sample.

STATISTICAL PROCESS CONTROL (SPC)

Statistical process control (SPC) is a statistical technique that is widely used to ensure that processes are meeting standards. All processes are subject to a certain degree of variability. Walter Shewhart of Bell Laboratories, while studying process data in the 1920s, made the distinction between the common and special causes of variation. Many people now refer to these variations as *natural* and *assignable* causes. He developed a simple but powerful tool to separate the two—the control chart.

We use statistical process control to measure performance of a process. A process is said to be operating in statistical control when the only sources of variation are common (natural) causes. The process must first be brought into statistical control by detecting and eliminating special (assignable) causes of variation.[1] Then its performance is predictable, and its ability to meet customer expectations can be assessed. The *objective* of a process control system is *to provide a statistical signal when assignable causes of variation are present.* Such a signal can quicken appropriate action to eliminate assignable causes.

natural variations

NATURAL VARIATIONS. Natural variations affect almost every production process and are to be expected. **Natural variations** are the many sources of variation within a process that is in statistical control. They behave like a constant system of chance causes. Although individual values are all different, as a group they form a pattern that can be described as a distribution. When these distributions are *normal,* they are characterized by two parameters. These parameters are

- Mean, μ (the measure of central tendency—in this case, the average value).
- Standard deviation, σ (variation, the amount by which the smaller values differ from the larger ones).

[1]Removing assignable causes is work. As W. Edwards Deming observed, "a state of statistical control is not a natural state for a manufacturing process. It is instead an achievement, arrived at by elimination, one by one, by determined effort, of special causes of excessive variation." See W. Edwards Deming, "On Some Statistical Aids Toward Economic Production," *Interfaces* 5, no. 4 (1975): 5.

As long as the distribution (output precision) remains within specified limits, the process is said to be "in control," and the modest variations are tolerated.

ASSIGNABLE VARIATIONS. Assignable variation in a process can be traced to a specific reason. Factors such as machine wear, misadjusted equipment, fatigued or untrained workers, or new batches of raw material are all potential sources of **assignable variations.**

assignable variations

NOTE
Random chance → natural
Specific cause → assignable variable

Natural and assignable variations distinguish two tasks for the operations manager. The first is to ensure that the process will have only natural variation that is capable of operating under control. The second is, of course, to identify and eliminate assignable variations so that the processes will remain under control.

SAMPLES. Because of natural and assignable variation, statistical process control uses averages of small samples (often of five items or parts) as opposed to data on individual parts. Individual pieces tend to be too erratic to make trends quickly visible.

Figure S3.1 provides a detailed look at the important steps in determining process variation. The horizontal scale can be weight (as in the number of ounces

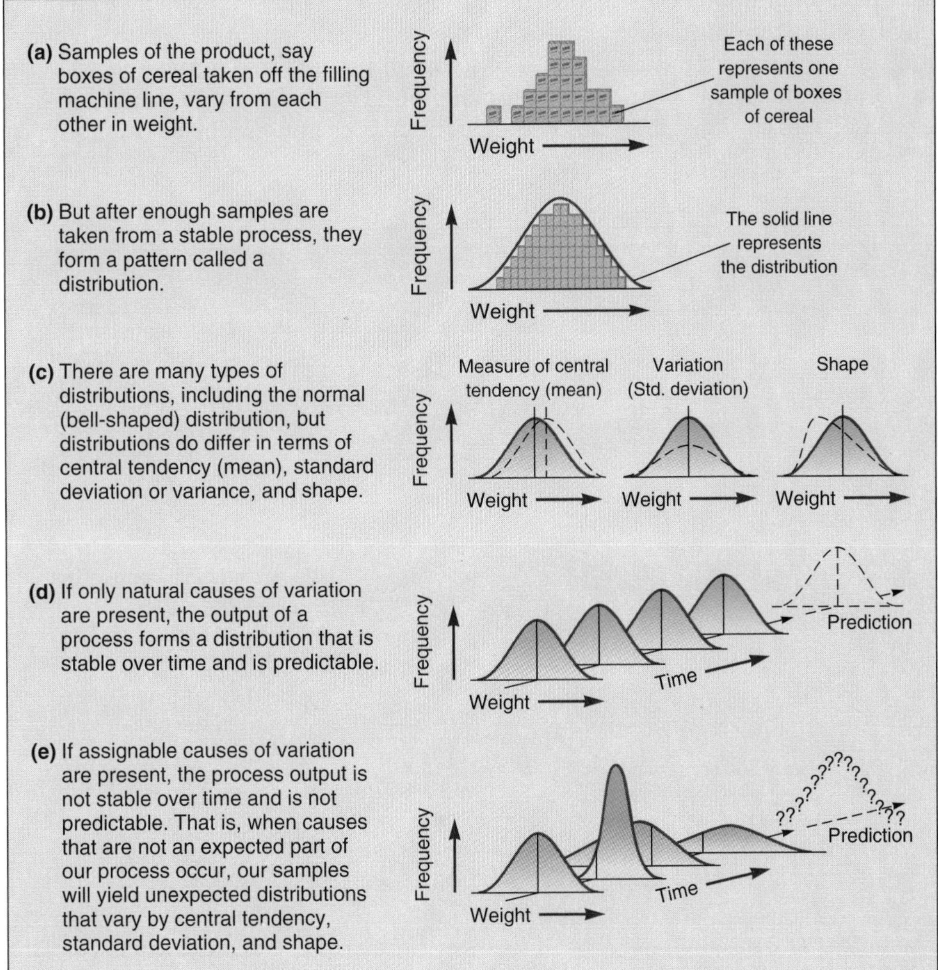
(a) Samples of the product, say boxes of cereal taken off the filling machine line, vary from each other in weight.
Frequency
Weight
Each of these represents one sample of boxes of cereal
(b) But after enough samples are taken from a stable process, they form a pattern called a distribution.
Frequency
Weight
The solid line represents the distribution
(c) There are many types of distributions, including the normal (bell-shaped) distribution, but distributions do differ in terms of central tendency (mean), standard deviation or variance, and shape.
Measure of central tendency (mean)
Variation (Std. deviation)
Shape
Frequency
Weight
Weight
Weight
(d) If only natural causes of variation are present, the output of a process forms a distribution that is stable over time and is predictable.
Frequency
Weight
Time
Prediction
(e) If assignable causes of variation are present, the process output is not stable over time and is not predictable. That is, when causes that are not an expected part of our process occur, our samples will yield unexpected distributions that vary by central tendency, standard deviation, and shape.
Frequency
Weight
Time
Prediction

FIGURE S3.1
NATURAL AND ASSIGNABLE VARIATION

in boxes of cereal), or length (as in fence posts), or any physical measure. The vertical scale is frequency.

CONTROL CHARTS. The process of building control charts is based on the concepts presented in Figure S3.2. This figure shows three distributions that are the result of outputs from three types of processes. We plot small samples and then examine characteristics of the resulting data to see if the process is within "control limits." The purpose of control charts is to help distinguish between natural variations and variations due to assignable causes. As seen in Figure S3.2, a process is (a) in control *and the process is capable of producing within established control limits*, (b) in control, *but the process is not capable of producing within established limits*, or (c) out of control. We now look at how to build control charts that help the operations manager keep a process under control.

NOTE
"It is a capital mistake to theorize before you have the data." Sherlock Holmes (Sir Arthur Conan Doyle)

Control Charts for Variables

Variables are characteristics that have continuous dimensions. They have an infinite number of possibilities. Examples are weight, speed, length, or strength. Control charts for the mean, $\bar{x}$, and the range, R, are used to monitor processes that have continuous dimensions. The $\bar{x}$-(x-bar) **chart** tells us whether changes have occurred in the central tendency of a process. This might be due to such factors as tool wear, a gradual increase in temperature, a different method used on the second shift, or new and stronger materials. The ***R*-chart** values indicate that a gain or loss in uniformity has occurred. Such a change might be due to worn

$\bar{x}$-chart

***R*-chart**

FIGURE S3.2

PROCESS CONTROL: THREE TYPES OF PROCESS OUTPUTS

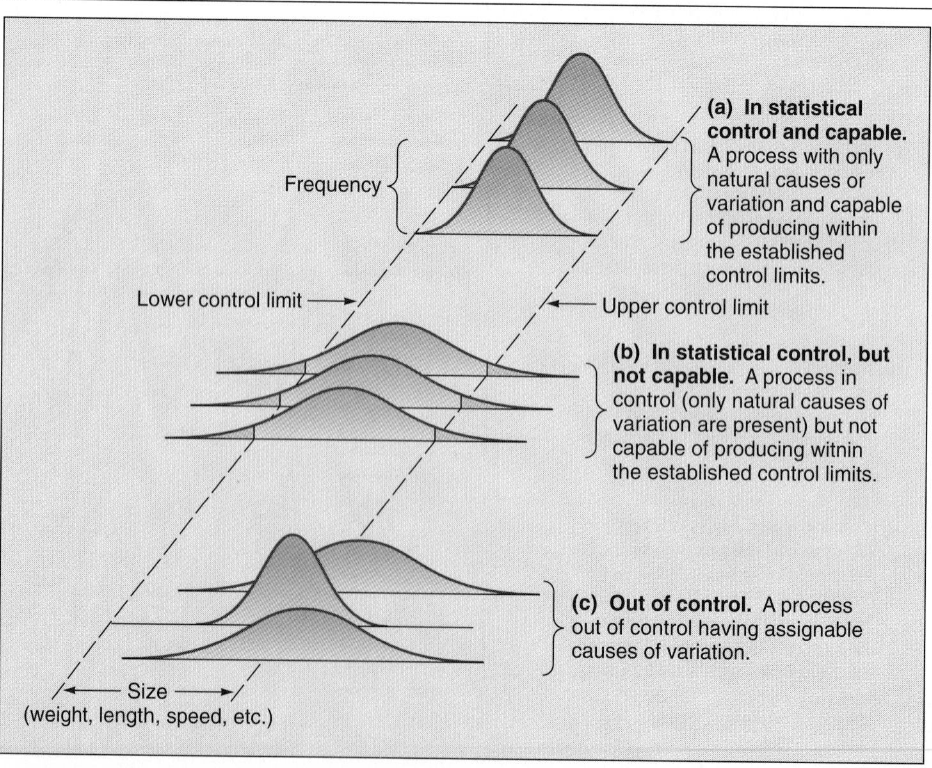
Frequency
(a) In statistical control and capable. A process with only natural causes or variation and capable of producing within the established control limits.
Lower control limit
Upper control limit
(b) In statistical control, but not capable. A process in control (only natural causes of variation are present) but not capable of producing witnin the established control limits.
(c) Out of control. A process out of control having assignable causes of variation.
Size
(weight, length, speed, etc.)

bearings, a loose tool part, an erratic flow of lubricants to a machine, or to sloppiness on the part of a machine operator. The two types of charts go hand in hand when monitoring variables.

The Central Limit Theorem

central limit theorem

The theoretical foundation for $\bar{x}$-charts is the **central limit theorem.** In general terms, this theorem states that regardless of the distribution of the population of all parts or services, the distribution of $\bar{x}$s (each of which is a mean of a sample drawn from the population) will tend to follow a normal curve. And, fortunately, even if the sample (n) is fairly small (say, 4 or 5), the distributions of the averages will still roughly follow a normal curve. The theorem also states that (1) the mean of the distribution of the $\bar{x}$s (called $\bar{\bar{x}}$) will equal the mean of the overall population (called μ); and (2) the standard deviation of the sampling distribution, $\sigma_{\bar{x}}$, will be the population standard deviation, σ_x, divided by the square root of the sample size, n. In other words,

NOTE
The two parameters are:
Mean → measure of central tendency.
Range → measure of dispersion

$$\bar{\bar{x}} = \mu \quad \text{and} \quad \sigma_{\bar{x}} = \frac{\sigma_x}{\sqrt{n}}$$

Figure S3.3 shows three possible population distributions, each with its own mean, μ, and standard deviation σ_x. If a series of random samples ($\bar{x}_1$, $\bar{x}_2$, $\bar{x}_3$, $\bar{x}_4$, and so on) each of size n is drawn from any one of these, the resulting distribution of $\bar{x}_1$s will appear as in the bottom graph of that figure. Because this is a normal distribution, we can state that

1. 99.7% of the time, the sample averages will fall within $\pm 3\sigma_{\bar{x}}$ if the process has only random variations; and
2. 95.5% of the time, the sample averages will fall within $\pm 2\sigma_{\bar{x}}$ if the process has only random variations.

If a point on the control chart falls outside of the $\pm 3\sigma_{\bar{x}}$ control limits, then we are 99.7% sure the process has changed. This is the theory behind control charts.

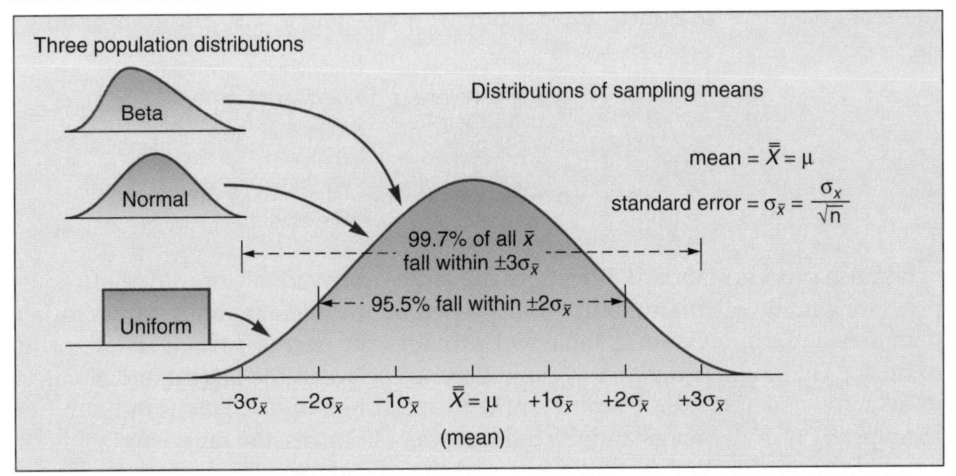

Regardless of the population distribution (beta, normal, or uniform), each with its own mean (μ) and standard deviation (σ_x), the distribution of sample means is always normal.

FIGURE S3.3

THE RELATIONSHIP BETWEEN POPULATION AND SAMPLING DISTRIBUTIONS

Setting Mean Chart Limits ($\bar{x}$ Charts)

If we know, through past data, the standard deviation of the process population, σ_x, we can set upper and lower control limits by these formulas:

$$\text{Upper control limit (UCL)} = \bar{\bar{x}} + z\sigma_{\bar{x}} \qquad \text{(S3.1)}$$

$$\text{Lower control limit (LCL)} = \bar{\bar{x}} - z\sigma_{\bar{x}} \qquad \text{(S3.2)}$$

where

$\bar{\bar{x}}$ = Mean of the sample means

z = Number of normal standard deviations (2 for 95.5% confidence, 3 for 99.7%)

$\sigma_{\bar{x}}$ = Standard deviation of the sample means $= \dfrac{\sigma_x}{\sqrt{n}}$

n = Sample size

Example S1 shows how to set control limits for sample means using standard deviations.

EXAMPLE S1

The weights of boxes of Oat Flakes within a large production lot are sampled each hour. To set control limits that include 99.7% of the sample means, samples of nine boxes are randomly selected and weighed. Here are the results for the past 12 hours:

HOUR	AVG. OF 9 BOXES	HOUR	AVG. OF 9 BOXES	HOUR	AVG. OF 9 BOXES
1	17.1	5	16.5	9	16.3
2	16.8	6	16.4	10	16.5
3	14.5	7	15.2	11	14.2
4	14.8	8	16.4	12	17.3

The average mean of all 12 of the samples is easily calculated to be exactly 16 ounces and the population standard deviation is calculated to be 1 ounce. We therefore have $\bar{\bar{x}} = 16$ ounces, $\sigma_x = 1$ ounce, $n = 9$, and $z = 3$. The control limits are:

$$UCL_{\bar{x}} = \bar{\bar{x}} + z\sigma_{\bar{x}} = 16 + 3\left(\frac{1}{\sqrt{9}}\right) = 16 + 3\left(\frac{1}{3}\right) = 17 \text{ ounces}$$

$$LCL_{\bar{x}} = \bar{\bar{x}} - z\sigma_{\bar{x}} = 16 - 3\left(\frac{1}{\sqrt{9}}\right) = 16 - 3\left(\frac{1}{3}\right) = 15 \text{ ounces}$$

Because process standard deviations are either not available or difficult to compute, we usually calculate control limits based on the average range values rather than on standard deviations. Table S3.1 provides the necessary conversion for us to do so. The range is defined as the difference between the largest and smallest items in one sample. For example, if the heaviest box of Oat Flakes in hour 1 of Example S1 was 19 ounces and the lightest was 14 ounces, the range for that hour would be 5 ounces. We use Table S3.1 and the equations

$$UCL_{\bar{x}} = \bar{\bar{x}} + A_2\bar{R} \qquad \text{(S3.3)}$$

TABLE S3.1 FACTORS FOR COMPUTING CONTROL CHART LIMITS

SAMPLE SIZE, n	MEAN FACTOR, A_2	UPPER RANGE, D_4	LOWER RANGE, D_3
2	1.880	3.268	0
3	1.023	2.574	0
4	.729	2.282	0
5	.577	2.114	0
6	.483	2.004	0
7	.419	1.924	0.076
8	.373	1.864	0.136
9	.337	1.816	0.184
10	.308	1.777	0.223
12	.266	1.716	0.284
14	.235	1.671	0.329
16	.212	1.636	0.364
18	.194	1.608	0.392
20	.180	1.586	0.414
25	.153	1.541	0.459

SOURCE: Reprinted by permission of American Society for Testing Materials. Copyright 1951. Taken from Special Technical Publication 15-C, "Quality Control of Materials," pp. 63, 72.

and

$$\text{LCL}_{\bar{x}} = \bar{\bar{x}} - A_2\bar{R} \qquad \text{(S3.4)}$$

where

$\bar{R}$ = Average range of the samples

A_2 = Value found in Table S3.1

$\bar{\bar{x}}$ = Mean of the sample means

Example S2 shows how to set control limits for sample means using Table S3.1 and the average range.

EXAMPLE S2

Super Cola bottles soft drinks labeled "net weight 16 ounces." An overall process average of 16.01 ounces has been found by taking several batches of samples in which each sample contained five bottles. The average range of the process is .25 ounce. Determine the upper and lower control limits for averages in this process.

Looking in Table S3.1 for a sample size of 5 in the mean factor A_2 column, we find the number .577. Thus, the upper and lower control chart limits are:

$$\begin{aligned}\text{UCL}_{\bar{x}} &= \bar{\bar{x}} + A_2\bar{R} \\ &= 16.01 + (.577)(.25) \\ &= 16.01 + .144 \\ &= 16.154 \text{ ounces}\end{aligned}$$

$$\begin{aligned}\text{LCL}_{\bar{x}} &= \bar{\bar{x}} - A_2\bar{R} \\ &= 16.01 - .144 \\ &= 15.866 \text{ ounces}\end{aligned}$$

To satisfy customers, AVX, a maker of electronic chip components, has declared war on defects. The Japanese-owned company's objective is zero defects at very low tolerance for variable data and nearly zero defects for parts per million (ppm) for attribute data. Here process capability indexes take into consideration both process variation vs. specification limits and process mean location vs. targets.

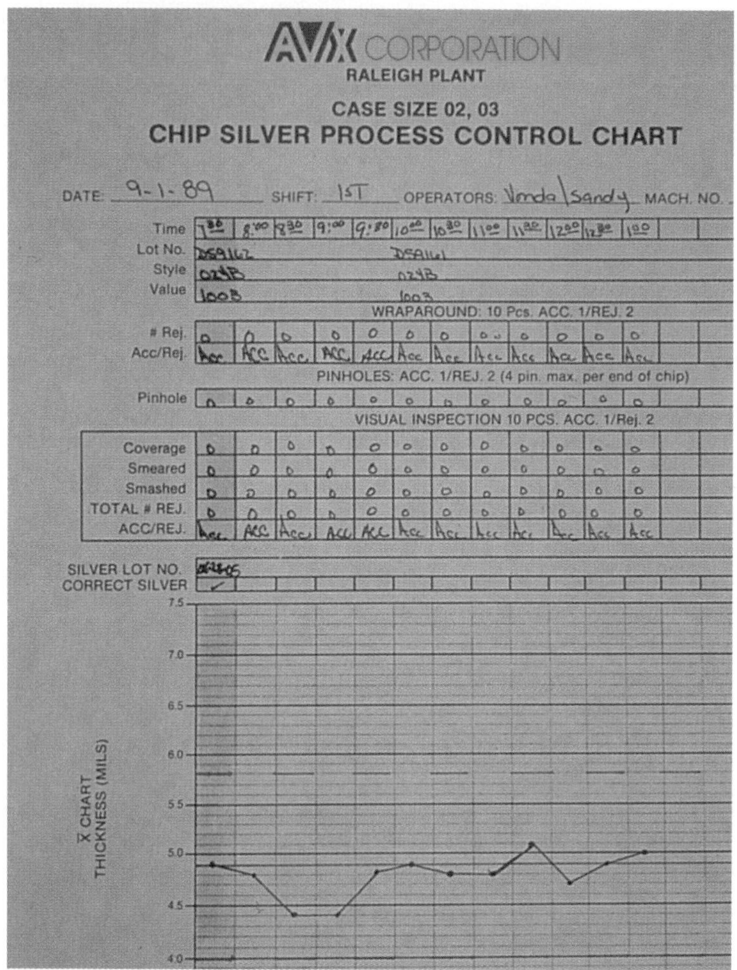

Setting Range Chart Limits (*R*-Charts)

In Examples S1 and S2, we determined the upper and lower control limits for the process *average*. In addition to being concerned with the process average, operations managers are interested in the process *dispersion*, or *variability*. Even though the process average is under control, the variability of the process may not be. For example, something may have worked itself loose in a piece of equipment. As a result, the average of the samples may remain the same, but the variation within the samples could be entirely too large. For this reason, operations managers use control charts for *ranges* in order to monitor the process variability, as well as control charts for the process *average*, which monitor the process average. The theory behind the control charts for ranges is the same as that for the process average control charts. Limits are established that contain $\pm$ 3 standard deviations of the distribution for the average range $\overline{R}$. We can use the following equation to set the upper and lower control limits for ranges:

$$\text{UCL}_R = D_4\bar{R} \tag{S3.5}$$

$$\text{LCL}_R = D_3\bar{R} \tag{S3.6}$$

where

UCL_R = Upper control chart limit for the range

LCL_R = Lower control chart limit for the range

D_4 and D_3 = Values from Table S3.1

Example S3 shows how to set control limits for sample ranges using Table S3.1 and the average range.

EXAMPLE S3

The average *range* of a process is 5.3 pounds. If the sample size is 5, determine the upper and lower control chart limits.

Looking in Table S3.1 for a sample size of 5, we find that $D_4 = 2.114$ and $D_3 = 0$. The range control limits are

$$\begin{aligned}\text{UCL}_R &= D_4\bar{R}\\ &= (2.114)(5.3 \text{ pounds})\\ &= 11.2 \text{ pounds}\\ \text{LCL}_R &= D_3\bar{R}\\ &= (0)(5.3 \text{ pounds})\\ &= 0\end{aligned}$$

STEPS TO FOLLOW IN USING CONTROL CHARTS. Five steps are generally followed when using $\bar{x}$-charts and R-charts:

1. Collect 20 to 25 samples of $n = 4$ or $n = 5$ each from a stable process and compute the mean and range of each.
2. Compute the overall means ($\bar{\bar{x}}$ and $\bar{R}$), set appropriate control limits, usually at the 99.7% level, and calculate the preliminary upper and lower control limits. If the process is not currently stable, use the desired mean, μ, instead of $\bar{\bar{x}}$ to calculate limits.
3. Graph the sample means and ranges on their respective control charts and determine whether they fall outside the acceptable limits.
4. Investigate points or patterns that indicate the process is out of control. Try to assign causes for the variation and then resume the process. Refer back to Chapter 3's Figure 3.7 on page 105 for patterns to look for on control charts.
5. Collect additional samples and, if necessary, revalidate the control limits using the new data.

Control Charts for Attributes

Control charts for $\bar{x}$ and R do not apply when we are sampling *attributes*, which are typically classified as defective or nondefective. Measuring defectives involves counting them (for example, number of bad light bulbs in a given lot or number of letters or data-entry records typed with errors), whereas *variables* are usually measured for length or weight. There are two kinds of attribute control charts: (1) those that measure the percent defective in a sample—called p-charts, and (2) those that count the number of defects—called c-charts.

***p*-charts**

P-CHARTS. Using ***p*-charts** is the chief way to control attributes. Although attributes that are either good or bad follow the binomial distribution, the normal distribution can be used to calculate p-chart limits when sample sizes are large. The procedure resembles the $\bar{x}$-chart approach, which was also based on the central limit theorem.

The formulas for p-chart upper and lower control limits follow:

$$\text{UCL}_p = \bar{p} + z\sigma_{\hat{p}} \quad \text{(S3.7)}$$

$$\text{LCL}_p = \bar{p} - z\sigma_{\hat{p}} \quad \text{(S3.8)}$$

where

$\bar{p}$ = Mean fraction defective in the sample

z = Number of standard deviations ($z = 2$ for 95.5% limits; $z = 3$ for 99.7% limits)

$\sigma_{\hat{p}}$ = Standard deviation of the sampling distribution

$\sigma_{\hat{p}}$ is estimated by the formula:

$$\sigma_{\hat{p}} = \sqrt{\frac{\bar{p}(1-\bar{p})}{n}} \quad \text{(S3.9)}$$

where n = size of each sample.

Example S4 shows how to set control limits for p-charts for these standard deviations.

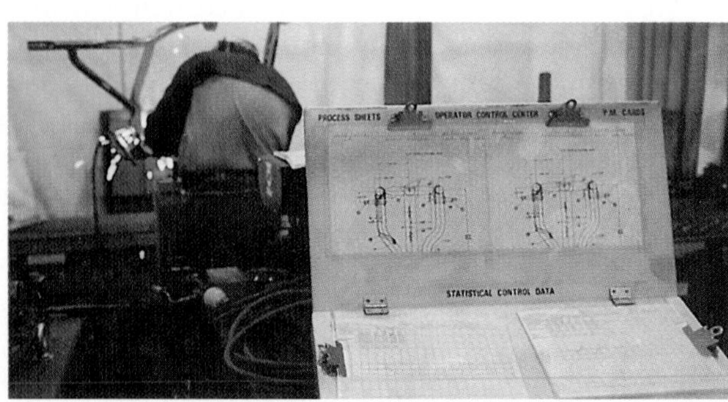

Harley-Davidson, like other world-class firms, makes extensive use of statistical process control (SPC). At the work cell shown here, an employee measures the dimensions of a part and posts the data on the control chart.

EXAMPLE S4

Data-entry clerks at ARCO key in thousands of insurance records each day. Samples of the work of 20 clerks are shown in the table. One hundred records entered by each clerk were carefully examined to make sure they contained no errors. The fraction defective in each sample was then computed.

Set the control limits to include 99.7% of the random variation in the entry process when it is in control.

SAMPLE NUMBER	NUMBER OF ERRORS	FRACTION DEFECTIVE	SAMPLE NUMBER	NUMBER OF ERRORS	FRACTION DEFECTIVE
1	6	.06	11	6	.06
2	5	.05	12	1	.01
3	0	.00	13	8	.08
4	1	.01	14	7	.07
5	4	.04	15	5	.05
6	2	.02	16	4	.04
7	5	.05	17	11	.11
8	3	.03	18	3	.03
9	3	.03	19	0	.00
10	2	.02	20	4	.04
				80	

$$\bar{p} = \frac{\text{Total number of errors}}{\text{Total number of records examined}} = \frac{80}{(100)(20)} = .04$$

$$\sigma_{\hat{p}} = \sqrt{\frac{(.04)(1-.04)}{100}} = .02$$

(*Note:* 100 is the size of each sample $= n$)

$$\text{UCL}_p = \bar{p} + z\sigma_{\hat{p}} + .04 + 3(.02) = .10$$

$$\text{LCL}_p = \bar{p} - z\sigma_{\hat{p}} = .04 - 3(.02) = 0$$

(because we cannot have a negative percent defective)

When we plot the control limits and the sample fraction defectives, we find that only one data-entry clerk (number 17) is out of control. The firm may wish to examine that individual's work a bit more closely to see if a serious problem exists (see Figure S3.4).

FIGURE S3.4

p-CHART FOR DATA ENTRY FOR EXAMPLE S4

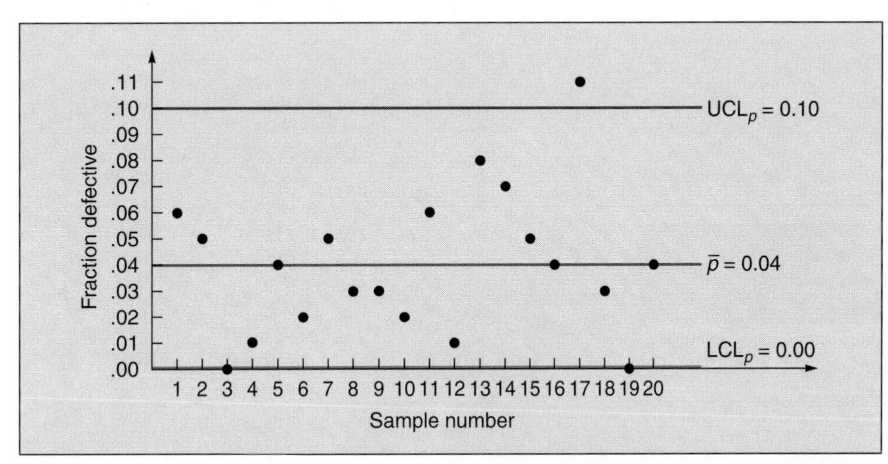

Space-age robotics and computerized analytical equipment are used by Waste Management to protect groundwater. Waste Management processing and disposal centers analyze up to 60,000 samples annually in its attempt to assure the highest standards of environmental quality.

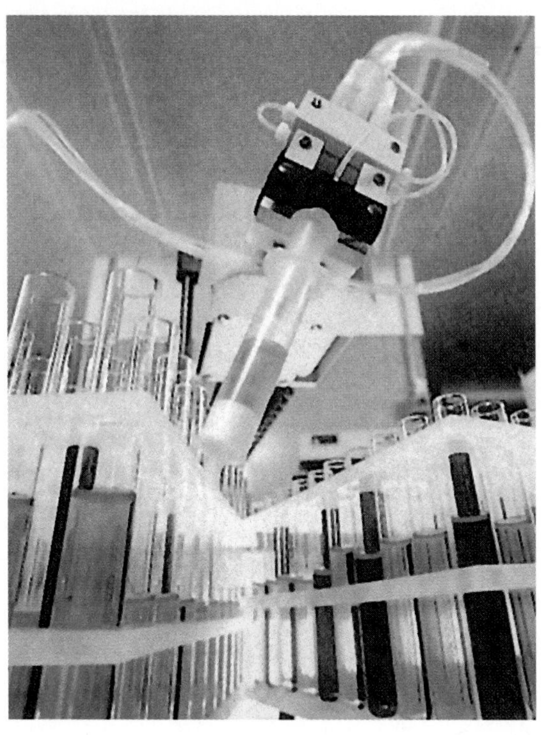

c-charts

C-CHARTS. In Example S4, we counted the number of defective records entered. A defective record was one that was not exactly correct. A bad record may contain more than one defect, however. We use **c-charts** to control the *number* of defects per unit of output (or per insurance record in the preceding case).

Control charts for defects are helpful for monitoring processes in which a large number of potential errors can occur but the actual number that do occur is relatively small. Defects may be errors in newspaper words, bad circuits in a microchip, blemishes on a table, or missing pickles on a fast-food hamburger.

The Poisson probability distribution, which has a variance equal to its mean, is the basis for *c*-charts. Because *c* is the mean number of defects per unit, the standard deviation is equal to $\sqrt{\bar{c}}$. To compute 99.7% control limits for $\bar{c}$, we use the formula

$$\bar{c} \pm 3\sqrt{\bar{c}} \qquad \text{(S3.10)}$$

Example S5 shows how to set control limits for a $\bar{c}$-chart.

EXAMPLE S5

Red Top Cab Company receives several complaints per day about the behavior of its drivers. Over a nine-day period (where days are the units of measure), the owner received the following numbers of calls from irate passengers: 3, 0, 8, 9, 6, 7, 4, 9, 8, for a total of 54 complaints.

To compute 99.7% control limits, we take

$$\bar{c} = \frac{54}{9} = 6 \text{ complaints per day}$$

Thus,

$$UCL_c = \bar{c} + 3\sqrt{\bar{c}} = 6 + 3\sqrt{6} = 6 + 3(2.45) = 13.35$$
$$LCL_c = \bar{c} - 3\sqrt{\bar{c}} = 6 - 3\sqrt{6} = 6 - 3(2.45) = 0$$

After the owner plotted a control chart summarizing these data and posted it prominently in the drivers' locker room, the number of calls received dropped to an average of three per day. Can you explain why this occurred?

Note that although we have discussed process charts and control limits, a focus on the *target* value, not the limits, is best.

ACCEPTANCE SAMPLING

acceptance sampling

Acceptance sampling is a form of testing that involves taking random samples of "lots" or batches of finished products and measuring them against predetermined standards. Sampling is more economical than 100% inspection. The quality of the sample is used to judge the quality of all items in the lot. Although either attributes or variables can be inspected by acceptance sampling, attribute inspection is more commonly used in business and is illustrated in this section.

Acceptance sampling can be applied when raw materials arrive at a plant during a production process, or in final inspection, but it is usually used to control incoming lots of purchased products. A lot of items rejected, based on an unacceptable level of defects found in the sample, can (1) be returned to the supplier or (2) be 100% inspected to cull out all defects, with the cost of this screening usually billed to the supplier. However, acceptance sampling is not a substitute for adequate process controls. In fact, the current approach is to build statistical quality controls at the supplier level so that acceptance sampling can be eliminated.

NOTE
"Quality is never an accident; it is always the result of intelligent effort."
John Ruskin

Operating Characteristic Curve

operating characteristic (OC) curve

The **operating characteristic (OC) curve** describes how well an acceptance plan discriminates between good and bad lots. A curve pertains to a specific plan, that is, a combination of n (sample size) and c (acceptance level). It is intended to show the probability that the plan will accept lots of various quality levels.

producer's risk

consumer's risk

In acceptance sampling, two parties are usually involved: the producer of the product and the consumer of the product. In specifying a sampling plan, each party wants to avoid costly mistakes in accepting or rejecting a lot. The producer wants to avoid the mistake of having a good lot rejected **(producer's risk).** This is because the producer usually has the responsibility of replacing all defects in the rejected lot or of paying for a new lot to be shipped to the customer. On the other hand, the customer or consumer wants to avoid the mistake of accepting a bad lot because defects found in a lot that has already been accepted are usually the responsibility of the customer **(consumer's risk).** The OC curve shows the features of a particular sampling plan, including the risks of making a wrong decision.[2]

[2]Note that sampling always runs the danger of leading to an erroneous conclusion. Let us say in this example that the total population under scrutiny is a load of 1,000 computer chips, of which in reality only 30 (or 3%) are defective. This means that we would want to accept the shipment of chips, since 4% is the allowable defect rate. But if a random sample of $n = 50$ chips were drawn, we could conceivably end up with 0 defects and accept that shipment (that is, it is OK) or we could find all 30 defects in the sample. If the latter happened, we could wrongly conclude that the whole population was 60% defective and reject them all.

Figure S3.5 can be used to illustrate one sampling plan in more detail. Four concepts are illustrated in this figure.

acceptable quality level (AQL)

The **acceptable quality level (AQL)** is the poorest level of quality we are willing to accept. We wish to accept lots that have this level of quality. If an acceptable quality level is 20 defects in a lot of 1,000 items or parts, then AQL is 20/1,000 = 2% defectives.

lot tolerance percent defective (LTPD)

The **lot tolerance percent defective (LTPD)** is the quality level of a lot we consider bad. We wish to reject lots that have this level of quality. If it is agreed that an unacceptable quality level is 70 defects in a lot of 1,000, then the LTPD is 70/1,000 = 7% defective.

To derive a sampling plan, the producer and the consumer must define not only "good lots" and "bad lots" through the AQL and LTPD, but they must also specify risk levels.

Producer's risk (α) is the probability that a "good" lot will be rejected. This is the risk of taking a random sample that results in a much higher proportion of defects than the population of all items. A lot with an acceptable quality level of AQL still has an α chance of being rejected. Sampling plans are often designed to have the producer's risk set at $\alpha = .05$, or 5%.

FIGURE S3.5

AN OPERATING CHARACTERISTIC (OC) CURVE SHOWING PRODUCER'S AND CONSUMER'S RISK

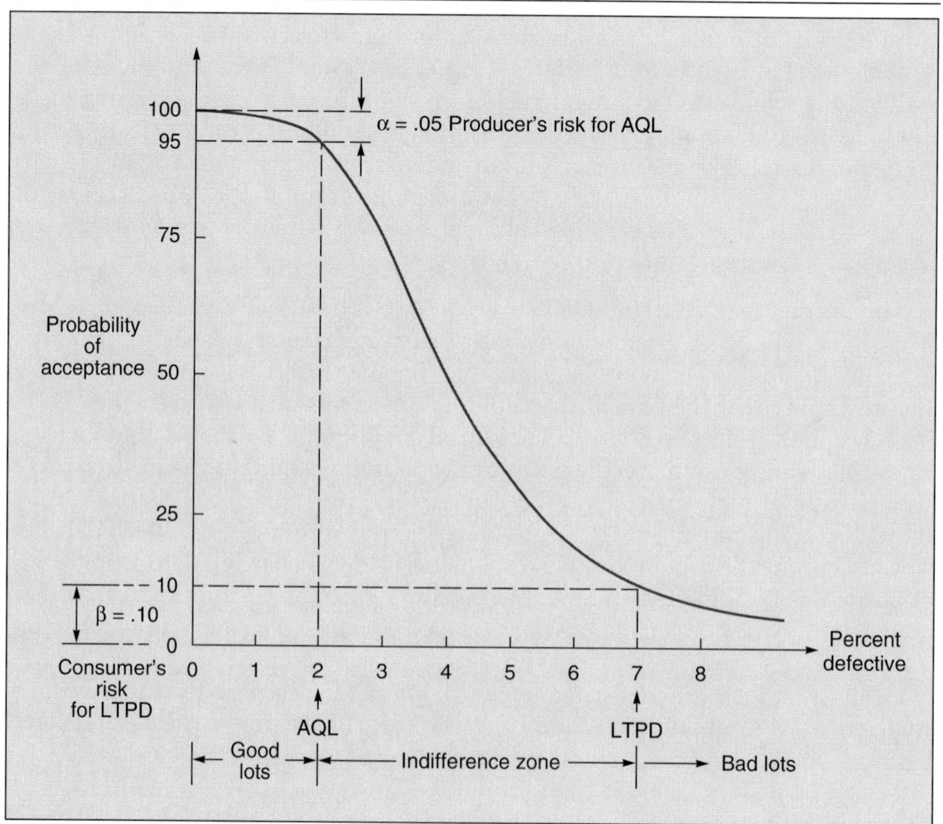

A good lot for this particular acceptance plan has less than or equal to 2% defectives. A bad lot has 7% or more defectives.

Consumer's risk (β) is the probability that a "bad" lot will be accepted. This is the risk of taking a random sample that results in a lower proportion of defects than the overall population of items. A common value for consumer's risk in sampling plans is $\beta = .10$, or 10%.

In statistics, the probability of rejecting a good lot is called a **type I error.** The probability of a bad lot being accepted is referred to as a **type II error.**

type I error

type II error

Sampling plans and OC curves can be developed by computer (as seen in the software available with this text), by published tables such as the U.S. Military Standard MIL-STD-105 or Dodge-Romig table, or by calculation, using the binomial or Poisson distributions.[3]

Average Outgoing Quality

In most sampling plans, when a lot is rejected, the entire lot is inspected and all of the defective items are replaced. Use of this replacement technique improves the average outgoing quality in terms of percent defective. In fact, given (1) any sampling plan that replaces all defective items encountered and (2) the true incoming percent defective for the lot, it is possible to determine the **average outgoing quality (AOQ)** in percent defective. The equation for AOQ is:

average outgoing quality (AOQ)

$$\text{AOQ} = \frac{(P_d)(P_a)(N - n)}{N} \qquad \text{(S3.11)}$$

where

P_d = True percent defective of the lot

P_a = Probability of accepting the lot

N = Number of items in the lot

n = Number of items in the sample

The maximum value on the AOQ curve corresponds to the highest average percent defective or the lowest average quality for the sampling plan. It is called the *average outgoing quality limit (AOQL).*

Acceptance sampling is useful for screening incoming lots. When the defective parts are replaced with good parts, acceptance sampling helps to increase the quality of the lots by reducing the outgoing percent defective.

SUMMARY

Statistical process control and acceptance sampling are major statistical tools of quality control. Control charts for SPC help the operations manager distinguish between natural and assignable variations. The $\bar{x}$-chart and the R-chart are used for variable sampling and the p-chart and the c-chart for attribute sampling. Operating characteristic (OC) curves facilitate acceptance sampling and provide the manager with tools to evaluate the quality of a production run or shipment.

[3]The two most frequently used tables for acceptance plans are: *Military Standard Sampling Procedures and Tables for Inspection by Attributes* (MIL-STD-105D)(Washington, D.C.: U.S. Government Printing Office, 1963); and H. F. Dodge and H. G. Romig, *Sampling Inspection Tables—Single and Double Sampling,* 2nd ed. (New York: Wiley and Sons, 1959).

KEY TERMS

Control chart *(p. 116)*
Natural variations *(p. 116)*
Assignable variations *(p. 117)*
$\bar{x}$-chart *(p. 118)*
R-chart *(p. 118)*
Central limit theorem *(p. 119)*
p-charts *(p. 124)*
c-charts *(p. 126)*
Acceptance sampling *(p. 127)*
Operating characteristic (OC) curve *(p. 127)*
Producer's risk *(p. 127)*
Consumer's risk *(p. 127)*
Acceptable quality level (AQL) *(p. 128)*
Lot tolerance percent defective (LTPD) *(p. 128)*
Type I error *(p. 129)*
Type II error *(p. 129)*
Average outgoing quality (AOQ) *(p. 129)*

USING POM FOR WINDOWS

POM for Windows' Quality Control module has the ability to compute all of the SPC control charts we introduced in this supplement. To illustrate, Program S3.1 uses the *p*-chart data for ARCO found in Example S4. It computes *p*-bar, the standard deviation, and the upper and lower control limits. Students need only enter the number of defects for each of the 20 samples.

PROGRAM S3.1

POM for Windows, Analysis of ARCO's Data to Compute *p*-Chart Control Limits

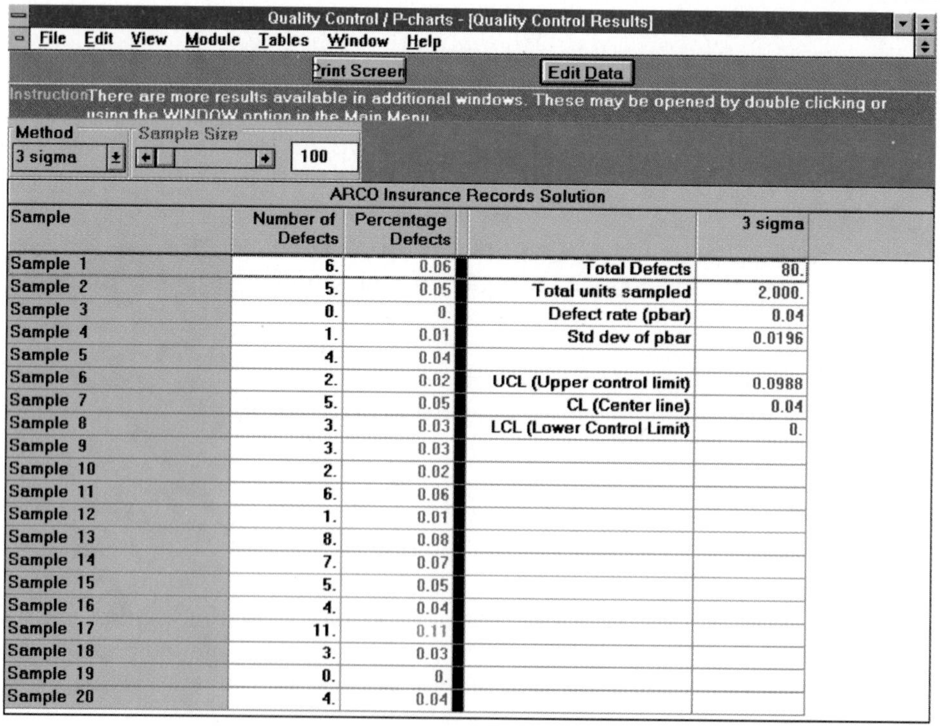

Quality Control / P-charts - [Quality Control Results]

File Edit View Module Tables Window Help

Print Screen Edit Data

Instruction There are more results available in additional windows. These may be opened by double clicking or using the WINDOW option in the Main Menu

Method: 3 sigma Sample Size: 100

ARCO Insurance Records Solution

Sample	Number of Defects	Percentage Defects		3 sigma
Sample 1	6.	0.06	Total Defects	80.
Sample 2	5.	0.05	Total units sampled	2,000.
Sample 3	0.	0.	Defect rate (pbar)	0.04
Sample 4	1.	0.01	Std dev of pbar	0.0196
Sample 5	4.	0.04		
Sample 6	2.	0.02	UCL (Upper control limit)	0.0988
Sample 7	5.	0.05	CL (Center line)	0.04
Sample 8	3.	0.03	LCL (Lower Control Limit)	0.
Sample 9	3.	0.03		
Sample 10	2.	0.02		
Sample 11	6.	0.06		
Sample 12	1.	0.01		
Sample 13	8.	0.08		
Sample 14	7.	0.07		
Sample 15	5.	0.05		
Sample 16	4.	0.04		
Sample 17	11.	0.11		
Sample 18	3.	0.03		
Sample 19	0.	0.		
Sample 20	4.	0.04		

USING EXCEL SPREADSHEETS FOR STATISTICAL PROCESS CONTROL

Excel and other spreadsheets are extensively used in industry to maintain control charts. Programs S3.2 and S3.3 illustrate an Excel spreadsheet approach to computing control limits for the Oat Flakes company of Example S1.

The "tricky" part of this spreadsheet is understanding the IF functions in column C of Program S3.2. The IF formula in cell C4 has two components. The test condition B4 > $F$9 returns a true if the actual sample weight exceeds the calculated upper control limit, or a false if it is under the upper control limit. Excel uses the second IF function to test to see if the actual sample weight is less than the lower control limit. The use of these nested IF functions allows Excel to perform If-Then analysis which involves more than 2 possibilities (for example, the sample is over, under, or within the control limits.) See Excel's help on the IF function for a thorough explanation of nested IF functions.

Notice how column C of Program S3.3 tells the operator whether a point is within the control limits. For instance, cell C4 displays "over" because the sample weight (17.1) is above the UCL (17.0).

Excel also contains a built-in graphing ability. A graph of Program S3.3 can be made by first selecting cells A3 through B15. Then, the chart wizard can be called to build a line chart, using the first column for the X-values and the first row for axis labels.

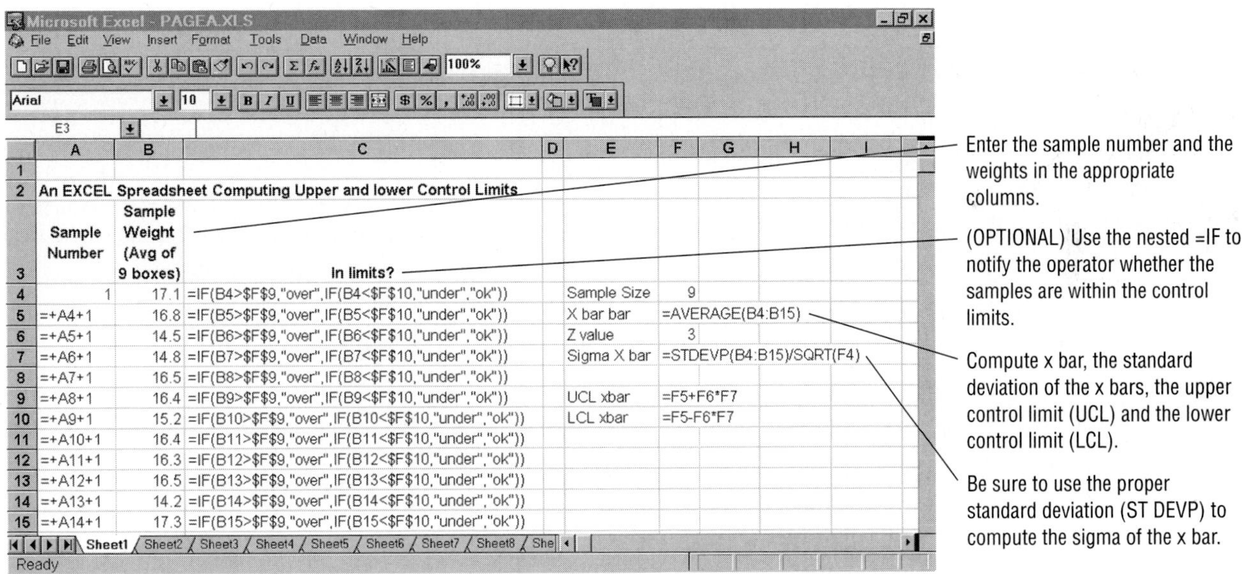

	A	B	C	D	E	F
1						
2	An EXCEL Spreadsheet Computing Upper and lower Control Limits					
3	Sample Number	Sample Weight (Avg of 9 boxes)	In limits?			
4	1	17.1	=IF(B4>$F$9,"over",IF(B4<$F$10,"under","ok"))		Sample Size	9
5	=+A4+1	16.8	=IF(B5>$F$9,"over",IF(B5<$F$10,"under","ok"))		X bar bar	=AVERAGE(B4:B15)
6	=+A5+1	14.5	=IF(B6>$F$9,"over",IF(B6<$F$10,"under","ok"))		Z value	3
7	=+A6+1	14.8	=IF(B7>$F$9,"over",IF(B7<$F$10,"under","ok"))		Sigma X bar	=STDEVP(B4:B15)/SQRT(F4)
8	=+A7+1	16.5	=IF(B8>$F$9,"over",IF(B8<$F$10,"under","ok"))			
9	=+A8+1	16.4	=IF(B9>$F$9,"over",IF(B9<$F$10,"under","ok"))		UCL xbar	=F5+F6*F7
10	=+A9+1	15.2	=IF(B10>$F$9,"over",IF(B10<$F$10,"under","ok"))		LCL xbar	=F5-F6*F7
11	=+A10+1	16.4	=IF(B11>$F$9,"over",IF(B11<$F$10,"under","ok"))			
12	=+A11+1	16.3	=IF(B12>$F$9,"over",IF(B12<$F$10,"under","ok"))			
13	=+A12+1	16.5	=IF(B13>$F$9,"over",IF(B13<$F$10,"under","ok"))			
14	=+A13+1	14.2	=IF(B14>$F$9,"over",IF(B14<$F$10,"under","ok"))			
15	=+A14+1	17.3	=IF(B15>$F$9,"over",IF(B15<$F$10,"under","ok"))			

PROGRAM S3.2 Excel Spreadsheet Formulas for Oat Flakes Example S1

PROGRAM S3.3

OUTPUT USING EXCEL TO SOLVE OAT FLAKES EXAMPLE S1 USING PROGRAM S3.2 AS INPUT

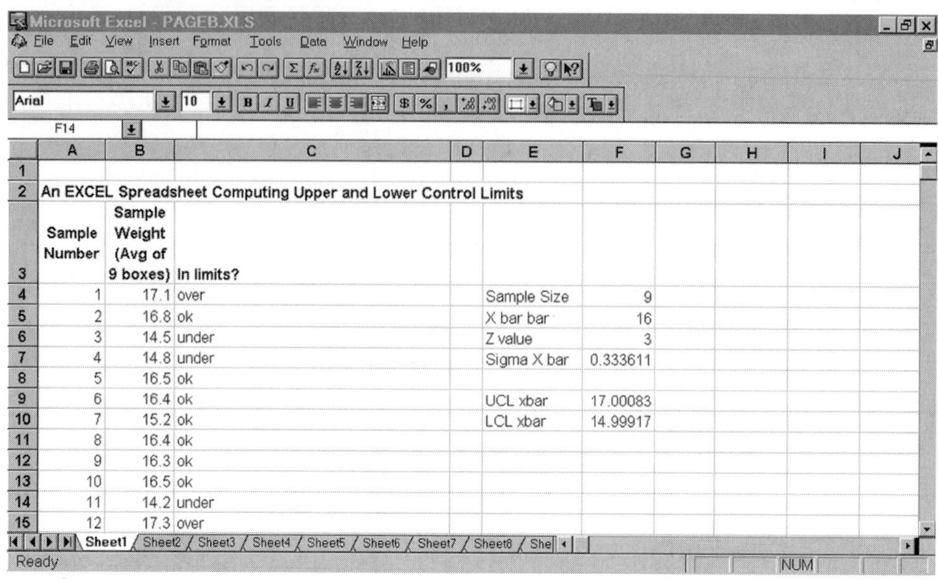

An EXCEL Spreadsheet Computing Upper and Lower Control Limits

Sample Number	Sample Weight (Avg of 9 boxes)	In limits?		
1	17.1	over	Sample Size	9
2	16.8	ok	X bar bar	16
3	14.5	under	Z value	3
4	14.8	under	Sigma X bar	0.333611
5	16.5	ok		
6	16.4	ok	UCL xbar	17.00083
7	15.2	ok	LCL xbar	14.99917
8	16.4	ok		
9	16.3	ok		
10	16.5	ok		
11	14.2	under		
12	17.3	over		

SOLVED PROBLEM S3.1

The manufacturer of precision parts for drill presses produces round shafts for use in the construction of drill presses. The average diameter of a shaft is .56 inch. The inspection samples contain six shafts each. The average range of these samples is .006 inch. Determine the upper and lower control chart limits.

SOLUTION

The mean factor A_2 from Table S3.1 where the sample size is 6, is seen to be .483. With this factor, you can obtain the upper and lower control limits:

$$UCL_{\bar{x}} = .56 + (.483)(.006)$$
$$= .56 + .0029$$
$$= .5629$$
$$LCL_{\bar{x}} = .56 - .0029$$
$$= .5571$$

SOLVED PROBLEM S3.2

Nocaf Drinks, Inc., a producer of decaffeinated coffee, bottles Nocaf. Each bottle should have a net weight of 4 ounces. The machine that fills the bottles with coffee is new, and the operations manager wants to make sure that it is properly adjusted. Bonnie Crutcher, the operations manager, takes a sample of $n = 8$ bottles and records the average and range in ounces for each sample. The data for several samples is in the following table. Note that every sample consists of 8 bottles.

SAMPLE	SAMPLE RANGE	SAMPLE AVERAGE	SAMPLE	SAMPLE RANGE	SAMPLE AVERAGE
A	.41	4.00	E	.56	4.17
B	.55	4.16	F	.62	3.93
C	.44	3.99	G	.54	3.98
D	.48	4.00	H	.44	4.01

Is the machine properly adjusted and in control?

SOLUTION

We first find that $\overline{\overline{x}} = 4.03$ and $\overline{R} = .51$. Then, using Table S3.1, we find:

$$UCL_{\overline{x}} = \overline{\overline{x}} + A_2\overline{R} = 4.03 + (.373)(.51) = 4.22$$

$$LCL_{\overline{x}} = \overline{\overline{x}} - A_2\overline{R} = 4.03 - (.373)(.51) = 3.84$$

$$UCL_R = D_4\overline{R} = (1.864)(.51) = .95$$

$$LCL_R = D_3\overline{R} = (.136)(.51) = .07$$

It appears that the process average and range are both in control.

SOLVED PROBLEM S3.3

Altman Electronics, Inc., makes resistors, and among the last 100 resistors inspected, the percent defective has been .05. Determine the upper and lower limits for this process for 99.7% confidence.

SOLUTION

$$UCL_p = \overline{p} + 3\sqrt{\frac{\overline{p}(1-\overline{p})}{n}} = .05 + 3\sqrt{\frac{(.05)(1-.05)}{100}}$$

$$= .05 + 3(0.0218) = .1154$$

$$LCL_p = \overline{p} - 3\sqrt{\frac{\overline{p}(1-\overline{p})}{n}} = .05 - 3(.0218)$$

$$= .05 - .0654 = 0$$ (because percent defective cannot be negative)

DISCUSSION QUESTIONS

1. Why is the central limit theorem so important in statistical quality control?
2. Why are $\overline{x}$- and R-charts usually used hand in hand?
3. Explain the differences among the four types of control charts.
4. What might cause a process to be out of control?
5. Explain why a process can be out of control even though all samples fall within the upper and lower control limits.
6. What do the terms *producer's risk* and *consumer's risk* mean?
7. Define type I and type II errors.

SELF-TEST ■ SUPPLEMENT 3

- *Before taking the self-test* refer back to the learning objectives listed at the beginning of the supplement and the key terms listed at the end of the supplement.
- Use the key at the back of the text to *correct* your answers.
- *Restudy* pages that correspond to any questions you answered incorrectly or material you feel uncertain about.

1. The basic issues relating to inspection include
   a. how much and how often to inspect
   b. where to inspect
   c. when to inspect
   d. all of the above

2. The type of inspection that classifies items as being either good or defective is
   a. variable inspection
   b. attribute inspection
   c. fixed inspection
   d. all of the above

3. The type of chart used to control the number of defects per unit of output is
   a. $\bar{x}$-bar chart
   b. *R*-chart
   c. *p*-chart
   d. all of the above
   e. none of the above

4. Control charts for attributes are
   a. *p*-charts
   b. $\bar{c}$-charts
   c. *R*-charts
   d. $\bar{x}$-charts

5. C-charts are based on the
   a. Poisson distribution
   b. normal distribution
   c. Erlang distribution
   d. hyper Erlang distribution
   e. binomial distribution

6. If a sample of parts are measured and the mean of the sample measurement is outside the tolerance limits,
   a. the process is out of control and the cause can be established
   b. the process is in control, but not capable of producing within the established control limits
   c. the process is within the established control limits with only natural causes of variation
   d. all of the above are true

7. If a sample of parts are measured and the mean of the sample measurement is in the middle of the tolerance limits but some parts measure too low and other parts measure too high,
   a. the process is out of control and the cause can be established
   b. the process is in control, but not capable of producing within the established control limits
   c. the process is within the established control limits with only natural causes of variation
   d. all of the above are true

8. Acceptance sampling
   a. may involve inspectors taking random samples (or batches) of finished products and measuring them against predetermined standards
   b. may involve inspectors taking random samples (or batches) of incoming raw materials and measuring them against predetermined standards
   c. is more economical than 100% inspection
   d. may be of either a variable or attribute type, although attribute inspection is more common in the business environment
   e. all of the above are true

9. The ______________ risk is the probability that a lot will be rejected despite the quality level exceeding or meeting the ______________.

10. If a 95.5% level of confidence is desired, the $\bar{x}$-chart limits will be set plus or minus ______________.

11. The two techniques discussed to find and resolve assignable variations in process control are the ______________ and the ______________.

12. ______________ inspection is used to determine good parts from defectives, while ______________ inspection actually measures the values of the dimensions of inspected parts.

OPERATIONS IN PRACTICE EXERCISE

When Nashua Corp., a large paper company, had quality problems, they called noted quality guru W. Edwards Deming. Deming discovered that the Nashua technicians did not understand natural variations. They frequently stopped the paper-coating machinery to make adjustments to the coating head. But by assuming any variation had to be corrected, they were inadvertently *increasing* the variation. What they did was the equivalent of trying to adjust a scale while someone was jumping up and down on it. When they stopped meddling with the machine, it turned out to be in fairly good statistical control. The special (assignable) cause of variation was eliminated. Nashua then went back to work at reducing the common (natural) causes of variation in the machine.[4]

Prepare a brief explanation for foremen at Nashua Corp. of special (assignable) versus common (natural) variations.

PROBLEMS

• **S3.1.** The overall average on a process you are attempting to monitor is 75 units. The average range is 6 units. What are the upper and lower control limits if you choose to use a sample size of 10?

• **S3.2.** The overall average on a process you are attempting to monitor is 50 units. The average range is 4 units. What are the upper and lower control limits if you choose to use a sample size of 5?

• **S3.3.** Your supervisor, Austine Heldman, has asked that you check and report on the output of a machine on the factory floor. This machine is supposed to be producing optical lenses that have a mean weight of 50 grams, and a range of 3.5 grams. The table contains the data for a sample size of n = 10 taken during the past three hours:

SAMPLE NUMBER	SAMPLE AVERAGE	SAMPLE RANGE
1	55	3
2	47	1
3	49	5
4	50	3
5	52	2
6	57	6
7	55	3
8	48	2
9	51	2
10	56	3

Prepare your report.

• **S3.4.** Food Storage Technologies produces refrigeration units for food producers and retail food establishments. The overall average temperature that these units maintain is 46° Fahrenheit. The average range is 2° Fahrenheit. Samples of six are taken to monitor the process. Determine the upper and lower control-chart limits for averages and ranges for these refrigeration units.

• **S3.5.** When set at the standard position, Autopitch can throw hard balls toward a batter at an average speed of 60 mph. Autopitch devices are made for both major- and minor-league teams to help them improve their batting averages. Autopitch executives take samples of ten Autopitch devices at a time to monitor these devices and to maintain the highest quality. The average range is 3 mph. Using control-chart techniques, determine control-chart limits for averages and ranges for Autopitch.

[4]Adapted from Jeremy Maine, *Quality Wars* (New York: Free Press, 1994), p. 110.

S3.6. Major Products, Inc., produces granola cereal, granola bars, and other natural food products. Its natural granola cereal is sampled to ensure proper weight. Each sample contains eight boxes of cereal. The overall average for the samples is 17 ounces. The range is only 0.5 ounces. Determine the upper and lower control-chart limits for averages for the boxes of cereal.

S3.7. Small boxes of NutraFlakes cereal are labeled "net weight 10 ounces." Each hour, random samples of size $n = 4$ boxes are weighed to check process control. Five hours of observations yielded the following:

	WEIGHTS			
Time	*Box 1*	*Box 2*	*Box 3*	*Box 4*
9 A.M.	9.8	10.4	9.9	10.3
10 A.M.	10.1	10.2	9.9	9.8
11 A.M.	9.9	10.5	10.3	10.1
Noon	9.7	9.8	10.3	10.2
1 P.M.	9.7	10.1	9.9	9.9

Using these data, construct limits for $\bar{x}$- and R-charts. Is the process in control? What other steps should the QC department follow at this point?

S3.8. Sampling four pieces of precision-cut wire (to be used in computer assembly) every hour for the past 24 hours has produced the following results:

HOUR	$\bar{x}$	R	HOUR	$\bar{x}$	R
1	3.25″	.71″	13	3.11″	.85″
2	3.10	1.18	14	2.83	1.31
3	3.22	1.43	15	3.12	1.06
4	3.39	1.26	16	2.84	.50
5	3.07	1.17	17	2.86	1.43
6	2.86	.32	18	2.74	1.29
7	3.05	.53	19	3.41	1.61
8	2.65	1.13	20	2.89	1.09
9	3.02	.71	21	2.65	1.08
10	2.85	1.33	22	3.28	.46
11	2.83	1.17	23	2.94	1.58
12	2.97	.40	24	2.64	.97

Develop appropriate control charts and determine whether there is any cause for concern in the cutting process.

S3.9. In the past, the defect rate for your product has been 1.5%. What are the upper and lower control chart limits if you wish to use a sample size of 500 and $z = 3$?

S3.10. In the past, the defect rate for your product has been 3.5%. What are the upper and lower control chart limits if you wish to use a sample size of 500 and $z = 3$?

S3.11. You are attempting to develop a quality monitoring system for some parts purchased from Warton & Kotha Manufacturing Co. These parts are either good or defective. You have decided to take a sample of 100 units. Develop a table of the appropriate upper and lower control chart limits for various values of the fraction defective in the sample taken. The values for p in this table should range from 0.02 to 0.10 in increments of 0.02. Develop the upper and lower control limits for a 99.7% confidence level.

S3.12. Due to the poor quality of various semiconductor products used in their manufacturing process, Microlaboratories has decided to develop a quality control program. Because the semiconductor parts it gets from suppliers are either good or defective, George Haverty has decided to develop control charts for attributes. The total number of semiconductors in every sample is 200. Furthermore, George would like to determine the upper control chart limit and the lower control chart limit for various values of the fraction defective (p) in the sample taken. To allow more flexibility, he has decided to develop a table that lists values for p, UCL, and LCL. The values for p should range from .01 to 0.10, incrementing by .01 each time. What are the UCLs and the LCLs for 99.7% confidence?

S3.13. For the last two months, Mary Hart has been concerned about the number 5 machine at the West Factory. In order to make sure that the machine is operating correctly, samples are taken, and the average and range for each sample is computed. Each sample consists of 12 items produced from the machine. Recently 12 samples were taken, and for each, the sample range and average were computed. The sample range and sample average were 1.1 and 46 for the first sample, 1.31 and 45 for the second sample, .91 and 46 for the third sample, and 1.1 and 47 for the fourth sample. After the fourth sample, the sample averages increased. For the fifth sample, the range was 1.21 and the average was 48; for sample number 6 it was .82 and 47; for sample number 7, it was .86 and 50; and for the eighth sample, it was 1.11 and 49. After the eighth sample, the sample average continued to increase, never getting below 50. For sample number 9, the range and average were 1.12 and 51; for sample number 10, they were .99 and 52; for sample number 11, they were .86 and 50; and for sample number 12, they were 1.2 and 52.

During installation, the supplier set an average of 47 for the process with an average range of 1.0. It was Mary's feeling that something was definitely wrong with machine number 5. Do you agree?

S3.14. Pet Products, Inc., caters to the growing market for cat supplies, with a full line of products ranging from litter to toys to flea powder. One of its newer products, a tube of fluid that prevents hairballs in long-haired cats, is produced by an automated machine that is set to fill each tube with 63.5 grams of paste.

To keep this filling process under control, four tubes are pulled randomly from the assembly line every four hours. After several days, the data shown in the table below resulted. Set control limits for this process and graph the sample data for both the $\bar{x}$- and R-charts.

	SAMPLE NUMBER												
	1	2	3	4	5	6	7	8	9	10	11	12	13
$\bar{x}$	63.5	63.6	63.7	63.9	63.4	63.0	63.2	63.3	63.7	63.5	63.3	63.2	63.6
R	2.0	1.0	1.7	0.9	1.2	1.6	1.8	1.3	1.6	1.3	1.8	1.0	1.8

	SAMPLE NUMBER											
	14	15	16	17	18	19	20	21	22	23	24	25
$\bar{x}$	63.3	63.4	63.4	63.5	63.6	63.8	63.5	63.9	63.2	63.3	64.0	63.4
R	1.5	1.7	1.4	1.1	1.8	1.3	1.6	1.0	1.8	1.7	2.0	1.5

• **S3.15.** The smallest defect in a computer chip will render the entire chip worthless. Therefore, tight quality-control measures must be established to monitor these chips. In the past, the percentage defective for these chips for a California-based company has been 1.1%. The sample size is 1,000. Determine upper and lower control chart limits for these computer chips. Use $z = 3$.

: **S3.16.** Chicago Supply Company manufactures paper clips and other office products. Although inexpensive, paper clips have provided the firm with a high margin of profitability. The percentage defective for paper clips produced by Chicago Supply Company has been averaging 2.5%. Samples of 200 paper clips are taken. Establish upper and lower control chart limits for this process at 99.7% confidence.

: **S3.17.** Daily samples of 100 power drills are removed from Drill Master's assembly line and inspected for defects. Over the past 21 days, the following information has been gathered. Develop a 3 standard deviation (99.7% confidence) *p* chart and graph the samples. Is the process in control?

DAY	NUMBER OF DEFECTIVE DRILLS	DAY	NUMBER OF DEFECTIVE DRILLS
1	6	12	5
2	5	13	4
3	6	14	3
4	4	15	4
5	3	16	5
6	4	17	6
7	5	18	5
8	3	19	4
9	6	20	3
10	3	21	7
11	7		

: **S3.18.** A random sample of 100 Modern Art dining room tables that came off the firm's assembly line is examined. Careful inspection reveals a total of 2,000 blemishes. What are the 99.7% upper and lower control limits for the number of blemishes? If one table had 42 blemishes, should any special action be

Internet Data Base Application See our website at http://www.prenhall.com/renderpom for a challenging, computer-based problem.

CASE STUDY

SPC at the Gazette

Accurate typesetting is critical to a newspaper. To assure typesetting quality, a Quality Improvement Team was established in the printing department at the *Gazette* in Geronimo, Texas. The team developed a procedure for monitoring the performance of typesetters over a period of time. Such a procedure involves sampling output, establishing control limits, comparing the *Gazette's* accuracy with that of the industry, and occasionally updating the information.

The team randomly selected 30 of the *Gazette's* newspapers published during the preceding 12 months. From each paper, 100 paragraphs were randomly chosen and were read for accuracy. The number of paragraphs with errors in each paper was recorded, and the fraction of paragraphs with errors in each sample was determined.

The following table shows the results of the sampling:

SAMPLE	PARAGRAPHS WITH ERRORS	FRACTION OF PARAGRAPHS WITH ERRORS (per 100)	SAMPLE	PARAGRAPHS WITH ERRORS	FRACTION OF PARAGRAPHS WITH ERRORS (per 100)
1	2	.02	16	2	.02
2	4	.04	17	3	.03
3	10	.10	18	7	.07
4	4	.04	19	3	.03
5	1	.01	20	2	.02
6	1	.01	21	3	.03
7	13	.13	22	7	.07
8	9	.09	23	4	.04
9	11	.11	24	3	.03
10	0	.00	25	2	.02
11	3	.03	26	2	.02
12	4	.04	27	0	.00
13	2	.02	28	1	.01
14	2	.02	29	3	.03
15	8	.08	30	4	.04

DISCUSSION QUESTIONS

1. Plot the overall fraction of errors (p) and the upper and lower control limits on a control chart using a 95.45% confidence level.
2. Assume the industry upper and lower control limits are .10 and .04, respectively. Plot them on the control chart.
3. Plot the fraction of errors in each sample. Do all fall within the firm's control limits? When one falls outside the control limits, what should be done?

SOURCE: Professor Jerry Kinard, Western Carolina University.

Internet Case Study See our Internet home page at http://www.prenhall.com/renderpom for this additional case study: Bayfield Mud Company.

BIBLIOGRAPHY

Besterfield, D. H. *Quality Control*, 2nd ed. Englewood Cliffs, NJ: Prentice Hall, 1986.

Kumar, S., and Y. P. Gupta. "Statistical Process Control at Motorola's Austin Assembly Plant." *Interfaces* 23, no. 2 (March-April 1993): 84–92.

Runger, G. C., and D. C. Montgomery. "Adaptive Sampling Enhancements for Shewhart Control Charts." *IIE Transactions* 25, no. 3 (May 1993): 41–51.

See additional references at the end of Chapter 3.

Design of Goods and Services

4

CHAPTER OUTLINE

Goods and Services Selection

Product Options ■ Generation of New Product Opportunities ■ Product Life ■ Time-Based Competition

Product Development

Product-by-Value

Defining and Documenting the Product

Make or Buy ■ Group Technology ■ Computer-Aided Design and Computer-Aided Manufacture

Documents for Production

Service Design

Documents for Services

Product Reliability

Improving Individual Components ■ Providing Redundancy

Transition to Production

Summary ■ *Key Terms* ■ *Using POM for Windows for Reliability Analysis* ■ *Solved Problems* ■ *Discussion Questions* ■ *Operations in Practice Exercise* ■ *Self-Test Chapter 4* ■ *Problems* ■ *Case Study: GE's Rotary Compressor* ■ *Bibliography*

LEARNING OBJECTIVES

When you complete this chapter you should be able to:

IDENTIFY OR DEFINE:

Product life cycle
Product development team
Value engineering
Value analysis
Group technology
Configuration management
Time-based competition

DESCRIBE OR EXPLAIN:

Product-by-value analysis
Product documentation
Reliability concepts
Quality robust design

Developing and designing great products are keys to success in business. Anything less than an excellent product strategy can be devastating to a firm. To maximize the potential for success, top companies focus on only a few products, and then concentrate on maintaining a high level of quality for those products. For instance, Honda's focus is engines. Virtually all of Honda's sales (autos, motorcycles, generators, lawn mowers) are based on its outstanding engine technology. Likewise, Intel's focus is on computer chips, while Microsoft's is PC software. However, since most products have a limited and even predictable life cycle, companies must constantly be looking for new products to design, develop and take to market. Good operations managers insist upon strong communication between customer, product, processes, and suppliers that results in a high success rate for their new products. Benchmarks, of course, vary by industry, but Rubbermaid does this very well and introduces a new product each day!

One product strategy is to build particular competence in customizing goods or services. This approach allows the customer to choose product variations while reinforcing the organization's strength. Dell Computers, for example, has built a huge market by delivering computers with the exact hardware and software desired by the end user. And Dell does it fast—it understands that speed to market is imperative to gain a competitive edge. Motorola also understands the importance of quick response and has built its pager business based on speed to market. That firm reduced the time from order to delivery from over a month to less than three hours!

Note that many service firms also refer to their offerings as products. For instance, when Allstate Insurance offers a new homeowner's policy, it is referred to as a new "product." Similarly, when Citicorp opens a mortgage department, it offers a number of new mortgage "products." So while the term *products* may often refer to tangible goods, it also refers to offerings by service organizations.

product decision

An effective product strategy links product decisions with investment, market share, product life cycle, and breadth of the product line. The objective of the **product decision** is to develop and implement a product strategy that meets the demands of the marketplace with a competitive advantage. In this chapter we look at how to make effective product decisions by looking at how to select, develop, and document products.

GOODS AND SERVICES SELECTION

Product Options

Management has many options in the selection, definition, and design of goods and services. Product selection is choosing the good or service to provide customers or clients. For instance, hospitals specialize in various types of patients and various types of medical procedures. They select their product when they decide what kind of hospital to be. A hospital's management may decide to operate a general-purpose hospital, a maternity hospital, or even a hospital specializing in hernias (as is the case with Canada's Shouldice Hospital). Numerous other options exist for hospitals, just as they exist for restaurants and automobile companies.

Product decisions are fundamental and have major implications throughout the operations function. They influence capital equipment cost, layout design, space requirements, the skills of people hired and trained, materials, and the processes used. GM's Pontiac Grand Am steering columns are a good example of the strong role product design has in both quality and efficiency. The new steering column has a simpler design, with about 30% fewer parts than its predecessor. The result: assembly time is one-third of the older column, and the new column's quality is about seven times higher. As an added bonus the new line's machinery costs a third less than that on the old line.

Generation of New Product Opportunities

Product selection, definition, and design take place on a continuing basis because so many new product opportunities exist. Five factors influencing market opportunities are

1. *Economic change,* which brings increasing levels of affluence in the long run but economic cycles and price changes in the short run. For instance, in the long run, more and more people can afford an automobile, but in the short run, a recession may alter the demand for automobiles.
2. *Sociological and demographic change,* which may appear in such factors as decreasing family size. This alters the size preference for homes, apartments, and automobiles.
3. *Technological change,* which makes possible everything from home computers to mobile phones to artificial hearts.
4. *Political/legal change,* which brings about new trade agreements, tariffs, and government contract requirements.
5. Other changes, which may be brought about through *market practice, professional standards, suppliers,* and *distributors.*

Operations managers must be aware of these factors and be able to anticipate changes in product opportunities, the products themselves, product volume, and product mix.

Product selection occurs in services as well as manufacturing. Shown here is Shouldice Hospital, renowned for its world-class specialization in hernia repair—no emergency room, no maternity ward, no open heart surgery, just hernias. Shouldice became world-class by selecting and then focusing on a product (service) at which it could excel. Discharging its patients three days earlier than other hospitals, Shouldice's cost is about one-third of general-purpose hospitals. Local anesthetics are used; patients enter and leave the operating room on their own; rooms are spartan, discouraging patients from remaining in bed; and all meals are served in a common dining room. As Shouldice has demonstrated, product selection impacts the entire production system.

Product Life

NOTE
Motorola went through 3,000 working models to develop its first pocket-size cellular telephone.

Products are born, they live, and they die. They are cast aside by a changing society. It may be helpful to think of a product's life as divided into four phases: introduction, growth, maturity, and decline.

The general phases of product life cycle are depicted in Figure 4.1. That figure also reveals the relative positions of five products: virtual reality, rollerblades, jet-skis, Sony Walkmen, and Boeing 727s.

Product life cycles may be a matter of a few hours (a newspaper), months (seasonal fashions), years (Betamax video recorders), or decades (Volkswagen Beetle). Regardless of the length of the cycle, the task for the operations manager is the same: to design a system that helps introduce new products successfully. If the operations function cannot perform effectively at this stage, the firm may be saddled with losers—products that cannot be produced efficiently and perhaps not at all.

NOTE
More than 30% of Rubbermaid sales each year come from products less than five years old.

An organization cannot survive without introducing new products. Older products are maturing and others in periods of decline must be replaced. This requires a constant successful introduction of new products and active participation by the operations manager. Successful firms have learned how to turn opportunities into successful products.

Product development goes through eight stages, starting with ideas and ending with delivery to market and then final evaluation. Figure 4.2 shows this progression. How well the development process is managed may well determine not

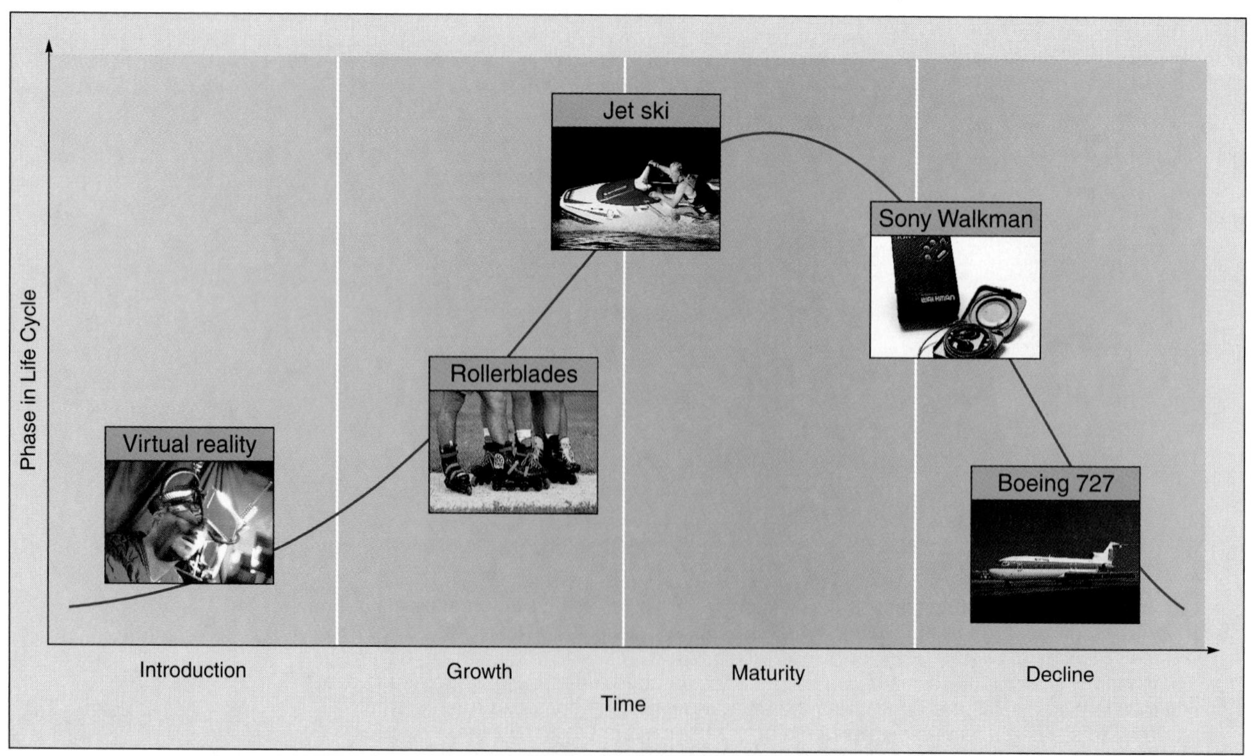

FIGURE 4.1 PRODUCTS IN VARIOUS STAGES OF LIFE CYCLE

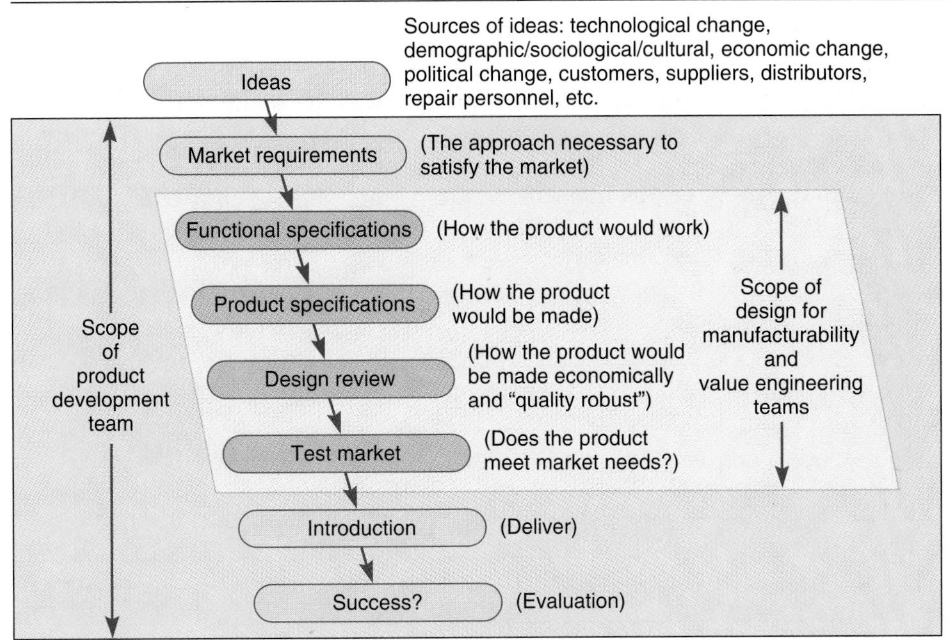

Product concepts are developed from a variety of sources, both external and internal to the firm. Concepts that survive the product idea stage progress through various stages with nearly constant review in a highly participative environment to minimize failure.

FIGURE 4.2

PRODUCT DEVELOPMENT STAGES

only product success but also the firm's future. A variety of sources contribute to the process. The emphasis can be external (market driven), internal (technology and innovation driven), or a combination of both.

In spite of all of the efforts that go into introducing new products, most do not succeed. For example, think about the turnover rate for television programming. Few shows are on the air more than one or two seasons before being replaced. Computer game software is another product category that sees a lot of winners and losers. Consequently, product development is an ongoing process. This means that the number of products that must be reviewed for production and, in some cases, actually produced, can be substantial. Operations managers must be able to accommodate this volume of new product ideas while keeping current products moving forward.[1]

NOTE
"Product development time is going to be a great competitive battleground in the 1990s—as intense, I would say, as the revolutionary push for quality in the eighties." Allan Gilmour, Executive VP Ford

Time-Based Competition

Product life cycles are becoming shorter. This increases the importance of product development. Therefore, faster developers of new products continually gain on slower developers and obtain a competitive advantage.[2] This concept is called **time-based competition.**

time-based competition

[1]See a discussion of this issue in Rosabeth Moss Kanter, "Swimming in New Streams: Mastering Innovation Dilemmas," *California Management Review* 31, 4 (Summer 1989): 45–69.

[2]See related discussion in George Stalk, Jr., "Time—The Next Source of Competitive Advantage," *Harvard Business Review* (July-August 1988): 41–51; Joseph Blackburn, *Time-Based Competition: The Next Battleground in American Manufacturing* (Homewood, IL: Irwin/Business One, 1990); "Manufacturing: About Time," *Economist* (April 11, 1990): 72. See also Kim Clark, as reported in James P. Womack, Daniel T. Jones, and Daniel Roos, *The Machine That Changed the World* (New York: Rawson Associates, 1990), p. 111.

FIGURE 4.3

TIME IT TAKES TO DEVELOP NEW VEHICLE FROM CONCEPT APPROVAL TO PRODUCTION

SOURCE: Valerie Reitman and Robert L. Simison, "Japanese Car Makers Speed Up Car Making," *The Wall Street Journal*, December 29, 1995, pp. B1–B13.

Auto Maker	Current Average (months)	Goal (months)	Record Time (model)
Mazda	21	15–18	17 months (Capella)
Toyota	27*	18*	15 months (Ipsum, Starlet)
Mitsubishi	24	18	19 months (FTO)
Nissan	30	20	Not available
Honda	36*	24*	24 months* (CR–V)
Chrysler Corp.	29	24	24 months (Sebring)
Ford	37	24	18 months (European Escort restyling)
GM	46	38	26 months (Yukon, Tahoe)

*Includes design time before concept approval

Shortening development time has become an increasingly important goal for the world's auto makers. Not only do faster development times cut costs by saving overhead and using engineering and production resources more efficiently, they make it possible for auto makers to get cars to market before trends and customer tastes change.

NOTE
Much of the current competitive battlefield is focused around the speed of product to market. If an organization loses here, catching up in other areas is very difficult.

As Figure 4.3 indicates, Japanese auto manufacturers are designing and introducing cars at a rapid rate, giving them a number of advantages. Those who can introduce products faster can use more recent technology. Additionally, those who introduce products faster gain experience in the numerous issues inherent in design, test, manufacture, and introduction of new products. Those who develop

FIGURE 4.4

PERCENT OF SALES FROM PRODUCTS INTRODUCED IN THE LAST FIVE YEARS

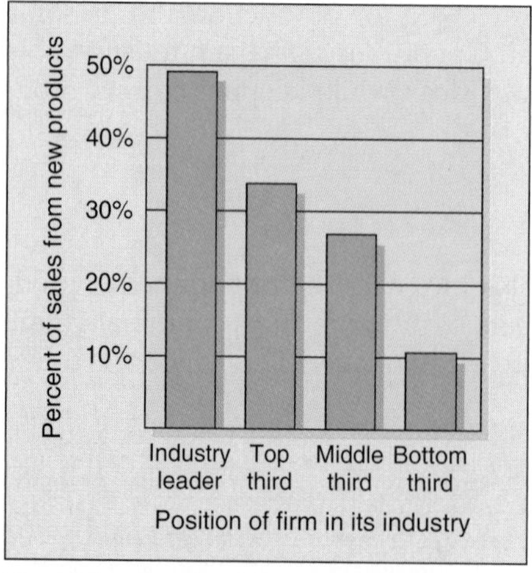

The higher the percentage of sales from products introduced in the last five years, the more likely the firm is to be a leader.

products faster are learning faster. Faster product introduction has a cumulative and positive effect not only in the marketplace but also on innovative design, quality improvements, and cost reduction. Figure 4.4 indicates the positive impact of rapid new-product development.

NOTE
Quality, price, and delivery are major determinants of market success; but quality is determined at design time.

PRODUCT DEVELOPMENT

The best product development approach seems to be a formal team approach. Such teams are known variously as product development teams, design for manufacturability teams, and value engineering teams. Successful product development teams typically have:

1. Support of top management.
2. Qualified, experienced leadership with decision-making authority.
3. Formal organization of the group or team.
4. Training programs to teach the skills and techniques of product development.
5. A diverse, cooperative team.
6. Adequate staffing, funding, and vendor assistance.

Product development teams are charged with the responsibility of moving from market requirements for a product to achieving a product success. This includes marketability, manufacturability, and serviceability. Use of such teams is also called **concurrent engineering** and implies a team representing all affected areas (known as a *cross functional* team). Concurrent engineering also implies speedier product development through simultaneous performance of various aspects of product development. A recent study suggests that the team approach is the dominant structure for product development by leading organizations in America.[3]

product development teams

concurrent engineering

Design for manufacturability and value engineering teams, on the other hand, have a somewhat narrower charge. They are charged with improvement of designs and specifications at the research, development, design, and production stages of product development. (Refer back to Figure 4.2.)

design for manufacturability and value engineering teams

BENEFITS. In addition to immediate and obvious cost reduction, design for manufacturability and value engineering may produce other benefits. These include:

1. Reduced complexity of the product.
2. Additional standardization of components.
3. Improvement of functional aspects of the products.
4. Improved job design.
5. Improved job safety.
6. Improved maintainability (serviceability) of the product.
7. Quality robust design.

Quality robust design means that the product is designed so that small variations in production or assembly do not adversely affect the product. For instance, AT&T developed an integrated circuit that could be used in many products to amplify voice signals. As originally designed, the circuit had to be manufactured very precisely to avoid variations in the strength of the signal.

quality robust design

[3]"Best Practices Survey 1994: Product Definition," *Target* 11, no. 3 (May-June 1995), pp. 22–24.

The new washer transmission designed by Maytag can switch from slow reciprocal motion of the agitator shaft during the wash cycle to fast rotary motion of the wash tub during the wring cycle. The new design using only 40 pieces is more reliable. The reduction in parts means a substantial reduction in cost with fewer designs and purchases, as well as less inventory and manufacturing expense.

Such a circuit would have been costly to make because of stringent quality controls needed during the manufacturing process. But AT&T's engineers, after testing and analyzing the design, realized that if the resistance of the circuit were reduced—a minor change with no associated costs—the circuit would be far less sensitive to manufacturing variations. The result was a 40% improvement in quality.[4]

Product development teams, design for manufacturability teams, and value engineering teams may be the best cost-avoidance technique available to operations management. They yield value improvement by defining the essential function(s) of the item and by achieving that function without lowering quality. Value engineering programs, when effectively managed, typically reduce cost between 15% and 70% without reducing quality. Some studies have indicated that for every dollar spent on value engineering, $10 to $25 in savings can be realized! The cost reduction achieved for a specific bracket via value engineering is shown in Figure 4.5.

value analysis

Value engineering takes place when the product is selected and designed. The corollary technique, **value analysis,** however, takes place during the production process when it is clear that a new product is a success. Improvement leads to either a better product or a product made more economically.

PRODUCT-BY-VALUE

product-by-value analysis

The effective operations manager directs efforts toward those items that show the greatest promise. This is the Pareto principle applied to product mix. Resources are invested in the critical few and not the trivial many. **Product-by-value analysis** lists products in descending order of their individual dollar contribution to the firm.[5] Product-by-value analysis also lists the total annual dollar contribution of the product. Low contribution on a per-unit basis by a particular product may look substantially different if it represents a large portion of the company's sales.

A product-by-value report allows management to evaluate possible strategies for each product. These might include increasing cash flow (for example, in-

FIGURE 4.5

COST REDUCTION OF A BRACKET VIA VALUE ENGINEERING AND VALUE ANALYSIS

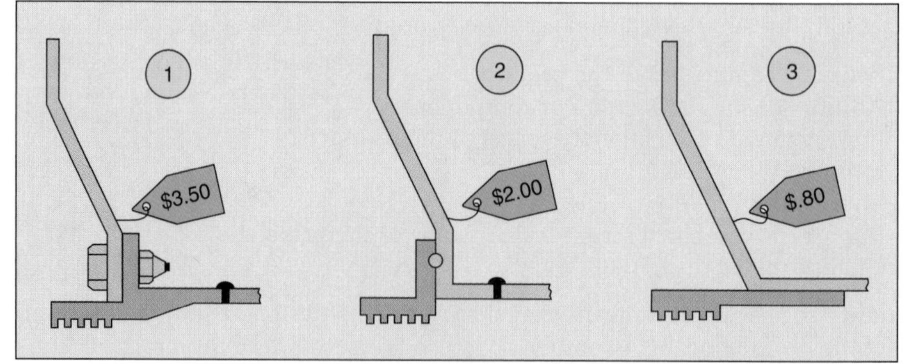

Adapted from Robert Goodell Brown, *Management Decisions for Production Operations* (Hinsdale, IL: The Dryden Press, Inc., 1971), p. 353.

[4]John Mayo, "Process Design as Important as Product Design," *The Wall Street Journal,* October 29, 1984, p. 32.
[5]Contribution is defined as the difference between direct cost and selling price. Direct costs are labor and material that go into the product.

creasing contribution by raising selling price or lowering cost), increasing market penetration (for example, improving quality and/or reducing cost or price), or reducing costs (for example, improving the production process). The report may also tell management which product offerings should be eliminated and which fail to justify further investment in research and development or capital equipment. The report focuses management's attention on opportunities for each product.

The success of the team approach at NCR corporation is indicated in their new 2760 electronic cash register. The cash register goes together with no screws or bolts. The entire terminal consists of just 15 vendor-produced components. The number of parts has been reduced by 85%, the number of suppliers by 65%, and the time to assemble by 25%.

Defining and Documenting the Product

Once new goods or services are selected for introduction, they must be defined. First, a good or service is defined in terms of its functions, that is, what it is to do. The product is then designed; that is, it is determined how the functions are to be achieved. Management typically has a variety of options as to how a product is to achieve its functional purpose. For instance, when producing an alarm clock, aspects of design such as the color, size, or location of buttons may make substantial differences in ease of manufacture, quality, and market acceptance.

Rigorous specifications of a good or service are necessary to assure efficient production. Equipment layout and human resources cannot be decided upon until the good or service is defined, designed, and documented. Therefore, every organization needs documents to define its products. This is true of everything from meat patties, to cheese, to computers, to a medical procedure. Indeed, written specifications or standard grades exist and provide the definition for many products. For instance, McDonald's Corp. has 60 specifications for potatoes that are to be made into McDonald's french fries.

In the case of an airplane, as in most manufactured items, a component is typically defined by a drawing, usually referred to as an engineering drawing. An **engineering drawing** shows the dimensions, tolerances, materials, and finishes of a component. The engineering drawing will be an item on a bill-of-material. An engineering drawing is shown in Figure 4.6, and a bill-of-material for a manufactured item is shown in Figure 4.7(a). The **bill-of-material (BOM)** lists the components, their description, and the quantity of each required to make one unit of a product. An engineering drawing shows how to make one item on the bill-of-material.

engineering drawing

bill-of-material (BOM)

In the food service industry, bills-of-material manifest themselves in portion control standards. The portion control standard for a "Juicy Burger" is shown in Figure 4.7(b). Products, in addition to being defined by a written specification, a portion control document, or bill-of-material, can be defined in other ways. For example, products such as chemicals, paints, or petroleums may be defined by formulas or proportions that describe how they are to be made. Movies are defined by scripts and insurance by legal documents, known as policies.

Make or Buy

For many products, firms have the option of producing components or purchasing them from outside sources. Choosing between these options is known as the make-or-buy decision. The **make-or-buy decision** distinguishes between what the firm is willing to produce and what it is willing to purchase. Many items can be purchased as a "standard item" produced by someone else. Such a standard item

make-or-buy decision

FIGURE 4.6

ENGINEERING DRAWINGS SUCH AS THIS ONE SHOW DIMENSIONS, TOLERANCES, MATERIALS, AND FINISHES

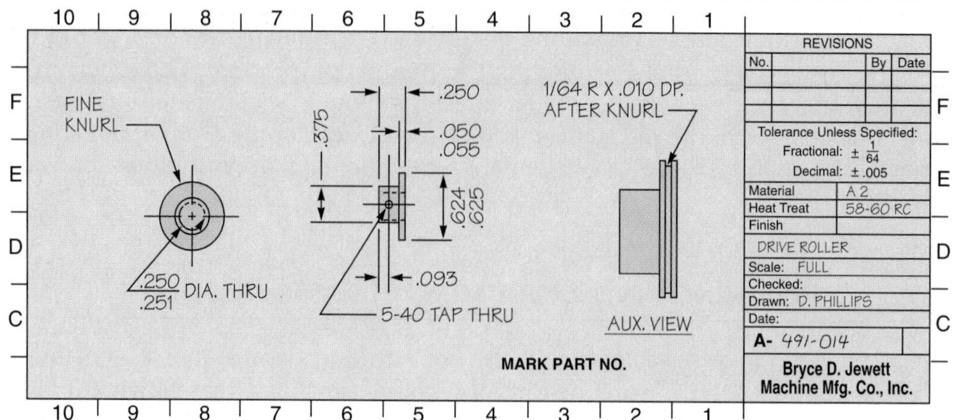

does not require its own bill-of-material or engineering drawing because its specification as a standard item is adequate. Examples are the standard nuts and bolts listed on the bill-of-material shown in Figure 4.7(a), for which there will be SAE (Society of Automotive Engineers) specifications. Therefore, there typically is no need for the firm to duplicate this specification in another document.

Group Technology

group technology

Modern engineering drawings will also include codes to facilitate group technology. **Group technology** requires that components be identified by a coding scheme

FIGURE 4.7

BILLS-OF-MATERIAL

(a) **Bill of Material for a Panel Weldment**

NUMBER	DESCRIPTION	QTY
A 60-71	PANEL WELDM'T	1
A 60-7	LOWER ROLLER ASSM.	1
R 60-17	ROLLER	1
R 60-428	PIN	1
P 60-97	BRASS WASHER	1
01-97-1150	WASHER	1
P 60-2	LOCKNUT	1
A 60-73	GUIDE ASSM. FR.	1
A 60-74	SUPPORT WELDM'T	1
R 60-99	WEAR PLATE	1
02-50-1150	BOLT	1
02-50-0020	LOCK NUT	1
11-65-3	BUMPER BLOCK	1
11-60-63	WIPER RING	1

(b) **Portion Control Standard for a Hamburger**

PRODUCT: Juicy Burger

DESCRIPTION	QTY
Buns	1
Cheese	1 slice
Meat patties	2
Pickle slice	2
Dehydrated onions	1/250 pkg.
Sauce	1/137.5
Lettuce	1/26 head

Bills-of-material take different forms in a manufacturing plant (a) and a fast-food restaurant (b), but in both cases the product must be defined.

The J. R. Simplot potato processing facility in Caldwell, Idaho, is responsible for making many of the billions of french fries McDonald's uses each year. Sixty specifications define how these strips of potatoes become french fries at McDonald's. These specifications define this product by first specifying a russet Burbank potato. The russet Burbank potato has a distinctive taste and high ratio of solids to water. It specifies a special blend of frying oil and a unique steaming process. The fries are then prefried and dried; the exact time and heat being covered by a patent. In lieu of dipping in sugar as are other fries, McDonald's fries are sprayed. This process causes the fries to brown evenly and appear more natural. The product is further defined by requiring that 40% of all fries be between two and three inches long and another 40% must be over three inches long. A few stubby ones constitute the final 20%.

that specifies the type of processing (such as drilling) and the parameters of the processing (such as size). An example of how families of parts may be grouped is shown in Figures 4.8(a) and (b). Machines can then process families of parts as a group, minimizing setups, routings, and material handling. Successful implementation of group technology leads to:

1. Improved design
2. Reduced raw material and purchases
3. Simplified production planning and control
4. Improved routing and machine loading
5. Development of work cells
6. Reduced tooling setup time, work-in-process, and production time.

The application of group technology helps the entire organization, as many costs are reduced.

FIGURE 4.8

(a) MANUFACTURED COMPONENTS (NOT GROUPED); (b) MANUFACTURED COMPONENTS (GROUPED) INTO FAMILIES WITH SIMILAR CHARACTERISTICS

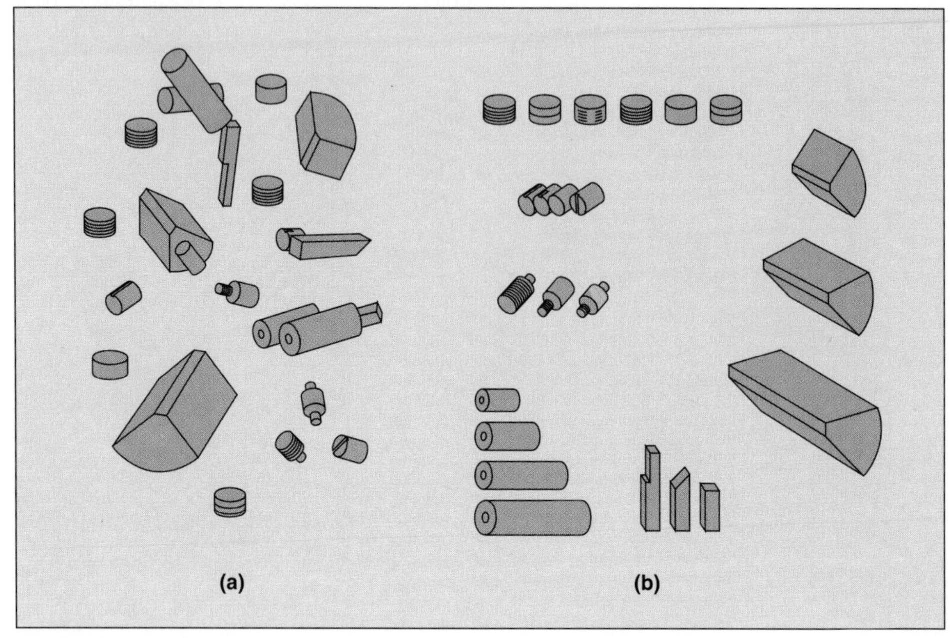

Computer-Aided Design and Computer-Aided Manufacture

computer-aided design (CAD)

NOTE
Computer-aided design (CAD) techniques are now used in mechanical engineering, electrical engineering, and even modeling large complex molecules.

Product design is greatly enhanced through the use of **computer-aided design (CAD).** Where CAD is used, a design engineer starts by developing a rough sketch or, conceivably, just an idea. The designer then utilizes a graphic display as a drafting board to construct the geometry of a design. As a geometric definition is completed, a sophisticated CAD system will allow the designer to determine various kinds of engineering data, such as strength or heat transfer. CAD will also allow the designer to ensure that parts fit together so there will be no interferences when parts are subsequently assembled. Thus, if the designer is sketching the fender for an automobile, the brackets and related panels are changed as the fender is changed. Analysis of existing, as well as new, designs can be done expediently and economically.

Once the designer is satisfied with the design, it becomes part of a drawing database on electronic media. The CAD system, through a library of symbols and details, also helps to ensure adherence to the drafting standards.

computer-aided manufacture (CAM)

NOTE
Proctor and Gamble used CAD when designing its Crest toothpaste pump dispenser.

The field of computer-aided design is merging with the field of **computer-aided manufacture (CAM).** Current CAD technology has branched out to provide tooling departments with data and to produce a computer program for numerically controlled machines. Thus we have the integration of computer-aided design (CAD) and computer-aided manufacturing (CAM), resulting in CAD/CAM. In this manner the initial programming generated at the design stage can be used to create a computer program that will be used not only by drafting departments, but also in tooling and manufacturing departments. Because the CAD data are available for subsequent use by others, tool design personnel and programmers of numerically controlled machines are aided. They can now proceed to design tooling and programs with confidence that they have the latest accurate engineering data and engineering drawings.

Computer-aided design (CAD) is available for a variety of applications, including electronic and mechanical design. CAD is used to design integrated circuits, toothpaste dispensers, and automobiles. The rule of thumb is that a state-of-the-art CAD work station not only speeds up development, but can improve engineering productivity by 400%. Here Control Data's mechanical CAD is displaying a three-dimensional view of Lamborghini Diablo chassis. Control Data's CAD shown on the left was indeed used to develop the Lamborghini Diablo shown on the right.

BENEFITS. The CAD/CAM approach has several benefits:

1. *Product quality.* CAD provides an opportunity for the designer to investigate more alternatives, potential problems, and dangers.
2. *Shorter design time.* Since time is money, the shorter the design phase, the lower the cost.
3. *Production cost reductions.* Faster implementation of design changes lowers costs.
4. *Database availability.* Consolidating product data so everyone is operating from the same information results in dramatic cost reductions.
5. *New range of capabilities.* CAD/CAM removes substantial detail work, allowing designers to concentrate on the conceptual and imaginative aspects of their task. This is a major benefit of CAD/CAM.

In addition to using CAD/CAM, many firms are also exploring another computer-based technology, *virtual reality,* to aid in the design and development of new products. While virtual reality is often thought of purely in terms of entertainment (many arcades now have virtual reality games and people have even been married in virtual reality settings), it actually has a number of applications for research and development. Economic sectors ranging from construction and architecture to entertainment, such as movies and theme-park developers, are finding that by first creating and testing a product or service in virtual reality, many pitfalls can be avoided. As with CAD/CAM, virtual reality allows designers to be more creative and imaginative.

DOCUMENTS FOR PRODUCTION

Once a product is selected and designed, its production is assisted by a variety of documents. We will briefly review some of these.

assembly drawing

An **assembly drawing** simply shows an exploded view of the product. An assembly drawing is usually a three-dimensional drawing, known as an isometric drawing; the relative locations of components are drawn in relation to each other to show how to assemble the unit (see Figure 4.9[a]).

assembly chart

The **assembly chart** shows in schematic form how a product is assembled. Manufactured components, purchased components, or a combination of both may be shown on an assembly chart. The assembly chart identifies the point of production where components flow into subassemblies and ultimately into a final product. An example of an assembly chart is shown in Figure 4.9(b).

route sheet

NOTE
Route sheets often show labor standards for each operation.

The **route sheet** lists the operations (including assembly and inspection) necessary to produce the component with the material specified in the bill-of-material. The route sheet for an item will have one entry for each operation to be performed on the item. When route sheets include specific methods of operation and labor standards, they are often known as *process sheets.*

work order

The **work order** is an instruction to make a given quantity of a particular item, usually to a given schedule. The ticket that a waiter writes in your favorite restaurant is a work order. In a hospital or factory the work order is a more formal order that provides authorization to draw various pharmaceuticals or items from

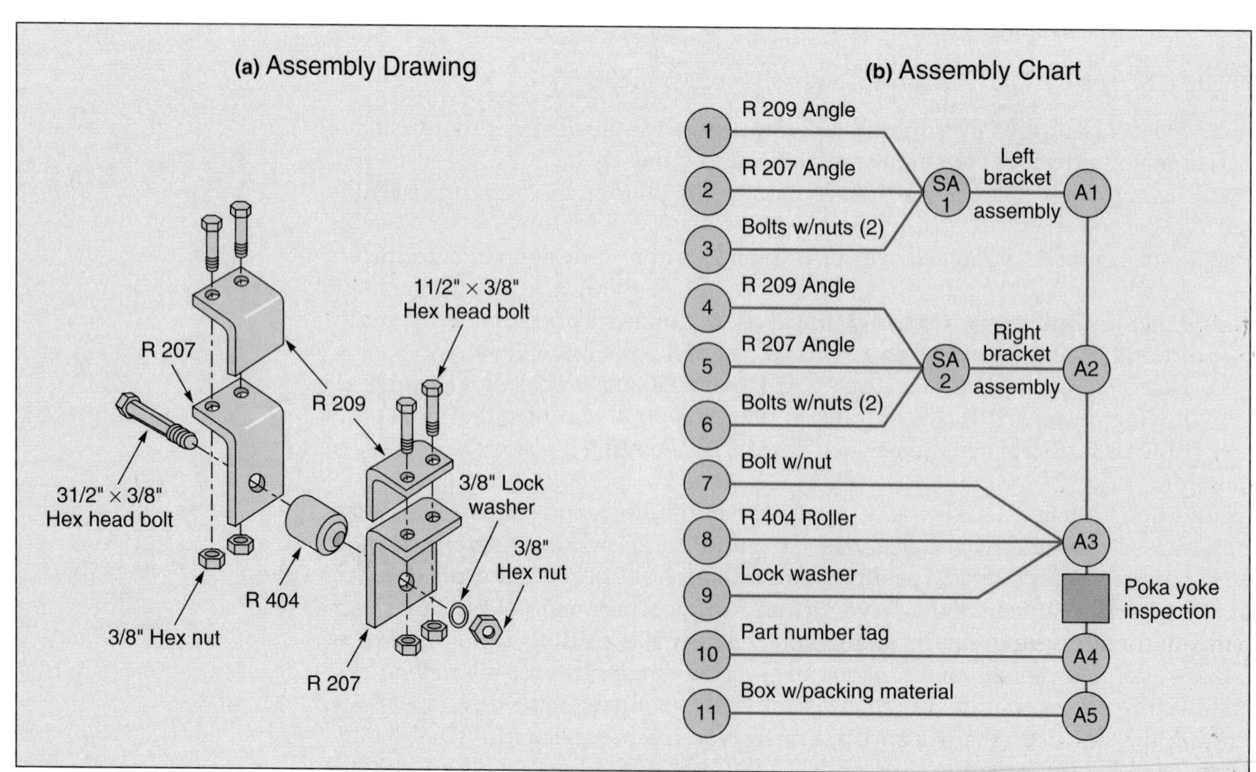

FIGURE 4.9 ASSEMBLY DRAWING AND ASSEMBLY CHART

inventory, to perform various functions, and to assign personnel to perform those functions.

Engineering change notices (ECNs) change some aspect of the product's definition or documentation, such as an engineering drawing or a bill-of-material. For a complex product that has a long manufacturing cycle, such as a Boeing 757, the changes may be so numerous that no two 757s are built exactly alike—which is indeed the case. Such dynamic design change has fostered the development of a discipline known as configuration management, which is concerned with product identification, control, and documentation. **Configuration management** is the system by which a product's planned and changing configurations are accurately identified and for which control and accountability of change are maintained.

engineering change notice (ECN)

configuration management

NOTE
Work orders are often computerized in modern facilities; entries via a computer terminal provide a record of a product's progress through a system.

SERVICE DESIGN

A lot of our discussion so far has focused on what we can call tangible products, that is, goods. On the other side of the product coin are, of course, services. Service industries include banking, finance, insurance, transportation, and communications. The "products" offered by service firms range from a medical procedure that leaves only the tiniest scar after an appendectomy, to a shampoo and cut at a hair salon, to a great movie.

Designing services to accommodate their unique characteristics is challenging. One reason productivity improvements in services are so low is because both the design and delivery of service products include customer interaction. When the customer participates in the design process, the service supplier may have a menu of services from which the customer selects options (see Figure 4.10[a]). At this point, the customer may also modify the design of the services. Design specifications may take the form of a contract or a narrative description with photos (such as for cosmetic surgery or a hair style). Similarly, the customer may be involved in the delivery of a service (see Figure 4.10[b]), or the customer may be involved in both design and delivery, which maximizes the product design challenge (see Figure 4.10[c]).

However, like goods, a large part of cost and quality of a service is defined at the design stage. Conveniently, there are a number of techniques *available when the service is designed* that can both reduce costs and provide a quality service. One technique is to design the product so that *customization is done as late in the process as possible.* This is the way a hair salon operates; shampoo and rinse are done in a standard way with lower-cost labor, and the tint and styling (customizing) are done last.

The second approach is to *modularize the product* so that customization takes the form of moving the modules around. This allows the modules to be designed as "fixed," standard entities. The modular approach to product design has applications in both manufacturing and service. Just as modular design allows you to buy a Harley-Davidson motorcycle or an automobile with just the features you want, this modular flexibility lets you buy meals, clothes, and insurance on a mix-and-match (modular) basis. Similarly, investment portfolios are put together in a modular basis. And certainly college curriculums are another example of how the modular approach can be used to customize services, in this case, education.

A third approach to the design of services is to divide the service into small parts and identify those parts that lend themselves to *automation* or *reduced customer interaction.* For instance, by isolating the check-cashing activity via ATM machines,

FIGURE 4.10

CUSTOMER PARTICIPATION IN THE DESIGN OF SERVICES

SOURCE: Robert Murdick, Barry Render, and Roberta Russell, *Service Operations Management* (Boston: Allyn & Bacon 1990).

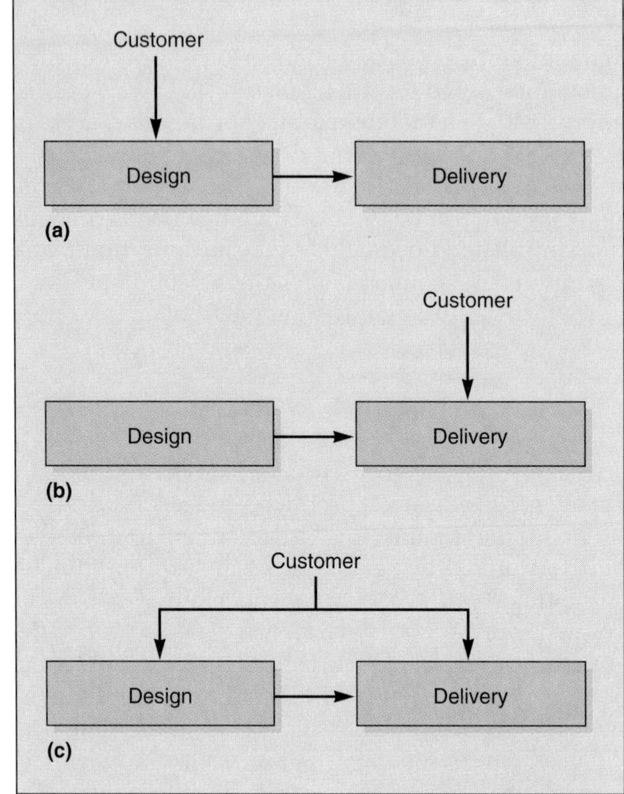

(a) Participation in design such as pre-arranged funeral services or cosmetic surgery
(b) Participation in delivery such as stress test for cardiac exam or delivery of a baby
(c) Participation in design and delivery such as counseling, seminar, financial management of personal affairs, or interior decorating

banks have been very effective at designing a product that both increases customer service and reduces costs. Similarly, Southwest Airlines has ticketless service. Because airlines spend $15 to $30 to produce a single ticket (including labor, printing, and travel agents' commission) the ticketless system could save the industry a billion dollars a year. If airlines are successful in reducing both costs and lines at airports, thereby increasing customer satisfaction, they will have win-win "product" design.

Because of the high customer interaction in many service industries, a fourth technique is to *focus design on the moment-of-truth.* Jan Carlzon, former president of Scandinavian Airways, believes that in the service industry there is a moment of truth when the relationship between the service provider and the customer is crucial.[6] At that moment the customer's satisfaction with that service is defined. The **moment-of-truth** is the moment that exemplifies, enhances, or detracts from the customer's expectations. That moment may be as simple as a smile or having the check-out clerk focus on you rather than talking over his shoulder to the clerk at the next counter. Moments-of-truth can occur when you order at McDonald's,

moment-of-truth

[6]Jan Carlzon, *Moments of Truth* (Cambridge: Ballinger Publishing Co., 1987).

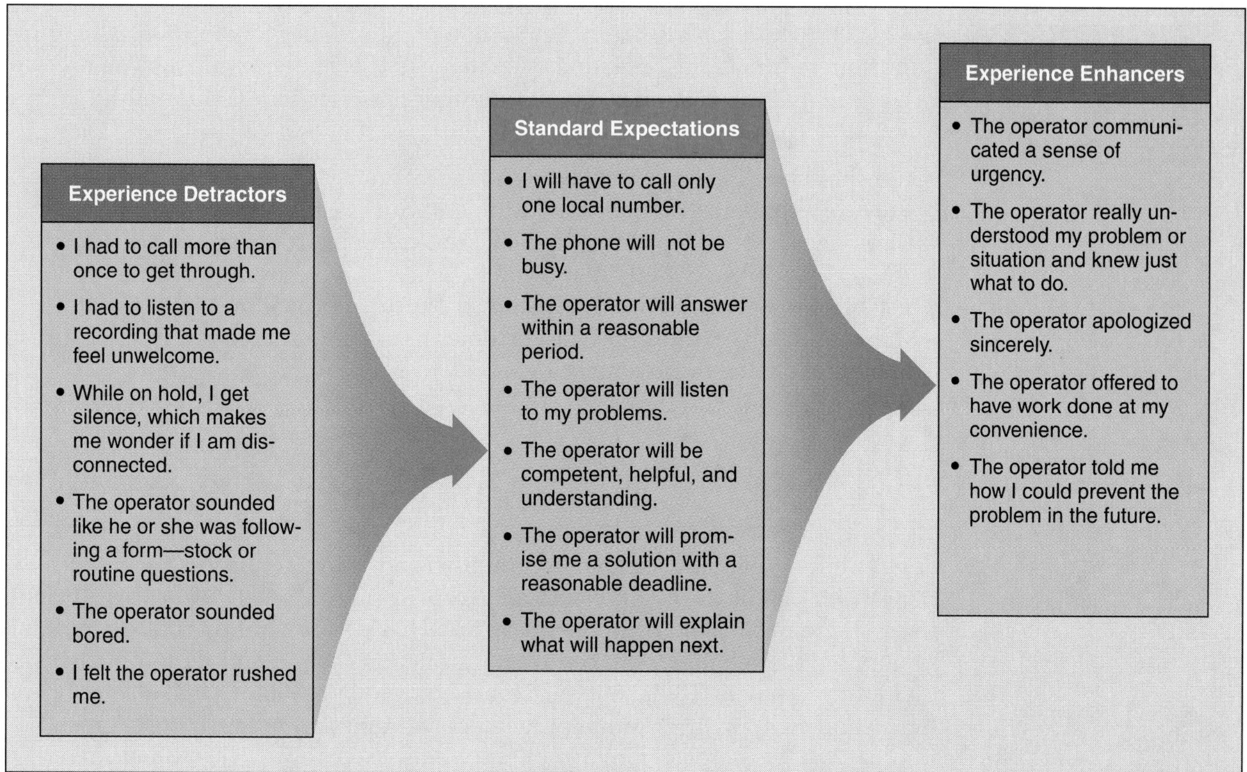

Experience Detractors
• I had to call more than once to get through.
• I had to listen to a recording that made me feel unwelcome.
• While on hold, I get silence, which makes me wonder if I am disconnected.
• The operator sounded like he or she was following a form—stock or routine questions.
• The operator sounded bored.
• I felt the operator rushed me.
Standard Expectations
• I will have to call only one local number.
• The phone will not be busy.
• The operator will answer within a reasonable period.
• The operator will listen to my problems.
• The operator will be competent, helpful, and understanding.
• The operator will promise me a solution with a reasonable deadline.
• The operator will explain what will happen next.
Experience Enhancers
• The operator communicated a sense of urgency.
• The operator really understood my problem or situation and knew just what to do.
• The operator apologized sincerely.
• The operator offered to have work done at my convenience.
• The operator told me how I could prevent the problem in the future.

FIGURE 4.11 **MOMENT-OF-TRUTH: THE CUSTOMER CONTACTS THE REPAIR ANSWERING CENTER AT GTE**

SOURCE: Adapted from Ron Zemke and Dick Schaaf, *The Service Edge* (New York: New American Library, 1989), p. 36.

get a haircut, or go through registration at college. Figure 4.11 shows a moment-of-truth analysis for a repair answering service at GTE. The operations manager's task is to identify the moments-of-truth and design a service that meets or exceeds the customer's expectations.

Documents for Services

Because of the high customer interaction for most services, the documents for moving the product to production are different. The documentation for a service to be produced will often take the form of the explicit job instructions that specify what is to happen at the moment-of-truth. For instance, regardless of how good the bank's products may be in terms of checking, savings, trusts, loans, mortgages, and so forth, if the moment-of-truth is not done well, the product may be poorly received. Example 1 shows the kind of documentation a bank may use to move a product (drive-up window banking) to "production." In a telemarketing service the product design and its related transmittal to production may take the form of telephone script, and a "story board" (similar to a cartoon strip) may be used for a motion picture.

EXAMPLE 1

Customers who use drive-up teller stations rather than walk-in lobbies may require different customer relations techniques. The distance and machinery between you and the customer raises communication barriers. Communication tips to improve customer relations at a drive-up window are:

- Be especially discreet when talking to the customer through the microphone.
- Provide written instructions for customers who must fill out forms you provide.
- Mark lines to be completed or attach a note with instructions.
- Always say "please" and "thank you" when speaking through the microphone.
- Establish eye contact with the customer if the distance allows it.
- If a transaction requires that the customer park the car and come into the lobby, apologize for the inconvenience.

SOURCE: Adapted from *Teller Operations*, (Chicago, IL: The Institute of Financial Education, 1987), p. 29.

PRODUCT RELIABILITY

reliability

High product reliability has an enormous positive impact on customer satisfaction. If any one of the components fails to perform, for whatever reason, the entire system can fail. And components do fail. Therefore, operations managers want to improve the reliability of their own production system and the products they build for customers. **Reliability** is expressed as the probability that a component (or several components working together) will function properly for a given period of time. When designing products, we use two approaches to improve reliability and reduce the likelihood of failure. These two approaches are:

1. To improve individual components.
2. To provide redundancy.

Let's first look at improving individual components and then at providing redundancy.

Improving Individual Components

Component reliability is often a design or specification issue for which product design personnel may be responsible. However, purchasing personnel may be able to improve components of systems by staying abreast of suppliers' products and research efforts. Purchasing personnel can also directly contribute to evaluation of supplier performance. Similarly, where high customer interaction is necessary, the human resource function may play a critical role in service reliability through hiring and training.

To measure system reliability (R_s) in which each individual part or component may have its own unique rate of reliability, we find the product of the individual reliabilities:

$$R_s = R_1 \times R_2 \times R_3 \times \ldots \times R_n \tag{4.1}$$

where

R_1 = Reliability of component 1

R_2 = Reliability of component 2

and so on.

Today's jetliners are expected to be designed so that one system's failure doesn't automatically cripple others. But the 1989 crash of this United Airlines DC-10 in Sioux City, Iowa, seems to indicate that the McDonnell Douglas plane's hydraulic systems aren't providing good enough protection. The DC-10 has three separate mazes of half-inch pipes running throughout the plane. Each pipe is designed to continuously pump fluid that operates control devices. But federal investigators think the pipes in the plane's tail were severed by flying tail engine parts. All hydraulic fluid then sprayed out causing loss of control and, ultimately, the crash.

This equation assumes that the reliability of an individual component does not depend on the reliability of other components (that is, each component is independent). Additionally, in this equation, as in most reliability discussions, reliabilities are presented as probabilities. A .90 reliability means that the unit will perform as intended 90% of the time. It also means that it will fail $1 - .90 = .10 = 10\%$ of the time. We can use this method to evaluate the reliability of a product, such as the one we examine in Example 2.

EXAMPLE 2

The National Bank of Greeley, Colorado, processes loan applications through three clerks set up in a series:

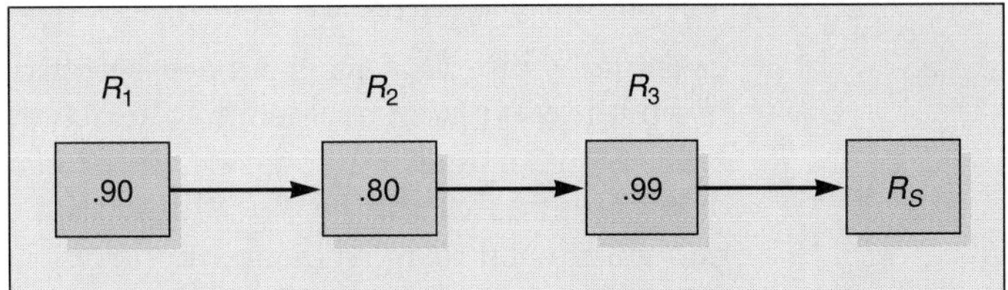

If the clerks have reliabilities of .90, .80, .99, then the reliability of the loan process is

$$R_s = R_1R_2R_3 = (.90)(.80)(.99) = .713 \text{ or } 71.3\%$$

Providing Redundancy

Redundancy is provided if one component fails and the system has recourse to another. To increase the reliability of systems, redundancy ("backing-up" the components) is added. For instance, if reliability of a component is .80 and we back it up with another component with reliability of .80, then the resulting reliability is the probability of the first component working plus the probability of the backup component working, multiplied by the probability of needing the backup component (1 − .8 = .2).

Therefore:

$$\begin{pmatrix}\text{Probability}\\ \text{of first}\\ \text{component}\\ \text{working}\end{pmatrix} + \left[\begin{pmatrix}\text{Probability}\\ \text{of second}\\ \text{component}\\ \text{working}\end{pmatrix} \times \begin{pmatrix}\text{Probability}\\ \text{of needing}\\ \text{second}\\ \text{component}\end{pmatrix}\right] =$$

$$(.8) \quad + \quad [(.8) \quad \times \quad (1 - .8)] \quad = .8 + .16 = .96$$

We demonstrate redundancy in Example 3.

EXAMPLE 3

National Bank is disturbed that its loan process has a reliability of only .713 (see Example 2). Therefore, the bank decides to provide redundancy for the two least reliable clerks. This results in the system shown below:

$$\begin{array}{ccc} R_1 & R_2 & R_3 \\ 0.90 & 0.8 & \\ \downarrow & \downarrow & \\ 0.90 \rightarrow & 0.8 \rightarrow & 0.99 \end{array}$$

$$\begin{aligned} &= [.9 + .9(1 - .9)] \times [.8 + .8(1 - .8)] \times .99 \\ &= [.9 + (.9)(.1)] \times [.8 + (.8)(.2)] \times .99 \\ &= .99 \times .96 \times .99 = .94 \end{aligned}$$

So by providing redundancy for two clerks, National Bank has increased reliability of the process from .713 to .94.

TRANSITION TO PRODUCTION

Eventually, our product has been selected, designed, and defined. The product has progressed from an idea, to a functional definition, and then to a prototype. Now, management must make a decision as to further development, production, or termination of the product idea. One of the arts of modern management is knowing when to move a product from development to production; this movement is known as *transition to production.*

Some companies appoint a project manager or use an ongoing product development team to ensure that the transition from the development phase to production is successful. This is often necessary because of the wide range of resources and talents that must be brought to bear to ensure satisfactory production of a product that is still in flux. Other firms use the design teams discussed earlier. And yet other firms find that integration of the product development and manufacturing organizations is advantageous. This allows for easy shifting of resources between the two organizations as needs change. The production manager's job is to make the transition from R & D to production smooth and without gaps.

SUMMARY

Selecting, designing, and defining a product and its related service have implications for all subsequent operations decisions. The operations manager must be imaginative and resourceful in the product development process. Products are defined by written specification, bills-of-material, and engineering drawings. Group technology, computer-aided design, and value engineering are helpful product design techniques. Assembly drawings, assembly charts, route sheets, and work orders assist the manager in defining a product for production. Reliable products are increasingly a necessity. Components' reliability can be increased and components can be put in parallel to improve reliability.

Once a product is in production, value analysis is appropriate for quality and production review. Configuration management allows the manager to track and document the product that has been produced.

As products move through their life cycle (introduction, growth, maturity, and decline) the options the operations manager should pursue change.

KEY TERMS

Product decision *(p. 142)*
Time-based competition *(p. 145)*
Product development teams *(p. 147)*
Concurrent engineering *(p. 147)*
Design for manufacturability and value engineering teams *(p. 147)*
Quality robust design *(p. 147)*
Value analysis *(p. 148)*
Product-by-value analysis *(p. 148)*
Engineering drawing *(p. 149)*
Bill-of-material (BOM) *(p. 149)*
Make-or-buy decision *(p. 149)*
Group technology *(p. 150)*
Computer-aided design (CAD) *(p. 152)*
Computer-aided manufacture (CAM) *(p. 152)*
Assembly drawing *(p. 154)*
Assembly chart *(p. 154)*
Route sheet *(p. 154)*
Work order *(p. 154)*
Engineering change notice (ECN) *(p. 155)*
Configuration management *(p. 155)*
Moment-of-truth *(p. 156)*
Reliability *(p. 158)*

USING POM FOR WINDOWS FOR RELIABILITY ANALYSIS

Program 4.1 illustrates POM for Window's Reliability Module applied to the National Bank in Example 3.

PROGRAM 4.1

POM FOR WINDOWS' RELIABILITY MODULE EXAMPLE

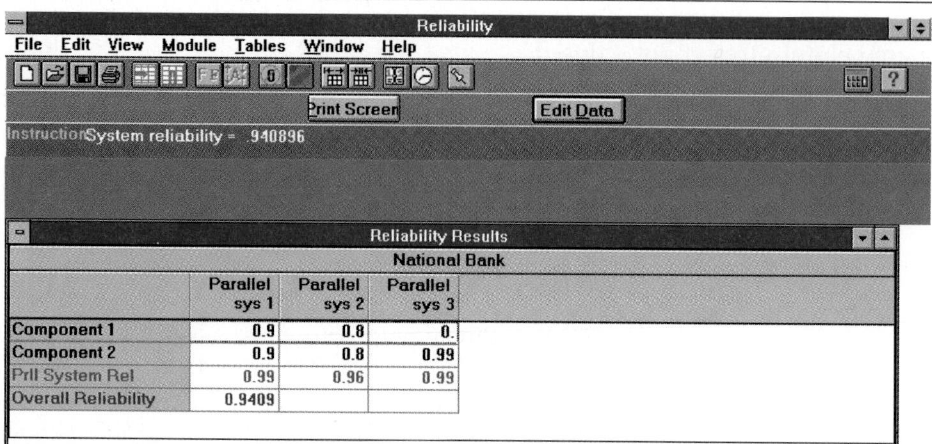

	Parallel sys 1	Parallel sys 2	Parallel sys 3
Component 1	0.9	0.8	0.
Component 2	0.9	0.8	0.99
Prll System Rel	0.99	0.96	0.99
Overall Reliability	0.9409		

The entries for reliability are: 1. *number of systems* (components) in the series (1 through 10); 2. *number of backup* or parallel components (1 through 12); 3. *component reliability.* Enter the reliability of each component in the body of the table. Series data are entered across the table, and backup or parallel data down the table. The program will disregard any zeroes in the table.

SOLVED PROBLEM 4.1

The semiconductor used in the Sullivan Wrist Calculator has five parts, each of which has its own reliability rate. Component 1 has a reliability of .90; component 2, .95; component 3, .98; component 4, .90; and component 5, .99. What is the reliability of one semiconductor?

SOLUTION

Semiconductor reliability $R_s = R_1R_2R_3R_4R_5$

$= (.90)(.95)(.98)(.90)(.99)$

$= .7466$

SOLVED PROBLEM 4.2

A recent engineering change at Sullivan Wrist Calculator places a backup component in each of the two least reliable transistor circuits. The new circuit will look like the following:

What is the reliability of the new system?

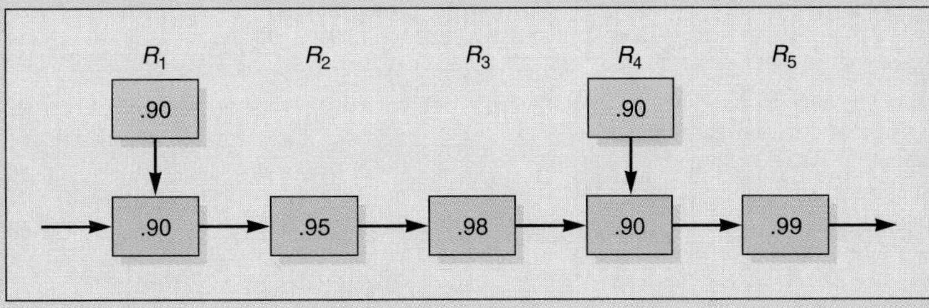

SOLUTION

$$\text{Reliability} = [.9 + .9 \times (1 - .9)] \times .95 \times .98 \times [.90 + .9 \times (1 - .9)] \times .99$$

$$= [.9 + .09] \times .95 \times .98 \times [.90 + .09] \times .99$$

$$= .99 \times .95 \times .98 \times .99 \times .99$$

$$= .903$$

DISCUSSION QUESTIONS

1. What management techniques may prove helpful in making the transition from design to production?
2. Why is it necessary to document a product explicitly?
3. What techniques do we use to document a product?
4. Configuration management has proved particularly useful in what industries? Why?
5. How does computer-aided design help other departments?
6. What is group technology and why is it proving helpful in our quest for productivity improvement?
7. What savings can be expected by computer-aided design?
8. How does computer-aided design help computer-aided manufacture?
9. What are the four phases of the product life cycle?
10. How does product selection (and design) affect quality?
11. Once a product is defined, what documents are used to assist production personnel in the manufacture of that product?
12. How does configuration management manifest itself when you ask for service on your automobile?
13. What are the similarities and dissimilarities between a manufactured product and a new type of life insurance policy referred to by the salesperson as a new "product."

OPERATIONS IN PRACTICE EXERCISE

Rubbermaid's record of new product innovation is remarkable. With almost 5,000 products, the firm continues to crank out a new one almost every day, with great success. Rubbermaid has divided its product line into four dozen categories. Then it creates entrepreneurial teams of five to seven members in each category. Each team includes a product manager, research and manufacturing engineers, and financial sales and marketing executives. The teams conceive their own products, shepherding them from design stage to the marketplace.

Compare Rubbermaid's product approach to other approaches discussed in this chapter.

SELF-TEST ■ CHAPTER 4

- *Before taking the self-test* refer back to the learning objectives listed at the beginning of the chapter and the key terms listed at the end of the chapter.
- Use the key at the back of the text to *correct* your answers.
- *Restudy* pages that correspond to any questions you answered incorrectly or material you feel uncertain about.

1. A product's life cycle is divided into four stages, which include:
a. introduction
b. growth
c. maturity
d. all of the above

2. Which of the following would likely cause a change in market opportunities based upon family size?
a. economic change
b. technological change
c. political change
d. sociological and demographic change

3. Listing products in descending order of their individual dollar contribution to the firm is called
a. product-by-value analysis
b. value analysis
c. value engineering
d. all of the above

4. The benefits of CAD/CAM include
a. shorter design time
b. production cost reductions
c. product quality improvement
d. design database availability
e. all of the above

5. A route sheet
a. lists the operations necessary to produce the component
b. is an instruction to make a given quantity of a particular item
c. shows in schematic form how a product is assembled
d. all of the above

6. An application of the Pareto principle is
a. the first customers to arrive are the first customers served
b. the shortest distance between two points is a straight line
c. resources are invested in the critical few and not the trivial many
d. the good things in life are free

7. An assembly chart is
a. an exploded view of the product
b. a schematic showing how the product is assembled
c. a list of the operations necessary to produce the component
d. an instruction to make a given quantity of a particular item
e. a set of detailed instructions about how to perform a task

8. If a system has a component with less than 100% reliability, we can make the system 100% reliable by adding redundancy.
a. True **b.** False

9. As we increase the number of non-redundant components in a system, all other things being equal, the reliability of the system usually
a. increases
b. stays the same
c. decreases
d. increases, then decreases

10. Four techniques that are available when a service is designed are
a. recognize political or legal change, technological change, sociological demographic change, and economic change
b. understand product introduction, growth, maturity, and decline
c. recognize functional specifications, product specifications, design review, and test markets
d. ensure customization is done as late in the process as possible, modularize the product, reduce customer interaction, focus on the moment-of-truth

11. The probability that a machine, part, or product will function properly for a given period of time is called
a. maintenance
b. quality control
c. reliability
d. all of the above

12. A product-by-value analysis report is ______________
______________________________.

13. Products must be continually developed because ______
______________________________.

14. Products are documented by ______________
______________________________.

PROBLEMS

- **4.1.** Prepare a bill-of-material for a ballpoint pen.
- **4.2.** Draw an assembly chart for a ballpoint pen.
- **4.3.** Prepare a bill-of-material for a simple table lamp. Identify the items that you, as manufacturer of the body and related components, are likely to make and that you are likely to purchase. Justify your decision for each.
- **4.4.** Prepare an assembly chart for the table lamp in Problem 4.3.
- **4.5.** As a library project, find a series of group technology codes.
- **4.6.** Given the contribution made on each of the three products below, prepare a product-by-value report. What does the report tell you?

PRODUCT	PRODUCT CONTRIBUTION (percent of selling price)	COMPANY CONTRIBUTION (percent of total annual contribution divided by total annual sales)	POSITION IN LIFE CYCLE
Portable computer	30	40	Growth
Laptop computer	30	50	Introduction
Hand calculator	50	10	Decline

- **4.7.** You have a system composed of four components in series. The reliability of each component is 0.95. What is the reliability of the system?
- **4.8.** You have a system composed of a serial connection of four components with the following reliabilities:

COMPONENT	RELIABILITY
1	0.90
2	0.95
3	0.80
4	0.85

What is the reliability of the system?

- **4.9.** You have a system composed of three components in parallel (if any one of the components work, the system will work). The components have the following reliabilities: $R_1 = 0.90$, $R_2 = 0.95$, $R_3 = 0.85$.

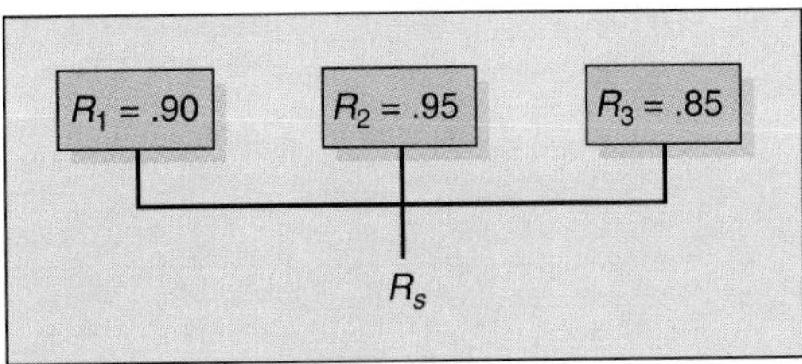

What is the reliability of the system?

- **4.10.** A hydraulic control system has three components in series with individual reliabilities (R_1, R_2, and R_3) as shown below.

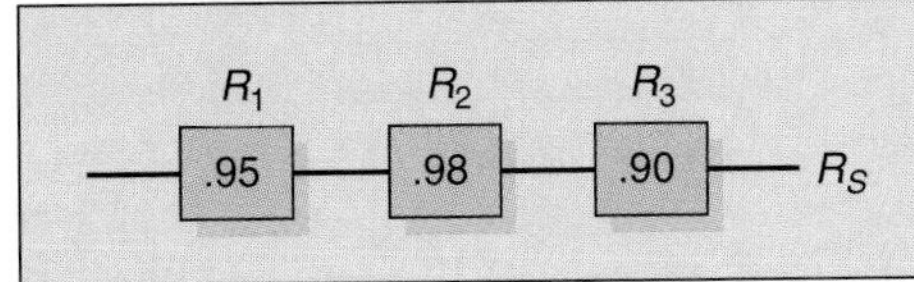

What is the reliability of the system?

: **4.11.** What is the reliability of the system shown below?

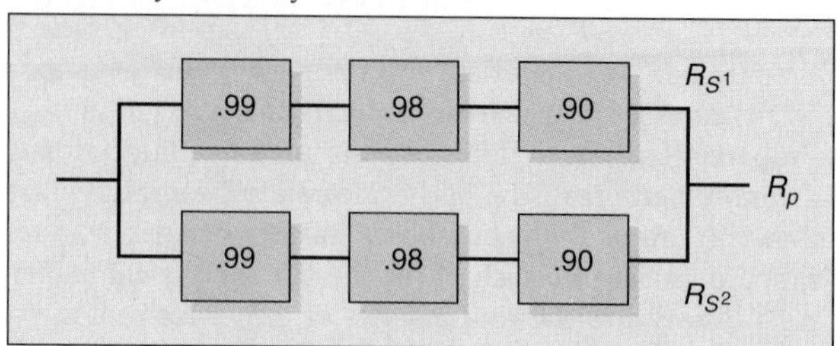

: **4.12.** What is the impact on reliability if the hydraulic control system shown in Problem 4.10 is changed to the parallel system shown in problem 4.11?

. **4.13.** Your design team has proposed the following system with component reliabilities as indicated.

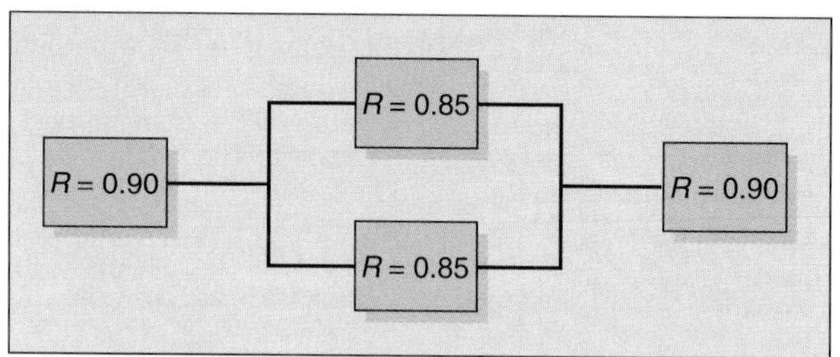

What is the reliability of the system?

: **4.14.** The Beta II computer's electronic processing unit contains five components in series. The average reliability of each component is .99. Determine the overall reliability of the processing unit.

. **4.15.** Alain Prost, salesman for Wave Soldering Systems, Inc. (WSSI), has provided you with a proposal for improving the temperature control on your present machine. The present machine uses a hot-air knife to remove cleanly excess solder from printed circuit boards; this is a great concept, but the hot-air temperature control lacks reliability. The engineers at WSSI have, says Alain, improved the reliability of the critical temperature controls. The new system still has the four sensitive integrated circuits controlling the temperature, but the new machine has a backup for each. The four integrated circuits have reliabilities of .90, .92, .94, and .96. The four backup circuits all have a reliability of .90.

a. What is the reliability of the new temperature controller?

b. If you pay a premium, Alain says he can improve all four of the backup units to .93. What is the reliability of this option?

CASE STUDY

GE's Rotary Compressor

In 1981, market share and profits in General Electric's appliance division were falling. The company's technology was antiquated compared to foreign competitors. For example, making refrigerator compressors required 65 minutes of labor in comparison to 25 minutes for competitors in Japan and Italy. Moreover, GE's labor costs were higher. The alternatives were obvious: Either purchase compressors from Japan or Italy or design and build a better model.

By 1983, the decision to build a new rotary compressor in-house was made, along with a commitment for a new $120 million factory. GE was not a novice in rotary compressor technology; it had invented the technology and had been using it in air conditioners for many years. A rotary compressor weighed less, had one-third fewer parts, and was more energy efficient than the current reciprocating compressors. The rotary compressor took up less space, thus providing more room inside the refrigerator and better meeting customer requirements.

Some engineers argued to the contrary, citing the fact that rotary compressors run hotter. This is not a problem in most air conditioners because the coolant cools the compressor. In a refrigerator, however, the coolant flows only one-tenth as fast, and the unit runs about four times longer in one year than an air conditioner. GE had problems with the early rotary compressors in air conditioners. Although the bugs had been eliminated in smaller units, GE quit using rotaries in larger units due to frequent breakdowns in hot climates.

GE managers and design engineers were concerned about other issues. Rotary compressors make a high-pitched whine, and managers were afraid that this would adversely affect consumer acceptance. Many hours were spent on this issue by managers and consumer test panels. The new design also required key parts to work together with a tolerance of only 50 millionths of an inch. Nothing had been mass produced with such precision before, but manufacturing engineers felt sure they could do it.

The compressor they finally designed was nearly identical to that used in air conditioners, with one change. Two small parts inside the compressor were made out of powdered metal, rather than the hardened steel and cast iron used in air conditioners. This material was chosen because it could be machined to much closer tolerances, and it reduced machining costs. Powdered metal had been tried a decade earlier on air conditioners but did not work. The design engineers who were new to designing compressors did not consider the earlier failure important.

A consultant suggested that GE consider a joint venture with a Japanese company that had a rotary refrigerator compressor already on the market. The idea was rejected by management. The original designer of the air-conditioner rotary compressor, who had left GE, offered his services as a consultant. GE declined his offer, writing him that they had sufficient technical expertise.

About 600 compressors were tested in 1983 without a single failure. They were run continuously for two months under elevated temperatures and pressures that were supposed to simulate five years' operation. GE normally conducts extensive field testing of new products; its original plan to test models in the field for two years was reduced to nine months due to time pressure to complete the project.

The technician who disassembled and inspected the parts thought they did not look right. Parts of the motor were discolored, a sign of excessive heat. Bearings were worn, and it appeared that high heat was breaking down the lubricating oil. The technician's supervisors discounted these findings and did not relay them to upper levels of management. Another consultant who evaluated the test results believed that something was wrong because only one failure was found in two years and recommended that test conditions be intensified. This suggestion was also rejected by management.

By 1986, only two and a half years after board approval, the new factory was producing compressors at a rate of ten per minute. By the end of the year, more than 1 million had been produced. Market share rose and the new refrigerator appeared to be a success. But in July 1987, the first compressor failed. Soon after, reports of other failures in Puerto Rico arrived. By September, the appliance division knew it had a major problem. In December, the plant stopped making the compressor. Not until 1988 was the problem diagnosed as excessive wear in the two powdered-metal parts that burned up the oil. The cost in 1989 alone was $450 million. By mid-1990, GE had voluntarily replaced nearly 1.1 million compressors with ones purchased from six suppliers, five of them foreign.

DISCUSSION QUESTIONS

1. What factors in the product development process caused this disaster? What individuals were responsible?
2. How might this disaster have been prevented? What lessons do you think GE learned for the future?
3. On what basis was GE attempting to achieve a competitive advantage? How did they fail?

SOURCE: James Dean and James Evans, *Total Quality* (St. Paul: West Publishing, 1994) pp. 256–257.

BIBLIOGRAPHY

Berliner, C., and J. A. Brimson. *Cost Management for Today's Advanced Manufacturing*. Boston: Harvard Business School Press, 1988.

Burt, D. N., and W. R. Soukup. "Purchasing's Role in New Product Development." *Harvard Business Review* 63 (September-October 1985): 90–97.

Canton, I. D. "Learning to Love the Service Economy." *Harvard Business Review* 62 (May-June 1984): 89–97.

Choi, M., and W. E. Riggs. "GT Coding and Classification Systems for Manufacturing Cell Design." *Production and Inventory Management Journal* 32 (First Quarter 1991): 28.

Clark, K., and S. Wheelwright. "Organizing and Leading 'Heavyweight' Development Teams." *The California Management Review* (Spring 1992).

Cooper, Robin, and W. Bruce Chew. "Control Tomorrow's

Costs Through Today's Designs," *Harvard Business Review* 74 (January/February 1996): 88–97.

Eppen, G. D., W. A. Hanson, and R. K. Martin. "Bundling-New Products, New Markets, Low Risk." *Sloan Management Review* 32 (Summer 1991): 7.

Iansiti, M. "Real-World R&D: Jumping the Product Generation Gap." *Harvard Business Review* 71, (May-June 1993): 131–147.

Mosier, C. T., and R. E. Janaro. "Toward a Universal Classification and Coding System for Assemblies." *Journal of Operations Management* 9 (January 1990): 44.

Neibel, B. W., and A. B. Draper. *Product Design and Process Engineering*. New York: McGraw-Hill, 1974.

Smith, P. G., and D. G. Reinertsen. *Developing Products in Half the Time*. New York: Van Nostrand Reinhold, 1991.

Souder, W. E. *Managing New Product Innovations*. Lexington, MA: Lexington Books, 1987.

Takeuchi, H., and I. Nonaka. "The New Product Development Game." *Harvard Business Review* 64 (January-February 1986): 137–146.

Wheelwright, S. C., and W. E. Sasser, Jr. "The New Product Development Map." *Harvard Business Review* 67 (May-June 1989): 112–125.

Process and Capacity Design 5

CHAPTER OUTLINE

Three Process Strategies

Process Focus ■ Product Focus ■ Repetitive Focus ■ Moving Toward Lean Production ■ Comparison of Process Choices

Machinery, Equipment, and Technology

Numerical Control ■ Process Control ■ Robots ■ Automated Guided Vehicles (AGVs) ■ Flexible Manufacturing System (FMS) ■ Computer-Integrated Manufacture (CIM)

Process Reengineering

Time-Function Mapping ■ Work-Flow Analysis

Choosing a Service Process Strategy

Service-Sector Considerations ■ Customer Interaction and Process Strategy ■ Other Service Process Opportunities

Capacity

Capacity Management ■ Forecasting Capacity Requirements ■ Demand Management

Break-Even Analysis

Making the Investment

Strategy-Driven Investments ■ Investment, Variable Cost, and Cash Flow

Summary ■ *Key Terms* ■ *Solved Problems* ■ *Discussion Questions* ■ *Self-Test Chapter 5* ■ *Operations in Practice Exercise* ■ *Problems* ■ *Case Study: Service at Minit-Lube, Inc.* ■ *Bibliography*

LEARNING OBJECTIVES

When you complete this chapter you should be able to:

IDENTIFY OR DEFINE:

Process focus
Repetitive focus
Product focus

DESCRIBE OR EXPLAIN:

Lean production
The capacity issue
Break-even analysis
Financial considerations
Process reengineering

In Chapter 4 we examined the need for the selection, definition, and design of goods and services. We now turn to their production. A major decision for the operations manager is finding the best way to produce. This chapter looks at ways to help managers design a process.

process decision

A **process** (or transformation) **decision** is the approach that an organization takes to transform resources into goods and services. We use both terms, *process* and *transformation,* to describe this strategy. The *objective of a process design* is to find a way to produce goods and services that meet customer requirements and product specifications within cost and other managerial constraints. The process selected will have a long-run effect on efficiency and production, as well as the flexibility, cost, and quality of the goods produced. Therefore much of a firm's strategy is determined at the time of this process decision.

THREE PROCESS STRATEGIES

Virtually every good or service is made by using some variation of one of three process strategies: process focus, repetitive focus, and product focus.

In Crawfordsville, Indiana, Nucor, probably the world's most efficient steel producer, produces sheet steel in a new state-of-the-art mill. Selection and investment in this process has eliminated a substantial amount of reheating prior to rolling the steel into its final shape. Additionally, the process used at Crawfordsville results in high labor productivity and high quality. In this photo, a ladle, which is equipped with magnetic stirring and vacuum degassing features, is opened, and steel exits into the continuous caster. Steel pours from the ladle via a ceramic nozzle into a metering vessel and then to a special mold that can adjust the slab's dimensions.

In 1947, McDonald's, like most restaurants, paid out between 35% and 40% of gross income as wages. In December 1948, Richard and Mac McDonald switched their process to a limited and rigidly standardized menu. The new process was based on meticulous attention to detail. The McDonald brothers developed specific portions to be served with each menu item. This included such things as dispensers that put an exact amount of catsup or mustard on each bun and paper goods to replace glassware and china. The new process with such innovations reduced wasted ingredients, motion, and time. By 1952 it took 20 seconds for McDonald's to serve a customer a hamburger, a drink, french fries, and ice cream; labor costs had dropped to 17% of gross income, and McDonald's was on its way to becoming the leading fast-food restaurant.

Process Focus

NOTE
When manufacturing is built around processes, it is called *process*-focused manufacturing.

Perhaps as much as 75% of production is accomplished in a setting of very small volume or batches of different products in places called "job shops." Low-volume products may be as diverse as oceangoing tugboats, gourmet French meals, heart transplants, or a special set of ornate hinges for the front door of a house of worship. These low-volume, high-variety processes are also known as **intermittent processes.** The facilities are organized around *process*; they have a **process focus.**

intermittent processes
process focus

Product Focus

High-volume, low-variety processes are **product focused.** The facilities are organized around *products.* They are also called **continuous processes.** They have very long, continuous production runs, hence the name. Products such as glass, paper, tin sheets, light bulbs, and nuts and bolts are made via a continuous process. Some products, such as light bulbs, are discrete; others, such as rolls of paper, are nondiscrete. It is only with standardization (as popularized by Eli Whitney) and statistical quality control (as introduced by Walter Shewhart) that firms have established product-focused facilities. An organization producing the same light bulb

product focus
continuous processes

NOTE
When manufacturing is built around the product, it is called *product*-focused manufacturing.

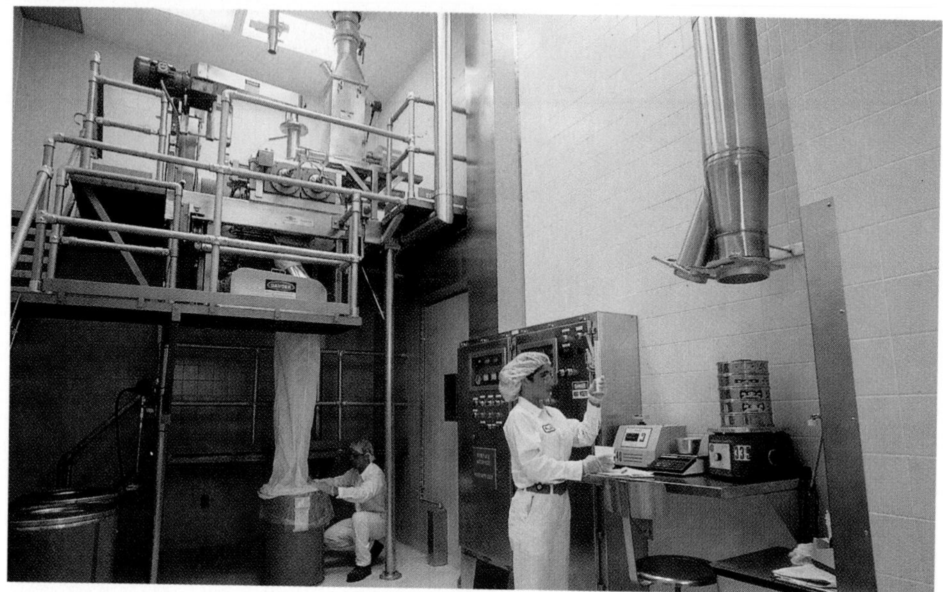

Mylan Laboratories uses just three manufacturing processes for all 79 of its products. Low capital investment and flexible scheduling allow Mylan to hold down costs and meet any order within five days.

or hot dog bun day after day can organize around a product. Such an organization has an inherent ability to set standards and maintain a given quality, as opposed to an organization that is producing unique products every day.

Repetitive Focus

repetitive processes

modules

Production need not be at either of the above extremes of the process continuum but may be a repetitive process that falls somewhere in between. **Repetitive processes** use modules. **Modules** are parts or components previously prepared, often in a continuous process.

The repetitive process line is the classic assembly line. The repetitive process is widely used, including the assembly of virtually all automobiles and household appliances. The repetitive strategy has more structure and consequently less flexibility than a process-focused facility.

Fast-food firms are an example of a repetitive process using modules. This type of production allows more customizing than a continuous process; so modules (for example, meat, cheese, sauce, tomatoes, onions) are assembled to get a quasi-custom product, a cheeseburger. In this manner, the firm obtains both the economic advantages of the continuous model (where many of the modules are prepared) and the custom advantage of the low-volume, high-variety model.

Moving Toward Lean Production

lean producers

Lean Producers[1] is the term used to describe leading repetitive producers.[2] The lean producer's mission is to achieve perfection. Lean production calls for con-

[1]John Krafcik is given credit for coining the term *lean production*.

[2]*Synchronous manufacturing* is another term currently in vogue to describe efficient repetitive processes. General Motors has gone so far as to add the title synchronous manufacturing manager to its lexicon.

TABLE 5.1 SUMMARY OF AUTOMOTIVE ASSEMBLY PLANT PERFORMANCE

	LEAN PRODUCERS	OTHERS		
	Japanese in Japan	*Japanese in North America*	*American in North America*	*All Europe*
Inventories (days for eight sample parts)	.2	1.6	2.9	2.0
Quality (assembly defects/100 vehicles)	60.0	65.0	82.3	97.0
Space (sq. ft./vehicle/year)	5.7	9.1	7.8	7.8
Supplier share of engineering	51%	14%	37%	32%
Workforce:				
Productivity (hours/veh.)	16.8	21.2	25.1	36.2
% of Workforce in teams	69.3	71.3	17.3	.6
Number of job classes	11.9	8.7	67.1	14.8
Training of new production workers (hours)	380.3	370.0	46.4	173.3
Suggestions/employee	61.6	1.4	.4	.4
Absenteeism	5.0	4.8	11.7	12.1

SOURCE: Adapted from James P. Womack, Daniel T. Jones, and Daniel Roos, *The Machine That Changed the World* (New York: Macmillan, 1990), pp. 92, 118.

tinuous learning, creativity, and teamwork. It requires the full commitment and application of everyone's capabilities.

The advantages held by lean producers are spectacular (see Table 5.1). The documented attributes of lean producers include the following:

- They remove waste by focusing on *inventory reduction.* They eliminate virtually all inventory. The removal of inventory removes the safety nets that allow a poor product to make its way through the production process.
- They use *just-in-time* techniques to reduce inventory and the waste caused by inventory. They drive down the time and cost of switching production from one product to another.
- They *build systems that help employees* produce a perfect part every time.
- They *reduce space requirements.* The technique is to minimize the distance a part travels.
- They *develop close relationships with suppliers;* suppliers understand their needs and their customers' needs.
- They *educate suppliers* to accept responsibility for helping meet customer needs.
- They strive for continually declining costs by *eliminating all but value-added activities.* They eliminate material handling, inspection, inventory, and rework jobs because they do not add value to the product.
- They *develop the workforce.* They constantly improve job design, training, employee participation and commitment, and work teams.
- They *make jobs more challenging,* pushing responsibility to the lowest level possible. They reduce the number of job classes.

Viewed in this context, we see that traditional production techniques have *limited* goals. For instance, traditionally, managers have accepted the production of some defective parts and some safety stock inventory. Lean producers, on the other hand, set their sights on perfection; no bad parts and no inventory. Lean production requires a commitment to remove continuously those activities that do not add value to the product. It is a learning organization that is constantly improving to produce better, low-cost products faster.

Comparison of Process Choices

Figure 5.1 compares three processes. Advantages exist across the continuum. Unit costs will be less in the continuous process case if high volume exists. While the theoretical cost per unit may be less, we do not always use the continuous processes (that is, specialized equipment and specialized facility). That is too expensive for low volumes and may reduce the ability to customize products. A low-volume, unique good or service is more economical when produced under process focus. However, the idea is to move to the right as far as possible to reduce costs while maintaining the necessary product customization.

NOTE
We are at the beginning of the era where it's practical and economical to build many things one at a time.

FIGURE 5.1

PROCESS CONTINUUM

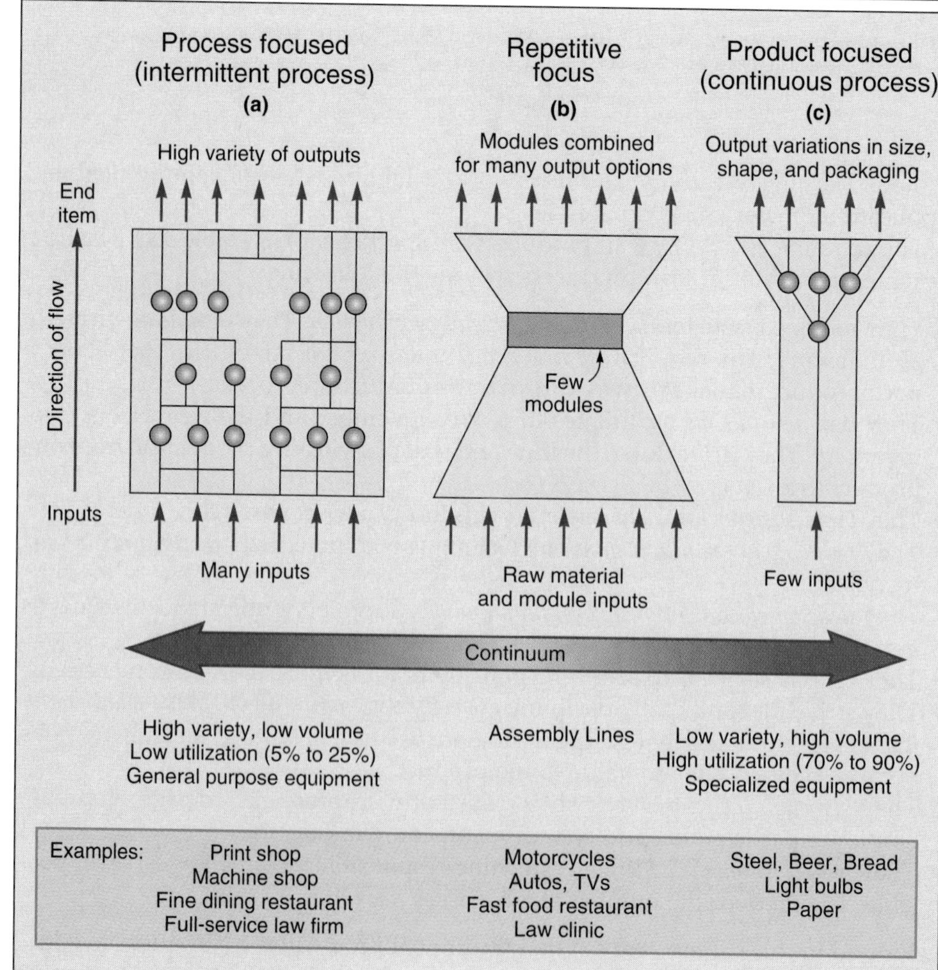

NOTE
McDonald's started the fast-food industry by moving from the left (Process focused) to the right (Product focused) in Figure 5.1.

Restaurants are considered service businesses, but Darden's Red Lobster restaurants are simply the end of a long production line. At the beginning of the line, raw material goes in: at Red Lobster that means 60 million pounds of seafood a year. The seafood is purchased from all over the world. The shrimp arrives in frozen boxes from Ecuador and Thailand at a Red Lobster processing plant in St. Petersburg, Florida. There the shrimp is loaded onto a conveyor belt to be peeled, deveined, cooked, quick frozen (left), sorted (right), and repacked for ultimate delivery to individual restaurants.

MACHINERY, EQUIPMENT, AND TECHNOLOGY

Alternate methods of production are present in virtually all operations functions, whether they are hospitals, restaurants, or manufacturing facilities.

The selection of machinery and equipment can provide competitive advantage. Many firms, for instance, develop a unique machine or technique within the established processes that provides an advantage that can result in added flexibility in meeting customer requirements, lower cost, or higher quality. Modification might also allow for a more stable production process that takes less adjustment, maintenance, and training of operators. In any case, a competitive advantage for winning orders has been developed. For example, Chicago's AM Manufacturing has developed a unique system that can produce a pizza crust that is as crunchy and chewy as the handiwork of a pizza parlor. Untouched by human hands, AM's six-step assembly line takes only three minutes to bake. The crusts are sold in grocery stores for people who want to make their pizzas at home.

Numerical Control

Recent microprocessor developments allow increased flexibility of equipment, particularly when manufacturing discrete items. This is a result of the ease with which the machines can now be reprogrammed because of information technology. The transition from manual and mechanical controls to electronic control has allowed this flexibility. Machines without computer memory but controlled by magnetic tape are called **numerical control (NC)** machines. Machines with their own memory are called **computer numerical control (CNC)** machinery. Electronic

numerical control (NC)

computer numerical control (CNC)

Technology can result in new processes. Shown here is a process developed by Floyd Hammer (right) that converts plastic into weather-resistant park benches, parking lot curbs, and landscaping timbers. Hammer's company, Plastic Recycling Corp., based in Iowa Falls, expects to grow from only 2 plants to more than 16 as this new process provides an environmentally friendly product.

control is accomplished by writing computer programs to control a machine. The computer program is written much as one might write a program to produce a paycheck.

Process Control

process control

Process control is the use of information technology to control a physical process. For instance, process control is used to measure the moisture content and thickness of paper as it travels through a paper machine at a thousand feet per minute. Process control is also used to determine temperatures, pressures, and quantities in petroleum refineries, petrochemical processes, cement plants, steel mills, nuclear reactors, and other continuous processes.

Robots

robot

Where a machine is flexible and has the ability to hold, move, and perhaps "grab" items, we tend to use the word **robot.** However, in spite of movies and cartoons about robots, they are not mechanical people. They are mechanical devices that may have a few electronic impulses stored on a semiconductor chip that will activate motors or switches. When robots are part of a transformation system, they usually provide the movement of material between machines. They may also be used effectively to perform tasks that are especially monotonous, or dangerous, or where the task can be improved by the substitution of mechanical for human effort. This would be the case where consistency, accuracy, speed, or the necessary strength or power can be enhanced by the substitution of machines for people.

Operations managers find competitive advantage wherever they can in the transformation process. For instance, since weekly news magazine printing is simple, the competitive advantage comes from better service when the magazine is distributed. So Britain's Watmough Plc. developed a specialized process that builds pinwheels of magazines holding 14,000 copies each. The pinwheels fit into a newspaper's own binding and sorting machines, so as each newspaper is folded and stacked, a copy of the magazine section is automatically inserted.

Automated Guided Vehicles (AGVs)

automated guided vehicles (AGVs)

Automated material handling can take the form of monorails, conveyers, robots, or automated guided vehicles. **Automated guided vehicles (AGVs)** are electronically guided and controlled carts used in manufacturing to move parts and equipment. They are also used in offices to move mail and in hospitals and jails to deliver meals.

NOTE

Advantages of FMS include: ■ improved capital utilization ■ lower direct labor cost ■ reduced inventory ■ consistent quality

Disadvantages of FMS include: ■ limited ability to adapt to changes in product ■ substantial preplanning and capital ■ tooling and fixture requirements

Flexible Manufacturing System (FMS)

In the sophisticated case, material handling equipment is used to complement direct numerical control (DNC) machines. The material handling equipment can be robots, transfer machines, or automated guided vehicles; it moves materials from one workstation to another. The material handling equipment and the workstation may be connected to a common centralized computer facility, which provides the instructions for routing jobs to the appropriate workstation and the instructions for each workstation. Such an arrangement is an automated work cell or, as it is more commonly known, a **flexible manufacturing system (FMS).**

flexible manufacturing system (FMS)

Robots are used not only for labor savings, but more importantly, for those jobs that are dangerous, monotonous, or require consistency, as in the even spraying of paint on an automobile.

NOTE
Because of capital and technological problems related to network communication, fully operational computer-integrated manufacturing systems (CIM) are still rare.

computer-integrated manufacturing (CIM)

Computer-Integrated Manufacture (CIM)

A flexible manufacturing system can be extended backward electronically into the engineering (computer-aided design), production, and inventory control departments. In this way, computer-aided drafting can ultimately generate the necessary electronic code (instructions) to control a direct numerically controlled (DNC) machine. If this machine is connected to others and to material-handling equipment as a part of a flexible manufacturing system, then the entire system would be **computer-integrated manufacturing (CIM)** (see Figure 5.2).

PROCESS REENGINEERING

reengineering

Process **reengineering** is the fundamental rethinking and radical redesign of business processes to bring about dramatic improvements in performance.[3] Reengineering asks such questions as:

- Is the process designed to create customer value?
- Do we achieve competitive advantage in terms of quality, product, speed of delivery, or price?
- Does the process help us to win orders?
- Does the process maximize the customer's perception of value?

---

[3]Michael Hammer and Steven Stanton, *The Reengineering Revolution* (New York: HarperCollins, 1995), p. 3.

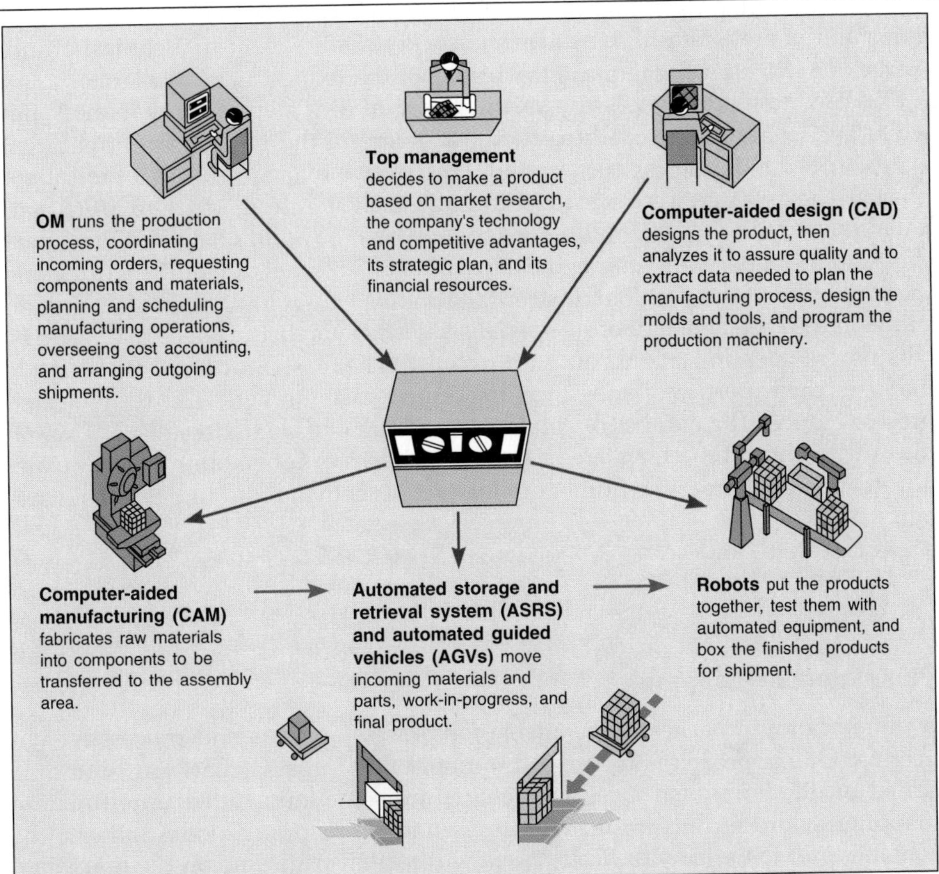

Top management decides to make a product based on market research, the company's technology and competitive advantages, its strategic plan, and its financial resources.
OM runs the production process, coordinating incoming orders, requesting components and materials, planning and scheduling manufacturing operations, overseeing cost accounting, and arranging outgoing shipments.
Computer-aided design (CAD) designs the product, then analyzes it to assure quality and to extract data needed to plan the manufacturing process, design the molds and tools, and program the production machinery.
Computer-aided manufacturing (CAM) fabricates raw materials into components to be transferred to the assembly area.
Automated storage and retrieval system (ASRS) and automated guided vehicles (AGVs) move incoming materials and parts, work-in-progress, and final product.
Robots put the products together, test them with automated equipment, and box the finished products for shipment.

FIGURE 5.2

COMPUTER-INTEGRATED MANUFACTURING (CIM)

Computer-aided design (CAD), computer-aided manufacturing (CAM), and flexible manufacturing systems (FMSs), brought together with automated storage and retrieval systems (ASRSs) and automated guided vehicles (AGVs).

Process reengineering means reevaluating the purpose of the process and questioning those purposes and assumptions. Process reengineering only works if the basic process and objectives are reexamined. Often a firm finds that the initial assumptions of its process are no longer valid.

By focusing on business *processes* we focus on those activities that cross functional lines. Because managers are usually in charge of specific "functions" or a specialized area of responsibility, those activities (processes) that cross from one function or specialty to another may be neglected. Therefore, process reengineering often finds a fertile ground in these areas. Reengineering casts aside all notions of how the process is currently being done and focuses on dynamic improvements in cost, time, or customer service. Any process is a candidate for radical redesign. The process can be a factory layout, a purchasing procedure, or a new way of processing credit applications at IBM as described in Example 1.

EXAMPLE 1

The traditional IBM credit application process took many steps. The first step consisted of 14 people answering phones and logging calls from field sales personnel who were requesting credit for their customers. After receiving the calls, the phone personnel made paper notations that they sent upstairs to credit personnel for a credit check. Then the paper went down the hall to the business practice's group where they entered the data into a computer for determination of terms and interest rates. From there the packet of data went to a clerical group. A week or two after the request, the results of the request were available.

IBM tried to fix the process by keeping a log of each step of every request. But while this logging allowed them to know where in the process the application was, it added a day to the turnaround. Finally, two managers tried a radical approach. They walked a loan request through each step from office to office, and found that it took only 90 minutes of actual work. The additional week was spent shuttling the paperwork among the departments. This meant that the work along the way was not the problem. Instead, the *process* was at fault. Reengineering resulted in IBM replacing all of its specialists with generalists, called case workers, who process an application from start to finish. The firm also developed software that uses the expertise of specialists to support case workers. The reengineered process reduced the number of employees and achieved better results. The week-plus turn-around time for a credit request is down to four hours. The company now handles 100 times the number of loan requests than it did under the old system.

Adapted from: Michael Hammer and James Campy, *Reengineering the Corporation, A Manifesto for Business Revolution* (New York: HarperCollins, 1993).

Time-Function Mapping

time-function mapping

process mapping

A number of approaches are available for process analysis and process reengineering. One approach is to use a traditional flow process chart but with time added on the horizontal axis. Such charts are sometimes called **time-function mapping** or **process mapping.** With time-function mapping, nodes indicate the activities and the arrows indicate the flow direction with time on the horizontal

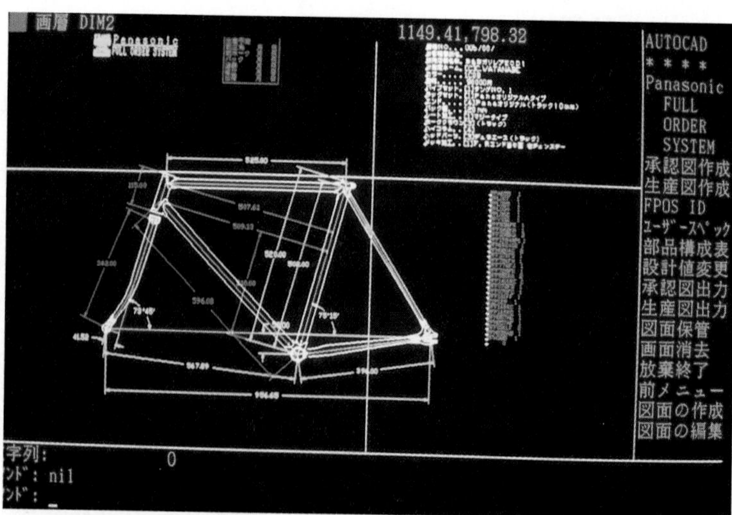

Flexible manufacturing can improve customer service and provide a competitive advantage. National Bicycle's customized Panasonic bicycle production process begins by defining individual customer needs. The customer mounts the special frame in a Panasonic bicycle store from which measurements are taken. These custom measurements are sent to the factory where CAD software produces a blueprint in about three minutes. At the same time, a bar-code label is prepared that will identify bicycle components as they move through production. Time—from beginning to end—is only three hours.

(a)

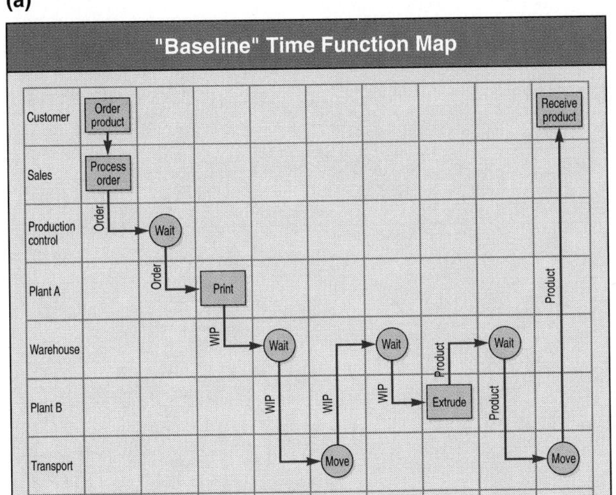

(b)

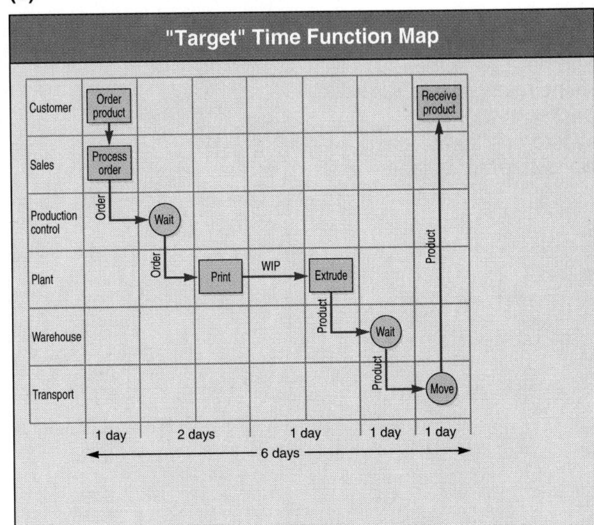

FIGURE 5.3 TIME-FUNCTION MAPPING (PROCESS MAPPING) FOR A PRODUCT REQUIRING PRINTING AND EXTRUDING OPERATIONS AT AMERICAN NATIONAL CAN COMPANY

This example shows that 46 days can be eliminated for a product that requires printing and extruding operations.

SOURCE: Elaine J. Labach, "Faster, Better, and Cheaper." *Target* 7, no. 5 (Winter 1991): 43.

axis. This type of analysis provides identification of waste in the form of extra steps, duplication, and time so that they can be eliminated. Figure 5.3(a) shows the use of process mapping prior to reengineering and Figure 5.3(b) shows the process after reengineering. In this example, process reengineering at American National Can Co. resulted in a savings of 46 days.

Work-Flow Analysis

A second reengineering technique, known as work-flow analysis, mimics the way people communicate. The idea is that everyone in an organization is a customer or a performer depending on the precise transaction. **Work-flow analysis** documents a network of transactions between customers and performance. The objective of each transaction is to achieve customer satisfaction. Work-flow analysis involves four phases:

work-flow analysis

1. *Request* from a customer or an offer to provide services by a performer.
2. *Negotiation,* which allows the customer and the performer to agree on how the work should be done and what will constitute customer satisfaction.
3. *Performance* of the assignment and completion.
4. *Acceptance,* which closes the transaction provided the customer expresses satisfaction and agrees that the conditions were met.

Transactions can be very complex in a large organization with a multitude of loops between customers and performers. Therefore this type of analysis is typically

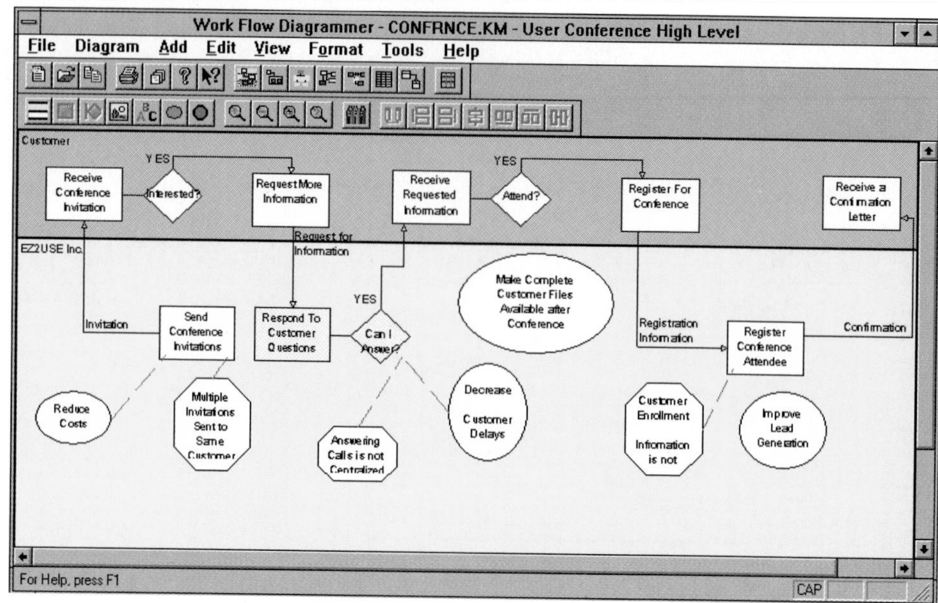

A number of computer software packages exist to help with work flow modeling and business process reengineering. One such package is *Key for Workgroup* from Sterling Software, Inc., Atlanta.

done with computer programs that help chart various work flows. (See photo of work-flow software by Sterling Software, Inc.)

CHOOSING A SERVICE PROCESS STRATEGY

Figure 5.1 can be applied to services as well as manufacturing. For instance, empirical evidence suggests that much of the service industry is producing in very small lots. This is probably true for legal services, medical services, dental services, and restaurants. They are often producing in lot sizes as small as one. Such organizations would be to the left of Figure 5.1.

Service-Sector Considerations

As Figure 5.1 indicates, in process-focused facilities, equipment utilization is low—perhaps as low as 5%. This is true not only for manufacturing but also for services. An x-ray machine in a dentist's office and much of the equipment in a fine dining restaurant have low utilization. Hospitals, too, can be expected to be in that range, which would suggest why their costs are considered high. Why such low utilization? In part because excess capacity for peak loads is desirable. Hospital administrators, as well as managers of other service facilities and their patients and customers, expect equipment to be available as needed. Another reason utilization is low is poor scheduling (although substantial efforts have been made to forecast demand in the service industry) and the resulting imbalance in the use of facilities.

The service industry moves to the right of Figure 5.1 by establishing fast-food restaurants, legal clinics, auto lubrication shops, auto tune-up shops, and so on. As the variety of services is reduced, we would expect per-unit cost to drop also. This is typically what happens.

Customer Interaction and Process Strategy

Customer interaction is an important variable in process decisions. In a process that directly interfaces with the customer, one expects the customer to affect process performance adversely. Activities in the service sector are a good example. In a restaurant, a medical facility, a law office, or a retail store, too much interaction between the customer and the process keeps the process from operating as smoothly as it otherwise might. Individual attention and customizing of the product or service for the customer can play havoc with a process. The more the process can be insulated from the customer's unique requirements, the lower will be the cost.

While services can be thought of as falling on the process continuum shown in Figure 5.1, the four quadrants in Figure 5.4 (a) and (b) provide more insight into service processes. The ten operations management decisions we introduced in Chapter 2 are used with a different emphasis in each of these quadrants. For instance:

- In the upper sections (quadrants) of *mass service* and *professional service*, where *labor intensity is high*, we expect the manager to focus extensively on human resources. This is particularly true in the quadrant with *high interaction and customization*. These quadrants require that managers find ways of addressing unique issues to satisfy these customers. This is often done with very personalized service, some of which requires high labor intensity and therefore significant selection and training issues in the human resources area.
- The quadrants with *low interaction and low customization* may be able to: (1) standardize or restrict some offerings of the service, as do fast food restaurants, (2)

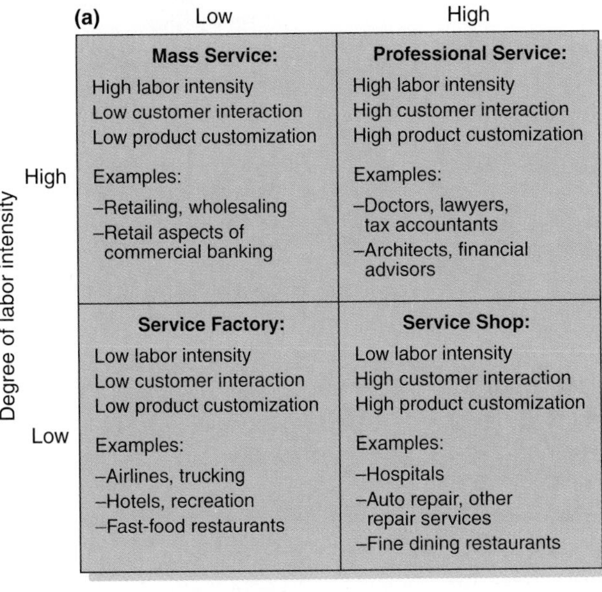

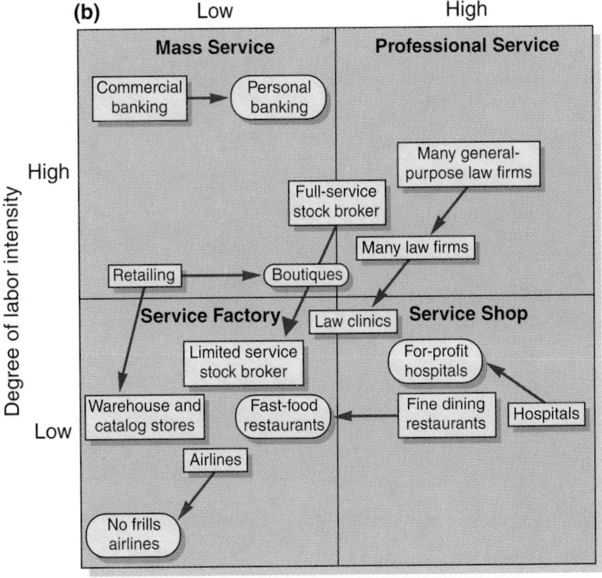

FIGURE 5.4 **(a) THE SERVICE PROCESS MATRIX (b) OPERATION CHANGES WITHIN THE SERVICE PROCESS MATRIX**

SOURCE: Adapted from work by Roger Schmenner, "How Can Service Business Survive and Prosper?" *Sloan Management Review* (Spring 1986): 21–32.

automate, as have some airlines which have ticket vending machines, or (3) remove some services, such as seat assignments, as has Southwest Airlines. Off-loading some aspect of the service through automation may require innovations in process design as well as capital investment. Such was the case with airline ticket vending and bank ATMs. This move to standardization and automation may require added capital expenditure, as well as putting operations managers under pressure to develop new skills for the purchase and maintenance of such equipment. A reduction in a customization capability will require added strength in other areas.

- Because customer feedback is lower in the quadrants with low interaction, tight control may be required to maintain quality standards.
- Those operations with a *low labor intensity* may lend themselves particularly well to innovations in process, technology, and scheduling capability.

These service process strategies can be summarized as: (1) separation of unique customer requirements from the high cost personal service, (2) automation, (3) excellent scheduling, and (4) outstanding training. Some of these ideas are shown in Table 5.2.

TABLE 5.2 TECHNIQUES USED TO IMPROVE OPERATIONS PRODUCTIVITY IN SERVICES

STRATEGY	TECHNIQUE	EXAMPLE
Separation	*Restricting* the offerings	Limited-menu restaurant
	Customizing at delivery	Customizing vans at delivery rather than at production
	Structuring service so customers must go where the service is offered	Banks where customers go to a manager to open a new account, to loan officers for loans, and to tellers for deposits
	Self-service so customers examine, compare, and evaluate at their own pace	Supermarkets or department stores
	Modular selection of service	Investment and insurance selection
Automation	*Separating services* that may lend themselves to some type of automation	Automatic teller machines
Scheduling	Precise personnel *scheduling*	Scheduling ticket counter personnel at 15-minute intervals at airlines
Training	*Clarifying the service* options	Investment counselor, funeral directors
	Explaining problems	After-sale maintenance personnel

Other Service Process Opportunities

LAYOUT. Layout is an integral part of any production process, particularly in retailing, banking, and dining. In retailing it can provide not only product exposure, but also customer education and product enhancement. In restaurants, layout can enhance the dining experience as well as provide an effective flow in both the kitchen and dining area. In banks, layout provides security as well as work flow and personal comfort. Because layout is such an integral part of many services, it provides continuing opportunity for winning orders. Similarly, staffing and training, because of high customer-client interaction and high labor intensity in some services, also provides another opportunity for competitive advantage.

TECHNOLOGY. Technology can also help improve services. Andersen Windows of Bayport, Minnesota, the world's largest maker of wooden windows and patio doors, is improving the service part of its manufacturing business through automation. Much in the way automatic teller machines improve customer banking services, Andersen Windows has developed computer software that enables customers to design their own window specifications. The customer, with user-friendly software, calls up a product information guide, promotion material, gallery of designs, and sketch pad to create the designs desired. The software also allows customers to determine their likely energy savings and see a graphic view of their home with the new window. It goes so far as to determine the product numbers and create a price and order list that initiates the order entry process.

Process improvement takes place in the agriculture industry as well as in services and manufacturing. Here is a machine that uses a hollow tube to punch a hole in an egg shell, pushes the tube an inch inside the egg, and squirts in vaccine. Then the tube pulls out to be sterilized and reused. The result is a vaccination line that processes eggs instead of live chicks. Vaccination of eggs means no traumatized chicks, which results in faster growing chicks that are better able to resist infections. Additionally, automation has lowered cost by reducing the manpower required for vaccination.

Similarly, computers and electronic communications in retail stores download prices quickly to reflect changing costs or market conditions. For instance, when devaluation struck Mexico, Farmacias Benavides[4] used computer systems to immediately stop the reorders of higher priced items and to stock up instead on lower cost generic product lines.

In the remainder of this chapter we deal with three issues that help managers choose the correct process. Those issues are capacity, break-even analysis, and the investment itself.

CAPACITY

After considering the process options, a number of issues remain. Because determining the size of a facility is critical to a firm's success, we now investigate the concepts and techniques of capacity planning. First, we note how a firm can manage its demand, given that a certain capacity exists. We then use forecasting to help us evaluate capacity requirements.

Capacity Management

capacity

Capacity is the maximum output of a system in a given period. Capacity is normally expressed as a rate, such as the number of tons of steel that can be produced per week, per month, or per year. For many companies, measuring capacity can be straightforward. It is the maximum number of units that can be produced in a specific time. However, for some organizations, determining capacity can be more difficult. Capacity can be measured in terms of beds (a hospital), active members (a church), or the number of counselors (a drug abuse program). Other organizations use total work time available as a measure of overall capacity.

Most organizations operate their facilities at a rate less than the capacity. They do so because they have found that they can operate more efficiently when their resources are not stretched to the limit. Instead they operate at perhaps 92% of capacity. This concept is called effective capacity or utilization.

effective capacity or utilization

Effective capacity or utilization is simply the percent of design capacity actually expected. It can be computed from the following formula:

$$\text{Effective capacity or utilization} = \frac{\text{Expected capacity}}{\text{Capacity}}$$

Effective capacity or utilization is the capacity a firm can *expect* to achieve given its product mix, methods of scheduling, maintenance, and standards of quality.

Another consideration is efficiency. Depending on how facilities are used and managed, it may be difficult or impossible to reach 100% efficiency. Typically,

efficiency

efficiency is expressed as a percentage of the effective capacity. Efficiency is a measure of actual output over effective capacity:

$$\text{Efficiency} = \frac{\text{Actual output}}{\text{Effective capacity}}$$

[4]"Who's Afraid of Wal-Mart?" *Forbes*, July 31, 1995, p. 81.

The **rated capacity** is a measure of the maximum usable capacity of a particular facility. Rated capacity will always be less than or equal to the capacity. The equation used to compute rated capacity is given below:

rated capacity

$$\text{Rated capacity} = (\text{Capacity})(\text{Utilization})(\text{Efficiency})$$

We determine rated capacity in the following example.

EXAMPLE 2

The Sara James Bakery has a plant for processing breakfast rolls. The facility has an efficiency of 90%, and the utilization is 80%. Three process lines are used to produce the rolls. The lines operate seven days a week and three eight-hour shifts per day. Each line was designed to process 120 standard (that is, plain) rolls per hour. What is the rated capacity?

SOLUTION

In order to compute the rated capacity, we multiply the design capacity (which is equal to the number of lines times the number of hours times the number of rolls per hour) times the utilization times the efficiency. Each facility is used seven days a week, three shifts a day. Therefore, each process line is utilized for 168 hours per week (168 = 7 days × 3 shifts per day × 8 hours per shift). With this information, the rated capacity can be determined. This is done below.

$$\begin{aligned}\text{Rated capacity} &= (\text{Capacity})(\text{Utilization})(\text{Efficiency})\\ &= [(3)(168)(120)](.8)(.9) = 43{,}546 \text{ rolls per week}\end{aligned}$$

Forecasting Capacity Requirements

Determining future capacity requirements can be a complicated procedure, one based in large part on future demand. When demand for goods and services can be forecasted with a reasonable degree of precision, determining capacity requirements can be straightforward. It normally requires two phases. During the first phase, future demand is forecasted with traditional methods. During the second phase, this forecast is used to determine capacity requirements.

Once the rated capacity has been forecasted, the next step is to determine the incremental size of each addition to capacity. At this point the assumption is made that management knows the technology and the *type* of facilities to be employed to satisfy these future demand requirements.

Figure 5.5 reveals how new capacity can be planned for future demand growth. As seen in Figure 5.5(a), new capacity is acquired at the beginning of year one. This capacity will be sufficient to handle increased demand until the beginning of year two. At the beginning of year two, new capacity is again acquired, which will allow the organization to meet demand until the beginning of year three. This process can be continued indefinitely into the future.

The capacity plan shown in Figure 5.5(a) is only one of an almost limitless number of plans to satisfy future demand. In this figure, new capacity was acquired at the beginning of year one and at the beginning of year two. In Figure 5.5(b), a large increase in capacity is acquired at the beginning of year one, which will satisfy future demand until the beginning of year three.

FIGURE 5.5

TWO APPROACHES TO ADDING CAPACITY

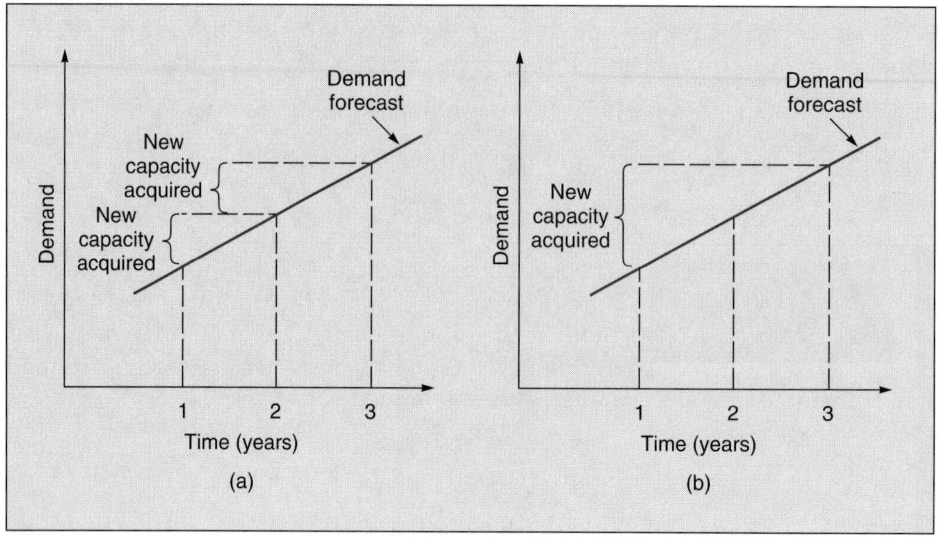

Figures 5.5(a) and 5.5(b) reveal only two possible alternatives. In some cases, deciding between alternatives can be relatively easy. The total cost of each alternative can be computed, and the alternative with the least total cost can be selected. In other cases, determining the capacity of future facilities can be much more complicated. In most cases, numerous subjective factors are difficult to quantify and measure. These factors include technological options; actions by competitors; building restrictions; cost of capital; human resource options; and local, state, and federal laws and regulations.

Demand Management

A manager may have the ability to alter demand. In the case where *demand exceeds capacity,* the firm may be able to curtail demand simply by raising prices, scheduling long lead times (which may be inevitable), and discouraging marginally profitable business. In the case where capacity *exceeds demand,* the firm may want to stimulate demand through price reductions or aggressive marketing, or accommodate the market in a better way through product changes.

Unused facilities (that is, excess capacity) mean excess fixed costs; inadequate facilities reduce revenue below what is possible. Therefore, various tactics for matching capacity to demand exist. Internal changes include adjusting the process to a given volume through:

1. Staffing changes.
2. Adjusting equipment and processes, which might include purchasing additional machinery or selling or leasing existing equipment.
3. Improving methods to increase throughput.
4. Redesigning the product to facilitate more throughput.

Another capacity issue with which management may be confronted is a seasonal or cyclical pattern of demand. In such cases management may find it helpful to find products with complementing demand patterns, that is, products for which the demand is the opposite. For example, in Figure 5.6 the firm is adding

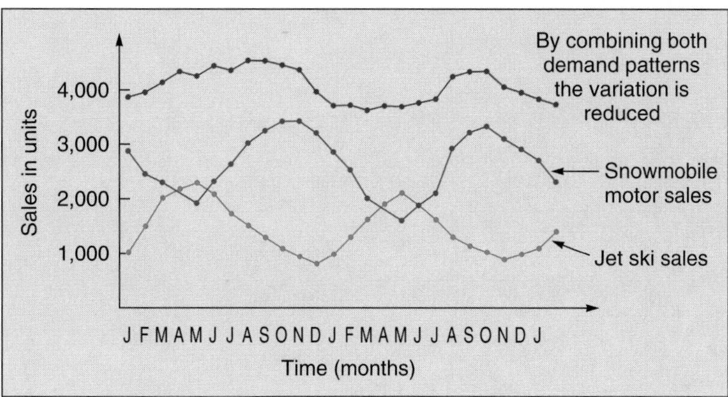

FIGURE 5.6

By Combining Products That Have Complementary Seasonal Patterns, Capacity Can Be Better Utilized

A smoother demand for sales also contributes to improved scheduling and better human resource strategies.

a line of snowmobile engines to its line of Jet Skis to smooth demand. With appropriate complementing products, perhaps the utilization of facility, equipment, and personnel can be smoothed.

Break-Even Analysis

break-even analysis

The objective of **break-even analysis** is to find the point, in dollars and units, at which costs equal revenues. This point is the break-even point. Break-even analysis requires an estimation of fixed cost, variable cost, and revenue. We will proceed by first defining the fixed and variable costs and then the revenue function.

fixed costs

variable costs

Fixed costs are costs that continue even if no units are produced. Examples include depreciation, taxes, debt, and mortgage payments. **Variable costs** are those that vary with the volume of units produced. The major components of variable costs are labor and materials. However, other costs, such as the portion of the utilities that varies with volume, are also variable costs.

revenue function

Another element in break-even analysis is the **revenue function.** It begins at the origin and proceeds upward to the right, increasing by the selling price of each unit. This revenue line is shown in Figure 5.7. Where the revenue function crosses the total cost line is the break-even point, with a profit corridor to the right and a loss corridor to the left. The profit-and-loss corridors are also shown in Figure 5.7.

NOTE
Fixed costs do not remain constant over all volume; new warehouses and new overhead charges result in step functions in fixed cost.

ASSUMPTIONS. A number of assumptions underlie this basic break-even model. Notably, costs and revenue are shown as straight lines. They are shown to increase linearly, that is, in direct proportion to the volume of units being produced. However, neither fixed costs nor variable costs (nor, for that matter, the revenue function) need be a straight line. For example, fixed costs change as more capital equipment or warehouse space is used; labor costs change with overtime or as marginally skilled workers are employed; and the revenue function may change with such factors as volume discounts.

NOTE
Virtually *no* variable costs are linear, but we make that assumption here.

FIGURE 5.7

BASIC BREAK-EVEN ANALYSIS

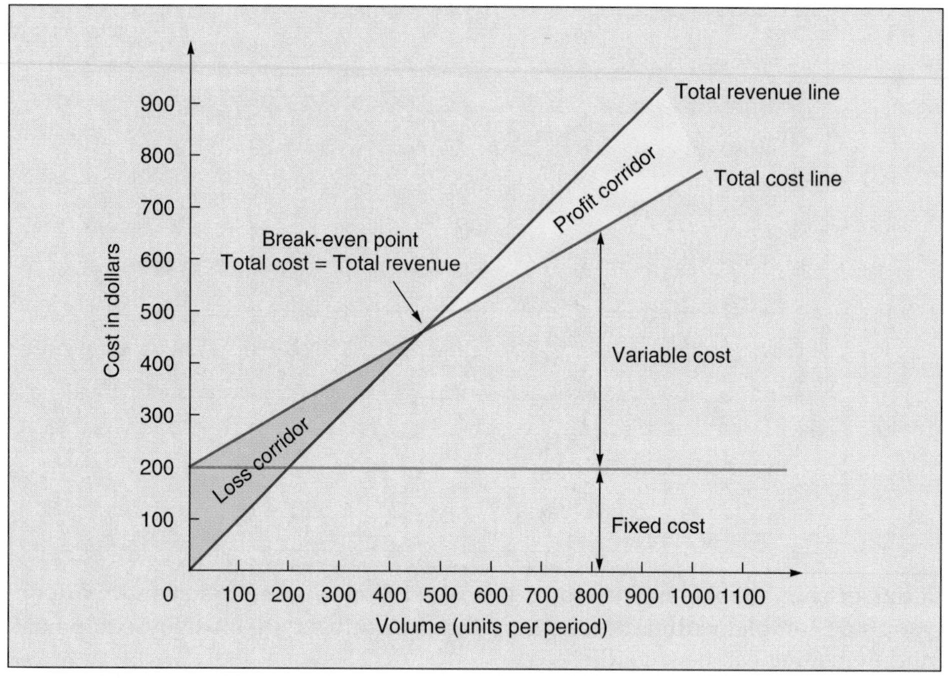

GRAPHIC APPROACH. The first step in the graphic approach to break-even analysis is to define those costs that are fixed and sum them. The variable costs are then estimated by an analysis of labor, materials, and other costs connected with the production of each unit. The fixed costs are drawn as a horizontal line beginning at that dollar amount on the vertical axis. The variable costs are then shown as an incrementally increasing cost, originating at the intersection of the fixed cost on the vertical axis and increasing with each change in volume as we move to the right on the volume (or horizontal) axis. Both fixed and variable cost information is usually available from a firm's cost accounting department, although an industrial engineering department may also maintain cost information.

ALGEBRAIC APPROACH. The respective formulas for the break-even point in units and dollars are shown below. Let:

$BEP(x)$ = Break-even point in units

$BEP(\$)$ = Break-even point in dollars

P = Price per unit (dollars received per unit after all discounts)

x = Number of units produced

TR = Total revenue = Px

F = Fixed costs

V = Variable costs per unit

TC = Total costs = $F + Vx$

Setting total revenue equal to total costs, we get

$$TR = TC$$

or

$$Px = F + Vx$$

Solving for x, we get

$$BEP(x) = \frac{F}{P - V}$$

and

$$\begin{aligned} BEP(\$) &= BEP(x)P \\ &= \frac{F}{P - V} P = \frac{F}{(P - V)/P} \\ &= \frac{F}{1 - V/P} \end{aligned}$$

$$\begin{aligned} \text{Profit} &= TR - TC \\ &= Px - (F + Vx) \\ &= Px - F - Vx \\ &= (P - V)x - F \end{aligned}$$

Using these equations, we can solve directly for break-even point and profitability. The two formulas that are of particular interest are:

$$\text{Break-even in units} = \frac{\text{Total fixed cost}}{\text{Price} - \text{Variable cost}} \qquad (5.1)$$

$$\text{Break-even in dollars} = \frac{\text{Total fixed cost}}{1 - \dfrac{\text{Variable cost}}{\text{Selling price}}} \qquad (5.2)$$

CROSSOVER CHARTS. Break-even analysis can aid process selection by identifying the processes with the lowest total cost for the volume expected. Such analysis will, of course, also indicate the largest profit corridor. We are, therefore, able to address two issues: the low-cost process and the absolute amount of profit. Only by directly addressing both issues can the process decision be successful. Figure 5.8 shows three alternative processes compared on a single chart. Such a chart is sometimes called a **crossover chart.** Process A has the lowest cost for volumes below V_1, process B has the lowest cost between V_1 and V_2, and process C has the lowest cost at volumes above V_2.

crossover chart

In Example 3 we determine the break-even point in dollars and units for one product.

FIGURE 5.8

CROSSOVER CHARTS

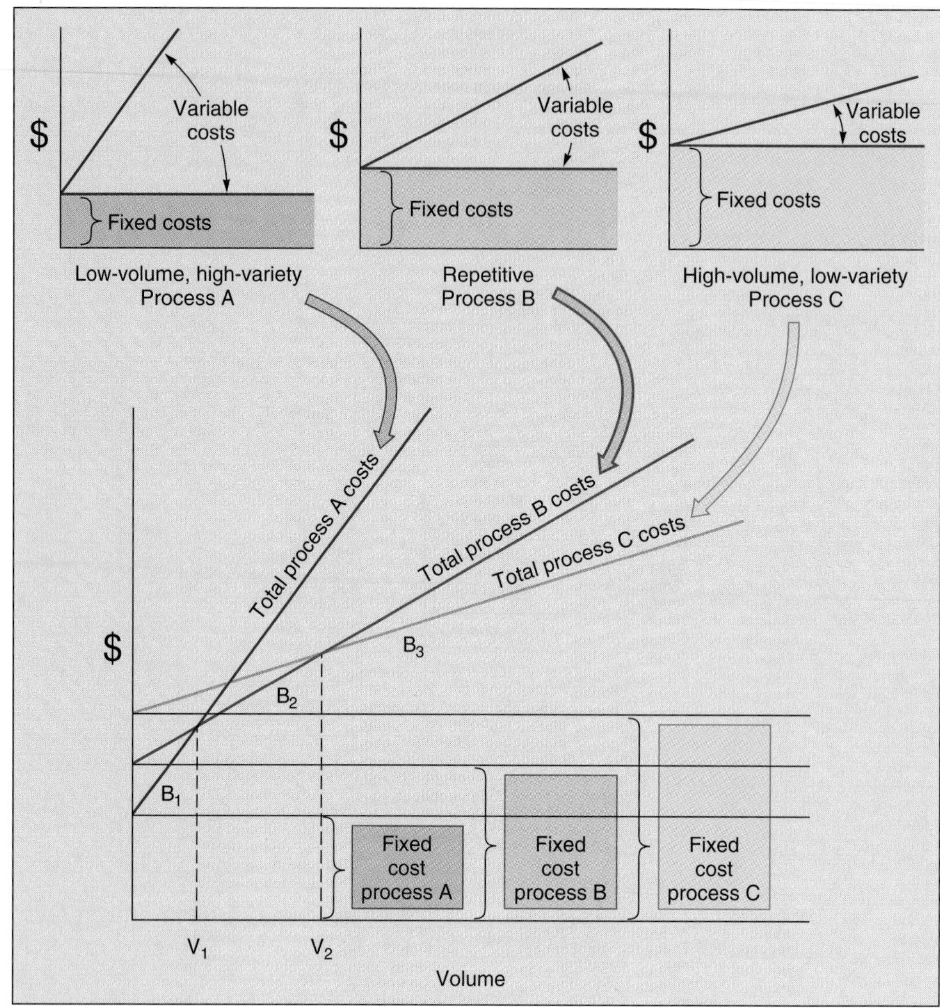

Three different processes can be expected to have three different costs. However, at any given volume, only one will have the lowest cost.

EXAMPLE 3

Smith, Inc., has fixed costs of $10,000 this period. Direct labor is $1.50 per unit, and material is $.75 per unit. The selling price is $4.00 per unit.

The break-even point in dollars is computed as follows:

$$BEP(\$) = \frac{F}{1 - (V/P)} = \frac{\$10{,}000}{1 - [(1.50 + .75)/(4.00)]} = \frac{\$10{,}000}{.4375} = \$22{,}857.14$$

and the break-even point in units is:

$$BEP(x) = \frac{F}{P - V} = \frac{\$10{,}000}{4.00 - (1.50 + .75)} = 5{,}714$$

Note that, in this example, we must use the *total* variable costs (that is, both labor and material).

BREAK-EVEN ANALYSIS APPLIED TO CAPACITY DECISIONS. The impact of capacity decisions can be shown through the use of break-even analysis. This is shown in Figure 5.8. If the forecast volume is lower than actual volume, the firm may have chosen the wrong process. Then higher per-unit cost will result because the firm is operating with the wrong process, say point B_1, rather than at point B_2 or B_3. A capacity decided upon at the time the process was selected is difficult to change.

Additionally, the farther to the right of the continuum (referring back to Figure 5.1), the more likely it is that equipment and process units will be in large and costly chunks. If demand fluctuates or is uncertain, then process flexibility may be particularly important. Altering the size of a continuous-oriented process often means a major redesign and substantial expense. There is more flexibility on the left of the continuum, where modest changes are possible.

MAKING THE INVESTMENT

Increasingly, managers realize that sustained profits come from building competitive advantage, not from a good financial return on a specific process.[5] A good

NOTE
The production manager in large part may be the one held responsible for return on investment.

These paper machines, recently upgraded at a cost of $500 million by International Paper in Texarkana, Texas, produce bleached board. Bleached board is used in cigarette cartons, signs, pharmaceutical boxes, and so on. International Paper is one of the world's largest and most efficient producers of bleached board. This huge capital expenditure will result in a high fixed cost but will allow production of these products at a very low variable cost. The production manager's job is to maintain utilization above the break-even point to achieve profitability.

[5]For an excellent discussion on investments that support competitive advantage, see Terry Hill, *Manufacturing Strategy: Text and Cases* (Homewood, IL: Irwin, 1989). Also see "Selling Rockwell on Automation," *Business Week*, June 6, 1988, p. 104.

financial return is only one criterion for a new investment. Improving competitive position in the long run is the primary criterion. A short-term focus on financial return is usually self-defeating. Proposals to invest in processes that increase production flexibility, product quality, or breadth of the product line may be difficult to support if the focus is solely on return on investment.

Strategy-Driven Investments

We recommend that the traditional approach to investment analysis (just looking at financial returns) be enhanced by strategic considerations. Specifically, we suggest the following strategic considerations:

1. That investments be made as *part of a coordinated strategic plan.* Where are these investments taking the organization? Investments should not be made as isolated expenditures, but as part of a coordinated strategic plan that will place the firm in an advantageous position. The question to be asked is, "Will these investments eventually win customers?"
2. That investments *yield a competitive advantage* (flexibility of process, speed of delivery, quality, and so on).
3. That investments *consider product life cycles.*
4. That a *variety of operating factors be included in the financial return analysis* (for instance, reductions in scrap, rework, floor space, and inventory increase returns).
5. That investments be *tested in light of several revenue projections* to ensure that upside potential and down-side risk are considered.

Once the strategy implications of potential investments have been considered, traditional investment analysis is appropriate.

Investment, Variable Cost, and Cash Flow

NOTE
Capital investment requires cash flow, as well as an evaluation of return on investments.

Because process alternatives exist, so do options with regard to capital investment and variable cost. Managers must choose from among different financial alternatives as well as process alternatives. The number of initial alternatives may be large, but analysis of six major factors (cost, volume, human resource constraints, technology, quality, and reliability) typically reduces the number of alternatives to a few. Analysis should show the capital investment, variable cost, and cash flows for each alternative. The impact of cash flows, as well as the absolute investment, may influence process selection.

In addition to capital, variable cost, and cash flow considerations, management may want to consider the time value of money when evaluating investments. This can be done via net present value, payback, or internal rate-of-return. We will leave further discussion of those topics to a finance text.

SUMMARY

The processes that operations managers use to perform transformations can be as important as the products themselves. Transformation processes determine much of the cost, as well as quantity and quality of the product. The process decision can result in selection of a transformation system that is process focused or product focused or someplace in between. However, it must be of a capacity and technology that will provide a competitive advantage with a strategy of faster, better, or less expensive.

Good forecasting, break-even analysis, crossover charts, and capacity decisions are particularly useful to operations managers when making the process decision.

KEY TERMS

Process decision *(p. 170)*
Intermittent processes *(p. 171)*
Process focus *(p. 171)*
Product focus *(p. 171)*
Continuous process *(p. 171)*
Repetitive processes *(p. 172)*
Modules *(p. 172)*
Lean producers *(p. 172)*
Numerical control (NC) *(p. 175)*
Computer numerical control (CNC) *(p. 175)*
Process control *(p. 176)*
Robot *(p. 176)*
Automated guided vehicles (AGVs) *(p. 177)*
Flexible manufacturing system (FMS) *(p. 177)*
Computer-integrated manufacturing (CIM) *(p. 178)*
Reengineering *(p. 178)*
Time-function mapping *(p. 180)*
Process mapping *(p. 180)*
Work-flow analysis *(p. 181)*
Capacity *(p. 186)*
Effective capacity or utilization *(p. 186)*
Efficiency *(p. 186)*
Rated capacity *(p. 187)*
Break-even analysis *(p. 189)*
Fixed costs *(p. 189)*
Variable costs *(p. 189)*
Revenue function *(p. 189)*
Crossover chart *(p. 191)*

SOLVED PROBLEM 5.1

Joe Biggs works part-time making canoe paddles in Wisconsin. His annual fixed cost is \$10,000, direct labor is \$3.50 per paddle, and material is \$4.50 per paddle. The selling price will be \$12.50 per paddle. What is break-even in dollars? What is break-even in units?

SOLUTION

$$BEP(\$) = \frac{F}{1 - V/P} = \frac{\$10{,}000}{1 - (\$8.00/\$12.50)} = \frac{\$10{,}000}{.36} = \$27{,}777$$

$$BEP(x) = \frac{F}{P - V} = \frac{\$10{,}000}{\$12.50 - \$8.00} = \frac{\$10{,}000}{\$4.50} = 2{,}222 \text{ units}$$

SOLVED PROBLEM 5.2

Sara James Bakery, described earlier in Examples 1 and 2, has decided to increase its facilities by adding one additional process line. The firm will have four process lines, each working seven days a week, three shifts per day, eight hours per shift. Utilization is 90%. This addition, however, will reduce their overall system efficiency to 85%. Compute the new rated capacity with this change in facilities.

SOLUTION

Rated capacity

$$= \text{Capacity} \times \text{Utilization} \times \text{Efficiency}$$

$$= [(120)(4 \times 7 \times 3 \times 8)] \times (.9) \times (.85)$$

$$= (80{,}640) \times (.9) \times (.85)$$

$$= 61{,}689.6 \text{ per week}$$

or

$$= 120 \times 4 \times .9 \times .85$$

$$= 367.2 \text{ per hour.}$$

SOLVED PROBLEM 5.3

Chazen Yogurt's new store in Demarest, New Jersey, sells several thousand pounds of yogurt each month. Because of expanding sales, Cynthia Chazen would like to know when to schedule delivery of the next display freezer. She wants to have a freezer for each 1,000 pounds sold in a month. She now has five display freezers. Using least square regression (a topic explored in Chapter 2 Supplement), determine in which month she needs the next freezer (that is, in which month will she exceed her 5,000-lb capacity?).

Sales for months 1 to 5 are (in 1,000 lbs): 4.2, 4.1, 4.4, 4.6, and 4.5.

SOLUTION

We now determine the intercept, a, the slope, b, and the regression equation to solve for the forecasted value, $\hat{y}$, which equals a + bx, ie, $\hat{y} = a + bx$

$$\text{Slope} = b = \frac{\Sigma xy - n\overline{x}\overline{y}}{\Sigma x^2 - n\overline{x}^2}$$

and y intercept $= a = \overline{y} - b\overline{x}$

x (month)	y (lbs in 1000)	x^2	xy
1	4.2	1	4.2
2	4.1	4	8.2
3	4.4	9	13.2
4	4.6	16	18.4
5	4.5	25	22.5
$\Sigma x = 15$	$\Sigma y = 21.8$	$\Sigma x^2 = 55$	$\Sigma xy = 66.5$

$$\overline{x} = \frac{\Sigma x}{n} = \frac{15}{5} = 3 \qquad \overline{y} = \frac{\Sigma y}{n} = \frac{21.8}{5} = 4.36$$

$$b = \frac{(66.5) - (5)(3)(4.36)}{(55) - (5)(9)} = \frac{66.5 - 65.4}{10} = \frac{1.1}{10} = .11$$

(or 110 lbs. slope)

$$a = 4.36 - (.11)(3) = 4.36 - (.33) = 4.03$$

(or 4,030-lb intercept)

She now has capacity for 5,000 lbs, which is 970 lbs above the intercept.

At 110 lbs increase per month, how many months will it take to get to 970 lbs? The answer is 970/110 = 8.82 months.

Therefore, during month 8 Chazen will need her additional freezer.

DISCUSSION QUESTIONS

1. What are the advantages of standardization? How do we obtain variety while maintaining standardization?
2. What type of process is used for each of the following?
   a. beer
   b. business cards
   c. automobiles
   d. telephone
   e. "Big Macs"
   f. custom homes
3. In an affluent society, how do we produce a wide number of options for products at low cost?
4. What products would you expect to have made by a repetitive process?
5. Where does the manager obtain data for break-even analysis?
6. What keeps plotted variable and fixed-cost data from falling on a straight line?
7. What keeps plotted revenue data from falling on straight line?
8. What are the assumptions of break-even analysis?
9. How might we isolate the production/operations process from the customer?
10. Identify two services located at the process focus side of the process continuum (Figure 5.1).
11. Distinguish between flexible manufacturing systems (FMS) and computer-integrated manufacturing (CIM).

SELF-TEST ■ CHAPTER 5

- *Before taking the self-test* refer back to the learning objectives listed at the beginning of the chapter and the key terms listed at the end of the chapter.
- Use the key at the back of the text to *correct* your answers.
- *Restudy* pages that correspond to any questions you answered incorrectly or material you feel uncertain about.

1. Low-volume, high-variety processes are also known as
   a. continuous processes
   b. intermittent processes
   c. repetitive processes
   d. product focused

2. Efficiency is given by
   a. expected capacity divided by capacity
   b. capacity divided by utilization
   c. actual output divided by effective capacity

3. Advantages of a flexible manufacturing system (FMS) include
   a. lower direct labor cost
   b. consistent and perhaps better quality
   c. reduced inventory
   d. all of the above

4. The maximum output of a system in a given period is called
   a. the break-even point
   b. the capacity
   c. all of the above

5. Costs that continue even if no units are produced are called
   a. fixed costs
   b. variable costs
   c. marginal costs
   d. all of the above

6. Lean producers remove waste by
   a. focusing on inventory reduction
   b. using JIT techniques
   c. reducing space requirements
   d. developing close relationships with suppliers
   e. all of the above

7. Repetitive process lines
   a. use modules
   b. are the classic assembly lines
   c. have more structure and less flexibility than a job shop layout
   d. include the assembly of basically all automobiles
   e. all of the above

8. As the quantity produced increases and you move toward product-focused production
   a. the variable cost per unit increases
   b. the total fixed cost for the production operation
   c. the equipment utilization rate decreases
   d. more general purpose equipment is used
   e. all of the above

9. Characteristics of a modular production process include
   a. the use of just-in-time procurement techniques
   b the use of just-in-time inventory control techniques
   c. the use of just-in-time movement of modules
   d. materials are moved by such means as conveyors, transfer machines, and automated guided vehicles
   e. all of the above

10. Two of the new techniques to address process reengineering are
    a. Compact and APT
    b. time and motion study
    c. work-flow analysis and time-function mapping
    d. work-flow analysis and motion study

11. Computer-integrated manufacturing (CIM) includes manufacturing systems that have
    a. computer-aided design, direct numerical control machines, material handling equipment controlled by automation
    b. transaction processing, management information system, and decision support systems
    c. automated guided vehicles, robots, and process control
    d. robots, automated guided vehicles, and transfer equipment

12. Advantages of flexible manufacturing systems include all of the following except
    a. lower set-up costs
    b. ability to adapt to wide range of sizes and configuration
    c. high utilization of facilities
    d. lower direct labor costs
    e. all of the above are advantages

13. Process control is used to control physical processes in
    a. discrete manufacturing facilities
    b. repetitive manufacturing facilities
    c. intermittent facilities
    d. job shops
    e. product-oriented facilities

OPERATIONS IN PRACTICE EXERCISE

In our high-tech world, pigs, cows, and chickens often lead lives in small, confining stalls or cages. In the case of pigs, at Premium Standard Farm Inc.'s Princeton, Missouri, complex, sows are impregnated and must wait for 40 days in metal stalls so small that they cannot turn around. After an ultrasound test, they wait another 67 days in a similar stall until they give birth. Two weeks after giving birth to 10 or 11 piglets, the sows are moved back to the breeding rooms for another cycle. After three years, the sow is slaughtered. Animal-welfare advocates say such confinement drives pigs crazy. Premium Standard replies that its hogs must be comfortable, because only 1% die before Premium Standard wants them to. Discuss the business and ethical implications of this industry and these two divergent opinions.

PROBLEMS

• **5.1.** River Road Medical Clinic, which runs an optometrist lab, has been blessed with substantial growth over the last decade. Additionally, they were able to buy additional increments of lens-grinding equipment in relatively small units. Since their growth has been steady and constant, data analysis suggests that regression analysis is adequate to determine their capacity demands. Data for the past decade are shown in the following table:

YEAR	1987	1988	1989	1990	1991	1992	1993	1994	1995	1996
UNITS PRODUCED (in thousands)	15.0	15.5	16.25	16.75	16.9	17.24	17.5	17.3	17.75	18.1

a. Determine their capacity needs in units for 1997, 1999, and 2003.

b. If each machine is capable of producing 2,500 lenses, how many machines should they expect to have in 1999?

• **5.2.** Assume River Road Medical Clinic (Problem 5.1) in 1997 has eight machines, each capable of producing 2,500 lenses per year. However, the new and best machine then on the market has the capability of producing 5,000 per year.

a. What is the status of capacity at the firm in the year 2003 if they buy one new machine in 1997?

b. What is the status of capacity at the firm in the year 2003 if they buy one more standard machine with a capacity of 2,500?

• **5.3.** Collins Manufacturing intends to increase capacity by overcoming a bottleneck operation through addition of new equipment. Two vendors have presented proposals. The fixed costs for Proposal A is $50,000 and for Proposal B $70,000. The variable cost for A is $12 and for B, $10. The revenue generated by each of these units is $20.

a. What is the break-even point in units for Proposal A?

b. What is the break-even point in units for Proposal B?

• **5.4.** Given the data in Problem 5.3:

a. What is the break-even point in dollars for Proposal A?

b. What is the break-even point in dollars for Proposal B?

• **5.5.** Given the data in Problem 5.3, at what volume (units) of output would the two alternatives yield the same profit?

• **5.6.** Using the same data in Problem 5.3:

a. If the expected volume is 8,500 units, which alternative should be chosen?

b. If the expected volume is 15,000 units, which alternative should be chosen?

• **5.7.** A work center operates two shifts per day five days per week (eight hours per shift) and has four machines of equal capability. If the machines are utilized 80% of the time at a system efficiency of 95%, what is the rated output in standard hours per week?

5.8. The time (in minutes) available for the next quarter of 1997 at Milt Chortkoff Mfg. in Waco, Texas, for each of three departments is shown below. Recent data on utilization and efficiency are also shown.

DEPARTMENT	MINUTES AVAILABLE	EFFECTIVE UTILIZATION	RECENT EFFICIENCY
Design	93,600	.92	.95
Fabrication	156,000	.95	1.03
Finishing	62,400	.96	1.05

Compute the expected capacity for the next quarter for each department.

5.9. An electronics firm is currently manufacturing an item that has a variable cost of $0.50 per unit and a selling price of $1.00 per unit. Fixed costs are $14,000. Current volume is 30,000 units. The firm can substantially improve the product quality by adding a new piece of equipment at an additional fixed cost of $6,000. Variable cost would increase to $0.60, but volume should jump to 50,000 units due to a higher-quality product. Should the company buy the new equipment?

5.10. The electronics firm in Problem 5.9 is now considering the new equipment with a price increase to $1.10 per unit. With the higher-quality product, the new volume is expected to be 45,000 units. Under these circumstances, should the company purchase the new equipment and increase the selling price?

5.11. Given the following data, calculate *BEP*(*x*), *BEP*($), and the profit at 100,000 units:

$$P = \$8/\text{unit} \qquad V = \$4/\text{unit} \qquad F = \$50{,}000$$

5.12. Tom Miller and Jeff Vollman have opened a copy service on Commonwealth Avenue. They estimate their fixed cost at $12,000 and their variable cost of each copy sold at $.01. They expect their selling price to average $.05.

a. What is their break-even point in dollars?
b. What is their break-even point in units?

5.13. Dr. Aleda Roth, a prolific author, is considering starting her own publishing company. She will call it DSI Publishing, Inc. DSI's estimated costs are
Fixed = $250,000
Variable cost per book = $20
Selling price per book = $30
How many books must DSI sell to break even?

5.14. In addition to the costs in Problem 5.13, Dr. Roth wants to pay herself a salary of $50,000 per year.

a. Now what is her break-even point in units?
b. What is her break-even point in dollars?

CASE STUDY

Service at Minit-Lube, Inc.

In recent years a substantial market has developed for automobile tune-up and lubrication shops. This demand came about because of the change in consumer buying patterns as self-service gas stations proliferated. Consumers acquired the habit of pumping their own gas; this has made a second stop necessary for oil and lubrication. Consequently, Minit-Lube and Jiffy-Lube developed a strategy to accommodate this opportunity.

Minit-Lube stations perform oil changes, lubrication, and interior cleaning in a spotless environment. The buildings are clean, painted white, and surrounded by neatly trimmed landscaping. To facilitate fast service, cars can be driven through three abreast. At Minit-Lube the customer is greeted by service representatives who are graduates of the Minit-Lube school in Salt Lake City. The Minit-Lube school is not unlike McDonald's Hamburger University near Chicago, or Holiday Inn's training school in Memphis, Tennessee. The greeter takes the order, which typically includes fluid checks (oil, water, brake fluid, transmission fluid, differential grease) and the necessary lubrication, as well as filter changes for air and oil. Service personnel in neat uniforms move into action; the standard three-person team has one person checking fluid levels under the hood; another is assigned interior vacuuming and window cleaning; the third is in the garage pit, removing the oil filter, draining the oil, checking the differential and transmission, and lubricating as necessary. Precise task assignments and good training are designed to put the car in and out of the bay in ten minutes. The idea is to charge no more, and hopefully less, than gas stations, automotive repair chains, and auto dealers, while providing better service.

DISCUSSION QUESTIONS

1. What service does Minit-Lube provide?
2. How would we measure productivity (a) at Minit-Lube and (b) in this industry?
3. Is it likely that Minit-Lube or Jiffy-Lube have increased productivity over their more traditional competitors? Why?
4. What is the production process used at Minit-Lube? Where does it fit on our process continuum?

Internet Case Study See our Internet home page at http://www.prenhall.com/renderpom for this additional case study: Rochester Manufacturing.

BIBLIOGRAPHY

Berry, Leonard L. *Great Service*, New York: The Free Press, 1995.

Berry, W. L., C. C. Bozarth, T. J. Hill, and J. E. Klompmaker. "Factory Focus: Segmenting Markets from an Operations Perspective." *Journal of Operations Management* 10, no. 3 (August 1991): 363.

Burbidge, J. L. "Production Flow Analysis for Planning Group Technology." *Journal of Operations Management* 10, no. 1 (January 1991): 5–27.

Ettlie, J. E. "What Makes a Manufacturing Firm Innovative." *The Executive* (November 1990): 10.

Ettlie, J. E., and E. M. Reza. "Organizational Integration and Process Innovation." *The Academy of Management Journal* (October 1992): 795.

Heizer, J. H. "Manufacturing Productivity: Japanese Techniques Not Enough." *Industrial Management* (September-October 1986): 21–23.

Hounshell, D. A. *From the American System to Mass Production, 1800–1932.* Baltimore: Johns Hopkins University Press, 1984.

Mansfield, E. "The Diffusion of Flexible Manufacturing Systems in Japan, Europe, and the United States." *Management Science* 39, no. 2 (February 1993): 149–159.

McCutcheon, D. M., A. S. Raturi, and J. R. Meredith. "The Customization-Responsiveness Squeeze." *Sloan Management Review* 35, no. 2 (Winter 1994): 89–100.

Morris, J. S., and R. J. Tersine. "A Simulation Analysis of Factors Influencing the Attractiveness of Group Technology Cellular Layout." *Management Science* 36 (December 1990): 1567–1578.

Parsaei, H. R., and A. Mital. *Economic Aspects of Advanced Production and Manufacturing Systems.* New York: Van Nostrand Reinhold, 1991.

Pine, B. J., II. *Mass Customization: The New Frontier in Business Competition.* Boston: Harvard Business School Press, 1993.

Primrose, P. *Investment in Manufacturing Technology.* New York: Van Nostrand Reinhold, 1991.

Russell, R. S., P. Y. Huang, and Y. Leu. "A Study of Labor Allocation Strategies in Cellular Manufacturing." *Decision Sciences* 22 (July-August 1991): 594.

Schonberger, Richard. *Building a Chain of Customers.* New York: The Free Press, 1995.

Selecting the Location

6

CHAPTER OUTLINE

The Strategic Importance of Location

Factors That Affect Location Decisions

Labor Productivity ■ Exchange Rates ■ Costs ■ Attitudes

Methods of Evaluating Location Alternatives

The Factor-Rating Method ■ Locational Break-Even Analysis ■ Center-of-Gravity Method ■ The Transportation Model

Service Location Strategy

How Hotel Chains Select Sites ■ The Telemarketing Industry

Summary ■ *Key Terms* ■ *Using POM for Windows* ■ *Using Excel Spreadsheets to Solve a Factor-Rating Problem* ■ *Solved Problems* ■ *Discussion Questions* ■ *Self-Test Chapter 6* ■ *Operations in Practice Exercise* ■ *Problems* ■ *Case Study: Southern Recreational Vehicle Company* ■ *Bibliography*

LEARNING OBJECTIVES

When you complete this chapter you should be able to:

IDENTIFY OR DEFINE:

Objective of location strategy
International location issues

EXPLAIN:

Three methods of solving the location problem:

- Factor-rating method
- Locational break-even analysis
- Center-of-gravity method

THE STRATEGIC IMPORTANCE OF LOCATION

When Mercedes-Benz announced its plans to build its first major overseas plant in Vance, Alabama, it ended a year of competition among 170 sites in 30 states and two countries.[1] When Quality Coils Inc. pulled the plug on Juarez and reopened its old electromagnetic coil factory in Connecticut, it ended four years of losing money in low-wage Mexico.[2] And when McDonald's opened in Pushkin Square in Moscow, it ended a six-year advance preparation of developing a Russian "food town" to supply its desired quality of ingredients.[3]

One of the most important strategic decisions companies like Mercedes-Benz, Quality Coil, and McDonald's make is where to locate their operation. The international aspect of these decisions is an indication of the global nature of location decisions. With the opening up of the Soviet and Chinese blocs a great transformation is taking place. Business is restructuring globally. World markets have doubled.

Firms throughout the world are using the concepts and techniques of this chapter to address the location decision, because location greatly affects costs, both fixed and variable. It has a major impact on the overall profit of the company. For instance, depending on the product and type of production or service taking place, transportation costs alone can total as much as 25% of the product's selling price. That is, one-fourth of the total revenue of a firm may be needed just to cover freight expenses of the raw materials coming in and the finished product going out. Other costs that may be influenced by location include taxes, wages, raw material costs, and rents.

Once management is committed to a specific location, many costs are firmly in place and difficult to reduce. For instance, if a new factory location is in a region with high energy costs, even good management with an outstanding energy strategy is starting at a disadvantage. Management is in a similar bind with its human resource strategy if labor in the selected location is expensive, ill-trained, or has a poor work ethic. Consequently, hard work to determine an optimal facility location is a good investment.

The strategic decision often depends on the type of business. For industrial location decisions the strategy is usually minimizing costs, whereas for retail and professional service organizations the strategy focuses on maximizing revenue. Warehouse location strategy, however, may be driven by a combination of cost and speed of delivery. In general, the *objective of location strategy* is to maximize the benefit of location to the firm.

NOTE
List the factors most important to *you* in selecting a city in which to live.

Companies make location decisions relatively infrequently, usually because demand has outgrown the current plant's capacity or because of changes in labor productivity, exchange rates, costs, or local attitudes. Companies may also relocate their manufacturing or service facility because of shifts in customer demand.

Location options include (1) not moving, but instead expanding an existing facility, (2) maintaining current sites, but adding another facility elsewhere, or (3) closing the existing facility and moving to another location.

---

[1] *The Economist*, January 8, 1994, p. 32.
[2] *The Wall Street Journal*, September 15, 1993, p. A-1.
[3] P. Ritchie, "McDonald's: A Winner Through Logistics," *International Journal of Physical Distribution and Logistics Management* 20, no. 3 (1990): 21–24.

FACTORS THAT AFFECT LOCATION DECISIONS

Selecting a facility location is becoming much more complex with the globalization of the workplace. Globalization has taken place because of the development of (1) market economics as well as: (2) better international communications; (3) more rapid, reliable travel and shipping; (4) ease of capital flow between countries; and (5) high differences in labor costs. Many firms now consider opening new offices, factories, retail stores, or banks outside their own country. Location decisions transcend national borders. In fact, as Figure 6.1 shows, the sequence of location decisions often begins with choosing a country in which to operate. Before Germany's Mercedes-Benz chose Alabama, it first considered Mexico. In the end, the fear of marketing a $50,000 Mercedes that was "Made in Mexico" drove the firm back to the United States.

Once a firm decides which country is best for its location, it focuses on a region of the chosen country and a community. In the United States, the South has become a popular destination for a variety of reasons, including the hospitality so often found in smaller towns.

The final step in the location decision process is choosing a specific site within a community. The company must pick the one location that is best suited for shipping and receiving, zoning, utilities, size, and cost. Again, Figure 6.1 summarizes this series of decisions and the factors that affect them.

Besides globalization, a number of other factors affect the location decision. Among these are labor productivity, foreign exchange, and changing attitudes toward the industry, unions, employment, zoning, pollution, taxes, and so forth.

Assembly plants operating along the Mexican side of the border, from Texas to California, are called *maquiladoras*. Some 2,000 firms and industrial giants, such as General Motors, Zenith, Hitachi, and GE, operate these plants, which were designed to help both sides of the impoverished border region. After the 1982 devaluation of the peso, the number of *maquiladoras* nearly tripled, and it is believed that by the year 2005 as many as 3 million workers will be employed in these cross-border plants. Mexican wages are low, and at current exchange rates, companies don't look to the Far East as they once did.

Labor Productivity

When deciding on a location, management may be tempted by an area's low wage rates (see Table 6.1 for a comparison of hourly manufacturing costs in 16 countries). However, wage rates cannot be considered by themselves, as Quality Coils discovered when it opened its plant in Mexico. Management must also consider productivity.

As discussed in Chapter 1, differences exist in productivity in various countries. What management is really interested in is the combination of productivity and the wage rate. For example, if Quality Coils pays $70 per day with 60 units produced per day in Connecticut, it will spend less on labor than its Mexican plant which pays $25 per day with a productivity of 20 units per day.

$$\frac{\text{Labor cost per day}}{\text{Productivity (that is, units per day)}} = \text{cost per unit}$$

Case 1: Connecticut plant

$$\frac{\$70 \text{ Wages per day}}{60 \text{ Units produced per day}} = \frac{\$70}{60} = \$1.17 \text{ per unit}$$

Case 2: Juarez, Mexico, plant

$$\frac{\$25 \text{ Wages per day}}{20 \text{ Units produced per day}} = \frac{\$25}{20} = \$1.25 \text{ per unit}$$

NOTE
In most cases, it is cheaper to make clothes in Korea, Taiwan, or Hong Kong and ship them to the United States than it is to produce them in the United States. But final cost is the critical factor and low productivity can negate low cost.

Employees with poor training, poor education, or poor work habits may not be a good buy even at low wages. By the same token, employees who cannot or

FIGURE 6.1

SOME CONSIDERATIONS AND FACTORS THAT AFFECT LOCATION DECISIONS

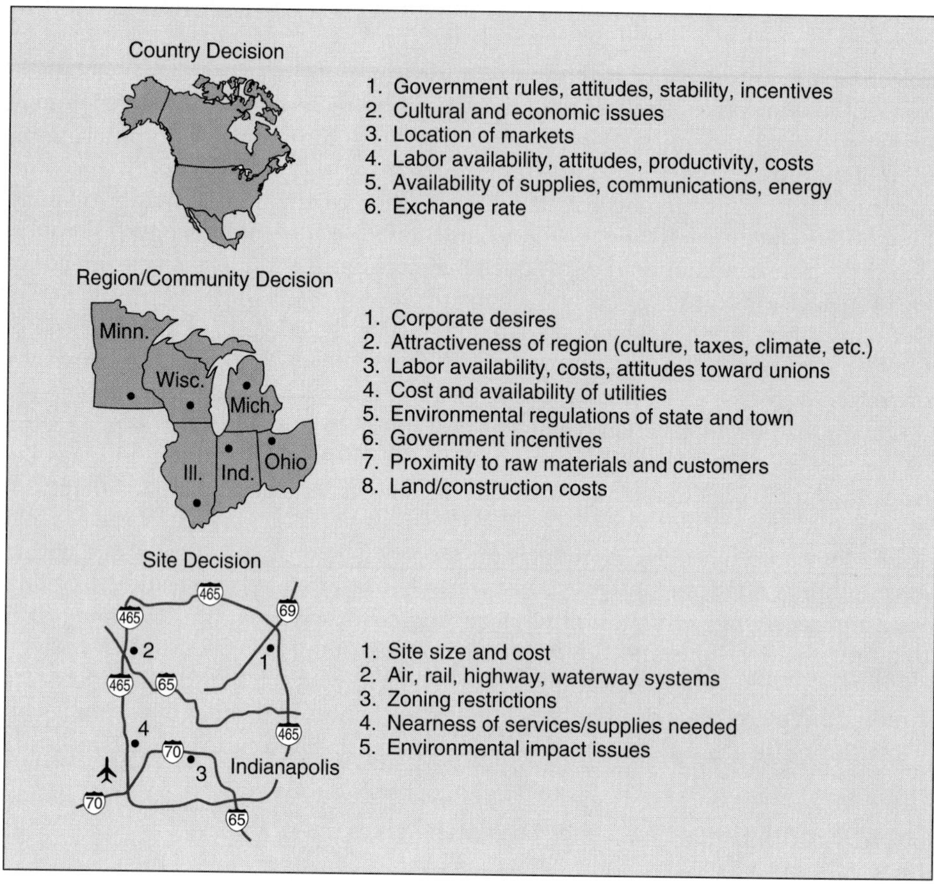

NOTE

Labor costs in many underdeveloped countries are now one-third of those in developed nations. But, when labor costs are only 15% of manufacturing costs, the difference may not overcome many other disadvantages of low-labor-cost countries.

will not always reach their place of work are not much good to the organization even at low wages. Labor cost per unit is sometimes called the *labor content* of the product.

Exchange Rates

Although wage rates and productivity may make different countries seem economical, unfavorable exchange rates might negate any savings. Sometimes,

TABLE 6.1 LABOR COSTS AROUND THE GLOBE

HOURLY COMPENSATION—MANUFACTURING WORKERS (1994)

Germany* $27.37	Belgium $22.91	Japan $21.38	Sweden $18.81	United States $17.10	France $17.10	Italy $16.25	Canada $15.73
Britain $13.68	Australia $13.68	Spain $11.46	Israel $9.06	Korea $6.33	Taiwan $5.47	Hong Kong $4.79	Mexico $2.57

*WEST GERMANY

SOURCE: *Business Week*, November 20, 1995, p. 38.

Even with reduced tax benefits and a saturated hotel market, opportunities still exist when hotel/motel locations are right. Good sites include those near hospitals and medical centers. As medical complexes in metropolitan areas continue to increase, so does the need for hotels to house patients' families. Additionally, medical services such as outpatient care, shorter hospital stays, and more diagnostic tests increase the need for hotels near hospitals.

though, companies can take advantage of a particularly favorable exchange rate by relocating or exporting to a foreign country. However, the values of foreign currencies continually rise and fall in most countries. Such changes could well make what was a good location in 1996 a disastrous one in 2001. Many of the *maquiladora* plants, U.S.-owned factories in Juarez, Tijuana, and Matamoros, Mexico, opened shortly after the Mexican peso decreased by 200% in relation to the dollar in the 1980s.

NOTE
The Texas city of Amarillo recently sent checks for $8 million apiece to 1,350 businesses as a "bribe." To cash the check, the business would have to set up shop in Amarillo and employ 800 workers. Only three takers so far. Why?

Costs

We can divide location costs into two categories, tangible and intangible. **Tangible costs** are those costs that are readily identifiable and precisely measured. They include utilities, labor, material, taxes, depreciation, and other costs the accounting department and management can identify. In addition, such costs as transportation of raw materials, transportation of finished goods, and site construction are all factored into the overall cost of a location.

tangible costs

Intangible costs are less easily quantified. They include quality of education, public transportation facilities, community attitudes toward the industry and the company, and quality and attitude of prospective employees. They also include quality-of-life variables, such as climate and sports teams, that may influence personnel recruiting.

intangible costs

Attitudes

Attitudes of national, state, and local governments toward private property, zoning, pollution, and employment stability may be in flux. Governmental attitudes at the time a location decision is made may not be lasting ones. Moreover, management may find that these attitudes can be influenced by leadership.

"May I have my allowance in Deutsche Marks, Dad?"

METHODS OF EVALUATING LOCATION ALTERNATIVES

Four major methods are used for solving location problems: the factor-rating method, locational break-even analysis, center-of-gravity method, and the transportation model. This section describes these approaches.

The Factor-Rating Method

factor-rating method

There are many factors, both qualitative and quantitative, to consider in choosing a location. Some of these factors are more important than others, so managers can use weightings to make the decision process more objective. The **factor-rating method** is popular because a wide variety of factors from education to recreation to labor skills can be included. Table 6.2 lists a few of the many factors that affect location decisions.

The factor-rating method has six steps:

1. Develop a list of relevant factors (such as those in Table 6.2).
2. Assign a weight to each factor to reflect its relative importance in the company's objectives.
3. Develop a scale for each factor (for example, 1 to 10 or 1 to 100 points).
4. Have management score each location for each factor, using the scale in step 3.
5. Multiply the score by the weights for each factor, and total the score for each location.
6. Make a recommendation based on the maximum point score, considering the results of quantitative approaches as well.

NOTE
The numbers used in factor weighting can be subjective and the model's results are not "exact" even though this is a quantitative approach.

TABLE 6.2 FACTORS AFFECTING LOCATION SELECTION
Labor costs (including wages, unionization, productivity)
Labor availability (including attitudes, age, distribution, skills)
Proximity to raw materials and suppliers
Proximity to markets
State and local government fiscal policies (including incentives, taxes, unemployment compensation)
Environmental regulations
Utilities (including gas, electric, water, and their costs)
Site costs (including land, expansion, parking, drainage)
Transportation availability (including rail, air, water, interstate roads)
Quality-of-life issues in the community (including all levels of education, cost of living, health care, sports, cultural activities, transportation, housing, entertainment, religious facilities)
Foreign exchange (including rates, stability)
Quality of government (including stability, honesty, attitudes toward new business—whether overseas or local)

NOTE
A recent Grant Thornton study showed North Dakota, Nebraska, and South Dakota as the best places to locate and Montana, Ohio, and Michigan as the worst.

EXAMPLE 1

Five Flags Over Florida, a U.S. chain of ten family-oriented theme parks, has decided to expand overseas by opening its first park in Europe. The rating sheet in Table 6.3 provides a list of qualitative factors that management has decided are important; their weightings and their rating for two possible sites—Dijon, France, and Copenhagen, Denmark—are shown.

TABLE 6.3 WEIGHTS, SCORES, AND SOLUTION

		SCORES (out of 100)		WEIGHTED SCORES	
FACTOR	WEIGHT	*France*	*Denmark*	*France*	*Denmark*
Labor availability and attitude	.25	70	60	(.25)(70) = 17.5	(.25)(60) = 15.0
People-to-car ratio	.05	50	60	(.05)(50) = 2.5	(.05)(60) = 3.0
Per capita income	.10	85	80	(.10)(85) = 8.5	(.10)(80) = 8.0
Tax structure	.39	75	70	(.39)(75) = 29.3	(.39)(70) = 27.3
Education and health	.21	60	70	(.21)(60) = 12.6	(.21)(70) = 14.7
Totals	1.00			70.4	68.0

Table 6.3 also indicates use of weights to evaluate alternative site locations. Given the option of 100 points assigned to each factor, the French location is preferable. By changing the points or weights slightly for those factors about which there is some doubt, we can analyze the sensitivity of the decision. For instance, we can see that changing the scores for "labor availability and attitude" by 10 points can change the decision.

When a decision is sensitive to minor changes, further analysis of either the weighting or the points assigned may be appropriate. Alternatively, management may conclude that these intangible factors are not the proper criteria on which to base a location decision. Managers therefore place primary weight on the more quantitative aspects of the decision.

Locational Break-Even Analysis

locational break-even analysis

Locational break-even analysis is the use of cost-volume analysis to make an economic comparison of location alternatives. By identifying fixed and variable costs and graphing them for each location, we can determine which one provides the lowest cost. Locational break-even analysis can be done mathematically or graphically. The graphic approach has the advantage of providing the range of volume over which each location is preferable.

The three steps to locational break-even analysis are:

1. Determine the fixed and variable cost for each location.
2. Plot the costs for each location, with costs on the vertical axis of the graph and annual volume on the horizontal axis.
3. Select the location that has the lowest total cost for the expected production volume.

EXAMPLE 2

A manufacturer of automobile carburetors is considering three locations—Akron, Bowling Green, and Chicago—for a new plant. Cost studies indicate that fixed costs per year at the sites are \$30,000, \$60,000, and \$110,000, respectively; and variable costs are \$75 per unit, \$45 per unit, and \$25 per unit, respectively. The expected selling price of the carburetors produced is \$120. The company wishes to find the most economical location for an expected volume of 2,000 units per year.

For each of the three, we can plot the fixed costs (those at a volume of zero units) and the total cost (fixed costs + variable costs) at the expected volume of output. These lines have been plotted in Figure 6.2.

FIGURE 6.2

CROSSOVER CHART FOR LOCATIONAL BREAK-EVEN ANALYSIS

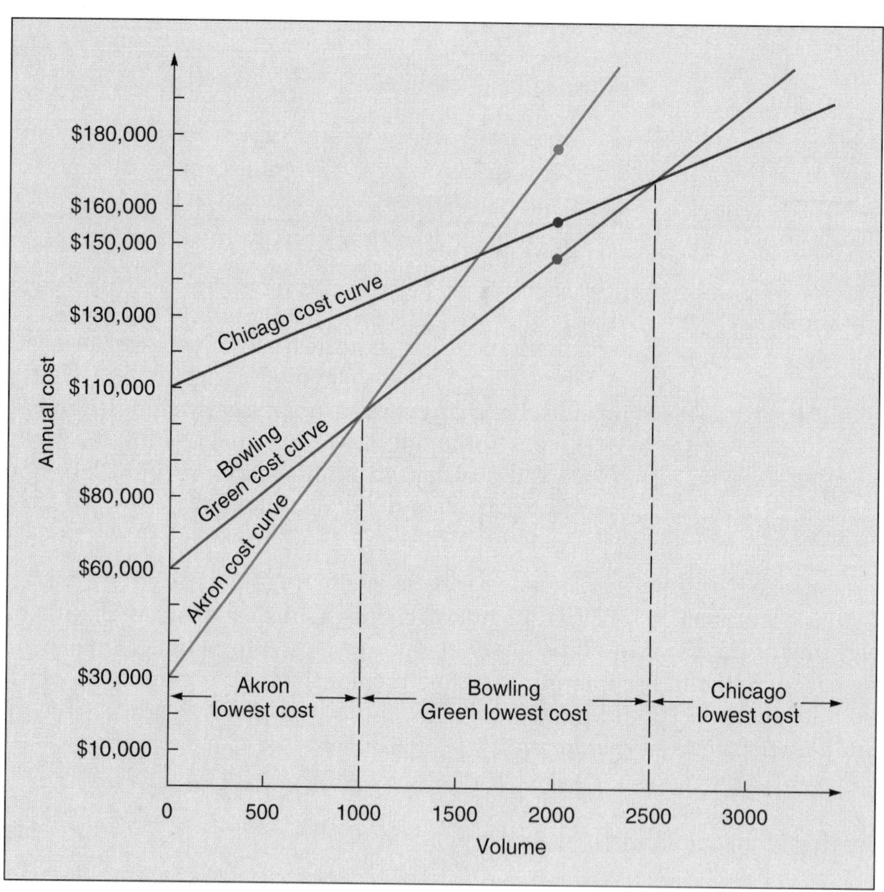

For Akron,

$$\text{Total cost} = \$30{,}000 + \$75(2{,}000) = \$180{,}000$$

For Bowling Green,

$$\text{Total cost} = \$60{,}000 + \$45(2{,}000) = \$150{,}000$$

For Chicago,

$$\text{Total cost} = \$110{,}000 + \$25(2{,}000) = \$160{,}000$$

With an expected volume of 2,000 units per year, Bowling Green provides the lowest cost location. The expected profit is:

$$\text{Total revenue} - \text{Total cost} = \$120(2{,}000) - \$150{,}000 = 90{,}000 \text{ per year}$$

The chart also tells us that for a volume of less than 1,000, Akron would be preferred, and for a volume greater than 2,500, Chicago would yield the greatest profit. The crossover points are 1,000 and 2,500.

Center-of-Gravity Method

center-of-gravity method

The **center-of-gravity method** is a mathematical technique used for finding the location of a distribution center that will minimize distribution costs. The method takes into account the location of markets, the volume of goods shipped to those markets, and shipping costs in finding the best location for a distribution center.

The first step in the center-of-gravity method is to place the locations on a coordinate system. This will be illustrated in Example 3. The origin of the coordinate system and the scale used are arbitrary, just as long as the relative distances are correctly represented. This can be done easily by placing a grid over an ordinary map. The center of gravity is determined by Equations 6.1 and 6.2:

$$C_x = \frac{\sum_i d_{ix} W_i}{\sum_i W_i} \tag{6.1}$$

$$C_y = \frac{\sum_i d_{iy} W_i}{\sum_i W_i} \tag{6.2}$$

where

C_x = x-coordinate of the center of gravity

C_y = y-coordinate of the center of gravity

d_{ix} = x-coordinate of location i

d_{iy} = y-coordinate of location i

W_i = Volume of goods moved to or from location i

Note that Equations 6.1 and 6.2 include the term W_i, the volume of supplies transferred to or from location i.

Since the number of containers shipped each month affects cost, distance alone should not be the principal criterion. The center-of-gravity method assumes that cost is directly proportional to both distance and volume shipped. The ideal location is that which minimizes the weighted distance between the warehouse and its retail outlets, where the distance is weighted by the number of containers shipped.

Masaki Kaneho, plant manager of Motorola's integrated semiconductor plant in Aizu, Japan, with author Jay Heizer. As a world-class manufacturer, Motorola has located facilities throughout the world. Where labor costs are a significant part of product cost, Southeast Asia may be appropriate. For other countries, such as Japan, exchange rates or a local presence may be critical. While a Southeast Asian worker can wire 120 integrated circuits to metal frames each hour, an automated machine can do 640. And one worker can monitor eight machines for a total hourly production of 5,120. Clearly, in integrated-circuit production direct labor costs have become less critical and other considerations relatively more important.

EXAMPLE 3

Consider the case of Quain's Discount Department Stores, a chain of four large Kmart-type outlets. The firm's store locations are in Chicago, Pittsburgh, New York, and Atlanta; they are currently being supplied out of an old and inadequate warehouse in Pittsburgh, the site of the chain's first store. Data on demand rates at each outlet are shown in Table 6.4.

TABLE 6.4 DEMAND FOR QUAIN'S DISCOUNT STORES

STORE LOCATION	NUMBER OF CONTAINERS SHIPPED PER MONTH
Chicago	2,000
Pittsburgh	1,000
New York	1,000
Atlanta	2,000

The firm has decided to find some "central" location in which to build a new warehouse. Its current store locations are shown in Figure 6.3. For example, location 1 is Chicago, and from Table 6.4 and Figure 6.3, we have:

$$d_{1x} = 30$$

$$d_{1y} = 120$$

$$W_1 = 2,000$$

FIGURE 6.3

COORDINATE LOCATIONS OF FOUR QUAIN'S DEPARTMENT STORES AND CENTER OF GRAVITY

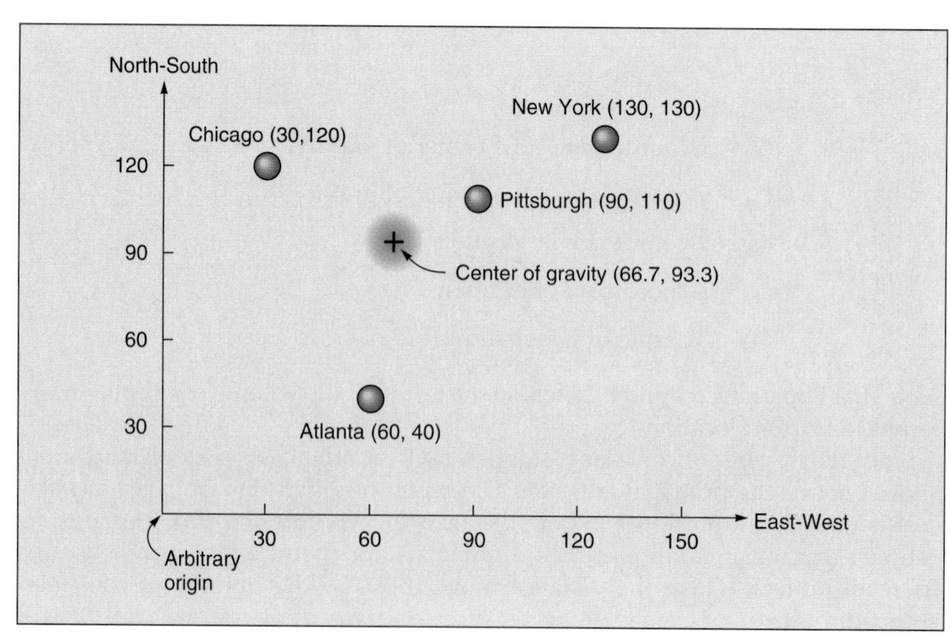

Using the data in Table 6.4 and Figure 6.3 for each of the other cities, in Equations 6.1 and 6.2 we find:

$$C_x = \frac{(30)(2000) + (90)(1000) + (130)(1000) + (60)(2000)}{2000 + 1000 + 1000 + 2000} = \frac{400{,}000}{6{,}000}$$

$$= 66.7$$

$$C_y = \frac{(120)(2000) + (110)(1000) + (130)(1000) + (40)(2000)}{2000 + 1000 + 1000 + 2000} = \frac{560{,}000}{6{,}000}$$

$$= 93.3$$

This location (66.7, 93.3) is shown by the crosshair in Figure 6.3. By overlaying a U.S. map on this exhibit, we find that this location is near central Ohio. The firm may well wish to consider Columbus, Ohio, or a nearby city as an appropriate location.

The Transportation Model

transportation model

The objective of the **transportation model** is to determine the best pattern of shipments from several points of supply (sources) to several points of demand (destinations) so as to minimize total production and transportation costs. Every firm with a network of supply-and-demand points faces such a problem. The complex Volkswagen supply network (shown in Figure 6.4) provides one such illustration.

Although the linear programming (LP) technique can be used to solve this type of problem, more efficient, special-purpose algorithms have been developed for the transportation application. The transportation model finds an initial feasible solution and then makes step-by-step improvement until an optimal solution is reached.

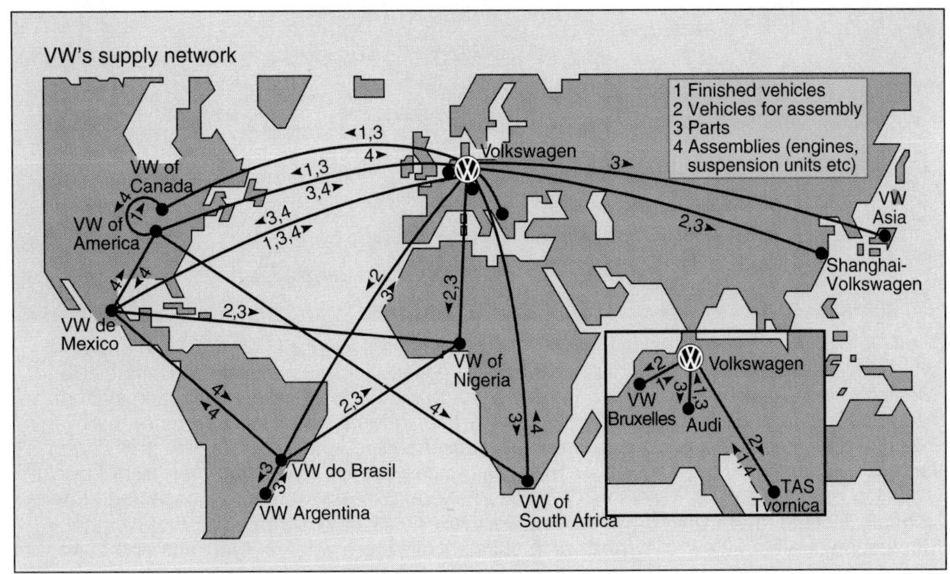

FIGURE 6.4

WORLDWIDE DISTRIBUTION OF VOLKSWAGENS AND PARTS

SOURCE: *The Economist, Ltd.* Distributed by *The New York Times*/Special Features.

SERVICE LOCATION STRATEGY

While the focus in industrial-sector location analysis is on minimizing cost, the focus in the service sector is on maximizing revenue. This is because manufacturing costs tend to vary substantially between locations, but in service firms location often has more impact on revenue than cost. Therefore, for the service firm, a specific location often influences revenue more than it does cost. This means that the location focus for service firms should be on determining the volume of business and revenue. There are eight major components of volume and revenue for the service firm. These are:

NOTE
It is often desirable to locate near competition; large department stores often attract more shoppers when they are close by. The same applies to shoe stores, fast-food restaurants, and others.

1. Purchasing power of the customer drawing area.
2. Service and image compatibility with demographics of the customer drawing area.
3. Competition in the area.
4. Quality of the competition.

Fred Smith, founder and president of Federal Express, received a C on a college paper in which he proposed the central "hub" distribution concept for small packages. Smith selected Memphis and has proved that the hub provides a unique and effective distribution system. About 100 Federal Express aircraft converge by midnight each evening with more than 700,000 documents and packages. Sorting and exchanging in the huge facility (the size of 33 football fields) is completed by 4 A.M. Then planes can depart, typically to their city of origin.

Why a hub in Memphis? Memphis provides Federal Express with an uncongested airport, centrally located in the United States, with very few hours of closure because of weather. Competing carriers fly out of airports with substantially more weather problems and often with a less-desirable location relative to their customers. Location may be a contributor to the Federal Express safety record of no crashes in 20 years.

As Figure 6.4 indicates, Volkswagen has found substantial local markets in many nations outside of Germany. The market in Mexico or Brazil may not be big enough to support a major company, but VW moved in and invested heavily because the market tomorrow is going to be 100 million people. Global location strategy demands bases that can reach the world's massive markets.

5. Uniqueness of the firm's and competitor's locations.
6. Physical qualities of facilities and neighboring businesses.
7. Operating policies of the firm.
8. Quality of management.

Realistic analysis of these factors can provide a reasonable picture of the revenue expected. The techniques used in the service sector include correlation analysis, traffic counts, demographic analysis, purchasing power analysis, the factor-rating method, and the center-of-gravity method. Table 6.5 provides a summary of location strategies for both service and industrial organizations.

How Hotel Chains Select Sites

One of the most important decisions a lodging chain makes is location. Hotel chains that pick good sites more accurately and quickly than competitors have a distinct strategic advantage. La Quinta Motor Inns, headquartered in San Antonio, Texas, is a moderately priced chain of 150 inns oriented toward frequent business travelers. To model motel selection behavior and predict success of a site, La Quinta turned to statistical regression analysis.[4]

The hotel started by testing 35 independent variables, trying to find which of them would have the highest correlation with predicted profitability, the dependent variable. "Competitive" independent variables included the number of hotel rooms in the vicinity and average room rates. "Demand generator" variables were such local attractions as office buildings and hospitals that drew potential customers to a four-mile-radius trade area. "Demographic" variables, such as local population and unemployment rate, can also affect the success of a hotel.

[4]Sheryl Kimes and James Fitzsimmons, "Selecting Profitable Hotel Sites at La Quinta Motor Inns," *Interfaces* (March-April 1990): 12–20.

TABLE 6.5 LOCATION STRATEGIES—SERVICE VERSUS INDUSTRIAL ORGANIZATIONS

SERVICE/RETAIL/PROFESSIONAL	INDUSTRIAL LOCATION
Revenue Focus	*Cost Focus*
Volume/revenue	**Tangible costs**
Drawing area; purchasing power	Transportation cost of raw material
Competition; advertising/pricing	Shipment cost of finished goods
	Energy and utility cost; labor; raw material; taxes, and so on
Physical quality	
Parking/access; security/lighting; appearance/image	
	Intangible and future costs
	Attitude toward union
Cost determinants	Quality of life
Management caliber	Education expenditures by state
Operation policies	Quality of state and local government
Techniques	*Techniques*
Regression models to determine importance of various factors	Transportation method
Factor-rating method	Factor-rating method
Traffic counts	Locational break-even analysis
Demographic analysis of drawing area	Crossover charts
Purchasing power analysis of area	
Center-of-gravity method	
Assumptions	*Assumptions*
Location is a major determinant of revenue	Location is a major determinant of cost
High customer-contact issues are critical	Most major costs can be identified explicitly for each site
Costs are relatively constant for a given area; therefore, the revenue function is critical	Low customer contact allows focus on the identifiable costs
	Intangible costs can be evaluated

"Market awareness" factors, such as the number of inns in a region were a fourth category. Finally, "physical characteristics" of the site, such as ease of access or sign visibility, provided the last group of the 35 independent variables.

In the end, the regression model chosen, with a coefficient of determination (r^2) of 51%, included just four predictive variables. They are the price of the inn, median income levels, the state population per inn, and the location of nearby colleges (which serves as a proxy for other demand generators). La Quinta then used the regression model to predict profitability and developed a cutoff that gave the best results for predicting success or failure of a site. A spreadsheet is now used to implement the model, which applies the decision rule and suggests "build" or "don't build."

NOTE
Where to locate telemarketers? Sixteen states now use prisoners to pitch products, conduct surveys, or answer hotel/airline reservation systems.

The Telemarketing Industry

Those industries and office activities that require neither face-to-face contact with the customer nor movement of material broaden the location options substantially. A case in point is the telemarketing industry, in which our traditional variables (as noted earlier) are no longer relevant. Where the electronic movement of information is good, the cost and availability of labor may drive the location decision. For instance, Fidelity Investments recently relocated many of its employees from Boston to Covington, Kentucky.[5] Now employees in the low-cost Covington region connect, by inexpensive fiber-optic phone lines, to their colleagues in the Boston office at a cost of less than a penny per minute. That is less than Fidelity spends on local connections.

The changes in location criteria may also affect a number of other businesses. For instance, states with smaller tax burdens and owners of property in fringe suburbs and scenic rural areas should come out ahead. And so should e-mail providers (like MCI), telecommuting software makers (like IBM/Lotus), videoconferencing firms (like Picture-Tel), makers of office electronic equipment (like Dell and Hewlett-Packard), and delivery firms (like UPS and Federal Express).

SUMMARY

Location may determine up to 10% of the total cost of an industrial firm. Location is also a critical element in determining revenue for the service, retail, or professional firm. Industrial firms need to consider both tangible and intangible costs. We typically address industrial location problems via a factor-rating method, locational break-even analysis, the center-of-gravity method, and the transportation method of linear programming.

For service, retail, and professional organizations, analysis is typically made of a variety of variables including purchasing power of a drawing area, competition, advertising and promotion, physical qualities of the location, and operating policies of the organization.

KEY TERMS

Tangible costs *(p. 205)*
Intangible costs *(p. 205)*
Factor-rating method *(p. 206)*
Locational break-even analysis *(p. 207)*
Center-of-gravity method *(p. 209)*
Transportation model *(p. 211)*

[5] *Forbes,* November 23, 1992, pp. 184–190.

USING POM FOR WINDOWS

The facility location (plant location) module in POM for Windows includes two different models. The first, the qualitative weighting model (also known as the factor-rating method), is used to solve Example 1 (see Program 6.1). The second, two-dimensional siting, is applied to the center-of-gravity problem described in Example 3 (see Program 6.2).

PROGRAM 6.1

POM FOR WINDOW'S FACTOR RATING (PLANT LOCATION) MODEL, APPLIED TO EXAMPLE 1 DATA (FIVE FLAGS OVER FLORIDA)

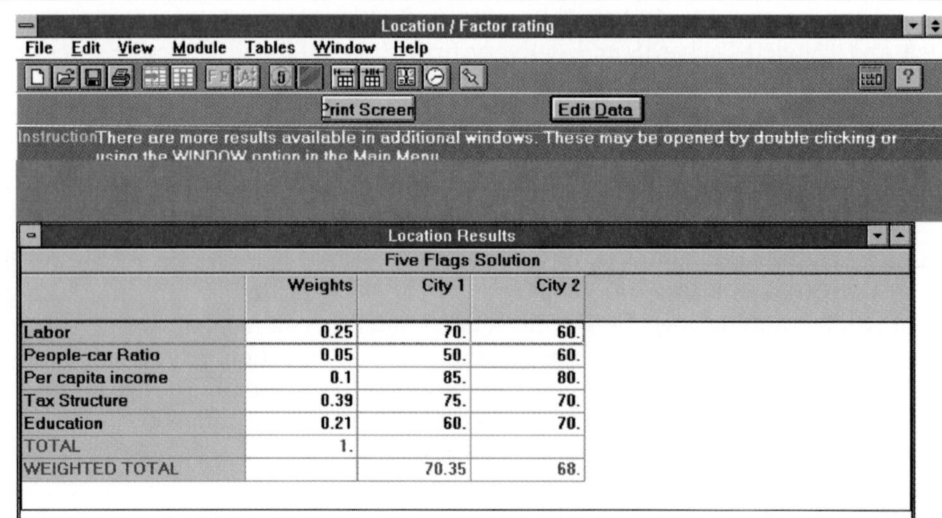

Five Flags Solution

	Weights	City 1	City 2
Labor	0.25	70.	60.
People-car Ratio	0.05	50.	60.
Per capita income	0.1	85.	80.
Tax Structure	0.39	75.	70.
Education	0.21	60.	70.
TOTAL	1.		
WEIGHTED TOTAL		70.35	68.

PROGRAM 6.2

POM FOR WINDOW'S PLANT LOCATION/ CENTER-OF-GRAVITY METHOD, APPLIED TO EXAMPLE 3 DATA (QUAIN DISCOUNT DEPARTMENT STORE)

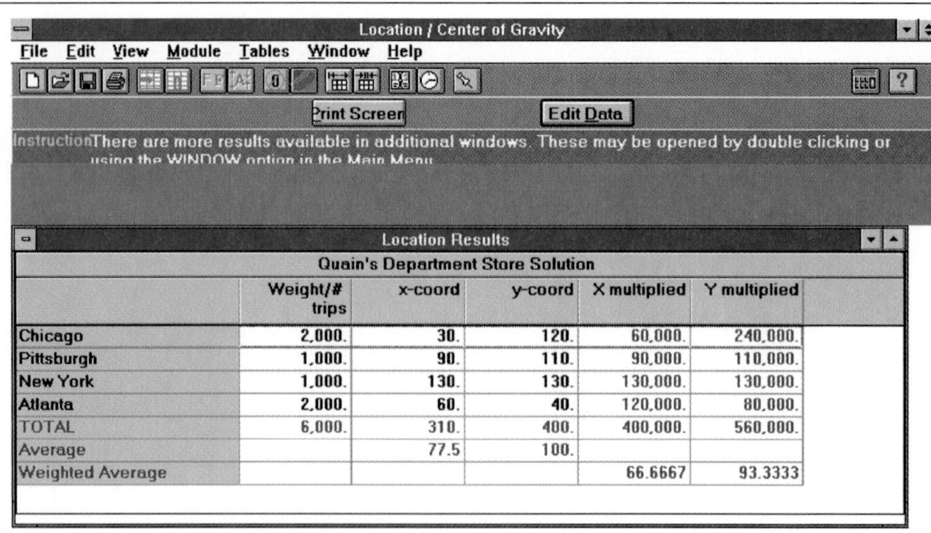

Quain's Department Store Solution

	Weight/# trips	x-coord	y-coord	X multiplied	Y multiplied
Chicago	2,000.	30.	120.	60,000.	240,000.
Pittsburgh	1,000.	90.	110.	90,000.	110,000.
New York	1,000.	130.	130.	130,000.	130,000.
Atlanta	2,000.	60.	40.	120,000.	80,000.
TOTAL	6,000.	310.	400.	400,000.	560,000.
Average		77.5	100.		
Weighted Average				66.6667	93.3333

USING EXCEL SPREADSHEETS TO SOLVE A FACTOR-RATING PROBLEM

Program 6.3 provides an Excel spreadsheet alternative to Program 6.1. Program 6.3 illustrates how straightforward it is to solve a factor-rating problem with spreadsheet formulas. Cells E5 through F11 show the formulas needed to compute the weighted scores for France and Denmark. France is weighted highest using these criteria.

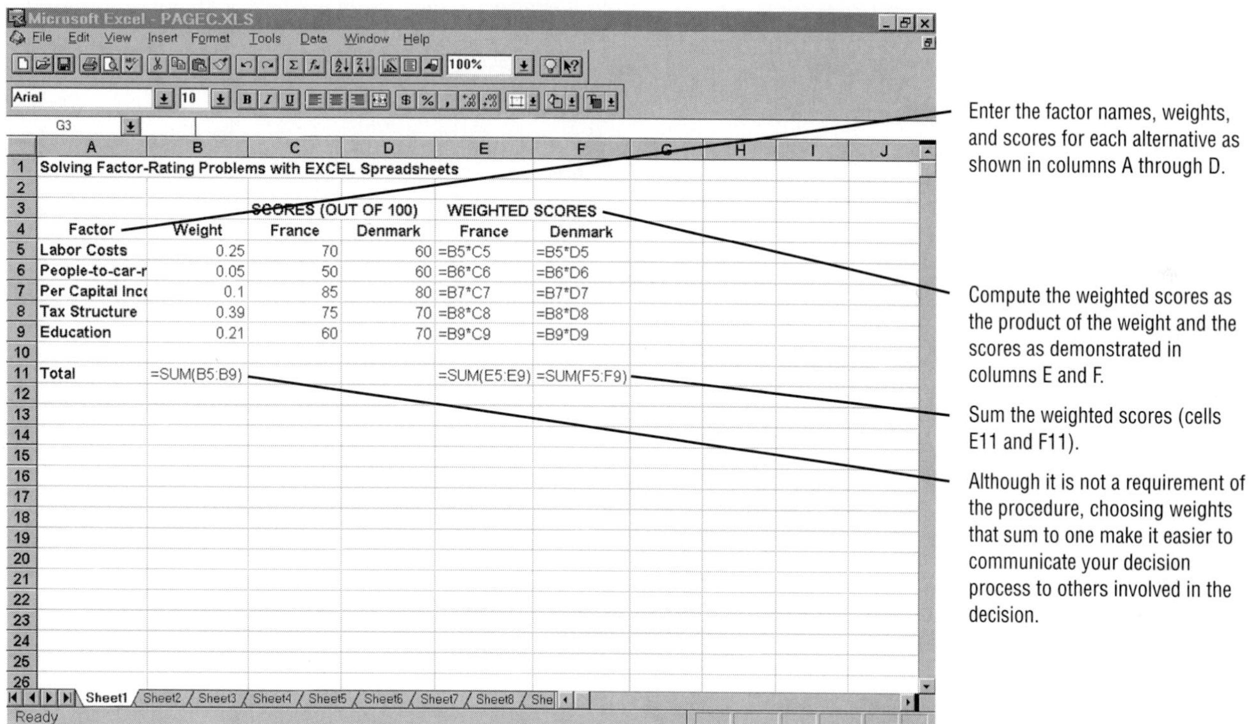

	A	B	C	D	E	F
1	Solving Factor-Rating Problems with EXCEL Spreadsheets					
2						
3			SCORES (OUT OF 100)		WEIGHTED SCORES	
4	Factor	Weight	France	Denmark	France	Denmark
5	Labor Costs	0.25	70	60	=B5*C5	=B5*D5
6	People-to-car-r	0.05	50	60	=B6*C6	=B6*D6
7	Per Capital Inc(	0.1	85	80	=B7*C7	=B7*D7
8	Tax Structure	0.39	75	70	=B8*C8	=B8*D8
9	Education	0.21	60	70	=B9*C9	=B9*D9
10						
11	Total	=SUM(B5:B9)			=SUM(E5:E9)	=SUM(F5:F9)

Microsoft Excel - PAGEC.XLS
File Edit View Insert Format Tools Data Window Help
Arial 10 100%
G3
Sheet1 Sheet2 Sheet3 Sheet4 Sheet5 Sheet6 Sheet7 Sheet8
Ready
Enter the factor names, weights, and scores for each alternative as shown in columns A through D.
Compute the weighted scores as the product of the weight and the scores as demonstrated in columns E and F.
Sum the weighted scores (cells E11 and F11).
Although it is not a requirement of the procedure, choosing weights that sum to one make it easier to communicate your decision process to others involved in the decision.

PROGRAM 6.3 USING EXCEL TO ANALYZE THE FIVE FLAGS DATA IN EXAMPLE 1

SOLVED PROBLEM 6.1

Just as cities and communities can be compared for location selection by the weighted approach model, as we saw earlier in this chapter, so can actual site decisions within those cities be helped. Table 6.6 illustrates four factors of importance to Washington, D.C., health officials charged with opening that city's first public AIDS clinic. Of primary concern (and given a weight of 5) was location of the clinic so it would be as accessible as possible to the largest number of patients. The annual lease cost also was of some concern due to a tight budget. A suite in the new City Hall, at 14th and U Streets, was highly rated because its rent would be free. An old office building near the downtown bus station received a much lower rating because of its cost. Equally important as lease cost was the need for confidentiality of patients and, therefore, for a relatively inconspicuous clinic. Finally, because so many of the staff at the AIDS clinic would be donating their time, the safety, parking, and accessibility of each site were of concern as well.

(continued on next page)

SOLUTION

From the three rightmost columns in Table 6.6, the weighted scores are summed. The bus terminal area has a low score and can be excluded from further consideration. The other two sites are virtually identical in total score. The city may now want to consider other factors, including political ones, in selecting between the two remaining sites.

SOURCE: R. Murdick, B. Render, and R. Russell, *Service Operations Management*. Copyright ©1990 by Allyn & Bacon. Reprinted by permission.

TABLE 6.6 POTENTIAL AIDS CLINIC SITES IN WASHINGTON, D.C.

		POTENTIAL LOCATIONS*			WEIGHTED SCORES		
Factor	*Importance Weight*	*Homeless Shelter (2nd and D, SE)*	*City Hall (14th and U, NW)*	*Bus Terminal Area (7th and H, NW)*	*Homeless Shelter*	*City Hall*	*Bus Terminal Area*
Accessibility for infectives	5	9	7	7	45	35	35
Annual lease cost	3	6	10	3	18	30	9
Inconspicuous	3	5	2	7	15	6	21
Accessibility for health staff	2	3	6	2	6	12	4
			Total scores:		84	83	69

*All sites are rated on a 1 to 10 basis, with 10 as the highest score and 1 as the lowest.

SOLVED PROBLEM 6.2

Chuck Bimmerle is considering opening a new foundry in Denton, Texas, Edwardsville, Illinois, or Fayetteville, Arkansas, to produce high-quality rifle sights. He has assembled the following fixed- and variable-cost data:

		PER UNIT COSTS		
Location	*Fixed Cost per Year*	*Material*	*Labor*	*Variable Overhead*
Denton	$200,000	$ .20	$ .40	$ .40
Edwardsville	$180,000	$ .25	$ .75	$ .75
Fayetteville	$170,000	$1.00	$1.00	$1.00

a. Graph the total cost lines.

b. Over what range of annual volume is each facility going to have a competitive advantage?

c. What is the volume at the intersection of Edwardsville and Fayetteville?

SOLUTION

a. A graph of the total cost lines is shown in Figure 6.5.

b. Below 8,000 units, the Fayetteville facility will have a competitive advantage (lowest cost); between 8,000 units and 26,666 units, Edwardsville has an advantage; and above 26,666, Denton has the advantage. (We have made the assumption in this problem that other costs, that is, delivery and intangible factors, are constant regardless of the decision.)

c. From the chart, we can see that the cost line for Fayetteville and the cost line for Edwardsville cross at about 8,000. We can also determine this point with a little algebra:

$$\$180{,}000 + 1.75Q = \$170{,}000 + 3.00Q$$

$$\$10{,}000 = 1.25Q$$

$$8{,}000 = Q$$

FIGURE 6.5

GRAPH OF TOTAL COST LINES FOR CHUCK BIMMERLE

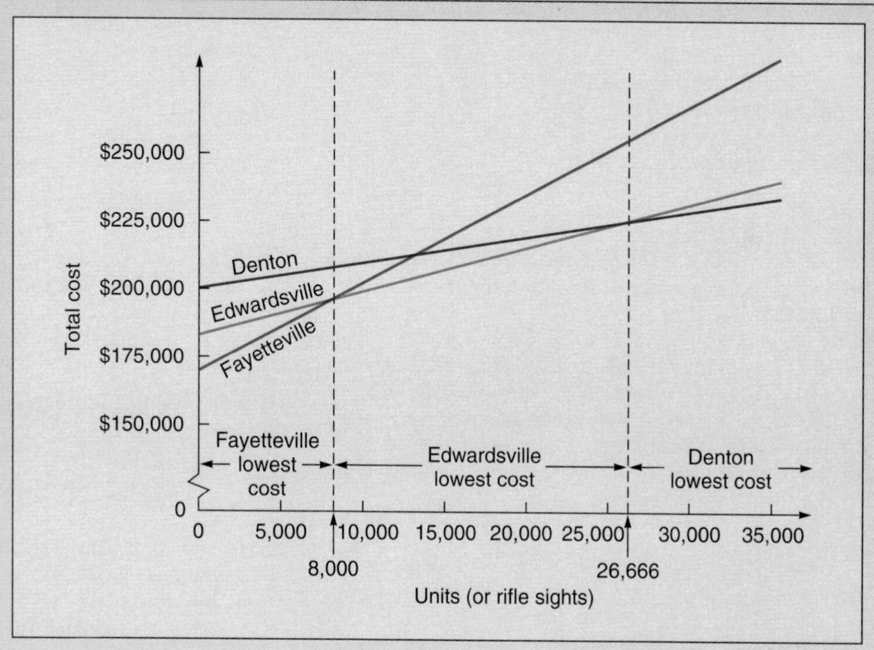

DISCUSSION QUESTIONS

1. In terms of the strategic objective, how do industrial and service location decisions differ?
2. In recent years, the federal government has increased the latitude that railroads have in setting rates and has deregulated much of the rate-setting structure of trucks and airlines. What will be the long-range impact of this deregulation on location strategies?
3. Beth Wood, city manager of a large eastern city, responding to a group of manufacturers who were complaining about the impact of increased taxes, said that taxes levied by a city were not an important consideration to a new business contemplating moving to that city. If you were president of the local chamber of commerce, how would you respond? If you are a person who is concerned about the unemployment rate in the inner city, how would you respond?
4. Explain the assumptions behind the center-of-gravity method. How can the model be used in a service facility location?
5. How do service facility location decisions differ from industrial location decisions in terms of the techniques used to analyze them?
6. What is the objective of location strategy?
7. What are the three steps to locational break-even analysis?
8. What are the major factors firms consider when choosing a country in which to locate?
9. What factors affect region/community location decisions?
10. Name several factors that affect site location.
11. How can quantitative and qualitative factors both be considered in a location decision?

SELF-TEST ■ CHAPTER 6

- *Before taking the self-test* refer back to the learning objectives listed at the beginning of the chapter and the key terms listed at the end of the chapter.
- Use the key at the back of the text to *correct* your answers.
- *Restudy* pages that correspond to any questions you answered incorrectly or material you feel uncertain about.

1. Which of the following methods best considers intangible costs related to a location decision?
   a. weighted methods
   b. locational break-even analysis
   c. transportation method
   d. assignment method
   e. none of the above

2. What is the major difference in focus between location decisions in the service sector and in the manufacturing sector?
   a. there is no difference in focus
   b. the focus in manufacturing is revenue maximization, while the focus in service is cost minimization
   c. the focus in service is revenue maximization, while the focus in manufacturing is cost minimization
   d. the focus in manufacturing is on raw materials, while the focus in service is on labor

3. Service/retail/professional locational analysis typically has a:
   a. cost focus
   b. revenue focus
   c. labor focus
   d. environmental focus

4. The factors involved in location decisions include
   a. foreign exchange
   b. attitudes
   c. labor productivity
   d. all of the above
   e. none of the above

5. Industrial locational analysis typically has a
   a. cost focus
   b. revenue focus
   c. labor focus
   d. environmental focus

6. The major types of methods used to solve location problems are
   a. ________ b. ________ c. ________ d. ________

7. The objective of location strategy is to
   ____

8. The three steps to locational break-even analysis are
   a. ____________ b. ____________ c. ____________

9. Hotel chains find regression analysis useful in site location.
   a. True b. False

10. The telemarketing industry seeks locations that have
    a. good electronic movement of data
    b. low cost labor
    c. adequate availability of labor
    d. all of the above

11. Factors affecting location decisions include
    a. proximity to markets, proximity to suppliers, proximity to athletic facilities
    b. site costs, transportation availability, labor availability
    c. average age of labor force, labor costs, number of females in college
    d. utility costs, zoning, altitude of city
    e. all of the above

OPERATIONS IN PRACTICE EXERCISE

In this chapter, we have discussed a number of location decisions, including Mercedes-Benz's selection of Vance, Alabama, for its first U.S. plant. Similarly, United Airlines recently announced its competition to select a town for a new billion dollar aircraft repair base. The bidding for the prize of 7,000 jobs was fast and furious, with Orlando offering $154 million in incentives, and Denver more than twice that amount. Kentucky's Governor Wilkinson angrily rescinded Louisville's offer of $300 million, likening the bidding to "squeezing every drop of blood out of a turnip." What are the ethical, legal, and economic implications of location wars such as these? Who pays for such giveaways? Are local citizens allowed to vote on offers made by their cities, counties, or states? Should there be limits on these incentives?

PROBLEMS

6.1. Consolidated Refineries, headquartered in Houston, must decide among three sites for the construction of a new oil processing center. The firm has selected the six factors listed below as a basis for evaluation and has assigned rating weights from 1 to 5 on each factor.

FACTOR	FACTOR NAME	RATING WEIGHT
1	Proximity to port facilities	5
2	Power-source availability and cost	3
3	Workforce attitude and cost	4
4	Distance from Houston	2
5	Community desirability	2
6	Equipment suppliers in area	3

Management has rated each location for each factor on a 1 to 100 point basis.

FACTOR	LOCATION A	LOCATION B	LOCATION C
1	100	80	80
2	80	70	100
3	30	60	70
4	10	80	60
5	90	60	80
6	50	60	90

What site will be recommended?

6.2. The fixed and variable costs for four potential plant sites for a ski equipment manufacturer are shown below.

SITE	FIXED COST PER YEAR	VARIABLE COST PER UNIT
Atlanta	$125,000	$ 6
Burlington	75,000	5
Cleveland	100,000	4
Denver	50,000	12

a. Graph the total cost lines for the four potential sites.
b. Over what range of annual volume is each location the preferable one (that with lowest expected cost)?
c. If expected volume of the ski equipment is 5,000 units, which location would you recommend?

6.3. A Detroit seafood restaurant is considering opening a second facility in the suburb of West Bloomfield. The table below shows its ratings of five factors at each of four potential sites. Which site should be selected?

FACTOR	WEIGHT	SITE *1*	*2*	*3*	*4*
Affluence of local population	10	70	60	85	90
Construction and land cost	10	85	90	80	60
Traffic flow	25	70	60	85	90
Parking availability	20	80	90	90	80
Growth potential	15	90	80	90	75

6.4. When placing a new medical clinic, county health offices wish to consider three sites. The pertinent data are given in the table below. Which is the best site?

LOCATION FACTOR	SCORES *Weight*	*Downtown*	*Suburb A*	*Suburb B*
Facility utilization	9	9	7	6
Average time per emergency trip	8	6	6	8
Employee preferences	5	2	5	6
Accessibility to major roadways	5	8	4	5
Land costs	4	2	9	6

6.5. The main post office in Tampa, Florida, is due to be replaced with a much larger, more modern facility that can handle the tremendous flow of mail that has followed the city's growth since 1970. Since all mail, incoming or outgoing, travels from the seven regional post offices in Tampa through the main post office, its site selection can mean a big difference in overall delivery and movement efficiency. Using the data in the following table, calculate the center of gravity for the proposed new facility.

REGIONAL POST OFFICE	MAP COORDINATES (x, y)	TRUCK ROUND TRIPS PER DAY
Ybor City	(10, 5)	3
Davis Island	(3, 8)	3
Dale-Mabry	(4, 7)	2
Palma Ceia	(15, 10)	6
Bayshore	(13, 3)	5
Temple Terrace	(1, 12)	3
Hyde Park	(5, 5)	10

6.6. Laurie Shader owns two exclusive women's clothing stores in Miami. In her plan to expand to a third location, she has narrowed her decision down to three sites—one in a downtown office building, one in a shopping mall, and one in an old Victorian house in the suburban area of Coral Gables. She feels that rent is absolutely the most important factor to be considered, while walk-in traffic is 90% as important as rent. Further, the more distant the new store is from her two existing stores the better, she thinks. She weights this factor to be 80% as important as walk-in traffic. Laurie developed the table below, where she graded each site on the same system used in her MBA program in college. Which site is preferable?

	DOWNTOWN	SHOPPING MALL	CORAL GABLES HOUSE
Rent	D	C	A
Walk-in traffic	B	A	D
Distance from existing stores	B	A	C

6.7. The following table gives the map coordinates and the shipping loads for a set of cities that we wish to connect through a central "hub." Near what map coordinates should the hub be located?

CITY	MAP COORDINATE (*x*, *y*)	SHIPPING LOAD
A	(5, 10)	5
B	(6, 8)	10
C	(4, 9)	15
D	(9, 5)	5
E	(7, 9)	15
F	(3, 2)	10
G	(2, 6)	5

6.8. Nancy Evans Retailers is attempting to decide upon a location for a new retail outlet. At the moment, they have three alternatives—stay where they are, but enlarge the facility; locate along the main street in nearby Newbury; or locate in a new shopping mall in Hyde Park. They have selected the four factors listed in the following table as the basis for evaluation and have assigned weights as shown:

FACTOR	FACTOR DESCRIPTION	WEIGHT
1	Average community income	.30
2	Community growth potential	.15
3	Availability of public transportation	.20
4	Labor availability, attitude, and cost	.35

Evans has rated each location for each factor, on a 100-point basis. These ratings are given below:

	LOCATION		
FACTOR	*Present Location*	*Newbury*	*Hyde Park*
1	40	60	50
2	20	20	80
3	30	60	50
4	80	50	50

Which site should be recommended?

6.9. The fixed and variable costs for three potential manufacturing plant sites for a rattan chair weaver are shown below:

SITE	FIXED COST PER YEAR	VARIABLE COST PER UNIT
1	$ 500	$11
2	1000	7
3	1700	4

a. Over what range of production is each location optimal?
b. For a production of 200 units, which site is best?

Internet Data Base Application See our website at http://www.prenhall.com/renderpom for a challenging, computer-based problem.

CASE STUDY

Southern Recreational Vehicle Company

In October 1996, top management of Southern Recreational Vehicle Company of St. Louis, Missouri, announced its plans to relocate its manufacturing and assembly operations by constructing a new plant in Ridgecrest, Mississippi. The firm, a major producer of pickup campers and camper trailers, had experienced five consecutive years of declining profits as a result of spiraling production costs. The costs of labor and raw materials had increased alarmingly, utility costs had gone up sharply, and taxes and transportation expenses had climbed upward steadily. In spite of increased sales, the company suffered its first net loss since operations were begun in 1977.

When management initially considered relocation, they closely scrutinized several geographic areas. Of primary importance to the relocation decision were the availability of adequate transportation facilities, state and municipal tax structures, an adequate labor supply, positive community attitudes, reasonable site costs, and financial inducements. Although several communities offered essentially the same incentives, the management of Southern Recreational Vehicle Company was favorably impressed by the efforts of the Mississippi Power and Light Company to attract "clean, labor-intensified" industry and the enthusiasm exhibited by state and local officials who actively sought to bolster the state's economy by enticing manufacturing firms to locate within its boundaries.

Two weeks prior to the announcement, management of Southern Recreational Vehicle Company finalized its relocation plans. An existing building in Ridgecrest's industrial park was selected (the physical facility had previously housed a mobile home manufacturer that had gone bankrupt due to inadequate financing and poor management); initial recruiting was begun through the state employment office; and efforts to lease or sell the St. Louis property were initiated. Among the inducements offered Southern Recreational Vehicle Company to locate in Ridgecrest were:

1. Exemption from county and municipal taxes for five years.
2. Free water and sewage services.
3. Construction of a second loading dock—free of cost—at the industrial site.
4. An agreement to issue $500,000 in industrial bonds for future expansion.
5. Public-financed training of workers in a local industrial trade school.

In addition to these inducements, other factors weighed heavily in the decision to locate in the small Mississippi town. Labor costs would be significantly less than those incurred in St. Louis; organized labor was not expected to be as powerful (Mississippi is a right-to-work state); and utility costs and taxes would be moderate. All in all, management of Southern Recreational Vehicle Company felt that its decision was sound.

On October 15, the following announcement was attached to each employee's paycheck:

> To: Employees of Southern Recreational Vehicle Company
> From: Gerald O'Brian, President
>
> The Management of Southern Recreational Vehicle Company regretfully announces its plans to cease all manufacturing operations in St. Louis on December 31. Because of increased operating costs and the unreasonable demands forced upon the company by the union, it has become impossible to operate profitably. I sincerely appreciate the fine service that each of you has rendered to the company during the past few years. If I can be of assistance in helping you find suitable employment with another firm, please let me know. Thank you again for your cooperation and past service.

DISCUSSION QUESTIONS

1. Evaluate the inducements offered Southern Recreational Vehicle Company by community leaders in Ridgecrest, Mississippi.
2. What problems would a company experience in relocating its executives from a heavily populated industrialized area to a small rural town?
3. Evaluate the reasons cited by O'Brian for relocation. Are they justifiable?
4. What responsibilities does a firm have to its employees when a decision to cease operations is made?

SOURCE: Professor Jerry Kinard (Western Carolina University).

BIBLIOGRAPHY

Craig, C. S., et al., "Models of the Retail Location Process." *Journal of Retailing* 60 (April 1984): 5–36.

DeForest, M. E. "Thinking of a Plant in Mexico?" *The Academy of Management Executive* 8, no. 1 (February 1994): 33–40.

Domich, P. D., K. L. Hoffman, R. H. F. Jackson, and M. A. McClain. "Locating Tax Facilities: A Graphics-Based Microcomputer Optimization Model." *Management Science* 37 (August 1991): 960.

Drezner, Z. *Facility Location: A Survey of Applications and Methods,* Secaucus, NJ: Springer-Verlag, 1995.

Fitzsimmons, J. A. "A Warehouse Location Model Helps Texas Comptroller Select Out-of-State Audit Officers." *Interfaces* 13 (October 1983): 40–45.

Murdick, R., B. Render, and R. Russell. *Service Operations Management.* Boston: Allyn & Bacon, 1990.

Price, W. L., and M. Turcotte. "Locating a Blood Bank." *Interfaces* 16 (September-October 1986): 17–26.

Reed, R. *Plant Location, Layout, and Maintenance.* Homewood, IL: Richard D. Irwin, 1967.

Render, B., and R. M. Stair. *Introduction to Management Science.* Boston: Allyn & Bacon, 1992.

Render, B., and R. M. Stair. *Quantitative Analysis for Management,* 6th ed. Upper Saddle River, NJ: Prentice-Hall, 1997.

Schmenner, R. W. "Look Beyond the Obvious in Plant Location." *Harvard Business Review* 57 (January-February 1979): 126–132.

Vargas, G. A., and T. W. Johnson. "An Analysis of Operational Experience in the U.S./Mexico Production Sharing (Maquiladora) Program." *Journal of Operations Management* 11, no. 1 (March 1993): 17–34.

Zarrillo, M. J. "Strategies for Selecting a Mixed-Use Corporate Site." *Industrial Development* (March-April 1986).

People and Work Systems

7

CHAPTER OUTLINE

People and Work Systems

Constraints on People and Work Systems ■ Job Classifications and Work Rules

Job Design

Labor Specialization ■ Job Expansion ■ Psychological Components of Job Design ■ Self-Directed Teams ■ Motivation and Incentive Systems ■ Ergonomics and Work Methods

Labor Standards and Work Measurement

Historical Experience ■ Time Studies ■ Predetermined Time Standards ■ Work Sampling

Summary ■ Key Terms ■ Using Excel Spreadsheets for Time Study ■ Solved Problems ■ Self-Test Chapter 7 ■ Discussion Questions ■ Operations in Practice Exercise ■ Problems ■ Case Studies: The Fleet That Wanders; Lincoln Electric's Incentive Pay System ■ Bibliography

LEARNING OBJECTIVES

When you complete this chapter you should be able to:

IDENTIFY OR DEFINE:

Labor specialization
Core job characteristics
Tools of methods analysis
Ergonomics
Job design
Lean production
Labor standards

DESCRIBE OR EXPLAIN:

Requirements of good job design
Requirements of good labor standards

At 9 A.M. the assembly line has been moving for only one hour, but already the day is dragging. In position five on line four, Annette Fullbright catches the next circuit board crawling down the line. At the current pace, one board passes her workstation every minute and a half. Forty down, 280 left to go today. Over in quality control, Ismael Hernandez puts his soldering gun back in its holster, fidgets with his left shirt sleeve and steals a quick glance at his watch. Thirty more minutes before coffee break. Two and a half hours to lunch. Seven and a half more until quitting time.[1]

Scenes such as these are repeated a thousand times every day all over the world. Why are Annette's and Ismael's jobs like this? Why do firms have such jobs? In this chapter we will examine these and related questions.

PEOPLE AND WORK SYSTEMS

Human performance is crucial to an organization's performance. An organization does not function without people. It does not function well without competent people. It does not excel without competent, motivated people. Consequently, how the operations manager formulates a human resource strategy determines the talents available to operations. Moreover, people are expensive; in many organizations, a third of total cost is in wages and salaries. Therefore, this chapter considers human resource strategy options.

As we focus on people and work systems, we want to ensure that people:

1. Are efficiently utilized within the constraints of other operations management actions.
2. Have a reasonable quality of work life in an atmosphere of mutual commitment and trust.

quality of work life

mutual commitment

mutual trust

By reasonable **quality of work life** we mean a job that not only is reasonably safe and for which the pay is equitable, but also achieves an appropriate level of both physical and psychological requirements. By **mutual commitment** we mean both management and employee strive to meet common objectives. By **mutual trust** we mean reasonable, documented employment policies that are honestly and equitably implemented to the satisfaction of both management and employee.[2] When management has a genuine respect for its employees and their contribution to the firm, establishing a reasonable quality of work life and mutual trust is not particularly difficult.

This chapter is devoted to how the operations manager can achieve an effective human resource strategy.

Constraints on People and Work Systems

As Figure 7.1 suggests, many decisions that are made about people are constrained by other decisions. First, the product mix may determine seasonality and stability of employment. Second, technology, equipment, and processes may have implications for safety and job content. Third, the location decision may have an im-

[1] Roger Thurow, "Life on the Job," *The Wall Street Journal*, June 1, 1981, p. 1.

[2] With increasing frequency we find companies calling their employees *associates, individual contributors,* or members of a particular team.

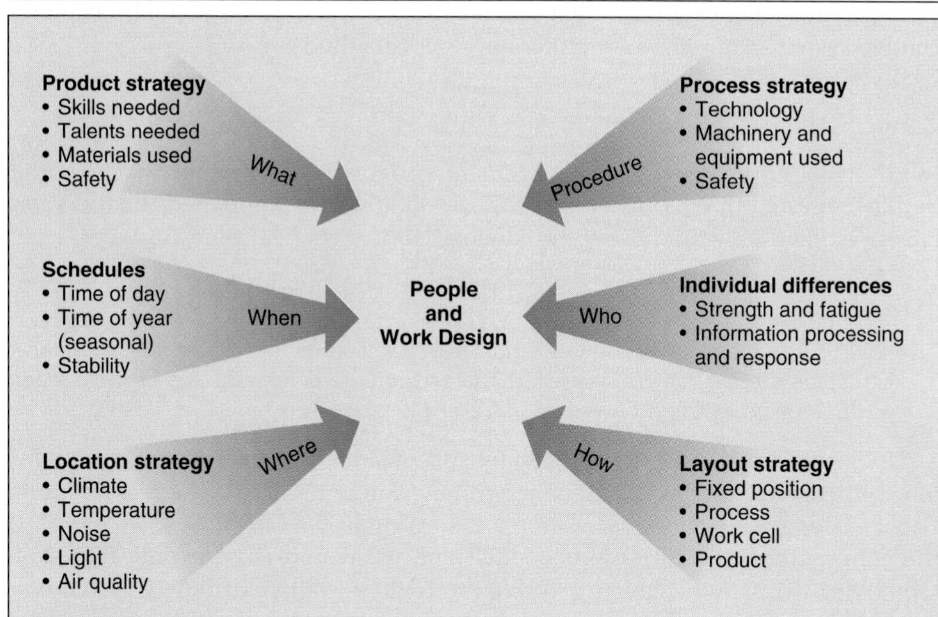

The effective operations manager understands how decisions blend together to constrain the work design.

FIGURE 7.1

CONSTRAINTS ON PEOPLE AND WORK DESIGN

pact on the ambient environment in which the employees work. Finally, decisions regarding layout may dictate, in large part, job content.

Knowledge of the technology available, combined with location and layout decisions, and the proper capital investment decisions may yield efficiency and a tolerable, if not an ideal, quality of work life. The trade-offs are difficult. Consequently, it behooves a prudent manager to ensure that such decisions are considered simultaneously. The manager blends ingredients so that the result is an effective, efficient system where individuals have optimum job design.

Job Classifications and Work Rules

Many organizations have strict job classifications and work rules that specify who can do what, when they can do it, and under what conditions they can do it. These job classifications and work rules restrict employee flexibility on the job, which in turn reduces the flexibility of the production/operations function. But part of an operations manager's task is to manage the unexpected. Therefore, the more flexibility a firm has when staffing and establishing work schedules, the more efficient it can be. Building morale and meeting staffing requirements that result in an efficient production function are easier if managers have fewer job classifications and work-rule constraints.

JOB DESIGN

Job design specifies the tasks that constitute a job for an individual or a group. We examine six components of job design: (1) labor specialization, (2) job expan-

job design

sion, (3) psychological components, (4) self-directed teams, (5) motivation and incentive systems, and (6) ergonomics and work methods.

Labor Specialization

labor specialization

Job design's importance as a management variable is credited to Adam Smith.[3] Smith suggested that a division of labor, also known as **labor specialization** and job specialization, would assist in reducing labor costs in several ways:

1. *Development of dexterity* and faster learning by the employee because of repetition.
2. *Less loss of time* because the employee would not be changing jobs or tools.
3. *Development of specialized tools* and the reduction of investment because each employee has only a few tools needed for a particular task.

Charles Babbage determined that a fourth consideration was also important for labor efficiency.[4] Because pay tends to follow skill with a rather high correlation, Babbage suggested *paying exactly the wage needed for the particular skill required.* If the entire job consists of only one skill, then we would pay for only that skill. Otherwise, we would tend to pay for the highest skill contributed by the employee. These four advantages of labor specialization are still valid today.

A classic example of labor specialization is the assembly line, as described in the opening paragraph of this chapter. Such systems are often very efficient, although they may require employees to do repetitive, mind-numbing jobs. The wage rate for many of these jobs, however, is very good. Given the relatively high wage rate for the modest skills required in many of these jobs, there is often a large pool of employees from which to choose. This is not an incidental consideration for the manager with responsibility for staffing the operations function. However, only 2% to 3% of the workforce in industrialized nations perform highly specialized, repetitive, assembly-line jobs. The traditional way of developing and maintaining worker commitment under labor specialization has been good selection (matching people to the job), good wages, and incentive systems.

Job Expansion

NOTE
An enlarged job may only give employees a number of boring things to do.

job enlargement

job rotation

job enrichment

In recent years, there has been an effort to improve the quality of work life by moving from labor specialization toward a more varied job design. The theory is that variety makes the job "better" and the employee therefore finds a higher quality of work life. This in turn benefits the employee and the organization. We modify jobs in a variety of ways. The first approach is **job enlargement,** which occurs when we add tasks of similar skill to the existing job. **Job rotation** is a version of job enlargement that occurs when the job per se is not enlarged, but rather the employee is allowed to move from one specialized job to another. Variety has been added to the employee's perspective of the job. Another approach is **job enrichment,** which adds planning and control to the job. Job enrichment can be thought of as *vertical expansion,* as opposed to job enlargement, which is *horizontal.* These ideas and others are shown in Figure 7.2.

---

[3]Adam Smith, *On the Creation of the Wealth of Nations* (London, 1876).

[4]Charles Babbage, *On the Economy of Machinery and Manufacturers* (London, 1832), chap. 18.

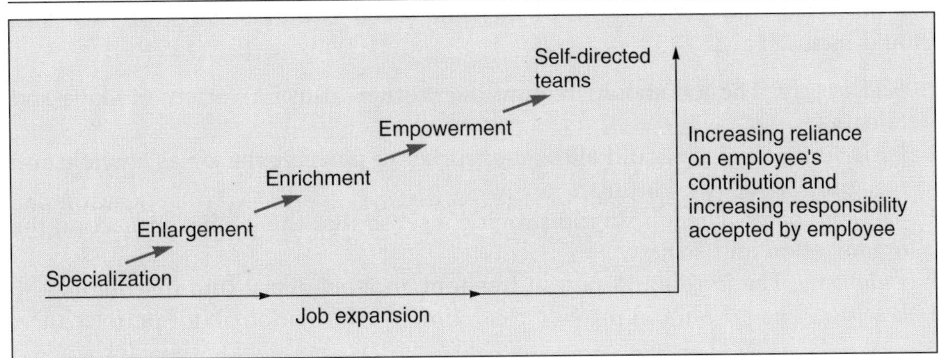

FIGURE 7.2
JOB DESIGN CONTINUUM

Employee empowerment is the practice of enriching jobs so employees accept responsibility for a variety of decisions normally associated with staff specialists.[5] Employee empowerment is a popular extension of job enrichment. Empowering employees helps them take ownership of their jobs and promotes a personal interest in improving performance. At the Ritz-Carlton hotel chain the authority of front-desk clerks and sales managers has been extended so they are empowered to spend up to $2,000 and $5,000, respectively, of company money—to ensure that guests leave satisfied.

employee empowerment

Psychological Components of Job Design

An effective human resources strategy also requires consideration of the psychological components of job design. Psychological components of job design focus on how to design jobs that meet some minimum psychological requirements.

NOTE
"We hired workers and human beings came instead." Max Frisch

HAWTHORNE STUDIES. The Hawthorne studies introduced psychology to the workplace. They were conducted in the late 1920s at GE's Hawthorne Plant near Chicago. Publication of the findings in 1939[6] showed conclusively that a dynamic social system exists at the workplace. Ironically, these studies were initiated to determine the impact of lighting on productivity. Instead they found the social system and distinct roles played by employees to be more important than the intensity of the lighting. They also found that individual differences may be dominant in what employees expect from their jobs and what employees think their contributions to their jobs should be.

The GE process for empowering employees is generating ideas in offices and on factory floors. Here at Appliance Park in Louisville, Kentucky, for example, employees, like utility operator Leo Porter (left) and shop steward Ron Rowe of IUE Local 761, are constantly coming up with ideas—and putting them into action.

CORE JOB CHARACTERISTICS. In the six decades since the Hawthorne studies, substantial research regarding the psychological components of job design has taken place.[7] Hackman and Oldham have incorporated much of that work into

[5]See W. C. Byham, *Zapp! The Lightning of Empowerment* (New York: Ballantine, 1992).
[6]F. J. Roethlisberger and William J. Dickinson, *Management and the Workers* (New York: John Wiley, 1964, copyright 1939, by the President & Fellows of Harvard College).
[7]See, for instance, the work of Abraham H. Maslow, "A Theory of Human Motivation," *Psychological Review* 50 (1943): 370–396; and Frederick Herzberg, B. Mausner, and B. B. Snyderman, *The Motivation to Work* (New York: John Wiley, 1965).

five desirable characteristics of job design.[8] Their summary suggests that jobs should include:

1. *Skill variety.* The job should require the worker to use a variety of skills and talents.
2. *Job identity.* The job should allow the worker to perceive the job as a whole and recognize a start and a finish.
3. *Job significance.* The job should provide a sense that the job has impact on the organization and society.
4. *Autonomy.* The job should permit freedom, independence, and discretion.
5. *Feedback.* The job should provide clear, timely information about performance.

Including these five ingredients in job design is consistent with job enlargement, job enrichment, and employee empowerment. We now look at teams as a way to expand jobs and achieve these five job characteristics.

Self-Directed Teams

self-directed team

Many world-class organizations have adopted teams to foster mutual trust and commitment and provide the core job characteristics. One team concept of particular note is the self-directed team. A **self-directed team** is a group of empowered individuals working together to reach a common goal. These teams may be organized for long-term or short-term objectives. Teams are effective because they can easily provide employee empowerment, core job characteristics, and many of the psychological needs of team members.[9] Teamwork is reinforced at many world-class plants, including Mazda's Flat Rock, Michigan, plant where interpersonal skills and team participation are stressed from initial employment and training through evaluation.

Of course, many good job designs can provide these psychological needs. Therefore, to maximize team effectiveness, managers do more than just form "teams." For instance, they (1) ensure that those who have a legitimate contribution are on the team, (2) provide management support, (3) ensure the necessary training, and (4) endorse a clear objective for the team. Successful teams should also receive rewards and recognition. Finally, managers must recognize that teams have a life cycle and that achieving an objective may suggest disbanding the team. However, teams may be renewed with a change in members or new assignments. Empowered employees working in teams can make a powerful contribution to world-class performance.

Teams and other approaches to job expansion should not only improve the quality of work life and job satisfaction, but also motivate employees to achieve organizational objectives. Both managers and employees need to be committed to achieving organizational objectives. However, employee contribution is fostered in a variety of ways, including organizational climate, supervisory action, *and* job design.

Expanded job designs allow the employee to accept more responsibility. For employees who accept this responsibility, we may well expect some enhancement in productivity and product quality. Among the other positive aspects of job ex-

---

[8]See "Motivation Through the Design of Work," in Jay Richard Hackman and Greg R. Oldham, *Work Redesign* (Reading, MA: Addison-Wesley, 1980).

[9]Per H. Engelstad, "Sociotechnical Approach to Problems of Process Control," in Louis E. Davis and James C. Taylor, eds., *Design of Jobs* (Santa Monica: Goodyear Publishing, 1979), pp. 184–205.

pansion are reduced turnover, tardiness, and absenteeism. Managers who expand jobs and build communication systems that elicit suggestions from employees have an added potential for efficiency.

Sleep Inn is showing the world that big gains in productivity can be made not only by manufacturers but in the service industry as well. Designed with labor efficiency in mind, Sleep Inn is staffed with 13% fewer employees than similar budget hotels. Its features include a laundry room that is almost completely automated, round shower stalls that eliminate dirty corners, and closets that have no doors for maids to open and shut.

LIMITATIONS OF JOB EXPANSION. If job designs that enlarge, enrich, empower, and use teams are so good, why are they not universally used? Let us identify some limitations of these expanded job designs:

1. *Higher capital cost.* Job expansion requires facilities that cost more than a conventional layout. This extra expenditure must be generated through savings (greater efficiency) or through higher prices.
2. *Many individuals prefer simple jobs.* Some studies indicate that many employees opt for the less-complex jobs.[10] In a discussion about improving the quality of work life, we cannot forget the importance of individual differences. Differences in individuals provide latitude for the resourceful operations manager when designing jobs.
3. *Higher wage rates are required.* People often receive wages for their highest skills, not their lowest.[11] So, expanded jobs may well require a higher average wage than jobs that are not.
4. *Smaller labor pool exists.* Because expanded jobs require more skill and acceptance of more responsibility, the job requirements have increased. Depending upon the availability of labor, this may be a constraint.
5. *Increased accident rates may occur.* Expanded jobs may contribute to a higher accident rate.[12] This indirectly increases wages, insurance costs, and workmen's compensation.
6. *Current technology may not lend itself to job expansion.* The "disassembly" jobs at a slaughterhouse and computer assembly jobs are that way because alternative technologies (if any) are thought to be unacceptable.

These six points provide the constraints on job expansion. These practices increase costs. Therefore, for the firm to have a competitive advantage, its savings must be greater than its cost. It is not always obvious that such is the case. The strategic decision is not an easy one.

LEAN PRODUCTION. When mutual trust and commitment are combined with good job designs, lean production may be possible. Under **lean production,** highly trained employees are committed to removing waste and doing only those activities where value is added. Empowered employees analyze every detail of serving the customer and are increasingly successful in squeezing out waste. The concept of lean production varies substantially from a more traditional effort to make jobs ever more simple and require ever less training. Indeed, when effectively implemented, lean production utilizes the employee's *mental* as well as physical attributes to continually improve the production system. Because of a reasonable quality of work life and mutual trust, the employee buys into mutual commitment. In this way, the production process is constantly improving, and higher levels of efficiency are achieved. Under lean production, the employee is not a ro-

lean production

NOTE
"What should be obvious from the outset is that people perform to the standards of their leaders. If management thinks people don't care, then people won't care."
Quality control expert, Philip Crosby

[10]Michell Fein, "Job Enrichment Does Not Work," *Atlanta Economic Review* (November-December 1975): 50–54.
[11]Charles Babbage, *On the Economy of Machinery and Manufacturers* (London, 1832), chap. 18.
[12]J. Tsaari and J. Lahtella, "Job Enrichment: Cause of Increased Accidents?" *Industrial Engineering* (October 1978): 41–45.

bot; he or she is an empowered member of the organization who uses both mental and physical abilities to help serve the customer through ever higher levels of productivity.

learning organization

Using an empowered employee's mental as well as physical attributes suggests a *learning organization.* A **learning organization** is a constantly improving lean producer where mutual trust and commitment exist. In a high technology society operations managers need to think in terms of building and managing learning organizations.

NOTE
Roger Penske, president of Detroit Diesel, which he purchased from GM, has used good relations with employees and a profit-sharing system to turn his firm around.

Motivation and Incentive Systems

Our discussion of psychological components of job design provides insight into the factors that may contribute to job satisfaction and motivation. In addition to these psychological factors, there are monetary factors. Money often serves as a psychological, as well as a financial motivator. Monetary rewards take the form of bonuses, profit and gain sharing, and incentive systems.

bonus

profit sharing

gain sharing

Bonuses, typically in cash or stock options, are often used at executive levels to reward management. **Profit-sharing** systems provide some part of the profit for distribution to employees. A variation of profit sharing is gain sharing. **Gain-sharing** techniques reward employees for improvements made in an organization's performance. The most popular of these is the Scanlon plan, where any reduction in the cost of labor is shared between management and labor.

The gain-sharing approach used by Panhandle Eastern Corp. of Houston, Texas, allows for employees to receive a bonus of 2% of their salary at year end if the company earns at least $2.00 per share. When Panhandle earns $2.10 per share, the bonus climbs to 3%. Employees have become much more sensitive about costs since the plan began.

incentive system

Incentive systems based on individual or group productivity are used in close to half of the manufacturing firms in America. These systems are often based on the employee or crew achieving production above a predetermined standard. The standard can be based on a standard time per task or number of pieces made.

measured daywork

piece rate

Standard time systems are sometimes called **measured daywork,** where employees are paid based on the amount of standard time accomplished. A **piece-rate** system assigns a standard time for each piece, and the employee is paid based on the number of pieces made. Both measured daywork and piece-rate systems typically guarantee the employee at least a base rate for the shift.

Ergonomics and Work Methods

SCIENTIFIC MANAGEMENT. You may recall from the discussion of scientific management in Chapter 1 that, in the late 1880s, Frederick W. Taylor began the era of scientific management.[13] He and his contemporaries began to examine personnel selection, work methods, work standards, and motivation. They examined the role of management and employees at the workplace and were concerned with the following:

[13]Frederick W. Taylor, *Scientific Management* (New York: Harper & Row, 1911), p. 204.

Ergonomics and an understanding of human capability provide an opportunity to improve human performance. The left photo shows traditional round analog dials and gauges that can present a lot of difficult-to-interpret information. They are being replaced by cockpits with less clutter because of fewer dials and gauges and heads-up displays. The heads-up display allows images and critical flight information to be projected on a fold-down screen, as shown on the right, so the pilot can fly heads-up. The new improvement in pilot-response time may save lives.

1. Matching employees to the task (individual differences).
2. Work methods (improving task performance).
3. Work standards (so both employee and employer would know what was to be done and what constituted a fair day's work).

With the foundation provided by Taylor and his contemporaries, we have developed a body of knowledge about people's capabilities and limitations. This

Ergonomics issues occur in the office as well as in the factory. Here an ergonomics consultant is measuring the angle of a terminal operator's neck. Posture, which is related to desk height, chair height and position, keyboard placement, and computer screen, is an important factor in reducing back and neck pain that can be caused by extended hours at a computer.

knowledge is useful because humans are a hand-eye animal possessing exceptional capabilities and some limitations. Because managers must design jobs that can be done, we are now going to introduce briefly a few of the issues related to people's capabilities and limitations.

ergonomics

The operations manager is interested in building a good interface between human and machine. Studies of this interface are known as **ergonomics.** *Ergonomics* means "the study of work." (*Ergo* is from the Greek word for *work.*) In America the term *human factors* is often substituted for the word *ergonomics.*

Male and female adults come in limited configurations. Therefore, design of the workplace depends on biomechanics and anthropometric data. Biomechanical and anthropometric data provide the basic strength and measurement data needed to design tools and the workplace. The design of tools and the workplace can make jobs easy or impossible.

NOTE
Many bicycle riders have seats set too low. The correct height is 103% of crotch to foot distance.

Let us look briefly at one problem resulting from poor ergonomic design. The current typewriter keyboard was purposely arranged to slow down typists. The mechanical lever arrangement of early typewriters would "jam" when an outstanding typist went to work. So the answer was to place the keys in an inconvenient arrangement. The result is the familiar QWERTY keyboard. However, even with a poor keyboard, the operator performed a variety of activities from manually returning the carriage to changing and aligning paper. The operator's hands and wrists were exercised. But with the advent of the word processor, the opportunity for typists to exercise hands and wrists was severely curtailed. The re-

Because the proper, comfortable tools are important to people, including those who use telephone headsets, engineers at Plantronics took an ergonomic look at ears. They took plaster casts of 700 different ears to develop the perfect fit. The new unit is lightweight, doesn't mess one's hair, is only four inches long, and can be worn all day without discomfort.

FIGURE 7.3 JOB DESIGN AND THE KEYBOARD

Apple Computers' adjustable keyboard is divided into two hinged sections that can be customized. (Apple Computers, Cupertino, California)

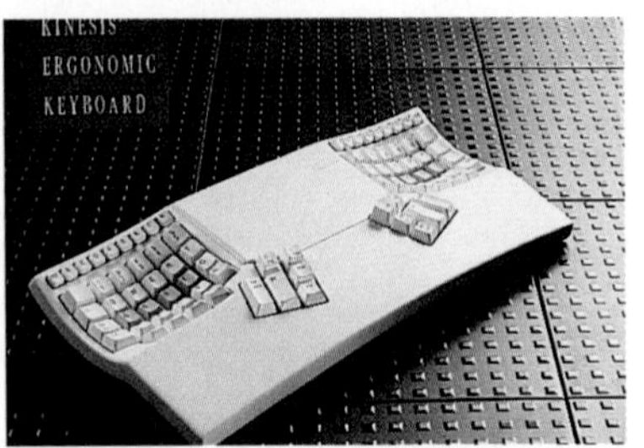

Tests indicate that this keyboard is less physically demanding and more comfortable to use than a traditional computer keyboard. The keyboard is a closer fit to the natural shape of the hand. (Kinesis Corp., Bellevue, WA)

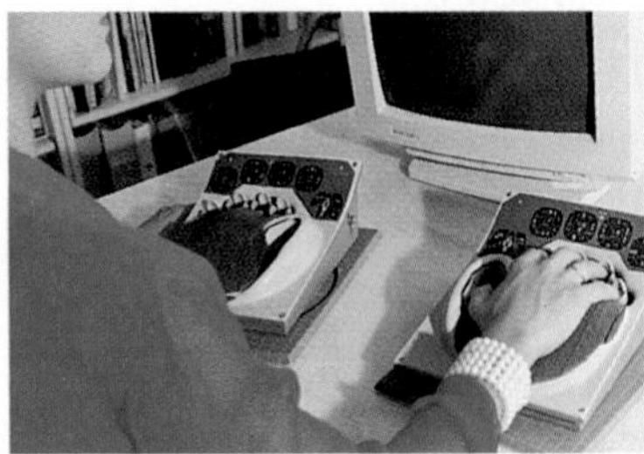

The "Data-Hand" keyboard allows each hand to rest on its own ergonomically shaped and padded palm support. Five keys surround each finger tip and thumb. (Industrial Innovations, Inc., Scottsdale, AZ)

sult is a huge increase in carpal tunnel syndrome, a painful nerve condition stemming from repetitive, abnormal use of the wrist. As Figure 7.3 shows, efforts are being made to address the problem. How operations managers design the workplace does make a difference.

THE WORK ENVIRONMENT. The physical environment in which employees work affects their performance, safety, and quality of work life. Illumination, noise and vibration, temperature, humidity, and air quality are work environment factors under the control of the organization and the operations manager. The manager must approach them as controllable.

Illumination is necessary, but the proper level depends upon the work being performed. Figure 7.4 provides some guidelines. However, other factors of lighting are important. These other factors include reflective ability, contrast of the work surface with surroundings, glare, and shadows.

Noise of some form is usually present in the work area, and many employees seem to adjust well. However, high levels of sound will damage hearing.

FIGURE 7.4

LEVELS OF ILLUMINATION RECOMMENDED FOR VARIOUS TASK CONDITIONS

Task Condition	Type of Task or Area	Illumination Level (FT-C)*	Type of Illumination
Small detail, extreme accuracy	Sewing, inspecting dark materials	100	Overhead ceiling lights and desk lamp
Normal detail, prolonged periods	Reading, parts assembly, general office work	20–50	Overhead ceiling lights
Good contrast, fairly large objects	Recreational facilities	5–10	Overhead ceiling lights
Large objects	Restaurants, stairways, warehouses	2–5	Overhead ceiling lights

*FT-C (the footcandle) is a measure of illumination.
(*Source:* C. T. Morgan, J. S. Cook III, A. Chapanis, and M. W. Lund, eds., *Human Engineering Guide to Equipment Design* (New York: McGraw-Hill, 1963)).

FIGURE 7.5

DECIBEL LEVELS (dB) AND SOUND-POWER RATIOS FOR VARIOUS SOUNDS

SOURCE: A. P. G. Peterson and E. E. Gross, Jr., *Handbook of Noise Measurement*, 7th ed. (New Concord, MA: General Radio Co.), as presented in Ernest J. McCormick, *Human Factors in Engineering and Design* (New York: McGraw-Hill, 1976) p. 116.

Sound–Power Ratio	Decibels	Environment Noises	Specific Noise Sources	Decibels
1,000,000,000,000	120		Jet takeoff (200 ft)	120
100,000,000,000	110	Casting shakeout area	Riveting machine*	110
10,000,000,000	100	Electric furnace area	Cutoff saw* Pneumatic peen hammer*	100
1,000,000,000	90	Boiler room Printing press plant	Textile weaving plant* Subway train (20 ft)	90
100,000,000	80	Tabulating room Inside sports car (50 mph)	Pneumatic drill (50 ft)	80
10,000,000	70	Near freeway (auto traffic) Large store	Freight train (100 ft) Vacuum cleaner (10 ft) Speech (1 ft)	70
1,000,000	60	Accounting office Private business office Light traffic (100 ft)		60
100,000	50	Average residence	Large transformer (200 ft)	50
10,000	40	Minimum levels, residential areas in Chicago at night		40
1,000	30	Studio (speech)	Soft whisper (5 ft)	30

*At operator's position

Decibel levels are *A*-weighted sound levels measured with a sound-level meter.

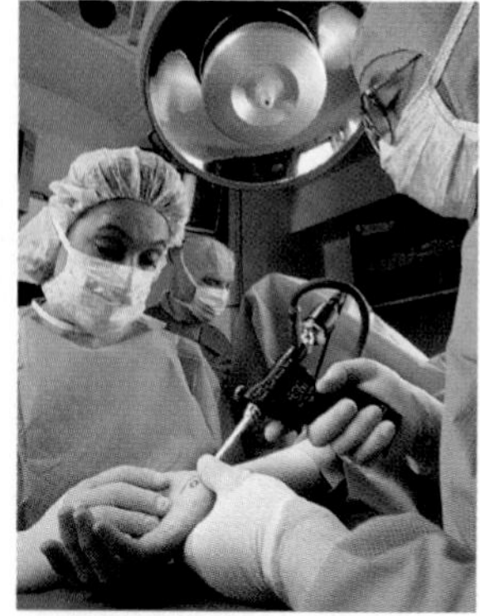

Carpal tunnel syndrome is a wrist disorder that afflicts 23,000 workers annually and costs employers and insurers an average of $30,000 per affected worker. Many of the tools, handles, and typewriter keyboards now in use put the wrists in an unnatural position. An unnatural position combined with extended repetition can cause carpal tunnel syndrome. One of the medical procedures for carpal tunnel syndrome is the operation shown here that reduces the symptoms—but the cure is in the ergonomics of workplace and tool design.

Figure 7.5 provides indications of the sound generated by various activities. (Note that decibel scales are log scales, not linear ones.) Extended periods of exposure to decibel levels above 90dB have been judged to be permanently damaging to hearing. The Occupational Safety and Health Administration (OSHA) requires ear protection above this level if exposure equals or exceeds eight hours. Even at low levels, noise and vibration can be distracting. Therefore most managers make substantial effort to reduce noise and vibration through good machine design, enclosures, or segregation of sources of noise and vibration.

Temperature and humidity parameters have been well established. Managers with activities operating outside of the established comfort zone should expect some adverse effect on performance.

CONTROLLING (ADJUSTING AND PROVIDING INPUT TO THE MACHINE). Any operator response to a machine, be it via hand tools, pedals, levers, or buttons, needs to be evaluated. Does the operator have the strength, reflexes, perception, and mental capacity to provide the necessary control?

Similarly, feedback to operators is provided by *sight, sound,* and *feel.* Selection of feedback to operators should not be left to chance. A rich body of research regarding the proper displays for use under various conditions is available to the operations manager.[14]

METHODS ANALYSIS. Methods analysis focuses on *how* a task is accomplished. Whether controlling a machine or making or assembling components, how a task

[14]Henry Dreyfuss, *The Measure of Man* (New York: Whitney Library of Design, 1960).

is done makes a difference in performance, safety, and quality. Using knowledge from ergonomics and methods analysis, methods engineers are charged with ensuring that quality and quantity standards are achieved efficiently and safely. Methods analysis and related techniques are useful in office environments as well as in the factory. Methods techniques are used to analyze:

1. Movement of individuals or material. The analysis is performed using *flow diagrams* and *process charts* with varying amounts of detail.
2. Activity of human and machine and crew activity. This analysis is performed using *activity charts* (also known as man-machine charts and crew charts).
3. Body movement (primarily arms and hands). This analysis is performed using *micro-motion charts.*

Flow diagrams are schematics (drawings) used to investigate movement of people or material. As shown for Britain's Paddy Hopkirk Factory in Figure 7.6, they provide a systematic procedure for looking at long-cycle repetitive tasks. The old method is shown in Figure 7.6(a) and a new method is shown in Figure 7.6(b).

flow diagrams

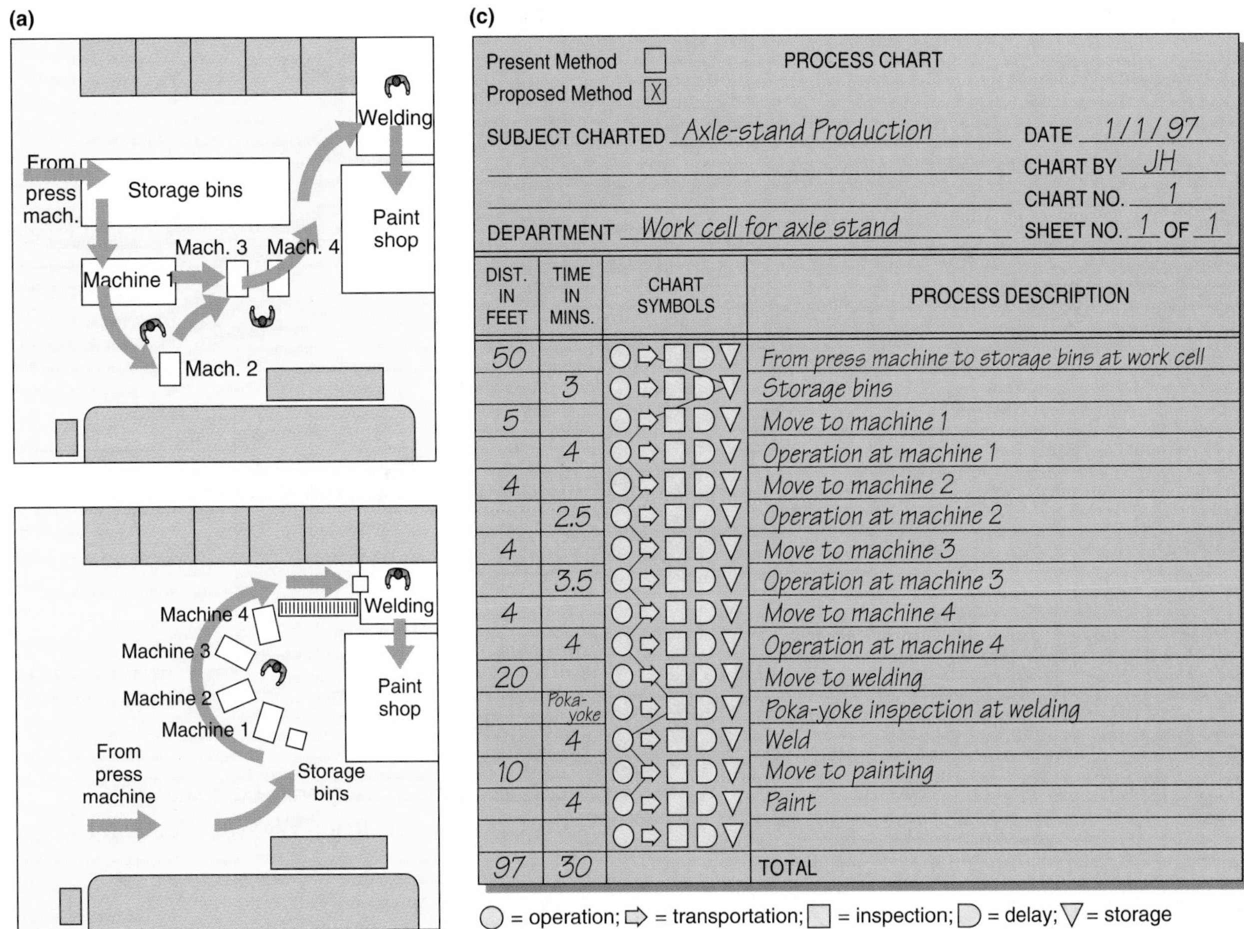

Present Method ☐
Proposed Method ☒
PROCESS CHART

SUBJECT CHARTED Axle-stand Production
DATE 1/1/97
CHART BY JH
CHART NO. 1
DEPARTMENT Work cell for axle stand
SHEET NO. 1 OF 1

DIST. IN FEET	TIME IN MINS.	CHART SYMBOLS	PROCESS DESCRIPTION
50		○ ⇨ □ D ▽	From press machine to storage bins at work cell
	3	○ ⇨ □ D ▽	Storage bins
5		○ ⇨ □ D ▽	Move to machine 1
	4	○ ⇨ □ D ▽	Operation at machine 1
4		○ ⇨ □ D ▽	Move to machine 2
	2.5	○ ⇨ □ D ▽	Operation at machine 2
4		○ ⇨ □ D ▽	Move to machine 3
	3.5	○ ⇨ □ D ▽	Operation at machine 3
4		○ ⇨ □ D ▽	Move to machine 4
	4	○ ⇨ □ D ▽	Operation at machine 4
20		○ ⇨ □ D ▽	Move to welding
	Poka-yoke	○ ⇨ □ D ▽	Poka-yoke inspection at welding
	4	○ ⇨ □ D ▽	Weld
10		○ ⇨ □ D ▽	Move to painting
	4	○ ⇨ □ D ▽	Paint
		○ ⇨ □ D ▽	
97	30		TOTAL

○ = operation; ⇨ = transportation; □ = inspection; D = delay; ▽ = storage

FIGURE 7.6 FLOW DIAGRAM OF AXEL-STAND PRODUCTION LINE AT PADDY HOPKIRK FACTORY

(a) Old Method; (b) New Method; (c) Process chart of axle-stand production using Paddy Hopkirk's new method (shown in a).

process charts

Process charts use symbols,[15] as in Figure 7.6(c), to help us understand the movement of people or material. In this way, movement and delays can be reduced and operations made more efficient. Figure 7.6(c) is a process chart used to supplement the flow diagram shown in Figure 7.6(b).

activity charts

Activity charts are used to study and improve utilization of an operator and a machine or some combination of operators (a "crew") and machines. Through observation, the analyst records the present method and then on a second chart the proposed improvement (see Figure 7.7).

operations chart

Body movement is analyzed by an **operations chart.** It is designed to show economy of motion by pointing out wasted motion and idle time (delay). The operations chart (also known as right-hand/left-hand chart) is shown in Figure 7.8.

LABOR STANDARDS AND WORK MEASUREMENT

labor standards

Effective management of people requires knowledge of labor standards. **Labor standards** are the amount of time required to perform a job or part of a job. Every firm has labor standards, although they may vary from those established via informal methods to those established by professionals. Labor standards are necessary to determine the following:

ACTIVITY CHART
SOUTHERN TECHNICAL INSTITUTE
MARIETTA, GEORGIA 30060

	MAN TIME	MAN %	MACHINE TIME	MACHINE %
WORK	6	43%	19	100%
IDLE	8	57	0	0

OPERATION:
EQUIPMENT:
OPERATOR:
STUDY NO.: ANALYST:

SUBJECT Semi-Auto Machine DATE 11-6
PRESENT / PROPOSED DEPT. SHEET 1 OF 1 CHART BY LSA

	TIME	Operator	TIME	Machine	TIME
	2, 4	Load machine		Being loaded	
	6, 8, 10, 12	Idle		Run	
	14	Unload		Being unloaded	
Repeat cycle	16, 18	Load machine		Being loaded	

FIGURE 7.7

ACTIVITY CHART

SOURCE: L. S. Aft, *Productivity Measurement and Improvement* (Upper Saddle River, NJ: Prentice-Hall, 1992), pp. 67, 76. Adapted by permission of Prentice-Hall, Inc.

LEFT-HAND / RIGHT-HAND CHART
SOUTHERN TECHNICAL INSTITUTE
MARIETTA, GEORGIA 30060

SYMBOLS	PRESENT LH	PRESENT RH	PROPOSED LH	PROPOSED RH	DIFFERENCE LH	DIFFERENCE RH
○ OPERATIONS	5	10				
⇨ TRANSPORTATIONS						
□ INSPECTIONS						
D DELAYS	10	5				
▽ STORAGES						
TOTALS	15	15				

PROCESS Bolt Washer Assembly
STUDY NO.
OPERATOR SRA
ANALYST
DATE 11/ 6 / 97 SHEET NO. 1 of 1
METHOD (PRESENT PROPOSED)
REMARKS

LEFT-HAND ACTIVITY Present METHOD	DIST.	SYMBOLS	SYMBOLS	DIST.	RIGHT-HAND ACTIVITY Present METHOD
1 Reach for bolt		●⇨□D▽	○⇨□◗▽		Idle
2 Grasp bolt		●⇨□D▽	○⇨□◗▽		Idle
3 Move bolt to		●⇨□D▽	○⇨□◗▽		Idle
work area		○⇨□D▽	○⇨□D▽		
4 Hold bolt		○⇨□◗▽	○⇨□D▽		Reach for washer
5 Hold bolt		○⇨□◗▽	○⇨□D▽		Grasp washer
6 Hold bolt		○⇨□◗▽	○⇨□D▽		Move washer to bolt
7 Hold bolt		○⇨□◗▽	○⇨□D▽		Assemble washer
		○⇨□◗▽	○⇨□D▽		on bolt

FIGURE 7.8

OPERATION CHART (RIGHT-HAND/LEFT-HAND CHART) FOR BOLT-WASHER ASSEMBLY

SOURCE: Adapted from L. S. Aft, *Productivity Measurement and Improvement* (Upper Saddle River, NJ: (Prentice-Hall, 1992), p. 5. Reprinted by permission of Prentice-Hall, Inc.

[15]The standard American Society of Mechanical Engineers (ASME) process symbols are ○ = operation; ⇨ = transportation; □ = inspection; D = delay; ▽ = storage.

Performance during a pit stop makes a difference between winning and losing a race. Activity charts are used to orchestrate the movement of members of a pit crew, an operating room staff, or machine operators in a factory.

1. Labor content of items produced (the labor cost).
2. Staffing needs of organizations (how many people it will take to make the required production).
3. Cost and time estimates prior to production (to assist in a variety of decisions from developing cost estimates for customers to the make-or-buy decision).
4. Crew size and work balance (who does what on a group activity or assembly line).
5. Production expected (both manager and worker should know what constitutes a fair day's work).
6. Basis of wage-incentive plans (what provides a reasonable incentive).
7. Efficiency of employees and supervision (a standard is necessary against which to determine efficiency).

Ergonomics shows-up in some unusual places. Here Jerry Rice is wearing a *Breathe Right* strip. The strips allow more air through the nose, to the lungs, and then to the muscles. This increases the oxygen supply to stressed muscles; so many athletes are now wearing them.

Properly set labor standards represent the amount of time it should take an average employee to perform specific job activities under normal working conditions. Labor standards are set in four ways:

1. Historical experience.
2. Time studies.
3. Predetermined time standards.
4. Work sampling.

The following sections cover each of these techniques.

Historical Experience

historical experience

Labor standards can be estimated based on **historical experience,** that is, how many labor-hours were required to do a task the last time it was performed.

Historical standards have the distinct advantage of being relatively easy and inexpensive to obtain. They are usually available from employee time cards or production records. But they are not objective. And we do not know their accuracy. Do they represent a reasonable work pace or a poor work pace? Are unusual occurrences included? Because these variables are unknown, their use is not recommended. Instead, we will stress the three work-measurement methods that are preferred to set labor standards.

Time Studies

time study

The classical stopwatch study, or time study, originally proposed by Frederick W. Taylor in 1881, is still the most widely used time-study method. A **time study** involves timing a sample of a worker's performance and using it to set a standard. A trained and experienced person can establish a standard by following these eight steps:

NOTE
Labor standards exist for telephone operators, auto mechanics, and UPS drivers, as well as factory workers.

1. Define the task to be studied (after methods analysis has been conducted).
2. Break down the task into precise elements (parts of a task that often take no more than a few seconds).
3. Decide how many times to measure the task (the number of cycles or samples needed).
4. Time and record the elemental times and ratings of performance.
5. Compute the average actual cycle time. The **average actual cycle time** is the arithmetic mean of the times for *each* element measured, adjusted for unusual influences for each element:

average actual cycle time

$$\text{Average actual cycle time} = \frac{\text{Sum of the times recorded to perform each element}}{\text{Number of cycles observed}} \tag{7.1}$$

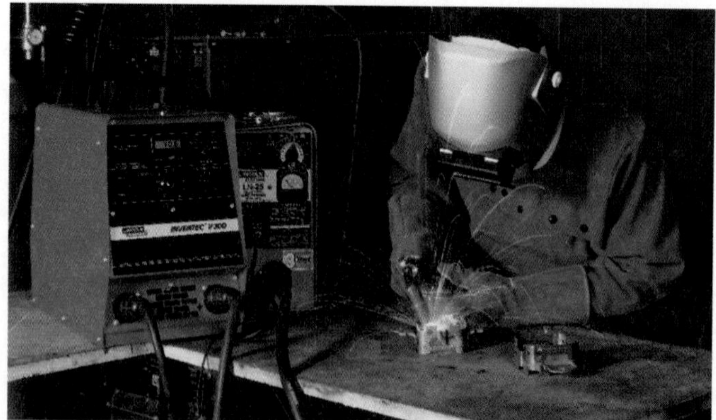

Lincoln Electric pays its employees according to actual production results. Through a sophisticated point system, each employee is evaluated on performance. Managers at Lincoln Electric are held responsible for building a work environment that allows employees to perform at their maximum. Employees work diligently at improving work methods and production systems at a level of productivity that makes Lincoln Electric a world-class producer of arc-welding equipment. In this way, employees, stockholders, and customers benefit.

6. Compute the **normal time** for each element. This measure is a "performance rating" for the particular worker pace observed:

normal time

$$\text{Normal time} = (\text{Average actual cycle time}) \times (\text{Rating factor}) \qquad (7.2)$$

The performance rating adjusts the observed time to what a normal worker could expect to accomplish. For example, a normal worker should be able to walk three miles per hour. He or she should also be able to deal a deck of 52 cards into four equal piles in 30 seconds. There are numerous videos specifying work pace on which professionals agree; and activity benchmarks have been established by the Society for the Advancement of Management. However, performance rating is still something of an art.

NOTE
It is important to let a worker who is going to be observed know about the study in advance in order to avoid misunderstanding or suspicion.

7. Sum the normal times for each element to develop a total normal time for the task.
8. Compute the **standard time.** This adjustment to the total normal time provides for allowances such as *personal* needs, unavoidable work *delays,* and worker *fatigue:*

standard time

$$\text{Standard time} = \frac{\text{Total normal time}}{1 - \text{allowance factor}} \qquad (7.3)$$

Personal time allowances are often established in the range of 4% to 7% of total time, depending upon nearness to restrooms, water fountains, and other facilities. Delay standards are often set as a result of the actual studies of the delay that occurs. Fatigue standards are based on our growing knowledge of human energy expenditure[16] under various physical and environmental conditions. A sample set of personal and fatigue allowances is shown in Figure 7.9. One organization, NASA has established a 6% personal allowance for all tasks and a 3% allowance for unavoidable delays.[17]

EXAMPLE 1

The time study of a work operation yielded an average actual cycle time of 4.0 minutes. The analyst rated the observed worker at 85%. This means the worker performed at 85% of normal when the study was made. The firm uses a 13% allowance factor. We want to compute the standard time.

SOLUTION:

$$\text{Average actual time} = 4.0 \text{ min.}$$

$$\begin{aligned}\text{Normal time} &= (\text{Average actual cycle time}) \times (\text{Rating factor}) \\ &= (4.0)(.85) \\ &= 3.4 \text{ minutes}\end{aligned}$$

$$\begin{aligned}\text{Standard time} &= \frac{\text{Normal time}}{1 - \text{allowance factor}} = \frac{34}{1 - .13} = \frac{3.4}{.87} \\ &= 3.9 \text{ minutes}\end{aligned}$$

[16]Ernest J. McCormick, *Human Factors in Engineering and Design* (New York: McGraw-Hill, 1976), pp. 171–178. Also see Haim Gershoni, "Allowances for Heat Stress," *Industrial Engineering* (September 1979): 2–24.

[17]Susan L. Murray, Amanda M. Mitskevich, and Robert R. Safford, "Work Measurement at Kennedy Space Center," *IIE Solutions,* (July 1995), pp. 18–20.

1. Constant allowances:
   - a) Personal allowance. 5
   - b) Basic fatigue allowance. 4
2. Variable allowances:
   - A) Standing allowance. 2
   - B) Basic fatigue allowance:
     - a) Slightly awkward. 0
     - b) Awkward (bending). 2
     - c) Very awkward (lying, stretching). 7
   - C) Use of force, or muscular energy, in lifting, pulling, pushing
     - Weight lifted (pounds):
     - 10. 1
     - 20. 3
     - 30. 5
     - 40. 9
     - 50. 13
     - 60. 17
   - D) Bad light:
     - a) Slightly below recommended. 0
     - b) Well below. 2
     - c) Quite inadequate. 5
   - E) Atmospheric conditions (head and humidity):
     - Variable. 0–10
   - F) Close attention:
     - a) Fairly fine work. 0
     - b) Fine or exacting. 2
     - c) Very fine or exacting. 5
   - G) Noise level:
     - a) Continuous. 0
     - b) Intermittent—loud. 2
     - c) Intermittent—very loud or high-pitched. 5
   - H) Mental strain:
     - a) Fairly complex process. 1
     - b) Complex or wide span of attention. 4
     - c) Very complex. 8
   - I) Tediousness:
     - a) Rather tedious. 0
     - b) Tedious. 2
     - c) Very tedious. 5

FIGURE 7.9 REST ALLOWANCES (IN PERCENTAGE) FOR VARIOUS CLASSES OF WORK

SOURCE: Excerpted from B. W. Niebel, *Motion and Time Study*, 9th ed. (Homewood, IL: Richard D. Irwin, 1993), p. 446. Reprinted by permission.

Let us now look at an example in which we are given a series of actual stopwatch times for each element.

EXAMPLE 2

Management Science Associates promotes its management development seminars by mailing thousands of individually typed letters to various firms. A time study has been done on the task of preparing letters for mailing. On the basis of the observations below, Management Science Associates wants to develop a time standard for the task. The firm's personal, delay, and fatigue allowance factor is 15%.

	CYCLE OBSERVED (in minutes)					
JOB ELEMENT	*1*	*2*	*3*	*4*	*5*	PERFORMANCE RATING
A. Type letter	8	10	9	21*	11	120%
B. Type envelope address	2	3	2	1	3	105%
C. Stuff, stamp, seal, and sort envelopes	2	1	5*	2	1	110%

The procedure after the data have been collected is as follows:

1. Delete all unusual or nonrecurring observations, such as those marked with an asterisk (*), (they might be due to personal interruption, a conference with the boss, or a mistake of an unusual nature; these are not part of the job).

2. Compute the average cycle time for each job element:

$$\text{Average time for A} = \frac{8 + 10 + 9 + 11}{4}$$

$$= 9.5 \text{ minutes}$$

$$\text{Average time for B} = \frac{2 + 3 + 2 + 1 + 3}{5}$$

$$= 2.2 \text{ minutes}$$

$$\text{Average time for C} = \frac{2 + 1 + 2 + 1}{4}$$

$$= 1.5 \text{ minutes}$$

3. Compute the normal time for each job element:

$$\text{Normal time for A} = (\text{Average actual time}) \times (\text{Rating})$$

$$= (9.5)(1.2)$$

$$= 11.4 \text{ minutes}$$

$$\text{Normal time for B} = (2.2)(1.05)$$

$$= 2.31 \text{ minutes}$$

$$\text{Normal time for C} = (1.51)(1.10)$$

$$= 1.65 \text{ minutes}$$

   Normal times are computed for each element because the rating factor may vary for each element, which it did in this case.

4. Add the normal times for each element to find the total normal time (the normal time for the whole job):

$$\text{Total normal time} = 11.40 + 2.31 + 1.65$$

$$= 15.36 \text{ minutes}$$

5. Compute the standard time for the job:

$$\text{Standard time} = \frac{\text{Total normal time}}{1 - \text{allowance factor}} = \frac{15.36}{1 - .15}$$

$$= 18.07 \text{ minutes}$$

Thus, 18.07 minutes is the time standard for this job.

Time study is a sampling process, and the question of sampling error in the average actual cycle time naturally arises. Error, according to statistics, varies inversely with sample size. In order to determine just how many cycles should be timed, consideration of the variability of each element in the study is necessary.

To determine an adequate sample size, three items must be considered:

1. How accurate we want to be (that is, is ±5% of actual close enough?).
2. The desired level of confidence (that is, the z value; is 95% adequate or is 99% required?).

TABLE 7.1

DESIRED CONFIDENCE (percent)	z VALUE (standard deviation required for desired level of confidence)
90.0	1.65
95.0	1.96
95.4	2.00
99.0	2.58
99.7	3.00

3. How much variation exists within the job elements (that is, if the variation is large, a larger sample will be required).

The formula for finding the appropriate sample size given these three variables is:

$$n = \left(\frac{zs}{h\bar{x}}\right)^2 \qquad (7.4)$$

where

h = Accuracy level desired in percent of the job element, expressed as a decimal (5% = .05)

z = Number of standard deviations required for desired level of confidence (90% confidence = 1.65; see Table 7.1 for the more common z values)[18]

s = Standard deviation of the initial sample

$\bar{x}$ = Mean of the initial sample

We demonstrate with Example 3.

EXAMPLE 3

Bob Swan Mfg., has asked you to check a labor standard prepared by a recently terminated analyst. Your first task is to determine the correct sample size. Your accuracy is to be within 5% and your confidence level to be 95%. The standard deviation of the sample is 1.0 and the mean is 3.00.

SOLUTION:

$$h = .05 \qquad \bar{x} = 3.00 \qquad s = 1.0$$

$$z = 1.96 \text{ (from Table 7.1 or Appendix A)}$$

$$n = \left(\frac{zs}{h\bar{x}}\right)^2$$

$$n = \left(\frac{(1.96 \times 1.0)}{(.05 \times 3)}\right)^2 = 170.74 \approx 171$$

Therefore, you recommend a sample size of 171.

[18]The values of z for any desired confidence level can be found in Appendix A, "Normal Curve Areas and How to Use the Distribution." These values in Appendix A represent a one-tail analysis, whereas Table 7.1 is a two-tail analysis.

Let's look at two variations of Example 3. First, if h, the desired accuracy, is expressed as an absolute amount of error (say one minute of error is acceptable) then substitute e, for $h\bar{x}$, and the appropriate formula is

$$n = \left(\frac{zs}{e}\right)^2 \tag{7.5}$$

where e = absolute amount of acceptable error.

Secondly, for those cases when s, the standard deviation of the sample, is not provided (which is typically the case outside the classroom), it must be computed. The formula for doing so is

$$s = \sqrt{\frac{\Sigma(x_i - \bar{x})^2}{n - 1}} = \sqrt{\frac{\Sigma(\text{Each sample observation } - \bar{x})^2}{\text{Number in sample } - 1}} \tag{7.6}$$

where

x_i = Value of each observation

$\bar{x}$ = Mean of the observations

n = Number of observations

An example of this computation is provided in Solved Problem 7.5 at the end of the chapter.

Time studies provide accuracy in setting labor standards, but they have two disadvantages. First, they require a trained staff of analysts. Second, labor standards cannot be set before the task is actually performed. This leads us to two alternative work measurement techniques.

Predetermined Time Standards

A third way to set production standards is to use predetermined time standards. **Predetermined time standards** divide manual work into small basic elements that have established times (based on very large samples of workers). To estimate the time for a particular task, the time factors for each basic element of that task are added together. For any given firm to develop a comprehensive system of predetermined time standards would be prohibitively expensive. Consequently, a number of systems are commercially available. The most common predetermined time standard is *methods time measurement* (MTM), which is a product of the MTM Association.[19]

predetermined time standards

Predetermined time standards are an outgrowth of basic motions called therbligs. The term *therblig* was coined by Frank Gilbreth (*Gilbreth* spelled backwards with the *t* and *h* reversed). Therbligs include activities such as select, grasp, position, assemble, reach, hold, rest, and inspect. These activities are stated in terms of time-measurement units (TMUs), which are each equal to only .00001 hour or .0006 minute. MTM values for various therbligs are specified in very detailed tables.

Labor standards in the service sector are also addressed by a variety of MTM standards. The GET and PLACE standards of Figure 7.10 are a part of the health care and clerical standards (MTM-HC and MTM-C). To use GET and PLACE (the

[19]MTM is really a family of products available from the Methods Time Measurement Association.

FIGURE 7.10

SAMPLE MTM TABLE FOR GET MOTION. TIME VALUES ARE IN TMUS.

SOURCE: Used with permission of MTM Association for Standards and Research.

GET AND PLACE			Distance range in inches	<8	>8 <20	>20 <32
Weight	Conditions of get	Place accuracy	Code	1	2	3
<2 lbs.	Easy	Approximate	AA	20	35	50
		Loose	AB	30	45	60
		Tight	AC	40	55	70
	Difficult	Approximate	AD	20	45	60
		Loose	AE	30	55	70
		Tight	AF	40	65	80
	Handful	Approximate	AG	40	65	80
>2 lbs. <18 lbs.		Approximate	AH	25	45	55
		Loose	AJ	40	65	75
		Tight	AK	50	75	85
>18 lbs. <45 lbs.		Approximate	AL	90	106	115
		Loose	AM	95	120	130
		Tight	AN	120	145	160

most complex motion in the MTM system), one needs to know what is "gotten," its approximate weight, and where and how far it is placed. Example 4 helps clarify this concept.

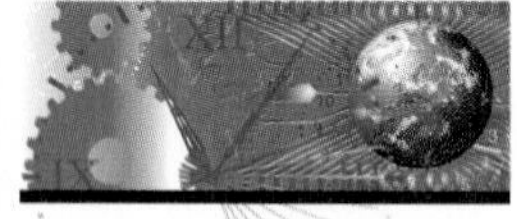

EXAMPLE 4

Pouring a tube specimen in a hospital lab is a repetitive task for which the MTM data in Figure 7.10 may be used to develop standard times. The sample tube is in a rack and the centrifuge tubes are in a nearby box. A technician removes the sample tube from the rack, uncaps it, gets the centrifuge tube, pours, and places both tubes in the rack.

The first work element involves getting the tube from the rack. Suppose the conditions for GETTING the tube and PLACING it in front of the technician are

- weight (less than 2 pounds)
- conditions of GET (easy)
- place accuracy (approximate)
- distance range (8 to 20 inches)

Then the MTM element for this activity is AA2 (as seen from Figure 7.10). The rest of Table 7.2 is developed from similar MTM tables.

TABLE 7.2 MTM-HC ANALYSIS: POURING TUBE SPECIMEN

ELEMENT DESCRIPTION	ELEMENT	TIME	FREQUENCY	TOTAL
Get tube from rack	AA2	35	1	35
Get stopper, place on counter	AA2	35	1	35
Get centrifuge tube, place at sample tube	AD2	45	1	45
Pour (3 seconds)	PT	83	1	83
Place tubes in rack (simultaneously)	PC2	40	1	40
			Total TMU	238

$.0006 \times 238$ = Total standard minutes = .14

SOURCE: A. S. Helms, B. W. Shaw, and C. A. Lindner, "The Development of Laboratory Workload Standards Through Computer-Based Work Measurement Technique, Part 1," *Journal of Methods-Time Measurement* 12: 43. Used with permission of MTM Association for Standards and Research.

Most MTM calculations, by the way, are computerized, so the user need only type in the appropriate MTM codes, such as AA2 in Example 4.

Predetermined time standards have several advantages relative to direct time studies. First, they may be established in a laboratory environment, which will not upset production activities (which time studies tend to do). Second, the standard can be set before a task is done and can be used for planning. In addition, no performance ratings are necessary—and the method is widely accepted by unions as a fair means of setting standards. Predetermined time standards are particularly effective in firms that do substantial numbers of studies where the tasks are similar. Some firms use both time studies and predetermined time standards to ensure accurate labor standards.

NOTE
Many firms use a combination of stopwatch studies and predetermined time standards when they are particularly interested in verifying results.

Work Sampling

The fourth method of developing labor or production standards, work sampling, was developed by an Englishman, L. Tippet, in the 1930s. **Work sampling** estimates the percentage of the time that a worker spends working on various tasks. The method involves random observations to record the activity that the worker is performing (see Figure 7.11). Work sampling is used in:

work sampling

1. *Ratio delay studies.* These estimate the percentage of time employees spend in unavoidable delays. The results are used to investigate work methods, to estimate activity costs, and to set allowances in labor standards.
2. *Setting labor standards.* For setting standard task times, the observer must be experienced enough to rate the worker's performance.
3. *Measuring worker performance.* Sampling can develop a performance index for workers for periodic evaluations.

The work-sampling procedure can be summarized in seven steps:

1. Take a preliminary sample to obtain an estimate of the parameter value (such as percent of time a worker is busy).

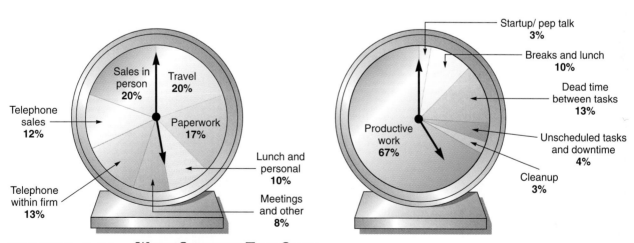

Sales in person 20%
Travel 20%
Telephone sales 12%
Paperwork 17%
Lunch and personal 10%
Telephone within firm 13%
Meetings and other 8%

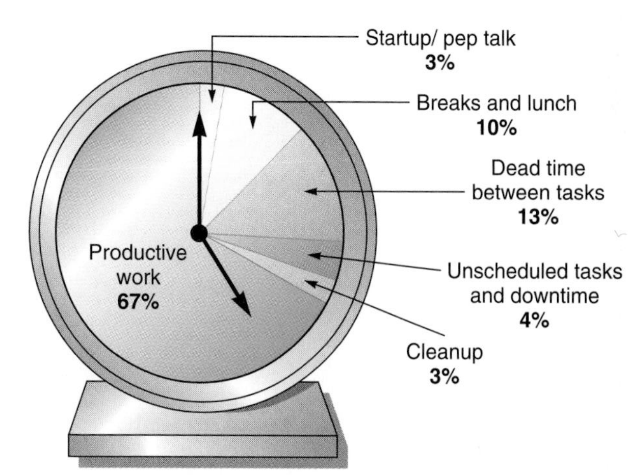

FIGURE 7.11 WORK SAMPLING TIME STUDY

These two work-sampling time studies were done to determine what salespeople do at a wholesale electronic distributor (left) and a composite of several auto assembly line employees (right).

SOURCE: McKinsey & Co. Small Business Reports, as published in *Forbes*, April 24, 1995.

2. Compute the sample size required.
3. Prepare a schedule for observing the worker at appropriate times. The concept of random numbers is used to provide for random observation.
4. Observe and record worker activities; rate the worker's performance.
5. Record the number of units produced during the applicable portion of the study.
6. Compute the normal time per part.
7. Compute the standard time per part.

To determine the number of observations required, management must make a statement about the desired confidence level and accuracy. But first the work analyst must select a preliminary value of the parameter under study (step 1). The choice is usually based on a small sample of perhaps 50 observations. The following formula then gives the sample size for a desired confidence and accuracy:

$$n = \frac{Z^2\, p(1 - p)}{h^2} \tag{7.7}$$

where

n = Required sample size

Z = Standard normal deviate for the desired confidence level $Z = 1$ for 68% confidence, $Z = 2$ for 95.45% confidence, and $Z = 3$ for 99.7% confidence—these values are obtained from Table 7.1 or the normal table in Appendix A

p = Estimated value of sample proportion (of time worker is observed busy or idle)

h = Accuracy level desired, in percent

EXAMPLE 5

The supervisor of a large data entry group estimates that the clerks are idle 25% of the time. The supervisor would like to take a work sample that would be accurate within 3% and wants to have 95.45% confidence in the results.

In order to determine how many observations should be taken, the supervisor applies the equation:

$$n = \frac{Z^2\, p(1 - p)}{h^2}$$

where

n = Sample size required

Z = 2 for 95.45% confidence level

p = Estimate of idle proportion = 25% = .25

h = Accuracy desired of 3% = .03

It is found that:

$$n = \frac{(2)^2(.25)(.75)}{(.03)^2} = 833 \text{ observations}$$

Thus, 833 observations should be taken. If the percent idle time noted is not close to 25% as the study progresses, then the number of observations may have to be recalculated and increased or decreased as appropriate.

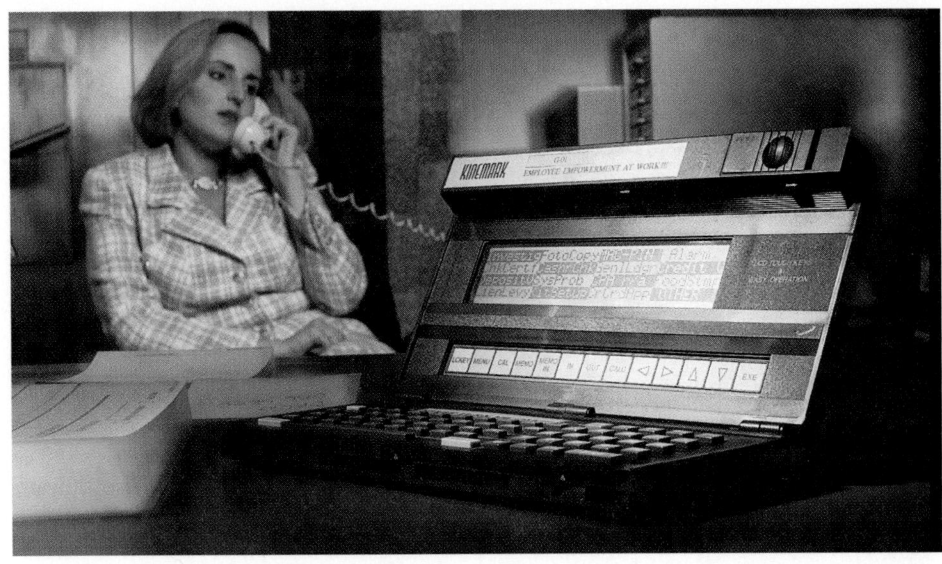

To reduce the cost of work sampling, Kinemark, a Parsippany, New Jersey, firm, developed this small computer with options for 48 everyday office tasks. As each task is completed, the operator presses the appropriate key. After a week of such reporting, a rather complete picture of what is going on is available.

Work sampling is used to set labor standards in a fashion similar to that used in time studies. The analyst, however, simply records whether a worker is busy or idle during the observation. After all the observations have been recorded, the worker rated, and the units produced counted (steps 4 and 5), we can determine the normal time by the formula:

$$\text{Normal time} = \frac{\begin{pmatrix}\text{Total study}\\ \text{time}\end{pmatrix} \times \begin{pmatrix}\text{Percent of time employee}\\ \text{observed working}\end{pmatrix} \times \begin{pmatrix}\text{Performance}\\ \text{rating factor}\end{pmatrix}}{\text{Number of pieces produced}}$$

The standard time is the normal time adjusted by the allowance factor, computed as:

$$\text{Standard time} = \frac{\text{Normal time}}{1 - \text{Allowance factor}}$$

EXAMPLE 6

A work-sample study conducted over the 80 hours (or 4,800 minutes) of a two-week period yielded the following data. The number of parts produced was 225 by an operator who was performance rated at 100%. The operator's idle time was 20%, and the total allowance given by the company for this task is 25%.

$$\text{Normal time} = \frac{\begin{pmatrix}\text{Total}\\ \text{time}\end{pmatrix} \times \begin{pmatrix}\text{Percent of time}\\ \text{working}\end{pmatrix} \times \begin{pmatrix}\text{Rating}\\ \text{factor}\end{pmatrix}}{\text{Number of units completed}}$$

$$= \frac{(4{,}800 \text{ min.})(.80)(1.00)}{225} = 17.07 \text{ minutes per part}$$

$$\text{Standard time} = \frac{\text{Normal time}}{1 - \text{allowance factor}}$$

$$= \frac{17.07}{1 - .25} = 22.76 \text{ minutes per part}$$

Work sampling offers several advantages over time-study methods. First, it is less expensive, because a single observer can observe several workers simultaneously. Second, observers usually don't require much training, and no timing devices are needed. Third, the study can be delayed temporarily at any time with little impact on the results. And fourth, because work sampling uses instantaneous observations over a long period, the worker has little chance of affecting the study's outcome.

The disadvantages of work sampling are: (1) it does not break down work elements as completely as time studies, (2) it can yield biased or incorrect results if the observer does not follow random routes of travel and observation, and (3) it is less effective than time studies when cycle times are short.

SUMMARY

How well a firm manages its human resources ultimately determines its success. The operations activity usually has a large role to play in achieving human resource objectives. The first objective is to achieve efficient use of people within the operations function. This is a major goal of a firm because labor is often a large part of the total cost of the product that can be controlled. The second objective is the design of jobs that are effective, safe, and provide a reasonable quality of work life for the employee in an atmosphere of mutual respect.

Labor standards are required for an efficient operations system. They are needed for production planning, labor planning, costing, and evaluating performance. They can also be used as a basis for incentive systems. They are used in both the factory and the office. Standards may be established via historical data, time studies, predetermined time standards, and work sampling.

KEY TERMS

Quality of work life *(p. 228)*
Mutual commitment *(p. 228)*
Mutual trust *(p. 228)*
Job design *(p. 229)*
Labor specialization *(p. 230)*
Job enlargement *(p. 230)*
Job rotation *(p. 230)*
Job enrichment *(p. 230)*
Employee empowerment *(p. 231)*
Self-directed team *(p. 232)*
Lean production *(p. 233)*
Learning organization *(p. 234)*
Bonus *(p. 234)*
Profit sharing *(p. 234)*
Gain sharing *(p. 234)*
Incentive system *(p. 234)*
Measured daywork *(p. 234)*
Piece rate *(p. 234)*
Ergonomics *(p. 236)*
Flow diagrams *(p. 239)*
Process charts *(p. 240)*
Activity charts *(p. 240)*
Operations chart *(p. 240)*
Labor standards *(p. 240)*
Historical experience *(p. 241)*
Time study *(p. 242)*
Average actual cycle time *(p. 242)*
Normal time *(p. 243)*
Standard time *(p. 243)*
Predetermined time standards *(p. 247)*
Work sampling *(p. 249)*

USING EXCEL SPREADSHEETS FOR TIME STUDY

The Excel equations in applying spreadsheets to Example 2 are relatively straightforward. The sum and count functions are used in Program 7.1 to demonstrate the count function; the average function would also work here. The calculated time standard is about 18 minutes. Note the blank cells (F6 and E8) did not influence this value.

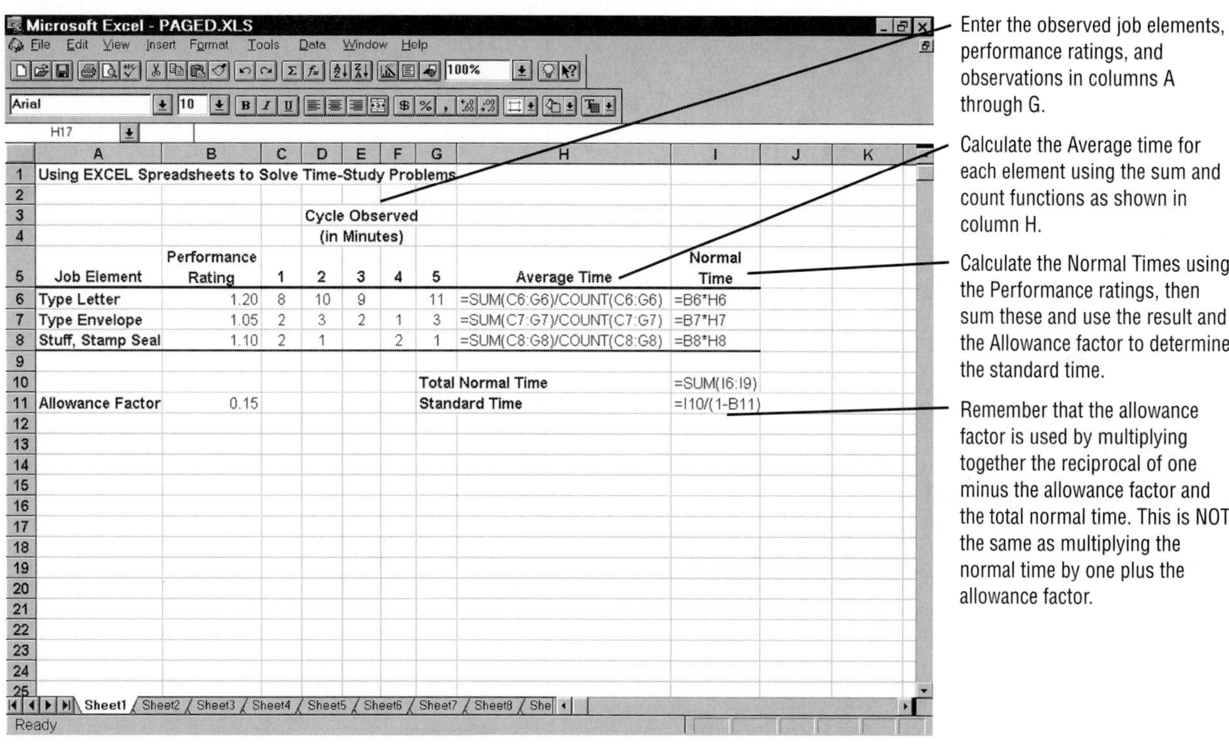
Microsoft Excel - PAGED.XLS
Using EXCEL Spreadsheets to Solve Time-Study Problems
Cycle Observed
(in Minutes)
Job Element | Performance Rating | 1 | 2 | 3 | 4 | 5 | Average Time | Normal Time
Type Letter | 1.20 | 8 | 10 | 9 | | 11 | =SUM(C6:G6)/COUNT(C6:G6) | =B6*H6
Type Envelope | 1.05 | 2 | 3 | 2 | 1 | 3 | =SUM(C7:G7)/COUNT(C7:G7) | =B7*H7
Stuff, Stamp Seal | 1.10 | 2 | 1 | | 2 | 1 | =SUM(C8:G8)/COUNT(C8:G8) | =B8*H8
Total Normal Time | =SUM(I6:I9)
Allowance Factor | 0.15
Standard Time | =I10/(1-B11)
Enter the observed job elements, performance ratings, and observations in columns A through G.
Calculate the Average time for each element using the sum and count functions as shown in column H.
Calculate the Normal Times using the Performance ratings, then sum these and use the result and the Allowance factor to determine the standard time.
Remember that the allowance factor is used by multiplying together the reciprocal of one minus the allowance factor and the total normal time. This is NOT the same as multiplying the normal time by one plus the allowance factor.

PROGRAM 7.1 USING EXCEL TO SOLVE THE MANAGEMENT SCIENCE ASSOCIATES PROBLEM OF EXAMPLE 2.

SOLVED PROBLEM 7.1

A work operation consisting of three elements has been subjected to a stopwatch time study. The observations recorded are shown below. By union contract, the allowance time for the operation is personal time 5%, delay 5%, and fatigue 10%. Determine the standard time for the work operation.

	CYCLE OBSERVATIONS (in minutes)						
JOB ELEMENT	*1*	*2*	*3*	*4*	*5*	*6*	PERFORMANCE RATING
A	.1	.3	.2	.9	.2	.1	90%
B	.8	.6	.8	.5	3.2	.7	110%
C	.5	.5	.4	.5	.6	.5	80%

continued on next page

SOLUTION

First, delete the two observations that are unusual (.9 minutes for job element A where a candy bar was opened, and 3.2 minutes for job element B where the candy bar was eaten). Then,

$$\text{A's average cycle time} = \frac{.1 + .3 + .2 + .2 + .1}{5} = .18 \text{ minute}$$

$$\text{B's average cycle time} = \frac{.8 + .6 + .8 + .5 + .7}{5} = .68 \text{ minute}$$

$$\text{C's average cycle time} = \frac{.5 + .5 + .4 + .5 + .6 + .5}{6} = .50 \text{ minute}$$

$$\text{A's normal time} = (.18)(.90) = .16 \text{ minute}$$

$$\text{B's normal time} = (.68)(1.10) = .75 \text{ minute}$$

$$\text{C's normal time} = (.50)(.80) = .40 \text{ minute}$$

$$\text{Normal time for job} = .16 + .75 + .40 = 1.31 \text{ minutes}$$

$$\text{Standard time} = \frac{1.31}{1 - .20} = 1.64 \text{ minutes}$$

SOLVED PROBLEM 7.2

A preliminary work sample of an operation indicates the following:

Number of times operator working	60
Number of times operator idle	40
Total number of preliminary observations	100

What is the required sample size for a 99.7% confidence level with ± 4% precision?

SOLUTION

$$n = \frac{Z^2\, p(1 - p)}{h^2} = \frac{(3)^2(.6)(.4)}{(.04)^2} = 1{,}350 \text{ sample size}$$

SOLVED PROBLEM 7.3

Each printed circuit board at Maggard Micro Manufacturing, Inc. (3M), has a semiconductor pressed into predrilled slots. The elemental motions for normal time used by 3M are:

Reach six inches for semiconductor	10.5 TMU
Grasp the semiconductor	8.0 TMU
Move semiconductor to printed circuit board	9.5 TMU
Position semiconductor	20.1 TMU
Press semiconductor into slots	20.3 TMU
Move board aside	15.8 TMU

Each time measurement unit is equal to .0006 minute.

Determine the normal time for this operation in minutes and in seconds.

SOLUTION

Add the time measurement units together:

$$10.5 + 8.0 + 9.5 + 20.1 + 20.3 + 15.8 = 84.2$$

$$\text{Time in minutes} = (84.2)(.0006 \text{ min.}) = .05052 \text{ minute}$$

$$\text{Time in seconds} = (.05052)(60 \text{ sec.}) = 3.0312 \text{ seconds}$$

SOLVED PROBLEM 7.4

To obtain the random sample needed for work sampling, a manager divides an 8-hour workday into 480 minutes. Using a random-number table to decide what time to go to an area to sample work occurrences, the manager records observations on a tally sheet such as the one that follows:

STATUS	TALLY	FREQUENCY
Productively working	~~IIII~~ ~~IIII~~ ~~IIII~~ I	16
Idle	IIII	4

SOLUTION

In this case, the supervisor made 20 observations and found that employees were working 80% of the time. So, out of 480 minutes in an office workday, 20%, or 96 minutes, was idle time, and 356 minutes was productive. Note that this procedure describes what a worker is doing, not necessarily what he or she *should* be doing.

SOLVED PROBLEM 7.5

Amor Manufacturing Co. of San Diego, California, has just studied a job in their laboratory in anticipation of releasing the job to the factory. They want rather good accuracy for costing and labor forecasting. Specifically, they want you to provide a 99% confidence level and a cycle time that is within 3% of the true value. How many observations should they make? The data collected so far are shown below.

OBSERVATION	CYCLE TIME
1	1.7
2	1.6
3	1.4
4	1.4
5	1.4

SOLUTION

First, solve for the mean, $\overline{x}$, and the sample standard deviation, s.

$$s = \sqrt{\frac{\Sigma(\text{Each sample observation} - \overline{x})^2}{\text{Number in sample} - 1}}$$

OBSERVATION	x_i	$\overline{x}$	$x_i - \overline{x}$	$(x_i - \overline{x})^2$
1	1.7	1.5	.2	0.04
2	1.6	1.5	.1	0.01
3	1.4	1.5	−.1	0.01
4	1.4	1.5	−.1	0.01
5	1.4	1.5	−.1	0.01
	$\overline{x} = 1.5$	7.5		$0.08 = \Sigma(x_i - \overline{x})^2$

$$s = \sqrt{\frac{.08}{n-1}} = \sqrt{\frac{.08}{4}} = .141$$

Then, solve for

$$n = \left(\frac{zs}{h\overline{x}}\right)^2 = \left[\frac{(2.58)(.141)}{(.03)(1.5)}\right]^2 = 65.3$$

where

$$\overline{x} = 1.5$$
$$s = .141$$
$$z = 2.58$$
$$h = .03$$

Therefore you recommend 65 observations.

SELF-TEST ■ CHAPTER 7

- *Before taking the self-test* refer back to the learning objectives listed at the beginning of the chapter and the key terms listed at the end of the chapter.
- Use the key at the back of the text to *correct* your answers.
- *Restudy* pages that correspond to any questions you answered incorrectly or material you feel uncertain about.

1. Methods analysis techniques are used to analyze
   a. movement of individuals or materials
   b. activity of man and machine and crew activity
   c. body movement
   d. all of the above

2. Micro hand motions devised by Frank and Lillian Gilbreth are
   a. flow diagrams
   b. activity charts
   c. therbligs
   d. SAE standards
   e. all of the above

3. When demand for your product fluctuates and yet you maintain a constant level of employment, some of your cost savings might include
   a. reduction in hiring costs
   b. reduction in firing costs and unemployment insurance costs
   c. lack of need to pay a premium wage to get workers to accept unstable employment
   d. having a trained workforce rather than having to retrain new employees each time you hire for an upswing in demand
   e. all of the above

4. Job enrichment
   a. includes job enlargement
   b. includes a modest increase in pay
   c. is a concept promoted by Adam Smith and Charles Babbage in books they wrote
   d. includes some of the planning and control necessary for job accomplishment
   e. includes all of the above

5. The difference between *job enrichment* and *job enlargement* is that
   a. enlarged jobs contain a larger number of similar tasks, while enriched jobs include some of the planning and control necessary for job accomplishment
   b. enriched jobs contain a larger number of similar tasks, while enlarged jobs include some of the planning and control necessary for job accomplishment
   c. enriched jobs enable an employee to do a number of boring jobs instead of just one
   d. all of the above

6. Ergonomics is the study of
   a. ergos
   b. the management of technology
   c. the man-machine interface
   d. the use of automation in a manufacturing organization

7. *Methods analysis* focuses on
   a. the design of the machines used to perform a task
   b. *how* a task is accomplished
   c. the raw materials that are consumed in performing a task
   d. reducing the number of steps required to perform a task

8. The Scanlon plan is a plan for rewarding improvements made in an organization's performance in which
   a. only the employees realize the gain from increased productivity
   b. both employees and management share the gain from improved productivity
   c. only management realizes the gain from increased productivity
   d. employees, on an individual basis only, realize the gains from increased productivity

9. The difference between the standard time or measured daywork system and the piece-rate system is
   a. there is no difference
   b. in general, the employee would make less money under the standard time system than under the piece-rate system
   c. they are fundamentally the same, but the effort required to change hourly rates under the piece-rate system is greater than under the standard time system
   d. in general, the employee would make less money under the piece-rate system than under the standard time system

10. Labor standards are necessary to determine which of the following?
    a. the steps necessary to perform a task
    b. cost and time estimates prior to production
    c. the amount of raw materials to be consumed in the process
    d. the machines required by the process

11. The least preferred method of establishing labor standards is
    a. time studies
    b. work sampling
    c. historical experience
    d. predetermined time standards

DISCUSSION QUESTIONS

1. What are some of the worst jobs you know about? Why are they bad jobs? Why do people want these jobs?
2. If you were redesigning the job described in question 1, what changes would you make? Are your changes realistic? Would they improve productivity (not just production, but productivity)?
3. How would you define a good "quality of work life"?
4. What is the difference between job enrichment, job enlargement, job rotation, and job specialization?
5. Do you know of any jobs that push the man-machine interface to the limits of human capabilities?
6. Why prepare flow diagrams and process charts for tasks that are poorly done?
7. What are the core characteristics of a good job design?
8. Why do operations managers require labor standards?
9. How do we establish a fair day's work?
10. Is a "normal" pace the same thing as a 100% pace?
11. What is the difference between "normal" and "standard" time?
12. What kind of work pace would you expect from an employee during a time study? Why?
13. As a new time-study engineer in your plant, you are engaged in studying an employee operating a drill press. Somewhat to your surprise, one of the first things you notice is that the drill-press operator is doing a lot of operations besides just drilling holes. Your problem is what to include in your time study. From the following examples, indicate how, as the individual responsible for labor standards in your plant, you would handle them.
    - **a.** Every so often, perhaps every 50th unit or so, the drill-press operator takes an extra-long look at the piece, which apparently is misshaped, and then typically throws it in the scrap barrel.
    - **b.** Approximately 1 out of 100 units has a rough edge and will not fit in the jig properly; therefore, the drill-press operator picks up the piece, hits the lower right-hand edge with a file a few times, puts the file down, and returns to normal operation.
    - **c.** About every hour or so, the drill-press operator stops to change the drill in the machine, even if the operator is in the middle of a job. (We can assume that the drill has become dull.)
    - **d.** Between every job and sometimes in the middle of jobs, the drill-press operator turns off the machine and goes for stock.
    - **e.** The drill-press operator is idle for a few minutes at the beginning of every job waiting for the setup person to complete the setup. Some of the setup time is used in going for stock, but the drill-press operator typically returns with stock before the setup person is finished with the setup.
    - **f.** The operator stops to talk to you.
    - **g.** The operator lights up a cigarette.
    - **h.** The operator opens his lunch pail (it is not lunch time), removes an apple, and takes an occasional bite.
    - **i.** The operator drops a part, and you pick it up and hand it to him. Does this make any difference in the time study? How?

OPERATIONS IN PRACTICE EXERCISE

The situation at the Lordstown, Ohio, airbag manufacturer was getting sticky. A skilled technician and member of the safety committee, Gregory White, suggested the line be shut down because of horrible fumes that were being created as employees inserted a chemical sensor into each airbag. The problem was that a new bonding agent for sealing the sensors was highly toxic as a liquid, but safe after drying. Additionally, the union steward was also questioning safety standards, saying that perhaps the bonding agent remained toxic when drying. A recently installed ventilation system made little difference in the odor, but all tests had shown the chemical parts per million to be below the OSHA standard of 100. Steve Goodman, the plant manager, had discussed the issue with Nancy Kirschberg, the plant health and safety manager, who advised that although the OSHA standard is 100 ppm, the American Conference of Governmental Industrial Hygienists' (ACGIH) standard is only 50 ppm. Goodman was also well aware that the new employee empowerment program was important, but the automobile assembly plant 15 miles away needed the airbags now. The automaker had no airbags in stock and depended on JIT delivery from this plant. Therefore, shutting down airbag assembly would also shut down the assembly plant. Goodman's plant's reputation and the jobs of his people depended upon timely airbag delivery.

First, what decision would you make? Then justify your position and that of the union and Gregory White. Finally, propose a solution to deal with the very immediate problem.

PROBLEMS

- **7.1.** Make a flow process chart for going from the living room to the kitchen for a glass, to the refrigerator for milk, and to a kitchen cabinet for cookies. Use a layout of your choosing. How can you make the task more efficient (that is, less time or fewer steps)?
- **7.2.** Draw an activity chart for a machine operator with the following operation. The relevant times are:

Prepare mill for loading (cleaning, oiling, and so on)	.50 min.
Load mill	1.75 min.
Mill operating (cutting material)	2.25 min.
Unload mill	.75 min.

- **7.3.** Draw an activity chart (a multiactivity chart) for a concert (for example, Phil Collins, Neil Diamond, Whitney Houston, Bruce Springsteen) and determine how to put the concert together so the star has reasonable breaks. For instance, at what point is there an instrumental number, a visual effect, a duet, a dance moment, that allows the star to pause and rest physically or at least rest his or her voice? Do other members of the show have moments of pause or rest?
- **7.4.** Make an operations chart of one of the following:
  - **a.** Putting a new eraser in (or on) a pencil.
  - **b.** Putting a paper clip on two pieces of paper.
  - **c.** Putting paper in a typewriter.
- **7.5.** Having made the operations chart in Problem 7.4 and now being told that you were going to do the task 10,000 times, how would you improve the procedure? Prepare an operations chart of the improved task. What motion, time, and effort have you saved over the life of the task by redesigning it?
- **7.6.** For a job you have had, rate each of Hackman and Oldham core job characteristics on a scale from 1 to 10. What is your total score? What about the job could have been changed so you would be inclined to give it a higher score?
- **7.7.** The cycle time for performing a certain task was clocked at ten minutes. The performance rating of the worker timed was estimated at 110%. Common practice in this department is to allow five minutes of personal time and three minutes of fatigue time per hour. In addition, it is estimated that there should be an extra allowance of two minutes per hour.
  - **a.** Find the normal time for the operation.
  - **b.** Compute the allowance factor and the standard time for the operation.
- **7.8.** A time study revealed an average cycle time of 5 minutes, with a standard deviation of 1.25 minutes. These figures were based on a sample of 75 cycles. Is this sample large enough that one can be 99% confident that the standard time is within 5% of the true value?
- **7.9.** The data in the following table represent time-study observations for an assembly process. On the basis of these observations, find the standard time for the process. Assume a 10% allowance factor.

		OBSERVATION (minutes per cycle)				
ELEMENT	PERFORMANCE RATING	*1*	*2*	*3*	*4*	*5*
1	100%	1.5	1.6	1.4	1.5	1.5
2	90%	2.3	2.5	2.1	2.2	2.4
3	115%	1.7	1.9	1.9	1.4	1.6
4	100%	3.5	3.6	3.6	3.6	3.2

: **7.10.** The following data represent observations for the cycle time of an assembly process. How many observations would be necessary for the observer to be 99% confident that the average cycle time is within 5% of the true value?

OBSERVATION (in minutes)				
1	2	3	4	5
1.5	1.6	1.4	1.5	1.5

Hint: Compute the sample standard deviation as shown in Solved Problem 7.5 shown earlier.

: **7.11.** A work sample taken over a 100-hour work-month produced the following results:

Units produced	200
Idle time	25%
Performance rating	110%
Allowance time	15%

What is the standard time for the job?

. **7.12.** An analyst clocked the cycle time for welding a part onto truck doors at 5.3 minutes. The performance rating of the worker timed was estimated at 105%. Find the normal time for this operation.

According to a local union contract, each welder is allowed three minutes of personal time per hour and two minutes of fatigue time per hour. Further, it is estimated that there should be an average delay allowance of one minute per hour. Compute the allowance factor, and then find the standard time for this welding activity.

: **7.13.** A time study of a factory worker revealed an average cycle time of 3.20 minutes, with a standard deviation of 1.28 minutes. These figures were based on a sample of 45 cycles observed.

Is this sample adequate in size for the firm to be 99% confident that the standard time is within 5% of the true value? If not, what should the proper number of observations be?

: **7.14.** The data in the following table represent time-study observations for a metalworking process. On the basis of these observations, find the standard time for the process, assuming a 25% allowance factor.

		OBSERVATIONS (minutes per cycle)						
ELEMENT	PERFORMANCE RATING	*1*	*2*	*3*	*4*	*5*	*6*	*7*
1	90%	1.80	1.70	1.66	1.91	1.85	1.77	1.60
2	100%	6.9	7.3	6.8	7.1	15.3*	7.0	6.4
3	115%	3.0	9.0*	9.5*	3.8	2.9	3.1	3.2
4	90%	10.1	11.1	12.3	9.9	12.0	11.9	12.0

*Disregard—unusual observation.

7.15. Based on a careful work study in the Smith and Johnson Company, the results shown in the table below are observed:

ELEMENT	PERFORMANCE RATING	CYCLE (in minutes) 1	2	3	4	5
Prepare daily reports	120%	35	40	33	42	39
Photocopy results	110%	12	10	36*	15	13
Label and package reports	90%	3	3	5	5	4
Distribute reports	85%	15	18	21	17	45†

*Photocopying machine broken.
†Power outage.

a. Compute the normal time for each work element.
b. If the allowance for this type of work is 15%, what is the standard time?
c. How many observations are needed for a 95% confidence level within 5% accuracy?
Hint: Calculate the sample size of each element.

7.16. The Division of Continuing Education at Virginia College promotes a wide variety of executive training courses for its audience of firms in the Arlington, Virginia, region. The division's director believes that individually typed letters add a personal touch to marketing. To prepare letters for mailing, she conducts a time study of her secretaries. On the basis of the observations shown in the following table, she wishes to develop a time standard for the whole job.

The college has an allowance factor of 12%. The director decides to delete all unusual observations from the time study.

ELEMENT	PERFORMANCE RATING	CYCLE OBSERVED (in minutes) 1	2	3	4	5	6
Typing letter	85%	2.5	3.5	2.8	2.1	2.6	3.3
Typing envelope	100%	.8	.8	.6	.8	3.1	.7
Stuffing envelope	95%	.4	.5	1.9	.3	.6	.5
Sealing, sorting	125%	1.0	2.9	.9	1.0	4.4	.9

7.17. A time study at the phone company observed a job that contained three elements. The times and ratings for 10 cycles are shown in the table below.

ELEMENT	PERFORMANCE RATING	OBSERVATIONS (minutes per cycle) 1	2	3	4	5	6	7	8	9	10
1	85%	.40	.45	.39	.48	.41	.50	.45	.39	.50	.40
2	88%	1.5	1.7	1.9	1.7	1.8	1.6	1.8	1.8	2.0	2.1
3	90%	3.8	3.4	3.0	4.8	4.0	4.2	3.5	3.6	3.7	4.3

a. Find the average cycle time for each element.
b. Find the normal time for each element.
c. Assuming an allowance factor for 20% of job time, determine the standard time for this job.

: **7.18.** The Dubuque Cement company packs 80-pound bags of concrete mix. Time-study data for the filling activity are shown in the table below.

The company's policy is a 20% allowance for workers. Compute the standard time for this work task. How many cycles are necessary for 99% confidence, within 5% accuracy?

		CYCLE TIME (seconds per cycle)				
ELEMENT	PERFORMANCE RATING	*1*	*2*	*3*	*4*	*5*
Grasp and place bag	110%	8	9	8	11	7
Fill bag	85%	36	41	39	35	112*
Seal bag	105%	15	17	13	20	18
Place bag on conveyor	90%	8	6	9	30†	35†

*Bag breaks open.
†Conveyor jams.

: **7.19.** An office worker is clocked performing three work elements, with the results shown in the table below. The allowance for tasks such as this is 15%.

		MINUTES FOR CYCLE					
ELEMENT	PERFORMANCE RATING	*1*	*2*	*3*	*4*	*5*	*6*
1	100%	13	11	14	16	51	15
2	110%	68	21	25	73	26	23
3	100%	3.0	3.3	3.1	2.9	3.4	2.8

a. Find the normal time.
b. Find the standard time.

: **7.20.** Installing mufflers at the Ross Garage in Queens, New York, involves five work elements. Richard Ross times workers performing these tasks seven times with the results shown in the table below.

		CYCLE OBSERVATIONS (minutes)						
JOB ELEMENT	PERFORMANCE RATING	*1*	*2*	*3*	*4*	*5*	*6*	*7*
1. Select correct mufflers	110%	4	5	4	6	4	15	4
2. Remove old muffler	90%	6	8	7	6	7	6	7
3. Weld/install new muffler	105%	15	14	14	12	15	16	13
4. Check/inspect work	100%	3	4	24	5	4	3	18
5. Complete paperwork	130%	5	6	8	—	7	6	7

By agreement with his workers, Ross allows a 10% fatigue factor and a 10% personal-time factor. To compute standard time for the work operation, Ross excludes all observations that appear to be unusual or nonrecurring. He does not want an error of more than 5%.

a. What is the standard time for the task?
b. How many cycles are needed to assure a 95% confidence level?

: **7.21.** Sample observations of an assembly line worker made over a 40-hour workweek revealed that the worker produced a total of 320 completed parts. The performance rating was 125%. The sample also showed that the worker was busy assembling the parts 80% of the time. Allowances for work on the assembly line total 10%. Find the normal time and standard time for this task.

• **7.22.** A bank wants to determine the percent of time its tellers are working and idle. It decides to use work sampling, and its initial estimate is that the tellers are idle 30% of the time. How many observations should be taken to be 95.45% confident that the results will not be more than 5% away from the true result?

: **7.23.** A work sample taken over a 160-hour work-month produced the following results. What is the standard time for the job?

Units manufactured	220
Idle time	20%
Performance rating	90%
Allowance time	10%

• **7.24.** Sharpening your pencil is an operation that may be broken down into eight small elemental motions. In MTM terms, each element may be assigned a certain number of TMUs, as shown below.

Reach four inches for the pencil	6 TMU
Grasp the pencil	2 TMU
Move the pencil six inches	10 TMU
Position the pencil	20 TMU
Insert the pencil into the sharpener	4 TMU
Sharpen the pencil	120 TMU
Disengage the pencil	10 TMU
Move the pencil six inches	10 TMU

What is the total normal time for sharpening one pencil? Convert this time to minutes and seconds.

CASE STUDY

The Fleet That Wanders

Bill Southard runs Southard Truck Lines. He recently purchased ten new tractors for his operation from ARC Trucks. His relations with his drivers have historically been excellent, but they do not like the new tractors. The complaint is that the new tractors are hard to control on the highway; they "wander." When the drivers have a choice, they choose the older tractors. Southard, after numerous discussions with the drivers, concludes that the new tractors do indeed have a problem. They get much better gas mileage, should have lower maintenance costs, and have the latest antilocking brakes. Since each tractor costs over $50,000, Mr. Southard has a total investment of over $500,000 in the new fleet. He is trying to improve his fleet performance by reducing maintenance and fuel costs. This has not happened. Additionally, he wants to keep his drivers happy. This has not happened either. Consequently, he has a rather serious talk with the manufacturer of the trucks.

The manufacturer, ARC Trucks of Canyon, Texas, redesigned the front suspension for this model of tractor. The firm tells him the new front end is great. Bill Southard finds out, however, that there have been minor changes in some front suspension parts on the model since he purchased his trucks.

ARC Trucks refuses to make any changes in the tractors Southard purchased. No one has suggested there is a safety problem, but the drivers are adamant that they have to work harder to keep the new tractors on the road. Mr. Southard has new tractors that spend much of their time sitting in the yard while drivers use the old tractors. His costs, therefore, are higher than they should be. He is considering court action, but legal counsel suggests that he document his case.

DISCUSSION QUESTIONS

1. What suggestions do you have for Southard?
2. Having been exposed to introductory material about ergonomics, can you imagine an analytical approach to documenting the problems reported by the drivers?

CASE STUDY

Lincoln Electric's Incentive Pay System

Cleveland's Lincoln Electric was founded by John C. Lincoln in 1895 to make an electric motor he had developed. When his brother James joined the organization in 1907, they began emphasizing employee motivation. Since that time, the company has endorsed the message that the business must prosper if employees are to benefit. Today, Lincoln is a $1 billion firm with 3,400 employees. About 90% of its sales come from manufacturing arc-welding equipment and supplies.

The company has encouraged workers to own a stake in its property by allowing them to buy stock at book value. (The employees are required to sell the stock at book value when they leave.) Approximately 70% of the employees own stock, and together they hold nearly 50% of the outstanding shares. Most of the remaining stock is held by members of the Lincoln family who are not involved in company operations.

Factory workers at Lincoln receive piece-rate wages with no guaranteed minimum hourly pay. After working for the firm for two years, employees begin to participate in the year-end bonus plan. Determined by a formula that considers the company's gross profits and the employees' base piece rate and merit rating, it might be the most lucrative bonus system for factory workers in the United States. The *average* size of the bonus over the past 56 years has been 95.5% of base wages. Some Lincoln factory workers make more than $100,000 a year. In recent good years, average employees have earned about $85,000 a year, well above the average for U.S. manufacturing workers as a whole. But in a bad year, Lincoln employees' average might fall as much as 40%.

The company has a guaranteed-employment policy that it put in place in 1958. Since that time, it has not laid off a single worker. In return for job security, however, employees agree to several things. During slow times, they will accept reduced work periods. They also agree to accept work transfers, even to lower-paid jobs, if that is necessary to maintain a minimum of 30 hours of work per week.

The company calls the low cost of high wages its incentive-pay system. Each employee inspects his or her own parts and must correct any imperfect work on personal time. Each is responsible for the quality of his or her own work. Records are maintained reflecting who worked on each piece of equipment. Should inferior work slip by and be discovered by Lincoln's quality control people or by customers, the worker's merit rating, bonus, and pay are lowered.

However, some employees feel the system can cause some unfriendly competition as well. Because a certain number of merit points is allotted to each department, an exceptionally high rating for one person may mean a lower rating for another.

But the pressure has been good for productivity. One company executive estimates that Lincoln's overall productivity is about double that of its domestic competitors. The company has earned a profit every year since the depths of the 1930s' depression and has never missed a quarterly dividend. Lincoln has one of the lowest employee turnover rates in U.S. industry. Recently, *Fortune* magazine cited Lincoln's two U.S. plants as among the ten best managed in the country.

DISCUSSION QUESTIONS

1. How are labor standards used to establish an incentive system such as this?
2. How and why does Lincoln's approach to motivating people work?
3. What problems might this system create for management?
4. What types of employee would be happy working at Lincoln?

SOURCE: *Business Week,* January 22, 1996, pp. 89–92; *HR Magazine* (November 1990): 73–76.

Internet Case Study See our Internet home page at http://www.prenhall.com/renderpom for this additional case study: Human Factors at Three Mile Island.

BIBLIOGRAPHY

Alexander, D. C. *Industrial Ergonomics: A Practitioner's Guide.* Norcross, GA: IE & MP Publishers, 1985.

Barnes, R. M. *Motion and Time Study, Design and Measurement of Work.* New York: John Wiley, 1968.

Berggren, C. *Alternatives to Lean Production: Work Organization in the Swedish Auto Industry.* Ithaca, NY: ILR Press, 1993.

———. "Point/Counterpoint: Nummi vs. Uddevalla." *Sloan Management Review* 35, no. 2 (Winter 1994): 37–50.

Bowen, David E. and Edward E. Lawler III, "Empowering Service Employees." *Sloan Management Review* 36, no. 4, (Summer 1995).

Carson, R. "Ergonomically Designed Tools: Selecting the Right Tool for the Job." *Industrial Engineering* 25, no. 7 (July 1993): 27–29.

Denton, D. K. "Redesigning a Job by Simplifying Every Task and Responsibility." *Industrial Engineering* 24, no. 8 (August 1992): 46.

Konz, S. *Work Design.* Columbia, OH: Grid, 1979.

McCormick, E. J. *Human Factors in Engineering and Design,* 4th ed. New York: McGraw-Hill, 1976.

Meyer, C. "How the Right Measures Help Teams Excel." *Harvard Business Review* (May-June 1994): 95.

Snell, S., and J. Dean. "Integrated Manufacturing and Human Resource Management: A Human Capital Perspective." *The Academy of Management Journal* 35, 3 (August 1992): 467–497.

Staughton, R. V. W., N. J. Kinnie, E. H. Davies, and R. L. C. Smith. "Modelling the Manufacturing Strategy Process: An Analysis of the Role Played by Human Resources Issues." *OM Review* 9, no. 2 (April 1992): 48–68.

Layout Designs

8

CHAPTER OUTLINE

Strategic Importance of Layout Decisions

Matching Layouts to Strategies—Some Examples

Types of Layouts

Fixed-Position Layout

Process-Oriented Layout

Cellular Layout ■ Focused Work Center and Focused Factory

Office Layout

Retail Store Layout

Warehousing and Storage Layouts

Crossdocking

Product-Oriented Layout

Assembly Line Balancing

Summary ■ *Key Terms* ■ *Using POM for Windows for Layout Design* ■ *Solved Problems* ■ *Self-Test Chapter 8* ■ *Discussion Questions* ■ *Operations in Practice Exercise* ■ *Problems* ■ *Case Studies: State Automobile License Renewals; Des Moines National Bank* ■ *Bibliography*

LEARNING OBJECTIVES

When you complete this chapter you should be able to:

IDENTIFY OR DEFINE:

Fixed-position layout
Process-oriented layout
Cellular layout
Focused work center
Focused factory
Retail/service layout
Warehouse layout
Crossdocking
Product-oriented layout
Assembly line factory

EXPLAIN:

How to achieve a good layout for the process case

How to balance production flow in a repetitive or product-oriented facility

STRATEGIC IMPORTANCE OF LAYOUT DECISIONS

Layout is one of the decisions that determines the long-run efficiency of operations. Layout has numerous strategic implications because it establishes a firm's competitive priorities in regard to capacity, processes, flexibility, and cost, as well as quality of work life. An effective layout can help a firm to achieve the following:

1. Higher utilization of space, equipment, and people.
2. Improved flow of information, materials, or people.
3. More convenience to the customer.
4. Improved employee morale and safer working conditions.

The objective of layout strategy is to develop an economic layout that will assist in these four areas while still meeting the firm's competitive requirements.

Matching Layouts to Strategies—Some Examples

Here are five examples of how vastly different organizations are using layout to their strategic advantage.

NOTE
Once the layout is set, it is not often changed, since it is very expensive to stop operations and alter the layout. Layout is a long-lasting decision.

PITTSBURGH INTERNATIONAL AIRPORT. Pittsburgh International's new X-shaped terminal and dual taxiways reduce airline delays, increase passenger convenience, cut fuel costs, and make the city a more attractive hub and business/conference site.

WAL-MART'S STORE IN ROGERS, ARKANSAS. With wide aisles, open displays, sitting areas for customers, and classy clothing racks, this new Wal-Mart looks like an upscale department store and shapes shoppers' inclinations to shop longer and spend more.

SQUARE D'S FACTORY OF THE FUTURE. At this $1.6 billion manufacturer's Lexington, Kentucky, location, the plant has been redesigned into a series of small factories (of 20 to 30-person teams) within a factory. The new plant's rejection rates are down 75%, and order processing time has dropped from six weeks to three days.

DENVER CONVENTION CENTER'S BATHROOMS. Creative layout has helped establish "potty parity" by installing movable walls to accommodate the ratio of men-to-women at each scheduled convention. This flexibility increases the center's ability to market itself.

KROGER'S MEMPHIS SUPERMARKETS. Kroger's store layouts include a fast-food restaurant, a deli, a photo lab, a video store, and, of course, groceries and drugs. They also include NCB branch banks that make loans and handle all consumer banking needs. This approach to layout makes the supermarkets an attractive one-stop shopper destination.

Pittsburgh International's X-shaped terminal reduces taxi time and improves gate access, thereby reducing airline fuel cost substantially. These dual taxiways contribute to reduced taxiing time for aircraft at the Pittsburgh airport as well as higher takeoff speeds. Layout criteria in airport design include reducing congestion, distance, and delays, as well as increasing passenger convenience, controlling costs, and providing for expandability.

TYPES OF LAYOUT

Layout decisions include the best placement of machines (in a production setting), offices and desks (in an office setting), or service centers (in settings such as hospitals or department stores). An effective layout facilitates the flow of materials, people, and information, within and between areas. Management's goal is to arrange (lay out) the system so that it operates at peak effectiveness and efficiency. To achieve these layout objectives, a variety of approaches have been developed. Among them are six that we will discuss in this chapter:

1. **Fixed-position layout**—addresses the layout requirements of large, bulky projects such as ships and buildings. **fixed-position layout**
2. **Process-oriented layout**—deals with low-volume, high-variety production (also called "job shop" or intermittent production). **process-oriented layout**
3. **Office layout**—positions workers, their equipment, and spaces/offices to provide for movement of information. **office layout**
4. **Retail/service layout**—allocates shelf space and responds to customer behavior. **retail/service layout**

TABLE 8.1 LAYOUT STRATEGIES

PROJECT (fixed-position)	JOB SHOP (process-oriented)	OFFICE	RETAIL (service/retail)	WAREHOUSE (storage)	REPETITIVE/ CONTINUOUS (product-oriented)
			Examples:		
Ingall Ship Building Co.	Shouldice Hospital	Allstate Insurance	Kroger's Supermarket	Federal-Mogul's warehouse	Sony's TV assembly line
Trump Plaza	Olive Garden Restaurants	Microsoft Corp.	Walgreens Bloomingdales	The Gap's distribution center	Dodge Caravan Minivans
			Problem:		
Move material to the limited storage areas around the site	Manage varied material flow for each product	Locate workers requiring frequent contact close to one another	Expose customer to high-margin items	Balance low-cost storage with low-cost material handling	Arrange product flow from one workstation to the next

warehouse layout

product-oriented layout

5. **Warehouse layout**—addresses trade-offs between space and material handling.
6. **Product-oriented layout**—seeks the best personnel and machine utilization in repetitive or continuous production.

Examples for each of these classes of layout problems are noted in Table 8.1.

Of these six layout strategies, only a few have undergone extensive mathematical analysis. The layout and design of physical facilities is still as much an art as it is a science. We introduce in this chapter some of the art as well as some of the science for effective and efficient layouts.

FIXED-POSITION LAYOUT

A *fixed-position layout* is one in which the project remains stationary and requires workers and equipment to come to one work area. Examples of this type of project are a ship, a highway, a bridge, a house, and a burning oil well.

The techniques for addressing the fixed-position layout are not well-developed. Construction sites and shipbuilding sites address this issue on an ad hoc basis. The construction industry usually has a "meeting of the trades" to assign space for various time periods. As you would suspect, this often yields less than an optimum solution, as the discussion may be more political than analytical. Shipyards, on the other hand, have loading areas called "platens" adjacent to the ship, which are loaded by a scheduling department.

The fixed-position layout is complicated by three factors:

1. Space is limited at virtually all sites.
2. At different stages in the construction process different materials are needed; therefore, different items become critical as the project develops. This adds the dynamics of scheduling to the layout problem.
3. The volume of materials needed is dynamic. For example, the rate of use of steel panels for the hull of a ship changes as the project progresses.

A house built via traditional fixed-position layout would be constructed on-site, with equipment, materials, and workers brought to that site. However, imaginative OM solutions allow this home to be built at a much lower cost. The house is built in two movable modules (shown joined here) in a factory where equipment and materials handling are expedited. The indoor work environment means no weather delays and no overnight thefts. Prepositioned work scaffolding and hoists mounted on the factory ceiling make the job easier, quicker, and cheaper.

Because the fixed-position layout is so difficult to solve well at the site, an alternative strategy is to complete as much of the project as possible off site. This approach is used in the shipbuilding industry when standard units, say pipeholding brackets, are assembled in a nearby assembly line process (a product-oriented facility). Ingall Ship Building Corporation has built similar sections of a ship (modules) or the same section of several similar ships in a product-oriented line. This is their strategy to bring added efficiency to shipbuilding. Similarly, other shipbuilding firms are experimenting with group technology (see Chapter 4) to produce components.

PROCESS-ORIENTED LAYOUT

The *process-oriented layout* can simultaneously handle a wide variety of products or services. In fact, it is most efficient when making products that have different requirements or when handling customers who have different needs. A process-oriented layout is typically the low-volume, high-variety strategy discussed in Chapter 5. In this job-shop environment, each product or each small group of products has a different sequence of operations. A product or small order is produced by moving it from one department to another in the sequence required for that product. A good example of the process-oriented layout is a hospital or clinic. Figure 8.1 illustrates the process at the emergency clinic in Chicago for two patients, A and B. A continuous inflow of patients, each with his or her own request, requires routing through admissions, laboratories, operating rooms, radiology, pharmacies, nursing beds, and so on.

NOTE
Process layouts are common not only in manufacturing, but in colleges, banks, auto repair shops, airlines, and libraries.

A big advantage of process-oriented layout is its flexibility in equipment and labor assignments. The breakdown of one machine, for example, need not halt an entire process; work can be transferred to other machines in the department.

FIGURE 8.1

AN EMERGENCY ROOM PROCESS LAYOUT SHOWING THE ROUTING OF TWO PATIENTS

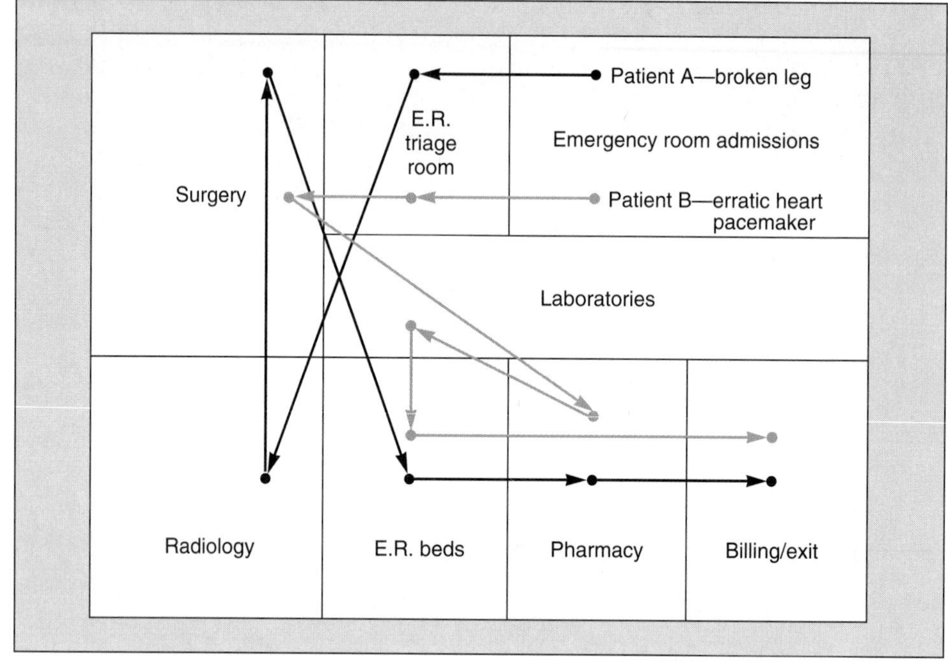

Patient A (broken leg) proceeds to E.R. triage, to radiology, to surgery, to a bed, to pharmacy, to billing. Patient B (pacemaker problem) moves to E.R. triage, to surgery, to pharmacy, to lab, to a bed, to billing.

job lots

Process-oriented layout is also especially good for handling the manufacture of parts in small batches, or **job lots,** and for the production of a wide variety of parts in different sizes or forms.

The disadvantages of process-oriented layout come from the general-purpose use of the equipment. Orders take more time and money to move through the system because of difficult scheduling, setups, and material handling. In addition, labor skill requirements and work-in-process inventories are higher because of larger imbalances in the production process. High labor skill needs increase the required level of training and experience; high work-in-process increases capital investment.

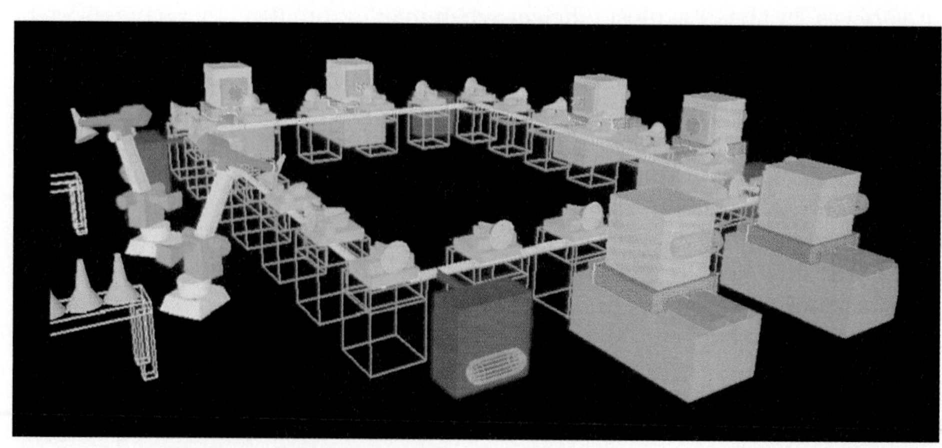

Historically, three-dimensional physical models were often built to address the layout problem. We now use three-dimensional computer models to achieve the same purpose but at greatly reduced cost. Here a transmission assembly line using AutoMod II is shown.

In process layout planning, the most common tactic is to arrange departments or work centers in the most economical locations. In many facilities, optimal placement in the most economical location means minimizing material handling costs. Process layout planning entails placing departments with large interdepartmental flows of parts or people next to one another. Material handling costs in this approach depend upon: (1) the number of loads (or people) to be moved during some period of time between two departments (*i* and *j*) and (2) the distance-related costs between departments. Cost can be a function of distance between departments. The *objective* can be expressed as follows:

$$\text{Minimize cost} = \sum_{i=1}^{n} \sum_{j=1}^{n} X_{ij}C_{ij}$$

where

n = Total number of work centers or departments

i, j = Individual departments

X_{ij} = Number of loads moved from department i to department j

C_{ij} = Cost to move a load between department i and department j

Process-oriented facilities (and fixed-position layouts as well) try to minimize the loads (or trips) times distance-related costs. The term C_{ij} combines the distance and a weighting factor into one factor. This assumes not only that the difficulty of movement is equal but also that the pickup and set-down costs are constant. This is not always the case, but for the moment we will summarize these data (that is, cost, difficulty, and pickup and set-down cost) into this one variable. The best way to understand the steps of process layout is to look at an example.

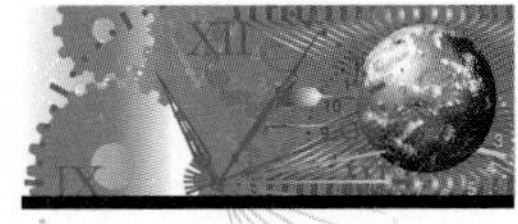

EXAMPLE 1

The Walters Company's management wants to arrange the six departments of its factory in a way that will minimize interdepartmental material handling costs. They make an initial assumption (to simplify the problem) that each department is 20 × 20 feet and that the building is 60 feet long and 40 feet wide. The process layout procedure that they follow involves six steps.

Step 1. *Construct a "from-to-matrix"* showing the flow of parts or materials from department to department (Figure 8.2).

Step 2. *Determine the space requirements* for each department. Figure 8.3 shows the available plant space.

Step 3. *Develop an initial schematic diagram* showing the sequence of departments through which parts will have to move. Try to place departments with a heavy flow of materials or parts next to one another (see Figure 8.4).

Step 4. *Determine the cost* of this layout by using the material-handling cost equation shown earlier; that is,

$$\text{Cost} = \sum_{i}^{n} \sum_{j}^{n} X_{ij}C_{ij}$$

For this problem, the Walters Company assumes that a forklift carries all interdepartmental loads. The cost of moving one load between adjacent departments

FIGURE 8.2

INTERDEPARTMENTAL FLOW OF PARTS

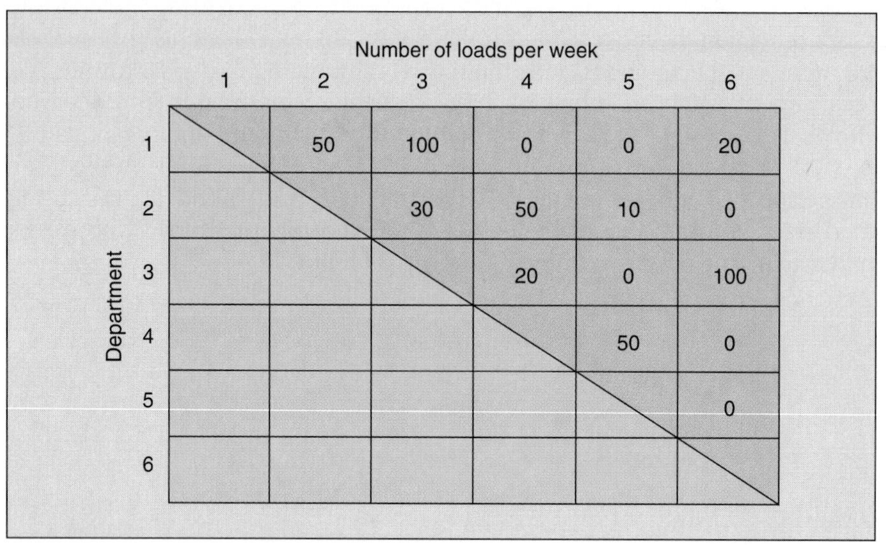

Number of loads per week

Department	1	2	3	4	5	6
1		50	100	0	0	20
2			30	50	10	0
3				20	0	100
4					50	0
5						0
6						

The high flows between 1 and 3, and 3 and 6, are immediately apparent. Departments 1, 3, and 6, therefore, should be close together.

FIGURE 8.3

BUILDING DIMENSIONS AND A POSSIBLE DEPARTMENT LAYOUT

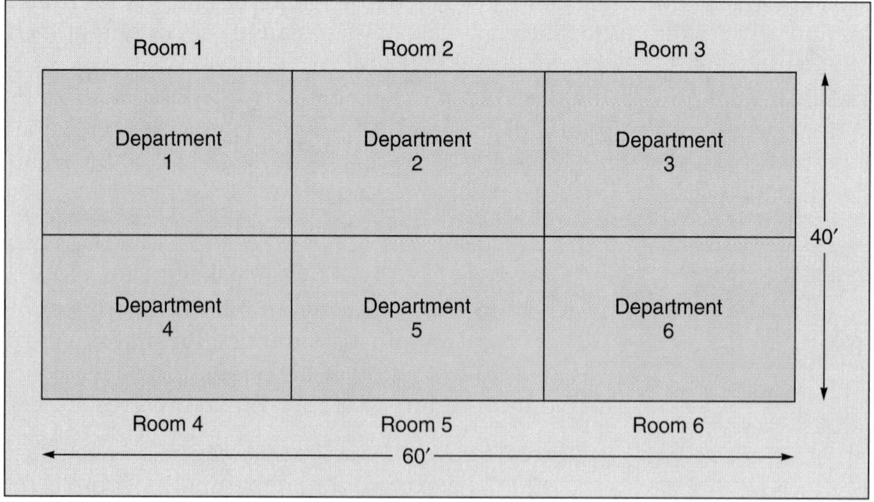

is estimated to be \$1. Moving a load between nonadjacent departments costs \$2. Hence, the handling cost between departments 1 and 2 is \$50 (\$1 × 50 loads), \$200 between departments 1 and 3 (\$2 × 100 loads), \$40 between departments 1 and 6 (\$2 × 20 loads), and so on. The total cost for the layout shown in Figure 8.4 then, is

$$\begin{aligned} \text{Cost} = {} & \underset{(1\text{ and }2)}{\$50} + \underset{(1\text{ and }3)}{\$200} + \underset{(1\text{ and }6)}{\$40} + \underset{(2\text{ and }3)}{\$30} + \underset{(2\text{ and }4)}{\$50} \\ & + \underset{(2\text{ and }5)}{\$10} + \underset{(3\text{ and }4)}{\$40} + \underset{(3\text{ and }6)}{\$100} + \underset{(4\text{ and }5)}{\$50} \\ = {} & \$570 \end{aligned}$$

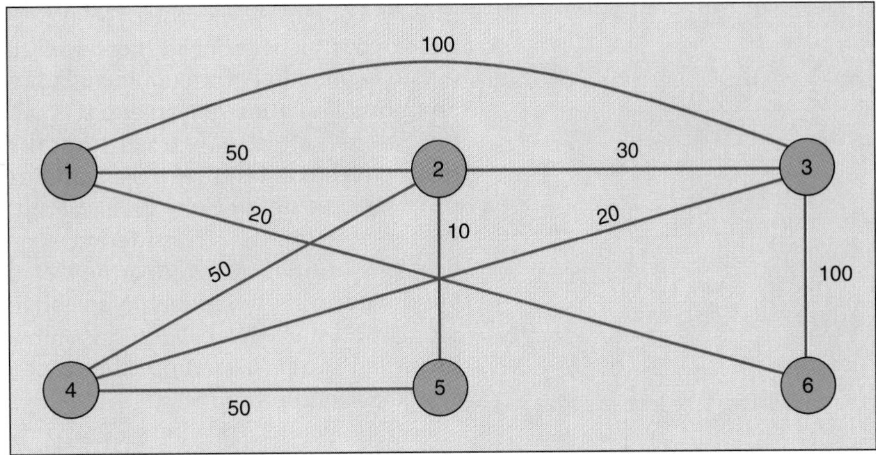

FIGURE 8.4

INTERDEPARTMENTAL FLOW GRAPH SHOWING NUMBER OF WEEKLY LOADS

Step 5. *Try to improve this layout* by trial and error (or by a more sophisticated computer program approach that we will discuss shortly) to establish a reasonably good arrangement of departments.

Looking at both the flow graph and the cost calculations, it appears desirable to place departments 1 and 3 closer together. They currently are nonadjacent, and the high volume of flow between them causes a large handling expense. Looking the situation over, we need to check the effect of shifting departments and possibly raising, instead of lowering, overall costs.

One possibility is to switch departments 1 and 2. This exchange produces the second departmental flow graph (Figure 8.5), which shows that it is possible to reduce the cost to \$480, a saving in material handling of \$90.

Cost = \$50 (1 and 2) + \$100 (1 and 3) + \$20 (1 and 6) + \$60 (2 and 3) + \$50 (2 and 4)

+ \$10 (2 and 5) + \$40 (3 and 4) + \$100 (3 and 6) + \$50 (4 and 5)

= \$480

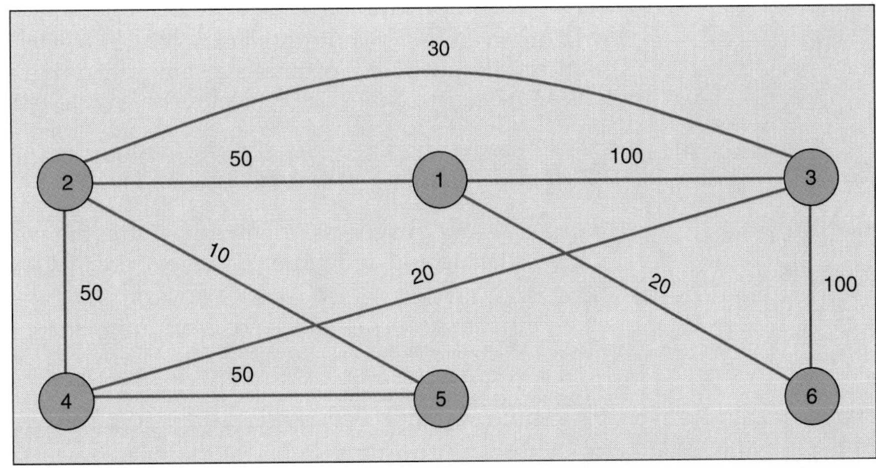

FIGURE 8.5

SECOND INTERDEPARTMENTAL FLOW GRAPH

This, of course, is only one of a large number of possible changes. For a six-department problem there are actually 720 (or $6! = 6 \times 5 \times 4 \times 3 \times 2 \times 1$) potential arrangements! In layout problems, we seldom reach an optimal solution and may have to be satisfied with a "reasonable" one reached after a few trials. Suppose the Walters Company is satisfied with the cost figure of $480 and the flow graph of Figure 8.5. The problem may not be solved yet. Often a sixth step is necessary.

Step 6. *Prepare a detailed plan* considering space or size requirements of each department; that is, arrange the departments to fit the shape of the building and its nonmovable areas (such as the loading dock, washrooms, and stairways). Often this step involves making certain that the final plan can be accommodated by the electrical system, floor loads, aesthetics, and other factors.

In the case of the Walters Company, space requirements are a simple matter (see Figure 8.6).

FIGURE 8.6

A FEASIBLE LAYOUT FOR THE WALTERS COMPANY

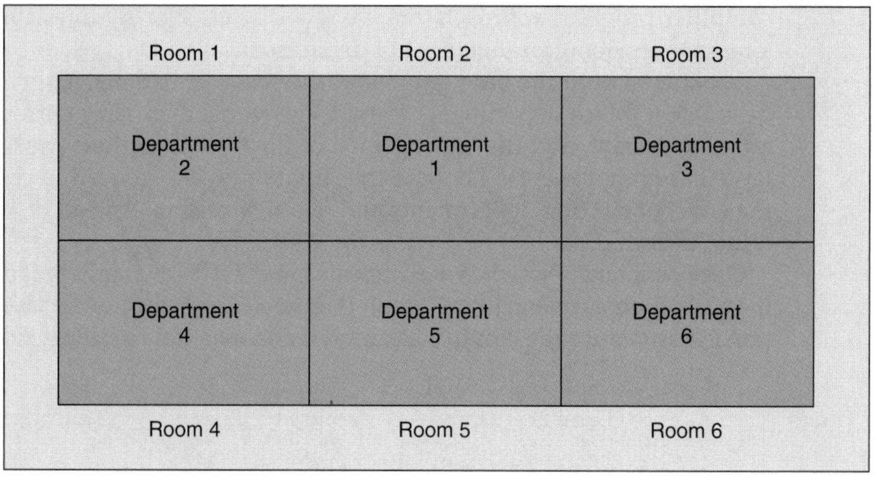

Room 1	Room 2	Room 3
Department 2	Department 1	Department 3
Department 4	Department 5	Department 6
Room 4	Room 5	Room 6

The graphic approach we have been discussing is adequate for small problems.[1] However, this method does not suffice for larger problems. When 20 departments are involved in a layout problem, over 600 *trillion* different department configurations are possible. Fortunately, computer programs such as CRAFT,[2] SPACECRAFT,[3] and Lay OPT have been written to handle large layouts.

Cellular Layout

work cell

A special case of process-oriented layout is the work cell. A **work cell** takes machines that would ordinarily be dispersed in various process departments and

[1]See also Richard Muther, *Systematic Layout Planning*, 2nd ed. (Boston: Cahners, 1976), for a similar approach to what the author calls simplified layout planning.

[2]E. S. Buffa, G. S. Armor, and T. E. Vollman, "Allocating Facilities with CRAFT," *Harvard Business Review* 42, no. 2 (March-April 1964): 136–159.

[3]R. V. Johnson, "SPACECRAFT for Multi-Floor Layout Planning," *Management Science* 28, no. 4 (1982): 407–417.

arranges them in a small group so that the advantages of product-oriented systems can be brought to bear on a particular batch or family of batches (Figure 8.7). The work cell is built around the product. The advantages of work cells are:

1. *Reduced work-in-process inventory* because the work cell is set up to provide a balanced flow from machine to machine.
2. *Less floor space* required because less space is needed between the machines to accommodate the work-in-process inventory.
3. *Reduced raw material and finished goods inventories* because less work in process allows more rapid movement of materials through the work cell.
4. *Reduced direct labor cost* because of better flow of material and improved scheduling. The time to move from one piece to another and from one batch within the family to another is substantially reduced.
5. *Heightened sense of employee participation* in the organization and the product because employees accept more responsibility for quality, since quality problems are readily identified with the work cell and the employee.
6. *Increased utilization of equipment and machinery* because of better scheduling and faster material flow.
7. *Reduced investment in machinery and equipment* because good facility utilization reduces the number of machines and the amount of equipment and tooling.

FIGURE 8.7

IMPROVING LAYOUTS BY MOVING TO THE WORK CELL CONCEPT

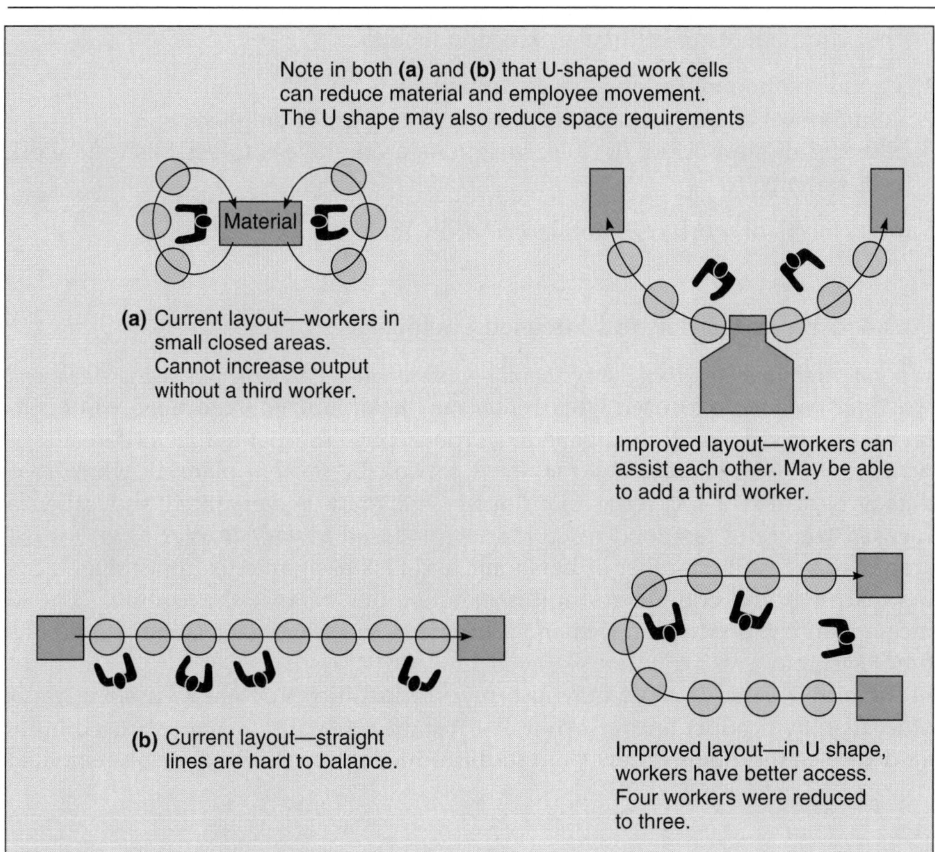

Note in both (a) and (b) that U-shaped work cells can reduce material and employee movement. The U shape may also reduce space requirements
Material
(a) Current layout—workers in small closed areas. Cannot increase output without a third worker.
Improved layout—workers can assist each other. May be able to add a third worker.
(b) Current layout—straight lines are hard to balance.
Improved layout—in U shape, workers have better access. Four workers were reduced to three.

TABLE 8.2 WORK CELLS, FOCUSED WORK CELLS, AND THE FOCUSED FACTORY

WORK CELL	FOCUSED WORK CENTER	FOCUSED FACTORY
A work cell is a temporary product-oriented arrangement of machines and personnel in what is ordinarily a process-oriented facility.	A focused work center is a permanent product-oriented arrangement of machines and personnel in what is ordinarily a process-oriented facility.	A focused factory is a permanent facility to produce a product or component in a product-oriented facility. Many of the focused factories currently being built were originally part of a process-oriented facility.
Example: A job shop with machinery and personnel rearranged to produce 30 unique control panels.	*Example:* Pipe bracket manufacturing at a shipyard.	*Example:* A plant to produce window mechanisms for automobiles.

The requirements of cellular production include:

1. Group technology codes or their equivalent.
2. A high level of training and flexibility on the part of employees.
3. Either staff support or flexible, imaginative employees to establish the work cells initially.

Various forms of work cells are described in Table 8.2.

Focused Work Center and Focused Factory

focused work center

focused factory

When a firm has *identified a large family of like products* and *the forecast is stable and of adequate volume,* a focused work center may be organized. A **focused work center** moves production from a general-purpose, process-oriented facility to a large work cell. The large work cell may be a part of the present plant, in which case it may be called a focused work center. Or it may be separated and called a **focused factory.** A fast-food restaurant is a focused factory. Burger King, for example, changes the number of personnel and task assignments rather than moving machines and equipment. In this manner, they balance the assembly line to meet changing production demands. In effect, the "layout" changes numerous times each day.

The term *focused factories* may also refer to facilities that are focused in ways other than by product line or layout. For instance, a facility may be focused in regard to meeting quality, new product introduction, or flexibility requirements.[4]

[4]See, for example, Wickham Skinner, "The Focused Factory," *Harvard Business Review* 52, no. 3 (May-June 1974): 113–121.

Focused facilities in manufacturing and in services appear to be better able to stay in tune with their customers, to produce quality products, and to operate at higher margins. This is true whether they are steel mills such as SMI, Nucor, or Chaparral, or restaurants such as McDonald's and Burger King.

OFFICE LAYOUT

The criteria for a rational approach to office layouts in terms of work flow are the same as those for manufacturing tangible goods. That is, we can organize around either processes or products. In most organizations, however, there is some middle ground where, for example, the accounts receivable department handles receivables, the order department handles incoming orders, and the accounts payable department handles results of purchases and other bills. This middle ground can be thought of as cellular organizations arranged and rearranged as work procedures and volumes change. The frequent rearrangement of offices is witness to the flexibility of this cellular relationship.

Figure 8.8 shows a relationship chart. It is an extremely effective way to plan office activities. This chart, prepared for an office of consulting engineers, indicates that Ms. Payne must be (1) near the engineers' area, (2) less near the secretary and central files, and (3) not at all near the photocopy or storage room.

There are additional layout considerations (some of which apply to a factory as well as to an office). These are considerations that have to do with teamwork, authority, and status. Should all or only part of the work area be air conditioned? Should all employees use the same entrance, rest rooms, lockers, and cafeteria? As mentioned earlier, layout decisions are part art and part science. The science part, flow of paper in an office, can be analyzed in the same manner as the flow of parts in a process layout.

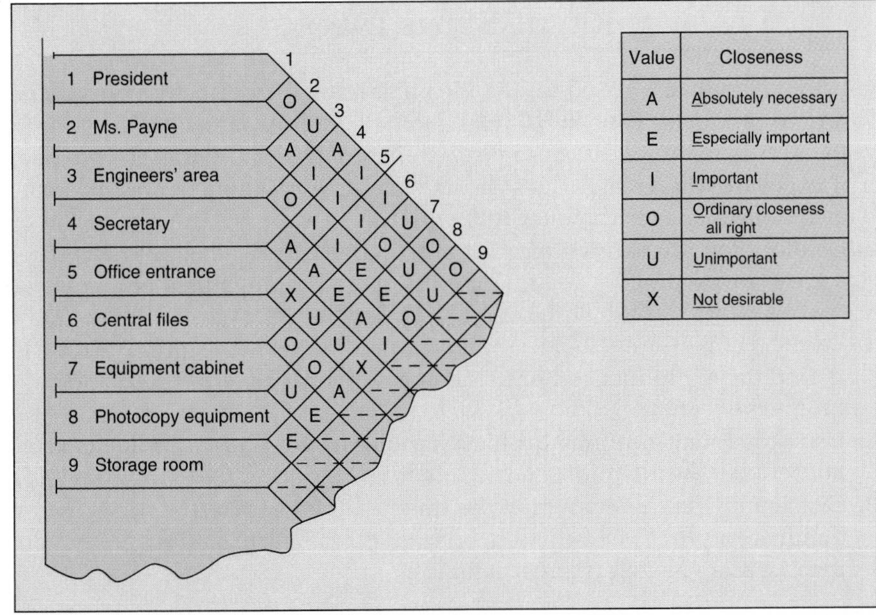

FIGURE 8.8

OFFICE RELATIONSHIP CHART

SOURCE: Adapted from Richard Muther, *Systematic Layout Planning*, 2nd ed. (Boston: Cahners Publishing Company, 1973).

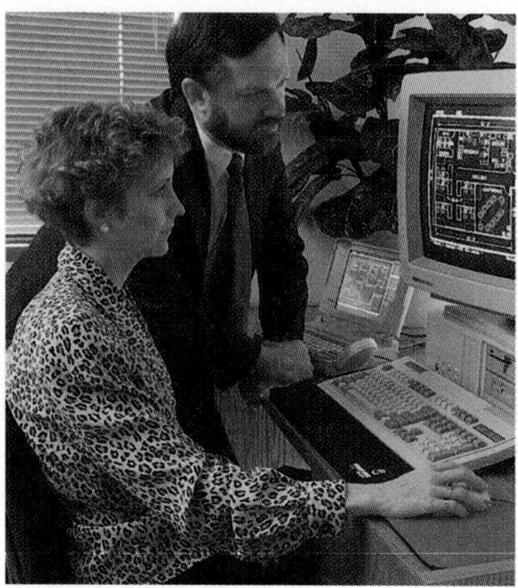

Once the material and information flows of any layout provide a general arrangement, the layout details must be added. This has traditionally been done on a drafting board, cardboard cutouts, or a 3-dimensional model. However, AutoDesk of Sausalito, California, has a new program, Office Layout, that has many of the features of a CAD (Computer-Aided Design) product that allows dimensions, walls dividers, and furniture, as well as people and even plants to be included and then printed.

As a final comment on the layout of offices, we should note two major trends. First, *technology*, such as cellular phones, beepers, faxes, the Internet, home offices, laptop computers, and personal digital assistants (PDAs), allows ever-increasing layout flexibility when information can be moved electronically. Second, *virtual companies* (discussed in Chapter 11 Supplement) create dynamic needs for space and services. These two changes require fewer office employees on site. For example, when Ernst & Young's Chicago office found that 30% to 40% of desks were empty at any given time, the firm developed its new "hoteling programs." Five hundred junior consultants lost their permanent offices; anyone who plans to be in the office (rather than out with clients) for more than half-a-day books an office through a "concierge," who hangs that consultant's name on the door for the day.

RETAIL STORE LAYOUT

Retail store layouts are based on the idea that sales vary directly with customer exposure to products. Thus, most retail store operations managers try to expose customers to as many products as possible. Studies do show that the greater the rate of exposure, the greater the sales and the higher the return on investment. The operations manager can alter *both* with the overall arrangement of the store and the allocation of space within that arrangement to various products.

Five ideas are helpful for determining the overall arrangement of many stores:

1. Locate the high-draw items around the periphery of the store. Thus, we tend to find dairy products on one side of a supermarket and bread and bakery products on another.
2. Use prominent locations for high-impulse and high-margin items such as housewares, beauty aids, and shampoos.
3. Distribute what are known in the trade as "power items"—items that may dominate a purchasing trip—to both sides of an aisle, and disperse them to increase the viewing of other items.

4. Use end aisle locations because they have a very high exposure rate.
5. Convey the image of the store by careful selection in the positioning of the lead-off department. Some stores will position the bakery and deli up front to appeal to convenience-oriented customers who want prepared foods.

The Gap strives for both high quality and low costs. It does this by (1) designing its own clothes, (2) ensuring quality control at the vendors, and (3) maintaining downward pressure on distribution costs. A new automatic distribution center near Baltimore allows The Gap to stock East Coast stores daily, rather than 3 times a week.

Once the overall layout of a retail store has been decided, the products need to be arranged for sale. Many considerations go into this arrangement. However, the main *objective of retail layout is to maximize profitability per square foot of shelf space* (some stores may base this profitability on linear foot of shelf space in lieu of square foot of shelf space). Big-ticket, or expensive, items may yield greater dollar sales, but the profit per square foot may be lower. A number of computerized programs exist that can assist managers in evaluating the profitability of various merchandise. One, SLIM (Store Labor and Inventory Management), can help store managers determine when shelf space is adequate to accommodate another full case. Another software package is COSMOS (Computerized Optimization and Simulation Modeling for Operating Supermarkets), which matches shelf space with delivery schedules, allocating sufficient space to minimize out-of-stock between receipts.

Warehousing and Storage Layouts

The objective of *warehouse layout* is to find the optimum trade-off between handling cost and warehouse space. Consequently, management's task is to maximize the utilization of the total "cube" of the warehouse—that is, utilize its full volume while maintaining low material-handling costs. We define material-handling costs as all the costs related to the incoming transport, storage, and outgoing transport of the material. These costs include equipment, people, material, supervision, insurance, and depreciation. Effective warehouse layout must, of course, also minimize the damage and spoilage of material within the warehouse. Management minimizes the sum of the resources spent on finding and moving material plus the deterioration and damage to the material itself. The variety of items stored and the number of items "picked" has direct bearing on the optimum layout. A warehouse storing a few items lends itself to higher density more than a warehouse storing a variety of items. Modern warehouse management is, in many instances, an automated procedure utilizing automatic stacking cranes, conveyors, and sophisticated controls that manage the flow of materials.

NOTE
Automated storage and retrieval systems are reported to improve productivity by an estimated 500% over manual methods.

An important component of warehouse layout is the relationship between the receiving/unloading area and the shipping/loading area. The facility design depends on the type of supplies unloaded, what they are unloaded from (trucks, rail cars, barges, and so on), and where they are unloaded. In some companies the receiving and shipping facilities, or docks, as they are called, are even the same area—sometimes they are receiving docks in the morning and shipping docks in the afternoon.

Crossdocking

crossdocking

The latest in strategic planning for warehousing involves crossdocking. **Crossdocking** is defined as the avoidance of placing materials or supplies in storage by processing them as they are received for shipment.[5] Wal-Mart, an early advocate, transfers goods from incoming trucks at the receiving dock to outgoing trucks at the shipping docks. Crossdocking has saved the firm a large amount of money and time by moving a large percentage of goods from one dock to another without the goods ever entering the warehouse.

PRODUCT-ORIENTED LAYOUT

Product-oriented layouts are organized around a product or a family of similar high-volume, low-variety products. The assumptions are:

1. Volume is adequate for high equipment utilization.
2. Product demand is stable enough to justify high investment in specialized equipment.
3. Product is standardized or approaching a phase of its life cycle that justifies investment in specialized equipment.
4. Supplies of raw material and components are adequate and of uniform quality (adequately standardized) to ensure they will work with the specialized equipment.

fabrication line

assembly line

One version of a product-oriented layout is a fabrication line; another is an assembly line. The **fabrication line** builds components, such as automobile tires or metal parts for a refrigerator, on a series of machines. An **assembly line** puts the fabricated parts together at a series of workstations. Both are the repetitive processes discussed in Chapter 5, and in both cases the line must be balanced. That is, the work performed on one machine must balance with the work performed on the next machine in the fabrication line, just as the work done at one workstation by an employee on an assembly line must balance with the work done at the next workstation by the next employee.

Fabrication lines tend to be machine paced and require mechanical and engineering changes to facilitate balancing. Assembly lines, on the other hand, tend to be paced by work tasks assigned to individuals or to workstations. Assembly lines, therefore, can be balanced by moving tasks from one individual to another. In this manner, the amount of time required by each individual or station is equalized.

assembly line balancing

The central problem in product-oriented layout planning is to balance the output at each workstation on the production line so that it is nearly the same, while obtaining the desired amount of output. Management's goal is to create a smooth, continuous flow along the assembly line with a minimum of idle time at each person's workstation. A well-balanced assembly line has the advantage of high personnel and facility utilization *and* equity between employees' work loads. Some union contracts include a requirement that work loads must be nearly equal among those on the same assembly line. The term most often used to describe this process is **assembly line balancing.** Indeed the *objective of the product-oriented layout is to minimize imbalance in the fabrication or assembly line.*

The main advantage of product-oriented layout is the low variable cost per unit usually associated with high-volume, standardized products. The product-oriented layout also keeps material handling costs low, reduces work-in-process in-

[5]James A. Tompkins, "Crossdocking: Lets Get It Right," *IE News* 27, no. 2 (January-March 1994): 1–4.

ventories, and makes training and supervision easier. These advantages often outweigh the disadvantages of product layout, namely:

1. High volume is required because of the large investment needed to set up the process.
2. Work stoppage at any one point ties up the whole operation.
3. Little flexibility exists when manufacturing a variety of products or production rates.

NOTE
Product layout can handle only a few products and process designs.

Since the problems of fabrication lines and assembly lines are similar, we will phrase our discussion in terms of an assembly line. On an assembly line, the product typically moves via automated means, such as a conveyor, through a series of workstations until completed (Figure 8.9). This is the way automobiles are assembled, television sets and ovens are produced, and fast-food hamburgers are made. Product-oriented layout uses more automated and specially designed equipment than is found in a process layout.

Assembly Line Balancing

Line-balancing is usually undertaken to minimize imbalance between machines or personnel while meeting a required output from the line. In order to produce at a specified rate, management must know the tools, equipment, and work methods used. Then the time requirements for each assembly task (such as drilling a hole, tightening a nut, or spray-painting a part) must be determined. Management also needs to know the precedence relationship among the activities, that is, the sequence in which various tasks need to be performed. Let us construct a precedence chart for the task data presented in Example 2.

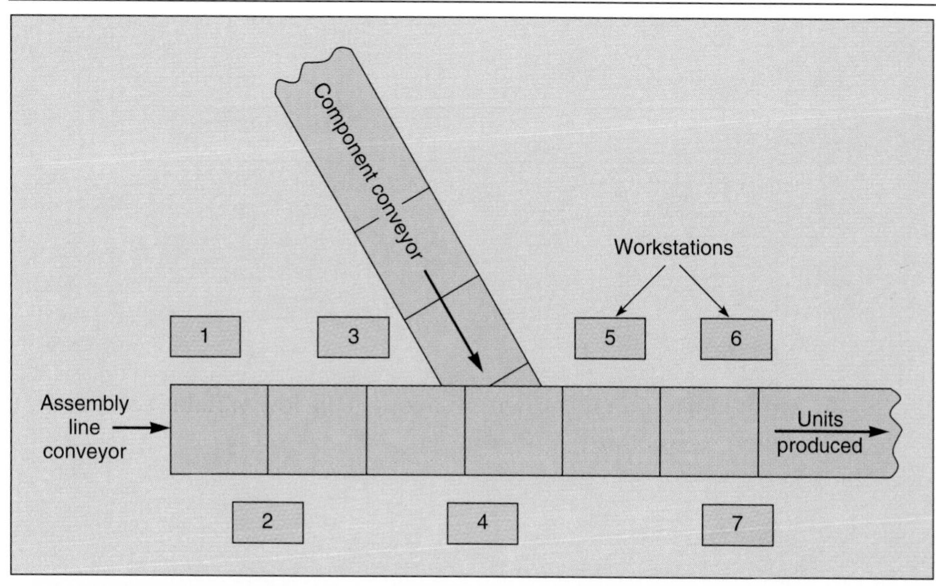

FIGURE 8.9

AN ASSEMBLY LINE LAYOUT

Boeing employs a modular construction to assemble its "parts." These "parts" of tail, aft body section, center body section, wings, front body, and nose are joined in a fixed-position layout. Landing gear is installed, and the airplane is ready for the first of its final five assembly line operations.

At the first position in the assembly line, hydraulics, wings, and air conditioning are installed. Next, cables are hooked up to wing flaps, slats, doors, and landing gear. At position 3, interiors (galleys, bathrooms, videos, safety slides) are installed. Then seats, overhead bins, and partitions are installed, along with jet engines, and cockpit avionics.

At the final assembly line station, interiors and engine connections are finalized and shakedown tests are held. The plane then moves to another building for a three-day paint job.

EXAMPLE 2

We want to develop a precedence diagram for an electrostatic copier that requires a total assembly time of 66 minutes. Table 8.3 and Figure 8.10 give the tasks, assembly times, and sequence requirements for the copier.

TABLE 8.3 PRECEDENCE DATA

TASK	PERFORMANCE TIME (minutes)	TASK MUST FOLLOW TASK LISTED BELOW
A	10	–
B	11	A
C	5	B
D	4	B
E	12	A
F	3	C, D
G	7	F
H	11	E
I	3	G, H
Total time	66	

This means that tasks B and E cannot be done until task A has been completed.

FIGURE 8.10

PRECEDENCE DIAGRAM

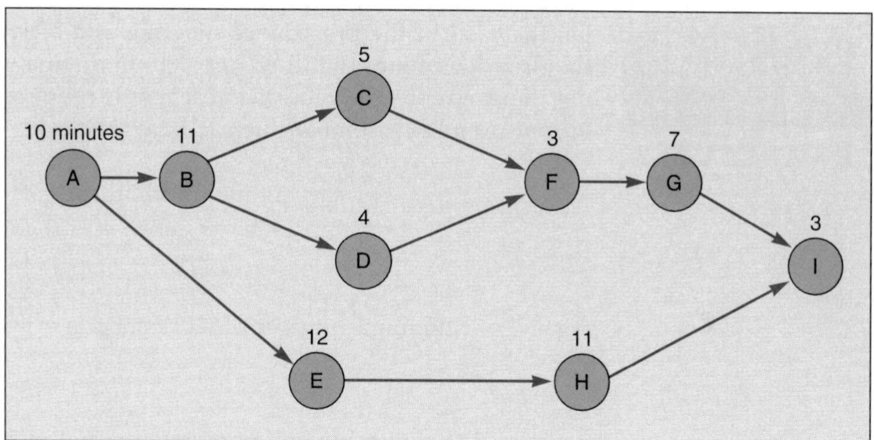

Once we have constructed a precedence chart summarizing the sequences and performance times, we turn to the job of grouping tasks into job stations to meet the specified production rate. This process involves three steps:

1. Take the demand (or production rate) per day and divide it into the productive time available per day (in minutes or seconds). This operation gives us what is called the **cycle time,** namely, the time the product is available at each workstation:

cycle time

$$\text{Cycle time} = \frac{\text{Production time available per day}}{\text{Demand per day or production rate per day}}$$

2. Calculate the theoretical minimum number of workstations. This is the total task-duration time divided by the cycle time. Fractions are rounded to the next higher whole number:

NOTE
The two goals in line balancing are maximizing the production rate and maximizing efficiency.

$$\text{Minimum number of workstations} = \frac{\sum_{i=1}^{m} \text{Time for task}}{\text{Cycle time}}$$

where m is the number of assembly tasks.

3. Perform the line balance by assigning specific assembly tasks to each workstation. An efficient balance is one that will complete the required assembly, follow the specified sequence, and keep the idle time at each workstation to a minimum. A formal procedure for doing this is
   - **a.** Identify a master list of work elements.
   - **b.** Eliminate those work elements that have been assigned.
   - **c.** Eliminate those work elements whose precedence relationship has not been satisfied.
   - **d.** Eliminate those elements for which inadequate time is available at the workstation.
   - **e.** Identify a unit of work that can be assigned, such as the first unit of work in the list, the last unit of work in the list, the unit of work with the shortest time, the unit of work with the longest time, a randomly selected unit of work, or some other criterion.
   - **f.** Repeat (that is, go to step a) until all elements have been assigned.

NOTE
Some tasks simply cannot be grouped together in one workstation. There may be a variety of physical reasons for this.

Example 3 illustrates a simple line-balancing procedure.

EXAMPLE 3

On the basis of the precedence diagram and activity times given in Example 2, the firm determines that there are 480 productive minutes of work available per day. Furthermore, the production schedule requires that 40 units be completed as output from the assembly line each day. Hence,

$$\text{Cycle time (in minutes)} = \frac{480 \text{ minutes}}{40 \text{ units}}$$

$$= 12 \text{ minutes per unit}$$

$$\text{Minimum number of workstations} = \frac{\text{Total task time}}{\text{Cycle time}} = \frac{66}{12}$$

$$= 5.5 \text{ or } 6 \text{ stations}$$

Figure 8.11 shows one solution that does not violate the sequence requirements and in which the tasks are grouped into six stations. To obtain it, appropriate activities were moved into workstations that use as much of the available cycle time of 12 minutes as possible. The first workstation consumes 10 minutes and has an idle time of 2 minutes.

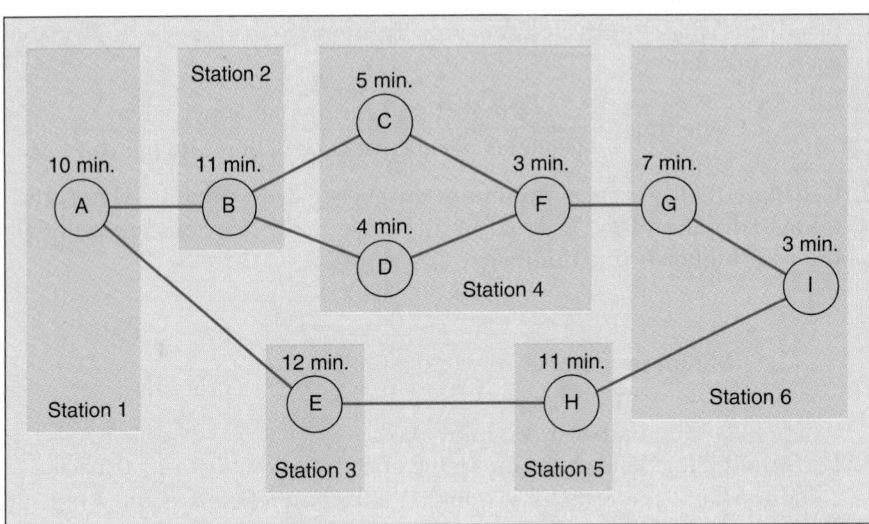

FIGURE 8.11
A SIX-STATION SOLUTION TO THE LINE-BALANCING PROBLEM

The second workstation uses 11 minutes, and the third consumes the full 12 minutes. The fourth workstation groups three small tasks and balances perfectly at 12 minutes. The fifth has 1 minute of idle time; the sixth (consisting of tasks G and I) has 2 minutes of idle time per cycle. Total idle time for this solution is 6 minutes per cycle.

We can compute the efficiency of a line balance by dividing the total task time by the product of the number of workstations times the assigned cycle time:

In the case of slaughtering operations, the assembly line is actually a disassembly line. The line-balancing procedures described in this chapter are the same as for an assembly line. The chicken processing plant shown here must balance the work of several hundred employees. Division of labor produces efficiency. Because one's skills develop with repetition, less time is lost in changing tools, and specialized tools are developed. The total labor content in each of the chickens processed is a few minutes. How long would it take you to process a chicken by yourself?

$$\text{Efficiency} = \frac{\Sigma\text{Task times}}{(\text{Number of workstations}) \times (\text{Assigned cycle time})}$$

Management often compares different levels of efficiency for various numbers of workstations. In this way, the firm can determine the sensitivity of the line to changes in the production rate and workstation assignments.

EXAMPLE 4

We can calculate the balance efficiency for Example 3 as follows:

$$\text{Efficiency} = \frac{66 \text{ minutes}}{(6 \text{ stations}) \times (12 \text{ minutes})} = \frac{66}{72} = 91.7\%$$

Opening a seventh workstation, for whatever reason, would decrease the efficiency of the balance to 78.6%:

$$\text{Efficiency} = \frac{66 \text{ minutes}}{(7 \text{ stations}) \times (12 \text{ minutes})} = 78.6\%$$

Large-scale line-balancing problems, like large process layout problems, are often solved by computers. Several different computer programs are available to handle the assignment of workstations on assembly lines with 100 (or more) individual work activities. Both the computer routine called COMSOAL (Computer Method for Sequencing Operations for Assembly Lines) and ASYBL (General Electric's assembly line configuration program) are widely used in larger problems to evaluate the thousands or millions of possible workstation combinations much more efficiently than could ever be done by hand.

SUMMARY

Layouts make a substantial difference in operating efficiency. The six classic layout situations are: (1) fixed position, (2) process-oriented, (3) office, (4) retail, (5) warehouse, and (6) product-oriented. A variety of techniques have been developed in attempts to solve these layout problems. Industrial firms focus on reducing material movement and assembly line balancing. Retail firms focus on product exposure. Storage layouts focus on the optimum trade-off between storage costs and material handling costs.

Often the variables in the layout problem are so wide-ranging and numerous as to preclude finding an optimal solution. For this reason, layout decisions, when having received substantial research effort, remain something of an art.

KEY TERMS

Fixed-position layout *(p. 267)*
Process-oriented layout *(p. 267)*
Office layout *(p. 267)*
Retail/service layout *(p. 267)*
Warehouse layout *(p. 268)*
Product-oriented layout *(p. 268)*
Job lots *(p. 270)*
Work cell *(p. 274)*
Focused work center *(p. 276)*
Focused factory *(p. 276)*
Crossdocking *(p. 279)*
Fabrication line *(p. 280)*
Assembly line *(p. 280)*
Assembly line balancing *(p. 280)*
Cycle time *(p. 283)*

USING POM FOR WINDOWS FOR LAYOUT DESIGN

■ *Solving Example 1 Using POM for Windows' Operations Layout Module*

POM for Windows' facility layout module can be used to place up to ten departments in ten rooms in order to minimize the total distance traveled as a function of the distances between the rooms and the flow between departments. The program performs pair-wise comparisons, exchanging departments until no exchange will reduce the total amount of movement.

The data screen in Program 8.1 consists of two tables of numbers—one for the flows and one for the distances. Output appears in Program 8.2.

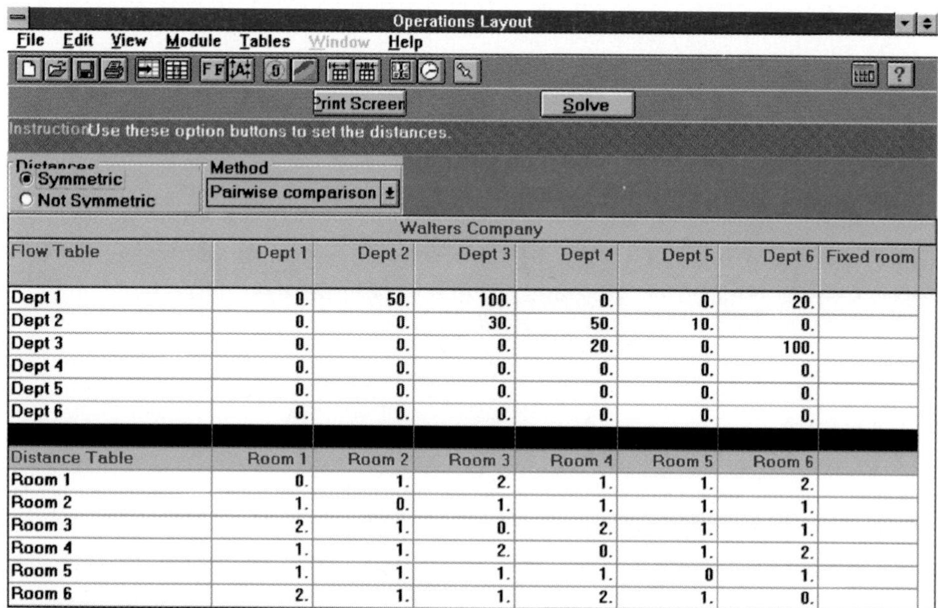

Flow Table	Dept 1	Dept 2	Dept 3	Dept 4	Dept 5	Dept 6	Fixed room
Dept 1	0.	50.	100.	0.	0.	20.	
Dept 2	0.	0.	30.	50.	10.	0.	
Dept 3	0.	0.	0.	20.	0.	100.	
Dept 4	0.	0.	0.	0.	0.	0.	
Dept 5	0.	0.	0.	0.	0.	0.	
Dept 6	0.	0.	0.	0.	0.	0.	

Distance Table	Room 1	Room 2	Room 3	Room 4	Room 5	Room 6
Room 1	0.	1.	2.	1.	1.	2.
Room 2	1.	0.	1.	1.	1.	1.
Room 3	2.	1.	0.	2.	1.	1.
Room 4	1.	1.	2.	0.	1.	2.
Room 5	1.	1.	1.	1.	0	1.
Room 6	2.	1.	1.	2.	1.	0.

Departments may be named in their columns.
Typically, the distance matrix will be symmetric. If not, all entries must be made. The solution appears in Program 8.2.

PROGRAM 8.1

POM for Windows' Operations Layout Program Applied to Walters Company's Data in Example 1

PROGRAM 8.2

SOLUTION TO PROGRAM 8.1 POM FOR WINDOWS' INPUT SCREEN FOR WALTER COMPANY DATA

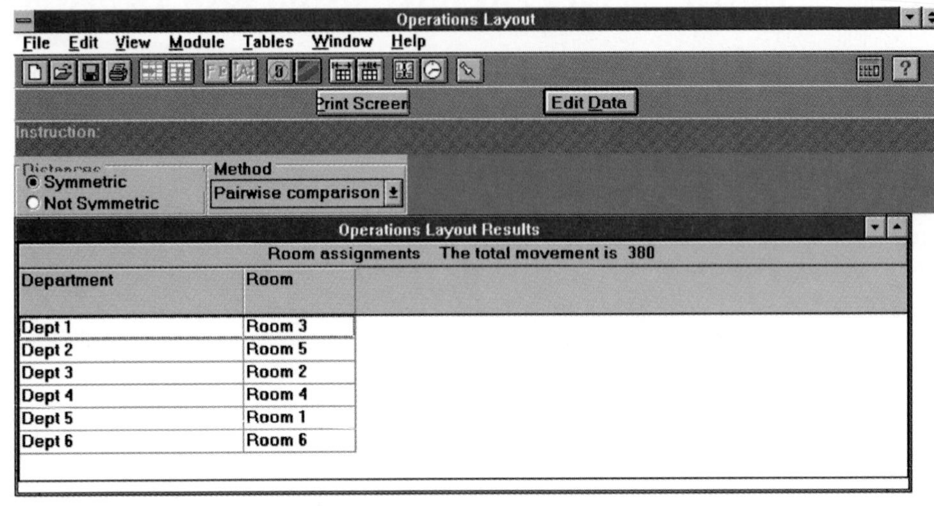

Department	Room
Dept 1	Room 3
Dept 2	Room 5
Dept 3	Room 2
Dept 4	Room 4
Dept 5	Room 1
Dept 6	Room 6

■ *Solving Examples 2, 3, and 4 Using POM for Windows' Assembly Line-Balancing Module*

POM for Windows' module for line balancing can handle a line with up to 99 tasks, each with up to six immediate predecessors. Programs 8.3 and 8.4 illustrate the input and output computer screens for this module applied to Examples 2, 3, and 4.

PROGRAM 8.3

POM FOR WINDOWS' ASSEMBLY LINE BALANCING PROGRAM DATA ENTRY SCREEN

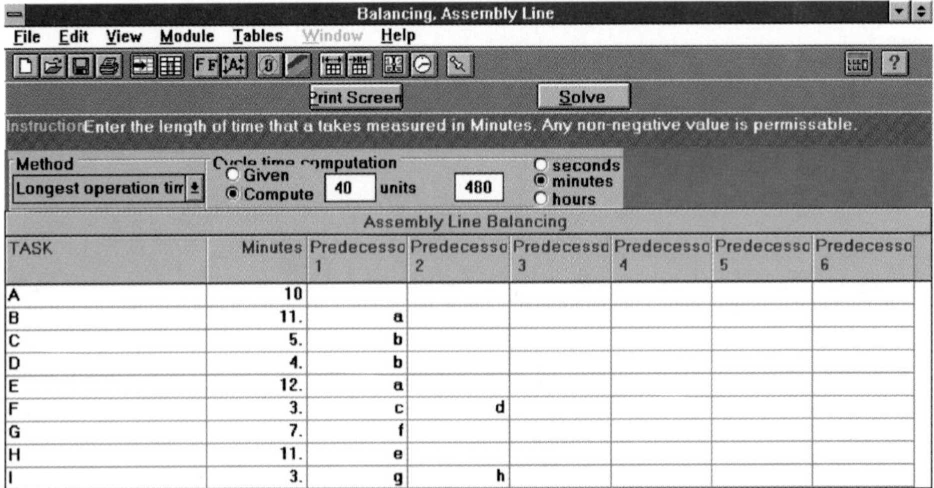

TASK	Minutes	Predecessor 1	Predecessor 2	Predecessor 3	Predecessor 4	Predecessor 5	Predecessor 6
A	10						
B	11.	a					
C	5.	b					
D	4.	b					
E	12.	a					
F	3.	c	d				
G	7.	f					
H	11.	e					
I	3.	g	h				

Cycle time can be entered in two ways: (1) either given if known or (2) demand rate can be entered with time available as shown. Five "heuristic rules" may be used: (1) longest operation time, (2) most following tasks, (3) ranked positional weight, (4) shortest operation time, and (5) least number of following tasks. No one rule can guarantee an optimal solution. The default rule is the longest operation time.

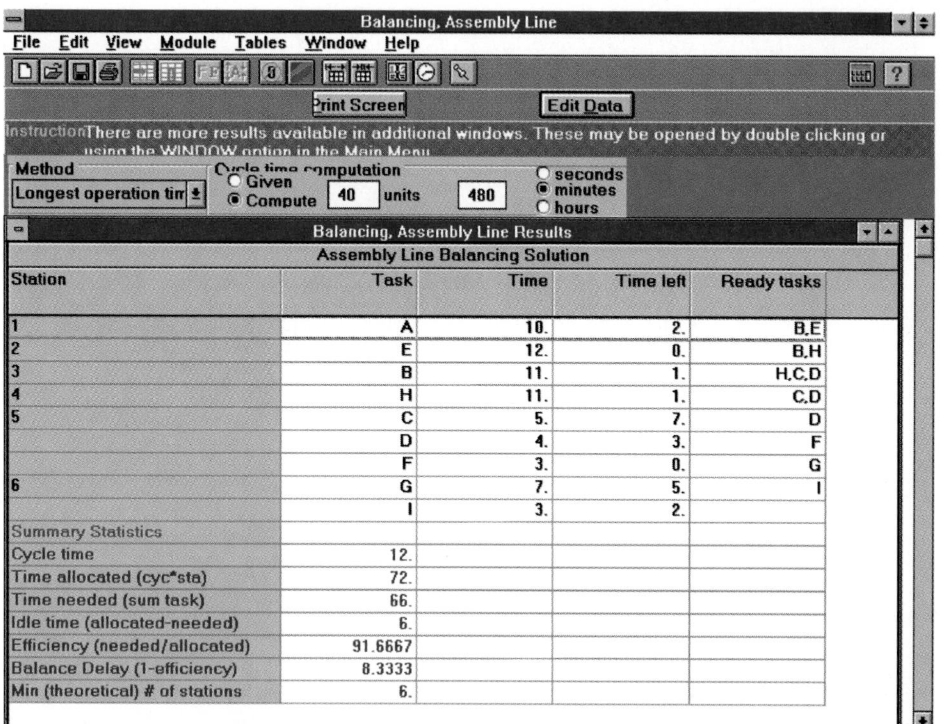

Balancing, Assembly Line

Method: Longest operation time — Cycle time computation: Compute 40 units 480 minutes

Balancing, Assembly Line Results

Assembly Line Balancing Solution

Station	Task	Time	Time left	Ready tasks
1	A	10.	2.	B,E
2	E	12.	0.	B,H
3	B	11.	1.	H,C,D
4	H	11.	1.	C,D
5	C	5.	7.	D
	D	4.	3.	F
	F	3.	0.	G
6	G	7.	5.	I
	I	3.	2.	
Summary Statistics				
Cycle time	12.			
Time allocated (cyc*sta)	72.			
Time needed (sum task)	66.			
Idle time (allocated-needed)	6.			
Efficiency (needed/allocated)	91.6667			
Balance Delay (1-efficiency)	8.3333			
Min (theoretical) # of stations	6.			

Note that longest operation time heuristic provides a different solution than the one we found in Figure 8.11.

PROGRAM 8.4

POM FOR WINDOWS' ASSEMBLY LINE BALANCING OUTPUT FOR EXAMPLES 2 THROUGH 4 AND PROGRAM 8.3

SOLVED PROBLEM 8.1

The Snow-Bird Hospital is a small emergency-oriented facility located in a popular ski resort area in northern Michigan. Its new administrator, Mary Lord, decides to reorganize the hospital, using the process-layout method she studied in business school. The current layout of Snow-Bird's eight emergency departments is shown in Figure 8.12.

The only physical restriction perceived by Lord is the need to keep the entrance and initial processing room in its current location. All other departments or rooms (each 10 feet square) can be moved if the layout analysis indicates it would be beneficial.

Mary's first step is to analyze records in order to determine the number of trips made by patients between departments in an average month. The data are shown in Figure 8.13. The objective, Ms. Lord

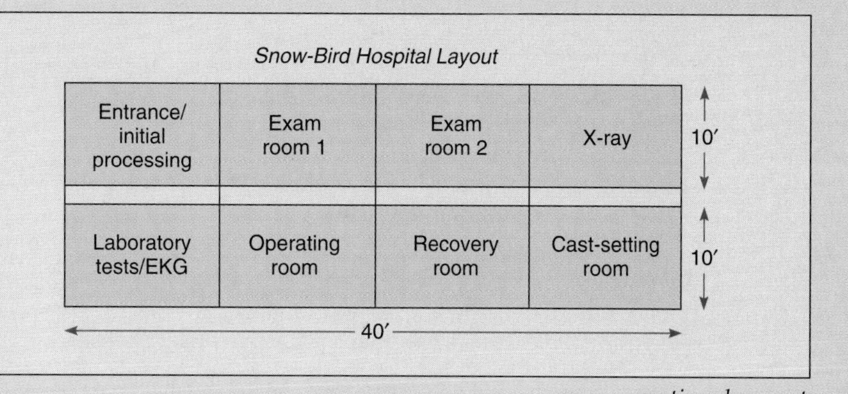

FIGURE 8.12

SNOW-BIRD HOSPITAL LAYOUT

continued on next page

FIGURE 8.13

NUMBER OF PATIENTS MOVING BETWEEN DEPARTMENTS IN ONE MONTH

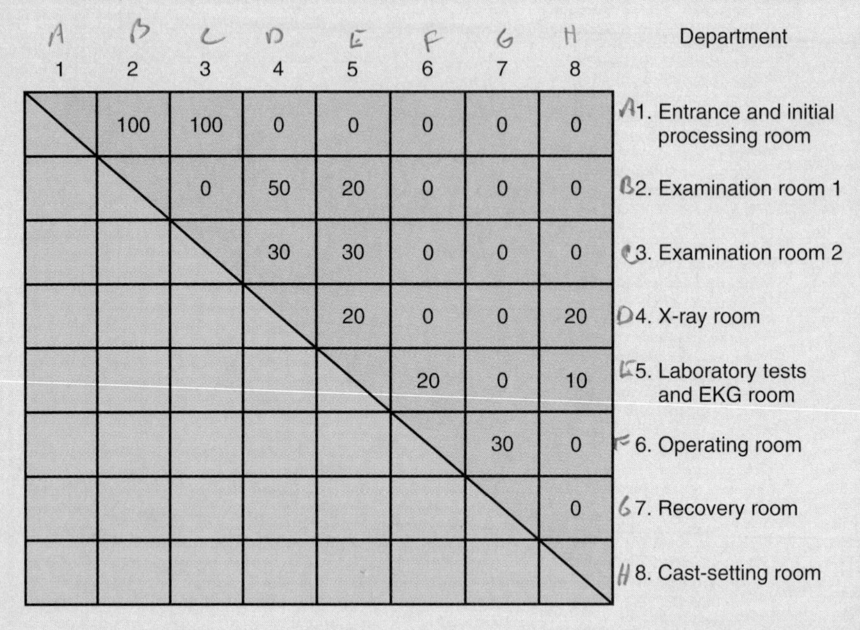

1	2	3	4	5	6	7	8	Department
	100	100	0	0	0	0	0	1. Entrance and initial processing room
		0	50	20	0	0	0	2. Examination room 1
			30	30	0	0	0	3. Examination room 2
				20	0	0	20	4. X-ray room
					20	0	10	5. Laboratory tests and EKG room
						30	0	6. Operating room
							0	7. Recovery room
								8. Cast-setting room

decides, is to lay out the rooms so as to minimize the total distance walked by patients who enter for treatment. She writes her objective as:

$$\text{Minimize patient movement} = \sum_{i=1}^{8}\sum_{j=1}^{8} X_{ij}C_{ij}$$

where

X_{ij} = Number of patients per month (loads or trips) moving from department i to department j

C_{ij} = Distance in feet between departments i and j (which, in this case, is the equivalent of cost per load to move between departments)

Note that this is only a slight modification of the cost objective equation shown earlier in the chapter.

Departments next to one another, such as entrance and examination room 1, are assumed to carry a walking distance of 10 feet. Diagonal departments are also considered adjacent and assigned a distance of 10 feet. Nonadjacent departments such as entrance and examination room 2 or entrance and recovery room are 20 feet apart, while nonadjacent rooms such as entrance and x-ray are 30 feet apart. (Hence, 10 feet is considered 10 units of cost, 20 feet is 20 units of cost, and 30 feet is 30 units of cost.)

Given the above information, redo the layout of Snow-Bird Hospital to improve its efficiency in terms of patient flow.

SOLUTION

First, establish Snow-Bird's current layout, as shown in Figure 8.14. Using Snow-Bird's current layout, the patient movement may be computed.

Total movement

$$= \underset{(1\text{ to }2)}{(100 \times 10')} + \underset{(1\text{ to }3)}{(100 \times 20')} + \underset{(2\text{ to }4)}{(50 \times 20')} + \underset{(2\text{ to }5)}{(20 \times 10')}$$

$$+ \underset{(3\text{ to }4)}{(30 \times 10')} + \underset{(3\text{ to }5)}{(30 \times 20')} + \underset{(4\text{ to }5)}{(20 \times 30')} + \underset{(4\text{ to }8)}{(20 \times 10')}$$

$$+ \underset{(5\text{ to }6)}{(20 \times 10')} + \underset{(5\text{ to }8)}{(10 \times 30')} + \underset{(6\text{ to }7)}{(30 \times 10')}$$

$$= 1{,}000 + 2{,}000 + 1{,}000 + 200 + 300 + 600 + 600$$

$$+ 200 + 200 + 300 + 300$$

$$= 6{,}700 \text{ feet}$$

It is not possible to prove a mathematically "optimal" solution, but you should be able to propose a new layout that will reduce the current figure of 6,700 feet. Two useful changes, for example, are to switch rooms 3 and 5 and to interchange rooms 4 and 6. This change would result in the schematic shown in Figure 8.15.

Figure 8.14

Current Snow-Bird Patient Flow

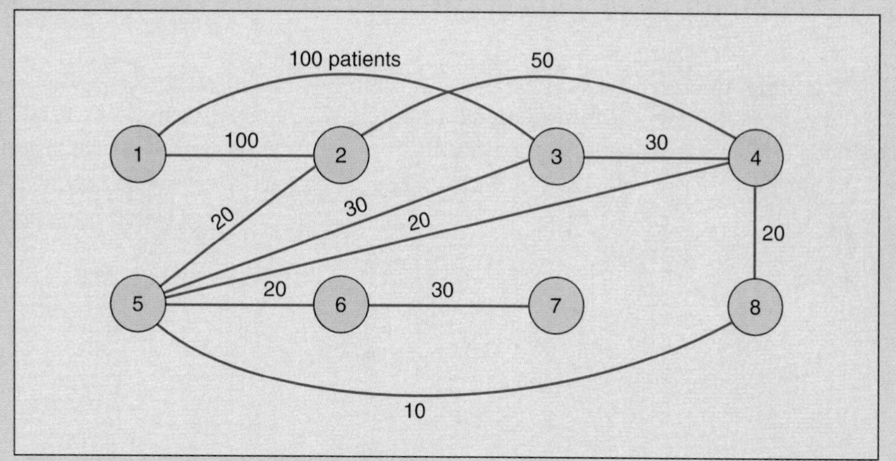

Total movement

$= (100 \times 10') + (100 \times 10') + (50 \times 10') + (20 \times 10')$
(1 to 2) (1 to 3) (2 to 4) (2 to 5)

$+ (30 \times 10') + (30 \times 20') + (20 \times 10') + (20 \times 20')$
(3 to 4) (3 to 5) (4 to 5) (4 to 8)

$+ (20 \times 10') + (10 \times 30') + (30 \times 10')$
(5 to 6) (5 to 8) (6 to 7)

$= 1{,}000 + 1{,}000 + 500 + 200 + 300 + 600 + 200 + 400 + 200 + 100 + 300$

$= 4{,}800$ feet

Do you see any room for further improvement? (See Homework Problem 8.2.)

Figure 8.15

Improved Layout

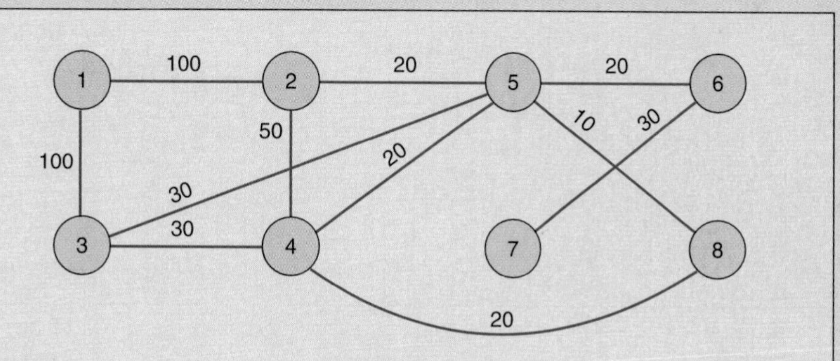

SOLVED PROBLEM 8.2

An assembly line, whose activities are shown in Figure 8.16, has an eight-minute cycle time. Draw the precedence graph and find the minimum possible number of workstations. Then arrange the work activities into workstations so as to balance the line. What is the efficiency of this line balance?

TASK	PERFORMANCE TIME (minutes)	TASK MUST FOLLOW THIS TASK
A	5	–
B	3	A
C	4	B
D	3	B
E	6	C
F	1	C
G	4	D, E, F
H	2	G
	28	

SOLUTION

The theoretical minimum number of workstations is

$$\frac{\Sigma t_i}{\text{Cycle time}} = \frac{28 \text{ minutes}}{8 \text{ minutes}} = 3.5 \text{ or } 4 \text{ stations}$$

The precedence graph and one good layout are shown in Figure 8.16.

Efficiency

$$= \frac{\text{Total task time}}{(\text{Number of workstations}) \times (\text{Cycle time})}$$

$$= \frac{28}{(4)(8)} = 87.5\%$$

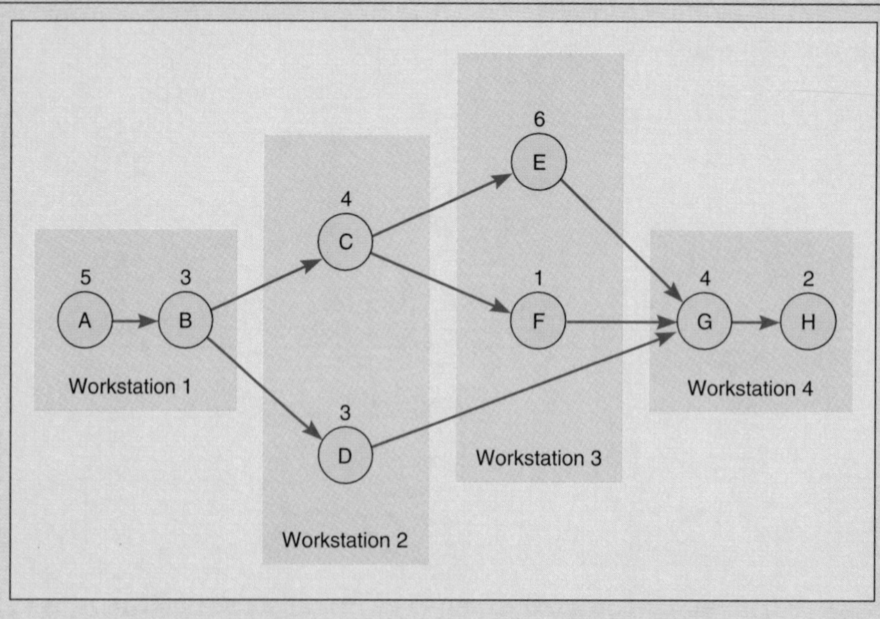

FIGURE 8.16

A FOUR-STATION SOLUTION TO THE LINE-BALANCING PROBLEM

SELF-TEST ■ CHAPTER 8

- *Before taking the self-test* refer back to the learning objectives listed at the beginning of the chapter and the key terms listed at the end of the chapter.
- Use the key at the back of the text to *correct* your answers.
- *Restudy* pages that correspond to any questions you answered incorrectly or material you feel uncertain about.

1. In process-oriented and fixed-position layouts, it is important to minimize the costs of
   a. raw material
   b. material handling
   c. special purpose machinery
   d. skilled labor

2. The same fundamental principles apply in the layout of an office as apply to the layout of a manufacturing process.
   a. True **b.** False

3. In a retail store layout, the manager has two fundamental variables that can be manipulated: the overall arrangement or flow pattern through the store and the allocation of space to individual products.
   a. True **b.** False

4. The objective of a warehouse layout is to find the optimum trade-off between handling costs and item unit costs.
   a. True **b.** False

5. A major assumption of stability of demand is important for justifying which of the following layout types?
   a. product layout
   b. process layout
   c. fixed-position layout
   d. all of the above

6. An assembly line is an example of a process-oriented layout.
   a. True **b.** False

7. To balance an assembly line, one can usually move tasks from one individual to another.
   a. True **b.** False

8. An assembly line is usually machine-paced and requires mechanical and engineering changes to facilitate balancing.
   a. True **b.** False

9. The *disadvantages* of product layout include
   a. high volume is required because of the large investment needed to set up the process
   b. work stoppage at any one point ties up the whole operation
   c. there is a lack of flexibility in handling a variety of products or production rates
   d. all of the above

10. We are seldom able to balance an assembly line so that it operates at 100% efficiency.
   a. True **b.** False

11. A fixed-position layout
   a. groups workers, their equipment, and spaces/offices to provide for movement of information
   b. addresses the layout requirements of large, bulky projects such as ships and buildings
   c. seeks the best personnel and machine utilization in repetitive or continuous production
   d. allocates shelf space and responds to customer behavior
   e. deals with low-volume, high-variety production

12. A process-oriented layout
   a. groups workers, their equipment, and spaces/offices to provide for movement of information
   b. addresses the layout requirements of large, bulky projects such as ships and buildings
   c. seeks the best personnel and machine utilization in repetitive or continuous production
   d. allocates shelf space and responds to customer behavior
   e. deals with low-volume, high-variety production

13. A product-oriented layout
   a. groups workers, their equipment, and spaces/offices to provide for movement of information
   b. addresses the layout requirements of large, bulky projects such as ships and buildings
   c. seeks the best personnel and machine utilization in repetitive or continuous production
   d. allocates shelf space and responds to customer behavior
   e. deals with low-volume, high-variety production

14. A big advantage of a process-oriented layout is
   a. its low cost
   b. its flexibility in equipment and labor assignment
   c. the simplified scheduling problem presented by this layout strategy
   d. the ability to employ low-skilled labor

15. The fundamental layout strategies include:
   a. ______ **b.** ______ **c.** ______ **d.** ______ **e.** ______

16. Various forms of "work cells" include
   a. ____________ **b.** ____________ **c.** ____________

17. For a focused work center or focused factory to be appropriate requires
   a. ____________ **b.** ____________ **c.** ____________

18. Before considering a product-oriented layout, we would wish to be certain that:
   a. ________ **b.** ________ **c.** ________ **d.** ________

DISCUSSION QUESTIONS

1. What is the layout strategy of your local print shop?
2. How would you go about collecting data to help a small business, like a print shop, improve its layout?
3. What are the six layout strategies presented in this chapter?
4. What are the advantages and disadvantages of product layout?
5. What are the advantages and disadvantages of process layout?
6. What are the advantages and disadvantages of work cells?
7. What layout innovations have you noticed recently in retail establishments?
8. What techniques can be used to overcome the inherent problems of fixed-position layout?
9. What layout variables might you want to consider as particularly important in an office layout where computer programs are written?

OPERATIONS IN PRACTICE EXERCISE

Offices in Japan tend to be considerably different from those in the United States. In the Tokyo office of Toyota, for example, about 110 people work in one large room. As is typical of Japanese offices, they work out in the open, with desks crammed together in clusters called islands. The islands are arranged in long rows; managers sit at the ends of the rows, with their subordinates in full view. (When important visitors arrive for meetings, they are ushered into special rooms and do not see these cramped offices.) Offices in Japan are also less automated and it is not uncommon for two workers to share a telephone. No one at Tokyo's Toyota office has his or her own PC; rather, there is an alcove of machines to share.

Discuss your perceptions of the importance of the U.S. and Japanese styles of office layout. Which yields greater productivity?

PROBLEMS

8.1. Given the following flow and distance matrices in Bob Dillman's job shop, what is the best layout? What is the "total movement" of this layout?

FLOW MATRIX

	DEPT. A	DEPT. B	DEPT. C	DEPT. D	DEPT. E	DEPT. F
Dept. A	0	100	50	0	0	50
Dept. B	25	0	0	50	0	0
Dept. C	25	0	0	0	50	0
Dept. D	0	25	0	0	20	0
Dept. E	50	0	100	0	0	0
Dept. F	10	0	20	0	0	0

DISTANCE MATRIX

	DEPT. A	DEPT. B	DEPT. C	DEPT. D	DEPT. E	DEPT. F
Dept. A	0	1	2	3	4	5
Dept. B	1	0	5	4	3	2
Dept. C	2	5	0	6	7	6
Dept. D	3	4	6	0	4	3
Dept. E	4	3	7	4	0	5
Dept. F	5	2	6	3	5	0

8.2. In Solved Problem 8.1 (shown earlier) we improved Snow-Bird's layout to 4,800 feet of movement. Is an improved layout possible? What is it?

8.3. Registration period at Southeastern University has always been a time of emotion, commotion, and lines. Students must move among four stations to complete the trying semiannual process. Last semester's registration, held in the fieldhouse, is described in Figure 8.17. You can see, for example, that 450 stu-

Interstation Activity Mix

	Pickup paperwork and forms (A)	Advising station (B)	Pickup class cards (C)	Verification of status and payment (D)
Paperwork/forms (A)	—	450	550	50
Advising (B)	250	—	200	0
Class cards (C)	0	0	—	750
Verification/payment (D)	0	0	0	—

Existing Layout

A	B	C	D

|——30′——|——30′——|——30′——|

FIGURE 8.17

REGISTRATION FLOW OF STUDENTS

dents moved from the paperwork station (A) to advising (B), while 550 went directly from A to picking up their class cards (C). Graduate students, who for the most part had preregistered, proceeded directly from A to the station where the registration was verified and payment collected (D). The layout used last semester is also shown in Figure 8.17. The registrar is preparing to set up this semester's stations and is anticipating similar numbers.

a. What is the "load × distance," or cost, of the layout shown?

b. Provide an improved layout and compute its cost.

8.4. You have just been hired as the director of operations for Bellas Chocolates, in Blacksburg, Virginia, a purveyor of exceptionally fine chocolates. Bellas Chocolates has two kitchen layouts under consideration for its recipe making and testing department. The strategy is to provide the best kitchen layout possible so the food scientists can devote their time and energy toward product improvement, not wasted effort in the kitchen. You have been asked to evaluate these two kitchen layouts and prepare a recommendation for your boss, Mr. Bellas, so that he can proceed with placing the contract for building the testing kitchens (see Figure 8.18 on the next page).

8.5. Bellas Chocolates (see Problem 8.4) is considering a third layout, which follows. Evaluate its effectiveness in trip-distance feet.

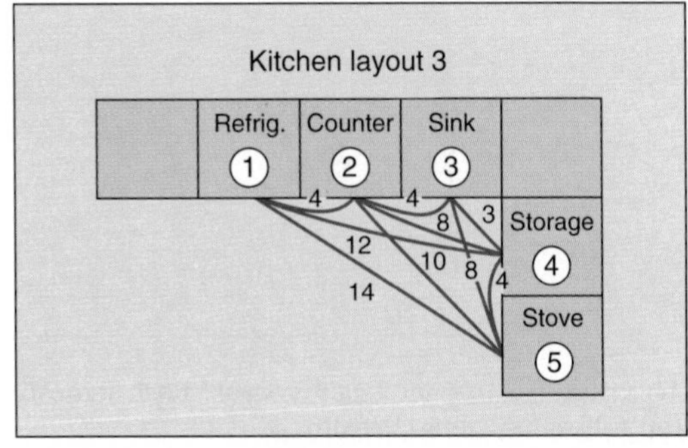

FIGURE 8.18

LAYOUT OPTIONS

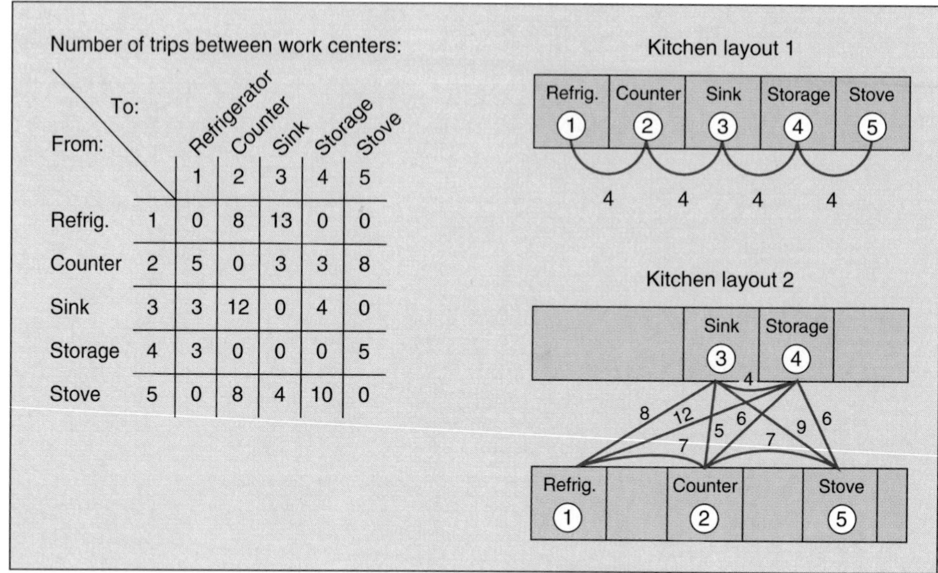

: **8.6.** Bellas Chocolates (see Problems 8.4 and 8.5) has yet a fourth layout to consider. This layout is shown. What is the total "trip-distance"?

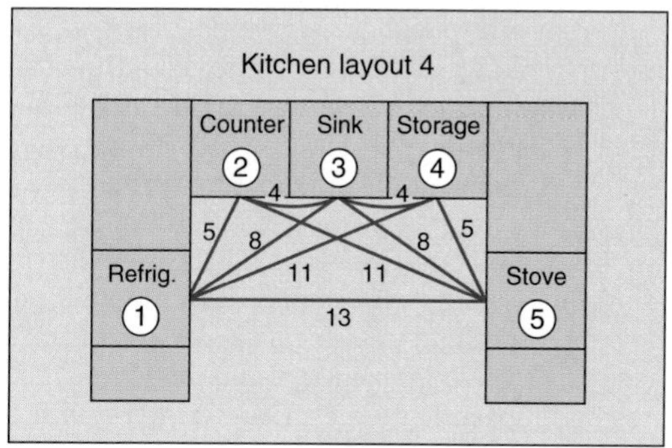

8.7. Given the following task, times, and sequence, develop a balanced line capable of operating with a 10-minute cycle time at John Coleman's company. What is the efficiency of that line?

TASK ELEMENT	TIME (minutes)	ELEMENT PREDECESSOR
A	3	–
B	5	A
C	7	B
D	5	–
E	3	C
F	3	B, D
G	5	D
H	6	G

: **8.8.** The preinduction physical examination given by the U.S. Army involves the following seven activities:

ACTIVITY	AVERAGE TIME (minutes)
Medical history	10
Blood tests	8
Eye examination	5
Measurements (weight, height, blood pressure)	7
Medical examination	16
Psychological interview	12
Exit medical evaluation	10

These activities can be performed in any order, with two exceptions: The medical history must be taken first and the exit medical evaluation is the final step. At present three paramedics and two physicians are on duty during each shift. Only a physician can perform the exit evaluation or conduct the psychological interview. Other activities can be carried out by either physicians or paramedics.

a. Develop a layout and balance the line. How many people can be processed per hour?

b. What activity is the current bottleneck?

c. If one more physician and one more paramedic can be placed on duty, how would you redraw the layout? What is the new throughput?

: **8.9.** A final assembly plant for Dictatape, a popular dictation company, produces the DT, a hand-held dictation unit. There are 400 minutes available in the final assembly plant for the DT, and the average demand is 80 units per day. The final assembly requires six separate tasks. Information concerning these tasks is given in the following table. What tasks should be assigned to various workstations, and what is the overall efficiency of the assembly line?

TASK	PERFORMANCE TIME (minutes)	TASK MUST FOLLOW TASK LISTED BELOW
1	1	–
2	1	1
3	4	1, 2
4	1	2, 3
5	2	4
6	4	5

: **8.10.** SCFI, South Carolina Furniture, Incorporated, produces all types of office furniture. The Executive Secretary is a chair that has been ergonomically designed to provide comfort during long work hours. The chair sells for \$130. There are 480 minutes available during the day for production, and the average daily demand has been 50 chairs. There are eight tasks. Given the following information, solve this assembly line balancing problem.

TASK	PERFORMANCE TIME (minutes)	TASK MUST FOLLOW TASK LISTED BELOW
1	4	–
2	7	1
3	6	1, 2
4	5	2, 3
5	6	4
6	7	5
7	8	5
8	6	6, 7

8.11. Tailwind, Inc., produces high-quality but expensive training shoes for runners. The Tailwind shoe, which sells for $110, contains both gas- and liquid-filled compartments to provide more stability and better protection against knee, foot, and back injuries. Manufacturing the shoes requires 10 separate tasks. How should these tasks be grouped into workstations? There are 400 minutes available for manufacturing the shoe in the plant each day. Daily demand is 60. The information for the tasks is as follows:

TASK	PERFORMANCE TIME (minutes)	TASK MUST FOLLOW TASK LISTED BELOW
1	1	–
2	3	1
3	2	2
4	4	2
5	1	3, 4
6	3	1
7	2	6
8	5	7
9	1	5, 8
10	3	9

8.12. Mach 10 is a one-person sailboat designed to be used in the ocean. Manufactured by Creative Leisure, Mach 10 can handle 40-mph winds and over 10-foot seas. The final assembly plant for Creative Leisure is in Cupertino, California. At this time, 200 minutes are available each day to manufacture Mach 10. The daily demand is 60 boats. Given the following information, how many workstations would you recommend?

TASK	PERFORMANCE TIME (minutes)	TASK MUST FOLLOW TASK LISTED BELOW
1	1	–
2	1	1
3	2	1
4	1	3
5	3	3
6	1	3
7	1	4, 5, 6
8	2	2
9	1	7, 8

8.13. Because of the expected high demand for Mach 10, Creative Leisure has decided to increase the manufacturing time available to produce the Mach 10 (see Problem 8.12). What impact would 300 available minutes per day have on the assembly line? What impact would 400 minutes have?

8.14. Nearbeer Products, Inc., manufactures drinks that taste the same as a good draft beer but do not contain any alcohol. With changes in drinking laws and demographics, interest has increased in Nearbeer Lite. Nearbeer Lite has fewer calories than the regular beer, is less filling, and tastes great. The final packing operation for Nearbeer Lite requires 13 tasks. Nearbeer bottles Nearbeer Lite five hours a day, five days a week. Each week there is a demand for 3,000 bottles of Nearbeer Lite. Given the following information, solve this assembly line balancing problem.

DATA FOR PROBLEMS 8.14 AND 8.15

TASK	PERFORMANCE TIME (minutes)	TASK MUST FOLLOW TASK LISTED BELOW
1	0.1	–
2	0.1	1
3	0.1	2
4	0.2	2
5	0.1	2
6	0.2	3, 4, 5
7	0.1	1
8	0.1	7
9	0.2	7, 8
10	0.1	9
11	0.2	6
12	0.2	10, 11
13	0.1	12

: **8.15.** Nearbeer's president, Bob Swan, believes that weekly demand for Nearbeer Lite could explode (see Problem 8.14). What would happen if demand doubled?

: **8.16.** Suppose production requirements in Solved Problem 8.2 increase and necessitate a reduction in cycle time from eight minutes to seven minutes. Balance the line once again using the new cycle time. Note that it is not possible to combine task times so as to group tasks into the minimum number of workstations. This condition occurs in actual balancing problems fairly often.

: **8.17.** Annie Engstrom, operations manager at Nesa Electronics, prides herself on excellent assembly line balancing. She has been told that the firm needs 1,400 electronic relays completed per day. There are 420 minutes of productive time in each working day (which is equivalent to 25,200 seconds). Group the assembly line activities shown in the following table into appropriate workstations and calculate the efficiency of the balance.

TASK	TIME (seconds)	MUST FOLLOW TASK	TASK	TIME (seconds)	MUST FOLLOW TASK
A	13	–	G	5	E
B	4	A	H	6	F, G
C	10	B	I	7	H
D	10	–	J	5	H
E	6	D	K	4	I, J
F	12	E	L	15	C, K

: **8.18.** Given the following data describing a line-balancing problem at Doug Brauer's company, develop a solution allowing a cycle time of three minutes. What is the efficiency of that line?

TASK ELEMENT	TIME (minutes)	ELEMENT PREDECESSOR
A	1	–
B	1	A
C	2	B
D	1	B
E	3	C, D
F	1	A
G	1	F
H	2	G
I	1	E, H

8.19. Southwestern University is in the process of designing a new 50,000-square-foot engineering research building. The dean has developed the following closeness ratings for the six departments the building will house. Assign the departments to fit in the space shown. Use the table in Figure 8.8 for closeness codes.

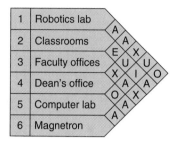

	Department
1	Robotics lab
2	Classrooms
3	Faculty offices
4	Dean's office
5	Computer lab
6	Magnetron

Pair	Rating	Pair	Rating	Pair	Rating
1–2	A	2–3	E	3–5	A
1–3	A	2–4	U	3–6	X
1–4	X	2–5	I	4–5	O
1–5	U	2–6	A	4–6	A
1–6	O	3–4	X	5–6	A

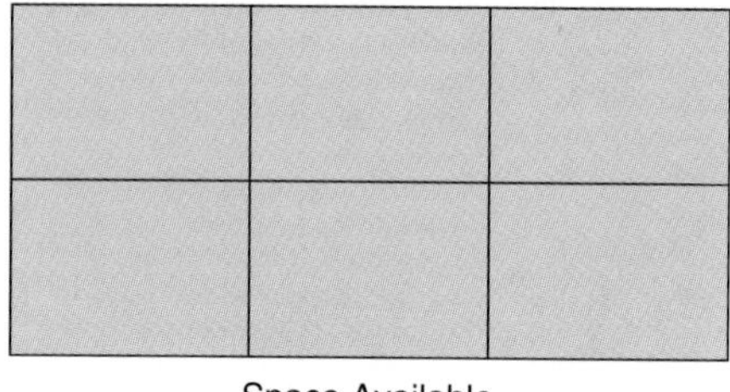

Space Available

Consider departments placed diagonally to be the same distance as those placed adjacent.

Internet Data Base Application See our website at http://www.prenhall.com/renderpom for a challenging, computer-based problem.

CASE STUDY

State Automobile License Renewals

Henry Coupe, the manager of a metropolitan branch office of the state Department of Motor Vehicles, attempted to perform an analysis of the driver's license renewal operations. Several steps were to be performed in the process. After examining the license renewal process, he identified the steps and associated times required to perform each step, as shown in the following table:

STATE AUTOMOBILE LICENSE RENEWALS PROCESS TIMES

STEP	AVERAGE TIME TO PERFORM (seconds)
1. Review renewal application for correctness	15
2. Process and record payment	30
3. Check file for violations and restrictions	60
4. Conduct eye test	40
5. Photograph applicant	20
6. Issue temporary license	30

Coupe found that each step was assigned to a different person. Each application was a separate process in the sequence shown above. Coupe determined that his office should be prepared to accommodate the maximum demand of processing 120 renewal applicants per hour.

He observed that the work was unevenly divided among the clerks, and the clerk who was responsible for checking violations tended to shortcut her task to keep up with the other clerks. Long lines built up during the maximum demand periods.

Coupe also found that jobs 1, 2, 3, and 4 were handled by general clerks who were each paid $6.00 per hour. Job 5 was performed by a photographer paid $8 per hour. Job 6, the issuing of a temporary license, was required by state policy to be handled by a uniformed motor vehicle officer. Officers were paid $9.00 per hour, but they could be assigned to any job except photography.

A review of the jobs indicated that job 1, reviewing the application for correctness, had to be performed before any other step could be taken. Similarly, job 6, issuing the temporary license, could not be performed until all the other steps were completed.

The branch offices were charged $5 per hour for each camera to perform photography.

Henry Coupe was under severe pressure to increase productivity and reduce costs, but he was also told by the regional director of the Department of Motor Vehicles that he had better accommodate the demand for renewals. Otherwise, "heads would roll."

DISCUSSION QUESTIONS

1. What is the maximum number of applications per hour that can be handled by the present configuration of the process?
2. How many applications can be processed per hour if a second clerk is added to check for violations?
3. Assuming the addition of one more clerk, what is the maximum number of applications the process can handle?
4. How would you suggest modifying the process in order to accommodate 120 applications per hour?

SOURCE: W. Sasser, R. Olson, and D. Wyckoff, *Management of Services Operations: Text, Cases, and Readings* (Boston: Allyn & Bacon, Inc., 1978).

CASE STUDY

Des Moines National Bank

Des Moines National Bank (DNB) recently finished construction on a new building in the downtown business district. Moving into a new building provides an opportunity to arrange the various departments to optimize the efficiency and effectiveness of the operations.

One primary operation of DNB is its check-processing division. This division acts as a clearinghouse for commercial and personal checks. These checks are received from the tellers downstairs as well as from other, smaller financial institutions with which DNB contracts for check processing. Checks are sorted to be sent to the bank from which they are drawn, using the magnetic-ink characters located at the bottom of the check. The reconcilement area ensures that the incoming and outgoing totals balance, and the crediting area makes the entries to complete the transaction. Finally, the sorted checks are bundled and shipped from the distribution area.

The personnel in this division are also responsible for processing government checks and for handling any returned checks coming back through the system. Because these checks require very different processing operations, they are placed in separate departments from the commercial check operations but are located on the same floor.

The service elevator only travels from the basement to the second floor; so it has been decided that the check-processing division will be located on the second floor of the new DNB building. The second floor is divided into eight equal-sized rooms, as shown in Figure 1. (We call them rooms even though they are not separated by walls.) Each room is 75 feet square. Fortunately, this will not be a concern to bank management as each of the eight departments to be located on this floor require roughly 5,000 square feet; these rooms will allow for some additional storage space and for future expansion.

The physical flow of materials—such as the checks being processed and computer printouts for the reconcilement and crediting areas—will be on aisles that run between the centers of the rooms, as shown in Figure 1. Since the checks will arrive and be distributed from the service elevator, it is necessary to put the distribution department in the room with the elevator. No other physical restrictions require any department to be placed in a particular room.

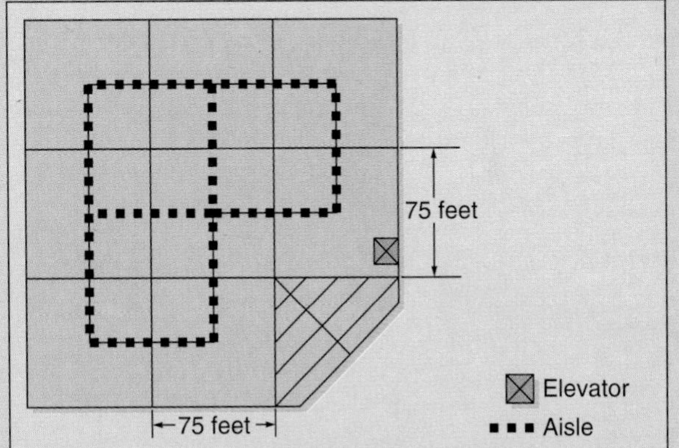

FIGURE 1 FLOOR PLAN OF THE SECOND FLOOR OF THE DNB BUILDING

The first step in this analysis required determining the amount of workflow between the departments. Data collected for several weeks determined the average daily traffic—measured in the number of trips between departments. Although some fluctuations exist in the number of checks processed during the different days of the week, these average figures provide a good estimate of the relative workflow between each pair of departments.

A review of the workflow data revealed that several important relationships were not being considered. For example, although no material flows directly between the commercial check-sorting area and the government check area, they use the same type of equipment. This equipment is very noisy and requires a "soundproof" wall to control the noise, necessitating keeping all of this equipment together to minimize the construction cost. Also,

continued on next page

TABLE 1 WORKFLOW AND CLOSENESS RELATIONSHIPS BETWEEN DEPARTMENTS

DEPARTMENT	1	2	3	4	5	6	7	8
1. Check sorting	–	50	0	250	0	0	0	0
2. Check reconcilement	X	–	50	0	0	0	0	0
3. Check crediting	X	A	–	0	0	0	0	10
4. Check distribution	U	U	U	–	40	60	0	0
5. Government checks	A	U	U	E	–	0	0	0
6. Returned checks	U	U	U	E	U	–	12	0
7. Credit adjustment	X	A	A	U	U	E	–	10
8. Offices	X	I	I	U	O	O	I	–

due to this noise, it is desirable to keep this department removed from areas that require concentration, such as the reconcilement area and the offices. To account for these types of concerns, closeness ratings were identified for each pair of departments using the following rating scheme:

A — Absolutely necessary
E — Especially important
I — Important
O — Ordinary closeness OK
U — Unimportant
X — Not desirable

Table 1 provides the average daily workflow between departments in the upper-right portion and the closeness ratings in the lower-left portion. For example, the workflow between the check sorting and reconcilement departments is 50 units per day, and there is a closeness rating of "X."

DISCUSSION QUESTIONS

1. Develop a layout that minimizes the total workflow.
2. Develop a layout using the relationships defined by the closeness ratings.
3. Develop a layout that considers both the workflow and closeness relationships between departments.
4. Comment on the various layouts developed.
5. Discuss any other factors that should be considered when developing a layout of the check-processing division.

SOURCE: Professor Timothy L. Urban, The University of Tulsa.

Internet Case Study See our Internet home page at http://www.prenhall.com/renderpom for this additional case study: Palm Beach Institute of Sports Medicine.

BIBLIOGRAPHY

Balakrishnan, J. "Notes: The Dynamics of Plant Layout." *Management Science* 39, no. 5 (May 1993): 654–655.

Ding, F., and L. Cheng. "An Effective Mixed-Model Assembly Line Sequencing Heuristic for Just-In-Time Production Systems." *Journal of Operations Management* 11, no. 1 (March 1993): 45–50.

Faaland, B. H., T. D. Klastorin, T. G. Schmitt, and A. Shtub. "Assembly Line Balancing with Resource Dependent Task Times." *Decision Sciences* 23, no. 2 (March-April 1992): 343.

Francis, R. L., L. F. McGinnis, and J. A. White. *Facility Layout and Location*, 2nd ed. Englewood Cliffs, NJ: Prentice Hall, 1992.

Huang, P. Y., and B. L. W. Houck. "Cellular Manufacturing: An Overview and Bibliography." *Production and Inventory Management* 26 (Fourth Quarter 1985): 83–92.

Joshi, S., and M. Sudit. "Procedures for Solving Single-Pass Strip Layout Problems." *IIE Transactions* 26, no. 1 (January 1994): 27–37.

Leung, J. "A New Graph-Theoretic Heuristic for Facility Layout." *Management Science* 38, no. 4 (April 1992): 594.

Makens, P. K., D. F. Rossin, and M. C. Springer. "A Multivariate Approach for Assessing Facility Layout Complexity." *Journal of Operations Management* 9, no. 2 (April 1990): 185.

Montreuil, B., U. Venkatadri, and H. D. Ratliff. "Generating a Layout from a Design Skeleton." *Industrial Engineering Research & Development* 25, no. 1 (January 1993): 3–15.

Morris, J. S., and R. J. Tersine. "A Comparison of Cell Loading Practices in Group Technology." *Journal of Manufacturing and Operations Management* 2, no. 4 (Winter 1989): 299.

Vakharia, A. J., and B. K. Kaku. "Redesigning a Cellular Manufacturing System to Handle Long-Term Demand Changes: A Methodology and Investigation." *Decision Sciences* 24, no. 5 (September-October 1993): 909.

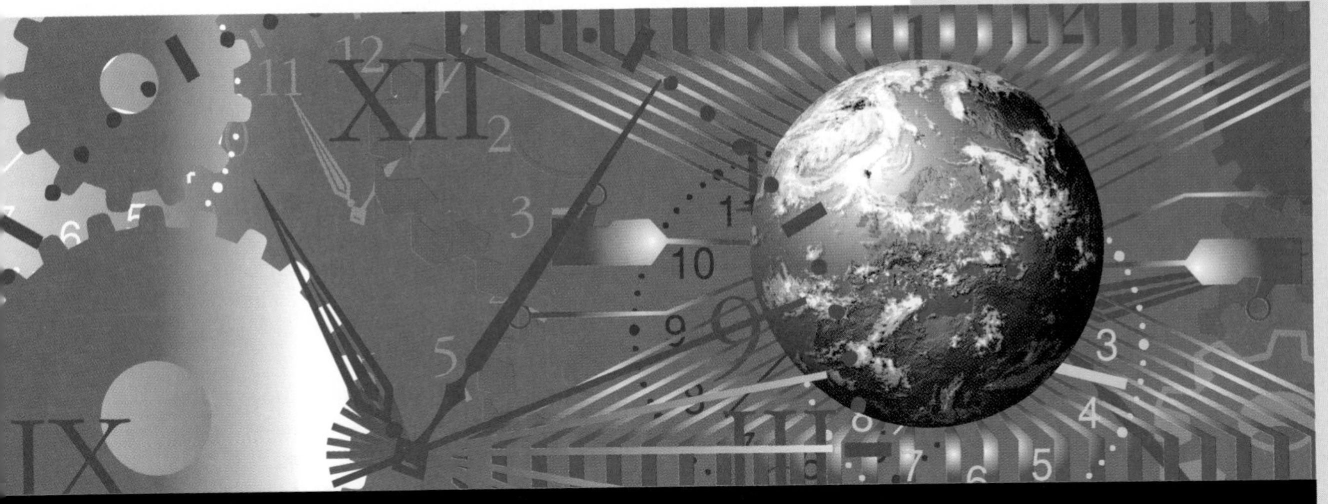

Inventory for Independent Demand

9

CHAPTER OUTLINE

Functions of Inventory

Types of Inventory

Inventory Management

ABC Analysis ■ Record Accuracy ■ Cycle Counting ■ Control of Services Inventories

Inventory Models

Independent versus Dependent Demand ■ Holding, Ordering, and Setup Costs

Inventory Models for Independent Demand

The Basic Economic Order Quantity (EOQ) Model ■ Minimize Costs ■ Reorder Points ■ Production Order Quantity Model ■ Quantity Discount Models

Probabilistic Models with Constant Lead Time

Fixed-Period Systems

Summary ■ Key Terms ■ Using POM for Windows ■ Using Excel Spreadsheets to Solve Inventory Problems ■ Solved Problems ■ Discussion Questions ■ Operations in Practice Exercise ■ Problems ■ Self-Test Chapter 9 ■ Case Studies: Sturdivant Sound Systems; Martin-Pullin Bicycle Corporation ■ Bibliography

LEARNING OBJECTIVES

When you complete this chapter you should be able to:

IDENTIFY OR DEFINE:

ABC analysis
Cycle counting
Holding, ordering, and setup costs
Independent and dependent demand
Record accuracy

DESCRIBE OR EXPLAIN:

The functions of inventory and basic inventory models

Inventory is one of the most expensive assets of many companies, representing as much as 40% of total invested capital. Operations managers around the globe have long recognized that good inventory management is crucial. On one hand, a firm can reduce costs by reducing on-hand inventory levels. On the other hand, customers become dissatisfied when an item is frequently out of stock. Thus, companies must strike a balance between inventory investment and customer service levels.

All organizations have some type of inventory planning and control system. A bank has methods to control its inventory of cash. A hospital has methods used to control blood supplies and pharmaceuticals. Government agencies, schools, and, of course, virtually every manufacturing and production organization are concerned with inventory planning and control.

In cases of physical products, the organization must determine whether to produce goods or to purchase them. Once this has been determined, the next step is to forecast demand, as discussed in the Supplement to Chapter 2. Then operations managers determine the inventory necessary to service that demand. In this chapter, we discuss the functions, types, and management of inventory. We then address two basic inventory issues: how much to order and when to order.

Functions of Inventory

Inventory can serve several important functions that add flexibility to the operation of a firm. Six uses of inventory are:

1. To provide a stock of goods to *meet anticipated demand* by customers.
2. To *decouple production from distribution*. For example, if product demand is high only during the summer, a firm may build up stock during the winter and thus avoid the costs of shortages and stockouts in the summer. Similarly, if a firm's supplies fluctuate, extra raw materials of inventory may be needed to "decouple" production processes.
3. To take advantage of *quantity discounts*, since purchases in larger quantities can substantially reduce the cost of goods.
4. To *hedge against inflation* and price changes.
5. To *protect against shortages* that can occur due to weather, supplier shortages, quality problems, or improper deliveries. "Safety stocks," namely, extra goods on hand, can reduce the risk of stockouts.
6. To *permit operations to continue smoothly* with the use of "work-in-process" inventory. This is because it takes time to make goods and because a pipeline of inventories are stocked throughout the process.

Types of Inventory

Firms maintain four types of inventories: (1) raw material inventory, (2) work-in-process inventory, (3) maintenance/repair/operating supply (MRO) inventory, and (4) finished goods inventory.

raw material inventory

Raw material inventory has been purchased, but not processed. The items can be used to separate suppliers from the production process. However, the preferred approach is to eliminate supplier variability in quality, quantity, or delivery time so that separating is not needed. **Work-in-process (WIP) inventory** has undergone some change but is not completed. WIP exists because of the time it takes for a product to be made (called *cycle time*). Reducing the cycle time reduces inventory. Often this is not difficult, for most of the time a product is "being made,"

work-in-process inventory

it is in fact sitting idle. Actual work time or "run" time is a small portion of the material flow time, perhaps as low as 5%. **MROs** are inventories devoted to **maintenance/repair/operating** supplies. They exist because the need and timing for maintenance and repair of some equipment are unknown. Although the demand for MRO inventories is often a function of maintenance schedules, other MRO demands must be anticipated. Similarly, **finished goods inventory** is completed and awaiting shipment. Finished goods may be inventoried because customer demands for a given time period may be unknown.

MRO

finished goods inventory

INVENTORY MANAGEMENT

Operations managers establish systems for managing inventory. In this section we briefly examine ingredients of such systems: (1) how inventory items can be classified (called ABC analysis) and (2) how accurate inventory records can be maintained. We will then look at inventory control in the service sector.

ABC Analysis

ABC analysis divides on-hand inventory into three classifications on the basis of annual dollar volume.[1] ABC analysis is an inventory application of what is known as the Pareto principle. The Pareto principle states that there are a "critical few and trivial many".[2] The idea is to focus resources on the few critical inventory parts and not the many trivial ones.

ABC analysis

To determine annual dollar volume for ABC analysis, we measure the *annual demand* of each inventory item times the *cost per unit*. Class A items are those on which the annual dollar volume is high. Such items may represent only about 15% of the total inventory items, but they represent 70% to 80% of the total inventory cost. Class B items are those inventory items of medium annual dollar volume. These items may represent about 30% of the items and 15% to 25% of the value. Those with low annual dollar volume are class C, which may represent only 5% of the annual dollar volume but about 55% of the total items.

NOTE
Most automated inventory management systems include ABC analysis.

Graphically, the inventory of many organizations would appear as presented in Figure 9.1. An example of the use of ABC analysis is shown in Example 1.

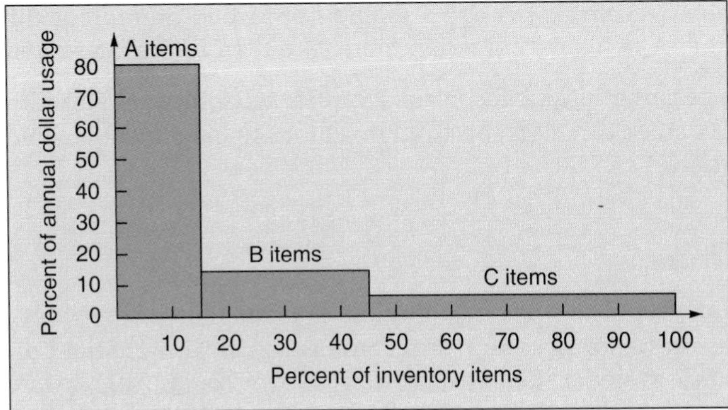

FIGURE 9.1

GRAPHIC REPRESENTATION OF ABC ANALYSIS

[1]H. Ford Dickie, *Modern Manufacturing* (formerly *Factory Management and Maintenance*) (July 1951).
[2]Vilfredo Pareto, nineteenth-century Italian economist.

EXAMPLE 1

Silicon Chips, Inc., maker of super-fast 1-meg chips, has organized its ten inventory items on an annual dollar volume basis. Shown below are the items, their annual demand, unit cost, annual dollar volume, and the percentage each item represents of the total. In the table below, we show these items grouped into ABC classifications.

ABC CALCULATION

ITEM STOCK NUMBER	PERCENT OF NUMBER OF ITEMS STOCKED	ANNUAL VOLUME (units)	UNIT COST	ANNUAL DOLLAR VOLUME	PERCENT OF ANNUAL DOLLAR VOLUME		CLASS
#10286	20%	1,000	$ 90.00	$90,000	38.8%	72%	A
#11526		500	154.00	77,000	33.2%		A
#12760	30%	1,550	17.00	26,350	11.4%	23%	B
#10867		350	42.86	15,001	6.5%		B
#10500		1,000	12.50	12,500	5.4%		B
#12572	50%	600	$ 14.17	8,502	3.7%	5%	C
#14075		2,000	.60	1,200	.5%		C
#01036		100	8.50	850	.4%		C
#01307		1,200	.42	504	.2%		C
#10572		250	.60	150	.1%		C
		8,550		$232,057	100.0%		

Criteria other than annual dollar volume can determine item classification. For instance, anticipated engineering changes, delivery problems, quality problems, or high unit cost may dictate upgrading items to a higher classification. The advantage of dividing inventory items into classes allows policies and controls to be established for each class.

Policies that may be based on ABC analysis include the following:

1. The purchasing resources expended on supplier development should be much higher for individual A items than for C items.
2. A items, as opposed to B and C items, should have tighter physical inventory control; perhaps they belong in a more secure area, and perhaps the accuracy of inventory records for A items should be verified more frequently.
3. Forecasting A items may warrant more care than forecasting other items.

Better forecasting, physical control, supplier reliability, and an ultimate reduction in safety stock can all result from inventory management techniques such as ABC analysis.

Record Accuracy

Good inventory policies are meaningless if management does not know what inventory is on hand. Accuracy of records is a critical ingredient in production and inventory systems. Record accuracy allows organizations to move away from being sure "some of everything" is in inventory to focusing on only those items that are needed. Only when an organization can determine accurately what it has on hand can it make precise decisions about ordering, scheduling, and shipping.

Cycle Counting

Even though an organization may have gone to substantial efforts to record inventory accurately, these records must be verified through a continuing audit. Such audits are known as **cycle counting.** Historically, many firms took annual physical inventories. This often meant shutting down the facility and having inexperienced people counting parts and material. Inventory records should instead be verified via cycle counting. Cycle counting uses inventory classifications developed through ABC analysis. With cycle counting procedures, items are counted, records are verified, and inaccuracies are periodically documented. The cause of inaccuracies is then traced and appropriate remedial action taken in accordance with the classification of the item. A items will be counted frequently, perhaps once a month; B items will be counted less frequently, perhaps once a quarter; and C items will be counted perhaps once every six months.

cycle counting

Control of Service Inventories

Management of service inventories deserves some special considerations. Although we tend to think of services as not having inventory, that is not the case. For instance, extensive inventory is held in wholesale and retail businesses, making inventory management crucial. In the food service business, for example, control of inventory can make the difference between success and failure. Moreover, inventory that is in transit or idle in a warehouse is lost value. Similarly, inventory which is damaged or stolen prior to sale is a loss. In retailing, inventory that is unaccounted for between receipt and time of sale is known as **shrinkage.** Shrinkage occurs from theft as well as sloppy paperwork. In the retail business, theft is also known as **pilferage.** Retail inventory losses of 1% of sales is considered good, as losses in many stores exceed 3%. The impact on profitability is substantial, consequently inventory accuracy and control is critical. The applicable techniques include:

shrinkage

pilferage

1. Good personnel selection, training, and discipline. These are never easy, but very necessary in food service, wholesale, and retail operations where employees have access to directly consumable merchandise.
2. Tight control of incoming shipments. This is being addressed by many firms through the use of bar-code systems that read every incoming shipment and automatically check the tallies against the purchase order. When properly designed, these systems are very hard to defeat.
3. Effective control of all goods leaving the facility. This is done with bar codes or items being shipped, magnetic strips on merchandise, or personnel stationed at the exits and in potentially high-loss areas, such as Las Vegas casinos, via direct observation. Direct observation takes the form of one-way mirrors, video, and personal surveillance.

Inventory Models

We now examine a variety of inventory models and the costs associated with them.

Independent versus Dependent Demand

Inventory control models assume that demand for an item is independent of, or dependent on, the demand for other items. For example, the demand for refrigerators is *independent* of the demand for toaster ovens. However, the demand for toaster oven components is *dependent* on the production requirements of toaster ovens.

This chapter focuses on managing *independent* demand items. Chapter 10 presents the topic of *dependent* demand.

Holding, Ordering, and Setup Costs

holding costs

ordering cost

setup cost

Holding costs are the costs associated with holding or "carrying" inventory over time. Therefore, holding costs also include costs related to storage, such as insurance, extra staffing, and interest payments. Table 9.1 shows the kinds of costs that need to be evaluated to determine holding costs. Many firms fail to include all of the inventory holding costs. Consequently, inventory holding costs are often understated.[3] **Ordering cost** includes costs of supplies, forms, order processing, clerical support, and so forth. When orders are being manufactured, ordering costs also exist, but they are known as setup costs. **Setup cost** is the cost to prepare a machine or process for manufacturing an order. Operations managers can lower ordering costs by reducing setup costs and by using such efficient procedures as electronic ordering and payment.

setup time

In many environments setup cost is highly correlated with **setup time.** Setups usually require a substantial amount of work prior to an operation actually being accomplished at the work center. Much of the preparation required by a setup can be done prior to shutting down the machine or process. Setup times can be reduced substantially. Machines and processes that traditionally have taken hours to set up are now being set up in less than a minute by the more imaginative world-class manufacturers. As we shall see later in this chapter, reducing setup times is an excellent way to reduce inventory investment and to improve productivity.

Optical scanners at Giant Food Stores are used to read the codes on each item at the check-out counters. This procedure provides information for inventory control, quicker check-out, and monitoring of the cashier's speed. The food items and dollars rung by each cashier and the number of customers served are recorded on the printout.

[3]Jack G. Wacker, "Can Holding Costs Be Overstated for 'Just-in-Time' Manufacturing System?" *Production and Inventory Management* 27 (Third Quarter 1986): 11–14.

TABLE 9.1 DETERMINING INVENTORY HOLDING COSTS

CATEGORY	COST AS A PERCENT OF INVENTORY VALUE
Housing costs, such as building rent, depreciation, operating cost, taxes, insurance	6% (3–10%)
Material handling costs, including equipment, lease or depreciation, power, operating cost	3% (1–3.5%)
Labor cost from extra handling	3% (3–5%)
Investment costs, such as borrowing costs, taxes, and insurance on inventory	11% (6–24%)
Pilferage, scrap, and obsolescence	3% (2–5%)
Overall carrying cost	26%

NOTE: All numbers are approximate, as they vary substantially depending on the nature of the business, location, and current interest rates. Any inventory holding cost of less than 15% is suspect, but annual inventory holding costs often approach 40% of the value of inventory.

INVENTORY MODELS FOR INDEPENDENT DEMAND

In this section, we introduce three inventory models that address two important questions: *when to order* and *how much to order.* These *independent* demand models are:

1. Basic economic order quantity (EOQ) model.
2. Production order quantity model.
3. Quantity discount model.

This store takes four weeks to get an order for Levis 501 jeans filled by the manufacturer. If the store sells 10 pairs of size 30-32 Levis a week, the store manager could set up two containers, keep 40 pairs of jeans in the second container, and place an order whenever the first container is empty. This would be a fixed-point reordering system. It is also called a "two-bin" system and is an example of a very elementary, but effective, inventory approach.

FIGURE 9.2

INVENTORY USAGE OVER TIME

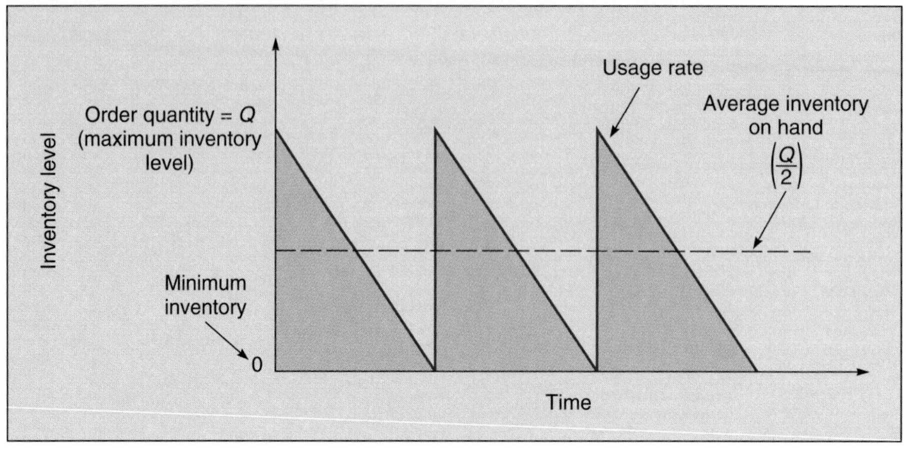

The Basic Economic Order Quantity (EOQ) Model

The economic order quantity (EOQ) is one of the oldest and most commonly known inventory control techniques.[4] This technique is relatively easy to use but is based on several assumptions:

1. Demand is known and constant.
2. Lead time, that is, the time between the placement of the order and the receipt of the order, is known and constant.
3. Receipt of inventory is instantaneous. In other words, the inventory from an order arrives in one batch, at one time.
4. Quantity discounts are not possible.
5. The only variable costs are the cost of setting up or placing an order (setup cost) and the cost of holding or storing inventory over time (holding or carrying cost). These costs were discussed in the previous section.
6. Stockouts (shortages) can be completely avoided if orders are placed at the right time.

With these assumptions, the graph of inventory usage over time has a sawtooth shape, as in Figure 9.2. In Figure 9.2, Q represents the amount that is ordered. If this amount is 500 dresses, all 500 dresses arrive at one time (when an order is received). Thus, the inventory level jumps from 0 to 500 dresses. In general, an inventory level increases from 0 to Q units when an order arrives.

Because demand is constant over time, inventory drops at a uniform rate over time. (Refer to the sloped line in Figure 9.2.) When the inventory level reaches 0, the new order is placed and received, and the inventory level again jumps to Q units (represented by the vertical lines). This process continues indefinitely over time.

Minimize Costs

The objective of most inventory models is to minimize the total costs. With the assumptions just given, the significant costs are the setup (or ordering) cost and

[4]The research on EOQ dates back to 1915; see Ford W. Harris, *Operations and Cost* (Chicago: A. W. Shaw, 1915).

the holding (or carrying) cost. All other costs, such as the cost of the inventory itself, are constant. Thus, if we minimize the sum of the setup and holding costs, we will also be minimizing the total costs. To help you visualize this, in Figure 9.3 we graph total costs as a function of the order quantity, Q. The optimal order size, Q^*, will be the quantity that minimizes the total costs. As the quantity ordered increases, the total number of orders placed per year will decrease. Thus, as the quantity ordered increases, the annual setup or ordering cost will decrease. But as the order quantity increases, the holding cost will increase due to larger average inventories that are maintained.

You should note that in Figure 9.3 the optimal order quantity occurred at the point where the ordering cost curve and the carrying cost curve intersected. This was not by chance. With the EOQ model, the optimal order quantity will occur at a point where the total setup cost is equal to the total holding cost.[5] We use this fact to develop equations that solve directly for Q^*. The necessary steps are:

1. Develop an expression for setup or ordering cost.
2. Develop an expression for holding cost.
3. Set setup cost equal to holding cost.
4. Solve the equation for the best order quantity.

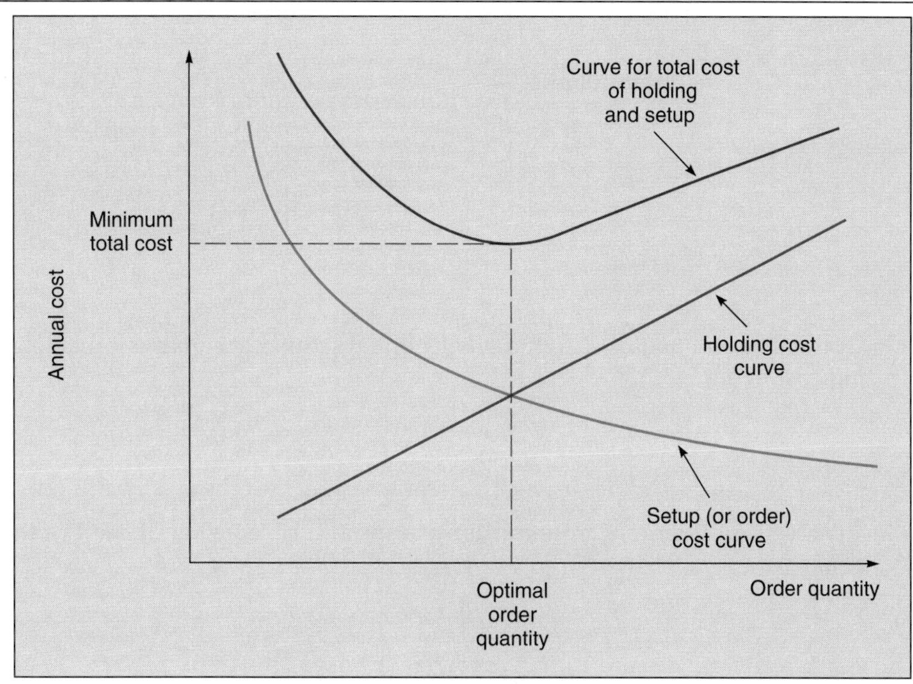

FIGURE 9.3

TOTAL COST AS A FUNCTION OF ORDER QUANTITY

[5]The minimum total cost occurs because the slope of the total cost curve is zero.

Using the following variables we can determine setup and holding costs and solve for Q^*:

Q = Number of pieces per order

Q^* = Optimum number of pieces per order (EOQ)

D = Annual demand in units for the inventory item

S = Setup or ordering cost for each order

H = Holding or carrying cost per unit per year

1. Annual setup cost = (Number of orders placed per year)(Setup or order cost per order)

$$= \left(\frac{\text{Annual demand}}{\text{Number of units in each order}}\right)(\text{Setup or order cost per order})$$

$$= \left(\frac{D}{Q}\right)(S)$$

$$= \frac{D}{Q}S$$

2. Annual holding cost = (Average inventory level) (Holding cost per unit per year)

$$= \left(\frac{\text{Order quantity}}{2}\right)(\text{Holding cost per unit per year})$$

$$= \left(\frac{Q}{2}\right)(H)$$

$$= \frac{Q}{2}H$$

3. Optimal order quantity is found when annual setup cost equals annual holding cost, namely,

$$\frac{D}{Q}S = \frac{Q}{2}H$$

4. To solve for Q^*, simply cross-multiply terms and isolate Q on the left of the equal sign.

$$2DS = Q^2H$$

$$Q^2 = \frac{2DS}{H}$$

$$Q^* = \sqrt{\frac{2DS}{H}} \qquad (9.1)$$

Now that we have derived equations for the optimal order quantity, Q^*, it is possible to solve inventory problems directly, as is done in Example 2.

EXAMPLE 2

Sharp, Inc., a company that markets painless hypodermic needles to hospitals, would like to reduce its inventory cost by determining the optimal number of hypodermic needles to obtain per order. The annual demand is 1,000 units; the setup or ordering cost is \$10 per order; and the holding cost per unit per year is \$.50. Using these figures, we can calculate the optimal number of units per order:

$$Q^* = \sqrt{\frac{2DS}{H}}$$

$$Q^* = \sqrt{\frac{2(1{,}000)(10)}{0.50}} = \sqrt{40{,}000} = 200 \text{ units}$$

We can also determine the expected number of orders placed during the year (N) and the expected time between orders (T) as follows:

$$\text{Expected number of orders} = N = \frac{\text{Demand}}{\text{Order quantity}} = \frac{D}{Q^*} \quad (9.2)$$

$$\text{Expected time between orders} = T = \frac{\text{Number of working days per year}}{N} \quad (9.3)$$

EXAMPLE 3

Using the data from Sharp, Inc., in Example 2, and a 250-day working year, we find the number of orders (N) and the expected time between orders (T) as:

$$N = \frac{\text{Demand}}{\text{Order quantity}}$$

$$= \frac{1{,}000}{200} = 5 \text{ orders per year}$$

$$T = \frac{\text{Number of working days per year}}{\text{Expected number of orders}}$$

$$= \frac{250 \text{ working days per year}}{5 \text{ orders}} = 50 \text{ days between orders}$$

As mentioned earlier in this section, the total annual inventory cost is the sum of the setup and holding costs:

$$\text{Total annual cost} = \text{Setup cost} + \text{Holding cost} \quad (9.4)$$

In terms of the variables in the model, we can express the total cost TC as:

$$TC = \frac{D}{Q}S + \frac{Q}{2}H \quad (9.5)$$

EXAMPLE 4

Again using the Sharp, Inc., data (Examples 2 and 3), we determine that the total annual inventory costs are

$$TC = \frac{D}{Q}S + \frac{Q}{2}H$$

$$= \frac{1{,}000}{200}(\$10) + \frac{200}{2}(\$.50)$$

$$= (5)(\$10) + (100)(\$.50)$$

$$= \$50 + \$50 = \$100$$

Often the total inventory cost expression is written to include the actual cost of the material purchased. If we assume that the annual demand and the price per hypodermic are known values (for example, 1,000 hypodermics per year at $P = \$10$), total annual cost should include purchase cost. Material cost does not depend on the particular order policy found to be optimal, since regardless of how many units are ordered each time, we still incur an annual material cost of $D \times P = (1{,}000)\ (\$10) = \$10{,}000$. (Shortly, we will discuss the case in which this may not be true, namely, when a quantity discount is available to the customer who orders a certain amount each time.)

Reorder Points

Now that we have decided how much to order, we shall look at the second inventory question, when to order. Simple inventory models assume that receipt of an order is instantaneous. In other words, they assume that a firm will wait until its inventory level for a particular item reaches zero before placing an order, and that it will receive the items immediately. However, the time between the placement and receipt of an order, called the **lead time** or delivery time, can be as short as a few hours to as long as months. Thus, the when-to-order decision is usually expressed in terms of a reorder point, the inventory level at which an order should be placed (see Figure 9.4).

lead time

The **reorder point (ROP)** is given as:

reorder point (ROP)

$$\text{ROP} = (\text{Demand per day})(\text{Lead time for a new order in days})$$

$$= d \times L \qquad (9.6)$$

This equation for ROP *assumes that demand is uniform and constant.* When this is not the case, extra stock, often called **safety stock,** should be added.

safety stock

The demand per day, d, is found by dividing the annual demand, D, by the number of working days in a year:

$$d = \frac{D}{\text{Number of working days in a year}}$$

Computing the reorder point is demonstrated in Example 5.

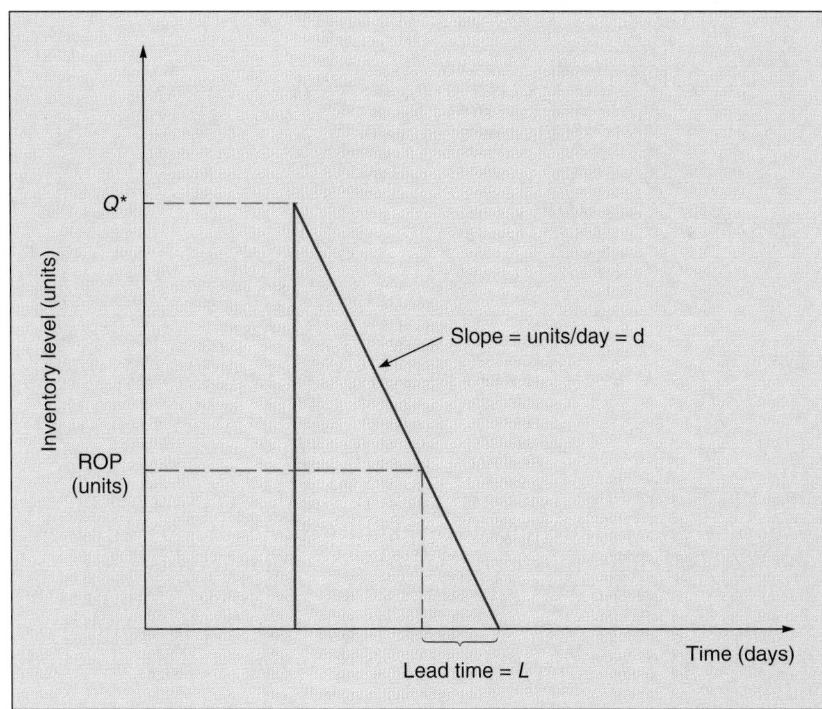

FIGURE 9.4

THE REORDER POINT (ROP) CURVE

EXAMPLE 5

Electronic Assembler, Inc., has a demand for 8,000 VCRs per year. The firm operates a 200-day working year. On the average, delivery of an order takes three working days. We calculate the reorder point as

$$d = \frac{D}{\text{Number of working days in a year}} = \frac{8{,}000}{200}$$

$$= 40$$

$$\text{ROP} = \text{Reorder point} = d \times L = 40 \text{ units per day} \times 3 \text{ days}$$

$$= 120 \text{ units}$$

Hence, when the inventory stock drops to 120, an order should be placed. The order will arrive three days later, just as the firm's stock is depleted.

Production Order Quantity Model

In the previous inventory model, we assumed that the entire inventory order was received at one time. There are times, however, when the firm may receive its inventory over a period of time. Such cases require a different model, one that does not require the instantaneous receipt assumption. This model is applicable when inventory continuously flows or builds up over a period of time after an order has been placed or when units are produced and sold simultaneously. Under these circumstances, we take into account the daily production (or inventory flow) rate and the daily demand rate. Figure 9.5 shows inventory levels as a function of time.

FIGURE 9.5

CHANGE IN INVENTORY LEVELS OVER TIME FOR THE PRODUCTION MODEL

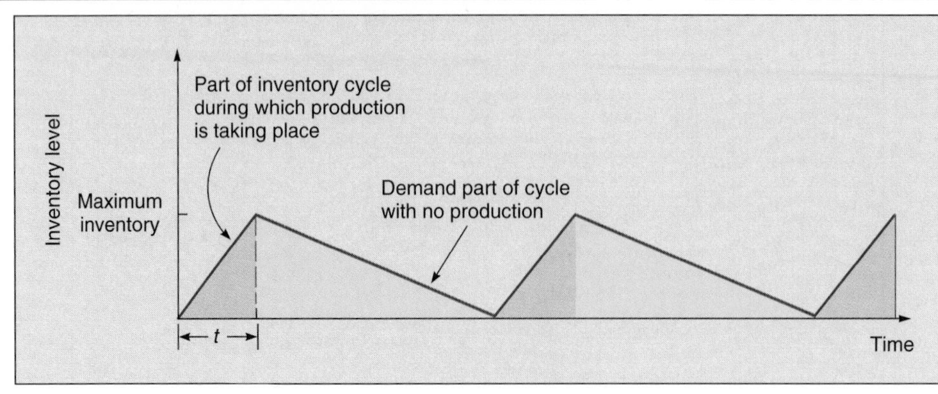

production order quantity model

Because this model is especially suitable for the production environment, it is commonly called the **production order quantity model.** It is useful when inventory continuously builds up over time and the traditional economic order quantity assumptions are valid. We derive this model by setting ordering or setup costs equal to holding costs and solving for Q^*. Using the following symbols, we can determine the expression for annual inventory holding cost for the production run model:

Litton Industries uses bar-code readers to automate inventory control at its production and distribution facilities. Bar coding makes the data collection process more accurate as well as faster and cheaper. With rapidly obtained data, shipments can be checked against production records and sales invoices to verify inventory accuracy and reduce losses. The scanning device shown is linked to the central computer by wireless data transmission.

$$Q = \text{Number of pieces per order}$$
$$H = \text{Holding cost per unit per year}$$
$$p = \text{Daily production rate}$$
$$d = \text{Daily demand rate, or usage rate}$$
$$t = \text{Length of the production run in days}$$

1. $$\begin{pmatrix}\text{Annual inventory}\\\text{holding cost}\end{pmatrix} = (\text{Average inventory level}) \times \begin{pmatrix}\text{Holding cost}\\\text{per unit per year}\end{pmatrix}$$
$$= (\text{Average inventory level}) \times H$$

2. $$\begin{pmatrix}\text{Average inventory}\\\text{level}\end{pmatrix} = (\text{Maximum inventory level})/2$$

3. $$\begin{pmatrix}\text{Maximum}\\\text{inventory level}\end{pmatrix} = \begin{pmatrix}\text{Total produced during}\\\text{the production run}\end{pmatrix} - \begin{pmatrix}\text{Total used during}\\\text{the production run}\end{pmatrix}$$
$$= pt - dt$$

But Q = total produced = pt, and thus $t = Q/p$. Therefore,

$$\text{Maximum inventory level} = p\left(\frac{Q}{p}\right) - d\left(\frac{Q}{p}\right)$$
$$= Q - \frac{d}{p}Q$$
$$= Q\left(1 - \frac{d}{p}\right)$$

4. Annual inventory holding cost (or simply holding cost) =

$$\frac{\text{Maximum inventory level}}{2}(H) = \frac{Q}{2}\left[1 - \left(\frac{d}{p}\right)\right]H$$

NOTE
A major difference between this model and the basic EOQ model is the annual holding cost, which is reduced in the production run model.

Using the expression for holding cost above and the expression for setup cost developed in the basic EOQ model, we solve for the optimal number of pieces per order by equating setup cost and holding cost:

$$\text{Setup cost} = (D/Q)S$$

$$\text{Holding cost} = \tfrac{1}{2}\,HQ\,[1 - (d/p)]$$

Set ordering cost equal to holding cost to obtain Q^*_p:

$$\frac{D}{Q}S = \tfrac{1}{2}\,HQ[1 - (d/p)]$$

$$Q^2 = \frac{2DS}{H[1 - (d/p)]}$$

$$Q^*_p = \sqrt{\frac{2DS}{H[1 - (d/p)]}} \qquad (9.7)$$

We can use the above equation, Q^*_p, to solve for the optimum order or production quantity when inventory is consumed as it is produced. We do so in Example 6.

EXAMPLE 6

Nathan Manufacturing, Inc., makes and sells specialty hubcaps for the retail automobile aftermarket. Nathan's forecast for its wire-wheel hubcap is 1,000 units next year, with an average daily demand of 6 units. However, the production process is most efficient at 8 units per day. So the company produces 8 per day but uses only 6 per day. Given the following values, solve for the optimum number of units per order. (Note: This plant operates to produce hubcaps only 167 days per year.)

$$\text{Annual demand} = D = 1{,}000 \text{ units}$$

$$\text{Setup cost} = S = \$10$$

$$\text{Holding cost} = H = \$0.50 \text{ per unit per year}$$

$$\text{Daily production rate} = p = 8 \text{ units daily}$$

$$\text{Daily demand rate} = d = 6 \text{ units daily}$$

$$Q^*_p = \sqrt{\frac{2DS}{H[1 - (d/p)]}}$$

$$Q^*_p = \sqrt{\frac{2(1{,}000)(10)}{0.50[1 - (6/8)]}}$$

$$= \sqrt{\frac{20{,}000}{0.50(1/4)}} = \sqrt{160{,}000}$$

$$= 400 \text{ hubcaps}$$

You may want to compare this solution with the answer in Example 2. Eliminating the instantaneous receipt assumption, where $p = 8$ and $d = 6$, has resulted in an increase in Q^* from 200 in Example 2 to 400. Also note that:

$$d = \frac{D}{\text{Number of days the plant is in operation}}$$

We can also calculate Q_p^* when annual data are available. When annual data are used, we can express Q_p^* as:

$$Q_p^* = \sqrt{\frac{2DS}{H[1 - (D/P)]}} \quad (9.8)$$

where

D = Annual demand rate

P = Annual production rate

Quantity Discount Models

quantity discount

To increase sales, many companies offer quantity discounts to their customers. A **quantity discount** is simply a reduced price (P) for the item when it is purchased in larger quantities. It is not uncommon to have a discount schedule with several discounts for large orders. A typical quantity discount schedule appears in Table 9.2.

As can be seen in the table, the normal price of the item is $5. When 1,000 to 1,999 units are ordered at one time, then the price per unit drops to $4.80; and when the quantity ordered at one time is 2,000 units or more, the price is $4.75 per unit. As always, management must decide when and how much to order. But with quantity discounts, how does the operations manager make these decisions?

As with other inventory models discussed so far, the overall objective will be to minimize the total cost. Since the unit cost for the third discount in Table 9.2 is the lowest, you might be tempted to order 2,000 units or more to take advantage of the lower product cost. Placing an order for that quantity with the greatest discount price, however, might not minimize the total inventory cost. As the discount quantity goes up, the product cost goes down, but the holding cost increases because the orders are large. Thus, the major trade-off when considering quantity discounts is between the reduced product cost and the increased holding cost. When we include the cost of the product, the equation for the total annual inventory cost becomes:

Total cost = Setup cost + Holding cost + Product cost

TABLE 9.2 A QUANTITY DISCOUNT SCHEDULE

DISCOUNT NUMBER	DISCOUNT QUANTITY	DISCOUNT (%)	DISCOUNT PRICE (P)
1	0 to 999	0	$5.00
2	1,000 to 1,999	4	$4.80
3	2,000 and over	5	$4.75

or

$$T_c = \frac{D}{Q}S + \frac{QH}{2} + PD \qquad (9.9)$$

where

Q = Quantity ordered

D = Annual demand in units

S = Ordering or setup cost per order or per setup

P = Price per unit

H = Holding cost per unit per year.

Now, we have to determine the quantity that will minimize the total annual inventory cost. Because there are several discounts, this process involves four steps:

Step 1. For each discount, calculate a value for Q^*, using the following equation:

$$Q^* = \sqrt{\frac{2DS}{IP}} \qquad (9.10)$$

You should note that the holding cost is IP instead of H. Because the price of the item is a factor in annual holding cost, we cannot assume that the holding cost is a constant when the price per unit changes for each quantity discount. Thus, it is common to express the holding cost (I) as a percentage of unit price (P) instead of as a constant cost per unit per year, H.

Step 2. For any discount, if the order quantity is too low to qualify for the discount, adjust the order quantity upward to the lowest quantity that will qualify for the discount. For example, if Q^* for discount 2 in Table 9.2 were 500 units, you would adjust this value up to 1,000 units. Look at the second discount in Table 9.2. Order quantities between 1,000 and 1,999 will qualify for the 4% discount. Thus, we will adjust the order quantity up to be 1,000 units if Q^* is below 1,000 units.

NOTE
Don't forget to adjust the order quantity upward if the quantity is too low to qualify for the discount.

The reasoning for step 2 may not be obvious. If the order quantity is below the quantity range that will qualify for a discount, a quantity within this range may still result in the lowest total cost.

As shown in Figure 9.6, the total cost curve is broken into three different total cost curves. There is a total cost curve for the first ($0 \le Q \le 999$), second ($1{,}000 \le Q \le 1{,}999$), and third ($2{,}000 \le Q$) discount. Look at the total cost (T_c) curve for discount 2. Q^* for discount 2 is less than the allowable discount range, which is from 1,000 to 1,999 units. As the figure shows, the lowest allowable quantity in this range, which is 1,000 units, is the quantity that minimizes the total cost. Thus, the second step is needed to ensure that we do not discard an order quantity that may indeed produce the minimum cost. Note that an order quantity computed in step 1 that is greater than the range that would qualify it for a discount may be discarded.

Step 3. Using the total cost equation above, compute a total cost for every Q^* determined in steps 1 and 2. If you had to adjust Q^* upward because

FIGURE 9.6

TOTAL COST CURVE FOR THE QUANTITY DISCOUNT MODEL

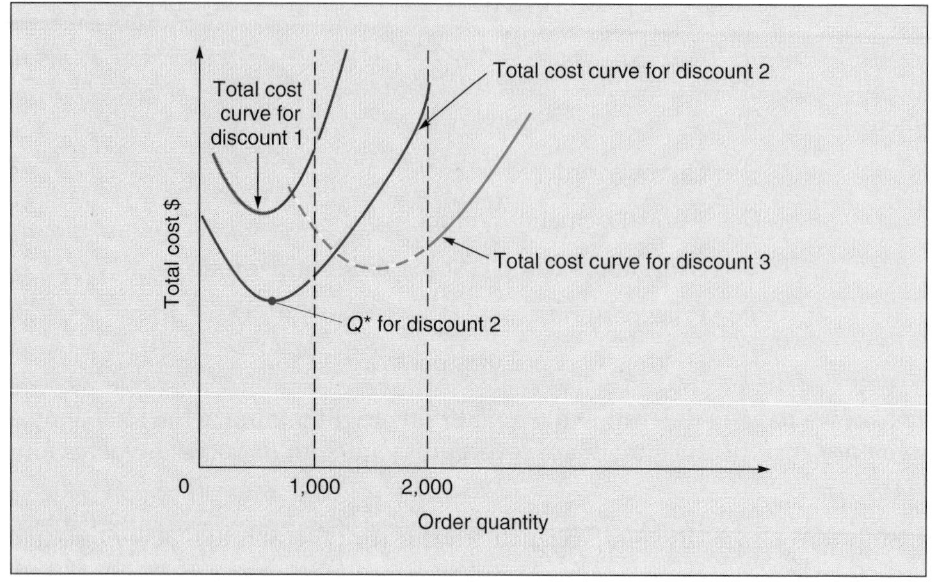

it was below the allowable quantity range, make sure to use the adjusted value for Q^*.

Step 4. Select that Q^* that has the lowest total cost as computed in step 3. It will be the quantity that will minimize the total inventory cost.

Let us see how this procedure can be applied with an example.

EXAMPLE 7

Wohl's Discount Store stocks toy race cars. Recently, they have been given a quantity discount schedule for the cars. This quantity schedule was shown in Table 9.2. Thus, the normal cost for the toy race cars is \$5. For orders between 1,000 and 1,999 units, the unit cost is \$4.80; and for orders of 2,000 or more units, the unit cost is \$4.75. Furthermore, the ordering cost is \$49 per order, the annual demand is 5,000 race cars, and the inventory carrying charge as a percentage of cost, I, is 20% or .2. What order quantity will minimize the total inventory cost?

The first step is to compute Q^* for every discount in Table 9.2. This is done as follows:

$$Q_1^* = \sqrt{\frac{2(5{,}000)(49)}{(.2)(5.00)}} = 700 \text{ cars order}$$

$$Q_2^* = \sqrt{\frac{2(5{,}000)(49)}{(.2)(4.80)}} = 714 \text{ cars order}$$

$$Q_3^* = \sqrt{\frac{2(5{,}000)(49)}{(.2)(4.75)}} = 718 \text{ cars order}$$

The second step is to adjust upward those values of Q^* that are below the allowable discount range. Since Q_1^* is between 0 and 999, it does not have to be adjusted. Q_2^* is below the allowable range of 1,000 to 1,999, and therefore, it must be adjusted to 1,000 units. The same is true for Q_3^*. It must be adjusted to 2,000 units. After this step, the following order quantities must be tested in the total cost equation:

$$Q_1^* = 700$$

$$Q_2^* = 1{,}000 - \text{adjusted}$$

$$Q_3^* = 2{,}000 - \text{adjusted}$$

The third step is to use the total cost equation and compute a total cost for each of the order quantities. This is accomplished with the aid of Table 9.3.

The fourth step is to select that order quantity with the lowest total cost. Looking at Table 9.3, you can see that an order quantity of 1,000 toy race cars will minimize the total cost. It should be recognized, however, that the total cost for ordering 2,000 cars is only slightly greater than the total cost for ordering 1,000 cars. Thus, if the third discount cost is lowered to $4.65, for example, then this order quantity might be the one that minimizes the total inventory cost.

TABLE 9.3 Total Cost Computations for Wohl's Discount Store

DISCOUNT NUMBER	UNIT PRICE	ORDER QUANTITY	ANNUAL PRODUCT COST	ANNUAL ORDERING COST	ANNUAL HOLDING COST	TOTAL
1	$5.00	700	$25,000	$350	$350	$25,700
2	$4.80	1,000	$24,000	$245	$480	$24,725
3	$4.75	2,000	$23,750	$122.50	$950	$24,822.50

Probabilistic Models with Constant Lead Time

All of the inventory models we have discussed so far make the assumption that the demand for a product is constant and uniform. We now relax this assumption. The following inventory models apply when product demand is not known but can be specified by means of a probability distribution. These types of models are called **probabilistic models.**

probabilistic models

An important concern of management is maintaining an adequate **service level** in the face of uncertain demand. The service level is the complement of the probability of a stockout. For instance, if the probability of a stockout is 0.05, then the service level is .95. Uncertain demand raises the possibility of a stockout. One method of reducing stockouts is to hold extra units in inventory to avoid this possibility. Such inventory is usually referred to as safety stock. It involves adding a number of units of safety stock as a buffer to the reorder point. As you recall from our previous discussion:

service level

NOTE
The cost of the inventory policy increases dramatically with an increase in service levels. Inventory costs increase exponentially as service level increases.

$$\text{Reorder point} = \text{ROP} = d \times L$$

$$d = \text{Daily demand}$$

$$L = \text{Order lead time, or number of working days it takes to deliver an order}$$

NOTE
Stockout costs are the sum of the units short × the probability × the stockout cost × the number of orders per year.

The inclusion of safety stock (*ss*) changes the expression to:

$$\text{ROP} = d \times L + ss \tag{9.11}$$

The amount of safety stock depends on the cost of incurring a stockout and the cost of holding the extra inventory. Example 8 shows how this is done for David Rivera Optical.

EXAMPLE 8

David Rivera Optical has determined that its reorder point for eyeglass frames is 50 ($d \times L$) units. Its carrying cost per frame per year is \$5, and stockout cost is \$40 per frame. The optical store has experienced the following probability distribution for inventory demand during the reorder period. The optimum number of orders per year is six.

	NUMBER OF UNITS	PROBABILITY
	30	.2
	40	.2
ROP →	50	.3
	60	.2
	70	.1
		1.0

How much safety stock should David Rivera Optical keep on hand?

The objective is to find the safety stock that minimizes the total additional inventory holding costs and stockout costs on an annual basis. The annual holding cost is simply the holding cost multiplied by the units added to the ROP. For example, a safety stock of 20 frames, which implies that the new ROP, with safety stock, is 70 (= 50 + 20) raises the annual carrying cost by \$5(20) = \$100.

The stockout cost is more difficult to compute. For any level of safety stock, the stockout cost is the expected cost of stocking out. We can compute it by multiplying the number of frames short by the probability by the stockout cost by the number of times per year the stockout can occur (or the number of orders per year). Then we add stockout costs for each possible stockout level for a given ROP. For zero safety stock, a shortage of 10 frames will occur if demand is 60, and a shortage of 20 frames will occur if the demand is 70. Thus the stockout costs for zero safety stock are

(10 frames short) (.2) (\$40 per stockout) (6 possible stockouts per year)
+ (20 frames short) (.1) (\$40) (6) = \$960

The following table summarizes the total costs for each alternative:

SAFETY STOCK	ADDITIONAL HOLDING COST	STOCKOUT COST		TOTAL COST
20	(20) (\$5) = \$100	\$0		\$100
10	(10) (\$5) = \$ 50	(10) (.1) (\$40) (6)	= \$240	\$290
0	\$0	(10) (.2) (\$40) (6) + (20) (.1) (\$40) (6)	= \$960	\$960

The safety stock with the lowest total cost is 20 frames. This safety stock changes the reorder point to 50 + 20 = 70 frames.

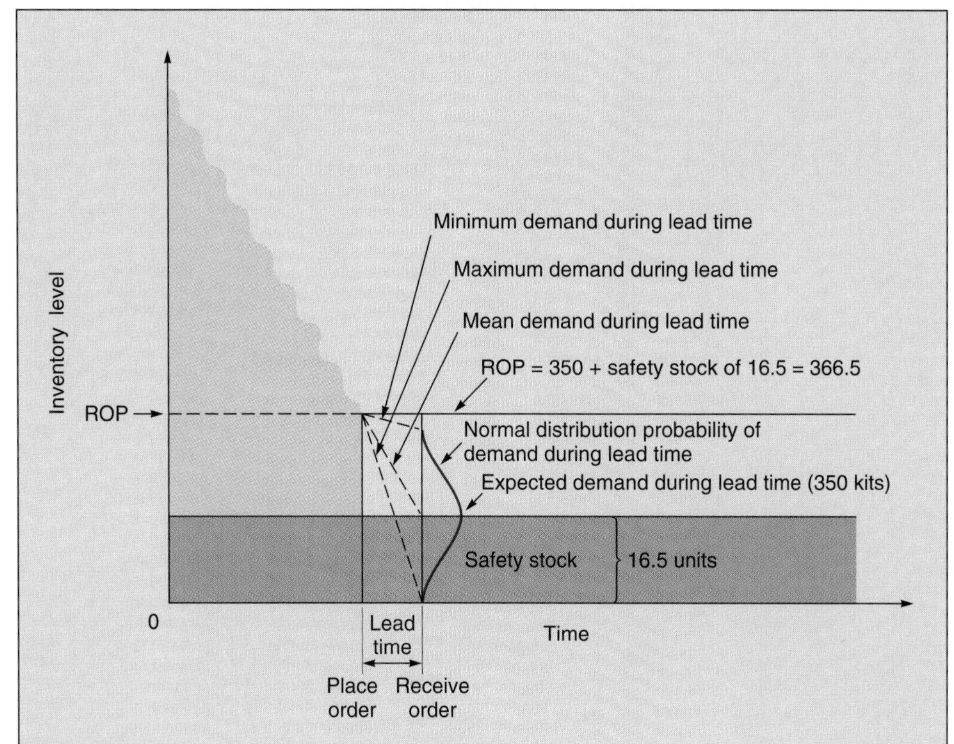

FIGURE 9.7

PROBABILISTIC DEMAND

When it is difficult or impossible to determine the cost of being out of stock, a manager may decide to follow a policy of keeping enough safety stock on hand to meet a prescribed customer service level. For instance, Figure 9.7 shows the use of safety stock when demand is probabilistic. We see that the safety stock in Figure 9.7 is 16.5, and the reorder point is also increased by 16.5.

The manager may want to define the service level as meeting 95% of the demand (or conversely having stockouts only 5% of the time). Assuming that demand during lead time (the reorder period) follows a normal curve, only the mean and standard deviation are needed to define the inventory requirements for any given service level. Sales data are usually adequate for computing the mean and standard deviation. In the following example we use a normal curve with a known mean (μ) and standard deviation (σ) to determine the safety stock necessary for a 95% service level.

NOTE
What are the ethical issues of setting service levels of emergency plasma or drug supplies in a hospital?

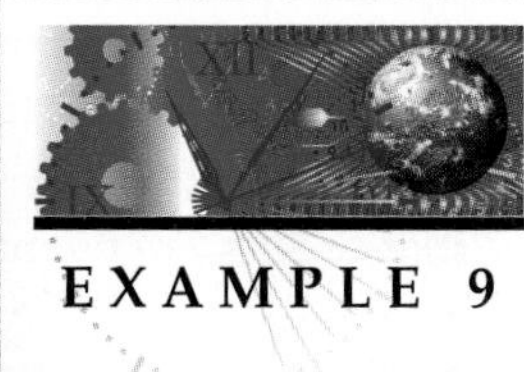

EXAMPLE 9

Memphis's Regional Hospital stocks a "code blue" resuscitation kit that has a normally distributed demand during the reorder period. The mean (average) demand during the reorder period is 350 kits, and the standard deviation is 10 kits. Regional Hospital wants to follow a policy that results in stockouts occurring only 5% of the time. How much safety stock should the hospital maintain? The following figure may help you visualize the example:

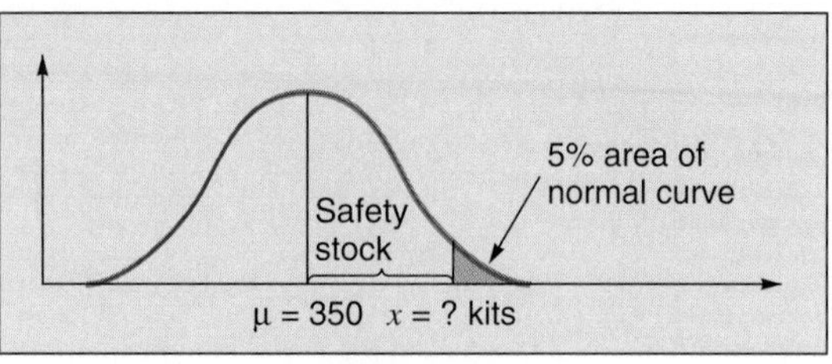

$$\mu = \text{Mean demand} = 350 \text{ kits}$$

$$\sigma = \text{Standard deviation} = 10 \text{ kits}$$

$$Z = \text{Number of standard normal deviates}$$

or

$$\text{Safety stock} = x - \mu$$

Since

$$Z = \frac{x - \mu}{\sigma}$$

Then

$$\text{Safety stock} = Z\sigma$$

We use the properties of a standardized normal curve to get a Z value for an area under the normal curve of .95 (or 1 − .05). Using a normal table (see Appendix A), we find a Z value of 1.65 standard deviations from the mean. Also:

$$Z = \frac{x - \mu}{\sigma} = \frac{\text{Safety stock}}{\sigma} \tag{9.12}$$

$$Z = 1.65 = \frac{\text{Safety stock}}{\sigma}$$

Solving for safety stock, as in Equation 9.12, gives

$$\text{Safety stock} = 1.65(10) = 16.5 \text{ kits}$$

This is the situation illustrated in Figure 9.7. The reorder point becomes (350 kits + 16.5 kits of safety stock =) 366.5, or 367 kits.

FIXED-PERIOD SYSTEMS

The inventory models we have considered so far in this chapter all fall into a class called *fixed-quantity systems*. That is to say, the same fixed amount is added to inventory every time an order for an item is placed. We saw that orders are event-triggered with the event triggering a reorder point occurring any time.

fixed-period system

In a **fixed-period system,** however, inventory is ordered at the end of a given

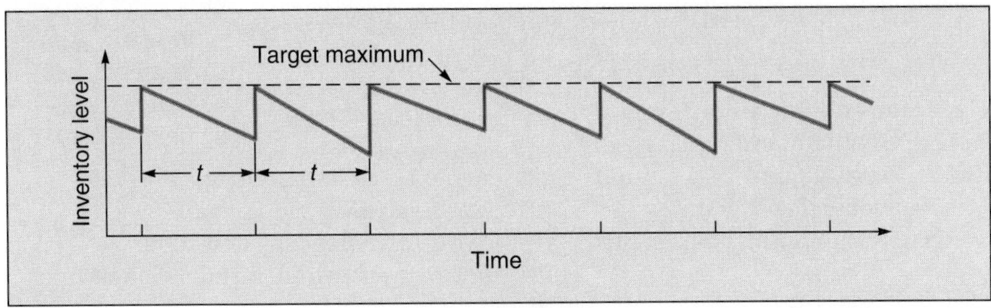

Various amounts are ordered based on the quantity necessary to bring inventory up to the target maximum.

FIGURE 9.8

INVENTORY LEVEL IN A FIXED-PERIOD SYSTEM

period. Then, and only then, on-hand inventory is counted. Only the amount necessary to bring total inventory up to a prespecified target level is ordered. Figure 9.8 illustrates this concept.

The advantage of the fixed-period system is that there is no physical count of inventory items after an item is withdrawn—this occurs only when the time for the next review comes up. This procedure is also convenient administratively, especially if inventory control is only one of several duties of an employee.

A fixed-period system is appropriate when vendors make routine (that is, at a fixed time interval) visits to customers to take fresh orders or when purchasers want to combine orders to save ordering and transportation costs (therefore, they will have the same review period for similar inventory items).

The disadvantage of this system is that since there is no tally of inventory during the review period, there is the possibility of a stockout during this time. This scenario is possible if a large order draws the inventory level down to zero right after an order is placed. Therefore, a higher level of safety stock (as compared to a fixed-quantity system) needs to be maintained to provide protection against stockout both during the time between reviews and the lead time.

SUMMARY

Inventory represents a major investment for many firms. This investment is often larger than it should be because firms find it easier to have "just-in-case" inventory rather than "just-in-time" inventory. Inventories are of four types:

1. Raw material and purchased components.
2. Work-in-process.
3. Maintenance, repair, and operating (MRO).
4. Finished goods.

In this chapter we discussed independent inventory, ABC analysis, record accuracy, and inventory models used to control independent inventories. The EOQ model, production run model, and the quantity discount model can all be solved using the POM for Windows software supplied with this text or with Excel spreadsheets. A summary of the inventory models presented in this chapter is shown in Table 9.4.

TABLE 9.4 STATISTICAL MODELS FOR INDEPENDENT DEMAND SUMMARIZED

Q = Number of pieces per order
EOQ = Optimum order quantity (Q^*)
ROP = Reorder point
D = Annual demand in units
S = Setup or ordering cost for each order
H = Holding or carrying cost per unit per year in dollars
p = Daily production rate
d = Daily demand rate
t = Length of production run in days
T_c = Total cost = Ordering cost + Carrying cost + Product cost

P = Price
I = Annual inventory carrying cost as a percentage of price
μ = Mean demand
σ = Standard deviation
x = Mean demand + Safety stock
ss = Safety stock
Z = Standardized value under the normal curve

EOQ

$$Q^* = \sqrt{\frac{2\,DS}{H}} \qquad (9.1)$$

EOQ production run model

$$Q_p^* = \sqrt{\frac{2\,DS}{H[1 - (d/p)]}} \qquad (9.7)$$

Total cost

T_c = Total cost

= Setup cost + Holding cost + Product cost

$$= \frac{D}{Q}S + \frac{QH}{2} + PD \qquad (9.9)$$

Quantity discount EOQ model

$$Q^* = \sqrt{\frac{2DS}{IP}} \qquad (9.10)$$

Probability model

$$Z = \frac{x - \mu}{\sigma} = \frac{ss}{\sigma} \qquad (9.12)$$

KEY TERMS

Raw material inventory *(p. 306)*
Work-in-process inventory *(p. 306)*
MRO *(p. 307)*
Finished goods inventory *(p. 307)*
ABC analysis *(p. 307)*
Cycle counting *(p. 309)*
Shrinkage *(p. 309)*
Pilferage *(p. 309)*
Holding cost *(p. 310)*
Ordering cost *(p. 310)*
Setup cost *(p. 310)*
Setup time *(p. 310)*
Lead time *(p. 316)*
Reorder point (ROP) *(p. 316)*
Safety stock *(p. 316)*
Production order quantity model *(p. 318)*
Quantity discount *(p. 320)*
Probabilistic models *(p. 323)*
Service level *(p. 323)*
Fixed-period system *(p. 326)*

USING POM FOR WINDOWS

The inventory model can solve all of the EOQ family of problems, as well as ABC inventory management. Programs 9.1 and 9.2 illustrate the software applied to Examples 6 and 7 respectively. The first is a production run model, while the second uses the Wohl quantity discount data. Input data are shown on the left side of each screen and output data on the right.

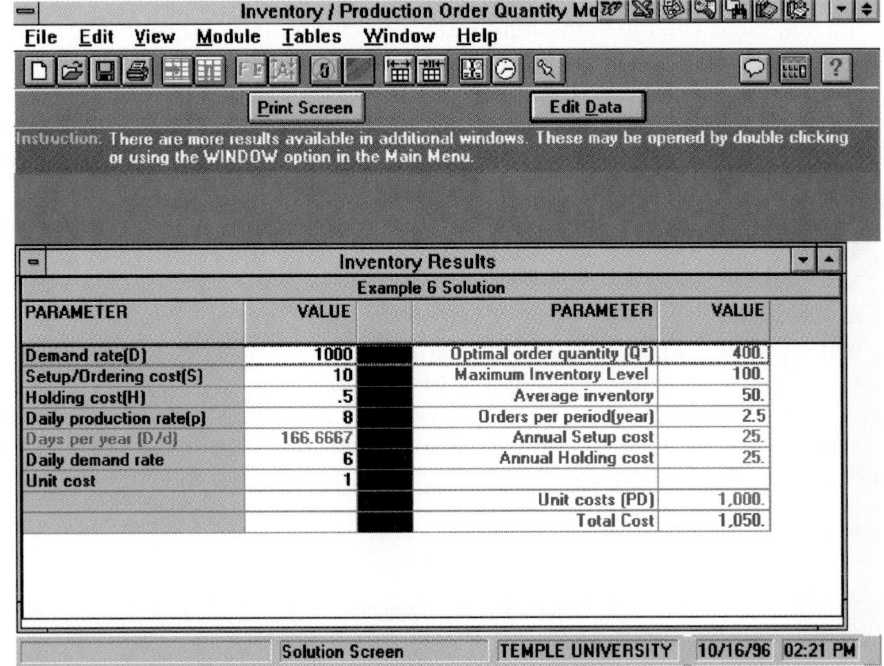

PROGRAM 9.1

POM FOR WINDOWS' PRODUCTION RUN MODEL USING EXAMPLE 6 DATA

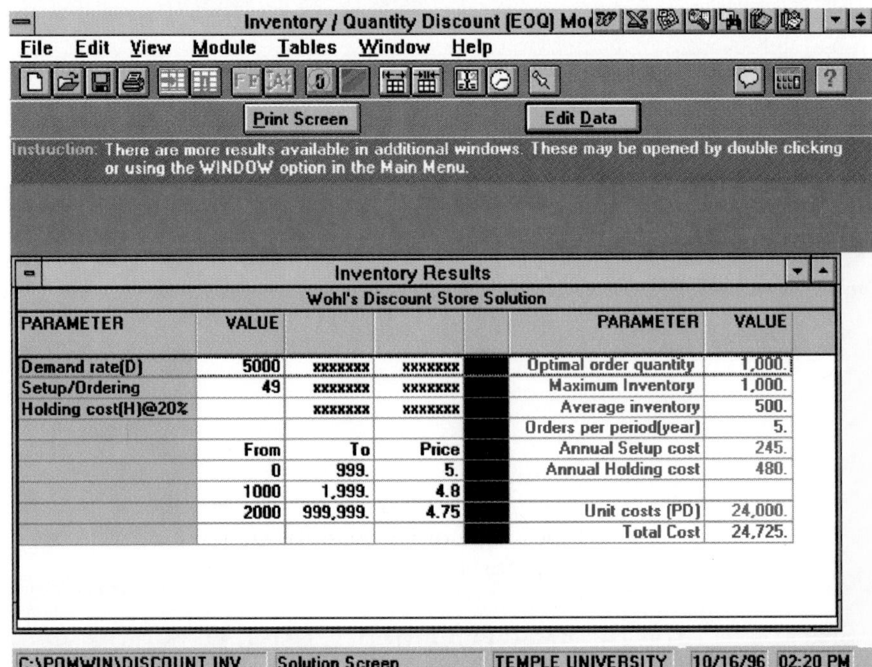

PROGRAM 9.2

USING POM FOR WINDOWS TO SOLVE THE QUANTITY DISCOUNT PROBLEM IN EXAMPLE 8

USING EXCEL SPREADSHEETS TO SOLVE INVENTORY PROBLEMS

Excel models the basic EOQ problem very easily, as we see in Program 9.3 (which uses the Sharp, Inc. data from Examples 2–5).

Spreadsheets become more complex as we extend Excel to solve a quantity discount problem, such as that of the Wohl Discount Store in Example 7. This example is illustrated in Program 9.4. Note the following:

1. The problem has been changed to reflect percentage discounts (as is typical in much of industry) rather than differing unit costs.
2. The spreadsheet uses the =CONCATENATE function to put together the headings of the columns.

An important reason for using spreadsheets is the better communication of information. The = CONCATENATE function is used to put together strings of text. In this case, it is used to put the value in Program 9.4's row 9, the minimum quantity ordered to achieve the discount, into the heading. In practice this is done to make the information more accessible, to increase the efficiency of the person doing the ordering, and (very importantly) to reduce errors.

The =IF function compares the calculated EOQ in row 12 to the minimum quantity required to get the discount (row 9). If the calculated value is less than the minimum, the minimum is used. If not, the calculated value is used.

Absolute addresses are used for ordering cost, annual demand, and the carrying cost formulas to make it easy to copy the formulas from column B into columns C and D.

The optional HLOOKUP function in row 20 identifies the best order quantity using the minimum of the total costs shown in row 17. To use this function it is necessary to have the quantity breaks *underneath* the costs, requiring the copying of the information from row 9 to row 18.

The spreadsheet in Program 9.5 reflects the values reached in the text. It could be easily modified to store several discount levels for many items.

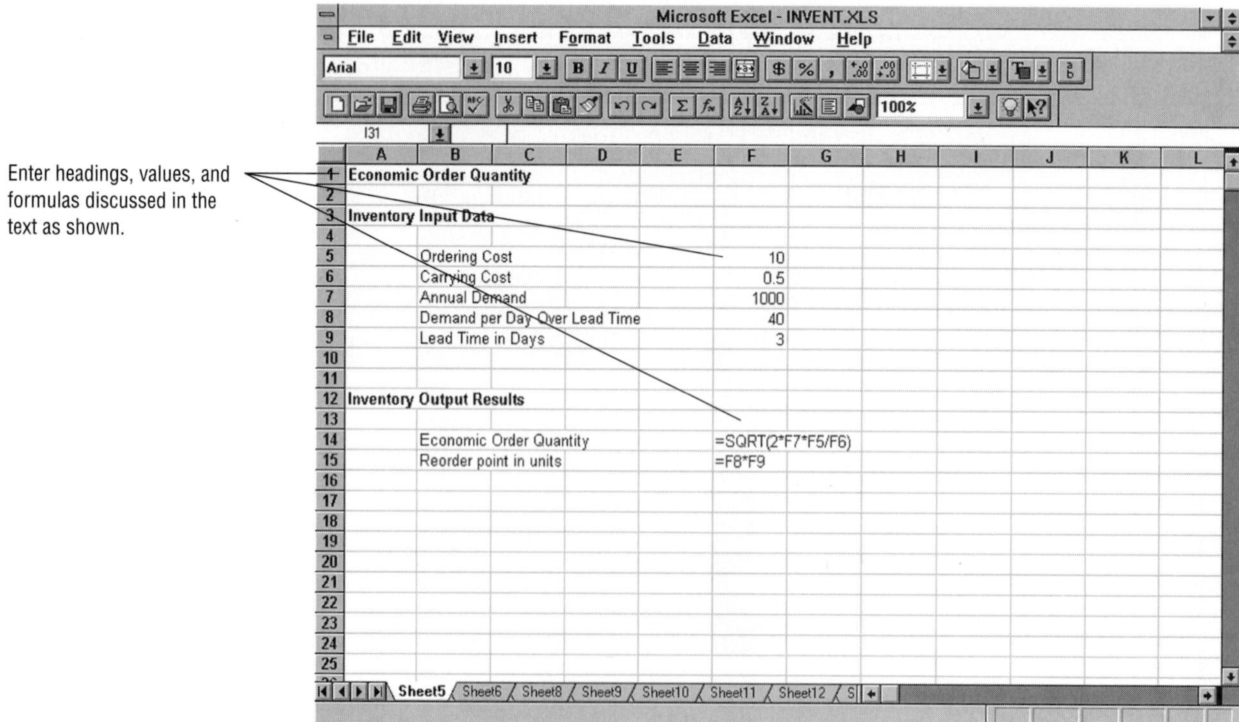

PROGRAM 9.3 EXCEL SPREADSHEET FOR THE BASIC EOQ MODEL, USING DATA FROM EXAMPLES 2–5

PROGRAM 9.4 AN EXCEL SPREADSHEET FOR THE QUANTITY DISCOUNT PROBLEM USING DATA FROM EXAMPLE 7

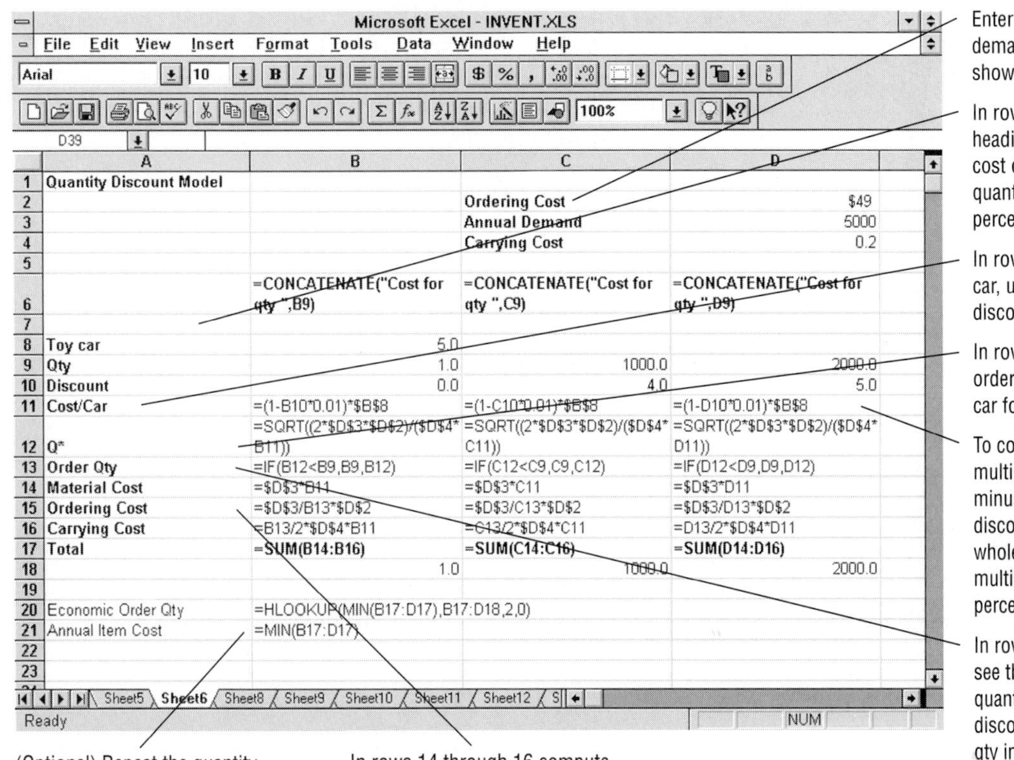

Microsoft Excel - INVENT.XLS

	A	B	C	D
1	Quantity Discount Model			
2			Ordering Cost	$49
3			Annual Demand	5000
4			Carrying Cost	0.2
5				
6		=CONCATENATE("Cost for qty ",B9)	=CONCATENATE("Cost for qty ",C9)	=CONCATENATE("Cost for qty ",D9)
7				
8	Toy car	5.0		
9	Qty	1.0	1000.0	2000.0
10	Discount	0.0	4.0	5.0
11	Cost/Car	=(1-B10*0.01)*$B$8	=(1-C10*0.01)*$B$8	=(1-D10*0.01)*$B$8
12	Q*	=SQRT((2*$D$3*$D$2)/($D$4*B11))	=SQRT((2*$D$3*$D$2)/($D$4*C11))	=SQRT((2*$D$3*$D$2)/($D$4*D11))
13	Order Qty	=IF(B12<B9,B9,B12)	=IF(C12<C9,C9,C12)	=IF(D12<D9,D9,D12)
14	Material Cost	=$D$3*B11	=$D$3*C11	=$D$3*D11
15	Ordering Cost	=$D$3/B13*$D$2	=$D$3/C13*$D$2	=$D$3/D13*$D$2
16	Carrying Cost	=B13/2*$D$4*B11	=C13/2*$D$4*C11	=D13/2*$D$4*D11
17	Total	=SUM(B14:B16)	=SUM(C14:C16)	=SUM(D14:D16)
18		1.0	1000.0	2000.0
19				
20	Economic Order Qty	=HLOOKUP(MIN(B17:D17),B17:D18,2,0)		
21	Annual Item Cost	=MIN(B17:D17)		

Enter the ordering cost, annual demand, and carrying costs as shown.

In rows 6, 8, 9, and 10 enter the headings for the columns, the cost of the car, the discount break quantities, and the discount percentage.

In row 11 calculate the cost of the car, using the qty 1 price and the discount.

In row 12 calculate the Q^* of the order, based on the price of the car found in row 11.

To compute the unit price we are multiplying the original price by 1 minus the discount. Since the discount in the spreadsheet is in whole numbers, it must be multiplied by .01 to convert it to a percentage.

In row 13 use an =IF to check to see that the Q^* is greater than the quantity needed to get the discount. If not, use the minimum qty instead of Q^*.

(Optional) Repeat the quantity breaks (row 9) in row 18. Use the =HLOOKUP and =MIN functions to report the minimum cost and best order quantity.

In rows 14 through 16 compute material, ordering, carrying, and total cost using the equations discussed in the text.

PROGRAM 9.5

EXCEL OUTPUT FOR PROGRAM 9.4, USING EXAMPLE 8 DATA

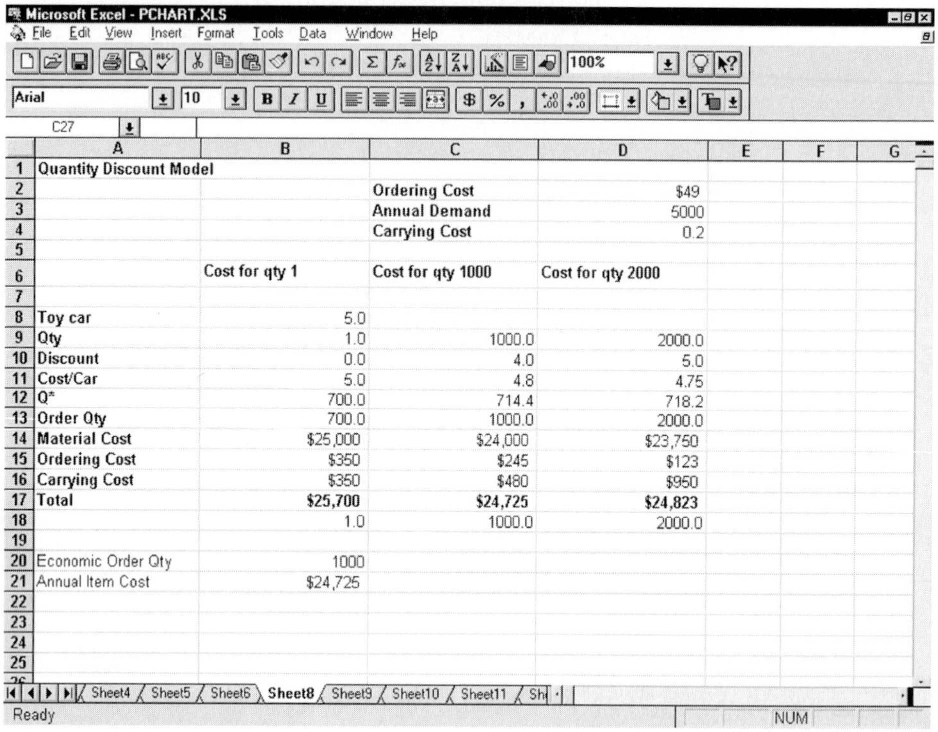

Microsoft Excel - PCHART.XLS

File Edit View Insert Format Tools Data Window Help

C27

	A	B	C	D
1	Quantity Discount Model			
2			Ordering Cost	$49
3			Annual Demand	5000
4			Carrying Cost	0.2
5				
6		Cost for qty 1	Cost for qty 1000	Cost for qty 2000
7				
8	Toy car	5.0		
9	Qty	1.0	1000.0	2000.0
10	Discount	0.0	4.0	5.0
11	Cost/Car	5.0	4.8	4.75
12	Q*	700.0	714.4	718.2
13	Order Qty	700.0	1000.0	2000.0
14	Material Cost	$25,000	$24,000	$23,750
15	Ordering Cost	$350	$245	$123
16	Carrying Cost	$350	$480	$950
17	Total	$25,700	$24,725	$24,823
18		1.0	1000.0	2000.0
19				
20	Economic Order Qty	1000		
21	Annual Item Cost	$24,725		

Sheet4 / Sheet5 / Sheet6 / Sheet8 / Sheet9 / Sheet10 / Sheet11

Ready NUM

SOLVED PROBLEM 9.1

The D. Saelens Computer Corporation purchases 8,000 transistors each year for use in the minicomputers it manufactures. The unit cost of each transistor is \$10, and the cost of carrying one transistor in inventory for a year is \$3. Ordering cost is \$30 per order.

What are the optimal order quantity, the expected number of orders placed each year, and the expected time between orders? Assume that Saelens operates a 200-day working year.

SOLUTION

$$Q^* = \sqrt{\frac{2DS}{H}} = \sqrt{\frac{2(8{,}000)(30)}{3}} = 400 \text{ units}$$

$$N = \frac{D}{Q^*} = \frac{8{,}000}{400} = 20 \text{ orders}$$

Time between orders = T

$$= \frac{\text{Number of working days}}{N} = \frac{200}{20}$$

$$= 10 \text{ working days}$$

Hence, an order for 400 transistors is placed every 10 days. Presumably, then, 20 orders are placed each year.

SOLVED PROBLEM 9.2

Annual demand for the notebook binders at Crone's Stationery Shop is 10,000 units. Heather Crone operates her business 300 days per year and finds that deliveries from her supplier generally take five working days. Calculate the reorder point for the notebook binders that she stocks.

Solution

$$L = 5 \text{ days}$$

$$d = \frac{10{,}000}{300} = 33.3 \text{ units per day}$$

$$\text{ROP} = d \times L = (33.3 \text{ units per day})(5 \text{ days}) = 166.7 \text{ units}$$

Thus, Heather should reorder when her stock of notebook binders reaches 167.

SOLVED PROBLEM 9.3

L. Alwayn, Inc., has an annual demand rate of 1,000 units but can produce at an average annual production rate of 2,000 units. Setup cost is \$10, and carrying cost is \$1.00. What is the optimal number of units to be produced each time?

Solution

$$Q^* = \sqrt{\frac{2DS}{H[1-(D/P)]}}$$

$$= \sqrt{\frac{2(1{,}000)(10)}{1[1-(1{,}000/2{,}000)]}} = \sqrt{\frac{20{,}000}{1/2}} = \sqrt{40{,}000}$$

$$= 200 \text{ units}$$

SOLVED PROBLEM 9.4

What safety stock should James Gilbert Corporation maintain if mean sales are 80 during the reorder period, the standard deviation is 7, and Gilbert can tolerate stockouts 10% of the time?

Solution

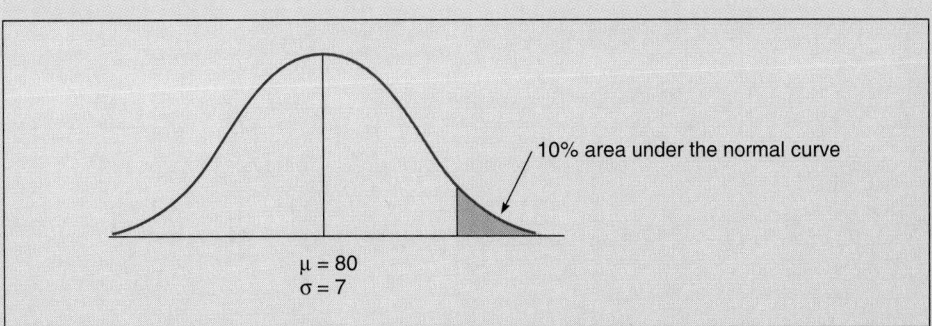

From Appendix A, Z at an area of .9 (or 1 − .10) = 1.28

$$Z = 1.28 = \frac{x-\mu}{\sigma} = \frac{ss}{\sigma}$$

$$ss = 1.28\sigma$$

$$= 1.28(7) = 8.96 \text{ units, or } 9 \text{ units}$$

DISCUSSION QUESTIONS

1. With the advent of low-cost computing, do you see alternatives to the popular ABC classifications?
2. What is the difference between the standard EOQ model and the production inventory model?
3. What are the main reasons that an organization has inventory?
4. Describe the costs that are associated with ordering and maintaining inventory.
5. What are the assumptions of the EOQ model?
6. How sensitive is EOQ to variations in demand or costs?
7. Does the production model or the standard EOQ model yield a higher EOQ if setup costs and holding costs are the same? Why?
8. When is a good time for cycle counting personnel to proceed with auditing a particular item?
9. What impact does a decrease in setup time have on EOQ?
10. What is meant by service level?
11. How would a firm go about determining a service level?
12. What happens to total inventory costs (and EOQ) if inventory holding costs per unit increase as inventory increases (that is, increase at an increasing rate)?
13. What happens to total inventory costs (and EOQ) if there is a fixed cost associated with inventory holding costs (for example, leasing the warehouse)?
14. Describe the difference between a fixed-quantity and a fixed-period inventory system.
15. Describe the four types of inventory.

OPERATIONS IN PRACTICE EXERCISE

Wayne Hills Hospital, in tiny Wayne, Nebraska, faces a problem common to large, urban hospitals as well as small, remote ones like itself. That problem is deciding how much of each type of whole blood to keep in stock. Because blood is expensive and has a limited shelf life (up to five weeks under 1–6°C refrigeration), Wayne Hills naturally wants to keep its stock as low as possible. Unfortunately, disasters such as a major tornado in 1986 and a train wreck in 1991 illustrated that lives would be lost because not enough blood was available to handle massive needs. The hospital administrator wants to set an 85% service level based on demand over the past decade. Discuss the implications of this decision. What is the hospital's responsibility with regard to stocking lifesaving medicines that have short shelf lives? How would you set the inventory level for a commodity such as blood?

PROBLEMS

• **9.1.** Trish Connor's company has compiled the following data on a small set of products:

SKU	ANNUAL DEMAND	UNIT COST
A	100	$250
B	75	$100
C	50	$ 50
D	200	$150
E	150	$ 75

Use her data to illustrate an ABC analysis.

(Problems continue on page 336)

SELF-TEST ■ CHAPTER 9

- *Before taking the self-test* refer back to the learning objectives listed at the beginning of the chapter and the key terms listed at the end of the chapter.
- Use the key at the back of the text to *correct* your answers.
- *Restudy* pages that correspond to any questions you answered incorrectly or material you feel uncertain about.

1. A use of inventory is
   a. to decouple production and distribution processes
   b. to provide a hedge against inflation
   c. to enable an organization to take advantage of quantity discounts
   d. all of the above

2. ABC analysis divides on-hand inventory into three classes based upon
   a. unit price
   b. the number of units on hand
   c. annual demand
   d. annual dollar values

3. Cycle counting
   a. provides a measure of inventory turnover
   b. assumes that all inventory records must be verified with the same frequency
   c. is a process by which inventory records are periodically verified
   d. all of the above

4. The service industry is improving inventory management by a number of ways. These include:
   a. shrinkage and pilferage
   b. good personnel selection
   c. bar coding of incoming and outgoing merchandise
   d. a and b above
   e. b and c above

5. Annual holding costs are often in the range of
   a. under 6% of inventory value
   b. 6% to 9% of inventory value
   c. 9% to 12% of inventory value
   d. 12% to 15% of inventory value
   e. over 15% of inventory value

6. For most items in inventory, yearly holding costs amount to only a few percent of the unit cost.
   a. True b. False

7. The major advantage of cycle counting is
   a. accurate inventory
   b. dispensing with the annual physical inventory
   c. the audit activity that accompanies cycle counting
   d. none of the above
   e. all of the above

8. Inventory models under conditions of dependent demand are quite different from those under conditions of independent demand.
   a. True b. False

9. In an EOQ model, the reorder point is determined by the average demand during the lead time.
   a. True b. False

10. The difference(s) between the basic EOQ model and the production order quantity model is(are) that
    a. the production order quantity model does not require the assumption of known, constant demand
    b. the EOQ model does not require the assumption of negligible lead time
    c. the production order quantity model does not require the assumption of instantaneous delivery
    d. all of the above

11. Extra units held in inventory to reduce stockouts are called
    a. reorder point
    b. safety stock
    c. just-in-time inventory
    d. all of the above

12. Inventory record accuracy can be improved by
    a. cycle counting
    b. reorder points
    c. ABC analysis
    d. all of the above

13. The two most important inventory-based questions answered by the typical inventory model are
    a. when to place an order and what is the cost of the order
    b. when to place an order and how much of an item to order
    c. how much of an item to order and what is the cost of the order
    d. how much of an item to order and with whom should the order be placed

14. The appropriate level of safety stock is typically determined by
    a. minimizing an expected stockout cost
    b. choosing the level of safety stock that assures a given service level
    c. carrying sufficient safety stock so as to eliminate all stockouts

9.2. Bell Enterprise has ten items in inventory. Greg Bell asks you, the recent OM graduate, to divide these items into ABC classifications. What do you report back to Mr. Bell?

ITEM	ANNUAL DEMAND	COST/UNIT
A2	3000	$ 50
B8	4000	12
C7	1500	45
D1	6000	10
E9	1000	20
F3	500	500
G2	300	1,500
H2	600	20
I5	1750	10
J8	2500	5

9.3. Sarita Uribe opened a new beauty products retail store. There are numerous items in inventory, and Sarita knows that there are costs associated with inventory. However, her time is limited so she cannot carefully evaluate the inventory policy for all products. Sarita wants to classify the items according to the dollars invested in them. The following table provides information about the ten items that she carries:

ITEM NUMBER	UNIT COST	DEMAND (UNITS)
E102	$4.00	800
D23	8.00	1200
D27	3.00	700
R02	2.00	1000
R19	8.00	200
S107	6.00	500
S123	1.00	1200
U11	7.00	800
U23	1.00	1500
V75	4.00	1500

Use ABC analysis to classify these items into categories A, B, and C.

9.4. It takes approximately two weeks (14 days) for an order of steel bolts to arrive once the order has been placed.

The demand for the bolts is fairly constant; on the average, the manager has observed that the hardware store sells 500 of these bolts each day. Since the demand is fairly constant, she believes she can avoid stockouts completely if she orders the bolts at the correct time. What is the reorder point?

9.5. Lead time for one of your fastest-moving products is 21 days. Demand during this period averages 100 units per day. What would be an appropriate reorder point?

9.6. Nancy Birdsong is attempting to perform an inventory analysis on one of her most popular products. Annual demand for this product is 5,000 units; unit cost is $200; carrying cost is considered to be approximately 25% of the unit price. Order costs for her company typically run nearly $30 per order and lead time averages 10 days. (Assume a 50-week year.)

a. What is the economic order quantity?

b. What is the reorder point?

c. What is the total inventory + ordering cost?

d. What is the optimal number of orders per year?
e. What is the optimal number of days between orders (assume 250 working days per year)?

9.7. Cynthia Chazen is the purchasing agent for Central Valve Company, which sells industrial valves and fluid-control devices. One of their most popular valves is the Western, which has an annual demand of 4,000 units. The cost of each valve is $90, and the inventory carrying cost is estimated to be 10% of the cost of each valve. Cynthia has made a study of the costs involved in placing an order for any of the valves that Central Valve stocks, and she has concluded that the average ordering cost is $25 per order. Furthermore, it takes about eight days for an order to arrive from the supplier. During this time, the demand per week for Central valves is approximately 80.
a. What is the economic order quantity?
b. What is the reorder point?
c. What is the total annual inventory cost (carrying cost + ordering cost)?
d. What is the optimal number of orders per year?
e. What is the optimal number of days between any two orders, assuming there are 200 working days per year?

9.8. Happy Pet, Inc., is a large pet store located in Long Beach Mall. Although the store specializes in dogs, it also sells fish, turtle, and bird supplies. Everlast Leader, a leather lead for dogs, costs Happy Pet $7.00 each. There is an annual demand for 6,000 Everlast Leaders. The manager of Happy Pet has determined that the ordering cost is $20 per order, and the carrying cost as a percentage of the unit cost is 15%. Happy Pet is now considering a new supplier of Everlast Leaders. Each lead would cost only $6.65; but in order to get this discount, Happy Pet would have to buy shipments of 3,000 Everlast Leaders at a time. Should Happy Pet use the new supplier and take this discount for quantity buying?

9.9. Doug Brauer uses 1,500 per year of a certain subassembly that has an annual holding cost of $45 per unit. Each order placed costs Doug $150. Doug operates 300 days per year and has found that an order must be placed with his supplier six working days before he can expect to receive that order. For this subassembly, find:
a. Economic order quantity.
b. Annual holding cost.
c. Annual ordering cost.
d. Reorder point.

9.10. Christina Reilly, of Reilly Plumbing, uses 1,200 of a certain spare part that costs $25 for each order and $24 annual holding cost. Calculate the total cost for order sizes of 25, 40, 50, 60, and 100. Identify the economic order quantity and consider the implications for making an error in calculating the economic order quantity.

9.11. Judy Shaw's Dream Store sells water beds and assorted supplies. The best-selling bed in the store has an annual demand of 400 units. The ordering cost is $40; the holding cost is $5 per unit per year. There are 250 working days per year, and the lead time is 6 days.
a. To minimize the total cost, how many units should be ordered each time an order is placed?
b. If the holding cost per unit were $6 instead of $5, what would the optimal order quantity be?

9.12. Norris Harrell's Computer Store in Houston sells a printer for $200. Demand for this is constant during the year, and annual demand is forecasted to be 600 units. The holding cost is $20 per unit per year, while the cost of ordering is $60 per order. Currently, the company is ordering 12 times per year (50 units each time). There are 250 working days per year and the lead time is 10 days.

a. Given the current policy of ordering 50 units at a time, what is the total of the annual ordering cost and the annual holding cost?

b. If the company used the absolute best inventory policy, what would the total of the ordering and holding costs be?

c. What is the reorder point?

9.13. Jan Kottas is the owner of a small company that produces electric knives used to cut fabric. The annual demand is for 8,000 knives, and Jan produces the knives in batches. On average, Jan can produce 150 knives per day; during the production process, demand for knives has been about 40 knives per day. The cost to set up the production process is $100.00, and it costs Jan $0.80 to carry a knife for one year. How many knives should Jan produce in each batch?

9.14. Don Williams, inventory control manager for Cal-Tex, receives wheel bearings from Wheel-Rite, a small producer of metal parts. Wheel-Rite can produce only 500 wheel bearings per day. Cal-Tex receives 10,000 wheel bearings from Wheel-Rite each year. Since Cal-Tex operates 200 working days each year, the average daily demand of wheel bearings by Cal-Tex is 50. The ordering cost for Cal-Tex is $40 per order, and the carrying cost is $0.60 per wheel bearing per year. How many wheel bearings should Cal-Tex order from Wheel-Rite at one time? Wheel-Rite has agreed to ship the maximum number of wheel bearings that it produces each day to Cal-Tex once an order has been received.

9.15. McLeavey Manufacturing has a demand for 1,000 pumps each year. The cost of a pump is $50. It costs McLeavey Manufacturing $40 to place an order, and the carrying cost is 25% of the unit cost. If pumps are ordered in quantities of 200, McLeavey Manufacturing can get a 3% discount on the cost of the pumps. Should McLeavey Manufacturing order 200 pumps at a time and take the 3% discount?

9.16. Jack McCanna Products offers the following discount schedule for its 4 feet by 8 feet sheets of quality plywood.

ORDER	UNIT COST
9 sheets or less	$18.00
10 to 50 sheets	$17.50
More than 50 sheets	$17.25

Home Sweet Home Company orders plywood from McCanna Products. Home Sweet Home has an ordering cost of $45. The carrying cost is 20%, and the annual demand is 100 sheets. What do you recommend?

9.17. Should the quantity discount be taken, given the following data on a hardware item stocked by the Niles Brothers Paint Store?

$$D = 2{,}000 \text{ units}$$

$$S = \$10$$

$$H = \$1$$

$$P = \$1$$

$$\text{Discount price} = \$.75$$

$$\begin{pmatrix}\text{Quantity needed to}\\ \text{qualify for discount}\end{pmatrix} = 2{,}000 \text{ units}$$

9.18. The regular price of a tape deck component is $20. On orders of 75 units or more, the price is discounted to $18.50. On orders of 100 units or more, the discount price is $15.75. At present, Sound Business, Inc., a manufacturer of stereo components, has an inventory carrying cost of 5% per unit per year, and its ordering cost is $10. Annual demand is 45 components. What should Sound Business, Inc., do?

9.19. A product is ordered once each year, and the reorder point without safety stock (dL) is 100 units. Inventory carrying cost is $10 per unit per year, and the cost of a stockout is $50 per unit per year. Given the following demand probabilities during the reorder period, how much safety stock should be carried?

	DEMAND DURING REORDER PERIOD	PROBABILITY
	0	.1
	50	.2
ROP →	100	.4
	150	.2
	200	.1
		1.0

9.20. Lori Smith, Inc., an organization that sells children's art sets, has an ordering cost of $40 for the BB-1 set. The carrying cost for BB-1 is $5 per set per year. In order to meet demand, Lori Smith orders large quantities of BB-1 seven times a year. The stockout cost for BB-1 is estimated to be $50 per set. Over the last several years, Lori Smith has observed the following demand during the lead time for BB-1.

DEMAND DURING LEAD TIME	PROBABILITY
40	.1
50	.2
60	.2
70	.2
80	.2
90	.1
	1.0

The reorder point for BB-1 is 60 units. What level of safety stock should be maintained for BB-1?

9.21. Yvette Angel's company produces a product for which the annual demand is 10,000. They operate 200 days per year so demand is about 50 per day. Daily production is 200 units. Holding costs are $1.00 per unit per year; setup costs are $200.00. If you wish to produce this product in batches, what size batch should be used?

9.22. A product is delivered to Malcolm Ward's company once a year. The reorder point, without safety stock, is 200 units. Carrying cost is $15 per unit per year, and the cost of a stockout is $70 per unit per year. Given the following demand probabilities during the reorder period, how much safety stock should be carried?

DEMAND DURING REORDER PERIOD	PROBABILITY
0	0.1
100	0.1
200	0.2
300	0.2
400	0.2

CASE STUDY

Sturdivant Sound Systems

Sturdivant Sound Systems manufactures and sells sound systems for both home and auto. All parts of the sound systems, with the exception of CD players, are produced in the Rochester, New York, plant. CD players used in the assembly of Sturdivant's systems are purchased from Morris Electronics of Concord, New Hampshire.

Mary Kim, purchasing agent for Sturdivant Sound Systems, submits a purchase requisition for the CD players once every four weeks. The company's annual requirements total 5,000 units (20 per working day), and the cost per unit is $60. (Sturdivant does not purchase in greater quantities because Morris Electronics, the supplier, does not offer quantity discounts.) Rarely does a shortage of CD players occur because Morris promises delivery within one week following receipt of a purchase requisition. (Total time between date of order and date of receipt is ten days.)

Associated with the purchase of each shipment are procurement costs. These costs, which amount to $20 per order, include the costs of preparing the requisition, inspecting and storing the delivered goods, updating inventory records, and issuing a voucher and a check for payment. In addition to procurement costs, Sturdivant Sound Systems incurs inventory carrying costs that include insurance, storage, handling, taxes, and so forth. These costs equal $6 per unit per year.

Beginning in August of this year, management of Sturdivant Sound Systems will embark on a companywide cost control program in an attempt to improve its profits. One area to be closely scrutinized for possible cost savings is inventory procurement.

DISCUSSION QUESTIONS

1. Compute the optimal order quantity of CD players.
2. Determine the appropriate reorder point (in units).
3. Compute the cost savings that the company will realize if it implements the optimal inventory procurement decision.
4. Should procurement costs be considered a linear function of the number of orders?

SOURCE: Professor Jerry Kinard, Western Carolina University.

CASE STUDY

Martin-Pullin Bicycle Corporation

Martin-Pullin Bicycle Corp. (MPBC), located in Dallas, is a wholesale distributor of bicycles and bicycle parts. Formed in 1981 by cousins Ray Martin and Jim Pullin, the firm's primary retail outlets are located within a 400-mile radius of the distribution center. These retail outlets receive the order from Martin-Pullin within two days after notifying the distribution center, provided the stock is available. However, if an order is not fulfilled by the company, then no backorder is placed; the retailers arrange to get their shipment from other distributors, and MPBC loses that amount of business.

The company distributes a wide variety of bicycles. The most popular model, and the major source of revenue to the company, is the AirWing. MPBC receives all the models from a single manufacturer overseas, and shipment takes as long as four weeks from the time an order is placed. With the cost of communication, paperwork, and customs clearance included, MPBC estimates that each time an order is placed, it incurs a cost of $65. The purchase price paid by MPBC, per bicycle, is roughly 60% of the suggested retail price for all the styles available, and the inventory carrying cost is 1% per month (12% per year) of the purchase price paid by MPBC. The retail price (paid by the customers) for the AirWing is $170 per bicycle.

MPBC is interested in making the inventory plan for 1997. The firm wants to maintain a 95% service level with its customers to minimize the losses on the lost orders. The data collected for the last two years are summarized in Table 1. A forecast for AirWing model sales in the upcoming year of 1997 has been developed and will be used to make an inventory plan for MPBC.

DISCUSSION QUESTIONS

1. Develop an inventory plan to help MPBC.
2. Discuss reorder points and total costs.
3. How can you address the demand that is not level for the planning horizon?

SOURCE: Professor Kala Chand Seal, Loyola Marymount University.

TABLE 1 DEMANDS FOR AIRWING MODEL

	YEAR		
MONTHS	*1995*	*1996*	*Forecast for 1997*
Jan.	6	7	8
Feb.	12	14	15
Mar.	24	27	31
Apr.	46	53	59
May	75	86	97
June	47	54	60
July	30	34	39
Aug.	18	21	24
Sept.	13	15	16
Oct.	12	13	15
Nov.	22	25	28
Dec.	38	42	47
Totals	343	391	439

Internet Case Study See our Internet home page at http://www.prenhall.com/renderpom for these additional case studies: La Place Power and Light Co. and Professional Video Management.

BIBLIOGRAPHY

Bowers, Melissa R., and Anurag Agarwal. "Lower In-Process Inventories and Better on Time Performance at Tanner Companies, Inc." *Interfaces* 25, no. 4 (July-August 1995): 30–43.

Brown, R. G. *Decision Rules for Inventory Management.* New York: Holt, Rinehart and Winston, 1967.

Freeland, J. R., J. P. Leschke, and E. N. Weiss. "Guidelines for Setup-Cost Reduction Programs to Achieve Zero Inventory." *Journal of Operations Management* 9 (January 1990): 85.

Groenevelt, H., L. Pintelon, and A. Seidmann. "Production Lot Sizing with Machine Breakdowns." *Management Science* 38, 1 (January 1992): 104.

Hall, R. *Zero Inventones.* Homewood, IL: Dow Jones-Irwin, 1983.

Jinchiro, N., and R. Hall. "Management Specs for Stockless Production." *Harvard Business Review* 63 (May-June 1983): 89–91.

Landvater, D. V. *World Class Production and Inventory Management.* Newburg, NH: Oliver Wight Publications, 1993.

Schniederjans, M. *Topics in Just-in-Time Management.* Boston: Allyn & Bacon, 1993.

Shingo, S. *A Revolution in Manufacturing: The SMED System.* Cambridge, MA: Productivity Press, 1986.

Vollmann, T. E., W. L. Berry, and D. C. Whybark. *Manufacturing Planning and Control Systems.* Homewood, IL: Irwin, 1988.

Wight, O. W. *Production and Inventory Management in the Computer Age.* Boston: Cahners, 1974.

Inventory for Dependent Demand

10

CHAPTER OUTLINE

Dependent Inventory Model Requirements

Master Production Schedule ■ Specifications or Bills-of-Material ■ Accurate Inventory Records ■ Purchase Orders Outstanding ■ Lead Times for Each Component

Benefits of MRP

MRP Structure

MRP Management

MRP Dynamics ■ MRP and JIT

Lot-Sizing Techniques

Extensions of MRP

MRP in Services

Restaurant Example ■ Distribution Example

Summary ■ *Key Terms* ■ *Using POM for Windows to Solve MRP Problems* ■ *Solved Problem* ■ *Self-Test Chapter 10* ■ *Discussion Questions* ■ *Operations in Practice Exercise* ■ *Problems* ■ *Case Study: Service, Inc.* ■ *Bibliography*

LEARNING OBJECTIVES

When you complete this chapter you should be able to:

IDENTIFY OR DEFINE:

Lot sizing
Low-level coding
Planning bills, pseudo bills, and kits
Phantom bills

DESCRIBE OR EXPLAIN:

Material requirements
Distribution requirements planning

The inventory models discussed in Chapter 9 assumed that the demand for one item was independent of the demand for another item. For example, the demand for refrigerators may be *independent* of the demand for anything else. Moreover, the demand today may be independent of the demand tomorrow.

However, demand for many items is dependent. By *dependent*, we mean the demand for one item is related to the demand for another item. Consider an auto manufacturer. The carmaker's demand for auto tires and radiators depends on the production of autos. Four tires and one radiator go into each finished car. Demand for items is *dependent* when the relationship between the items can be determined. Therefore, once management can make a forecast of the demand for the final product, quantities required for all components can be computed, because all components are *dependent* items. The Boeing Aircraft operations manager scheduling production of one plane per week, for example, knows the requirements down to the last rivet. For any product, all components of that product are *dependent* demand items. *More generally, for any item where a schedule can be established, dependent techniques should be used.*

NOTE
MRP is preferable in *dependent* manufacturing. Statistical techniques such as EOQ are preferable for *independent* demand items.

Dependent techniques, when they can be used, are preferable to the models of Chapter 9. This is true for all component parts, subassemblies, and supplies when a schedule is known. It is true not only for manufacturers and distributors, but also for a wide variety of firms from restaurants[1] to hospitals.[2] When dependent techniques are used in a production environment, they are called **material requirements planning (MRP).**

material requirements planning (MRP)

DEPENDENT INVENTORY MODEL REQUIREMENTS

In this chapter we examine the requirements of dependent inventory models. Then we look at how to use these models. Effective use of dependent inventory models requires that the operations manager know the following:

NOTE
Consider what happens to inventory if Wal-Mart orders Christmas trees with an EOQ system. Maybe the manager gets fired.

1. Master production schedule (what is to be made and when).
2. Specifications or bill-of-material (how to make the product).
3. Inventory availability (what is in stock).
4. Purchase orders outstanding (what is on order).
5. Lead times (how long it takes to get various components).

In this chapter each of these requirements is discussed in the context of material requirements planning (MRP).

Master Production Schedule

master production schedule

A **master production schedule** specifies what is to be made and when. The schedule must be in accordance with a production plan. Such plans include a variety of inputs, including financial plans, customer demand, engineering capabilities, labor availability, inventory fluctuations, supplier performance, and other considerations. Each contributes in its own way to the production plan, as shown in Figure 10.1, which shows the planning process from the production plan to exe-

[1]John G. Wacker, "Effective Planning and Cost Control for Restaurants: Making Resource Requirements Planning Work," *Production and Inventory Management* 26 (First Quarter 1985): 55–70.

[2]David W. Pentico, "Material Requirements Planning: A New Tool for Controlling Hospital Inventories," *Hospital Topics* 57 (May-June 1979): 40–43.

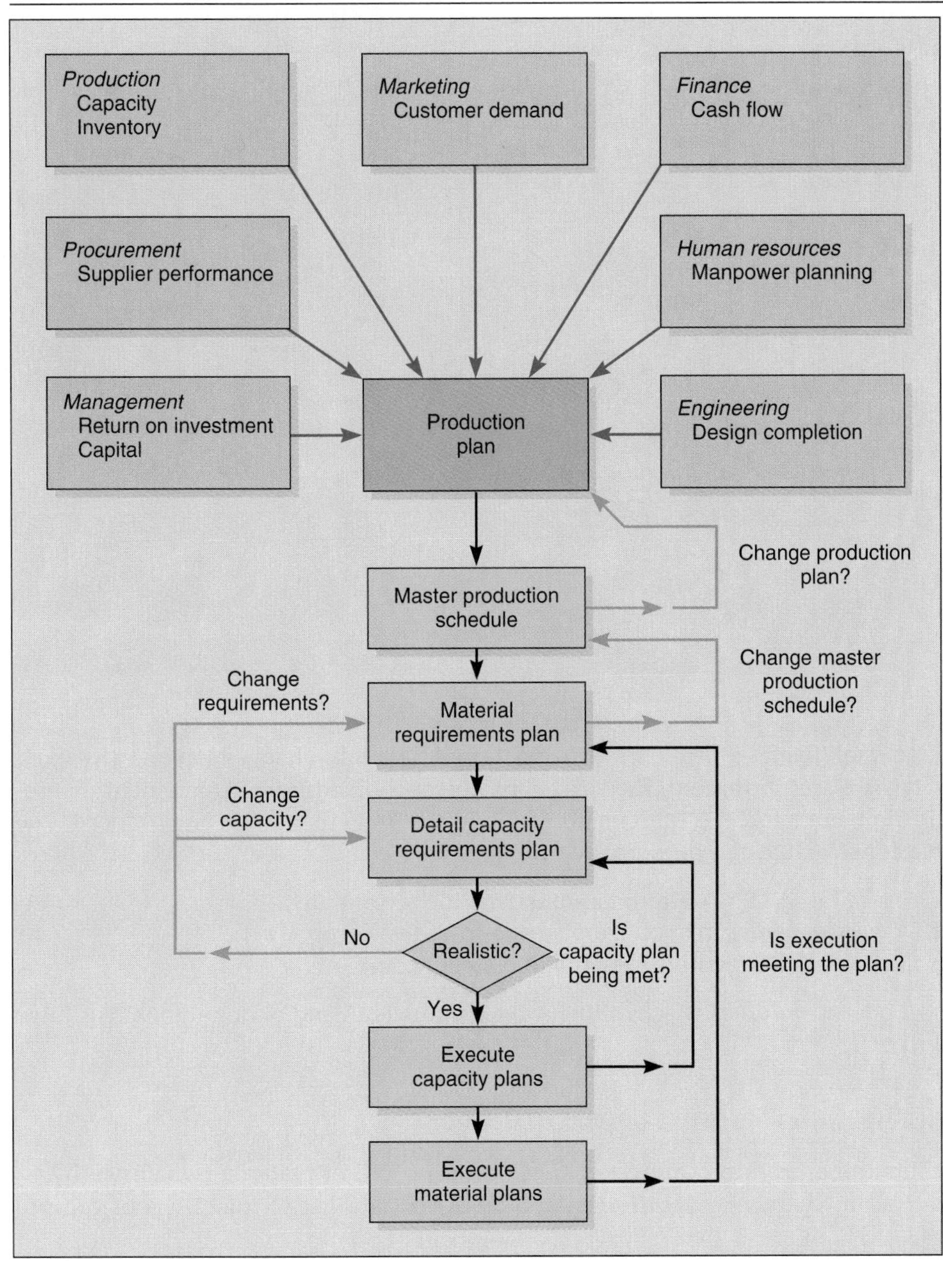

FIGURE 10.1

THE PLANNING PROCESS

NOTE
Regardless of the complexity of the planning process, the production plan and its derivative, the master production schedule, must be developed.

cution. Each of the lower-level plans must be feasible. When it is not, feedback to the next higher level is used to make the necessary adjustment. One of the major strengths of MRP is its ability to determine precisely the feasibility of a schedule within capacity constraints. The production plan sets the upper and lower bounds on the master production schedule.

The master production schedule tells us what is required to satisfy demand and meet the production plan. This schedule establishes what items to make and when. Many organizations establish a master production schedule and then "fix" the near-term portion of the plan. The fixed portion of the schedule is then referred

NOTE
MRP is tied into aggregate planning, purchasing, and scheduling systems, among others, in an organization.

Wheeled Coach Industries, headquartered in Orlando, Florida, is the world's largest ambulance manufacturer, with 20% of its vehicles marketed abroad. As this cutaway of one ambulance interior shows, a Wheeled Coach ambulance is a complex product, serving as the equivalent of a hospital emergency room in miniature. To complicate production, virtually every ambulance is custom ordered, with 7,000 different options available. Wheeled Coach uses an MRP system with daily updates. This firm uses MAPICS DB software on an IBM AS 400 minicomputer. The system has reduced inventory by over 30% in the past two years.

to as the "fixed," "firm," or "frozen" schedule. Only changes beyond the fixed schedule are permitted. The master production schedule is a statement of production, not a forecast of demand. It shows the units that are to be produced. The master schedule can be expressed in terms of:

1. An *end item* in a continuous (make-to-stock) company.
2. A *customer order* in a job shop (make-to-order) company.
3. *Modules* in a repetitive (assemble-to-stock) company.

A master production schedule for two products, A and S, might look like Table 10.1.

Specifications or Bills-of-Material

bill-of-material (BOM)

Units to be produced are often specified via a bill-of-material, which we introduced in Chapter 4. A **bill-of-material (BOM)** is a list of quantities of compo-

TABLE 10.1 MASTER PRODUCTION SCHEDULE FOR PRODUCTS A AND S

GROSS REQUIREMENTS FOR PRODUCT A										
Week	6	7	8	9	10	11	12	13	14	and so on
Amount	50		100	47	60		110	75		

GROSS REQUIREMENTS FOR PRODUCT S										
Week	7	8	9	10	11	12	13	14	15	16	and so on
Amount	100	200	150			60	75		100		

nents, ingredients, and materials required to make a product. A home kitchen recipe specifying ingredients and quantities and a full set of drawings for an airplane are both bills-of-material (although they do vary somewhat in scope). A bill-of-material for product A in Example 1 consists of items B and C. Items above any level are called *parents;* items below any level are called *components* or *children.* A bill-of-material provides the product structure. The following example shows how to develop the product structure and "explode" it to reveal the requirements for each component.

EXAMPLE 1

Fun Lawn's demand for product A is 50 units. Each unit of A requires two units of B and three units of C. Each unit of B requires two units of D and three units of E. Furthermore, each unit of C requires one unit of E and two units of F. And each F requires one unit of G and two units of D. Thus the demand for B, C, D, E, F, and G is completely dependent on the demand for A. Given this information, we can construct a product structure for the related inventory items:

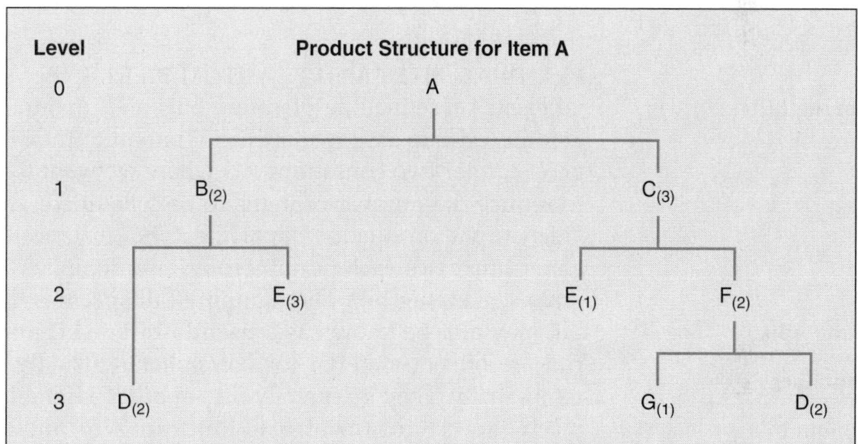

The structure has four levels: 0, 1, 2, and 3. There are four parents: A, B, C, and F. Each parent item has at least one level below it. Items B, C, D, E, F, and G are components because each item has at least one level above it. In this structure, B, C, and F are parents and components. The number in parentheses indicates how many units of that particular item are needed to make the item immediately above it. Thus $B_{(2)}$ means that it takes two units of B for every unit of A, and $F_{(2)}$ means that it takes two units of F for every unit of C.

Once we have developed the product structure, we can determine the number of units of each item required to satisfy demand as displayed in the following table:

Part B:	2 × number of As =	(2)(50) =	100
Part C:	3 × number of As =	(3)(50) =	150
Part D:	2 × number of Bs + 2 × number of Fs =	(2)(100) + (2)(300) =	800
Part E:	3 × number of Bs + 1 × number of Cs =	(3)(100) + (1)(150) =	450
Part F:	2 × number of Cs =	(2)(150) =	300
Part G:	1 × number of Fs =	(1)(300) =	300

Thus for 50 units of A, we will need 100 units of B, 150 units of C, 800 units of D, 450 units of E, 300 units of F, and 300 units of G.

Bills-of-material not only specify requirements, but are also useful for costing, and they can serve as a list of items to be issued to production or assembly personnel. When bills-of-material (BOM) are used in this way, they are usually called *pick lists*.

modular bills

MODULAR BILLS. Bills-of-material may be organized around product modules. Modules are not final products to be sold but are components that can be produced and assembled into units. They may be major components of the final product or product options. The bills-of-material for these modules are called **modular bills.** Bills-of-material are sometimes organized as modules (rather than as part of a final product) because production scheduling and production are often facilitated by organizing around relatively few modules rather than a multitude of final assemblies. For instance, a firm may make 138,000 different final products but have only 40 modules that are mixed and matched to produce the 138,000 final products.[3] The firm forecasts, prepares its master production schedule, and builds to the 40 modules, not the 138,000 configurations of the final product. The 40 modules can be assembled for specific orders at final assembly.

planning bills

pseudo bills

kit number

phantom bills-of-material

PLANNING BILLS AND PHANTOM BILLS. Other special kinds of bills-of-material exist. These include planning bills and phantom bills. **Planning bills** are created in order to assign an artificial parent to the bill-of-material. This is advantageous under two conditions: (1) where we want to group subassemblies together to reduce the number of items to be scheduled, and (2) where we want to issue "kits" to the production department. For instance, it may not be efficient to issue cotter pins with each of numerous subassemblies, so we call them a *kit* and generate a planning bill. The planning bill specifies the *kit* to be issued. A planning bill may also be known as a **pseudo bill** or **kit number. Phantom bills-of-material** are bills-of-material for components, usually subassemblies that exist only temporarily. They go directly into another assembly. Therefore, they are coded to receive special treatment; lead times are zero, and they are handled as an integral part of their parent item. They are never inventoried.

low-level coding

NOTE
Low-level coding ensures that an item is always at the lowest level of usage.

LOW-LEVEL CODING. Low-level coding of an item in a BOM is necessary when identical items exist at various levels in the BOM. **Low-level coding** means the item is coded at the lowest level at which it occurs. For example, item D in Example 1 is coded at the lowest level at which it is used. Item D could be coded as part of B and occur at level 2. But since D is also part of F, and F is level 2, item D becomes a level 3 item. Low-level coding allows easy computing of the requirements of an item. When the BOM has thousands of items and when requirements are frequently recomputed, the ease and speed of computation becomes a major concern.

Accurate Inventory Records

Knowledge of what is in stock is the result of good inventory management, as discussed in Chapter 9. Good inventory management is an absolute necessity for

[3]Dave Garwood, "Stop Before You Use the Bill Processor . . . ," *American Production and Inventory Control Society* (Second Quarter 1970): 73–75.

an MRP system to work. If the firm has not yet achieved at least 99% record accuracy, then material requirements planning will not work.

Purchase Orders Outstanding

Knowledge of outstanding orders should exist as a by-product of well-managed purchasing and inventory control departments. When purchase orders are executed, records of those orders and their scheduled delivery date must be available to production personnel. Only with good purchasing data can managers prepare good production plans and effectively execute an MRP system.

TABLE 10.2 LEAD TIMES FOR PRODUCT A

COMPONENT	LEAD TIME
A	1 week
B	2 weeks
C	1 week
D	1 week
E	2 weeks
F	3 weeks
G	2 weeks

Lead Times for Each Component

Management must determine when products are needed. Only then can it be determined when to purchase, produce, or assemble. This means operations personnel determine wait, move, queue, setup, and run times for each component. When grouped together, these times are called **lead times.** When the bill-of-material for item A (Example 1) is turned on its side and lead times (see Table 10.2) are added to each component (time on the horizontal axis), then we have a time-phased product structure. This is shown in Figure 10.2.

lead times

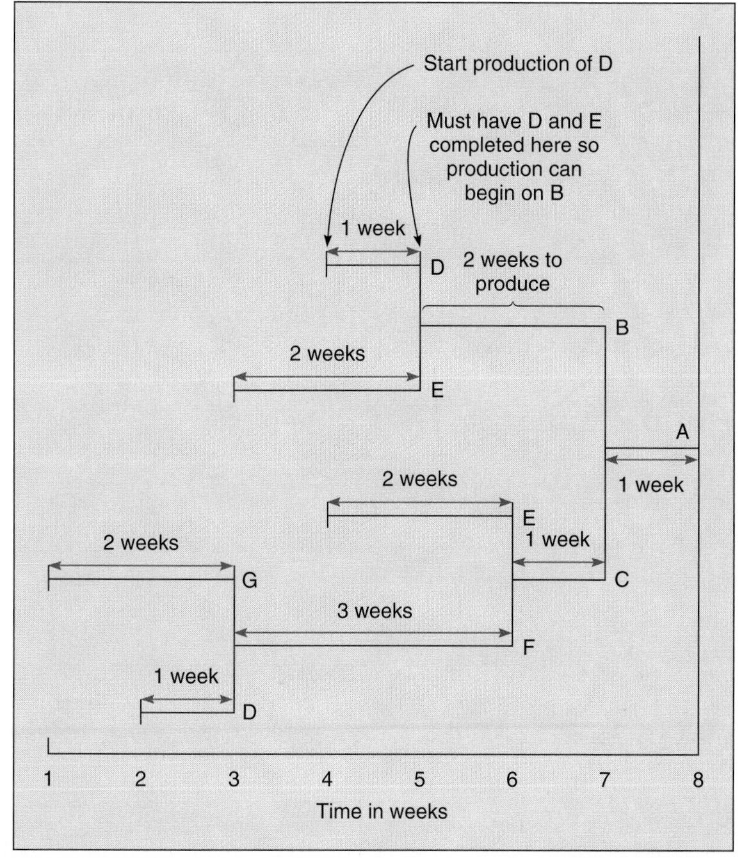

FIGURE 10.2

TIME-PHASED PRODUCT STRUCTURE

BENEFITS OF MRP

In the inventory models of Chapter 9, the questions answered were how much to order and when to order. While dependent demand makes inventory scheduling and planning more complex, it also makes it more beneficial. Some of the benefits of MRP are:

1. Increased customer service and satisfaction.
2. Improved utilization of facilities and labor.
3. Better inventory planning and scheduling.
4. Faster response to market changes and shifts.
5. Reduced inventory levels without reduced customer service.

When applied to repetitive manufacturing, outstanding MRP systems can yield an inventory turnover of 150 times per year.

MRP STRUCTURE

NOTE
MRP software programs are very popular since most manufacturers face dependent demand situations.

Although most MRP systems are computerized, the analysis is straightforward and similar from one computerized system to the next. A master production schedule, a bill-of-material, inventory and purchase records, and lead times for each item are ingredients of a material requirements planning system (see Figure 10.3).

FIGURE 10.3

STRUCTURE OF THE MRP SYSTEM

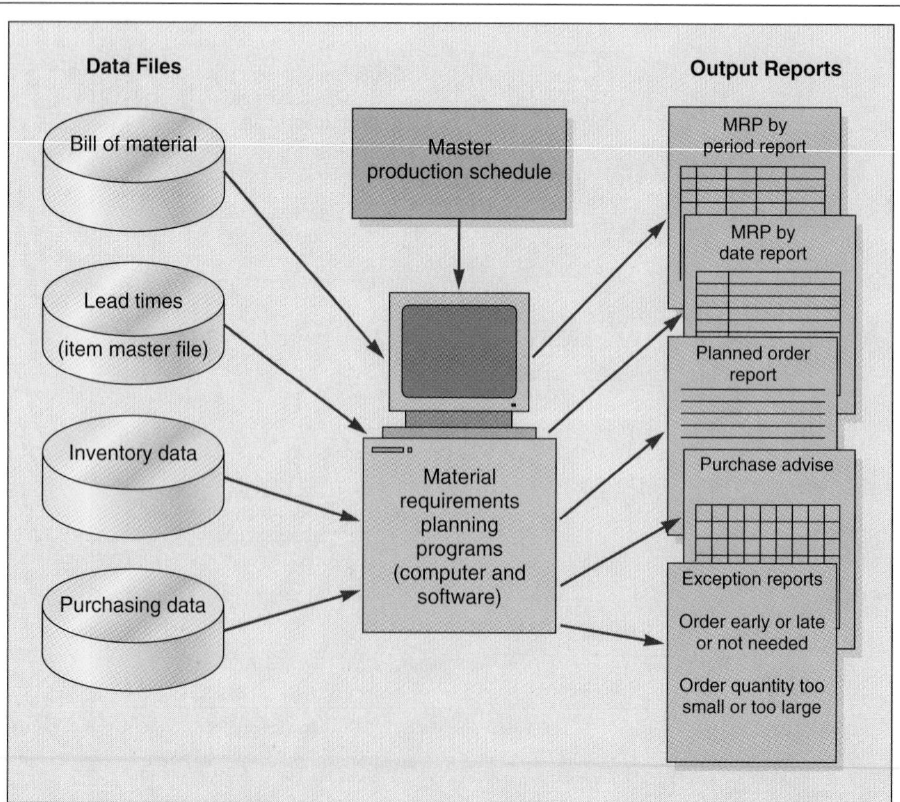

The next step is to construct a gross material requirements plan. The **gross material requirements plan** is a schedule that combines the master production schedule (Table 10.1) and the time-phased schedule (Figure 10.2). It shows when an item must be ordered from suppliers or when the production of an item must be started in order to satisfy the demand for the finished product by a particular date.

gross material requirements plan

EXAMPLE 2

Fun Lawns, Inc. (of Example 1), produces all of the items in product A. The lead times are shown in Table 10.2. Using this information, we construct the gross material requirements plan and draw up a production schedule that will satisfy the demand of 50 units of A by week 8 as shown in Table 10.3.

TABLE 10.3 GROSS MATERIAL REQUIREMENTS PLAN FOR 50 UNITS OF A

	WEEK								
	1	2	3	4	5	6	7	8	LEAD TIME
A. Required date								50	
Order releases							50		1 week
B. Required date							100		
Order releases					100				2 weeks
C. Required date							150		
Order releases						150			1 week
D. Required date					200				
Order releases				200					1 week
E. Required date					300	150			
Order releases			300	150					2 weeks
F. Required date						300			
Order releases			300						3 weeks
D. Required date			600						
Order releases		600							1 week
G. Required date			300						
Order releases	300								2 weeks

The interpretation of the gross material requirements is as follows: if you want 50 units of A at week 8, you must start assembling A in week 7. Thus, in week 7 you will need 100 units of B and 150 units of C. These two items take two weeks and one week, respectively, to produce. Production of B should start in week 5, and production of C should start in week 6 (lead time subtracted from the order release date for these items). Working backward, we can perform the same computations for all of the other items. The material requirements plan graphically reveals when production of each item should begin and end in order to have 50 units of A at week 8.

So far, we have considered *gross material requirements,* which assumes that no inventory is on hand. When inventory is on hand, we perform a *net requirements plan.* When considering on-hand inventory, we must realize that many items in inventory contain subassemblies or parts. If the gross requirement for lawn mowers is 100 units and 20 lawn mowers are on hand, the net requirement for lawn mowers is 80 (that is, 100 − 20). But each lawn mower on hand contains four wheels and one spark plug. As a result, the requirement for wheels drops by 80 wheels (20 lawn mowers on hand × 4 wheels per lawn mower), and the requirement for spark plugs drops by 20 (20 × 1). Therefore, if inventory is on hand for a parent item, the requirements for the parent item and *all its components decrease* because each lawn mower contains the components for lower-level items.

EXAMPLE 3

In Example 1 we developed a product structure from a BOM, and in Example 2 we developed a gross requirements plan. Given the following on-hand inventory, we now construct a net requirements plan.

ITEM	ON HAND
A	10
B	15
C	20
D	10

ITEM	ON HAND
E	10
F	5
G	0

A net material requirements plan includes gross requirements, on-hand inventory, net requirements, planned order receipt, and planned order release for each item. We begin with A and work backward through the components. Shown in the chart on the next page is the net material requirements plan for product A.

The construction of a net requirements plan is similar to construction of the gross requirements plan. Starting with item A, we work backward to determine net requirements for all items. To do these computations we refer to the product structure, on-hand inventory, and lead times. The gross requirement for A is 50 units in week 8. Ten items are on hand; therefore the net requirements and planned order receipt both are 40 items in week 8. Because of the one-week lead time, the planned order release is 40 items in week 7 (see the arrow connecting the order receipt and order release). Referring to week 7 and the product structure in Example 1, we can see 80 (2 × 40) items of B and 120 (3 × 40) items of C are required in week 7 in order to have a total for 50 items of A in week 8. The letter *A* to the right of the gross figure for items B and C was generated as a result of the demand for the parent, A. Performing the same type of analysis for B and C yields the net requirements for D, E, F, and G. Note the on-hand inventory in row E in week 6. It is zero because the on-hand inventory (10 units) was used to make B in week 5. By the same token, the inventory for D was used to make F in week 3.

NET MATERIAL REQUIREMENTS PLAN FOR PRODUCT A (EXAMPLE 3)

LOT SIZE	LEAD TIME (weeks)	ON HAND	SAFETY STOCK	ALLO-CATED	LOW-LEVEL CODE	ITEM IDENTI-FICATION			WEEK							
									1	2	3	4	5	6	7	8
Lot-for-Lot	1	10	—	—	0	A	Gross Requirements									50
							Scheduled Receipts									
							Projected On Hand	10	10	10	10	10	10	10	10	10
							Net Requirements									40
							Planned Order Receipts									40
							Planned Order Releases								40	
Lot-for-Lot	2	15	—	—	1	B	Gross Requirements								80[A]	
							Scheduled Receipts									
							Projected On Hand	15	15	15	15	15	15	15	15	
							Net Requirements								65	
							Planned Order Receipts								65	
							Planned Order Releases						65			
Lot-for-Lot	1	20	—	—	1	C	Gross Requirements								120[A]	
							Scheduled Receipts									
							Projected On Hand	20	20	20	20	20	20	20	20	
							Net Requirements								100	
							Planned Order Receipts								100	
							Planned Order Releases							100		
Lot-for-Lot	2	10	—	—	2	E	Gross Requirements						195[B]	100[C]		
							Scheduled Receipts									
							Projected On Hand	10	10	10	10	10	10			
							Net Requirements						185	100		
							Planned Order Receipts						185	100		
							Planned Order Releases				185	100				
Lot-for-Lot	3	5	—	—	2	F	Gross Requirements							200[C]		
							Scheduled Receipts									
							Projected On Hand	5	5	5	5	5	5	5		
							Net Requirements							195		
							Planned Order Receipts							195		
							Planned Order Releases				195					
Lot-for-Lot	1	10	—	—	3	D	Gross Requirements				390[F]		130[B]			
							Scheduled Receipts									
							Projected On Hand	10	10	10	10					
							Net Requirements				380		130			
							Planned Order Receipts				380		130			
							Planned Order Releases			380		130				
Lot-for-Lot	2	0	—	—	3	G	Gross Requirements				195[F]					
							Scheduled Receipts									
							Projected On Hand				0					
							Net Requirements				195					
							Planned Order Receipts				195					
							Planned Order Releases		195							
							Gross Requirements									
							Scheduled Receipts									
							Projected On Hand									
							Net Requirements									
							Planned Order Receipts									
							Planned Order Releases									

Examples 2 and 3 considered only product A and its completion only in week 8. Fifty units of A were required in week 8. Normally there is a demand for several products. When several product schedules exist, they contribute to one master production schedule and ultimately to one net material requirements plan as shown in Figure 10.4.

MRP MANAGEMENT

The material requirements plan is not static. And since the MRP system increasingly is integrated with JIT, we will now discuss these two issues.

MRP Dynamics

Bills-of-material and material requirements plans are altered by changes in design, schedules, and production processes. Similarly, alterations occur in an MRP system when changes are made to the master production schedule. Regardless of the cause of changes, the MRP model can be manipulated to reflect them. In this manner, up-to-date schedules are possible.

system nervousness

As nice as frequent recomputing of MRP may seem, many firms find they do not want to respond to minor changes even if they are aware of them. These frequent changes generate what is called **system nervousness.** Frequent changes can create havoc in purchasing and production departments if such changes are implemented. Consequently, operations personnel are expected to reduce the nervousness by evaluating the need and impact of changes prior to disseminating requests to other departments.

FIGURE 10.4

SEVERAL SCHEDULES CONTRIBUTING TO A GROSS REQUIREMENTS SCHEDULE FOR B

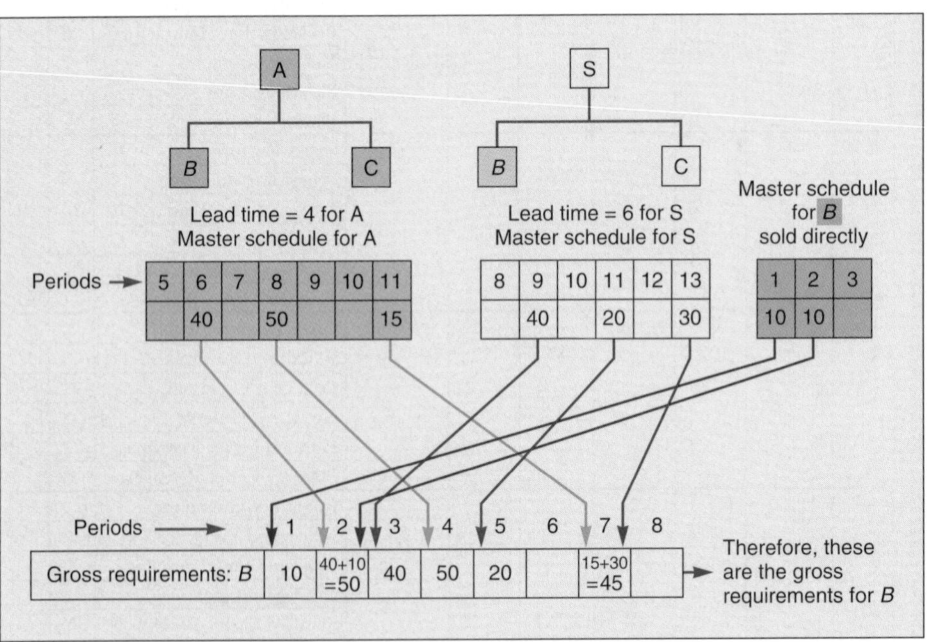

One "B" is in each A and one "B" in each S, and ten Bs are sold directly in week 1 and ten more are sold directly in week 2.

Operations personnel have two tools available to limit system nervousness. The first is the establishment of time fences. **Time fences** allow a segment of the master schedule to be designated as "not to be rescheduled." This segment of the master schedule is thus not changed during the periodic regeneration of schedules. The second tool available is pegging. **Pegging** means tracing upward in the BOM from the component to the parent item. By pegging upward, the production planner can determine the cause for the requirement and make a judgment about the necessity for a change in the schedule.

time fences

pegging

With MRP the operations manager *can* react to the dynamics of the real world. How frequently the manager wishes to impose those changes on the firm requires professional judgment.

MRP and JIT

MRP can be thought of as a planning and scheduling technique, and just-in-time (JIT) can be thought of as a way to move material expeditiously. They can very effectively be integrated. The first step is to reduce the MRP *buckets* from weekly to daily to perhaps hourly. **Buckets** are time units in an MRP system. The examples in this chapter have used weekly *time buckets,* although many firms now use daily or tenths-of-a-day time buckets. Secondly, the planned receipts that are part of a firm's planned orders in an MRP system are communicated to the assembly areas for production purposes and are used to sequence production. Third, inventory is moved through the plant on a JIT basis. Fourth, as products are completed, they are moved into inventory in the normal way. Receipt of these products reduces the quantities required for subsequent firm planned orders in the MRP system. Finally, a system known as **back flush** is used to reduce inventory balances. Back flushing means using the bill-of-materials to reduce inventory based upon completion of a product. In many respects an MRP system combined with JIT within the plant provides the best of both worlds. The combination provides a good master schedule and an accurate picture of requirements from the MRP system plus reduced work-in-process inventory from the use of JIT. However, just the use of MRP with small buckets can be very effective in reducing inventory.

buckets

back flush

Lot-Sizing Techniques

Thus far in our discussion of MRP we have used what is known as a *lot-for-lot* determination of our production units. This is evident in our planned order releases in Example 3 where we produced what we need, and no more and no less. The objective in an MRP system is to produce units only as needed, with no safety stock and no anticipation of further orders. Such a procedure is consistent with small lot sizes, frequent orders, low just-in-time inventory, and dependent demand. However, in cases where the setup costs are significant or where management has been unable to implement a philosophy of JIT, lot-for-lot can be an expensive technique. As we saw in Chapter 9, there are alternative ways of determining lot size, namely, economic order quantity (EOQ). Indeed, there are numerous ways of determining lot sizes in MRP systems. Many commercially available MRP systems include the option of a variety of lot-sizing techniques. We will review a few of them.

LOT-FOR-LOT. Example 3 used a **lot-for-lot** technique where we produced exactly what was required. Example 4 uses the lot-for-lot criterion and determines its cost.

lot-for-lot

EXAMPLE 4

Jet-Ski, Inc. wishes to compute its ordering and carrying cost of inventory on lot-for-lot criterion. The firm has determined that their professional model has a setup cost of $200 and its holding cost is $5.00 per period. The production schedule, as reflected in net requirements, is shown below:

MRP LOT-SIZING PROBLEM: LOT-FOR-LOT TECHNIQUE

		1	2	3	4	5	6
Gross Requirements		35	30	40	0	10	40
Scheduled Receipts							
Projected On Hand	35	0	0	0	0	0	0
Net Requirements		0	30	40	0	10	40
Planned Order Receipts			30	40		10	40
Planned Order Releases			30	40		10	40

Holding costs = $5 per unit per week; setup cost = $200; gross requirements average per week = 25.8; lead time = 0 (immediate delivery).

Shown is the lot-sizing solution using the lot-for-lot technique and its cost. The holding cost is zero, but four separate setups yield a total cost of $800.

ECONOMIC ORDER QUANTITY. As discussed in Chapter 9, EOQ can be used as a lot-sizing technique. But as we indicated there, EOQ is preferable where relatively constant independent demand exists, not where we know the demand. The assumption of our MRP procedure, remember, is that dependent demand is present. Operations managers should take advantage of this information, rather than assuming a constant demand. The EOQ formula *averages* demand over an extended time horizon. EOQ is examined in Example 5.

EXAMPLE 5

Jet Ski, Inc., with a setup cost of $200 and a per-week holding cost of $5, examines its cost with lot sizes based on EOQ criteria. The net requirements and lot sizes using the same requirements as in Example 4 are shown below:

MRP LOT-SIZING PROBLEM: EOQ TECHNIQUE

		1	2	3	4	5	6	7*
Gross Requirements		35	30	40	0	10	40	
Scheduled Receipts								
Projected On Hand	35	35	0	15	20	20	10	15*
Net Requirements		0	30	0	0	0	30	
Planned Order Receipts			45	45			45	
Planned Order Releases			45	45			45	

Holding costs = $5 per unit per week; setup cost = $200; gross requirements average per week = 25.8; lead time = 0 (immediate delivery).
*15 units held in inventory from week 6 to week 7.

Six-week usage equals 155 units; therefore, weekly usage equals 25.8, and 52 weeks (annual usage) equals 1,343 units. From Chapter 9 the EOQ model is:

$$Q^* = \sqrt{\frac{2DS}{H}}$$

where:

$$D = \text{Annual usage} = 1{,}343$$
$$S = \text{Setup cost} = \$200$$
$$H = \text{Holding (carrying) cost, on an annual basis per unit}$$
$$= \$5 \times 52 \text{ weeks} = \$260$$
$$Q^* = 45 \text{ units}$$
$$\text{Setups} = 1{,}343/45 \approx 30 \text{ per year}$$
$$\text{Setup cost} = 30 \times \$200 = \$6{,}000$$
$$\text{Holding cost} = \frac{45}{2} \times (\$5 \times 52 \text{ weeks}) = \$5{,}850$$
$$\text{Setup cost} + \text{Holding cost} = \$6{,}000 + 5{,}850 = \$11{,}850$$

The EOQ solution yields a computed six-week cost of $1,367:

$$\$11{,}850 \times (6 \text{ weeks}/52 \text{ weeks}) = \$1{,}367$$

Notice that Jet Ski's actual holding cost will vary from the computed $1,367, depending upon the rate of actual usage. From the table, we can see that in our six-week example costs really are $600 for three setups, plus a holding cost of 80 units at $5 per week for a total holding cost of $400 (for a total of $1,000). Because usage was not constant, the actual cost was less than the theoretical EOQ ($1,367) but more than the lot-for-lot rule ($800). If any stockouts had occurred, these costs too would need to be added to our actual EOQ of $1,000.

PART PERIOD BALANCING. **Part period balancing (PPB)** is a more dynamic approach to balance setup and holding cost. PPB uses additional information by changing the lot size to reflect requirements of the next lot size in the future. PPB attempts to balance setup and holding costs for known demands. Part period balancing develops an **economic part period (EPP),** which is the ratio of setup cost to holding cost. For Jet Ski, EPP = $200/$5 = 40 units. Therefore, holding 40 units for one period would cost $200, exactly the cost of one setup. Similarly, holding 20 units for two periods also costs $200 (2 periods × $5 × 20 units). PPB merely adds requirements until the number of part periods approximates the EPP, in this case 40. Our PC software, POM for Windows, has a Lot-Sizing module that includes a part-period algorithm. This software yields a net cost of $800 when used to solve for the data in Examples 4 and 5.

part period balancing (PPB)

economic part period (EPP)

WAGNER-WHITIN ALGORITHM. The **Wagner-Whitin procedure** is a dynamic programming model that adds some complexity to the lot-size computation. It assumes a finite time horizon beyond which there are no additional net requirements. It does, however, provide good results. The technique is seldom used in practice, but this may change with increasing understanding and software so-

Wagner-Whitin procedure

phistication. POM for Windows' Lot-Sizing module includes the Wagner-Whitin algorithm. When used to solve the data of Examples 4 and 5, the module yields a cost of $700.

LOT-SIZING SUMMARY. These examples should not lead operations personnel to hasty conclusions about the preferred lot-sizing technique. First, the cost can be altered by changing the scheduled requirements. The resulting costs may not follow the pattern of these examples. Second, in theory a new lot size should be computed with each change anywhere in the MRP hierarchy. In practice, this continuous instability in the planned order schedule is undesirable. The net result is that all lot sizes are wrong because the production system does not respond to such frequent changes. Such changes cause the system nervousness referred to earlier in this chapter.

In general, the lot-for-lot approach should be used wherever economical. Lot-for-lot is the goal. Lots can be modified as necessary for scrap allowances, process constraints (for example, a heat-treating process may require a lot of a given size), or raw material purchase lots (for example, a truckload of chemicals may be available in only one lot size). However, caution should be exercised prior to any modification of lot size because the modification can cause substantial distortion of actual requirements at lower levels in the MRP hierarchy. Where setup costs are significant and the demand is *not* particularly lumpy, part period balancing, Wagner-Whitin, or even EOQ should provide satisfactory results. Too much concern with lot sizing yields false accuracy because of MRP dynamics. A correct lot size can be determined only after the fact, based on what actually happened in terms of requirements.

EXTENSIONS OF MRP

Recent years have seen the development of a number of extensions of MRP. In this section, we review several of them.

CLOSED-LOOP MRP. Closed-loop material requirements planning implies an MRP system that provides feedback to scheduling from the inventory control system. Specifically, a **closed-loop MRP system** provides feedback to the capacity plan, master production schedule, and ultimately to the production plan (as shown earlier in this chapter in Figure 10.1). Virtually all commercial MRP systems are closed-loop.

closed-loop MRP system

CAPACITY PLANNING. In keeping with the definition of closed-loop MRP, load reports are required for each work center. **Load reports** show the resource requirements in a work center for all work currently assigned to the work center, all work planned, and expected orders. Figure 10.5 shows that the initial load in the milling center exceeds capacity in weeks 4 and 6. Closed-loop MRP systems allow production planners to move the work between time periods to smooth the load or at least bring it within capacity. The closed-loop MRP system can then reschedule all items in the net requirements plan. Tactics for smoothing the load and minimizing the impact of changed lead time include the following:

load reports

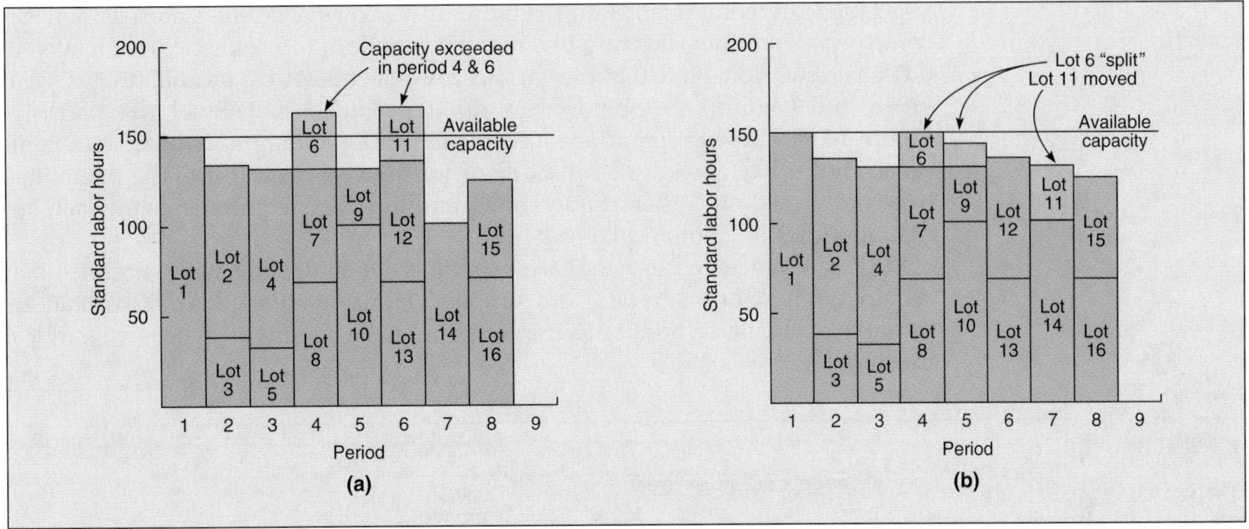

FIGURE 10.5 (a) INITIAL RESOURCE REQUIREMENTS PROFILE FOR A MILLING CENTER (b) SMOOTHED RESOURCE REQUIREMENTS PROFILE FOR A MILLING CENTER

1. *Overlapping*, which reduces the lead time, entails sending pieces to the second operation before the entire lot is completed on the first operation.
2. *Operations splitting*, which sends the lot to two different machines for the same operation. This involves an additional setup, but results in shorter throughput times, since only part of the lot is processed on each machine.
3. *Lot splitting*, which involves breaking up the order and running part of it ahead of schedule.

MATERIAL REQUIREMENTS PLANNING II. Material requirements planning II (MRP II) has substantial applications beyond scheduling and inventory management. It is an extremely powerful technique. Once a firm has MRP in place, inventory data can be augmented by labor hours, by material cost (rather than material quantity), by capital cost, or by virtually any resource variable. When MRP is used this way, it is usually referred to as MRP II, and *resource* is usually substituted for *requirements*. MRP then stands for material *resource* planning.

material requirements planning II (MRP II)

MRP IN SERVICES

The demand for components of many services is dependent. This is the case in institutional kitchens, hospitals, restaurants, and so forth. Additionally, MRP logic is widely used in distribution networks. We now introduce both of these applications.

Restaurant Example

In a restaurant each component of the meal, such as bread and vegetables, is dependent upon the demand for meals. The meal is an end item and the bread and vegetables are component items. Figure 10.6 shows a bill-of-materials and accompanying product structure tree for veal picante, a top-selling entree in a New Orleans restaurant. Note that the various components of veal picante (that is, veal, sauce, and linguini) are prepared by different kitchen personnel (see part *a* of Figure 10.6). These preparations also require different amounts of time to complete. Figure 10.6(c) shows a bill-of-labor for the veal dish. It lists the operations to be performed, the order of operations, and the labor requirements for each operation (types of labor and labor-hours).

MRP is also applied in hospitals, especially when dealing with surgeries that require equipment, materials, and supplies. Houston's Park Plaza Hospital, for example, uses the technique to improve the management of expensive surgical inventory.[4]

FIGURE 10.6

PRODUCT STRUCTURE TREE, BILL-OF-MATERIAL, AND BILL-OF-LABOR FOR VEAL PICANTE

SOURCE: Adapted from John G. Wacker, "Effective Planning and Cost Control for Restaurants," *Production and Inventory Management* (First Quarter 1985): 60.

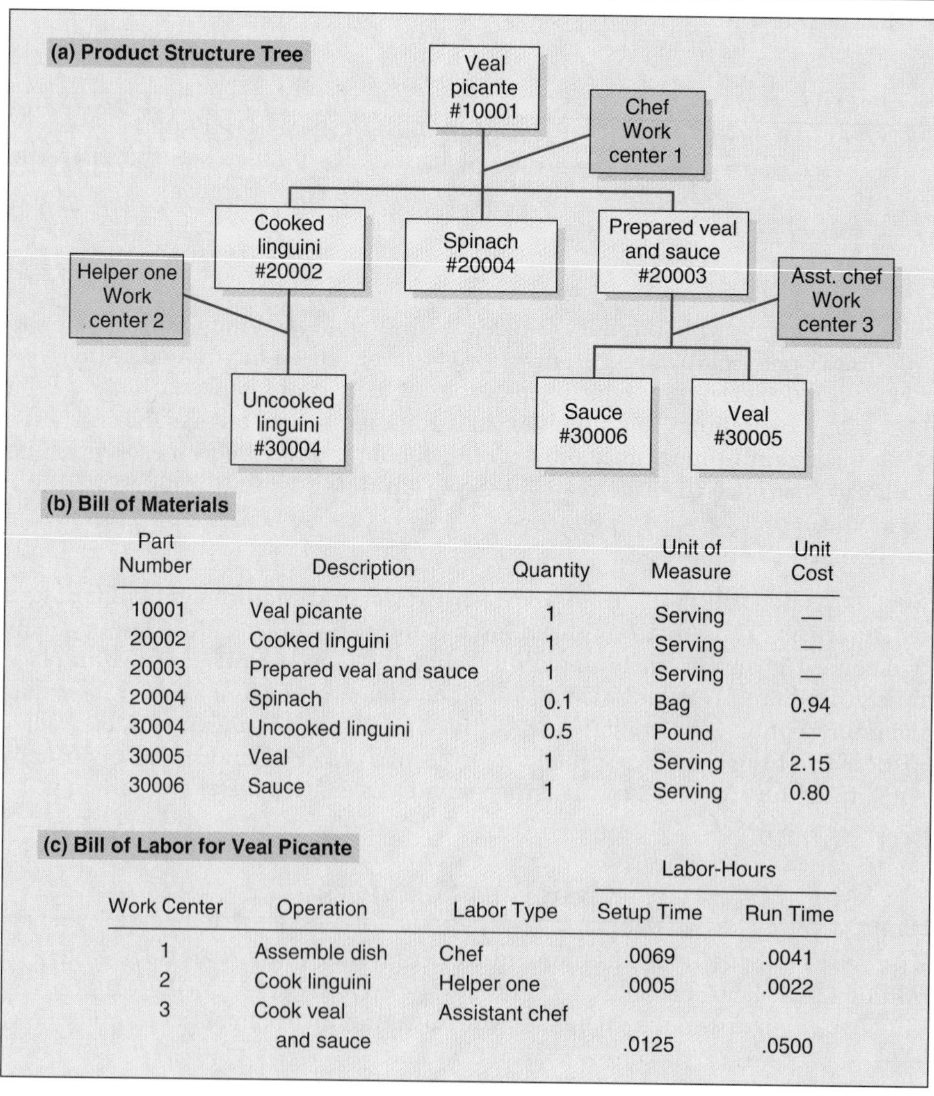

(b) Bill of Materials

Part Number	Description	Quantity	Unit of Measure	Unit Cost
10001	Veal picante	1	Serving	—
20002	Cooked linguini	1	Serving	—
20003	Prepared veal and sauce	1	Serving	—
20004	Spinach	0.1	Bag	0.94
30004	Uncooked linguini	0.5	Pound	—
30005	Veal	1	Serving	2.15
30006	Sauce	1	Serving	0.80

(c) Bill of Labor for Veal Picante

			Labor-Hours	
Work Center	Operation	Labor Type	Setup Time	Run Time
1	Assemble dish	Chef	.0069	.0041
2	Cook linguini	Helper one	.0005	.0022
3	Cook veal and sauce	Assistant chef	.0125	.0500

[4]See E. Steinberg, B. Khumawala, and R. Scamell, "Requirements Planning in the Health Care Environment," *Journal of Operations Management* 2, no. 4 (August 1982): 251–259.

Distribution Example

In a distribution network such as a chain of retail stores, the operations manager must keep the channel supplied with merchandise. The use of distribution resource planning provides a vehicle for doing so. **Distribution resource planning (DRP)** is a time-phased stock replenishment plan for all levels of *a* distribution network. Its procedures and logic are analogous to MRP. DRP requires:

distribution resource planning (DRP)

1. Gross requirements, which are the same as expected demand or sales forecasts.
2. Minimum levels of inventory to meet customer service levels.
3. Accurate lead time.
4. Definition of the distribution structure.

DRP STRUCTURE. When DRP is used, expected demand becomes gross requirements. Net requirements are determined by allocating available inventory to gross requirements. The DRP procedure starts with the forecast at the retail level (or the most distant point of the distribution network being supplied). All other levels are computed. As is the case with MRP, inventory is then reviewed with an aim to satisfying demand. So that stock will arrive when it is needed, net requirements are offset by the necessary lead time. A planned order release quantity becomes the gross requirement at the next level down the distribution chain. The system determines the requirements at each requesting location (say, each retail store) and the total system requirements. Then stock availability and production schedules determine replenishment based on both availability and system demand.

SUMMARY

Material requirements planning (MRP) is the preferred way to schedule production and inventory when demand is dependent. For MRP to work, management must have a master schedule, precise requirements for all components, accurate inventory and purchasing records, and accurate lead times. Production should often be lot-for-lot in an MRP system, given the constraints of ordering and transportation costs. MRP, when properly implemented, can contribute in a major way to reduction in inventory while at the same time improving customer service levels.

KEY TERMS

Material requirements planning (MRP) *(p. 344)*
Master production schedule *(p. 344)*
Bill-of-material (BOM) *(p. 346)*
Modular bills *(p. 348)*
Planning bills *(p. 348)*
Pseudo bills *(p. 348)*
Kit number *(p. 348)*
Phantom bills-of-material *(p. 348)*
Low-level coding *(p. 348)*
Lead times *(p. 349)*
Gross material requirements plan *(p. 351)*
System nervousness *(p. 354)*
Time fences *(p. 355)*
Pegging *(p. 355)*
Buckets *(p. 355)*
Back flush *(p. 355)*
Lot-for-lot *(p. 355)*
Part period balancing (PPB) *(p. 357)*
Economic part period (EPP) *(p. 357)*
Wagner-Whitin procedure *(p. 357)*
Closed-loop MRP system *(p. 358)*
Load reports *(p. 358)*
Material requirements planning II (MRP II) *(p. 359)*
Distribution resource planning (DRP) *(p. 361)*

USING POM FOR WINDOWS TO SOLVE MRP PROBLEMS

Programs 10.1 and 10.2 show the detailed input and output, respectively, for solving Examples 1 to 3 using POM for Windows. Here are the inputs used in Program 10.1:

1. *Item names.* The item names are entered in the left column. The same item name will appear in more than one row if the item is used by two parent items. Each item must follow its parents, as shown in Program 10.1.

2. *Item level.* The level in the indented BOM must be given here. The item *cannot* be placed at a level more than one below the item immediately above.

3. *Lead time.* The lead time for an item is entered here. The default is one week.

4. *Number per parent.* The number of units of this subassembly needed for its parent is entered here. The default is one.

5. *On-hand.* List current inventory on hand once, even if the subassembly is listed twice.

6. *Lot size.* The lot size can be specified here. A 0 or 1 will perform lot-for-lot ordering. If another number is placed here, then all orders for that item will be in integer multiples of that number.

7. *Demands.* The demands are entered in the end item row in the period in which the items are demanded.

8. *Scheduled receipts.* If units are scheduled to be received in the future, they should be listed in the appropriate time period (column) and item (row). (An entry here in level 1 is a demand; all other levels are receipts.)

PROGRAM 10.1

POM FOR WINDOWS' MRP MODULE APPLIED TO EXAMPLES 1, 2, AND 3

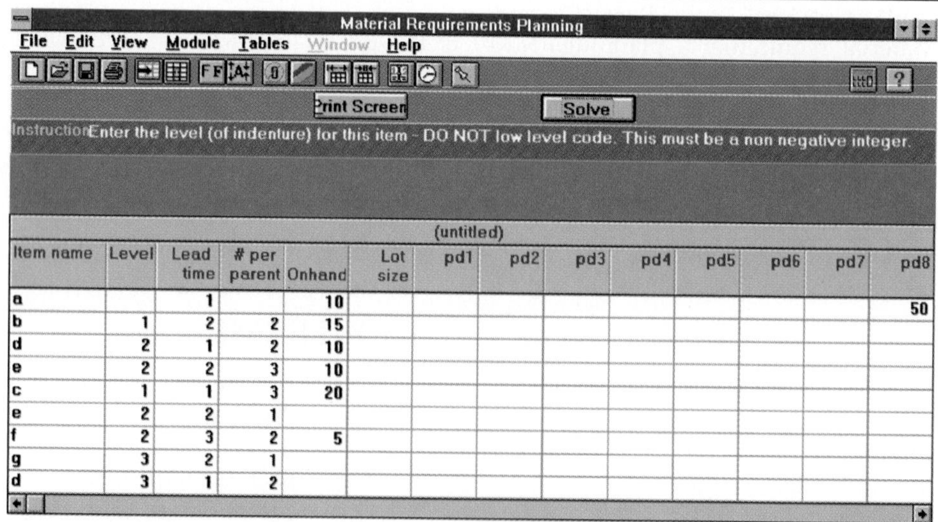

Item name	Level	Lead time	# per parent	Onhand	Lot size	pd1	pd2	pd3	pd4	pd5	pd6	pd7	pd8
a		1		10									50
b	1	2	2	15									
d	2	1	2	10									
e	2	2	3	10									
c	1	1	3	20									
e	2	2	1										
f	2	3	2	5									
g	3	2	1										
d	3	1	2										

POM for Windows' material requirements planning (MRP) module can be used to perform an MRP analysis for up to 18 periods. The data screen shown is generated by indicating the number of lines in the bill-of-materials. In our sample problem, we created a BOM with seven items but nine lines.

Material Requirements Planning - [Material Requirements Planning Results]

File Edit View Module Tables Window Help

Print Screen Edit Data

Instruction:

(untitled) Solution

Item name	pd1	pd2	pd3	pd4	pd5	pd6	pd7	pd8
a								
TOT.REQ.	0.	0.	0.	0.	0.	0.	0.	50.
ON HAND	10.	10.	10.	10.	10.	10.	10.	10.
SchdREC.	0.	0.	0.	0.	0.	0.	0.	0.
NET REQ	0.	0.	0.	0.	0.	0.	0.	40.
ORD REL.	0.	0.	0.	0.	0.	0.	40.	0.
b								
TOT.REQ.	0.	0.	0.	0.	0.	0.	80.	0.
ON HAND	15.	15.	15.	15.	15.	15.	15.	0.
SchdREC.	0.	0.	0.	0.	0.	0.	0.	0.
NET REQ	0.	0.	0.	0.	0.	0.	65.	0.
ORD REL.	0.	0.	0.	0.	65.	0.	0.	0.
d								
TOT.REQ.	0.	0.	390.	0.	130.	0.	0.	0.
ON HAND	10.	10.	10.	0.	0.	0.	0.	0.
SchdREC.	0.	0.	0.	0.	0.	0.	0.	0.
NET REQ	0.	0.	380.	0.	130.	0.	0.	0.
ORD REL.	0.	380.	0.	130.	0.	0.	0.	0.
e								
[illegible]	[illegible]	[illegible]	[illegible]	[illegible]	[illegible]	[illegible]	[illegible]	[illegible]

PROGRAM 10.2

SOLUTION TO MRP RUN ON EXAMPLES 1, 2, AND 3 DATA

The solution for items A, B, and D in Examples 1, 2, and 3 is shown in this output of Program 10.1. The meaning of each item on the left-hand column of the printed output is as follows:

1. *Total required.* The total number of units required in each week is listed in the first row. For the end item, the first row contains the demand schedule that was input on the data screen (Program 10.1). Other requirements are computed.
2. *On hand.* The number on hand is listed here. The on-hand amount starts as given on the data screen and is reduced according to needs.
3. *Scheduled receipt.* The amount that was scheduled in the original data screen is shown here.
4. *Net required.* The net amount required is the amount needed after the on-hand inventory is used.
5. *Order release.* Order release is the net amount required, offset by the lead time.

SOLVED PROBLEM 10.1

Determine the low-level coding and the quantity of each component necessary to produce ten bicycles. The product structure is shown below with the quantities of each component needed for each bicycle noted in parentheses.

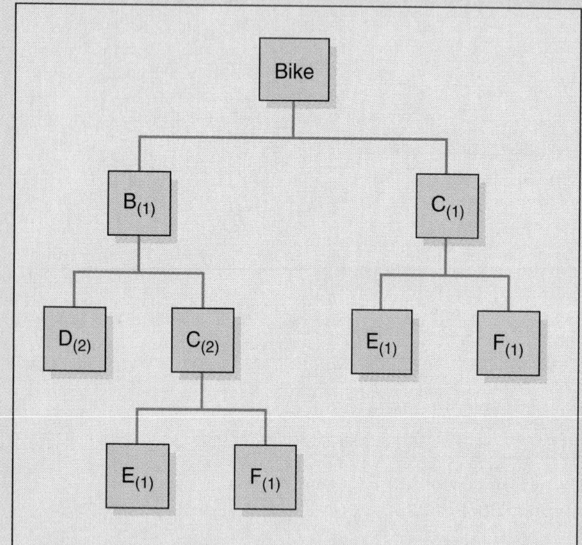

SOLUTION

Redraw the product structure with low-level coding. Then multiply down the structure until the requirements of each branch are determined. Then add across the structure until the total for each is determined.

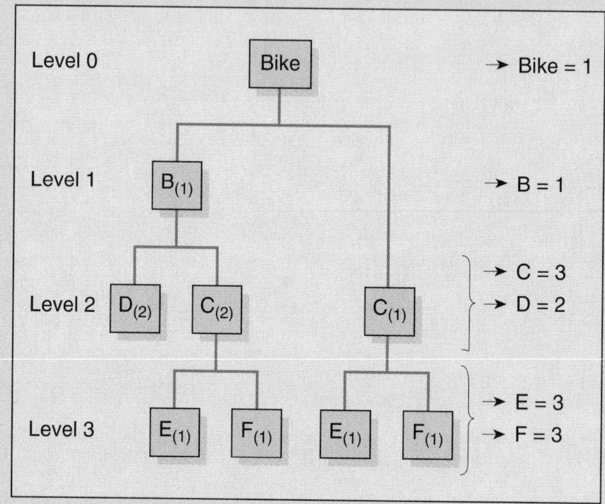

Es required for left branch:

$$(1_{\text{bike}} \times 1_B \times 2_C \times 1_E) = 2$$

plus Es required for right branch:

$$(1_{\text{bike}} \times 1_C \times 1_E) = \underline{1}$$

3 Es required

Then "explode" the requirements by multiplying each by 10 as shown in the following table:

LEVEL	ITEM	QUANTITY PER UNIT	TOTAL REQUIREMENTS FOR TEN BICYCLES
0	Bike	1	10
1	B	1	10
2	C	3	30
2	D	2	20
3	E	3	30
3	F	3	30

SELF-TEST ■ CHAPTER 10

- *Before taking the self-test* refer back to the learning objectives listed at the beginning of the chapter and the key terms listed at the end of the chapter.
- Use the key at the back of the text to *correct* your answers.
- *Restudy* pages that correspond to any questions you answered incorrectly or material you feel uncertain about.

1. Benefits of MRP include
   a. increased customer service and satisfaction
   b. better inventory planning and scheduling
   c. reduced inventory levels without reduced customer service
   d. all of the above
2. The list of quantities of components, ingredients, and materials required to produce a product is the
   a. bill-of-material
   b. engineering change notice
   c. purchase order
   d. all of the above
3. ________ allows a segment of the master schedule to be designated as "not to be rescheduled."
   a. regenerative MRP
   b. system nervousness
   c. pegging
   d. all of the above
   e. none of the above
4. A lot-sizing procedure that assumes a finite time horizon beyond which there are no additional net requirements is
   a. Wagner-Whitin algorithm
   b. part period balancing
   c. economic order quantity
   d. all of the above
5. Breaking up the order and running part of it ahead of schedule is known as
   a. overlapping
   b. operations splitting
   c. lot splitting
   d. all of the above
6. In a product structure diagram
   a. parents are only found at the top level of the diagram
   b. parents are found at every level in the diagram
   c. children are found at every level of the diagram except the top level
   d. all items in the diagrams are both parents and children
   e. all of the above are true
7. The difference between a gross material requirements plan (gross MRP) and a net materials requirements plan (net MRP) is
   a. the gross MRP may not be computerized, but the net MRP must be computerized
   b. the gross MRP includes consideration of the inventory on hand, whereas the net MRP doesn't include the inventory consideration
   c. the net MRP includes consideration of the inventory on hand, whereas the gross MRP doesn't include the inventory consideration
   d. the gross MRP doesn't take taxes into account, whereas the net MRP includes the tax considerations
   e. the net MRP is only an estimate, whereas the gross MRP is used for actual production scheduling
8. To effectively use dependent inventory models, the operations manager needs to know
   a. the master production schedule (which tells what is to be made and when)
   b. the specifications or bill-of-material (which tells how to make the product)
   c. the purchase orders outstanding (which tell what is on order)
   d. the lead times (or how long it takes to get various components)
   e. all of the above
9. A phantom bill-of-material is a bill-of-material developed for
   a. a final product for which production is to be discontinued
   b. a subassembly that exists only temporarily
   c. a module that is a major component of a final product
   d. the purpose of grouping subassemblies when we wish to issue "kits" for later use
10. Which of the following lot-sizing techniques is likely to prove the most complex to use?
    a. economic order quantity (EOQ)
    b. constant order quantity
    c. lot-for-lot
    d. the Wagner-Whitin algorithm
    e. part period balancing (PPB)
11. When a bill-of-material is used in order to assign an artificial parent to a bill-of-material, it is usually called a
    a. modular bill-of-material
    b. pick list
    c. phantom bill-of-material
    d. planning bill-of-material
12. The five requirements for an effective dependent inventory model (MRP) are
    a. ______, b. ______, c. ______, d. ______, e. ______.
13. A net material requirements plan differs from a gross requirements plan because it includes ________________.
14. The operations manager has several tools available to deal with MRP system nervousness; those tools are
    a. buckets and back flush
    b. net and gross requirements
    c. time fences and pegging
    d. pseudo bills and kits
15. If it is economical, the best lot-sizing technique to be used for MRP is ________________.

DISCUSSION QUESTIONS

1. How does the logic of DRP follow the logic of MRP?
2. Once a material requirements plan (MRP) has been established, what other managerial applications might be found for the technique?
3. How does MRP II differ from MRP?
4. Which is the best lot-sizing policy for manufacturing organizations?
5. What do we mean by closed-loop MRP?

OPERATIONS IN PRACTICE EXERCISE

The very structure of MRP systems suggests fixed lead times. However, many firms are moving toward JIT techniques. What are the issues and the impact of adding JIT inventory and purchasing techniques to an organization that has MRP?

PROBLEMS

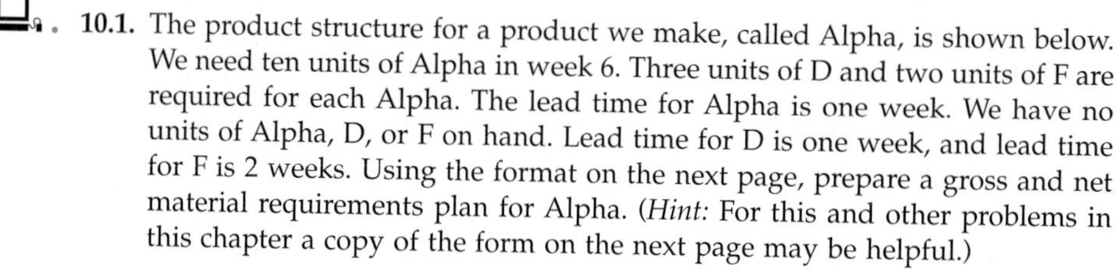

10.1. The product structure for a product we make, called Alpha, is shown below. We need ten units of Alpha in week 6. Three units of D and two units of F are required for each Alpha. The lead time for Alpha is one week. We have no units of Alpha, D, or F on hand. Lead time for D is one week, and lead time for F is 2 weeks. Using the format on the next page, prepare a gross and net material requirements plan for Alpha. (*Hint:* For this and other problems in this chapter a copy of the form on the next page may be helpful.)

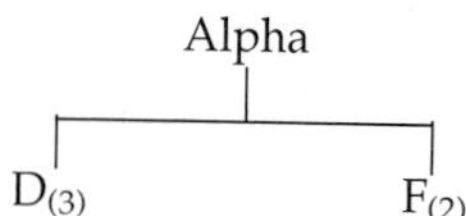

: **10.2.** The demand for subassembly S is 100 units in week 7. Each unit of S requires one unit of T and .5 units of U. Each unit of T requires one unit of V, two units of W, and one unit of X. Finally, each unit of U requires .5 units of Y and three units of Z. One firm manufactures all items. It takes two weeks to make S, one week to make T, two weeks to make U, two weeks to make V, three weeks to make W, one week to make X, two weeks to make Y, and one week to make Z.

a. Construct a product structure and a gross material requirements plan for the dependent inventory items. Identify all levels, parents, and components.

b. Construct a net material requirements plan from the product structure and the following on-hand inventory:

ITEM	ON-HAND INVENTORY	ITEM	ON-HAND INVENTORY
S	20	W	30
T	20	X	25
U	10	Y	15
V	30	Z	10

: **10.3.** In addition to 100 units of S (per Problem 10.2), there is also a demand for 20 units of U, which is a component of S. The 20 units of U are needed for maintenance purposes. These units are needed one week before S, in week 6. Modify the gross and net material requirements plan to reflect this change.

LOT SIZE	LEAD TIME (weeks)	ON HAND	SAFETY STOCK	ALLO-CATED	LOW-LEVEL CODE	ITEM IDENTI-FICATION		PERIOD (week, day)							
								1	2	3	4	5	6	7	8
							Gross Requirements								
							Scheduled Receipts								
							Projected On Hand								
							Net Requirements								
							Planned Order Receipts								
							Planned Order Releases								
							Gross Requirements								
							Scheduled Receipts								
							Projected On Hand								
							Net Requirements								
							Planned Order Receipts								
							Planned Order Releases								
							Gross Requirements								
							Scheduled Receipts								
							Projected On Hand								
							Net Requirements								
							Planned Order Receipts								
							Planned Order Releases								
							Gross Requirements								
							Scheduled Receipts								
							Projected On Hand								
							Net Requirements								
							Planned Order Receipts								
							Planned Order Releases								
							Gross Requirements								
							Scheduled Receipts								
							Projected On Hand								
							Net Requirements								
							Planned Order Receipts								
							Planned Order Releases								
							Gross Requirements								
							Scheduled Receipts								
							Projected On Hand								
							Net Requirements								
							Planned Order Receipts								
							Planned Order Releases								
							Gross Requirements								
							Scheduled Receipts								
							Projected On Hand								
							Net Requirements								
							Planned Order Receipts								
							Planned Order Releases								

10.4. Given the bill-of-material, master production schedule, and inventory status, on p. 368 develop: (a) a gross requirements plan for all items, and (b) net material requirements (planned order release) for all items.

MASTER PRODUCTION SCHEDULE: X1

PERIOD	7	8	9	10	11	12
GROSS REQUIREMENTS:		50		20		100

ITEM	LEAD TIME	ON HAND	ITEM	LEAD TIME	ON HAND
X1	1	50	C	3	10
B1	2	20	D	1	0
B2	2	20	E	1	0
A1	1	5			

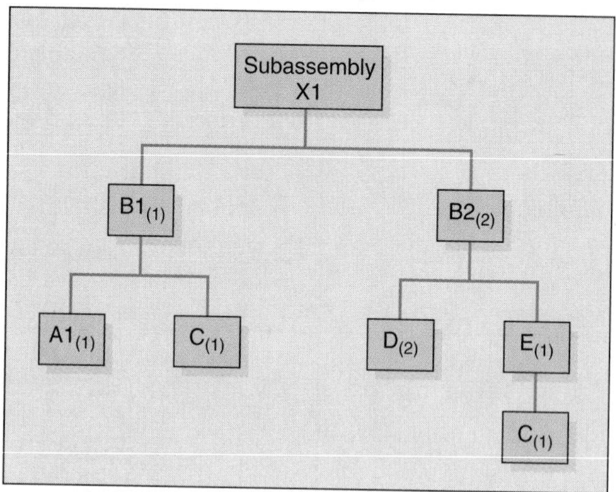

Problems 10.5 and 10.6 use the data shown below and on the top of the next page.

DATA FOR PROBLEMS 10.5 AND 10.6

PERIOD		8	9	10	11	12
GROSS REQUIREMENTS:	A	100		50		150
GROSS REQUIREMENTS:	H		100		50	

ITEM	ON HAND	LEAD TIME	ITEM	ON HAND	LEAD TIME
A	0	1	F	75	2
B	100	2	G	75	1
C	50	2	H	0	1
D	50	1	J	100	2
E	75	2	K	100	2

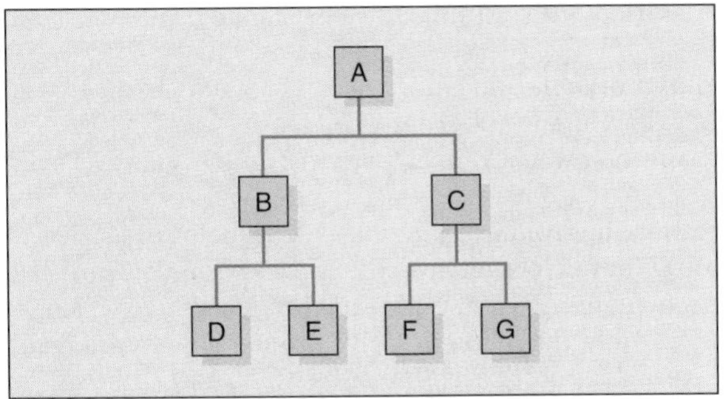

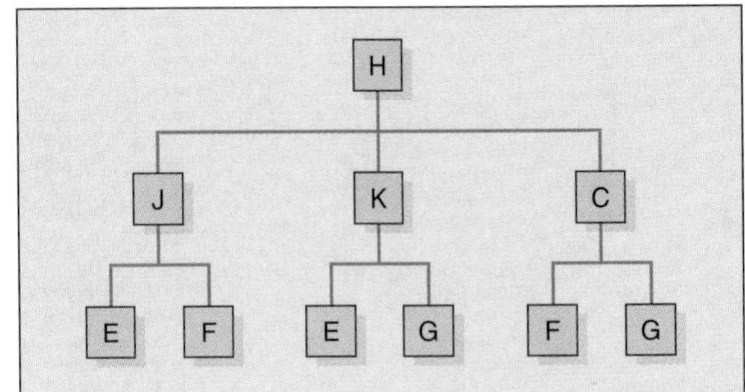

Figures for Problems 10.5 and 10.6.

10.5. Given the bill-of-material, master production schedule, and inventory status shown earlier, develop (a) a gross requirements plan for C, (b) a planned order release for C.

10.6. Based on the preceding data, complete a net planned order release schedule for all items (ten schedules in all).

Problems 10.7 and 10.8 are based on an item that has the gross requirements shown in the following table and a beginning inventory of 40 units.

DATA FOR PROBLEMS 10.7 AND 10.8

PERIOD	1	2	3	4	5	6	7	8	9	10	11	12
GROSS REQUIREMENTS:	30		40		30	70	20		10	80		50

Holding cost = \$2.50 per unit per week; setup cost = \$150; lead time = 1 week

10.7. Develop a lot-for-lot solution and calculate total relevant costs.

10.8. (a) Develop an EOQ solution and calculate total relevant costs. Stockout costs equal \$10 per unit. (b) Solve 10.8(a) with lead time = 0.

10.9. Given the following product tree:

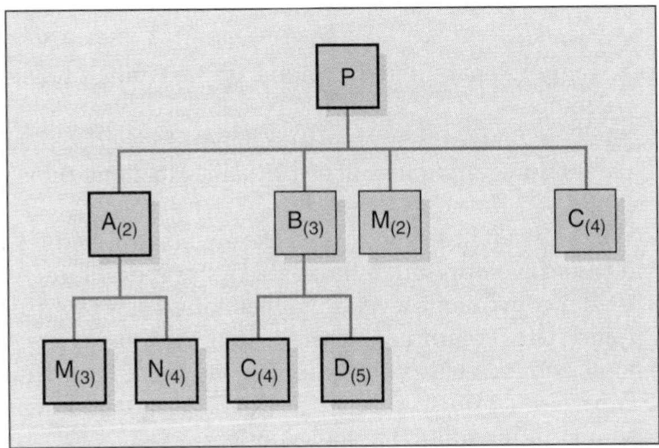

a. If 17 P's are needed and no on-hand inventory exists, how many C's are required?
b. If 17 P's are needed and on-hand inventory consists of 10 A's, 15 B's, 20 C's, 12 M's, and 5 N's, how many C's are required?
c. If 17 P's are needed and no on-hand inventory exists, how many M's are required?

10.10. Keebock, a maker of outstanding running shoes, keeps the soles of its size 13 running shoes in inventory for one period at a cost of $.25 per unit. The setup costs are $50. Beginning inventory is zero and lead time is one week; stock-out cost is $5 per unit. Shown in the following table are the net requirements per period. Determine Keebock's cost based on:
a. EOQ.
b. Lot-for-lot.

DATA FOR PROBLEM 10.10

PERIOD	0	1	2	3	4	5	6	7	8	9	10
NET REQUIREMENTS		35	30	45	0	10	40	30	0	30	55

Background for Problems 10.11 through 10.14
Problems 10.11 through 10.14 are based on the data shown in the following table. The parent item has a one-week lead time, and the lot-for-lot rule is employed. Beginning inventory is 20 units. The parent item has a component whose lead time is also one week and whose starting inventory position is 30 units. At the component level, production occurs in lot sizes to cover three periods of net requirements.

DATA FOR PROBLEMS 10.11 THROUGH 10.14

PERIOD	1	2	3	4	5	6	7	8	9	10
GROSS REQUIREMENTS	0	40	30	40	10	70	40	10	30	60

10.11. Develop the parent and component MRP tables to show the original planned positions.

10.12. At the parent level, gross requirements for period 2 are canceled. Develop the parent and component net MRP tables to show the net effect of this cancellation.

10.13. With the parent-level gross requirements canceled for period 2, what is the effect on inventory quantity, setup costs, and holding costs?

10.14. At the component level, there is enough capacity to produce 75 units in period 1. Gross requirements at the parent level increase from 40 units to 50 units in period 2. What problem arises? What solution would you recommend?

10.15. A part structure, lead time (weeks), and on-hand quantities for product A are shown in the following table.

DATA FOR PROBLEMS 10.15, 10.16, 10.17

PART	INVENTORY ON HAND
A	0
B	2
C	10
D	5
E	4
F	5
G	1
H	10

PART STRUCTURE TREE

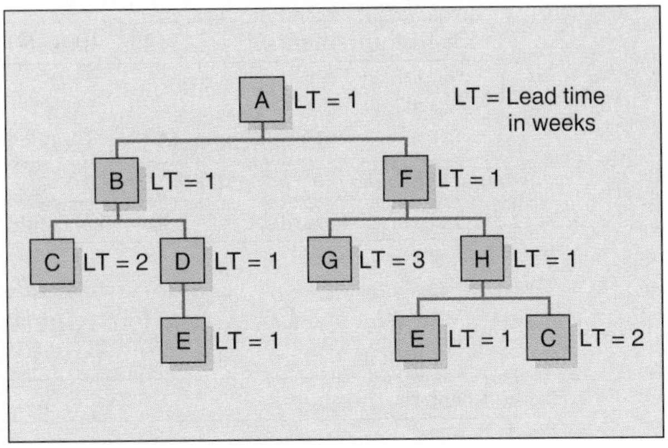

From the information shown, generate:

a. An indented bill-of-material for product A (see Figure 4.9a).
b. A bill-of-material showing the quantity of each part required to produce one A.
c. An exploded bill-of-material showing the quantity of each part required to produce ten A's.
d. Net requirements for each part to produce ten A's in week 8, using lot-for-lot.

(*Hint:* POM for Windows can help with b and c, but cannot produce an output other than in MRP format.)

10.16. You are product planner for product A (in Problem 10.15). The field service manager, "Speedy" Senna, has just called and told you that the requirements for B and F should each be increased by ten units for his repair requirements in the field.

a. Prepare an exploded bill-of-material showing the quantity of each part required to produce the requirements for the service manager and the production request of ten.
b. What are the net requirements (that is, exploded bill-of-material) less on-hand inventory?
c. Prepare a net requirement plan by date for the new requirements (for both production and field service), assuming that the field service manager wants his ten units in week 6 and the ten production units are still due in week 8.

10.17. You have just been notified via FAX that the lead time for component G of product A (Problem 10.16) has just been increased to four weeks.

a. Which items have changed and why?
b. What are the implications for the production plan?
c. As production planner, what can you do?

10.18. As director of operations, you have recently installed a distribution requirements planning (DRP) system. The company has an East Coast and a West Coast warehouse, as well as a main factory warehouse in Omaha, Nebraska. You have just received the orders for the next planning period from the managers at each of the three facilities. Their reports follow. The lead time to both the East Coast and the West Coast warehouses is two weeks and there is a one-week lead time to bring material to the factory warehouse. Shipments are in truckload quantities of 100 each. There is no initial inventory in the system.

The factory is having trouble installing the level of material work schedule and still has a lot size in multiples of 100.

DATA FOR EAST COAST WAREHOUSE

PERIOD	1	2	3	4	5	6	7	8	9	10	11	12
Forecast requirements			40	100	80	70	20	25	70	80	30	50

Lead time = 2 weeks

DATA FOR WEST COAST WAREHOUSE

PERIOD	1	2	3	4	5	6	7	8	9	10
Forecast requirements		30	45	60	70	40	80	70	80	55

Lead time = 2 weeks

DATA FOR FACTORY WAREHOUSE

PERIOD	1	2	3	4	5	6	7	8	9	10
Forecast requirements			30	40	10	70	40	10	30	60

Lead time = 1 week

a. Show the plan for *receipt* of orders from the factory.
b. If the factory requires two weeks to produce the merchandise, when must the orders be *released* to the factory?

Internet Data Base Application

See our website at http://www.prenhall.com/renderpom for a challenging, computer-based problem.

CASE STUDY

Service, Inc.

Service, Inc., is a distributor of automotive replacement parts. With no manufacturing capability, all products it sells are purchased, assembled, and repackaged. Service, Inc., does have extensive inventory and final assembly facilities. Among its products are private-label carburetor and ignition kits. The company has been experiencing difficulties for the last two years. First, profits have fallen considerably. Second, customer service levels have declined, with late deliveries now exceeding 25% of orders. Third, customer returns have been rising at a rate of 3% per month.

Bob Hass, vice president of sales, claims that most of the problem lies with the assembly department. He says that they are not producing the proper mix of the product, they have poor quality control, their productivity has fallen, and their costs are too high.

Dick Houser, the treasurer, believes that problems have arisen due to investment in the wrong inventories. He thinks that marketing has too many options and products. Houser also thinks that the purchasing department buyers have been hedging their inventories and requirements with excess purchasing commitments.

John Burnham, assembly manager, says, "The symptom is that we have a lot of parts in inventory, but no place to assemble them in the production schedule." An additional comment by Burnham was, "When we have the right part, it is not very good, but we use it anyway to meet the schedule."

Freddy Fearon, manager of purchasing, has taken the stance that purchasing has not let Service, Inc., down. He has stuck by his old suppliers, used historical data to determine requirements, maintained what he views as excellent prices from suppliers, and evaluated new sources of supply with an aim of lowering costs. Where possible, Fearon reacted to the increased pressure for profitability by emphasizing low cost and early delivery.

You are the president of Service, Inc., and must get the firm back on a course toward improved profitability.

DISCUSSION QUESTIONS

1. Identify both the symptoms and problems at Service, Inc.
2. What specific changes would you implement?

BIBLIOGRAPHY

Berry, W. L. "Lot Sizing Procedures for Requirements Planning Systems: A Framework for Analysis." *Production and Inventory Management* 13, no. 2 (1972).

Cerveny, R. P., and L. W. Scott. "A Survey of MRP Implementation." *Production and Inventory Management* 30, no. 3 (Third Quarter 1989): 31–34.

Dolinsky, L. R., T. E. Vollmann, and M. J. Maggard. "Adjusting Replenishment Orders to Reflect Learning in a Material Requirements Planning Environment." *Managerial Science* 36 (December 1990): 1532–1547.

Freeland, J. R., J. P. Leschke, and E. N. Weiss. "Guidelines for Setup Cost Reduction Programs to Achieve Zero Inventory." *Journal of Operations Management* 9 (January 1990): 85.

Haddock, J., and D. E. Hubicki. "Which Lot-Sizing Techniques Are Used in Material Requirements Planning?" *Production and Inventory Management* 30 (Third Quarter 1989): 57.

Karmarkar, U. "Getting Control of Just-in-Time." *Harvard Business Review* 71, (September-October 1989): 122–133.

Martin, A. J. *DRP: Distribution Resource Planning.* Englewood Cliffs, NJ: Prentice-Hall, 1983.

St. John, R. "The Evils of Lot Sizing in MRP." *Production and Inventory Management* 25 (Fourth Quarter 1984): 75–85.

Wagner, H. M., and T. M. Whitin. "Dynamic Version of the Economic Lot Size Model." *Management Science* 5, no. 1 (1958).

Just-in-Time Systems

11

CHAPTER OUTLINE

Just-in-Time Attacks Waste and Variability

Waste Reduction ■ Variability Reduction ■ Pull versus Push

Suppliers

Goals of JIT Partnerships ■ Concerns of Suppliers

JIT Layout

Distance Reduction ■ Increased Flexibility ■ Impact on Employees ■ Reduced Space and Inventory

Inventory

Hidden Variability ■ Inventory Reduction ■ Small Lots Essential ■ Setup Costs Driven Down

Scheduling

Level Material-Use Schedules ■ Kanban

Quality

Employee Empowerment

JIT in Services

Summary ■ *Key Terms* ■ *Discussion Questions* ■ *Self-Test Chapter 11* ■ *Operations in Practice Exercise* ■ *Case Study: Electronic Systems, Inc.* ■ *Bibliography*

LEARNING OBJECTIVES

When you complete this chapter you should be able to:

IDENTIFY OR DEFINE:

Kanban
Variability

DESCRIBE OR EXPLAIN:

Just-in-Time Philosophy
Pull systems
Push systems
The goals of JIT Partnerships
The impact of JIT on layout
How JIT affects quality and employees

just-in-time

Just-in-Time (JIT) is a philosophy of continuous and forced problem solving that drives out waste. Because the benefits of JIT are so pervasive, it can yield a competitive advantage. General Motors' tool and die plant in Lordstown, Ohio, is a typical example of the JIT drive for leanness. Thick rolls of steel, trucked in from the mills of Wheeling and Pittsburgh, arrive just as needed for the stamping out of Cadillac trunk lids, Saturn fenders, and Buick headlight brackets. To eliminate the costly stockpiling of parts, supplies are kept so tight that sometimes helicopters have to fly in and out with deliveries.[1] GM is using JIT, as are many other organizations, in its drive for continuous improvement.

JUST-IN-TIME ATTACKS WASTE AND VARIABILITY

As a continuous improvement system, JIT attacks waste and the variability that contributes to waste.

Waste Reduction

When we talk about waste in the production of goods or services, we are describing anything that does not add value. Products being stored, inspected, or delayed, products waiting in queues, and defective products do not add value; they are 100% waste. Moreover, any activity that does not add value to a product *from the customer's perspective* is waste. JIT speeds up production throughput, which allows faster delivery times and reduces work-in-process. Reducing work-in-process releases assets now in inventory for other more productive purposes.

Variability Reduction

variability

To achieve just-in-time material movement, managers *reduce variability caused by both internal and external factors.* **Variability** is any deviation from the optimum process that delivers perfect product on time every time. Inventory hides variability—a polite word for problems. The less variability in the system, the less waste in the system. Most variability is caused by tolerating waste or by poor management. Variability occurs because:

1. Employees, machines, and suppliers produce units that do not conform to standards, are late, or are not the proper quantity.
2. Engineering drawings or specifications are inaccurate.
3. Production personnel try to produce before drawings or specifications are complete.
4. Customer demands are unknown.

While these are some of the causes of variability, variability can often go unseen when inventory exists because inventory hides problems. This is why JIT is so effective. The JIT philosophy of continuous improvement removes variability. The removal of variability allows us to move good materials just-in-time for use. JIT reduces material throughout the supply chain. This reduces waste and helps us add value at each stage. Table 11.1 outlines the contributions of JIT; we discuss each of these concepts in this chapter.

[1] *The Wall Street Journal*, June 26, 1993, p. A-1.

TABLE 11.1 JIT Contributes to Competitive Advantage

JIT REQUIRES:	
Suppliers:	Reduced number of vendors Supportive supplier relationships Quality deliveries on time
Layout:	Work-cell layouts with testing at each step of the process Group technology Movable or changeable machinery High level of workplace organization and neatness Reduced space for inventory Delivery directly to work areas
Inventory:	Small lot sizes Low setup time Specialized bins for holding set number of parts
Scheduling:	Zero deviation from schedules Level schedules Suppliers informed of schedules Kanban techniques
Preventive maintenance:	Scheduled Daily routine Operator involvement
Quality production:	Statistical process control Quality by suppliers Quality within the firm
Employee empowerment:	Empowered and cross-trained employees Few job classifications to ensure flexibility of employees Training support
Commitment	Support of management, employees, and suppliers
	WHICH RESULTS IN:
	Queue and delay reduction, which speeds throughput, frees assets, and wins orders Quality improvement, which reduces waste and wins orders Cost reduction, which increases margin or reduces selling price Variability reduction in the workplace, which reduces wastes and wins orders Rework reduction, which reduces wastes and wins orders
	WHICH YIELDS:
	Faster response to the customer at lower cost and higher quality— A Competitive Advantage

Pull versus Push

pull system

The concept behind JIT is that of a "pull" system. JIT is a **pull system** that produces one unit *pulled* to where it is needed just as it is needed. A pull system uses signals to request delivery from upstream stations to the station that has production facilities available. These stations use signals to pull material as there is capacity to process the material. This concept is used within the immediate production process and with suppliers. By *pulling* material through the system in very small lots just as it is needed, the cushion of inventory that hides problems is removed. With inventory removed, problems become evident and continuous improvement is emphasized. By removing the cushion of inventory, both investment in inventory and manufacturing cycle time are reduced. **Manufacturing cycle time** is the time between when raw materials are received and when the finished product rolls out the door. For example, at Northern Telecom, a phone switching system producer, materials are pulled directly from qualified suppliers to the assembly line. This effort reduced Northern's receiving cycle time from three weeks to just four hours, the incoming inspection staff from 47 to 24, and problems on the shop floor caused by defective materials by 97%.[2]

manufacturing cycle time

push system

Many firms still move material through their facilities in a "push" fashion. A **push system** dumps orders on the processing department to be worked on when an opportunity presents itself. In a push system material is *pushed* into downstream workstations regardless of the resources available. Push systems are the antithesis of JIT.

SUPPLIERS

NOTE
To get JIT to work, the purchasing agent must communicate the company's goal to the supplier. This includes delivery, packaging, lot sizes, returns, etc.

In many production processes, incoming material is delayed at the shipping point, in transit, and at receiving departments. Similarly, finished goods are stored or held at warehouses prior to shipment to distributors or customers. Holding inventory in these ways is wasteful, and JIT is directed toward the reduction of waste. This includes waste present in the supply system, receiving, and incoming inspection. This waste often takes the form of excess inventory, poor quality, and delay.

JIT partnerships

JIT partnerships exist when supplier and purchaser work together with a mutual goal of removing the waste and driving down costs. Such relationships are critical for successful JIT. Every *moment* material is held should add value, and every *movement* of material should add value. To ensure this is the case, Xerox, like other leading organizations, views the supplier as an extension of its own organization. Because of this view, the Xerox staff expects suppliers to be as fully committed to improvement as Xerox. This requires a high degree of openness[3] by both supplier and purchaser. Table 11.2 shows the characteristics of JIT partnerships.

Goals of JIT Partnerships

The Goals of JIT Partnerships:

1. *Elimination of unnecessary activities.* For instance, receiving activity and incoming inspection activity are unnecessary under JIT with good suppliers.

[2]Roy Merrils, "How Northern Telecom Competes on Time," *Harvard Business Review* 67 (July-August 1989): 108–114.
[3]J. Douglas Blocher, Charles W. Lackey, and Vincent A. Mabert, "From JIT Purchasing to Supplier Partnerships at Xerox" *Target* 9, no. 3 (May-June 1993): 12–18.

TABLE 11.2 CHARACTERISTICS OF JIT PARTNERSHIPS

SUPPLIERS
Few suppliers
Nearby suppliers
Repeat business with same suppliers
Analysis to enable desirable suppliers to become or to stay price competitive
Competitive bidding mostly limited to new purchases
Buyer resists vertical integration and subsequent wipeout of supplier business
Suppliers encouraged to extend JIT buying to *their* suppliers
QUANTITIES
Steady output rate
Frequent deliveries in small-lot quantities
Long-term contract agreements
Minimal paperwork to release orders
Delivery quantities fixed for whole contract term
Little or no permissible overage or underage
Suppliers package in exact quantities
Suppliers reduce their production lot sizes (or store unreleased material)
QUALITY
Minimal product specifications imposed on supplier
Help suppliers to meet quality requirements
Close relationships between buyers' and suppliers' quality assurance people
Suppliers use process control charts instead of lot-sampling inspection
SHIPPING
Scheduling of inbound freight
Gain control by use of company-owned or contract shipping and warehousing

SOURCE: Adapted from Richard J. Schonberger and James P. Gilbert, "Just-in-Time Purchasing: a Challenge for U.S. Industry." Copyright © 1983 by The Regents of the University of California. Reprinted from the *California Management Review* 26, no. 1, by permission of The Regents.

2. *Elimination of in-plant inventory.* JIT delivers materials where and when needed. Raw material inventory is necessary only if there is reason to believe that suppliers are undependable. Likewise, parts or components for processing at some intermediate state should be delivered in small lots directly to the using department as needed.
3. *Elimination of in-transit inventory.* General Motors once estimated that at any given time over one-half of its inventory is in transit. Modern purchasing departments, such as General Motors, are now addressing in-transit inventory reduction by encouraging suppliers and prospective suppliers to locate near the plant and provide frequent small shipments. The shorter the flow of material in the resource "pipeline," the less inventory. Inventory can also be reduced by a technique known as *consignment.* Under a **consignment inventory** arrangement, the supplier maintains the title to the inventory until it is used. For instance, an assembly plant may find a hardware supplier that is willing to locate its warehouse where the user currently has its stockroom. In this manner, when hardware is needed, it is no farther than the stockroom, and the supplier can ship to other, perhaps smaller, purchasers from

consignment inventory

Many services have adopted JIT techniques as a normal part of their business. Most restaurants, and certainly all fine dining restaurants, expect and receive JIT deliveries. Both buyer and supplier expect fresh, high-quality produce delivered without fail just when it is needed. The system doesn't work any other way.

the "stockroom." The supplier bills the user based on the signed pick-up receipt or number of units shipped.

4. *Elimination of poor suppliers.* When a firm reduces the number of suppliers, it increases long-term commitments. To obtain improved quality and reliability, vendors and purchasers have mutual understanding and trust. Achieving deliveries only when needed, in the exact quantities needed, also requires perfect quality, or as it is also known, zero-defects, and of course, both the supplier and the delivery system must be excellent.

Concerns of Suppliers

To establish JIT partnerships, several supplier concerns[4] must be addressed. The supplier concerns include:

1. *Desire for diversification.* Many suppliers do not want to tie themselves to long-term contracts with one customer. The suppliers' perception is that they reduce their risk if they have a variety of customers.
2. *Poor customer scheduling.* Many suppliers have little faith in the purchaser's ability to reduce orders to a smooth, coordinated schedule.
3. *Engineering changes.* Frequent engineering changes, with inadequate lead time for suppliers to carry out tooling and process changes, play havoc with JIT.
4. *Quality assurance.* Production with "zero-defects" is not considered realistic by many suppliers.

[4]This summary is based on a study by Tom Schmitt and Mary Connors, "A Survey of Suppliers' Attitudes Toward the Establishment of JIT," *Operations Management Review* 3, no. 4 (Summer 1985): 36.

5. *Small lot sizes.* Suppliers often have processes designed for large lot sizes, and they see frequent delivery to the customer in small lots as a way to transfer holding costs to the supplier.
6. *Proximity.* Depending upon the customer's location, frequent supplier delivery of small lots may be seen as economically prohibitive.

For those who remain skeptical of the use of JIT partnerships, we would point out that virtually every restaurant in the world practices JIT, and with little staff support. Many restaurants order food for the next day in the middle of the night for delivery the next morning. They are ordering just *what* is needed, for delivery *when* it is needed, from reliable suppliers.

JIT Layout

JIT layouts allow us to reduce another kind of waste, movement. The movement of material (or paper in an office) does not add value. Consequently, we want flexible layouts that reduce the movement of people and material. JIT layouts move material directly to the location where needed. For instance, an assembly line

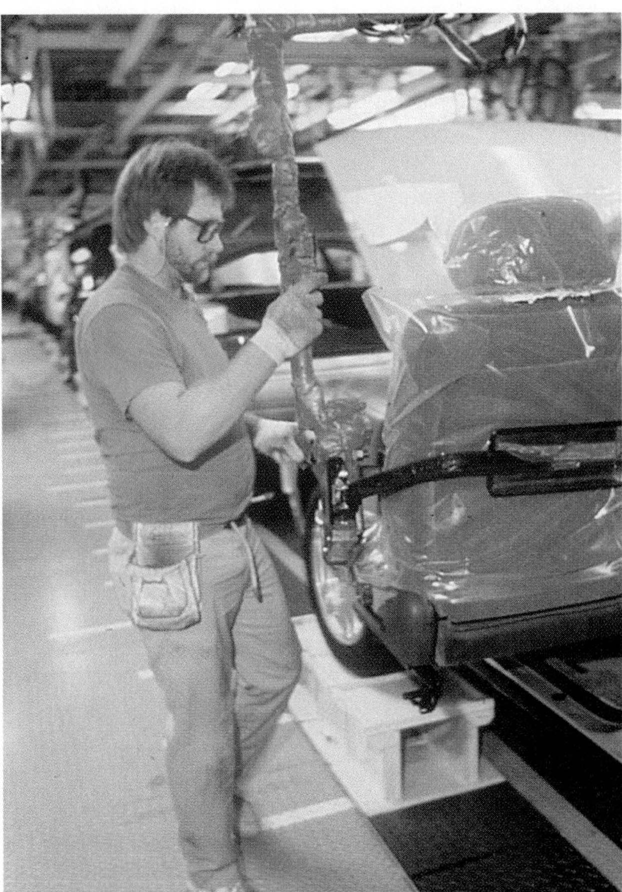

Little inventory is evident on this Toyota assembly line because inventory is waste and Toyota works aggressively with suppliers to reduce waste. Toyota and its suppliers share complete information about operations, including schedules, costs, and quality levels. *Partnership* is the word describing the relationship between manufacturer and supplier because both desire a long-term, stable relationship.

should be designed with delivery points next to the line so material need not be delivered to a receiving department elsewhere in the plant then moved again. This is what VF Corporation's Wrangler Division in Greensboro, North Carolina, did. Now denim is delivered directly to the line. When a layout reduces distance, we also save space and eliminate potential areas for unwanted inventory.

Distance Reduction

Reducing distance is a major contribution of work cells, work centers, and focused factories (see Chapter 8). The days of long production lines and huge economic lots, with goods passing through monumental, single-operation machines, are gone. Now we use work cells, often arranged in a U-shape, containing several machines performing different operations. These work cells are often based on group technology codes (as discussed in Chapter 4). Group technology codes help us identify components with similar characteristics so we can group them into families. Once the families are identified, we build work cells for those families. The result can be thought of as a small product-oriented facility where the product is a group of similar products. The cells produce one good unit at a time, and ideally they produce the units *only* after a customer orders them.

TABLE 11.3

LAYOUT TACTICS
Work cells for families of products
Distance minimized
Little space for inventory
Employee communication improved
Poka-yoke devices
Flexible or movable equipment
Cross-trained workers add flexibility

Increased Flexibility

Modern work cells are designed so they can easily be rearranged to adapt to changes in volume, product improvements, or even new designs. Almost nothing in these new departments is bolted down. This same concept of layout flexibility applies to office environments. Not only are most office furniture and equipment moveable, but so are office walls, computer connections, and telecommunications. Layout flexibility aids the changes that result from product *and* process improvements that are inevitable with a philosophy of continuous improvement.

Impact on Employees

NOTE
In a JIT system, each worker is inspecting the part as it comes to him or her. Each worker knows that the part must be good before it goes on to the next "customer."

Employees working together are cross-trained so they can add flexibility and efficiency to the work cell. Layouts should allow employees to work together so they can tell each other about problems and opportunities for improvement. Layouts provide for sequential operations so feedback can be immediate. Defects are waste. When workers produce units one at a time, they can test each product or component at each production stage. Machines in work cells with self-testing "poka-yoke" functions sense defects and stop automatically when defects occur. Before JIT, defective products were replaced from inventory. Since surplus inventory is not kept in a JIT facility, there are no such buffers. Getting it right the first time is critical.

Reduced Space and Inventory

Since JIT layouts reduce travel distance, they also contribute to a reduction in inventory by removing space for inventory. Because there is little space, inventory must be moved in very small lots or even single units. Units are always moving because there is no storage. For instance, each month Security Pacific

Corporation's focused facility sorts 7 million checks, processes 5 million statements, and mails 190,000 customer statements. With a JIT layout, mail processing time was reduced by 33%, salary costs reduced by $32,400 per year, floor space cut by 50%, and in-process waiting lines were reduced by 75% to 90%.[5] Storage, including shelves and drawers, has been removed. Table 11.3 provides a list of layout tactics.

INVENTORY

Inventories in production and distribution systems often exist "just in case" something goes wrong. That is, they are used just in case some variation from the production plan occurs. The "extra" inventory is then used to cover the variations or problems. Effective inventory tactics require "just in time," not "just in case." **Just-in-time inventory** is the minimum inventory necessary to keep a perfect system running. With just-in-time inventory, the exact amount of goods arrive at the moment they are needed, not a minute before or a minute after. Useful JIT inventory tactics are shown in Table 11.4.

just-in-time inventory

Hidden Variability

The idea behind JIT is to eliminate inventory that hides variability in the production system. This is illustrated on the next page in Figure 11.1, which shows a lake full of rocks. The water in the lake represents inventory flow, and the rocks represent problems such as late deliveries, machine breakdowns, and poor personnel performance. The water level in the lake hides variability and problems. Because inventory hides problems, they are hard to find.

Inventory Reduction

Operations managers move toward JIT by first removing inventory. Reducing inventory uncovers the "rocks" in Figure 11.1 that represent the variability and problems currently being tolerated. With reduced inventory, management chips away at the exposed problems until the lake is clear. After the lake is clear, managers make additional cuts in inventory and continue to chip away at the next level of exposed problems. Ultimately, there will be virtually no inventory and no problems (variability).

Perhaps the manager who said, "Inventory is the root of operations management evil" was not far from the truth. If inventory itself is not evil, it hides evil at great cost.

TABLE 11.4

JIT INVENTORY TACTICS

- A pull system to move inventory
- Ever smaller lots
- Just-in-time delivery from suppliers
- Deliveries directly to point of use
- Performance to schedule
- Setup reduction
- Group technology

Small Lots Essential

Just-in-time has also come to mean elimination of waste by reducing investment in inventory. The key to JIT is producing good product in small lot sizes. Reducing the size of batches can be a major help in reducing inventory and inventory costs. As we saw in Chapter 9, when inventory usage is constant, the average inven-

[5]Paul Jackson, "White Collar JIT at Security Pacific," *Target* 7, no. 1 (Spring 1991): 32–37.

FIGURE 11.1

Inventory Hides Problems, Just as Water in a Lake Hides the Rocks

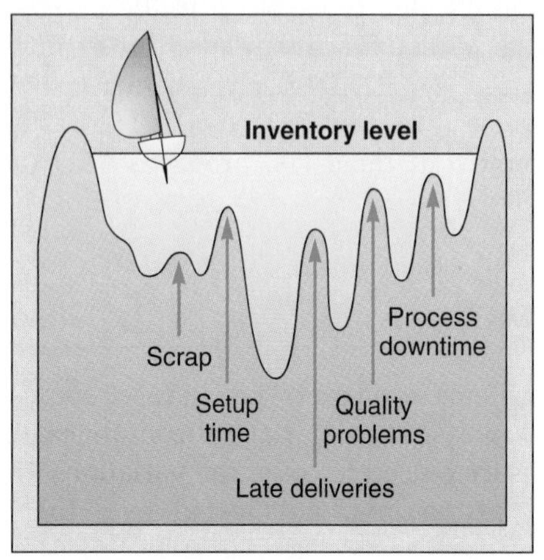

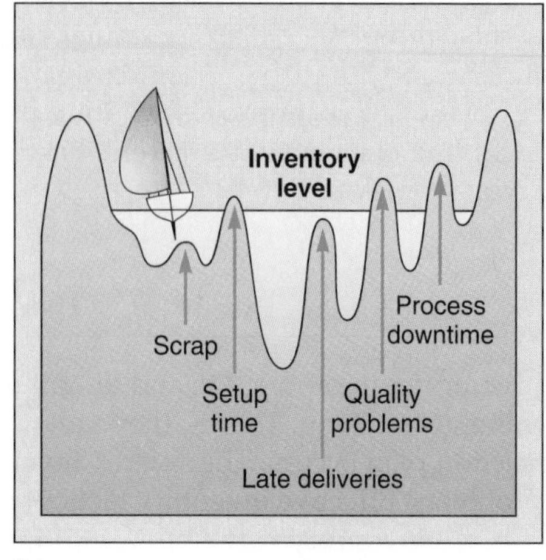

(a) (b)

(a) Reduce inventory so the problems can be found. (b) Solve those problems, then reduce inventory again. Eventually, as the inventory level is lowered, formerly tolerated problems surface so they can be eliminated.

tory level is the sum of the maximum inventory plus the minimum inventory divided by two. Figure 11.2(a) shows that lowering the order size increases the number of orders but drops inventory levels dramatically.

Setup Costs Driven Down

Inventory and the cost of holding that inventory goes down as the inventory reorder quantity drops because the maximum inventory level drops. But, since inventory requires incurring an ordering or setup cost that must be applied to the units produced, managers tend to purchase (or produce) large orders. With large orders, each unit purchased or ordered absorbs only a small part of the setup cost. Consequently, the way to drive down lot sizes and reduce average inventory is to reduce setup cost, which in turn lowers the optimum order size. The effect of reduced setup costs on total cost and lot size is shown in Figure 11.2(b). Moreover, smaller lot sizes hide fewer problems. Just as setup costs can be reduced at a machine in a factory, setup time can also be reduced when getting the order ready. It does little good to drive down factory setup time from hours to minutes if orders are going to take two weeks to process or "set up" in the office. This is exactly what happens in many organizations when we forget that JIT has applications in the office, shipping, and in nearly all services.

NOTE
Reduced lot sizes must be accompanied by reduced setup times, otherwise the setup cost must be assigned to fewer units.

In many environments, setup cost is highly correlated with setup time. Setups usually require a substantial amount of work prior to actually being accomplished at the work center. Much of the preparation required by a setup can be done prior to shutting down the machine or process. Setup times can be reduced substantially, as shown in Figure 11.3. Machines and processes that traditionally have taken hours to set up are now being set up in less than a minute by the more imaginative world-class manufacturers. Reducing setup times is an excellent way to reduce inventory investment and to improve productivity.

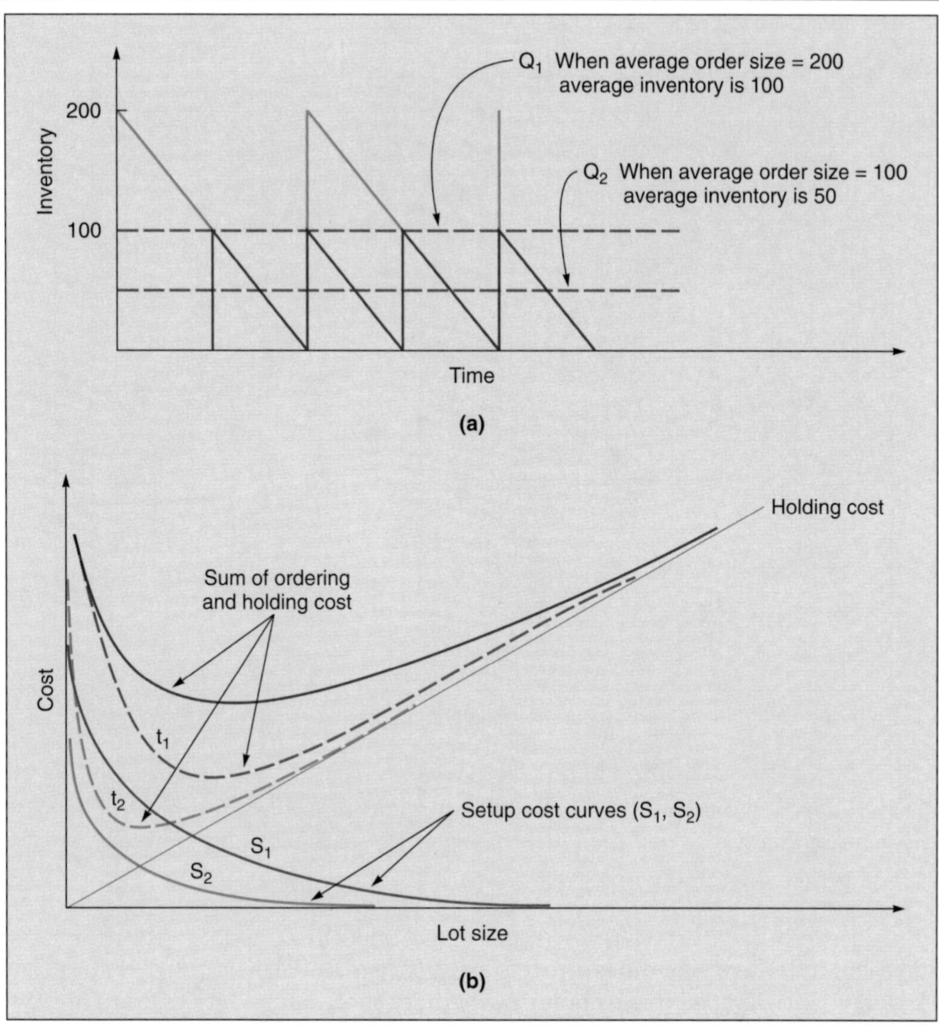

As the setup costs are lowered (lines S_1 and S_2) inventory cost also falls (lines t_1 and t_2).

FIGURE 11.2

(a) MORE FREQUENT ORDERS DRAMATICALLY REDUCE AVERAGE INVENTORIES (b) BUT MORE FREQUENT ORDERS REQUIRE REDUCING SETUP COSTS OR INVENTORY COSTS WILL RISE

SCHEDULING

Effective schedules, communicated within the organization and to suppliers, support JIT. Better scheduling also improves the ability to meet customer orders, drives down inventory by allowing smaller production lot sizes, and reduces work-in-process. For instance, Ford Motor Company now ties some suppliers to its final assembly schedule. Ford communicates its schedules to Polycon Industries from the Ford Oakville production control system. The scheduling system describes the style and color of the bumper needed for each vehicle moving down the final assembly line. The scheduling system transmits the information to portable terminals carried by warehouse personnel who load the bumpers onto conveyors leading to the loading dock. The bumpers are then trucked 50 miles to the Ford plant. Total time is four hours.[6] Table 11.5 suggests several items that can contribute to

TABLE 11.5

JIT SCHEDULING TACTICS

JIT Scheduling Tactics
Communicate the schedule to suppliers
Level schedules
Freeze part of the schedule
Plus-minus zero performance to schedule
Seek one-piece-make and one-piece-move
Eliminate waste
Small lots and kanban
Each operation makes a part that is perfect

[6]Mike Ngo and Paul Szucs, "Four Hours," *APICS—The Performance Advantage* 6, no. 1 (January 1996): 30–32.

FIGURE 11.3

STEPS TO REDUCE SETUP TIMES

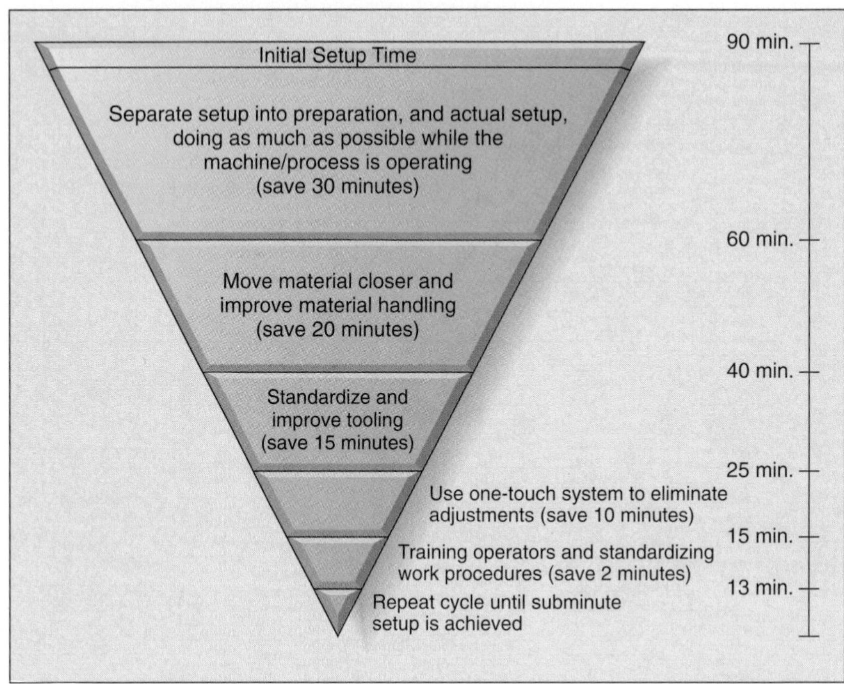

Reduced setup times are a major JIT component.

achieving these goals, but two techniques (in addition to communicating schedules) are paramount. They are level material-use schedules and kanban.

Level Material-Use Schedules

level material-use schedules

Level material-use schedules process frequent small batches rather than a few large batches. Because this technique schedules many small lots that are always changing, it has on occasion been called "jelly bean" scheduling. Figure 11.4 illustrates a traditional large-lot approach with large batches, and a JIT level material-use schedule with many small batches. The operations manager's task is to make and move small lots so the level material-use schedule is economical. The scheduler may find that *freezing* the portion of the schedule closest to due dates

FIGURE 11.4

SCHEDULING SMALL LOTS OF PARTS A, B, AND C INCREASES FLEXIBILITY TO MEET CUSTOMER DEMAND AND REDUCES INVENTORY

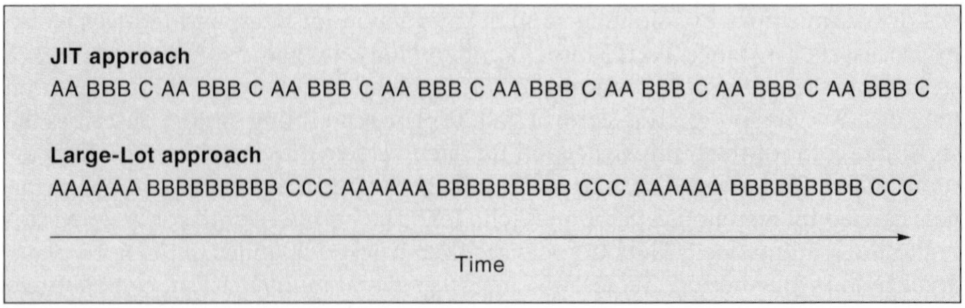

JIT approach

AA BBB C AA BBB C AA BBB C AA BBB C AA BBB C AA BBB C AA BBB C AA BBB C

Large-Lot approach

AAAAAA BBBBBBBBB CCC AAAAAA BBBBBBBBB CCC AAAAAA BBBBBBBBB CCC

Time →

The JIT approach to scheduling produces just as many of each model per time period as the large-lot approach, provided setup times are lowered.

Rather than produce motorcycle models in large batches, Harley-Davidson uses level material-use schedules to mix production of a wide variety of Harley motorcycles. In this way Harley drives down inventory, meets customer demand, and wins orders.

allows the production system to function and the schedule to be met. Freezing means not allowing changes to part of the schedule. Operations managers expect the schedule to be achieved with no deviations from the schedule.

Kanban

One way to achieve small lot sizes is to move inventory through the shop only as needed rather than *pushing* it on to the next workstation, whether the personnel there are ready for it or not. As noted earlier, when inventory is moved only as needed, it is referred to as a *pull* system and the ideal lot size is one. The Japanese call this system *kanban*.

kanban

Kanban is a Japanese word for "card." In their effort to reduce inventory, the Japanese use systems that "pull" inventory through the shop. They often use a "card" to signal the need for more material, hence the name kanban. The card is the authorization for the next batch of material to be produced. The kanban "pulls" the material through the plant.

NOTE
In a hospital with JIT, suppliers bring ready-to-use supplies directly to storage areas, nurses' stations, and operating rooms. Only a 24-hour reserve is maintained.

The system has been modified in many facilities so that, even though it is called a kanban, the card does not exist. In some cases, an empty position on the floor is indication that the next lot is needed. In other cases, some sort of signal, such as a flag or rag (Figure 11.5) is used to signify that it is time for the next batch.

The batches are typically very small, usually a matter of a few hours' worth of production. Such a system requires tight schedules. Small quantities must be produced several times a day. The process must run smoothly because any shortage has an almost immediate impact on the entire system. Kanban places added emphasis on meeting schedules, reducing the time and cost required by setups, and economical material handling.

Whether it is called kanban or not, the advantages of small inventory and *pulling* material through the plant only when needed are significant. For instance, small batches allow a very limited amount of faulty material. Numerous aspects of in-

FIGURE 11.5

DIAGRAM OF OUTBOUND STOCKPOINT WITH WARNING-SIGNAL MARKER

SOURCE: Robert W. Hall, *Zero Inventories* (Homewood, IL: Dow Jones-Irwin, 1983), p. 51.

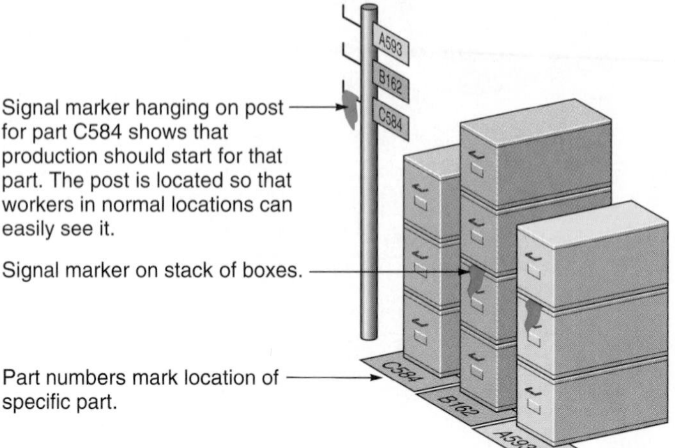
Signal marker hanging on post for part C584 shows that production should start for that part. The post is located so that workers in normal locations can easily see it.
Signal marker on stack of boxes.
Part numbers mark location of specific part.
A593
B162
C584
C584
B162
A593

NOTE
Manufacturers' inventory/sales ratio was substantially lower in the last recession than in earlier recessions, in large part thanks to JIT inventories.

ventory are bad, and only one aspect, availability, is good. Among the bad aspects are poor quality, obsolescence, damage, occupied space, committed assets, increased insurance, increased material handling, and increased accidents. All of these negative aspects add to the costs associated with holding (carrying) inventory.

In-plant kanban systems often use standardized, reusable containers that protect the specific quantities to be moved. Such containers are also desirable when shipping. Standardized containers reduce weight and disposal costs, generate less wasted space in trailers, and require less labor to pack, unpack, and prepare items. For instance, at American and Lufthansa airlines "Garment on Hanger" containers are used. Garments in special containers go from the manufacturer to the shipper to the retailer's display without repressing and rehanging costs.[7]

At some manufacturers, containers are specially made for individual parts, and many feature padding to protect the finish. Containers serve an important role in inventory reduction: the containers are the only place inventory is stored on the assembly line, so they serve as a kanban signal to supply new parts to the line. After all the pieces have been removed, the container is returned to its originating cell to signal the worker there to build more.

[7] Robert Millen, "JIT Logistics, Putting JIT on Wheels," *Target* 7, no. 2 (Summer 1991): 7.

QUALITY

The relationship between JIT and quality is a strong one.[8] They are related in three ways. First, JIT cuts the cost of obtaining good quality. This occurs because scrap, rework, inventory investment, and damage cost are buried in inventory. JIT forces down inventory; therefore, fewer bad units are produced and fewer units must be reworked. Inventory *hides* bad quality, while JIT immediately *exposes* bad quality.

Second, JIT improves quality. As JIT shrinks queues and lead time, it keeps evidence of errors fresh and limits the number of potential sources of error. JIT creates, in effect, an early warning system for quality problems so that fewer bad units are produced and feedback is immediate. This advantage can accrue both within the firm and with goods received from vendors.

Finally, better quality means fewer buffers are needed and, therefore, a better, easier-to-employ JIT system can exist. Often the purpose of keeping inventory is to protect against poor production performance resulting from unreliable quality. If consistent quality exists, JIT allows us to reduce all costs associated with inventory. Table 11.6 suggests some requirements for quality in a JIT environment.

TABLE 11.6

JIT QUALITY TACTICS

- Statistical process control
- Employee empowerment
- Failsafe methods (poka-yoke, checklists, and so on)
- Immediate feedback

Acceptable tolerance levels on auto body parts at this New United Motor Manufacturing (NUMMI) plant in Fremont, California, are so small that the company uses computers to see whether the process is in or out of control. Workers at NUMMI (which makes the Toyota Corolla and GM Prizm) are empowered to stop the entire production line by pulling the overhead cord if any quality problems are spotted. This Japanese practice called *andon* can eliminate production line inspectors and cut the number of supervisors.

EMPLOYEE EMPOWERMENT

Some techniques appropriate to developing a JIT philosophy require policy and strategy decisions, but many are part of the purview of empowered employees. Empowered employees can bring their involvement to bear on most of the daily operations issues that are so much a part of a just-in-time philosophy. Since the dawn of the industrial revolution, much of management has been concerned with improving performance through the simplification of work. This made good sense in an age when many employees were illiterate and communication was complicated because of a variety of languages in the immigrant-filled workplaces of America. However, in much of the world we now have the opportunity to hire literate employees. Consequently, communication problems are much less difficult than they were 100 or 200 years ago. This means that we can bring those tasks that have traditionally been assigned to staff and move them to empowered employees. Aided by aggressive cross-training and few job classifications, we can engage the mental, as well as physical, capacities of employees in the challenging task of improving the workplace.

Employee empowerment follows the management adage that no one knows the job better than those who do it. Firms not only train and cross-train, but need to take full advantage of that investment by enriching jobs.[9] For example, at a Thermofit plant in Britain, it once took machine operators two hours to change over their machines for a new product, a costly waste of time when entire production runs last only five or six hours. Now with training and the aid of videotaped changeovers and analysis by the employees themselves, the changeover has been reduced to 45 minutes.[10]

[8]See related discussion in Barbara B. Flynn, Sadao Sakakibara, and Roger G. Schroeder. "Relationship Between JIT and TQM: Practices and Performance," *Academy of Management Journal* 38, no. 5 (1995): 1325–1360.

[9]Richard J. Schonberger, "Human Resource Management Lessons from a Decade of Total Quality Management and Reengineering," *California Management Review* (Summer 1994): 109–123.

[10]Seth Lubove, "A Long, Last Mile," *Forbes*, October 10, 1994, pp. 66–69.

A kanban need not be as formal as signal lights or empty carts. In the photo shown above the cook in a fast food restaurant knows that when six cars are in line there are to be eight meat patties and six orders of french fries cooking.

JIT's philosophy of continuous improvement gives employees the opportunity to enrich their jobs and their lives. When empowerment is done successfully, we have mutual commitment and respect on the part of both employees and management so that all are working together for a more productive enterprise that wins orders.

JIT IN SERVICES

All of the JIT techniques for dealing with (1) suppliers, (2) layout, (3) inventory, and (4) scheduling are used in services.

SUPPLIERS. As we have noted, virtually every restaurant deals with their suppliers on a JIT basis. Those who do not are usually not successful. The waste is too evident—food spoils and the customers complain.

LAYOUTS. Layouts help JIT work in restaurant kitchens where cold food must be served cold and hot food hot. Layouts make a difference in airline baggage claim where customers expect their bags just-in-time.

INVENTORY. Every stock broker drives inventory down to close to zero. Most sell and buy orders occur on a JIT basis because an unexecuted sell or buy order is not acceptable to most clients. A broker may be in serious trouble if left holding an unexecuted trade.

SCHEDULES. At airline ticket counters the focus of a JIT system is customer demand, but rather than being satisfied by the inventory of a tangible product, that demand will be satisfied by personnel. Through elaborate scheduling, airline ticket counter personnel show up just-in-time to satisfy customer demand. They provide the service on a JIT basis. Personnel are scheduled, rather than 'things' inventoried. Schedules are critical. At a beauty salon the focus is only slightly different; the customer is scheduled to assure JIT service. Similarly, at a McDonald's restaurant (as in most fast-food restaurants) scheduling of personnel is down to 15-minute increments based on precise forecasting of demands. Additionally, production is done in small lots (no Big Mac sits more than ten minutes) to ensure that fresh, hot hamburgers are delivered just-in-time. Both personnel and production are scheduled on a JIT basis to meet a specific demand. The setup times are very low and the lot size very small, approaching one. McDonald's comes very close to the JIT idea of one good product delivered when and where the customer wants it.

Notice that in all three of these examples, the airline ticket counter, the beauty salon, and McDonald's, scheduling is a key ingredient to effective JIT. Excellent forecasts drive those schedules. Those forecasts may be very elaborate with seasonal, daily, and even hourly components in the case of the airline ticket counter (holiday sales, flight time, and so forth), or seasonal and weekly components at the beauty salon (holidays and Fridays creating special problems), or down to a few minutes at McDonald's.

With good methods analysis and the proper tools, the setup time for french fries at McDonald's has been made very short. The result is french fries prepared frequently (almost for each order) to ensure that the fries are delivered hot, just as the customer requests them.

Suppliers need to be good, inventories lean, cycle times short, and schedules nimble in order to deliver goods and services to customers under continuously changing demand. All of these are currently being done with great success in many firms regardless of their product. JIT techniques are widely used in both goods-producing and service-producing firms; they just look different.

SUMMARY

JIT is a philosophy of continuous improvement. It focuses on driving all waste out of the production process. Since waste is found in anything that does not add value, JIT facilities are adding value more efficiently than other facilities. Waste occurs when defects are produced within the production process or by suppliers. JIT attacks wasted space because of less-than-optimal layout, it attacks wasted time because of poor scheduling; it attacks waste in idle inventory, it attacks waste from poorly maintained machinery and equipment. JIT expects committed, empowered employees to work with committed management and suppliers to build systems that respond to customers with ever lower cost and ever higher quality. The success of JIT at driving out waste is shown in Figure 11.6.

KEY TERMS

Just-in-time (JIT) *(p. 376)*
Variability *(p. 376)*
Pull system *(p. 378)*
Manufacturing cycle time *(p. 378)*
Push system *(p. 378)*
JIT partnerships *(p. 378)*
Consignment inventory *(p. 379)*
Just-in-time inventory *(p. 383)*
Level material-use schedule *(p. 386)*
Kanban *(p. 387)*

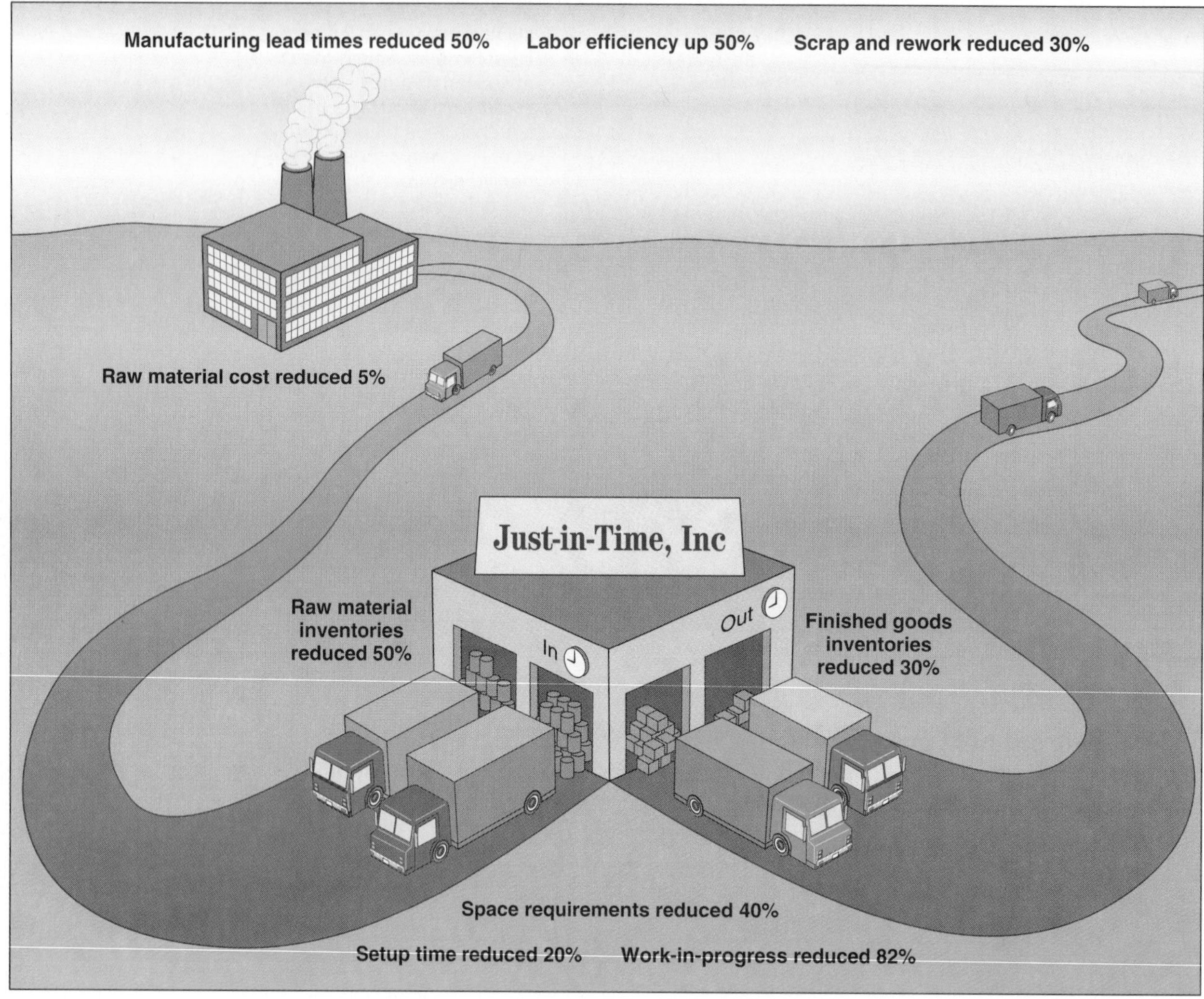

FIGURE 11.6 JIT WASTE REDUCTION

This data is based on performance at Hewlett-Packard's Vancouver Division and on work of the authors.

DISCUSSION QUESTIONS

1. What is meant by "a JIT philosophy?"
2. What are the characteristics of JIT partnerships?
3. What are the types of waste JIT is to remove?
4. What is the difference between a "pull" system and a "push" system?
5. What are the types of variability that JIT is expected to help us remove?
6. How does JIT help us reduce distance, space, and inventory?
7. How do empowered employees aid the JIT effort?
8. What is the impact of reducing setup costs on JIT?
9. Identify the results from a JIT system that should lead to and yield a competitive advantage.

SELF-TEST ■ CHAPTER 11

- *Before taking the self-test* refer back to the learning objectives listed at the beginning of the chapter and the key terms listed at the end of the chapter.
- Use the key at the back of the text to *correct* your answers.
- *Restudy* pages that correspond to any questions you answered incorrectly or material you feel uncertain about.

1. JIT is a philosophy of
  a. waste reduction
  b. variability reduction
  c. continuous improvement
  d. inspection improvement

2. Kanban design should consider
  a. size
  b. weight
  c. reuse
  d. quantity held
  e. all of the above

3. JIT is
  a. an execution technique
  b. a philosophy of continuous improvement
  c. an approach to waste reduction
  d. a process
  e. all of the above

4. Some reasons variability occurs are
  a. employees, machines, and suppliers produce units that do not conform to standards
  b. engineering drawings are inaccurate
  c. production begins prior to completion of design
  d. customer demands are unknown
  e. all of the above

5. An effective JIT effort should result in
  a. queue and delay reduction
  b. quality improvement
  c. cost reduction
  d. variability reduction
  e. all of the above

6. Which of the following issues are *not* important in the development of a JIT system?
  a. layout
  b. inventory
  c. a push system
  d. employee empowerment
  e. scheduling

7. Goals of JIT suppliers include
  a. elimination of unnecessary activities
  b. elimination of in-plant inventory
  c. elimination of in-transit inventory
  d. all of the above

8. Characteristics of just-in-time suppliers *do not* include
  a. scheduling of inbound freight
  b. short-term contract agreements
  c. few suppliers
  d. minimal release paperwork
  e. the purchaser actually helping the supplier to meet the quality requirements

9. Identify six types of waste that JIT is designed to remove, ______, ______, ______, ______, ______, ______.

10. JIT teaches us that ______% waste is found in storing, queues, inspection, adjusting, delays, and defects.

11. The key to just-in-time production is
  a. the elimination of all inventories
  b. to rely very heavily upon purchased items rather than in-house production
  c. production in large lot sizes
  d. the elimination of all or most product options

12. A production system in which inventory is "pulled" through the shop tends to require a larger work-in-process inventory than a system in which inventory is "pushed" through the shop.
  a. True **b.** False

13. The prime advantage of a just-in-time inventory system lies in the
  a. increased overall inventory value
  b. increased production rates
  c. use of a "pull" rather than "push" inventory system
  d. exposure of problems in the production/distribution system

OPERATIONS IN PRACTICE EXERCISE

As discussed earlier in this chapter, the Brea Operations Center of Security Pacific is a centralized "back office" operations center. One part of the center, the External Mail Services section, processes about 5 million customer statements, notices, and related mailings each month. About 80 full-time operations working on three shifts accomplish this processing. At the end of each month, 7 million customer checks are sorted, enclosed, and mailed to 190,000 customers. Most of these accounts are for business customers who average many more checks than do households. An additional 30,000 customer statements have so many checks that they must be prepared by hand. Discuss how to implement a JIT approach at the operations center of Security Pacific.

CASE STUDY

Electronic Systems, Inc.

Electronic System, Inc. (ESI) of Topeka, Kansas, is an electronic components manufacturer with a single production facility employing 2,000 assembly line workers, 1,200 skilled workers and 850 management and clerical personnel. Top management of ESI attended a JIT seminar offered by their major customer, the U.S. government. After some discussion, management sent down a dictum to first-line supervisors (plant foremen) that ESI was going to become a JIT operation.

ESI's components are used as replacement parts in military equipment and office equipment. The government purchases ESI's products in large lots and has no plans to change. The U.S. government's business represents about 80% of total sales for ESI.

Recently, government inspectors noticed that ESI's JIT-oriented competitors were improving quality, while ESI's quality decreased. ESI's past acceptance sampling methods simply did not catch all of the defective products, while similar products from the competitors were virtually defect free. Also, a growing number of new customers had in recent months placed pressure on ESI to adopt JIT methods that would permit quicker response from ESI on orders. The new customers expressed a desire to receive smaller lot sizes instead of the large lot size the ESI system had been designed to provide because of past government business. What's more, a foreign competitor recently entered the market and could provide a better quality product, at less cost, and in a more timely manner than ESI.

The task of learning what JIT was, devising an implementation plan, and implementing it was left entirely up to the first-line supervisors. ESI's management felt that the supervisors managing the workers who were going to be asked to perform JIT activities on the shop floor would be the best people to make the new system work. ESI management also realized converting to a more responsive and quality-conscious system had to be accomplished as soon as possible. They established a deadline for full implementation of JIT principles in 90 days. The foremen and supervisors were given 30 days to develop a plan, 30 more to train and install the plan, and 30 to work out any bugs. As an added inducement, management informed the workers that 100% of the savings from increased productivity would be given to them as a reward.

Supervisors felt that much of the JIT philosophy was based on identifying time-consuming, wasteful activities and reducing them where possible. At the same time, work activities that added value to the product should be identified, and where possible, have a renewed effort or an increased allocation of time invested in them. The first act by the supervisors was to publish the list presented in Table 11.7. This list was designed to identify targeted areas of improvement or waste removal.

DISCUSSION QUESTIONS

1. Do you think the ESI assignment to the first-line supervisors to implement the new JIT program was a correct move by management? Explain your answer.
2. What JIT key principles does the application in this case appear to violate? Which principles does it embrace?
3. Which of the items listed in Table 11.7 are waste and should be eliminated? Which add value to the product?
4. Do you think this JIT program will be successful? Give reasons why or why not.

SOURCE: Adapted from Marc J. Schniederjans, *Topics in Just-in-Time Management* (Boston: Allyn & Bacon, 1993), pp. 21–23.

TABLE 11.7 A LIST OF TARGETED ACTIVITIES

Try to reduce the time it takes to perform these activities since they represent a waste of time and add little to the value of our products:

Counting component parts
Counting boxes
Cutting material used in the product
Maintaining equipment
Switching machine on
Over-producing stock
Handling materials

Try to do a better job, even if it takes more time, in performing the following activities since they add value to our products:

Making sure components fit in subassemblies
Checking other workers' jobs
Checking orders to see they are correct
Cleaning up work centers
Moving boxes
Setting up machines for a production run

BIBLIOGRAPHY

Ansarl, A., and B. Modarress. "Just-in-Time Purchasing: Problems and Solutions." *Journal of Purchasing and Materials* 22 (Summer 1986): 11–15.

Chapman, S. N., and P. L. Carter. "Supplier/Customer Inventory Relationships under JIT." *Decision Sciences* (Winter 1990): 35–51.

Freeland, J. R. "A Survey of Just-in-Time Purchasing Practices in the United States." *Production and Inventory Management Journal* 32 (Second Quarter 1991): 43.

Freeland, J. R., J. P. Leschke, and E. N. Weiss. "Guidelines for Setup-Cost Reduction Programs to Achieve Zero Inventory." *Journal of Operations Management* 9 (January 1990): 85.

Golhar, D. Y. "JIT Purchasing Practices in Manufacturing Firms." *Production and Inventory Management Journal* 34, no. 3 (Third Quarter 1993): 75–79.

Hall, R. *Zero Inventories.* Homewood, IL: Dow Jones-Irwin, 1983.

Handfield, R. "A Resource Dependence Perspective of Just-in-Time Purchasing." *Journal of Operations Management* 11 (1993): 289–311.

Inman, R. A., and S. Mehra. "JIT Applications for Service Environments." *Production and Inventory Management Journal* 32, no. 3 (Third Quarter 1991): 16.

Jinchiro, N., and R. Hall. "Management Specs for Stockless Production." *Harvard Business Review* 63 (May-June 1983): 89–91.

Louis, R. S. *How to Implement Kanban for American Industry.* Cambridge, MA: Productivity Press, 1992.

Schniederjans, M. *Topics in Just-in-Time Management.* Boston: Allyn & Bacon, 1993.

Walleigh, R. C. "Getting Things Done. What's Your Excuse for Not Using JIT?" *Harvard Business Review* 64 (March-April 1986): 39–54.

Supply-Chain Management

Supplement 11

SUPPLEMENT OUTLINE

Strategic Importance of Supply-Chain Management

Purchasing

Operations Environment ■ Service Environments ■ Make or Buy

Purchasing Strategies

Many Suppliers ■ Few Suppliers ■ Vertical Integration ■ Keiretsu Networks ■ Virtual Companies

Purchasing Management

Vendor Relations ■ Purchasing Techniques

Materials Management

Distribution Systems

Benchmarking Supply-Chain Management

Summary ■ Key Terms ■ Self-Test Supplement 11 ■ Discussion Questions ■ Operations in Practice Exercise ■ Problems ■ Case Studies: Factory Enterprises, Inc.; Thomas Manufacturing Company ■ Bibliography

LEARNING OBJECTIVES

When you complete this supplement you should be able to:

IDENTIFY OR DEFINE:

Supply-chain management
Purchasing
Materials management
Virtual companies
Keiretsu

DESCRIBE OR EXPLAIN:

Purchasing strategies
Approaches to negotiations

No organization finds it economical to make all the materials it uses because the advantages of specializations are so overwhelming. Technology and economic efficiency demand specialization. Therefore, most items are purchased. Indeed many firms spend over 50% of their sales dollars on purchasing. This is true in all industrial and postindustrial societies. Because such a high percentage of an organization's costs are determined by purchasing, relationships with suppliers are increasingly long term. Joint efforts that will improve innovation, speed design, and reduce costs are common. Such joint efforts can dramatically improve both partners' competitiveness. Early involvement of suppliers in new product efforts can yield high dividends. Consequently, a discipline known as *supply-chain management* has developed.

supply-chain management

Supply-chain management is the management of the activities that procure raw materials, transform them into intermediate goods and final products, and deliver the products to customers through a distribution system. These activities include the traditional purchasing function plus many other activities that are important to the relationship with suppliers and distributors. Supply-chain management may include determining: (1) transportation vendors, (2) credit and cash transfers, (3) suppliers, (4) distributors and banks, (5) accounts payable and receivable, (6) warehousing, (7) order fulfillment, and (8) sharing information about forecasting, production, and inventory control activity. The idea is to focus on both reducing waste and maximizing value in the supply chain. Activities of supply-chain managers cut across accounting, finance, marketing, and the operations discipline. In this supplement we introduce aspects of supply-chain management that fall within the operations area with emphasis on purchasing, as it is the core of this activity.

STRATEGIC IMPORTANCE OF SUPPLY-CHAIN MANAGEMENT

NOTE
The distribution of goods to and from facilities can be 20% of the selling price.

Supply-chain management deals with the complete cycle of materials as they flow from suppliers, to production, to warehousing, to distribution, to the customer. As firms increase their competitiveness via product customization, high quality, cost reductions, and speed-to-market, added emphasis is placed on the supply chain (see Figure S11.1).

postponement

Many opportunities exist for good supply-chain management to enhance value at little cost. On the supplier side, JIT techniques and supplier cooperation that may help in distribution are part of supply-chain management. With design and supplier help, a manufacturer might maintain the generic nature of the product as long as possible. We know this technique as postponement. **Postponement** withholds any modifications or customization to the product as long as possible.[1] For instance, Hewlett-Packard (HP), after analyzing the supply chain for its printers, determined that if the printer's power supply was moved out of the printer itself and into a power cord, HP could ship the basic printer anywhere in the world. HP modified the printer, its power cord, its packaging, and its documentation so that only the power cord and documentation needed to be added at the final distribution point. This modification allowed the firm to manufacture and hold centralized inventories of the generic printer for shipment as demand changed. Only the unique power system and documentation had to be held in

[1]Hau L. Lee and Corey Billington, "The Evolution of Supply-Chain-Management Models and Practice at Hewlett-Packard," *Interfaces* 25, no. 5 (September-October 1995): 42–63.

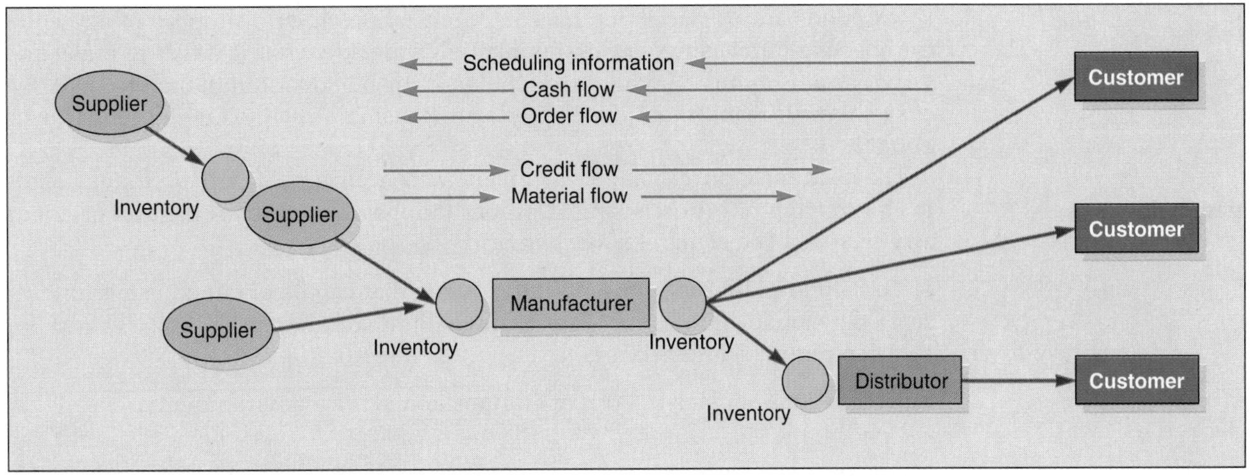

FIGURE S11.1 THE SUPPLY CHAIN

The supply chain includes all the interactions between suppliers, manufacturers, distributors, and customers. This includes transportation, scheduling information, cash and credit transfers, as well as material transfers between them.

each country. This understanding of the entire supply chain reduced both risk and investment in inventory.[2]

On the distribution side, one frequently used technique is to "drop ship." **Drop shipping** means the supplier will ship directly to the end consumer, rather than to the seller, saving both time and reshipping costs. Other common, but cost-saving measures include the use of special packaging, labels, and particular location of labels or bar codes. Another feature that might be added are size and number of units in each shipping container. Substantial savings can be obtained through management techniques such as these. Some of these techniques can be of particular benefit to wholesalers and retailers because they can help reduce shrinkage (lost, damaged, or stolen merchandise), as well as reduce handling cost.

drop shipping

Other techniques under the umbrella of supply-chain management are: (1) establishing lines of credit for suppliers, (2) reducing bank "float" (the time money is in transit), (3) coordinating production and shipping schedules with suppliers and distributors, and (4) making optimal use of warehouse space. The key to effective supply-chain management is to balance the production stream with ever changing customer demand.

PURCHASING

The supply chain receives such attention because purchasing is the most costly activity in most firms. The cost of purchases as a percent of sales, for both goods and services, is often substantial. Because such a huge portion of revenue is devoted to purchasing, an effective purchasing strategy is vital. Purchasing provides a major opportunity to reduce costs and increase contribution margins. Additionally, the quality of goods and services sold is directly related to the qual-

NOTE

INDUSTRY	% PURCHASED
All industry	54
Food	63
Lumber	60
Paper	54
Petroleum	83

[2]M. Eric Johnson and Tom Davis, "Gaining an Edge with Supply Chain Management," *APICS: The Performance Advantage* 5, no. 12 (December 1995): 26–31.

ity of goods and services purchased. Organizations have a number of strategies for effective purchasing, but first, a firm must decide what it wants to make and what it wants to buy. Having made the make-or-buy decision (which we will discuss shortly), firms must decide on a purchasing strategy for the items to be bought.

purchasing

The need for a purchasing strategy and accomplishment of that strategy leads to the creation of a purchasing function. **Purchasing** is the acquisition of goods and services. The *objective of the purchasing* activity is:

1. To help identify the products and services that can be obtained externally.
2. To develop, evaluate, and determine the best supplier, price, and delivery for those products and services.

Purchasing takes place in both operations and service environments.

Operations Environment

purchasing agent

In the operations environment, the purchasing function is usually managed by a **purchasing agent** who has legal authority to execute contracts on behalf of the firm. In a large firm, the purchasing agent may also have a staff that includes buyers and expediters. Buyers represent the company, performing all activities of the purchasing department except the signing of contracts. Expediters assist buyers in following up on purchases to ensure timely delivery. In *manufacturing* firms, the purchasing function is supported by product engineering drawings and specifications, quality control documents, and testing activities that evaluate the purchased items.

Service Environments

In many *service* environments, purchasing's role is diminished because the primary product is an intellectual one. In legal and medical organizations, for example, the main items to be procured are office facilities, furniture and equipment, autos, and supplies. However, in services such as transportation and restaurants, the purchasing function is critical. An airline that purchases planes that are not efficient for its route structure or a steak house that does not know how to buy steak is in trouble. In these and similar firms resources must be expended and training provided to ensure that purchasing is competently addressed.

buyer

In the wholesale and retail segment of services, purchasing is performed by a **buyer** who has responsibility for the sale of and profit margins on the purchased merchandise that will be resold. Buyers in this nonmanufacturing environment may have little support for standards and quality control other than historical customer behavior and standard grades. For instance, a USDA grade (such as AA eggs or U.S. choice meat), a textile standard or blend, or standard sizes may take the place of engineering drawings and quality control documents found in manufacturing environments.

Make or Buy

A wholesaler or retailer buys everything that it sells; a manufacturing operation hardly ever does. Manufacturers, restaurants, and assemblers of products buy components and subassemblies that go into final products. As we discussed in

Chapter 4, choosing products and services that can be advantageously obtained externally as opposed to produced internally is known as the **make-or-buy decision.** The purchasing department's role is to evaluate alternative suppliers and provide current, accurate, complete data that are relevant to the buy alternative. Table S11.1 lists a wide variety of considerations in the make-or-buy decision.

make-or-buy decision

Regardless of the decision, it should be reviewed periodically. Vendor competence and costs change, as do production capabilities and costs within the firm.

PURCHASING STRATEGIES

For those items to be purchased, companies must decide upon a purchasing strategy. One such strategy is the traditional American approach of *negotiating with many suppliers* and playing one supplier against another. A second strategy is to develop *long-term, "partnering"* relationships with a few suppliers who will work with the purchaser to satisfy the end customer. A third strategy is *vertical integration,* where firms may decide to use vertical backward integration by actually buying the supplier. A fourth variation is a combination of few suppliers and vertical integration, known as a "keiretsu." In a keiretsu, *suppliers become part of a company coalition.* Finally, the fifth strategy is to develop virtual companies *that use suppliers on an as-needed basis.* We will discuss each of these strategies next.

Many Suppliers

With the many-supplier strategy, the supplier responds to the demands and specifications of a "request for quotation" with the order usually going to the low bidder. This strategy plays one supplier against another and places the burden of meeting the demands of the buyer on the supplier. Suppliers aggressively compete with one another. While many approaches to negotiations can be used with

TABLE S11.1 CONSIDERATIONS FOR THE MAKE-OR-BUY DECISION

REASONS FOR MAKING	REASONS FOR BUYING
1. Lower production cost	1. Lower acquisition cost
2. Unsuitable suppliers	2. Preserve supplier commitment
3. Assure adequate supply (quantity or delivery)	3. Obtain technical or management ability
4. Utilize surplus labor facilities and make a marginal contribution	4. Inadequate capacity
5. Obtain desired quality	5. Reduce inventory costs
6. Remove supplier collusion	6. Ensure alternative sources
7. Obtain unique item that would entail a prohibitive commitment for a supplier	7. Inadequate managerial or technical resources
8. Maintain organizational talents and protect personnel from a layoff	8. Reciprocity
9. Protect proprietary design or quality	9. Item is protected by a patent or trade secret
10. Increase or maintain size of the company (management preference)	10. Frees management to deal with its primary business

Boeing 777. With an upfront investment of $4 billion, Boeing used suppliers from the United States and over a dozen countries in a "partnership" that spreads Boeing's risk. Purchasing personnel work closely with suppliers to develop contracts. These contracts ensure that quality components are delivered on time and within cost to Boeing's final assembly line in Everett, Washington.

this strategy, long-term "partnering" relationships are not the goal. This approach holds the supplier responsible for maintaining the necessary technology, expertise, and forecasting abilities plus cost, quality, and delivery competencies.

Few Suppliers

A strategy of few suppliers implies that rather than looking for short-term attributes, such as low cost, a buyer is better off forming a long-term relationship with dedicated suppliers. Long-term suppliers are more likely to understand the broad objectives of the firm and the end customer. Using few suppliers can create value by allowing suppliers to have economics of scale and a learning curve that yields both lower transaction costs and lower production costs.

Few suppliers, each with a large commitment to the buyer, may also be more willing to participate in JIT systems, as well as provide innovations and technological expertise. However, the most important factor may be the trust that comes with compatible organization cultures. A champion within one of the firms often promotes positive relationships between purchaser's and supplier's organization by committing resources toward advancing the relationship. Such a commitment can foster both formal and informal contact, which may contribute to the alignment of organization cultures between the two firms, further strengthening the partnership.

NOTE
Integrating suppliers, production, and distribution requires that production operations be as agile as possible.

Chrysler Corporation is using this approach for the Dodge Stratus. For instance, operations managers chose suppliers even before the parts for the Dodge Stratus were designed. Chrysler evaluated suppliers on many rigorous criteria but virtually eliminated traditional supplier bidding. As a part of this new process,

Chrysler has adopted contracts that run for at least the life of the model. By working with Chrysler as "partners," suppliers are to become more efficient, reducing prices as they move down the learning curve. This approach yields only a few suppliers, but Chrysler expects to develop long-term relationships with them. The success of this strategy is evident in Table S11.2.

NOTE
Nearly 80 years ago, Henry Ford surrounded himself with reliable suppliers, many on his own property, making his assembly operation close to self-sufficient.

Service companies like Marks and Spencer, a British retailer, have also demonstrated that cooperation with suppliers can yield cost savings for customers and suppliers alike. This strategy has resulted in suppliers that develop new products, winning customers for Marks and Spencer and the supplier.

Like all strategies, a down side exists. With few suppliers, the cost of changing partners is huge, so both buyer and supplier run the risk of becoming captives of the other. Poor supplier performance is only one risk the purchaser faces. The purchaser must also be concerned about the trade secrets and suppliers venturing out on their own. This happened when Schwinn Bicycle Co. taught Taiwan's Giant Manufacturing Company to make and sell bicycles.[3] Giant Manufacturing is now the largest bicycle manufacturer in the world and Schwinn filed for bankruptcy.

Vertical Integration

vertical integration

Purchasing can be extended to take the form of vertical integration. By **vertical integration,** we mean developing the ability to produce goods or services previously purchased, or actually buying a supplier or a distributor. Vertical integration can take the form of forward or backward integration, as shown in Figure S11.2.

Backward integration suggests a firm purchase its suppliers, as in the case of Ford Motor Company deciding to manufacture its own car radios. Forward inte-

TABLE S11.2 CHRYSLER'S SUPPLIER COST REDUCTION EFFORT (SCORE) HAS PRODUCED $161 MILLION IN SAVINGS IN TWO YEARS

SUPPLIER	SUGGESTION	MODEL	ANNUAL SAVINGS
Rockwell	Use passenger car door locks on Dodge trucks	Dodge trucks	$280,000
Rockwell	Simplify design and substitute materials on manual window-regulator systems	Various	$300,000
3M	Change tooling for wood-grain panels to allow three parts to be made in one die instead of two	Caravan, Voyager	$1,500,000
Trico	Change wiper-blade formulations to eliminate the disposable plastic shield used during assembly and shipping	Various	$140,000
Leslie Metal Arts	Exterior lighting suggestions	Various	$1,500,000

SOURCE: James Welch, Laddie Cook, and Joseph Blackburn, "The Bridge to Competitiveness, Building Supplier-Customer Linkages," *Target* (November-December 1992): 17–29. Reprinted from *Target* with permission of the Association for Manufacturing Excellence, Wheeling, IL.

[3]Andrew Tanzer, "Bury Thy Teacher," *Forbes*, December 21, 1992, pp. 90–95.

FIGURE S11.2

VERTICAL INTEGRATION CAN BE FORWARD OR BACKWARD

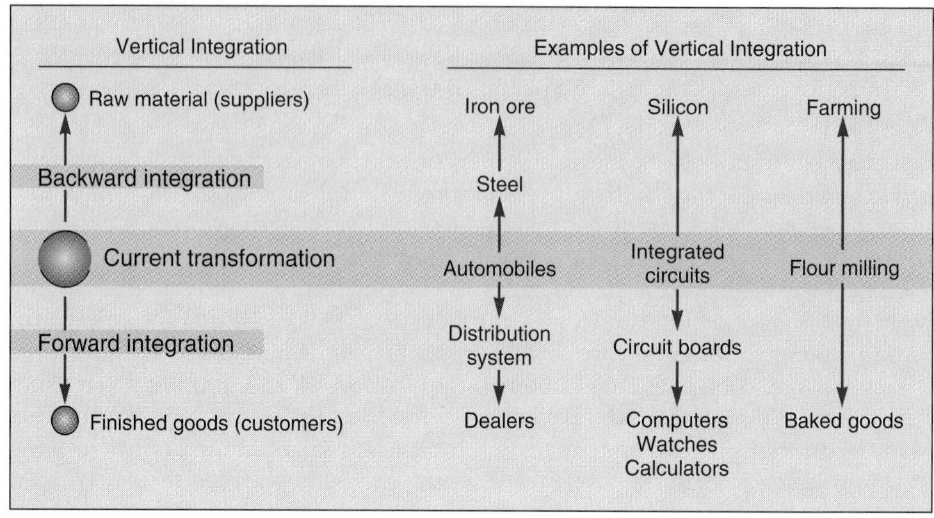

Sanford Corporation is one of America's largest producers of highlighters and markers. Sanford is vertically integrated, making its own inks, which gives it a research, development, quality, and product flexibility advantage.

gration, on the other hand, suggests that a firm make the finished product. An example is Texas Instruments, a manufacturer of integrated circuits; the firm also manufactures calculators and computers.

Vertical integration can offer a strategic opportunity for the operations manager. For firms whose internal analysis suggests that they have the necessary capital, managerial talent, and required demand, vertical integration may provide substantial opportunities for cost reduction. Other advantages in inventory reduction and scheduling can accrue to the company that effectively manages vertical integration or close, mutually beneficial relationships with suppliers.

Because purchased items represent such a large part of the costs of sales, it is obvious why so many organizations find interest in vertical integration. Vertical integration can yield cost reduction, quality adherence, and timely delivery. Additionally, vertical integration appears to work best when the organization has large market share or has the management talent to operate an acquired vendor successfully.[4] However, backward integration may be particularly dangerous for firms in industries undergoing technological change if management cannot keep abreast of those changes or invest the financial resources necessary for the next wave of technology.

Keiretsu Networks

keiretsu

Many large Japanese manufacturers have found a middle ground between purchasing from few suppliers and vertical integration. These manufacturers are often financial supporters of suppliers through ownership or loans. The supplier then becomes part of a company coalition known as a **keiretsu.** Members of the keiretsu are assured long-term relationships and are therefore expected to function as partners, lending technical expertise and stable quality production to the manufacturer. Members of the keiretsu may also operate as subcontractors to a chain of smaller suppliers.

[4]Robert D. Buzzell, "Is Vertical Integration Profitable?" *Harvard Business Review* 61, (January-February 1983): 92–102.

Virtual Companies

virtual companies

The limitations to vertical integration, as noted before, are severe. Moreover, our technological society continually demands more specialization that further complicates vertical integration. Rather than letting vertical integration lock an organization into businesses that it may not understand, another approach is to find good flexible suppliers. A firm that has a department or division for everything may be too bureaucratic to be world-class. **Virtual companies** rely on a variety of supplier relationships to provide services on demand.[5] Virtual companies have fluid, moving organizational boundaries that allow them to create a unique enterprise to meet changing market demands. These relationships may provide a variety of services that include doing the payroll, hiring personnel, designing products, providing consulting services, manufacturing components, conducting tests, or distributing products. The relationships may be short-term or long-term, true partners or only collaborators, or simply able suppliers and subcontractors. But whatever the formal relationship, the result can be lean world-class performance. The advantages of virtual companies include specialized management expertise, low capital investment, flexibility, and speed. The result is efficiency.

Each company in each industry makes its own judgment about the appropriate degree of vertical integration. Jaguar is changing its approach to vertical integration. In the past, Jaguar made virtually every part it could, even when it made little sense. It even manufactured some simple items such as washers. However, Jaguar is now focusing on those items that make a car unique: the body, engine, and suspension. Outside suppliers with their capabilities, expertise, and efficiencies provide most other components.

The apparel business provides a *traditional* example of virtual organizations. The designers of clothes seldom manufacture their designs; they license the manufacture. The manufacturer may then rent a loft, lease sewing machines, and contract for the labor. The result is an organization that has low overhead, is flexible, and can respond rapidly to the market.

A *contemporary* example is the semi-conductor industry, exemplified by two California companies, S3 Inc. in Santa Clara and Visioneer in Palo Alto. Both firms subcontract almost everything. At Visioneer software is written by several partners, hardware is manufactured by a subcontractor in Silicon Valley, printed circuit boards are made in Singapore and plastic cases are made in Boston, where units are tested and packed for shipment. In the virtual company, the purchasing function is demanding and dynamic.

PURCHASING MANAGEMENT

purchasing management

A firm that decides to buy material rather than make it must manage a purchasing function. **Purchasing management** considers numerous factors, such as inventory and transportation costs, availability of supply, delivery performance, and quality of suppliers. A firm may have some competence in all areas of purchasing management, and exceptional competence in only a few. However, an outstanding operations function requires excellent vendor relations.

Vendor Relations

Effective vendor relations require that purchasing conduct a three-stage process: (1) vendor evaluation, (2) vendor development, and (3) negotiations.

[5]Virtual companies are also known as *hollow corporations* or *network companies;* see *Business Week,* October 17, 1994, p. 86.

VENDOR EVALUATION. The first stage, vendor evaluation, involves finding potential vendors and determining the likelihood of their becoming good suppliers. This phase requires the development of evaluation criteria such as those in Figure S11.3. Both the criteria and the weights are dependent upon the needs of the organization. The selection of competent suppliers is critical. If good suppliers are not selected, then all other purchasing efforts are wasted. As firms move toward fewer longer-term suppliers, the issues of financial strength, quality, management, research, and technical ability play an increasingly important role. These attributes should be noted in the evaluation process.

VENDOR DEVELOPMENT. The second stage is *vendor development.* Assuming a firm wants to proceed with a particular vendor, how does it integrate this supplier into its system? Purchasing makes sure the vendor has an appreciation of quality requirements, engineering changes, schedules and delivery, the payment system, and procurement policies. Vendor development may include everything from training, to engineering and production help, to formats for electronic in-

FIGURE S11.3

VENDOR RATING FORM USED BY J. M. HUBER CORPORATION

SOURCE: Stuart F. Heinritz, Paul V. Farrell, Larry Giunipero, and Michael Kolchin, *Purchasing: Principles and Applications,* 8th ed. (Englewood Cliffs, NJ: Prentice Hall, 1992), p. 180.

VENDOR RATING REPORT J.M. HUBER CORPORATION

COMPANY TOTAL RATING

Company	Excellent (4)	Good (3)	Fair (2)	Poor (1)
Size and/or Capacity	4			
Financial Strength		3		
Operational Profit		3		
Manufacturing Range	4			
Research Facilities			2	
Technical Service		3		
Geographical Locations	4			
Management		3		
Labor Relations		3		
Trade Relations		3		
Total 32	12	18	2	
.63 x Total = 20.16				
Service				
Deliveries on Time	4			
Condition on Arrival		3		
Follow Instructions		3		
Number of Rejections	4			
Handling of Complaints		3		
Technical Assistance			2	
Emergency Aid		3		
Supply Up to Date Catalogues, Etc.				1
Supply Price Changes Promptly	4			
Total 27	12	12	2	1
.69 x Total = 18.63				

Products	Excellent (4)	Good (3)	Fair (2)	Poor (1)
Quality	4			
Price		3		
Packaging	4			
Uniformity		3		
Warranty	4			
Total 18	12	6		
1.25 x Total = 22.50				
Sales Personnel				
1. Knowledge				
His company		3		
His product	4			
Our industry		3		
Our Company		3		
2. Sales Calls				
Properly Spaced	4			
By Appointment		3		
Planned and Prepared		3		
Mutually Productive	4			
3. Sales-Service				
Obtain Information		3		
Furnish Quotations Promptly	4			
Follow Orders		3		
Expedite Delivery		3		
Handle Complaints		3		
Total 43	16	27		
.48 x Total = 20.64				

Evaluation categories are weighted according to importance (for example, "product" category is weighted 1.25; "service" is next at 0.69). Individual factors (for example, quality, delivery, and so on) have descending values, from 4 points for excellent to 1 point for poor. Total of points in each category is multiplied by the weight for that category.

formation transfer. Purchasing policies might include issues such as percent of business done with any one supplier or with minority businesses.

NEGOTIATIONS. The third stage is *negotiations.*[6] **Negotiation strategies** are of three classic types. First is the *cost-based price model.* This model requires that the supplier open its books to the purchaser. The contract price is then based on time and materials or on a fixed cost with an escalation clause to accommodate changes in the vendor's labor and materials cost.

negotiation strategies

NOTE
Purchasing negotiations should not be viewed as a win/lose game; it can be a win/win game.

Second is the *market-based price model.* In this model, price is based on a published price or index. Paperboard prices, for instance, are published weekly in the "yellow sheet,"[7] and nonferrous metal prices in *Metals Week.*[8]

The third method is *competitive bidding.* In cases where suppliers are not willing to discuss costs or where near-perfect markets do not exist, competitive bidding is often appropriate. Competitive bidding is the typical policy in many firms for the majority of their purchases. The policy usually requires that the purchasing agent have several potential suppliers of the product (or its equivalent) and quotations from each. The major disadvantage of this method, as mentioned earlier, is that the development of long-term relations between the buyer and seller are hindered. Competitive bidding may effectively determine cost. But it may also make difficult the communication and performance that are vital for engineering changes, quality, and delivery.

Yet a fourth approach is *to combine one or more* of the preceding negotiation techniques. The supplier and purchaser may agree on review of certain cost data, accept some form of market data for raw material costs, or agree that the supplier will "remain competitive."

A good supplier relationship is one where both partners have established a degree of mutual trust and a belief in the competence of each other.

As a world-class telecommunications company, AT&T has an aggressive supplier evaluation and quality improvement program. Part of this program requires that vendors provide company profile and capability information. Providing this information is often done in formal presentations, as Hitachi Cable Ltd. is doing here. Once vendors are approved and orders placed, AT&T tracks key supplier variables, such as order cycle time and quality yield, to determine effectiveness of the program.

Purchasing Techniques

BLANKET ORDERS. Blanket orders are unfilled orders with a vendor.[9] A blanket order is a contract to purchase certain items from the vendor. It is not an authorization to ship anything. Shipment is made only upon receipt of an agreed-upon document, perhaps a shipping requisition or shipment release.

INVOICELESS PURCHASING. Invoiceless purchasing is an extension of good purchaser-supplier relations. In an invoiceless purchasing environment, there is typically one supplier for all units of a particular product. If the supplier provides all four wheels for each lawn mower produced, then management knows how many wheels it purchased. It just multiplies the quantity of lawn mowers produced times four and issues a check to the supplier for that amount.

ELECTRONIC ORDERING AND FUNDS TRANSFER. Electronic ordering and funds transfer reduce paper transactions. Paper transactions consist of a purchase

[6]Gary J. Zenz, *Purchasing and the Management of Materials,* 7th ed. (New York: John Wiley, 1994).
[7]The "yellow sheet" is the commonly used name of the *Official Board Markets,* published by Magazines for Industry, Chicago. It contains announced paperboard prices for containerboard and boxboard.
[8]*Metals Week,* A. Patrick Ryan, editor and publisher, New York.
[9]Unfilled orders are also referred to as "open" orders or "incomplete" orders.

order, a purchase release, a receiving document, authorization to pay an invoice (which is matched with the approved receiving report), and finally the issuance of a check. Purchasing departments can reduce this barrage of paperwork by electronic ordering, acceptance of all parts as 100% good, and electronic funds transfer to pay for units received. Not only can electronic ordering reduce paperwork, but it also speeds up the traditionally long procurement cycle. General Motors has saved billions of dollars over the past few years through exactly this kind of electronic transfer.[10]

electronic data interchange (EDI)

Transactions between firms are increasingly done via electronic data interchange. **Electronic data interchange (EDI)** is a standardized data transmittal format for computerized communications between organizations. EDI provides data transfer for virtually any business application, including purchasing. Data are transmitted directly from electronic media of the sender via a third party (usually, the phone company) to electronic media of the receiver. For instance, under EDI, data for a purchase order, such as order date, due date, quantity, part number, purchase order number, address, and so forth, are fitted into the standard EDI format. The data are then sent, usually from one computer to another, by phone line. The receiving organization knows where the data are on the standardized format; a computer program is used to read those data into the receiving company's files.

STOCKLESS PURCHASING. The term *stockless purchasing* has come to mean that the supplier maintains the inventory for the purchaser. If the supplier can maintain the stock of inventory for a variety of customers who use the same product or whose differences are very minor, say, perhaps at the packaging stage, then there may be a net savings. Postponement and consignment inventories, discussed earlier in this chapter, are related options.

STANDARDIZATION. The purchasing department should make special efforts toward increased levels of standardization. That is, rather than obtaining a variety of very similar components with labeling, coloring, packaging, or perhaps even slightly different engineering specifications, the purchasing agent should endeavor to have those components standardized.

MATERIALS MANAGEMENT

materials management

Purchasing may be combined with various warehousing and inventory activities to form a materials management system. The purpose of **materials management** is to obtain efficiency of operations through the integration of all material acquisition, movement, and storage activities in the firm. When transportation and inventory costs are substantial on both the input and output side of the production process, an emphasis of materials management may be appropriate. The potential for competitive advantage is found via both reduced costs and improved customer service. Many manufacturing companies have moved to some form of material management structure.

Firms recognize that the distribution of goods to and from their facilities can represent as much as 25% of the cost of products. And total cost in the United

[10]See J. Carbonne, "G.M. After Lopez," *Electronic Business Buyer* (October 1993): 56–60.

States is over 10% of the gross national product (GNP).[11] Because of this high cost, firms constantly address their means of distribution. Five major means of distribution are trucking, railways, airfreight, waterways, and pipelines.

Distribution Systems

TRUCKING. The vast majority of manufactured goods moves by truck. The flexibility of shipping by truck is only one of its many advantages. Companies that have adopted JIT programs in recent years have put increased pressure on truckers to pick up and deliver on time, with no damage, with paperwork in order, and at low cost. Carriers such as Roadway Express and Skyway Freight Systems are now viewed as part of the chain of quality from supplier to processor to end customer. Trucking firms are increasingly using computers to monitor weather, find the most effective route, reduce fuel cost, and analyze the most efficient way to unload.

RAILROADS. Railroads in the United States employ close to 250,000 people and ship 60% of all coal, 67% of autos, 68% of paper products, and about one-half of all food, lumber, and chemicals in this country. Containerization has made intermodal shipping of truck trailers on railroad flat cars, often piggybacked as double-decks, a popular means of distribution. Over 4 million trailer loads are moved in the United States each year by rail. Norfolk and Southern uses piggybacked cars extensively to meet JIT demands of Detroit automakers. With the growth of JIT, rail transport has been the biggest loser because small-batch manufacture requires frequent, smaller shipments.

AIRFREIGHT. Airfreight represents only about 1% of tonnage shipped in the United States. But the recent proliferation of airfreight carriers such as Federal Express, UPS, and Purolator makes it the fastest growing mode of shipping. Clearly, for national and international movement of lightweight items such as medical and emergency supplies, flowers, fruits, and electronic components, airfreight offers quickness and reliability.

WATERWAYS. Waterways are one of the nation's oldest means of freight transportation, dating back to the start of construction of the Erie Canal in 1817. Included in U.S. waterways are the nation's rivers, canals, the Great Lakes, coastlines, and oceans connecting to other countries. The usual cargo on waterways is bulky, low-value cargo such as iron ore, grains, cement, coal, chemicals, limestone, and petroleum products. This distribution system is important when shipping cost is more important than speed.

PIPELINES. Pipelines are an important form of transport of crude oil, natural gas, and other petroleum and chemical products. An amazing 90% of the state of Alaska's budget is derived from the 1.5 million barrels of oil pumped daily through the pipeline at Prudhoe Bay.

---

[11]Robert Millen, "JIT Logistics, Putting JIT on Wheels," *Target* 7, no. 2 (Summer 1991): p. 4.

BENCHMARKING SUPPLY-CHAIN MANAGEMENT

As a strategic decision, many firms have moved to supply-chain management. These firms see themselves in supplier-customer relationships where 100% good quality is always expected. As Table S11.3 shows, world-class firms do indeed set world-class benchmarks. Supply-chain management reduces costs, but perhaps more importantly it can provide a competitive advantage by responding to a customer that is more demanding and sophisticated. Ninety-four percent of the respondents to a 1992 *Traffic Management* survey regularly monitor on-time delivery by their suppliers. An example of a firm that uses supply-chain management to develop a competitive edge is Wal-Mart. With its own fleet of almost 2,000 trucks, 19 distribution centers, and a satellite communication system, Wal-Mart replenishes its store shelves an average of twice per week. Competitors resupply every other week. Economical and speedy resupply means high levels of product availability and reductions in inventory investment.

TABLE S11.3 PERFORMANCE IN WORLD-CLASS FIRMS

	TYPICAL FIRMS	WORLD-CLASS FIRMS
Number of suppliers per purchasing agent	34	5
Purchasing costs as percent of purchases	3.3%	.8%
Lead time (weeks)	15	8
Time spent placing an order	42 minutes	15 minutes
Percentage of late deliveries	33%	2%
Percentage of rejected material	1.5%	.0001%
Number of shortages per year	400	4

SOURCE: Adapted from McKinsey & Company as reported in *Business Week*, November 30, 1992, p. 72.

SUMMARY

A substantial portion of the cost and quality of the products of many firms, including most manufacturing, restaurant, wholesale, and retail firms, is determined by how efficiently they manage the supply chain. Consequently, supply-chain management provides a great opportunity for such firms to develop a competitive advantage. Supply-chain management is an approach to managing suppliers that includes not only purchasing, but a comprehensive approach to developing maximum value for the supply chain. Five purchasing strategies have been identified. They are (1) many suppliers, (2) few suppliers, (3) keiretsu networks, (4) vertical integration, and (5) virtual companies. Leading companies determine the right purchasing strategy, and often develop a materials management organization to ensure effective warehousing and distribution.

KEY TERMS

Supply-chain management *(p. 398)*
Postponement *(p. 398)*
Drop shipping *(p. 399)*
Purchasing *(p. 400)*
Purchasing agent *(p. 400)*
Buyer *(p. 400)*
Make-or-buy decision *(p. 401)*
Vertical integration *(p. 403)*
Keiretsu *(p. 404)*
Virtual companies *(p. 405)*
Purchasing management *(p. 405)*
Negotiation strategies *(p. 407)*
Electronic data interchange (EDI) *(p. 408)*
Materials management *(p. 408)*

SELF-TEST ■ SUPPLEMENT 11

- *Before taking the self-test* refer back to the learning objectives listed at the beginning of the supplement and the key terms listed at the end of the supplement.
- Use the key at the back of the text to *correct* your answers.
- *Restudy* pages that correspond to any questions you answered incorrectly or material you feel uncertain about.

1. The classic types of negotiation strategies include
   a. cost-based price model
   b. market-based price model
   c. competitive bidding
   d. all of the above

2. Unfilled orders with a vendor are the result of
   a. blanket orders
   b. invoiceless purchasing
   c. electronic ordering and funds transfer
   d. stockless purchasing
   e. all of the above

3. People who assist buyers by following up on purchases to ensure timely delivery are known as
   a. purchasing agents
   b. expeditors
   c. purchasing assistants
   d. all of the above

4. In a production environment, the purchasing function is usually managed by
   a. an expediter
   b. a buyer
   c. a purchasing agent
   d. a lawyer

5. With regard to the *cost-based price model* of negotiation strategy, which of the following is true?
   a. potential vendors each submit quotations as to price, delivery, and so on
   b. prices are based in some way upon market standards agreed to by both vendor and purchaser
   c. prices are based upon vendor costs
   d. all of the above

6. *Invoiceless purchasing* and *stockless purchasing*
   a. mean the same thing
   b. both lead to vastly reduced overall purchasing costs for a particular item
   c. both tend to reduce the amount of paper involved in the transaction
   d. both require a multiplicity of suppliers
   e. none of the above

7. The term *vertical integration* means to
   a. develop the ability to produce products that complement or supplement the original product
   b. produce goods or services previously purchased
   c. develop the ability to produce the specified good more efficiently
   d. all of the above

8. Supply-chain management is
   a. concerned with developing new reliable suppliers
   b. all of the activities that procure raw materials, transforms them into intermediate goods and then final products, and delivers the products to customers through a distribution system
   c. the acquisition of goods and services
   d. integration of all-material acquisition, movement and storage activities of the firm

9. Materials management is
   a. concerned with developing new reliable suppliers
   b. all of the activities that procure raw materials, transforms them into intermediate goods and then final products, and delivers the products to customers through a distribution system
   c. the acquisition of goods and services
   d. integration of all material acquisition, movement and storage activities of the firm

10. Purchasing is
    a. concerned with developing new reliable suppliers
    b. all of the activities that procure raw materials, transforms them into intermediate goods and then final products, and delivers the products to customers through a distribution system
    c. the acquisition of goods and services
    d. integration of all material acquisition, movement and storage activities of the firm

11. Vendor relations is
    a. concerned with developing new reliable suppliers
    b. all of the activities that procure raw materials, transforms them into intermediate goods and then final products, and delivers the products to customers through a distribution system
    c. the acquisition of goods and services
    d. integration of all material acquisition, movement, and storage activities of the firm

12. The objective of the purchasing function is ________________.

13. Five purchasing strategies are ________, ________, ________, ________, ________.

14. Five techniques for improving purchasing efficiency are ________, ________, ________, ________, ________.

DISCUSSION QUESTIONS

1. Under what conditions might a firm decide to organize its purchasing function as a materials management function?
2. What is a keiretsu?
3. What information does purchasing receive from other functional areas of the firm?
4. How does a traditional adversarial relationship with suppliers change when a firm makes a decision to move to a few suppliers?
5. What are the three basic approaches to negotiations?
6. What can purchasing do to implement just-in-time deliveries?
7. How does a traditional adversarial relationship with suppliers change when a firm decides to move to just-in-time deliveries?
8. How do we distinguish between supplier management, supply-chain management, purchasing, and materials management?

OPERATIONS IN PRACTICE EXERCISE

What are the cultural impediments to establishing keiretsu networks in countries other than Japan? What would the antitrust division of the U.S. government think of such arrangements? What would the European Community's position be on such arrangements? Find an example of a firm that has a keiretsu network and describe its effectiveness.

PROBLEMS

: **S11.1.** As purchasing agent for Woolsey Enterprises in Golden, Colorado, you ask your buyer to provide you with a ranking of "excellent," "good," "fair," or "poor" for a variety of characteristics for two potential vendors. You suggest that the rankings be consistent with the vendor rating form shown in Figure S11.2. The buyer has returned the ranking shown below.

DONNA INC. = D VENDOR RATING:
KAY CORP. = K

Company	Excellent (4)	Good (3)	Fair (2)	Poor (1)
Size and/or capacity		K	D	
Financial strength			K	D
Operational profit			K	D
Manufacturing range			KD	
Research facilities	K		D	
Technical service		K	D	
Geographical locations		K	D	
Management		K	D	
Labor relations			K	D
Trade relations			KD	

Service	Excellent (4)	Good (3)	Fair (2)	Poor (1)
Deliveries on time		KD		
Condition on arrival		KD		
Follow instructions			D	K
Number of rejections				KD
Handling of complaints		KD		
Technical assistance		K	D	
Emergency aid				KD
Supply up-to-date catalogues, etc				KD
Supply price changes promptly				KD

Products	Excellent (4)	Good (3)	Fair (2)	Poor (1)
Quality	KD			
Price			KD	
Packaging			KD	
Uniformity			KD	
Warranty			KD	
Sales Personnel				
1. Knowledge				
His company			D	K
His products			K	D
Our industry			KD	
Our company			K	D
2. Sales calls				
Properly spaced			D	K
By appointment				KD
Planned and prepared			K	D
Mutually productive			K	D
3. Sales service				
Obtain information			D	K
Furnish quotations promptly		K		D
Follow orders			D	K
Expedite delivery			K	D
Handle complaints		KD		

How do you rank these potential vendors? (*Hint:* Figure S11.2 provides an excellent approach.)

S11.2. As a library assignment, identify organizations that are
- **a.** engaged in vertical integration
- **b.** engaged in reducing their vertical integration
- **c.** moving toward "virtual" companies

CASE STUDY

Factory Enterprises, Inc.

Factory Enterprises, Inc., makes automobile air conditioners for car dealer installation. The firm owns the patents and makes the product at a sizable markup. As a result, the 20-year-old company pays its private owners very well.

The enterprise shows growth in overseas sales at the very time that domestic market demand explodes. This exhausting situation calls for total effort by all company personnel: eight managers and supervisors, 30 factory workers, and six office employees.

Various people purchase materials and component parts, in addition to their regular duties. The production manager buys finned radiators and copper tubing. The shipping supervisor buys mounting assemblies, to which workers attach all of the component parts in the final process. The sales manager buys shipping cartons.

You have just joined the company as the purchasing manager.

DISCUSSION QUESTIONS

1. Describe for the president the materials management concept. What would it do for the company and what would it do to the company?
2. What action steps would you follow to install the materials management concept if the president decides to adopt it?
3. Explain how sales and purchasing can help each other by establishing a good relationship.
4. European customers insist on ISO 9000 compliance. How should the company respond?

SOURCE: Adapted from Gary J. Zenz, *Purchasing and the Management of Materials*, 7th ed. (New York: John Wiley & Sons, Inc., 1994) pp. 623–624.

CASE STUDY

Thomas Manufacturing Company

Mr. Thomas, president of Thomas Manufacturing Company, and Mr. McDonnell, the vice president, were discussing how future economic conditions would affect their product, home air purifiers. They were particularly concerned about cost increases. They increased selling prices last year and thought another price increase would have an adverse affect on sales. They wondered if there was some way to reduce costs in order to maintain the existing price structure.

McDonnell had attended a purchasing association meeting the previous night and heard a presentation by the president of a tool company on how they were approaching cost reduction. The tool company had just hired a purchasing agent with a business degree who was reducing costs by 15%. McDonnell thought some of the ideas might be applicable to Thomas Manufacturing. The present purchasing agent, Mr. Older, had been with the company for 25 years and they had no complaints. Production never stopped for lack of material. Yet a 15% cost reduction was something that could not be ignored. Thomas suggested that McDonnell look into this area and come up with a recommendation.

McDonnell contacted several business schools in the area. He said he would be interested in hiring a new graduate. One of the requirements for applicants was a paper on how to improve the company's purchasing function. Several applicants visited the plant and analyzed the purchasing department before they wrote their papers. The most dynamic paper was submitted by Tim Younger. He recommended:

1. Lower stock reorder levels (from 60 days to 45 days) for many items, thus reducing inventory.

continued on next page

2. Analyze specifications on many parts.
3. Standardize many of the parts to reduce the variety of items.
4. Analyze items to see whether more products can be purchased by blanket purchase orders, with the ultimate goal of reducing the purchasing staff.
5. Look for new and lower cost sources of supply.
6. Increase the number of requests for bids, to get still lower prices.
7. Be more aggressive in negotiations. Make fewer concessions.
8. Make sure all trade, quantity, and cash discounts are taken.
9. Buy from the lowest price source, disregarding local public relations.
10. Stop showing favoritism to customers who also buy from the company. Reciprocity comes second to price.
11. Purchase to current requirements rather than to market conditions. Too much money is tied up in inventory.

After reading all the papers McDonnell was debating with himself what he should recommend to Thomas. Just the previous week at the department meeting, Older was recommending many of the opposite actions. In particular, he recommended an increase in inventory levels anticipating future rising prices. Older also stressed the good relations the company had with all their suppliers and how they can be relied upon for good service and a possible extension of credit. Most of their suppliers bought their home air purifiers from Thomas Manufacturing. Yet Younger said the practice of favoring them was wrong and should be eliminated. McDonnell was hesitant about what action he should recommend; Thomas wanted a decision in the morning.

DISCUSSION QUESTIONS

1. What recommendation would you make if you were McDonnell? Why?
2. Analyze each of Younger's recommendations. Do you agree or disagree with them? Why?

Source: Professor Richard J. Tersine, University of Oklahoma.

Internet Case Studies See our Internet home page at http://www.prenhall. com/renderpom for these additional case studies: AT&T Buys a Printer, and Blue and Gray, Inc.

BIBLIOGRAPHY

Akin, U. "Selecting Venders in a Manufacturing Environment." *Journal of Operations Management* 11, no. 2 (June 1993): 104–122.

Arnold, J. R. T. *Introduction to Material Management*, 2nd ed. Upper Saddle River, NJ: Prentice-Hall, 1996.

Ballow, R. H. *Business Logistics Management,* 3rd ed. Upper Saddle River, NJ: Prentice-Hall, 1992.

Bhote, K. *Supply Management: How to Make U.S. Suppliers Competitive.* New York: American Management Association, 1987.

Blumenfeld, D. E., L. D. Burns, C. F. Daganzo, M. C. Frick, and R. W. Hall, "Reducing Logistics Costs at General Motors." *Interfaces* 17 (January-February 1987): 26–47.

Burt, D. N., and W. R. Soukup. "Purchasing's Role in New Product Development." *Harvard Business Review* 63 (September-October 1985): 90–97.

Chesbrough, Henry W., and David J. Teece. "When Is Virtual Virtuous? Organizing for Innovation." *Harvard Business Review* (January-February 1996): 65–73.

Dwyer, F., P. Schurr, and S. Oh (April 1987). "Developing Buyer-Seller Relationships." *Journal of Marketing* 51 (April 1987): 11–27.

Ellram, L. "A Managerial Guideline for the Development and Implementation of Purchasing Partnerships." *Internationals Journal of Purchasing* 11 (Summer 1991): 2–8.

Geoffrion, Arthur M., and Richard C. Grimes. "Twenty Years of Strategic Distribution System Design: An Evolutionary Perspective." *Interfaces* 25, no. 5 (1995).

Helper, S. "How Much Has Really Changed Between U.S. Automakers and Their Suppliers?" *Sloan Management Review* 32 (Summer 1991): 15.

Lewis, Jordan D. *The Connected Corporation: How Leading Companies Win Through Customer-Supplier Alliances.* New York: Free Press, 1996.

Magad, B. L., and J. M. Ames. *Total Material Management*, 2nd ed. New York: Chapman and Hall, 1995.

Min, Hokey, and Dooyoung Shin. "A Group Technology Classification and Coding System for Value-Added Purchasing." *Production and Inventory Management Journal* 35, no. 1 (First Quarter 1994).

Shapiro, Roy D. "Get Leverage from Logistics." *Harvard Business Review* 62 (May-June 1984): 119–126.

Aggregate Scheduling

12

CHAPTER OUTLINE

The Strategic Importance of Aggregate Scheduling

The Planning Process

The Nature of Aggregate Scheduling

Aggregate Planning Strategies

Capacity Options ■ Demand Options ■ Mixing Options to Develop a Plan ■ Level Scheduling

Methods for Aggregate Scheduling

Graphical and Charting Methods ■ Mathematical Approaches for Planning ■ Comparison of Aggregate Planning Methods

Disaggregation

Aggregate Scheduling in Services

Restaurants ■ Miscellaneous Services ■ National Chains of Small Service Firms ■ Airline Industry ■ Hospitals

A Case Study of Aggregate Scheduling in a Law Firm

Summary ■ Key Terms ■ Using POM for Windows for Aggregate Planning ■ Solved Problems ■ Discussion Questions ■ Self-Test Chapter 12 ■ Operations in Practice Exercise ■ Problems ■ Case Study: Southwestern State College ■ Bibliography

LEARNING OBJECTIVES

When you complete this chapter you should be able to:

IDENTIFY OR DEFINE:

Aggregate scheduling
Tactical scheduling
Graphic technique for aggregate planning
Mathematical techniques for planning

EXPLAIN:

How to do aggregate planning
How service firms develop aggregate plans

THE STRATEGIC IMPORTANCE OF AGGREGATE PLANNING

Manufacturers such as GE and Whirlpool face tough decisions when trying to schedule products like room air conditioners, which are heavily dependent on weather. If the firms increase output and a summer is warmer than usual, they stand to increase sales and market share. But if the summer is cool, GE and Whirlpool are stuck with expensive unsold machines. Developing plans that minimize costs connected with such forecasts is one of the main functions of an operations manager.

aggregate scheduling
aggregate planning

Aggregate scheduling (also known as **aggregate planning**) is concerned with determining the quantity and timing of production for the intermediate future, often from 3 to 18 months ahead. Operations managers try to determine the best way to meet forecasted demand by adjusting production rates, labor levels, inventory levels, overtime work, subcontracting rates, and other controllable variables. The *objective of the process usually is to minimize cost over the planning period.* However, other strategic issues may be more important than low cost. These strategies may be to smooth employment levels, drive down inventory levels, or to meet a high level of service regardless of cost.

For a manufacturer such as GE or Whirlpool, the aggregate schedule ties the firm's strategic goals to production plans for specific products. For a service organization, the aggregate schedule ties strategic goals with detailed schedules for the work force.

The purpose of this chapter is to describe the aggregate planning decision, to show how the aggregate plan fits into the overall planning process, and to describe several techniques that managers use in developing a plan. We stress both manufacturing and service-sector firms.

The Planning Process

NOTE
If top management did a poor or inconsistent job of long-term planning, problems will develop that make the aggregate planner's job very tough.

In the supplement to Chapter 2, we saw that demand forecasting can address short-, medium-, and long-range problems. Long-range forecasts help managers deal with capacity and strategic issues and are the responsibility of top management (see Figure 12.1). Top management formulates policy-related questions, such as facility location and expansion, new product development, research funding, and investment over a period of several years.

scheduling decisions

Medium-range planning begins once long-term capacity decisions are made. This is the job of the operations manager. **Scheduling decisions** include making monthly or quarterly plans, which address the problem of matching productivity to fluctuating demands. All of these plans need to be consistent with top management's long-range strategy and work within the resources allocated by earlier strategic decisions. The heart of the medium- (or "intermediate-") range plan is the aggregate production plan.

Short-range planning extends up to a year but is usually less than three months. This plan is also the responsibility of operations personnel, who work with supervisors and foremen, to "disaggregate" the intermediate plan into weekly, daily, and hourly schedules. Tactics for dealing with short-term planning involving loading, sequencing, expediting and dispatching are discussed in the next chapter.

Figure 12.1 illustrates the time horizons and features for short-, intermediate-, and long-range planning.

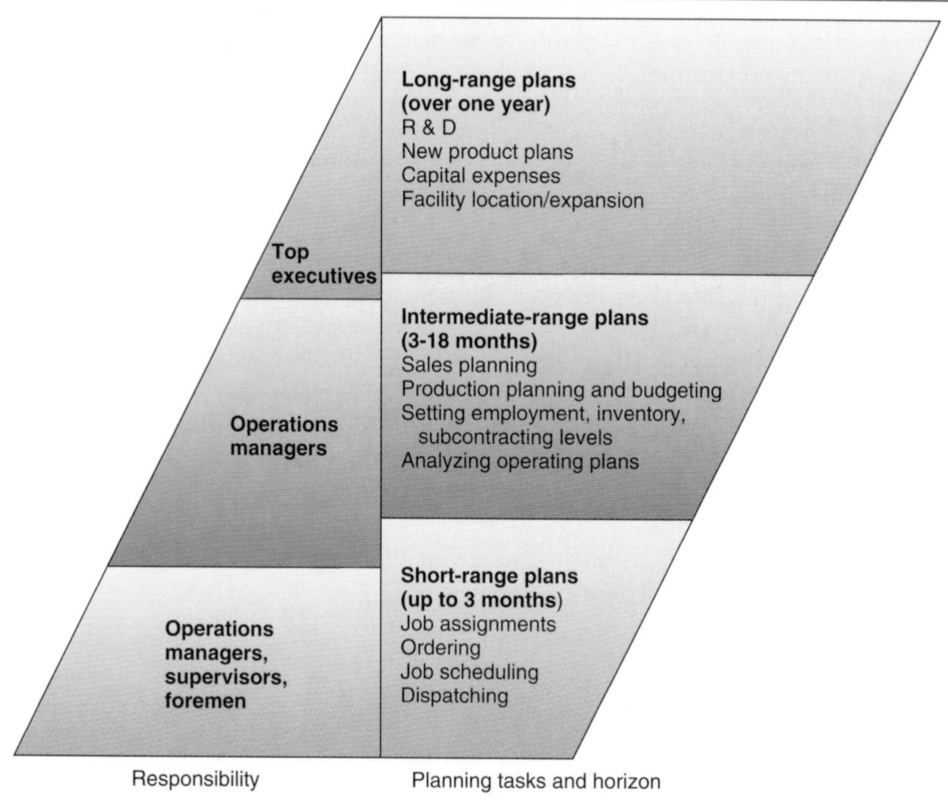

FIGURE 12.1

PLANNING TASKS AND RESPONSIBILITIES

THE NATURE OF AGGREGATE SCHEDULING

As the term *aggregate* implies, an aggregate plan means combining the appropriate resources into general, or overall, terms. Given the demand forecast, the facility capacity, inventory levels, the size of the workforce, and related inputs, the planner has to select the rate of output for the facility over the next 3 to 18 months. The plan can be for manufacturing firms such as GE and Whirlpool, hospitals, colleges, or Prentice-Hall, the company that published this textbook.

NOTE
Aggregate planning in the real world involves a lot of trial and error.

Take, for a manufacturing example, IBM or Compaq, each of which produces different models of microcomputers. They make (1) laptops, (2) desktops, (3) notebook computers, and (4) advanced technology machines with high-speed chips. The aggregate plan for IBM or Compaq might have the following output (in units of production) for this "family" of microcomputers each month in the upcoming three quarters:

QUARTER 1			QUARTER 2			QUARTER 3		
Jan.	Feb.	March	April	May	June	July	Aug.	Sept.
150,000	120,000	110,000	100,000	130,000	150,000	180,000	150,000	140,000

Note that the plan looks at production in the aggregate, not on a product-by-product breakdown.

An example from the service sector would be Computrain, a company that provides microcomputer training for managers. The firm offers courses on spreadsheets, graphics, data bases, word processing and the Internet, and employs several instructors to meet the demand from business and government for its services. Demand for training tends to be very low near holiday seasons and during summer, when many people take their vacations. To meet the fluctuating needs for courses, the company can perhaps hire and lay off instructors, advertise to increase demand in slow seasons, or subcontract its work to other training agencies during peak periods. Again, aggregate planning makes decisions about intermediate-range capacity, not specific courses or instructors.

Aggregate planning is part of a larger production planning system; therefore, understanding the interfaces between the plan and several internal and external factors is useful. Figure 12.2 shows that not only does the operations manager receive input from the marketing department's demand forecast, but he or she has to deal with financial data, personnel, capacity, and availability of raw materials as well. In a manufacturing environment, the resulting master production schedule provides input to material requirements planning (MRP) systems, which address the procurement or production of parts or components needed to make the

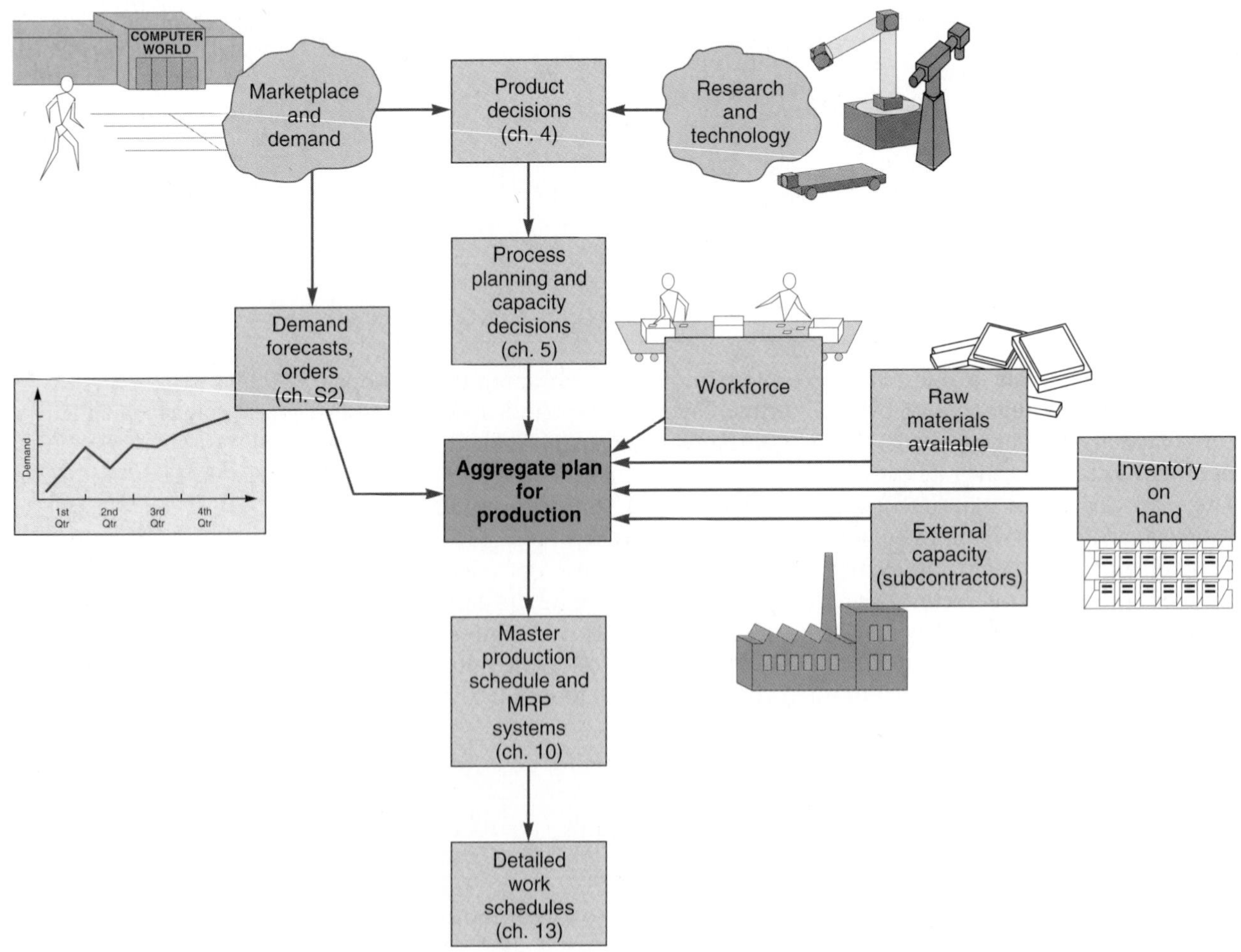

FIGURE 12.2 RELATIONSHIPS OF THE AGGREGATE PLAN

final product (see Chapter 10). Detailed work schedules for people and priority scheduling for products result as the final step of the production planning system (and are discussed in Chapter 13).

Federal Express's huge aircraft fleet is used to near capacity for nighttime delivery of packages but is 100% idle during the daytime. In an attempt to better utilize their capacity (and leverage their assets), Federal Express considered two services with opposite or countercyclical demand patterns to their nighttime service—commuter passenger service and passenger charter service. However, after a thorough analysis of these new services, the 12% to 13% return on investment was judged insufficient for the risks involved. Facing the same issues, however, UPS recently decided to begin a charter airline that operates on weekends.

AGGREGATE PLANNING STRATEGIES

There are several questions the operations manager must answer when generating an aggregate plan:

1. Should inventories be used to absorb changes in demand during the planning period?
2. Should changes be accommodated by varying the size of the workforce?
3. Should part-timers be used, or should overtime and idle time absorb fluctuations?
4. Should subcontractors be used on fluctuating orders so that a stable workforce can be maintained?
5. Should prices or other factors be changed to influence demand?

All of these are legitimate planning strategies available to management. They involve the manipulation of inventory, production rates, labor levels, capacity, and other controllable variables. We will now examine eight options in more detail. The first five are called *capacity options* because they do not try to change demand but attempt to absorb the fluctuations in it. The last three are *demand options* through which firms try to influence the demand pattern to smooth out its changes over the planning period.

Capacity Options

The basic capacity (supply) options that a firm can choose are the following:

1. *Changing inventory levels.* Managers can increase inventory during periods of low demand to meet high demand in future periods. If we select this pure strategy, costs associated with storage, insurance, handling, obsolescence, pilferage, and capital invested will increase. (These costs typically range from 15% to 40% of the value of an item annually.) On the other hand, when the firm enters a period of increasing demand, shortages can result in lost sales due to potentially longer lead times and poorer customer service.
2. *Varying workforce size by hiring or layoffs.* One way to meet demand is to hire or lay off production workers to match production rates. But often new employees need to be trained and the average productivity drops temporarily as they are absorbed into the firm. Layoffs or firings, of course, lower the morale of all workers and can lead to lower productivity.
3. *Varying production rates through overtime or idle time.* It is sometimes possible to keep a constant workforce but to vary working hours. When demand is on a large upswing, though, there is a limit on how much overtime is realistic. Overtime pay requires more money, and too much overtime can wear workers down to the point that their overall productivity drops off. Overtime also implies increased overhead associated with keeping the facility open. On the other hand, when there is a period of decreased demand,

the company must somehow absorb workers' idle time—usually a difficult process.

4. *Subcontracting.* A firm can also acquire temporary capacity by subcontracting some work during peak demand periods. Subcontracting, however, has several pitfalls. First, it is costly; second, it risks opening the door of your client to a competitor; and third, it is often hard to find the perfect subcontract supplier, one who always delivers the quality product on time.
5. *Using part-time workers.* Especially in the service sector, part-time workers can fill in for unskilled labor needs. This is evidenced in fast-food restaurants, retail stores, and supermarkets.

Demand Options

The basic demand options are the following:

1. *Influencing demand.* When demand is low, a company can try to increase demand through advertising, promotion, increased personal selling, and price cuts. Airlines and hotels have long offered weekend discounts and off-season rates; telephone companies charge less at night; some colleges give discounts to senior citizens to fill classes; and air conditioners are least expensive in winter. Special advertising, promotions, selling, and pricing are not always able, however, to balance the demand with the production capacity.
2. *Back ordering during high demand periods.* Back orders are orders for goods or services that a firm accepts but is unable (either on purpose or by chance) to fill at the moment. If customers are willing to wait without loss of their goodwill or order, back ordering is a possible strategy. Many auto dealers back order, but the approach often results in lost sales for many consumer goods and services.
3. *Counterseasonal product mixing.* A widely used active smoothing technique among manufacturers is to develop a product mix of counterseasonal items. Examples include companies that make both furnaces and air conditioners or lawn mowers and snowblowers. Service companies (and manufacturers also, for that matter) who follow this approach, however, may find themselves involved in services or products beyond their area of expertise or beyond their target market.

NOTE
Negative inventory means we owe units to customers. We either lose sales or we back order to make it up.

Mixing Options to Develop a Plan

Although each of the five capacity options and three demand options might produce a cost-effective aggregate schedule, a combination of them (called a **mixed strategy**) often works best. Mixed strategies involve the combination of two or more controllable variables to set a feasible production plan. For example, a firm might use a combination of overtime, subcontracting, and inventory leveling as its strategy. Since there can be a huge combination of different possible mixed strategies, managers find that aggregate planning can be a fairly challenging task. Finding the one "optimal" aggregate plan is not always possible.

The mix of strategy options is different for service firms than for manufacturing firms. For instance, stocking inventory may not be an option, and subcontracting may invite competition. Consequently, service firms often address aggregate scheduling via changes in personnel. They do this by changing labor requirements, cross-training, job rotation, and using part-time employees.

mixed strategy

NOTE
Mixed strategies are more complex than pure ones, but typically yield a better strategy.

NOTE
The most common options are regular time production, overtime production, and subcontracting.

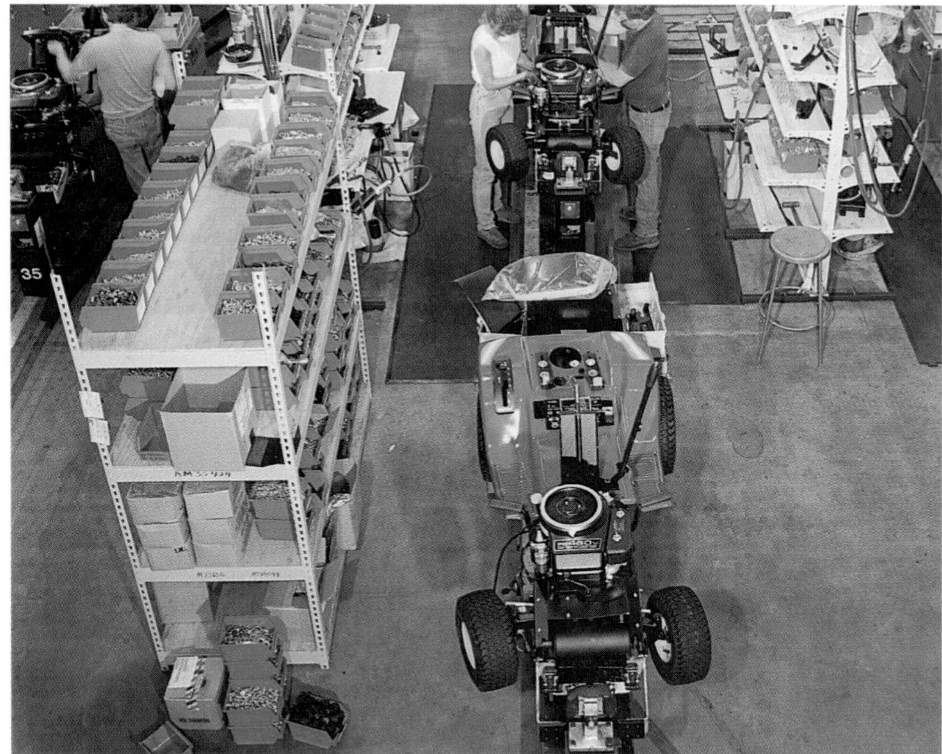

John Deere and Company, the "granddaddy" of farm equipment manufacturers, uses sales incentives to smooth demand. During the fall and winter off-seasons, sales are helped with price cuts and other incentives. About 70% of Deere's big machines are ordered in advance of seasonal use; this is about double the industry rate. The incentives hurt margins, but Deere keeps its market share and controls costs by producing more steadily all year long. Similarly, in service businesses such as L.L. Bean, some customers are offered free shipping on orders placed before the Christmas rush.

Level Scheduling

level scheduling

Level scheduling or level capacity planning, involves aggregate plans in which daily capacities from month to month are uniform. In effect, firms like Toyota and Nissan keep production systems at uniform levels and may let the finished goods inventory of autos go up or down to buffer the difference between monthly demand and production level or find alternative work for production employees. Their philosophy is that stable employment leads to better quality autos, less turnover, less absenteeism, and more employee commitment to corporate goals. Level scheduling works well when demand is reasonably stable.

Level scheduling usually results in lower production costs than other strategies. Workers tend to be more experienced, so supervision is easier; costs of hiring, firing, and overtime are minimized; and the operation is smoother with less dramatic startups and shutdowns.

Methods for Aggregate Scheduling

Some companies have no formal aggregate planning process. They use the same plan from year to year, making adjustments up or down just enough to fit the new demand. This method certainly does not provide much flexibility, and if the original plan was suboptimal, the entire production process will be locked into suboptimal performance.

In this section, we introduce several techniques operations managers use in developing more useful and appropriate aggregate plans. They range from the widely used charting (or graphical) method to a series of more formal mathematical approaches, including the transportation method of linear programming.

Graphical and Charting Methods

graphical and charting techniques

Graphical and charting techniques are popular because they are easy to understand and use. Basically, these plans work with a few variables at a time to allow planners to compare projected demand with existing capacity. They are trial-and-error approaches that do not guarantee an optimal production plan, but they require only limited computations and can be performed by clerical staff. The following are five steps in the graphical method:

1. Determine the demand in each period.
2. Determine what the capacity is for regular time, overtime, and subcontracting each period.
3. Find the labor costs, hiring and layoff costs, and inventory holding costs.
4. Consider company policy that may apply to the workers or to stock levels.
5. Develop alternative plans and examine their total costs.

These steps are illustrated in Examples 1 to 4.

Beer is produced in a product-focused facility where high utilization, because of high fixed cost, is critical. Operations personnel must match capacity to meet demand in the long, intermediate, and short runs. They must also effectively perform maintenance between batches to ensure schedules are maintained. Unused capacity is expensive, and inadequate capacity hurts market share. Shown here on the left are the brew kettles where wort, later to become beer, is boiled and hops are added. The canning line, shown on the right, imprints on each can a code that identifies the day, year, and 15-minute period of production, as well as the plant at which the product was brewed and packaged.

EXAMPLE 1

A Charlotte manufacturer of roofing supplies has developed monthly forecasts for an important product and presented the period January-June in Table 12.1.

TABLE 12.1

MONTH	EXPECTED DEMAND	PRODUCTION DAYS	DEMAND PER DAY (computed)
Jan.	900	22	41
Feb.	700	18	39
Mar.	800	21	38
Apr.	1,200	21	57
May	1,500	22	68
June	1,100	20	55
	6,200	124	

The demand per day is computed by simply dividing the expected demand by the number of production or working days each month.

To illustrate the nature of the aggregate planning problem, the firm also draws a graph (Figure 12.3) that charts the daily demand each month. The dotted line across the chart represents the production rate required to meet average demand. It is computed by:

$$\text{Average requirement} = \frac{\text{Total expected demand}}{\text{Number of production days}} = \frac{6{,}200}{124} = 50 \text{ units per day}$$

FIGURE 12.3

GRAPH OF FORECAST AND AVERAGE FORECAST DEMAND

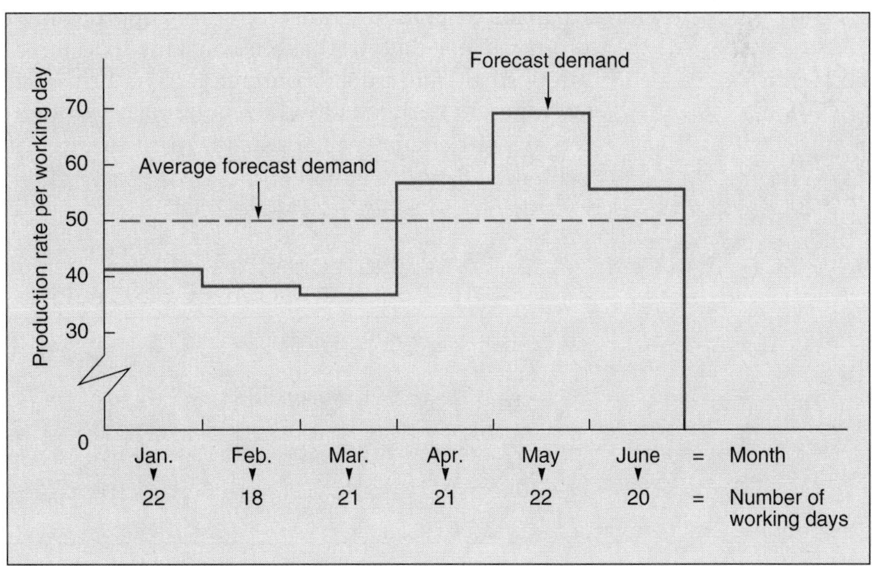

The graph in Figure 12.3 illustrates how the forecast differs from the average demand. Some strategies for meeting the forecast were listed earlier. The firm, for example, might staff to yield a production rate that meets the average demand (as indicated by the dashed line). Or it might produce a steady rate of, say, 30 units and then subcontract excess demand to other roofing suppliers. A third plan might be to combine overtime work with some subcontracting to absorb demand. Examples 2 to 4 illustrate three possible strategies.

EXAMPLE 2

One possible strategy (call it plan 1) for the manufacturer described in Example 1 is to maintain a constant workforce throughout the six-month period. A second (plan 2) is to maintain a constant workforce at a level necessary for the lowest demand month (March) and to meet all demand above this level by subcontracting. Yet a third plan is to hire and lay off workers as needed to produce exact monthly requirements. Table 12.2 provides cost information necessary for the analysis.

TABLE 12.2 COST INFORMATION

Inventory carrying cost	$5 per unit per month
Subcontracting cost per unit	$10 per unit
Average pay rate	$5 per hour ($40 per day)
Overtime pay rate	$7 per hour (above 8 hours)
Labor-hours to produce a unit	1.6 hours per unit
Cost of increasing production rate (training and hiring)	$10 per unit
Cost of decreasing production rate (layoffs)	$15 per unit

Analysis of plan 1. In analyzing this approach, which assumes that 50 units are produced per day, we have a constant workforce, no overtime or idle time, no safety stock, and no subcontractors. The firm accumulates inventory during the slack period of demand, which is January through March, and depletes it during the higher-demand warm season, April through June. We assume beginning inventory = 0, and planned ending inventory = 0.

MONTH	PRODUCTION AT 50 UNITS PER DAY	DEMAND FORECAST	MONTHLY INVENTORY CHANGE	ENDING INVENTORY
Jan.	1,100	900	+200	200
Feb.	900	700	+200	400
Mar.	1,050	800	+250	650
Apr.	1,050	1,200	−150	500
May	1,100	1,500	−400	100
June	1,000	1,100	−100	0
				1,850

Total units of inventory carried over from one month to the next month = 1,850 units

Workforce required to produce 50 units per day = 10 workers

Since each unit requires 1.6 labor-hours to produce, each worker can make 5 units in an eight-hour day. Hence to produce 50 units, 10 workers are needed.

Plan 1's costs are computed as follows:

COSTS		CALCULATIONS
Inventory carrying	$ 9,250	(= 1,850 units carried × $5 per unit)
Regular-time labor	49,600	(= 10 workers × $40 per day × 124 days)
Other costs (overtime, hiring, layoffs, subcontracting)	0	
Total cost	$58,850	

The graph for Example 2 was shown in Figure 12.3. Some planners prefer a *cumulative* graph to display visually how the forecast deviates from the average requirements. Such a graph is provided in Figure 12.4.

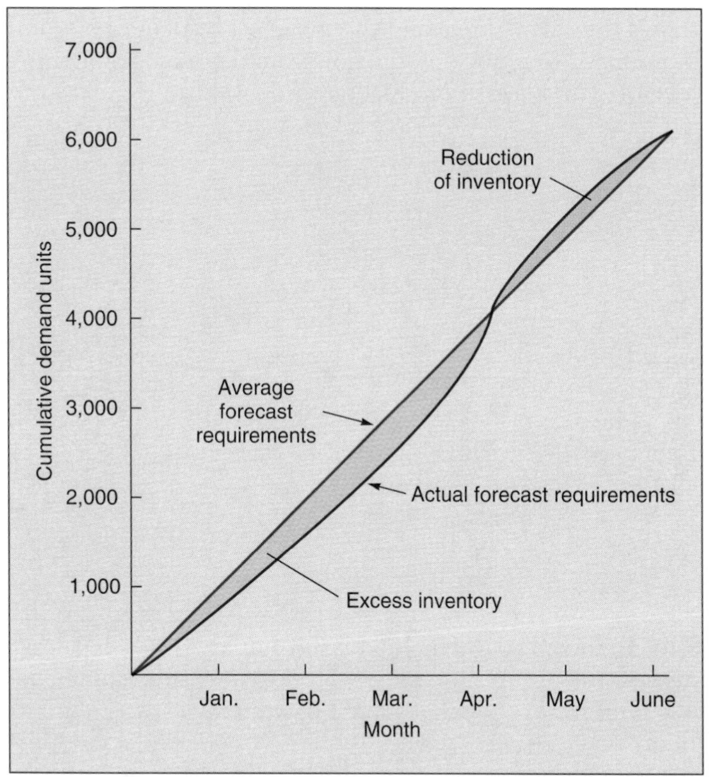

FIGURE 12.4

CUMULATIVE GRAPH FOR PLAN 1

EXAMPLE 3

Analysis of plan 2. A constant workforce is also maintained in plan 2, but set low enough to meet demand in March, the lowest month. To produce 38 units per day in-house, 7.6 workers are needed. (You can think of this as 7 full-time workers and 1 part-timer.) All other demand is met by subcontracting. Subcontracting is thus required in every other month. No inventory holding costs are incurred in plan 2.

Since 6,200 units are required during the aggregate plan period, we must compute how many can be made by the firm and how many subcontracted for:

$$\text{In-house production} = 38 \text{ units per day} \times 124 \text{ production days}$$
$$= 4{,}712 \text{ units}$$
$$\text{Subcontract units} = 6{,}200 - 4{,}712 = 1{,}488 \text{ units}$$

Plan 2's costs are:

COSTS		CALCULATIONS
Regular time labor	$37,696	(= 7.6 workers × $40 per day × 124 days)
Subcontracting	14,880	(= 1,488 units × $10 per unit)
Total cost	$52,576	

EXAMPLE 4

Analysis of plan 3. The final strategy, plan 3, involves varying the workforce size by hiring and firing as necessary. The production rate will equal the demand. Table 12.3 shows the calculations and the total cost of plan 3. Recall that it costs $15 per unit produced to reduce production from the previous month's level and $10 per unit change to increase production through hirings.

TABLE 12.3 COST COMPUTATIONS FOR PLAN 3

MONTH	FORECAST (units)	BASIC PRODUCTION COST (demand × 1.6 hrs per unit × $5 per hour)	EXTRA COST OF INCREASING PRODUCTION (hiring cost)	EXTRA COST OF DECREASING PRODUCTION (layoff cost)	TOTAL COST
Jan.	900	$ 7,200	—	—	$ 7,200
Feb.	700	5,600	—	$3,000 (= 200 × $15)	8,600
Mar.	800	6,400	$1,000 (= 100 × $10)	—	7,400
Apr.	1,200	9,600	4,000 (= 400 × $10)	—	13,600
May	1,500	12,000	3,000 (= 300 × $10)	—	15,000
June	1,100	8,800	—	$6,000 (= 400 × $15)	14,800
		$49,600	$8,000	$9,000	$66,600

The final step in the graphical method is to compare the costs of each proposed plan and to select the approach with the least total cost. A summary analysis is provided in Table 12.4. We see that plan 2 has the lowest cost and is the best of the three options.

Of course, many other feasible strategies can be considered in a problem like this, including combinations that use some overtime. Although charting and graphing is a popular management tool, its help is in evaluating strategies, not generating them. A systematic approach that considers all costs and produces an effective solution is needed.

Mathematical Approaches for Planning

This section briefly describes some of the mathematical approaches to aggregate planning that have been developed over the past 40 years.

TABLE 12.4 COMPARISON OF THE THREE PLANS

COST	PLAN 1 (constant work force of 10 workers)	PLAN 2 (workforce of 7.6 workers plus subcontract)	PLAN 3 (hiring and layoffs to meet demand)
Inventory carrying	$ 9,250	$ 0	$ 0
Regular labor	49,600	37,696	49,600
Overtime labor	0	0	0
Hiring	0	0	8,000
Layoffs	0	0	9,000
Subcontracting	0	14,880	0
Total cost	$58,850	$52,576	$66,600

THE TRANSPORTATION METHOD OF LINEAR PROGRAMMING. When an aggregate planning problem is viewed as one of allocating operating capacity to meet the forecasted demand, it can be formulated in a linear programming format. The **transportation method of linear programming** is not a trial-and-error approach like charting but produces an optimal plan for minimizing costs. It is also flexible in that it can specify the regular and overtime production in each time period, the number of units to be subcontracted, extra shifts, and the inventory carryover from period to period.

transportation method of linear programming

In Example 5, the supply consists of on-hand inventory and units produced by regular time, overtime, and subcontracting. Costs, in the upper right-hand corner of each cell of the matrix, relate to units produced in a given period or units carried in inventory from an earlier period.

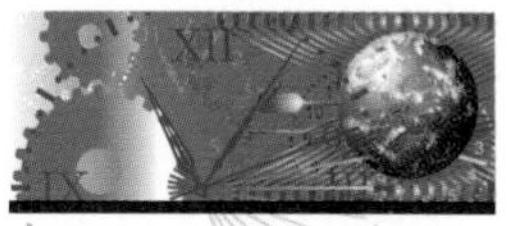

EXAMPLE 5

Farnsworth Tire Company developed data that relate to production, demand, capacity, and costs at its West Virginia plant, as shown in Table 12.5.

TABLE 12.5 FARNSWORTH'S PRODUCTION, DEMAND, CAPACITY, AND COST DATA

	SALES PERIOD		
	Mar.	*Apr.*	*May*
Demand	800	1,000	750
Capacity:			
Regular	700	700	700
Overtime	50	50	50
Subcontracting	150	150	130
Beginning inventory	100 tires		
	COSTS		
Regular time	$40 per tire		
Overtime	$50 per tire		
Subcontract	$70 per tire		
Carrying cost	$2 per tire per month		

Table 12.6 illustrates the structure of the transportation table and an initial feasible solution.

TABLE 12.6 FARNSWORTH'S TRANSPORTATION TABLE

SUPPLY FROM		DEMAND FOR *Period 1 (Mar.)*	*Period 2 (Apr.)*	*Period 3 (May)*	*Unused Capacity (Dummy)*	TOTAL CAPACITY AVAILABLE (supply)
Beginning inventory		0 / 100	2	4	0	100
Period 1	*Regular time*	40 / 700	42	44	0	700
	Overtime	50	52 / 50	54	0	50
	Subcontract	70	72 / 150	74	0	150
Period 2	*Regular time*		40 / 700	42	0	700
	Overtime		50 / 50	52	0	50
	Subcontract		70 / 50	72	0 / 100	150
Period 3	*Regular time*			40 / 700	0	700
	Overtime			50 / 50	0	50
	Subcontract			70	0 / 130	130
TOTAL DEMAND		800	1,000	750	230	2,780

You should note the following:

1. Carrying costs are $2/tire per month. Tires produced in one period and held one month will have a $2 higher cost. Since holding cost is linear, two months holdover costs $4.
2. Transportation problems require that supply equals demand; so, a dummy column called "unused capacity" has been added. Costs of not using capacity are zero.
3. Quantities in each column of Table 12.6 are the levels of inventory needed to meet demand requirements. Demand of 800 tires in March is met by using 100 tires from beginning inventory and 700 tires from regular time.

The transportation LP problem described here was originally formulated by E. H. Bowman in 1956.[1] Although it works well in analyzing the effects of holding inventories, using overtime, and subcontracting, it does not work when more fac-

[1]See E. H. Bowman, "Production Planning by the Transportation Method of Linear Programming," *Operations Research* 4, no. 1 (February 1956): 100–103.

tors are introduced. So, when hiring and layoffs are introduced, the more general method of simplex linear programming must be used.

LINEAR DECISION RULE.[2] The **linear decision rule (LDR)** is an aggregate planning model that attempts to specify an optimum production rate and workforce level over a specific period. It minimizes the total costs of payroll, hiring, layoffs, overtime, and inventory through a series of quadratic cost curves.

linear decision rule (LDR)

MANAGEMENT COEFFICIENTS MODEL. E. H. Bowman's **management coefficients model**[3] builds a formal decision model around a manager's experience and performance. The theory is that the manager's past performance is pretty good, so it can be used as a basis for future decisions. The technique uses a regression analysis of past production decisions made by managers. The regression line provides the relationship between variables (such as demand and labor) for future decisions. According to Bowman, managers' deficiencies were mostly inconsistencies in decision making.

management coefficients model

SIMULATION. A computer model called **scheduling by simulation** was developed in 1966 in R. C. Vergin.[4] This simulation approach used a search procedure to look for the minimum-cost combination of values for the size of the workforce and the production rate.

scheduling by simulation

Comparison of Aggregate Planning Methods

Although the search decision rule and other mathematical models have been found in research to work well under certain conditions and linear programming has found some acceptance in industry, the fact is that most sophisticated planning models are not widely used. Why is this the case? Perhaps it reflects the average manager's attitude about what he or she views as overly complex models. Planners, like all of us, like to understand how and why the models on which they are basing important decisions work. Additionally, operations managers need to make decisions quickly based on the changing dynamics of the workplace. This may explain why the simpler charting and graphical approach is more generally accepted.

DISAGGREGATION

The output of the aggregate planning process is usually a production schedule for family groupings of products. It tells an auto manufacturer how many cars to make, but not how many should be two-door versus four-door or red versus green. It tells a steel manufacturer how many tons of steel to produce, but does not differentiate plate steel from sheet steel. However, firms still need a plan dealing with specific products: What quantities should each one be produced in, and by what date? The process of breaking the aggregate plan down into greater detail is called **disaggregation.** Disaggregation results in a **master production schedule**

disaggregation

master production schedule (MPS)

[2]Because LDR was developed by Charles C. Holt, Franco Modigliani, John F. Muth, and Nobel Prize–winner Herbert Simon, it is popularly known as the HMMS rule. For details, see C. C. Holt *et al., Production Planning, Inventories, and Work Force* (Englewood Cliffs, NJ: Prentice-Hall, 1960).

[3]E. H. Bowman, "Consistency and Optimality in Managerial Decision Making," *Management Science* 9, no. 2 (January 1963): 310–321.

[4]R. C. Vergin, "Production Scheduling under Seasonal Demand," *Journal of Industrial Engineering* 17, no. 5 (May 1966): 260–266.

(MPS), which, as we saw in Chapter 10, specifies the sizing and timing of specific items produced and purchased.

AGGREGATE SCHEDULING IN SERVICES

Some service organizations conduct aggregate scheduling exactly the same way as we did in Examples 1 through 5 in this chapter. Most services pursue a number of the eight capacity and demand options discussed earlier in combination, resulting in a mixed aggregate planning strategy for meeting demand. In actuality, in some firms, such as banking, trucking, and fast foods, aggregate planning may be even easier than in manufacturing.

Controlling the cost of labor in service firms is critical.[5] It involves:

1. Close control of labor hours to assure quick response to customer.
2. Some form of on-call labor resource that can be added or deleted to meet unexpected demand.
3. Flexibility of individual worker skills that permits reallocation of available labor.
4. Individual worker flexibility in rate of output or hours of work to meet expanded demand.

These options may seem complex, but they are not unusual. Excess capacity is used to provide study and planning time by real estate and auto salespersons. Police and fire departments have provisions for calling in off-duty personnel for a major emergency. Where the emergency is extended, police or fire personnel may work longer hours and extra shifts. When business is unexpectedly light, restaurants and retail stores send personnel home early. Supermarket stock clerks work at the cash registers when checkout lines become too lengthy. Experienced waitresses increase their pace and efficiency of service as crowds of customers arrive.

Approaches to aggregate scheduling differ by the type of service provided. Here are five service scenarios.[6]

Restaurants

Aggregate scheduling in the case of a high-volume product output business such as a restaurant is directed toward (1) smoothing the production rate, (2) finding the size of the workforce to be employed, and (3) attempting to manage demand to keep equipment and employees working. The general approach usually requires building inventory during slack periods and depleting inventory during peak periods.

Since this is very similar to manufacturing, traditional aggregate planning methods may be applied to high-volume tangible services as well. One difference that should be noted is that in services, inventory may be perishable. In addition, the relevant units of time may be much smaller than in manufacturing. For example, in fast-food restaurants, peak and slack periods may be measured in hours and the "product" may be inventoried for only as long as ten minutes.

---

[5]Glenn Bassett, *Operations Management for Service Industries* (Westport, CT: Quorum Books, 1992), p. 77.

[6]The first four scenarios and their discussion are excerpted from R. Murdick, B. Render, and R. Russell, *Service Operations Management* (Boston: Allyn & Bacon, 1990), pp. 219–221.

Miscellaneous Services

Most "miscellaneous" services—financial services, hospitality services, transportation services, and many communication and recreation services—provide a high-volume but intangible output. Aggregate planning for these services deals mainly with planning for human resource requirements and managing demand. The goal is to level the demand peak and to design methods for fully utilizing labor resources during forecasted low-demand periods.

National Chains of Small Service Firms

With the advent of national chains of small service businesses such as funeral homes, fast-food outlets, photocopy/printing centers, and computer centers, the question of aggregate planning versus independent planning at each business establishment becomes an issue. Both output and purchasing may be centrally planned when demand can be influenced through special promotions. This approach to aggregate scheduling is advantageous because it reduces purchasing and advertising costs and helps manage cash flow at the independent sites.

Airline Industry

Another service example may be found in the airline industry. Consider an airline that has its headquarters in New York, two hub sites in cities such as Atlanta and Dallas, and 150 offices in airports throughout the country. Aggregate planning consists of tables or schedules of (1) number of flights in and out of each hub, (2) number of flights on all routes, (3) number of passengers to be serviced in all flights, and (4) number of air personnel and ground personnel required at each hub and airport.

This planning is considerably more complex than aggregate planning for a single site or a number of independent sites. Additional capacity decisions are focused on determining the percentage of seats to be allocated to various fare classes in order to maximize profit or yield. This type of capacity allocation problem is called **yield management.**

yield management

Hospitals

Hospitals face the aggregate planning problem by allocating money, staff, and supplies to meet the demands of patients for their medical services. Michigan's Henry Ford Hospital, for example, plans for bed capacity and personnel needs in light of a patient load forecast developed by moving averages. Its aggregate plan has led to the creation of a new floating staff pool serving each nursing pod.[7]

A CASE STUDY OF AGGREGATE SCHEDULING IN A LAW FIRM[8]

Klasson and Avalon, a medium-sized Tampa law firm of 32 legal professionals, has developed a three-month forecast for five categories of legal business it an-

[7] G. Buxey, "Production Planning for Seasonal Demand," *International Journal of Operations and Production Management* 13, no. 7 (1993): 4–21.

[8] Adapted from Glenn Bassett, *Operations Management for Service Industries* (Westport, CT: Quorum Books, 1992), p. 110.

TABLE 12.7 LABOR ALLOCATION AT KLASSON AND AVALON, ATTORNEYS-AT-LAW. FORECASTS FOR COMING QUARTER (1 LAWYER = 500 HOURS OF LABOR)

	LABOR HOURS REQUIRED			CAPACITY CONSTRAINTS	
(1) Category of Legal Business	*(2) Best Case (hours)*	*(3) Likely Case (hours)*	*(4) Worst Case (hours)*	*(5) Maximum Demand in People*	*(6) Number of Qualified Personnel*
Trial work	1,800	1,500	1,200	3.6	4
Legal research	4,500	4,000	3,500	9.0	32
Corporate law	8,000	7,000	6,500	16.0	15
Real estate law	1,700	1,500	1,300	3.4	6
Criminal law	3,500	3,000	2,500	7.0	12
Total hours	19,500	17,000	15,000		
Lawyers needed	39	34	30		

ticipates (see Table 12.7). Assuming a 40-hour work week and 100% of lawyer's hours billed, about 500 billable hours are available from each lawyer this fiscal quarter. Hours of billable time are forecast and accumulated for the quarter by the five categories of skill (column 1), then divided by 500 to provide a count of lawyers needed to cover the estimated business. Between 30 and 39 lawyers will be needed to cover the variations in level of business between the worst and best cases. (For example, best-case scenario of 19,500 total hours, divided by 500 hours per lawyer, equals 39 lawyers needed).

All 32 lawyers at Klasson and Avalon are qualified to perform basic legal research, so this skill area has maximum scheduling flexibility (column 6). The most highly skilled (and capacity constrained) categories are trial work and corporate law. In these areas, the firm's best-case forecast slightly more than covers trial work (with 3.6 lawyers needed—see column 5—and four qualified—see column 6), while corporate law is short one full person. Overtime can be used to cover the excess this quarter, but as business expands it might be necessary to hire or develop talent in both of these areas. Real estate and criminal practice are adequately covered by available staff, as long as other needs do not use their excess capacity.

With the current legal staff of 32, Klasson and Avalon's best-case forecast will increase the work load by 20% (assuming no new hires). This represents one extra day of work per lawyer per week. The worst case scenario will result in about a 6% underutilization of talent. For both these scenarios, the available staff is determined to provide adequate service.

SUMMARY

Aggregate scheduling provides companies with a competitive weapon to help capture market shares in the global economy. By looking at an intermediate planning horizon, the aggregate plan provides the ability to respond to changing customer demands while still producing at low-cost and high-quality levels.

The aggregate schedule sets levels of inventory, production, subcontracting, and employment over an intermediate time range, usually 3 to 18 months. This chapter describes several aggregate planning techniques ranging from the popular charting approach to a variety of mathematical and computer-oriented models such as linear programming.

The aggregate plan is an important responsibility of an operations manager and a key to efficient production. Output from the aggregate schedule leads to a more detailed master production schedule, which is the basis for disaggregation, job scheduling, and MRP systems.

Although the discussion in the early part of this chapter dealt mostly with the manufacturing environment, we just saw that aggregate plans for service systems are similar. Banks, restaurants, airlines, and auto repair facilities are all service systems that can employ the concepts developed here. Regardless of the industry or planning method, though, the most important issue is the implementation of the plan. Managers appear to be more comfortable with faster, less complex, and less mathematical approaches to planning.

KEY TERMS

Aggregate scheduling *(p. 416)*
Aggregate planning *(p. 416)*
Scheduling decisions *(p. 416)*
Mixed strategy *(p. 420)*
Level scheduling *(p. 421)*
Graphical and charting techniques *(p. 422)*
Transportation method of linear programming *(p. 427)*
Linear decision rule (LDR) *(p. 429)*
Management coefficients model *(p. 429)*
Scheduling by simulation *(p. 429)*
Disaggregation *(p. 429)*
Master production schedule (MPS) *(p. 429)*
Yield management *(p. 431)*

USING POM FOR WINDOWS FOR AGGREGATE PLANNING

POM for Windows' Aggregate Planning module performs aggregate or production planning for up to 12 time periods. Given a set of demands for future periods, you can try various plans to determine the lowest-cost plan based on holding, shortage, production, and changeover costs. Four methods are available for planning. More help is available on each of these methods after you choose the method.

Programs 12.1 and 12.2 illustrate the use of POM for Windows for analyzing plan 1 (the first strategy) for Example 2. That "user-defined" plan kept a constant workforce throughout the six-month planning period.

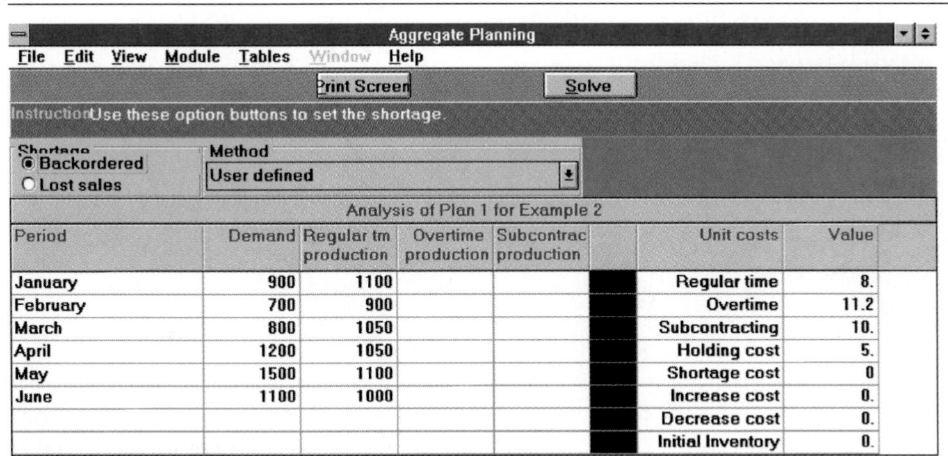

Period	Demand	Regular tm production	Overtime production	Subcontrac production		Unit costs	Value
January	900	1100				Regular time	8.
February	700	900				Overtime	11.2
March	800	1050				Subcontracting	10.
April	1200	1050				Holding cost	5.
May	1500	1100				Shortage cost	0
June	1100	1000				Increase cost	0.
						Decrease cost	0.
						Initial Inventory	0.

Note that "user-defined" method was chosen for this analysis.

PROGRAM 12.1

POM FOR WINDOWS' AGGREGATE PLANNING PROGRAM WITH DATA ENTRY SCREEN FOR PLAN 1 OF EXAMPLE 2

PROGRAM 12.2

POM FOR WINDOWS OUTPUT FOR AGGREGATE PLAN OF EXAMPLE 2

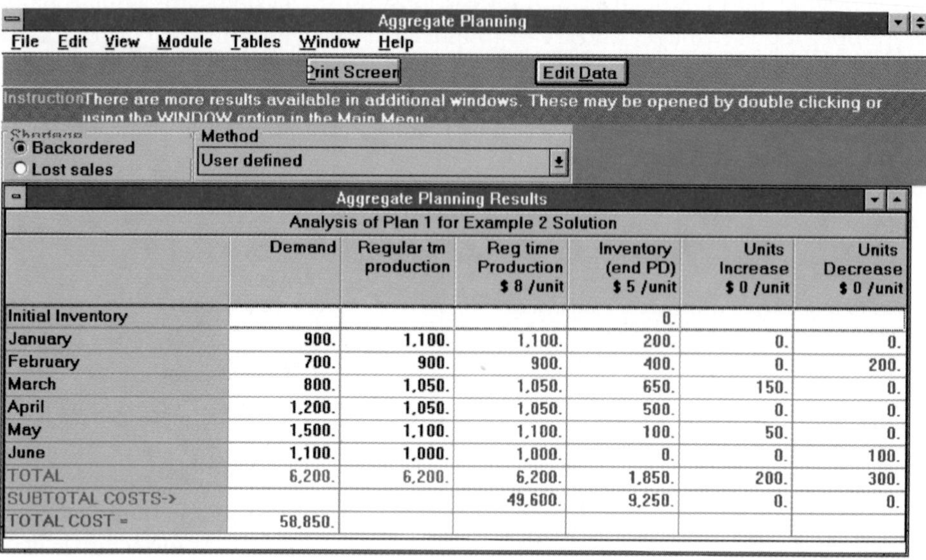

Aggregate Planning

File Edit View Module Tables Window Help

Print Screen | Edit Data

Instruction There are more results available in additional windows. These may be opened by double clicking or using the WINDOW option in the Main Menu.

Shortage: ● Backordered ○ Lost sales

Method: User defined

Aggregate Planning Results

Analysis of Plan 1 for Example 2 Solution

	Demand	Regular tm production	Reg time Production $ 8 /unit	Inventory (end PD) $ 5 /unit	Units Increase $ 0 /unit	Units Decrease $ 0 /unit
Initial Inventory				0.		
January	900.	1,100.	1,100.	200.	0.	0.
February	700.	900.	900.	400.	0.	200.
March	800.	1,050.	1,050.	650.	150.	0.
April	1,200.	1,050.	1,050.	500.	0.	0.
May	1,500.	1,100.	1,100.	100.	50.	0.
June	1,100.	1,000.	1,000.	0.	0.	100.
TOTAL	6,200.	6,200.	6,200.	1,850.	200.	300.
SUBTOTAL COSTS->			49,600.	9,250.	0.	0.
TOTAL COST =	58,850.					

SOLVED PROBLEM 12.1

The roofing manufacturer described earlier in this chapter in Examples 1 to 4 wishes to consider yet a fourth planning strategy (plan 4). This one maintains a constant workforce of eight people and uses overtime whenever necessary to meet demand. Use the cost information found in Table 12.2. Again, assume beginning and ending inventories are equal to zero.

SOLUTION

Employ eight workers and use overtime when necessary. Carrying costs will be encountered now.

MONTH	PRODUCTION AT 40 UNITS PER DAY	BEGINNING-OF-MONTH INVENTORY	FORECAST DEMAND THIS MONTH	OVERTIME PRODUCTION NEEDED	ENDING INVENTORY
Jan.	880	–	900	20	0
Feb.	720	0	700	0	20
Mar.	840	20	800	0	60
Apr.	840	60	1,200	300	0
May	880	0	1,500	620	0
June	800	0	1,100	300	0
				1240 units	80 units

Carrying cost totals = 80 units × \$5/unit/month = \$400

Regular pay:

8 workers × \$40/day × 124 days = \$39,680

To produce 1,240 units at overtime rate (of \$7/hour) requires 1,984 hours.

Overtime pay = \$7/hour × 1,984 hours = \$13,888

COSTS		PLAN 4 (workforce of eight plus overtime)
Carrying cost	$ 400	(80 units carried × $5/unit)
Regular labor	39,680	(8 workers × $40/day × 124 days)
Overtime	13,888	(1,984 hours × $7/hour)
Hiring or firing	0	
Subcontracting	0	
Total costs	$53,968	

SOLVED PROBLEM 12.2

A Dover, Delaware, plant has developed the accompanying supply, demand, cost, and inventory data. The firm has a constant workforce and meets all of its demand. Allocate the production capacity to satisfy demand at a minimum cost. What is the cost of this plan?

SUPPLY CAPACITY AVAILABLE (IN UNITS)

PERIOD	REGULAR TIME	OVERTIME	SUBCONTRACT
1	300	50	200
2	400	50	200
3	450	50	200

DEMAND FORECAST

PERIOD	DEMAND (units)
1	450
2	550
3	750

OTHER DATA

Initial inventory	50 units
Regular-time cost per unit	$50
Overtime cost per unit	$65
Subcontract cost per unit	$80
Carrying cost per unit per period	$1

continued on next page

SUPPLY FROM		DEMAND FOR Period 1	Period 2	Period 3	Unused Capacity (Dummy)	TOTAL CAPACITY AVAILABLE (supply)
		0	1	2	0	
Beginning inventory		50				50
		50	51	52	0	
Period 1	*Regular time*	300				300
		65	66	67	0	
Period 1	*Overtime*	50				50
		80	81	82	0	
Period 1	*Subcontract*	50			150	200
			50	51	0	
Period 2	*Regular time*		400			400
			65	66	0	
Period 2	*Overtime*		50			50
			80	81	0	
Period 2	*Subcontract*		100	50	50	200
				50	0	
Period 3	*Regular time*			450		450
				65	0	
Period 3	*Overtime*			50		50
				80	0	
Period 3	*Subcontract*			200		200
TOTAL DEMAND		450	550	750	200	1,950

SOLUTION

Cost of plan

Period 1: 50($0) + 300($50) + 50($65) + 50($80) = $22,250

Period 2: 400($50) + 50($65) + 100($80) = $31,250

Period 3: 50($81) + 450($50) + 50($65) + 200($80) = $45,800

Total cost $99,300

DISCUSSION QUESTIONS

1. What is the purpose of aggregate planning? Describe some demand and capacity options for implementing plans.
2. What is the difference between mixed production planning strategies and those eight demand and capacity options that are not mixed? Name four strategies that are not mixed.
3. Why are mathematical models not more widely used in aggregate planning?
4. What are the advantages and disadvantages of varying the size of the work force to meet demand requirements each period?
5. Why would some firms have longer planning horizons than others?
6. What is the relationship between the aggregate plan and the master production schedule?
7. Briefly describe four mathematical approaches to aggregate planning. (*Discussion Questions continued on p. 438*)

SELF-TEST ■ CHAPTER 12

- *Before taking the self-test* refer back to the learning objectives listed at the beginning of the chapter and the key terms listed at the end of the chapter.
- Use the key at the back of the text to *correct* your answers.
- *Restudy* pages that correspond to any questions you answered incorrectly or material you feel uncertain about.

1. Aggregate planning is concerned with determining the quantity and timing of production in
   a. short term
   b. intermediate term
   c. long term
   d. all of the above

2. The goal of the aggregate planning process is usually to minimize costs over the planning period.
   a. True b. False

3. Aggregate planning usually involves making a number of strategic decisions.
   a. True b. False

4. Graphical aggregate planning methods, while based upon trial and error, are useful because they require only limited computations and usually lead to optimal solutions.
   a. True b. False

5. One of the problems encountered when using the transportation algorithm for aggregate planning is that this method does not work well when one attempts to include the effect of hiring and layoffs in the model.
   a. True b. False

6. Managers typically do not use sophisticated planning models because
   a. these models do not provide information pertinent to the decision at hand
   b. they view these models as overly complex and do not fully understand them
   c. research has demonstrated that such models seldom work well
   d. the time periods addressed by such models are too long

7. Which of the following aggregate planning strategies requires employing relatively unskilled personnel to be most effective?
   a. varying production rates through overtime or idle time
   b. using part-time workers
   c. back ordering during high-demand periods
   d. subcontracting

8. Which of the following aggregate planning strategies is likely to have the least impact on quality?
   a. using part-time workers
   b. changing inventory level
   c. subcontracting
   d. varying production rates through overtime or idle time

9. The aggregate planning strategies of varying inventory level and back ordering during periods of high demand have which of the following disadvantages in common?
   a. customers may go elsewhere
   b. holding costs
   c. quality of output may suffer
   d. it is difficult to exactly match supply with demand

10. Level scheduling usually results in ______________ production costs than other strategies.
    a. higher
    b. the same
    c. lower

11. Approaches to aggregate planning in the service sector differ based upon the nature of the service provided.
    a. True b. False

12. In the service sector, aggregate planning for the production of high-volume intangible output is directed toward
    a. smoothing the production rate
    b. finding the size of the workforce to be employed
    c. attempting to manage demand to keep equipment and employees working
    d. planning for human resource requirements and managing demand

13. Aggregate planning strategies include:
    a. ____________, b. ____________, c. ____________,
    d. ____________, e. ____________, f. ____________,
    g. ____________.

9. Why are graphical aggregate planning methods useful?
10. What are major limitations of using the transportation method for aggregate planning?
11. What impact on quality do you think each of eight production planning strategies might have?
12. What are the disadvantages that the following two strategies have in common: (1) varying inventory levels and (2) back ordering during periods of high demand?

OPERATIONS IN PRACTICE EXERCISE

Many companies deal with aggregate scheduling by forcing overtime on their employees to adjust for the peaks of seasonal demand. For example, the *Wall Street Journal's* report on long and irregular hours in the United States (July 14, 1994, p. B1) highlights Angie Clark, a J.C. Penney supervisor in Springfield, Virginia. Clark works at least 44 hours a week, including evenings and frequent weekend shifts. Because of the recent recession, staffers are busier than five years earlier, when Clark had 38 salespeople instead of the current 28. The result of this pressure is a 40% turnover. Because employee turnover is so large, training consists of the bare minimum—mostly how to operate the cash registers.

Discuss the implications of a strategy of heavy use of overtime in retailing, as well as in other fields such as manufacturing, hospitals, and airlines. How does this U.S. approach compare to that in other countries?

PROBLEMS

: **12.1.** Develop another plan for the roofing manufacturer described in Examples 1 to 4 (in the chapter) and Solved Problem 12.1 (at the end of the chapter). For this plan, plan 5, the firm wishes to maintain a constant workforce of six and to pay overtime to meet demand. Is this plan preferable?

: **12.2.** The roofing manufacturer in Examples 1 to 4 (in this chapter) and Solved Problem 12.1 (at the end of the chapter) has yet a sixth plan. A constant workforce of seven is selected, and the remainder of demand is filled by subcontracting. Is this a better plan?

: **12.3.** The president of Daves Enterprises, Carla Daves, projects the firm's aggregate demand requirements over the next eight months as follows:

Jan.	1,400	May	2,200
Feb.	1,600	June	2,200
Mar.	1,800	July	1,800
Apr.	1,800	Aug.	1,400

Her operations manager is considering a new plan, which begins in January, with 200 units on hand. Stockout cost of lost sales is $100 per unit. Inventory holding cost is $20 per unit per month. Ignore any idle-time costs. The plan is called plan A.

Plan A. Vary the workforce level to meet exactly the demand requirements. The December rate of production is 1,600 units per month. The cost of hiring additional workers is $5,000 per 100 units. The cost of laying off workers is $7,500 per 100 units. Evaluate this plan.

: **12.4.** Refer to Problem 12.3. Daves Enterprises is now looking at plan B. Beginning inventory, stockout costs, and holding costs were provided in Problem 12.3.

Plan B. Produce at a constant rate of 1,400 units per month, which will meet minimum demands. Then it uses subcontracting, with additional units at a premium price of $75 per unit. Evaluate this plan.

: **12.5.** Beginning inventory, stockout costs, and holding costs were provided in Problem 12.3.

Plan C. Keep a stable workforce by maintaining a constant production rate equal to the average requirements and by varying inventory levels. Plot the demand with a histogram that also shows average requirements.

12.6. Daves' operations manager (see Problems 12.3 through 12.5) is also considering the following two mixed strategies:

Plan D. Keep the current workforce stable at 1,600 units per month. Permit a maximum of 20% overtime at an additional cost of $50 per unit. A warehouse now constrains the maximum allowable inventory on hand to 400 units or less.

Plan E. Keep the current workforce, which is producing 1,600 units per month, and subcontract to meet the rest of the demand. Evaluate these plans.

12.7. Certo and Herbert is a VCR manufacturer in need of an aggregate plan for July through December. The company has gathered the following data:

COSTS	
Holding cost	$8/VCR/month
Subcontracting	$80/VCR
Regular-time labor	$10/hour
Overtime labor	$16/hour for hours above 8 hours/worker/day
Hiring cost	$40/worker
Layoff cost	$80/worker

DEMAND	
July	400
Aug.	500
Sept.	550
Oct.	700
Nov.	800
Dec.	700

OTHER DATA	
Current workforce	8 people
Labor hours/VCR	4 hours
Workdays/month	20 days
Beginning inventory	150 VCRs

What will the two following strategies cost?

a. Vary the workforce to have exact production to meet the forecast demand. Begin with eight workers on board at the end of June.

b. Vary overtime only, and use a constant workforce of eight.

12.8. Develop your own aggregate plan for Certo and Herbert (see Problem 12.7). Justify your approach.

12.9. Sue Badger, the operations manager at Kimball Furniture, has received the following estimates of demand requirements.

APR.	MAY	JUNE	JULY	AUG.	SEPT.
1,000	1,200	1,400	1,800	1,800	1,600

Assuming stockout costs for lost sales are $100, and inventory carrying costs are $25 per unit per month, evaluate these two plans on an *incremental* cost basis:

Plan A. Produce at a steady rate (equal to minimum requirements) of 1,000 units per month and subcontract the additional units at a $60 per unit premium cost.

Plan B. Vary the workforce, which is at a current production level of 1,300 units per month. The cost of hiring additional workers is $3,000 per 100 units produced. The cost of layoffs is $6,000 per 100 units cut back.

12.10. Sue Badger (see Problem 12.9) is considering two more mixed strategies. Using the data in Problem 12.9, compare plans C and D with plans A and B and make a recommendation.

Plan C. Keep the current workforce steady at a level producing 1,300 units per month. Subcontract the remainder to meet demand. Assume 300 units remain from March that are available in April.

Plan D. Keep the current workforce at a level capable of producing 1,300 units per month. Permit a maximum of 20% overtime at a premium of $40 per unit. Assume warehouse limitations permit no more than a 180-unit carryover from month to month. This means that any time inventories reach 180, the plant is kept idle. Idle time per unit is $60. Any additional needs are subcontracted at a cost of $60 per incremental unit.

12.11. Consider the following aggregate planning problem for one quarter.

	REGULAR TIME	OVERTIME	SUBCONTRACTING
Production capacity/month	1,000	200	150
Production cost/unit	$5	$7	$8

Assume there is no initial inventory and a forecasted demand of 1,250 units in each of the three months. Carrying cost is $1 per unit per month. Solve this aggregate planning problem.

12.12. Mary Butler-Pearce's firm had developed the accompanying supply, demand, cost, and inventory data. Allocate the production capacity to meet demand at a minimum cost. What is the cost?

SUPPLY AVAILABLE

PERIOD	REGULAR TIME	OVERTIME	SUBCONTRACT	DEMAND FORECAST
1	30	10	5	40
2	35	12	5	50
3	30	10	5	40

Initial inventory	20 units
Regular-time cost per unit	$100
Overtime cost per unit	$150
Subcontract cost per unit	$200
Carrying cost per unit per month	$4

12.13. The production planning period of 100 megabyte RAM boards for CDM personal computers is four months. Cost data are as follows:

Regular-time cost per board	$70
Overtime cost per board	$110
Subcontract cost per board	$120
Carrying cost per board per month	$4

Capacity and demand for RAM boards for each of the next four months are:

	PERIOD			
	Month 1	*Month 2*	*Month 3**	*Month 4*
Demand	2,000	2,500	1,500	2,100
Capacity				
Regular time	1,500	1,600	750	1,600
Overtime	400	400	200	400
Subcontract	600	600	600	600

*Factory closes for two weeks of vacation.

CDM expects to enter the planning period with 500 RAM boards in stock. Back-ordering is not permitted (meaning, for example, that boards produced in the second month cannot be used in the first month). Set a production plan that minimizes costs.

12.14. Haifa Instruments, an Israeli producer of portable kidney dialysis units and other medical products, develops a four-month aggregate plan. Demand and capacity (in units) are forecast as follows:

CAPACITY SOURCE	MONTH 1	MONTH 2	MONTH 3	MONTH 4
Labor				
Regular time	235	255	290	300
Overtime	20	24	26	24
Subcontract	12	15	15	17
Demand	255	294	321	301

The cost of producing each dialysis unit is $985 on regular time, $1,310 on overtime, and $1,500 on a subcontract. Inventory carrying cost is $100 per unit per month. There is to be no beginning or ending inventory in stock. Set up a production plan that minimizes cost.

12.15. A Birmingham, Alabama, foundry produces cast-iron ingots according to a three-month capacity plan. The cost of labor averages $100 per regular shift hour and $140 per overtime (O.T.) hour. Inventory carrying cost is thought to be $4 per labor-hour of inventory carried. There are 50 direct labor-hours of inventory left over from March. For the next three months, demand and capacity (in labor-hours) are as follows:

	CAPACITY		
MONTH	*Regular Labor (hours)*	*O.T. Labor (hours)*	DEMAND
Apr.	2,880	355	3,000
May	2,780	315	2,750
June	2,760	305	2,950

Develop an aggregate plan for the three-month period.

12.16. A large Omaha feedmill prepares its six-month aggregate plan by forecasting demand for 50-pound bags of cattle feed as follows: January, 1,000 bags; February, 1,200; March, 1,250; April, 1,450; May, 1,400; and June, 1,400. The feedmill plans to begin the new year with no inventory left over from the previous year. It projects that capacity (during regular hours) for producing bags of feed will remain constant at 800 until the end of April, and then increase to 1,100 bags per month when a planned expansion is completed on May 1. Overtime capacity is set at 300 bags per month until the expansion, at which time it will increase to 400 bags per month. A friendly competitor in Sioux City, Iowa, is also available as a backup source to meet demand—but it insists on a firm contract and can provide only 500 bags total during the six-month period. Develop a six-month production plan for the feedmill.

Cost data are as follows:

Regular-time cost per bag (until April 30)	$12.00
Regular-time cost per bag (after May 1)	$11.00
Overtime cost per bag (during entire period)	$16.00
Cost of outside purchase per bag	$18.50
Carrying cost per bag per month	$1.00

12.17. The Kelly Chemical Supply Company manufactures and packages expensive vials of mercury. Given the following demand, supply, cost, and inventory data, allocate production capacity to meet demand at minimum cost. A constant workforce is expected, and no back orders are permitted.

	SUPPLY CAPACITY (in units)			
PERIOD	*Regular Time*	*Overtime*	*Subcontract*	DEMAND (in units)
1	25	5	6	32
2	28	4	6	32
3	30	8	6	40
4	29	6	7	40

OTHER DATA

Initial inventory	4 units
Ending inventory desired	3 units
Regular-time cost per unit	\$2,000
Overtime cost per unit	\$2,475
Subcontract cost per unit	\$3,200
Carrying cost per unit per period	\$200

12.18. Given the following information, solve for the minimum cost plan:

	PERIOD				
	1	*2*	*3*	*4*	*5*
Demand	150	160	130	200	210
Capacity					
Regular	150	150	150	150	150
Overtime	20	20	10	10	10

Subcontracting: 100 units available over the five-month period
Beginning inventory: 0 units
Ending inventory required: 20 units

COST

Regular-time cost per unit	\$100
Overtime cost per unit	\$125
Subcontract cost per unit	\$135
Inventory cost per unit per period	\$3

Assume that back orders are not permitted.

Internet Data Base Application See our website at http://www.prenhall.com/renderpom for a challenging, computer-based problem.

CASE STUDY

Southwestern State College

The campus police chief at Southwestern State College is attempting to develop a two-year plan for the department that involves a request for additional resources.

The department currently has 26 sworn officers. The size of the force has not changed over the past 15 years, but the following changes have prompted the chief to seek more resources:

- The college has expanded geographically, with some new facilities miles away from the main campus.
- Traffic and parking problems have increased.
- More portable, expensive computers with high theft potential are dispersed across the campus.
- Alcohol and drug problems have increased.
- The size of the athletic program has increased.
- The size of the surrounding community has doubled.
- The police need to spend more time on education and prevention programs.

The college is located in a small town. During the summer months, the student population is around 5,000. This number swells to 30,000 during fall and spring semesters. Thus demand for police and other services is significantly lower during the summer months. Demand for police services also varies by

- Time of day (peak time between 10 P.M. and 2 A.M.).
- Day of the week (weekends are the busiest).
- Weekend of the year (on football weekends, 50,000 extra people come to campus).
- Special events (check-in, check-out, commencement).

Football weekends are especially difficult to staff. Extra police services are typically needed from 8:00 A.M. to 5:00 P.M. on five football Saturdays. All 26 officers are called in to work double shifts. Over 40 law enforcement officers from surrounding locations are paid to come in on their own time, and a dozen state police lend a hand free of charge (when they are available). Twenty-five students and local residents are paid to work traffic and parking. During the last academic year (a nine-month period), overtime payments to campus police officers totaled over $30,000.

Other relevant data include the following:

- The average starting salary for a police officer is $18,000.
- Work-study, part-time students, and local residents who help with traffic and parking are paid $4.50 an hour.
- Overtime is paid to police officers who work over 40 hours a week at the rate of $13.00 an hour. Extra officers who are hired part-time from outside agencies also earn $13.00 an hour.
- There seems to be an unlimited supply of officers who will work for the college when needed for special events.
- With days off, vacations, and average sick leave considered, it takes five persons to cover one 24-hour, 7-day-a-week position.

The schedule of officers during fall and spring semesters is:

	WEEKDAYS	WEEKEND
First shift (7 A.M.–3 P.M.)	5	4
Second shift (3 P.M.–11 P.M.)	5	6
Third shift (11 P.M.–7 A.M.)	6	8

Staffing for football weekends and special events is *in addition to* the preceding schedule. Summer staffing is, on average, half that shown.

The police chief thinks that his present staff is stretched to the limit. Fatigued officers are potential problems for the department and the community. In addition, neither time nor personnel have been set aside for crime prevention, safety, or health programs. Interactions of police officers with students, faculty, and staff are minimal and usually negative in nature. In light of these problems, the chief would like to request funding for four additional officers, two assigned to new programs and two to alleviate the overload on his current staff. He would also like to begin limiting overtime to ten hours per week for each officer.

DISCUSSION QUESTIONS

1. Which variations in demand for police services should be considered in an aggregate plan for resources? Which variations can be accomplished with short-term scheduling adjustments?
2. Evaluate the current staffing plan. What does it cost? Are 26 officers sufficient to handle the normal workload?
3. What would be the additional cost of the chief's proposal? How would you suggest that the chief justify his request?
4. How much does it currently cost the college to provide police services for football games? What would be the pros and cons of subcontracting this work completely to outside law enforcement agencies?
5. Propose other alternatives.

SOURCE: From R. Murdick, Barry Render, and R. Russell, *Service Operations Management*. Copyright © 1990. Boston: Allyn & Bacon. Adapted by permission.

BIBLIOGRAPHY

Armacost, R. L., R. J. Penlesky, and S. C. Ross. "Avoiding Problems Inherent in Spreadsheet-Based Simulation Models—An Aggregate Planning Application." *Production and Inventory Management* 31 (Second Quarter 1990): 62–68.

Bowers, M. R., and J. P. Jarvis. "A Hierarchical Production Planning and Scheduling Model." *Decision Sciences* 23 (January-February 1992):144–157.

Buxey, G. "Production Planning and Scheduling for Seasonal Demand." *International Journal of Operations and Production Management* 13, no. 7 (1993): 4–21.

DeMatta, R., and T. Miller. "A Note on the Growth of a Production Planning System." *Interfaces* 23 (April 1993): 27–31.

Heskett, J., W. E. Sasser, and C. Hart. *Service Breakthroughs: Changing the Rules of the Game.* New York: Free Press, 1990.

Leone, R. A., and J. R. Meyer. "Capacity Strategies for the 1980's." *Harvard Business Review* 58 (November-December 1980): 133.

Murdick, R., B. Render, and R. Russell. *Service Operations Management.* Boston: Allyn & Bacon, 1990.

Sasser, W. E. "Match Supply and Demand in Service Industries." *Harvard Business Review* 54 (November-December 1976): 133–140.

Schmenner, Roger W. *Service Operations Management.* Upper Saddle River, NJ: Prentice Hall, 1995.

Vollmann, T. E., W. L. Berry, and D. C. Whybark. *Manufacturing Planning and Control Systems,* 3rd ed. Homewood, IL: Irwin, 1992.

Short-Term Scheduling

13

CHAPTER OUTLINE

Strategic Importance of Short-Term Scheduling

Scheduling Issues

Forward and Backward Scheduling ■ Scheduling Criteria

Scheduling Process-Focused Work Centers

Loading Jobs in Work Centers

Gantt Charts ■ Assignment Method

Sequencing Jobs in Work Centers

Priority Rules for Dispatching Jobs ■ Critical Ratio ■ Sequencing *N* Jobs on Two Machines: Johnson's Rule

Limitations of Rule-Based Systems

Finite Scheduling

Theory of Constraints

Bottleneck Work Centers

Repetitive Manufacturing

Scheduling for Services

Scheduling Nurses with Cyclical Scheduling

Summary ■ Key Terms ■ Using POM for Windows To Solve Scheduling Problems ■ Solved Problems ■ Discussion Questions ■ Operations in Practice Exercise ■ Self-Test Chapter 13 ■ Problems ■ Case Study: The NASA Space Shuttle ■ Bibliography

LEARNING OBJECTIVES

When you complete this chapter you should be able to:

IDENTIFY OR DEFINE:

Gantt charts
Assignment method
Sequencing rules
Johnson's rule

EXPLAIN:

Shop loading
Sequencing
Scheduling

STRATEGIC IMPORTANCE OF SHORT-TERM SCHEDULING

Scheduling machines, tools, and people to make aircraft parts at Northrop-Grumman's Dallas plant is the job of a mainframe computer. The computer downloads schedules for part production to a flexible machining system (FMS), where a manager makes the final scheduling decision. The FMS allows parts of many sizes or shapes to be made, in any order, without disrupting production. This versatility in scheduling results in parts ready on a Just-in-Time basis, with low setup times, little work-in-process, and high machine utilization. Efficient scheduling is how companies like Northrop-Grumman meet due dates promised to customers and face time-based competition.

Service firms also make schedules that match production to customer availability. American Airlines, for example, schedules over 500 aircraft, 8,000 pilots, and 16,000 flight attendants daily to accommodate thousands of passengers who wish to reach their destinations. This schedule, based on computer programs that took 15 man-years to develop, plays a major role in satisfying the customer. American finds competitive advantage with its flexibility for last minute adjustments to meet customer needs and weather disruptions.

The strategic implications of the importance of scheduling are clear to *all* firms:

1. By scheduling effectively, companies use assets more effectively and create greater capacity per dollar invested, which, in turn, *lowers cost.*
2. This added capacity and related flexibility provides *faster delivery* and therefore better customer service.
3. The third benefit of good scheduling is a competitive advantage through *dependable* delivery.

SCHEDULING ISSUES

Scheduling deals with the timing of operations. Table 13.1 illustrates scheduling decisions faced in four organizations. Scheduling begins with *capacity* planning,

TABLE 13.1 SCHEDULING DECISIONS

ORGANIZATION	MANAGERS MUST SCHEDULE THE FOLLOWING
Mount Sinai Hospital	Operating room use Patient admissions Nursing, security, maintenance staffs Outpatient treatments
Indiana University	Classrooms and audiovisual equipment Student and instructor schedules Graduate and undergraduate courses
Sony factory	Production of goods Purchases of materials Workers
American Airlines	Maintenance of aircraft Departure timetables Flight crews, catering, gate, and ticketing personnel

Northrop-Grumman maintains its world-class operation by automating the scheduling of people, machines, and tools at this flexible machine system (FMS). The computer screen at left aids the operator by showing a graphic display of the proper position for the material on the riser (which holds the fixtures). The second-floor control room in the background provides visual feedback to an on-site scheduler. Scheduling flexibility reduces delivery time and results in a strategic advantage for Northrop-Grumman.

which involves facility and equipment acquisition (discussed in Chapter 5). In the aggregate planning stage (Chapter 12), decisions regarding the *use* of facilities, inventory, people, and outside contractors are made. Then the master schedule breaks down the aggregate plan and develops an *overall* schedule for outputs. Short-term schedules then translate capacity decisions, intermediate planning, and master schedules into job sequences, specific assignments of personnel, materials, and machinery. In this chapter, we describe the narrow issue of scheduling goods and services in the *short run* (that is, on a weekly, daily, or hourly basis).

Forward and Backward Scheduling

Scheduling involves assigning due dates to specific jobs, but many jobs compete simultaneously for the same resources. To help address the difficulties inherent in scheduling, we can categorize scheduling techniques as (1) forward scheduling and (2) backward scheduling.

forward scheduling

Forward scheduling starts the schedule as soon as the requirements are known. Forward scheduling is used in a variety of organizations such as hospitals, clinics, fine-dining restaurants, and machine tool manufacturers. In these facilities, jobs are performed to customer order, and delivery is often requested as soon as possible. Forward scheduling is usually designed to produce a schedule that can be accomplished even if it means not meeting the due date. In many instances, forward scheduling causes a buildup of work-in-process inventory.

NOTE
Forward scheduling works well in firms where the supplier is usually behind in meeting schedules.

backward scheduling

Backward scheduling begins with the due date, scheduling the final operation first. Steps in the job are then scheduled, one at a time, in reverse order. By subtracting the lead time for each item, the start time is obtained. However, the resources necessary to accomplish the schedule may not exist. Backward scheduling is used in many manufacturing environments, as well as service environments such as catering a banquet or scheduling surgery. In practice, a combination of forward and backward scheduling is often used to find a reasonable trade-off between what can be achieved and customer due dates.

Machine breakdowns, absenteeism, quality problems, shortages, and other factors further complicate scheduling. Consequently, assignment of a date does not ensure that the work will be performed according to the schedule. Many specialized techniques have been developed to aid us in preparing reliable schedules.

Scheduling Criteria

The correct scheduling technique depends on the volume of orders, the nature of operations, and the overall complexity of jobs, as well as the importance placed on each of four criteria. Those four criteria are:

1. *Minimize completion time.* This is evaluated by determining the average completion time.
2. *Maximize utilization.* This is evaluated by determining the percent of the time the facility is utilized.
3. *Minimize work-in-process (WIP) inventory.* This is evaluated by determining the average number of jobs in the system. The relationship between the number of jobs in the system and WIP inventory is high. Therefore, the fewer the number of jobs that are in the system, the lower the inventory.
4. *Minimize customer waiting time.* This is evaluated by determining the average number of late days.

These four criteria are used in this chapter, as they are in industry, to evaluate scheduling performance. Additionally, good scheduling approaches should be simple, clear, easily understood, easy to carry out, flexible, and realistic. Given these considerations, *the objective of scheduling is to optimize the use of resources so the production objectives are met.* In this chapter, we examine scheduling in process-focused (intermittent) production, repetitive production, and the service sector.

SCHEDULING PROCESS-FOCUSED WORK CENTERS

Process-focused facilities (also known as intermittent or job shop facilities)[1] are high-variety, low-volume systems commonly found in manufacturing and service organizations. It is a production system in which products are made to order. Items made under this system usually differ considerably in terms of materials used, order of processing, processing requirements, time of processing, and setup requirements. Because of these differences, scheduling can be complex. To run a facility in a balanced and efficient manner, the manager needs a production planning and control system. This system should:

[1]Much of the literature on scheduling is about manufacturing; therefore, the traditional term *job shop scheduling* is often used.

1. Schedule incoming orders without violating capacity constraints of individual work centers.
2. Check the availability of tools and materials before releasing an order to a department.
3. Establish due dates for each job and check progress against need dates and order lead times.
4. Check work in progress as jobs move through the shop.
5. Provide feedback on plant and production activities.
6. Provide work efficiency statistics and monitor operator times for payroll and labor distribution analyses.

NOTE
A routing file describes the operation that should be performed in each work center and the standard for how long the operation should take for completion.

Whether the scheduling system is manual or automated, it must be accurate and relevant. This means it requires a production data base with both planning and control files.[2] Three types of **planning files** are (1) an *item master file,* which contains information about each component the firm produces or purchases; (2) a *routing file,* which indicates each component's flow through the shop; and (3) a *work center master file,* which contains information about the work center, such as capacity and efficiency. **Control files** track the actual progress made against the plan for each work order.

planning files

control files

LOADING JOBS IN WORK CENTERS

Loading means the assignment of jobs to work or processing centers. Operations managers assign jobs to work centers so that costs, idle time, or completion times are kept to a minimum. Loading work centers takes two forms.[3] One is oriented to capacity; the second is related to assigning specific jobs to work centers. We present two approaches used for loading: *Gantt charts* and the *assignment method* of linear programming.

loading

Gantt Charts

Gantt charts are visual aids that are useful in loading and scheduling. Their name is derived from Henry Gantt, who developed them in the late 1800s. The charts help describe the use of resources, such as work centers and overtime.

Gantt charts

When used in *loading,* Gantt charts show the loading and idle time of several departments, machines, or facilities. They display the relative workloads in the system so that the manager knows what adjustments are appropriate. For example, when one work center becomes overloaded, employees from a low-load center can be transferred temporarily to increase the workforce. Or if waiting jobs can be processed at different work centers, some jobs at high-load centers can be transferred to low-load centers. Versatile equipment may also be transferred among centers. Example 1 illustrates a simple Gantt load chart.

[2]For an expanded discussion, see *APICS Training Aid—Shop Floor Control* (Falls Church, VA: American Production and Inventory Control Society).

[3]Note that this discussion can apply to work centers that might be called a "shop" in a manufacturing firm, or a "ward" in a hospital, or a "department" in an office or large kitchen.

EXAMPLE 1

A New Orleans washing machine manufacturer accepts special orders for machines to be used in unique facilities such as submarines, hospitals, and large industrial laundries. The production of each machine requires varying tasks and durations. Figure 13.1 shows the load chart for the week of March 8.

The four work centers process several jobs during the week. This particular chart indicates that the metal works and painting centers are completely loaded for the entire week. The mechanical and electronic centers have some idle time scattered during the week. We also note that the metal works center is unavailable on Tuesday, perhaps for preventive maintenance.

FIGURE 13.1

GANTT LOAD CHART FOR THE WEEK OF MARCH 8

Work Center \ Day	Monday	Tuesday	Wednesday	Thursday	Friday
Metal works	Job 349	(not available)		Job 350	
Mechanical		Job 349		Job 408	
Electronics	Job 408			Job 349	
Painting	Job 295		Job 408	(not available)	Job 349

Processing

Center not available (for example, maintenance time, repairs, shortages)

The Gantt *load chart* does have some major limitations. For one, it does not account for production variability such as unexpected breakdowns or human errors that require reworking a job. The chart must also be updated regularly to account for new jobs and revised time estimates.

A Gantt *schedule chart* is used to monitor jobs in progress.[4] It indicates which jobs are on schedule and which are ahead of or behind schedule. In practice, many versions of the chart are found. The schedule chart in Example 2 places jobs in progress on the vertical axis and time on the horizontal axis.

EXAMPLE 2

JH Products Corporation uses the Gantt chart in Figure 13.2 to show the scheduling of three orders, jobs A, B, and C. Each pair of brackets on the time axis denotes the estimated starting and finishing of a job enclosed within it. The solid bars reflect the actual status or progress of the job. Job A, for example, is about one-half day behind schedule at the end of day 5. Job B was completed after equipment maintenance. Job C is ahead of schedule.

[4]Gantt charts are also used for project scheduling and are again noted in Chapter 14, "Project Scheduling."

FIGURE 13.2

GANTT SCHEDULING CHART FOR JOBS A, B, AND C

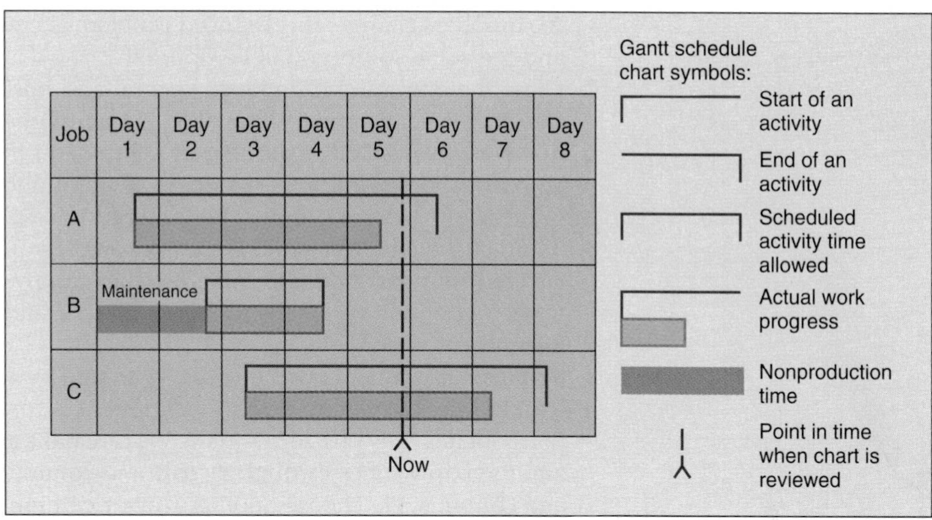

Assignment Method

The **assignment method** involves assigning tasks or jobs to resources. Examples include assigning jobs to machines, contracts to bidders, people to projects, and salespeople to territories. The objective is most often to minimize total costs or time required to perform the tasks at hand. One important characteristic of assignment problems is that only one job (or worker) is assigned to one machine (or project).

assignment method

Each assignment problem uses a table. The numbers in the table will be the costs or times associated with each particular assignment. For example, if a facility has three available machines (A, B, and C) and three new jobs to be completed, its table might appear as follows. The dollar entries represent the firm's estimate of what it will cost for each job to be completed on each machine.

JOB \ MACHINE	A	B	C
R-34	$11	$14	$6
S-66	$8	$10	$11
T-50	$9	$12	$7

The assignment method involves adding and subtracting appropriate numbers in the table in order to find the lowest *opportunity cost*[5] for each assignment. There are four steps to follow:

1. Subtract the smallest number in each row from every number in that row and then subtract the smallest number in each column from every number in that column. This step has the effect of reducing the numbers in the table until a series of zeros, meaning *zero opportunity costs,* appear. Even though

[5]Opportunity costs are those profits foregone or not obtained.

the numbers change, this reduced problem is equivalent to the original one, and the same solution will be optimal.

2. Draw the minimum number of vertical and horizontal straight lines necessary to cover all zeros in the table. If the number of lines equals either the number of rows or the number of columns in the table, then we can make an optimal assignment (see step 4). If the number of lines is less than the number of rows or columns, we proceed to step 3.
3. Subtract the smallest number not covered by a line from every other uncovered number. Add the same number to any number(s) lying at the intersection of any two lines. Return to step 2 and continue until an optimal assignment is possible.
4. Optimal assignments will always be at zero locations in the table. One systematic way of making a valid assignment is first to select a row or column that contains only one zero square. We can make an assignment to that square and then draw lines through its row and column. From the uncovered rows and columns, we choose another row or column in which there is only one zero square. We make that assignment and continue the procedure until we have assigned each person or machine to one task.

Example 3 (on page 453) shows how to use the assignment method.

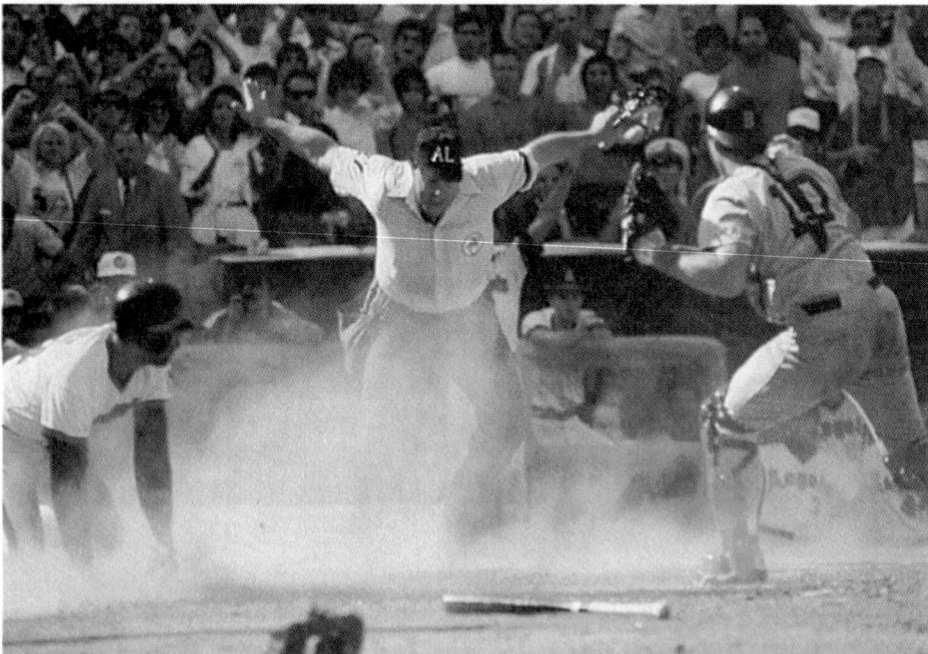

The problem of scheduling American League umpire crews from one series of games to the next is complicated by many restrictions on travel, ranging from coast-to-coast time changes, airline flight schedules, and night games running late. The league strives to achieve these two conflicting objectives: (1) balance crew assignments relatively evenly among all teams over the course of a season, and (2) minimize travel costs. Using the assignment problem formulation, the time it takes the league to generate a schedule has been significantly decreased, and the quality of the schedule has improved.

EXAMPLE 3

The cost table shown earlier in this section is repeated here. We find the minimum total cost assignment of jobs to machines by applying steps 1 through 4.

JOB \ MACHINE	A	B	C
R-34	$11	$14	$6
S-66	$8	$10	$11
T-50	$9	$12	$7

Step 1a. Using the previous table, subtract the smallest number in each row from every number in the row. The result is shown below (left).

JOB \ MACHINE	A	B	C
R-34	5	8	0
S-66	0	2	3
T-50	2	5	0

JOB \ MACHINE	A	B	C
R-34	5	6	0
S-66	0	0	3
T-50	2	3	0

Step 1b. Using the above (left) table, subtract the smallest number in each column from every number in the column. The result is shown above (right).

Step 2. Draw the minimum number of straight lines needed to cover all zeroes. Because two lines suffice, the solution is not optimal.

JOB \ MACHINE	A	B	C
R-34	5	6	0
S-66	0	0	3
T-50	(2)	3	0

Smallest uncovered number

Step 3. Subtract the smallest uncovered number (2 in this table) from every other uncovered number and add it to numbers at the intersection of two lines.

JOB \ MACHINE	A	B	C
R-34	3	4	0
S-66	0	0	5
T-50	0	1	0

Return to step 2. Cover the zeroes with straight lines again.

JOB \ MACHINE	A	B	C
R-34	3	4	0
S-66	0	0	5
T-50	0	1	0

Because three lines are necessary, an optimal assignment can be made (see step 4 on page 452). Assign R-34 to machine C, S-66 to machine B, and T-50 to machine A.

$$\text{Minimum cost} = \$6 + \$10 + \$9 = \$25$$

Note: If we had S-66 assigned to machine A, we could not assign T-50 to a zero location.

NOTE
Software such as POM for Windows can handle maximization problems as well as minimization ones.

Some assignment problems entail *maximizing* the profit, effectiveness, or payoff of an assignment of people to tasks or of jobs to machines. It is easy to obtain an equivalent minimization problem by converting every number in the table to an *opportunity loss.* To convert a maximizing problem to an equivalent minimization problem, we subtract every number in the original payoff table from the largest single number in that table. We then proceed to step 1 of the four-step assignment method. It turns out that minimizing the opportunity loss produces the same assignment solution as the original maximization problem.

SEQUENCING JOBS IN WORK CENTERS

sequencing

Scheduling provides a basis for assigning jobs to work centers. *Loading* is a capacity control technique that highlights overloads and underloads. **Sequencing** specifies the order in which jobs should be done at each center. For example, suppose that ten patients are assigned to a medical clinic for treatment. In what order should they be treated? Should the first patient to be served be the one who arrived first or the one who needs emergency treatment? Sequencing methods provide such detailed information. These methods are referred to as priority rules for dispatching jobs to work centers.

Priority Rules for Dispatching Jobs

priority rules

Priority rules provide guidelines for the sequence in which jobs should be worked. The rules are especially applicable for process-focused facilities such as clinics, print shops, and manufacturing job shops. We will examine a few of the most popular priority rules. Priority rules try to minimize completion time, number of jobs in the system, and job lateness, while maximizing facility utilization.

The most popular priority rules are:

first come, first served (FCFS)

- **FCFS: First come, first served.** The first job to arrive at a work center is processed first.

- **SPT: Shortest processing time.** The shortest jobs are handled first and completed.
- **EDD: Earliest due date.** The job with the earliest due date is selected first.
- **LPT: Longest processing time.** The longer, bigger jobs are often very important and are selected first.

shortest processing time (SPT)

earliest due date (EDD)

longest processing time (LPT)

Example 4 compares these rules.

EXAMPLE 4

Five sheet-metal jobs are waiting to be assigned at Ajax Company's Long Beach work center. Their work (processing) times and due dates are given in the following table. We want to determine the sequence of processing according to (1) FCFS, (2) SPT, (3) EDD, and (4) LPT rules. Jobs were assigned a letter in the order they arrived.

JOB	JOB WORK (processing) TIME (days)	JOB DUE DATE (days)
A	6	8
B	2	6
C	8	18

JOB	JOB WORK (processing) TIME (days)	JOB DUE DATE (days)
D	3	15
E	9	23

1. The *FCFS* sequence is simply A-B-C-D-E. The "flow time" in the system for this sequence measures the time each job spends waiting plus being processed. Job B, for example, waits 6 days while job A is being processed, then takes 2 more days of operation time itself; so it will be completed in 8 days—which is 2 days later than its due date.

JOB SEQUENCE	JOB WORK (PROCESSING) TIME	FLOW TIME	JOB DUE DATE	JOB LATENESS
A	6	6	8	0
B	2	8	6	2
C	8	16	18	0
D	3	19	15	4
E	9	28	23	5
	28	77		11

The first-come, first-served rule results in the following measures of effectiveness:

a. Average completion time $= \dfrac{\text{Sum of total flow time}}{\text{Number of jobs}}$

$$= \frac{77 \text{ days}}{5} = 15.4 \text{ days}$$

b. Utilization $= \dfrac{\text{Total job work (processing) time}}{\text{Sum of total flow time}}$

$$= \frac{28}{77} = 36.4\%$$

c. Average number of jobs in the system $= \dfrac{\text{Sum of total flow time}}{\text{Total job work (processing) time}}$

$$= \frac{77 \text{ days}}{28 \text{ days}} = 2.75 \text{ jobs}$$

d. Average job lateness $= \dfrac{\text{Total late days}}{\text{Number of jobs}} = \dfrac{11}{5} = 2.2$ days

2. The *SPT* rule results in the sequence B-D-A-C-E (see the following table). Orders are sequenced according to processing time, with the highest priority given to the shortest job.

JOB SEQUENCE	JOB WORK (processing) TIME	FLOW TIME	JOB DUE DATE	JOB LATENESS
B	2	2	6	0
D	3	5	15	0
A	6	11	8	3
C	8	19	18	1
E	9	28	23	5
	28	65		9

Measurements of effectiveness for SPT are:

a. Average completion time $= \dfrac{65}{5} = 13$ days

b. Utilization $= \dfrac{28}{65} = 43.1\%$

c. Average number of jobs in the system $= \dfrac{65}{28} = 2.32$

d. Average job lateness $= \dfrac{9}{5} = 1.8$ days

3. The *EDD* rule gives the sequence B-A-D-C-E. Note that jobs are ordered by earliest due date first.

JOB SEQUENCE	JOB WORK (processing) TIME	FLOW TIME	JOB DUE DATE	JOB LATENESS
B	2	2	6	0
A	6	8	8	0
D	3	11	15	0
C	8	19	18	1
E	9	28	23	5
	28	68		6

Measurements of effectiveness for EDD are:

a. Average completion time $= \dfrac{68}{5} = 13.6$ days

b. Utilization $= \dfrac{28}{68} = 41.2\%$

c. Average number of jobs in the system $= \frac{68}{28} = 2.42$

d. Average job lateness $= \frac{6}{5} = 1.2$ days

4. The *LPT* results in the order E-C-A-D-B.

JOB SEQUENCE	JOB WORK (processing) TIME	FLOW TIME	JOB DUE DATE	JOB LATENESS
E	9	9	23	0
C	8	17	18	0
A	6	23	8	15
D	3	26	15	11
B	2	28	6	22
	28	103		48

Measures of effectiveness for LPT are:

a. Average completion time $= \frac{103}{5} = 20.6$ days

b. Utilization $= \frac{28}{103} = 28.2\%$

c. Average number of jobs in the system $= \frac{103}{28} = 3.68$

d. Average job lateness $= \frac{48}{5} = 9.6$ days

The results of these four rules are summarized in the following table.

RULE	AVERAGE COMPLETION TIME (days)	UTILIZATION (%)	AVERAGE NUMBER OF JOBS IN SYSTEM	AVERAGE LATENESS (days)
FCFS	15.4	36.4	2.75	2.2
SPT	13.0	43.1	2.32	1.8
EDD	13.6	41.2	2.42	1.2
LPT	20.6	28.2	3.68	9.6

As we can see in Example 4, LPT is the least effective measurement of sequencing for the Ajax Company. SPT is superior in three measures and EDD in the fourth (average lateness). This is typically true in the real world also. We find that no one sequencing rule always excels on all criteria. Experience indicates the following:

1. Shortest processing time is generally the best technique for minimizing job flow and minimizing the average number of jobs in the system. Its chief disadvantage is that long-duration jobs may be continuously pushed back in priority in favor of short-duration jobs. Customers may view this dimly, and a periodic adjustment for longer jobs has to be made.

NOTE
The results of a dispatching rule change depending upon how full the facility is.

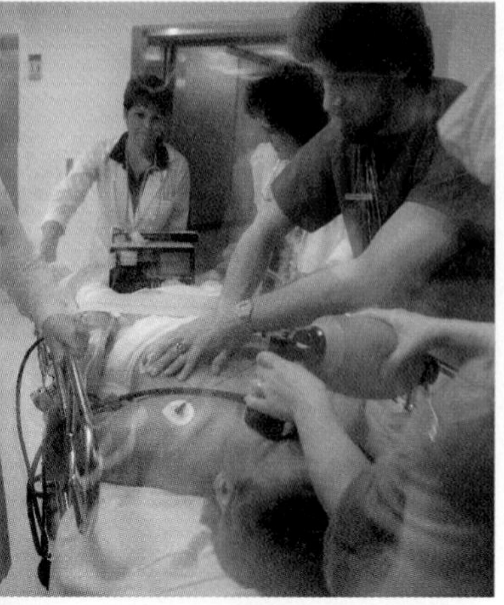

Your doctor may use a first-come, first-served priority rule satisfactorily. However, such a rule may be less than optimal for this emergency room. What priority rule might be best, and why? What priority rule was often used on the TV program M*A*S*H?

2. First come, first served does not score well on most criteria (but neither does it score particularly poorly). It has the advantage, however, of appearing fair to customers, which is important in service systems.

Critical Ratio

Another type of sequencing rule is the critical ratio. The **critical ratio (CR)** is an index number computed by dividing the time remaining until due date by the work time remaining. As opposed to the priority rules, critical ratio is dynamic and easily updated. It tends to perform better than FCFS, SPT, EDD, or LPT on the average job lateness criterion.

The critical ratio gives priority to jobs that must be done to keep shipping on schedule. A job with a low critical ratio (less than 1.0) is one that is falling behind schedule. If CR is exactly 1.0, the job is on schedule. A CR greater than 1.0 means the job is ahead of schedule and has some slack.

The formula for critical ratio is

$$\text{CR} = \frac{\text{Time remaining}}{\text{Work days remaining}} = \frac{\text{Due date} - \text{Today's date}}{\text{Work (lead) time remaining}}$$

Example 5 shows how to use the critical ratio.

EXAMPLE 5

Today is day 25 on Geraud Food's production schedule. Three jobs are on order, as indicated here:

JOB	DUE DATE	WORK DAYS REMAINING
A	30	4
B	28	5
C	27	2

We compute the critical ratios, using the formula for CR.

JOB	CRITICAL RATIO	PRIORITY ORDER
A	$(30 - 25)/4 = 1.25$	3
B	$(28 - 25)/5 = .60$	1
C	$(27 - 25)/2 = 1.00$	2

Job B has a critical ratio less than 1, meaning it will be late unless expedited. Thus, it has the highest priority. Job C is on time and job A has some slack.

The critical-ratio rule can help in most production scheduling systems to do the following:

1. Determine the status of a specific job.
2. Establish relative priority among jobs on a common basis.
3. Relate both stock and make-to-order jobs on a common basis.

4. Adjust priorities (and revise schedules) automatically for changes in both demand and job progress.
5. Dynamically track job progress.

"We've been at it all night, J.B., and we've narrowed it down to 36,000 possibilities. We should have today's schedule firmed up by noon."

SOURCE: CMCS News.

Sequencing *N* Jobs on Two Machines: Johnson's Rule

The next step in complexity is the case where *N* jobs (where *N* is 2 or more) must go through two machines or work centers in the same order. This is called the *N*/2 problem.

Johnson's rule can be used to minimize the processing time for sequencing a group of jobs through two facilities.[6] It also minimizes total idle time on the machines. *Johnson's rule* involves four steps:

Johnson's rule

1. All jobs are to be listed, and the time each requires on a machine is to be shown.
2. Select the job with the shortest activity time. If the shortest time lies with the first machine, the job is scheduled first. If the shortest time lies with the second machine, schedule the job last. Ties in activity times can be broken arbitrarily.
3. Once a job is scheduled, eliminate it.
4. Apply steps 2 and 3 to the remaining jobs, working toward the center of the sequence.

Example 6 shows how to apply Johnson's rule.

EXAMPLE 6

Five specialty jobs at a Fredonia, New York, tool and die shop must be processed through two work centers (drill press and lathe). The time for processing each job follows:

WORK (PROCESSING) TIME FOR JOBS (IN HOURS)

JOB	WORK CENTER 1 (drill press)	WORK CENTER 2 (lathe)
A	5	2
B	3	6
C	8	4
D	10	7
E	7	12

1. We wish to set the sequence that will minimize the total processing time for the five jobs. The job with the shortest processing time is A, in work center 2 (with a time of 2 hours). Because it is at the second center, schedule A last. Eliminate it from consideration.

				A

2. Job B has the next shortest time (3 hours). Because that time is at the first work center, we schedule it first and eliminate it from consideration.

B				A

[6] S. M. Johnson, "Optimal Two and Three Stage Production Schedules with Set-Up Times Included," *Naval Research Logistics Quarterly* 1, no. 1 (March 1954): 61–68.

3. The next shortest time is job C (4) on the second machine. Therefore, it is placed as late as possible.

B			C	A

4. There is a tie (at 7 hours) for the shortest remaining job. We can place E, which was on the first work center, first. Then D is placed in the last sequencing position.

B	E	D	C	A

The sequential times are:

Work center 1	3	7	10	8	5
Work center 2	6	12	7	4	2

The time phased flow of this job sequence is best illustrated graphically:

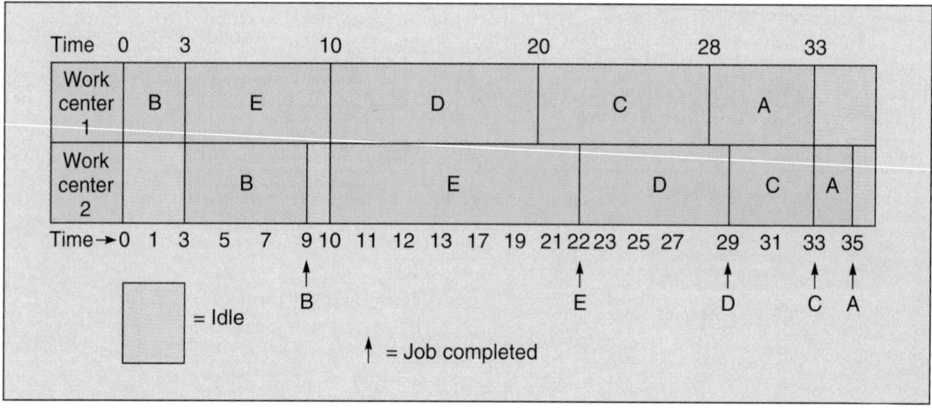

Thus, the five jobs are completed in 35 hours. The second work center will wait 3 hours for its first job, and it will also wait 1 hour after completing job B.

LIMITATIONS OF RULE-BASED SYSTEMS

NOTE
Scheduling can be complex to perform and still yield poor results—not a very fruitful combination. Even with sophisticated rules, good scheduling is very difficult.

The scheduling techniques just discussed are rule-based techniques, but rule-based systems have a number of limitations. Among those are:

1. Scheduling is dynamic; therefore, rules need to be revised to adjust to changes in process, equipment, product mix, and so forth.
2. Rules do not look upstream or downstream; idle resources and bottleneck resources in other departments may not be recognized.
3. Rules do not look beyond due dates. For instance, two orders may have the same due date. One order involves restocking a distributor and the other is a custom order that will shut down the customer's factory if not completed. Both may have the same due date, but clearly the custom order is more important.

In spite of these limitations, schedulers often use sequencing rules such as SPT, EDD, or critical ratio. They apply these methods periodically at each work center and then the scheduler modifies the sequence to deal with a multitude of real-world variables. They may do this manually or with finite scheduling software.

FINITE SCHEDULING

finite scheduling

A recent advance in short-term scheduling is interactive finite scheduling.[7] **Finite scheduling** overcomes the disadvantages of rule-based systems by providing the scheduler with graphical interactive computing. This system is characterized by the ability of the scheduler to make changes based on up-to-the-minute information. These schedules are often displayed in Gantt chart form (see Figure 13.2). The scheduler has the flexibility to handle any situation, including order, labor, or machine changes.

Finite scheduling allows delivery needs to be balanced against efficiency based on today's conditions and today's orders, not according to some predefined rule. Many of the current finite scheduling computer programs offer resource constraint features, a multitude of rules, and the ability of the scheduler to work interactively with the scheduling system to create a realistic schedule. These systems may also combine an expert system and simulation techniques and allow the scheduler to assign costs to various options. Finite scheduling helps the scheduler, but leaves it up to the scheduler to determine what constitutes a "good" schedule.[8]

THEORY OF CONSTRAINTS

theory of constraints (TOC)

Managers need to identify the operations that constrain output because it is throughput—that is, units through the facility and sold—that makes the difference. This has led to the use of the term *theory of constraints*. The **theory of constraints (TOC)** is that body of knowledge that deals with anything that limits an organization's ability to achieve its goals. Constraints can be physical (such as process or personnel availability, raw materials, or supplies) or non-physical (such as procedures, morale, training). Recognizing and managing these constraints through a five-step process is the basis of the theory of constraints.

Step 1. Identify the constraints.
Step 2. Develop a plan for overcoming the identified constraints.
Step 3. Focus resources on accomplishing step 2.
Step 4. Reduce the effects of the constraints by off-loading work or by expanding capability. Make sure that the constraints are recognized by all those who can have impact upon them.
Step 5. Once one set of constraints is overcome, go back to step 1 and identify new constraints.

---

[7]Andrew Gilman, "Interest in Finite Scheduling Is Growing . . . Why?" *APICS: The Performance Advantage* 4, no. 8 (August 1994): 45–48.

[8]Sam Anard, "Impact of a Decision Support and Finite Schedule of System on a Large Machine Shop," *Production and Inventory Management Journal* (Fourth Quarter 1994): 54–59.

Dr. Eliyahu Goldratt, a physicist, popularized the theory of constraints in a book he wrote with Jeff Cox, called *The Goal: A Process of Ongoing Improvement*.[9]

Bottleneck Work Centers

bottleneck

Bottleneck work centers limit the output of production. Bottlenecks have less capacity than the prior or following work centers. They constrain throughput. Bottlenecks are a common occurrence because even well-designed systems are seldom balanced for very long. Changing products, product mixes, and volumes often create multiple and shifting bottlenecks. Consequently, bottleneck work centers occur in nearly all process-focused facilities, from hospitals and restaurants to factories. Successful operations managers deal with bottlenecks by increasing the bottleneck's capacity, rerouting work, changing lot size, changing work sequence, or accepting idleness at other workstations. Substantial research has been done on the bottleneck issue.

To increase throughput, the bottleneck constraint must be maximized by imaginative management, well-trained employees, and a well-maintained process. Several techniques for dealing with the bottleneck are available. They include:

1. Increasing capacity of the constraint. This may require a capital investment or more people and take a while to implement.
2. Ensuring that well-trained and cross-trained employees are available to operate and maintain the constraint.
3. Developing alternate routings, processing procedures, or subcontractors.
4. Moving inspections and tests to a position just before the constraint. This approach has the advantage of rejecting any potential defects before they enter the bottleneck.
5. Scheduling throughput to match the capacity of the bottleneck: this may mean scheduling less.

REPETITIVE MANUFACTURING

The scheduling goals as defined at the beginning of this chapter are also appropriate for repetitive production. You may recall from Chapter 5 that repetitive producers make standard products from modules. Repetitive producers want to satisfy customer demands, lower inventory investment, reduce the batch (or lot) size, and utilize equipment and processes. The way to move toward these goals is to move to a level material-use schedule. **Level material use** means frequent, high-quality, small lot sizes that contribute to just-in-time production. This is exactly what world-class producers such as Harley-Davidson and John Deere do. The advantages of level material use are:

level material use

1. Lower inventory levels, which release capital for other uses.
2. Faster product throughput (that is, shorter lead times).

[9]Eliyahu M. Goldratt and Jeff Cox, *The Goal: A Process of Ongoing Improvement* (Croton-on-Hudson, NY: North River Press, 1986). For a more general discussion of the constraints, see James T. Low, "Strategic Linkages Between Purchasing and Production Management," *APICS—The Performance Advantage* 2 (December 1992): 33–34; and James T. Low, "A Model for Applying the Theory to Purchasing," *APICS—The Performance Advantage* 3 (January 1993): 38–41.

3. Improved component quality and hence improved product quality.
4. Reduced floor-space requirements.
5. Improved communication among employees because they are closer together (which can result in improved teamwork and *esprit de corps*).
6. Smoother production process because large lots have not "hidden" the problems.

Suppose a repetitive producer runs large monthly batches. With a level material use schedule, management would move toward shortening this monthly cycle. Management might run this cycle every week, day, or hour.

One way to develop a level material-use schedule is to determine first the minimum lot size that will keep the production process moving. Ideally, this is the one unit that is being moved from one adjacent process to the next. More realistically, analysis of the process, transportation time, and containers used for transport are considered when determining lot size. Such analysis typically results in a small lot size but a lot size larger than one. Once a lot size has been determined, the EOQ production-run model can be modified to determine the desired setup time. We saw in Chapter 9 that the production-run model takes the form

$$Q^* = \sqrt{\frac{2DS}{H[1 - (d/p)]}}$$

where

D = Annual demand

S = Setup cost

H = Holding cost

d = Daily demand

p = Daily production

Example 7 shows how Crate Furniture, Inc., a firm that produces rustic furniture, moves toward a level material-use schedule.

EXAMPLE 7

Crate Furniture's production analyst, Aleda Roth, determined that a two-hour production cycle would be acceptable between two departments. Further, she concluded that a setup time that would accommodate the two-hour cycle time could be achieved. Roth developed the following data and procedure to determine optimum setup time analytically:

D = Annual demand = 400,000 units

d = Daily demand = 400,000 per 250 days = 1,600 units per day

p = Daily production rate = 4,000 units per day

Q = EOQ desired = 400 (which is the two-hour demand, that is, 1,600 per day per four two hour periods)

H = Holding cost = \$20 per unit per year

S = Setup cost (to be determined)

Roth determines that the cost, on an hourly basis, of setting up equipment is \$30. Further, she computes that the setup cost per setup should be

$$Q = \sqrt{\frac{2DS}{H(1 - d/p)}}$$

$$Q^2 = \frac{2DS}{H(1 - d/p)}$$

$$S = \frac{(Q^2)(H)(1 - d/p)}{2D}$$

$$S = \frac{(400)^2(20)(1 - 1{,}600/4{,}000)}{2(400{,}000)}$$

$$= \frac{(3{,}200{,}000)(0.6)}{800{,}000} = \$2.40$$

$$\text{Setup time} = \$2.40/(\text{hourly labor rate})$$

$$= \$2.40/(\$30 \text{ per hour})$$

$$= 0.08 \text{ hour, or } 4.8 \text{ minutes}$$

Now, rather than producing components in large lots, Crate Furniture can produce in a two-hour cycle with the advantage of an inventory turnover of four *per day.*

Only two changes need to be made for this type of level material flow to work. First is the radical reduction in setup times, which is usually not difficult from a technical point of view. Second, changes may need to be made to improve material handling. With short production cycles, there can be very little wait time.

SCHEDULING FOR SERVICES

Scheduling service systems differs from scheduling manufacturing systems in several ways. First, in manufacturing, the scheduling emphasis is on materials; but in services, it is on staffing levels. Second, service systems seldom store inventories. Third, services are labor-intensive, and the demand for this labor can be highly variable.

Service systems try to match fluctuating customer demand with the capability to meet that demand. In some businesses, such as doctors' and lawyers' offices, an *appointment system* is the schedule. In retail shops, a post office, or a fast-food restaurant, a *first-come, first-served* rule for serving customers may suffice. Scheduling in these businesses is handled by bringing in extra workers, often part-timers, to help during peak periods. *Reservations systems* work well in rental car agencies, symphony halls, hotels, and some restaurants as a means of minimizing customer waiting time and avoiding disappointment over unfilled service.

HOSPITALS. A hospital is an example of a service facility that may use a scheduling system every bit as complex as one found in a job shop. Hospitals seldom use a machine shop priority system such as first come, first served (FCFS) for treating emergency patients. But they do schedule products (such as surgeries) just like a factory, even though finished goods inventories cannot be kept and capacities must meet wide variations in demand.

BANKS. Cross-training of the workforce in a bank allows loan officers and other managers to provide short-term help for tellers if there is a surge in demand. Banks also employ part-time personnel to effectively provide a variable capacity.

AIRLINES. Airlines face two constraints in scheduling flight crews: (1) a complex set of FAA work-time limitations and (2) union contracts that guarantee crew pay for some number of hours each day or each trip. Airline planners must build crew schedules that meet or exceed crews' pay guarantees.

To manage her hundreds of retail cookie outlets, Debbi Fields decided to capture her experience in a scheduling system that every store could access at any time. Her Retail Operations Intelligence System (ROIS) takes advantage of headquarter's expertise in scheduling minimum-wage employees, the predominant counter help. The software draws up a work schedule, including breaks, to best use hourly employees' time. ROIS also creates a full-day projection of the amount of dough to be processed and charts progress and sales on an hourly basis. It even tells staff when to cut back production and start offering free samples to passing customers.

Scheduling Nurses with Cyclical Scheduling

Head nurses in large hospitals often spend more than 20 hours a month establishing schedules for their departments. They consider a fairly long planning period (say, six weeks) and then need to set timely and efficient schedules so that adequate health care can be delivered to patients while keeping personnel happy with their hours. Although there are several ways of tackling this problem, one approach that is both workable yet simple is *cyclical scheduling*.[10]

Cyclical scheduling has seven steps:

1. Plan a schedule equal in length to the number of people being scheduled.
2. Determine how many of each of the least desirable off-shifts must be covered each week.
3. Begin the schedule for one nurse by scheduling the days off during the planning cycle (at a rate of two days per week on the average).
4. Assign off-shifts for that first nurse using step 2. Here is an example of one nurse's 42-day schedule, where X is the day off, D is the day shift, and E is the evening shift:

S	M	T	W	T	F	S
E	E	E	E	E	X	X

S	M	T	W	T	F	S
X	X	E	E	E	E	E

S	M	T	W	T	F	S
E	D	X	D	D	D	D

S	M	T	W	T	F	S
D	D	X	X	D	E	X

S	M	T	W	T	F	S
X	E	E	E	E	E	X

S	M	T	W	T	F	S
D	E	D	D	X	X	E

5. Repeat this pattern for each of the other nurses, but offsetting each one by one week from the previous one.
6. Allow each nurse to pick his or her "slot" or "line" in order of seniority.
7. Mandate that any changes from a chosen schedule are strictly between the personnel wanting to switch.

[10]For more details, see R. Murdick, B. Render, and R. Russell, *Service Operations Management* (Boston: Allyn & Bacon, 1990), pp. 336–340; or J. D. Megeath, "Successful Hospital Personnel Scheduling," *Interfaces* 8, no. 6 (February 1978): 55–59.

When this approach was applied at Colorado General Hospital, the head nurse saved an average of 10 to 15 hours a month and found these advantages: (1) no computer was needed, (2) the nurses were happy with the schedule, (3) the cycles could be changed during different seasons (to accommodate avid skiers), and (4) recruiting was easier because of predictability and flexibility.

SUMMARY

Scheduling involves the timing of operations to achieve the efficient movement of units through a system. This chapter addressed the issues of short-term scheduling in process-focused, repetitive, and service environments. We saw that process-focused facilities are production systems in which products are made to order, and that scheduling tasks in them can become complex. Several aspects and approaches to scheduling, loading, and sequencing of jobs were introduced. These ranged from Gantt charts and the assignment methods of scheduling to a series of priority rules, the critical-ratio rule, and Johnson's rule for sequencing. We also examined the use of level material flow in repetitive manufacturing environments.

Service systems generally differ from manufacturing systems. This leads to the use of appointment systems, first-come, first-served systems, and reservation systems, as well as to heuristics and mathematical programming approaches to servicing customers.

KEY TERMS

Forward scheduling *(p. 447)*
Backward scheduling *(p. 447)*
Planning files *(p. 449)*
Control files *(p. 449)*
Loading *(p. 449)*
Gantt charts *(p. 449)*
Assignment method *(p. 451)*
Sequencing *(p. 454)*
Priority rules *(p. 454)*
First come, first served (FCFS) *(p. 454)*
Shortest processing time (SPT) *(p. 455)*
Earliest due date (EDD) *(p. 455)*
Longest processing time (LPT) *(p. 455)*
Critical ratio (CR) *(p. 458)*
Johnson's rule *(p. 459)*
Finite scheduling *(p. 461)*
Theory of constraints (TOC) *(p. 461)*
Bottleneck *(p. 462)*
Level material use *(p. 462)*

USING POM FOR WINDOWS TO SOLVE SCHEDULING PROBLEMS

POM for Windows' Assignment module is used to solve the traditional one-to-one assignment problem of people to tasks, machines to jobs, and so on. Program 13.1 shows both the inputs and solution to the three-job, three-machine problem using the data in Example 3.

Program 13.2 illustrates POM for Windows' Job Shop Scheduling module, which can solve a one- or two-machine job shop problem. The data in Example 4 are used as input. Outputs appear on the same screen.

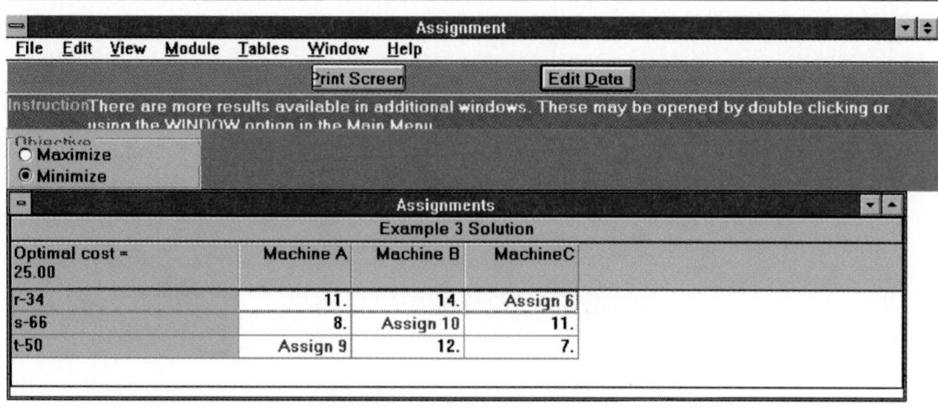

Assignment

File Edit View Module Tables Window Help

Print Screen | Edit Data

Instruction There are more results available in additional windows. These may be opened by double clicking or using the WINDOW option in the Main Menu

Objective: ○ Maximize ◉ Minimize

Assignments

Example 3 Solution

Optimal cost = 25.00	Machine A	Machine B	MachineC
r-34	11.	14.	Assign 6
s-66	8.	Assign 10	11.
t-50	Assign 9	12.	7.

The word *Assign* appears in boxes that yield an optimal solution.

PROGRAM 13.1

POM FOR WINDOWS' ASSIGNMENT MODEL PROGRAM USING EXAMPLE 3'S DATA

Job Shop Scheduling

File Edit View Module Tables Window Help

Print Screen | Edit Data

Instruction There are more results available in additional windows. These may be opened by double clicking or using the WINDOW option in the Main Menu

Method: SPT - Shortest Processing Time | Starting Day Number: 0

Job Shop Scheduling Results

Job Shop Scheduling

	Machine 1	Due Date	# Opns	Order	Flow time	Late
A	6.	8.	0.	third	11.	3.
B	2.	6.	0.	first	2.	0.
C	8.	18.	0.	fourth	19.	1.
D	3.	15.	0.	second	5.	0.
E	9.	23.	0.	fifth	28.	5.
TOTAL					65.	9.
AVERAGE					13.	1.8
Average # jobs in	2.3214					

Job Sequence
B, D, A, C, E,

Available priority rules include SPT, FCFS, EDD, and LPT. Each can be examined in turn once the data are all entered.

PROGRAM 13.2

POM FOR WINDOWS' JOB SHOP SCHEDULING PROGRAM USING EXAMPLE 4'S DATA

SOLVED PROBLEM 13.1

King Finance Corporation, headquartered in New York, wants to assign three recently hired college graduates, Julie Jones, Al Smith, and Pat Wilson, to regional offices. But the firm also has an opening in New York and would send one of the three there if it were more economical than a move to Omaha, Dallas, or Miami. It will cost $1,000 to relocate Jones to New York, $800 to relocate Smith there, and $1,500 to move Wilson. What is the optimal assignment of personnel to offices?

continued on next page

HIREE \ OFFICE	OMAHA	MIAMI	DALLAS
Jones	$800	$1,100	$1,200
Smith	$500	$1,600	$1,300
Wilson	$500	$1,000	$2,300

SOLUTION

a. The cost table has a fourth column to represent New York. To "balance" the problem, we add a "dummy" row (person) with a zero relocation cost to each city.

HIREE \ OFFICE	OMAHA	MIAMI	DALLAS	NEW YORK
Jones	$800	$1,100	$1,200	$1,000
Smith	$500	$1,600	$1,300	$ 800
Wilson	$500	$1,000	$2,300	$1,500
Dummy	0	0	0	0

b. Subtract the smallest number in each row and cover all zeroes (column subtraction will give the same numbers and therefore is not necessary).

HIREE \ OFFICE	OMAHA	MIAMI	DALLAS	NEW YORK
Jones	0	300	400	200
Smith	0	1,100	800	300
Wilson	0	500	1,800	1,000
Dummy	0	0	0	0

c. Subtract the smallest uncovered number (200), add it to each square where two lines intersect, and cover all zeroes.

HIREE \ OFFICE	OMAHA	MIAMI	DALLAS	NEW YORK
Jones	0	100	200	0
Smith	0	900	600	100
Wilson	0	300	1,600	800
Dummy	200	0	0	0

d. Subtract the smallest uncovered number (100), add it to each square where two lines intersect, and cover all zeroes.

HIREE \ OFFICE	OMAHA	MIAMI	DALLAS	NEW YORK
Jones	0	0	100	0
Smith	0	800	500	100
Wilson	0	200	1,500	800
Dummy	300	0	0	100

e. Subtract the smallest uncovered number (100), add it to squares where two lines intersect, and cover all zeroes.

HIREE \ OFFICE	OMAHA	MIAMI	DALLAS	NEW YORK
Jones	100	0	100	0
Smith	0	700	400	0
Wilson	0	100	1,400	700
Dummy	400	0	0	100

f. Because it takes four lines to cover all zeroes, an optimal assignment can be made at zero squares. We assign

Dummy (no one) to Dallas
Wilson to Omaha
Smith to New York
Jones to Miami

$$\text{Cost} = \$0 + \$500 + \$800 + \$1{,}100$$
$$= \$2{,}400$$

SOLVED PROBLEM 13.2

A defense contractor in Dallas has six jobs awaiting processing. Processing time and due dates are given in the following table. Assume jobs arrive in the order shown. Set the processing sequence according to FCFS and evaluate.

JOB	JOB PROCESSING TIME (days)	JOB DUE DATE (days)
A	6	22
B	12	14
C	14	30
D	2	18
E	10	25
F	4	34

SOLUTION

FCFS has the sequence A-B-C-D-E-F.

JOB SEQUENCE	JOB PROCESSING TIME	FLOW TIME	DUE DATE	JOB LATENESS
A	6	6	22	0
B	12	18	14	4
C	14	32	30	2
D	2	34	18	16
E	10	44	25	19
F	4	48	34	14
	48	182		55

1. Average completion time = 182/6 = 30.33.
2. Average number of jobs in system = 182/48 = 3.79.
3. Average job lateness = 55/6 = 9.16 days.
4. Utilization = 48/182 = 26.4%.

SOLVED PROBLEM 13.3

The Dallas firm noted in Solved Problem 13.2 wants also to consider job sequencing by the SPT priority rule. Apply SPT to the same data and provide a recommendation.

SOLUTION

SPT has the sequence D-F-A-E-B-C.

JOB SEQUENCE	JOB PROCESSING TIME	FLOW TIME	DUE DATE	JOB LATENESS
D	2	2	18	0
F	4	6	34	0
A	6	12	22	0
E	10	22	25	0
B	12	34	14	20
C	14	48	30	18
	48	124		38

1. Average completion time = 124/6 = 20.67 days.
2. Average number of jobs in system = 124/48 = 2.58.
3. Average job lateness = 38/6 = 6.33 days.
4. Utilization = 48/124 = 38.7%.

SPT is superior to FCFS in this case on all four measures. If we were to also analyze EDD, we would, however, find its average job lateness to be lowest at 5.5 days. SPT is a good recommendation. SPT's major disadvantage is that it makes long jobs wait, sometimes for a long time.

SOLVED PROBLEM 13.4

Use Johnson's rule to find the optimum sequence for processing the jobs shown on the right through two work centers. Times at each center are in hours.

JOB	WORK CENTER 1	WORK CENTER 2
A	6	12
B	3	7
C	18	9
D	15	14
E	16	8
F	10	15

SOLUTION

B	A	F	D	C	E

The sequential times are

Work center 1	3	6	10	15	18	16
Work center 2	7	12	15	14	9	8

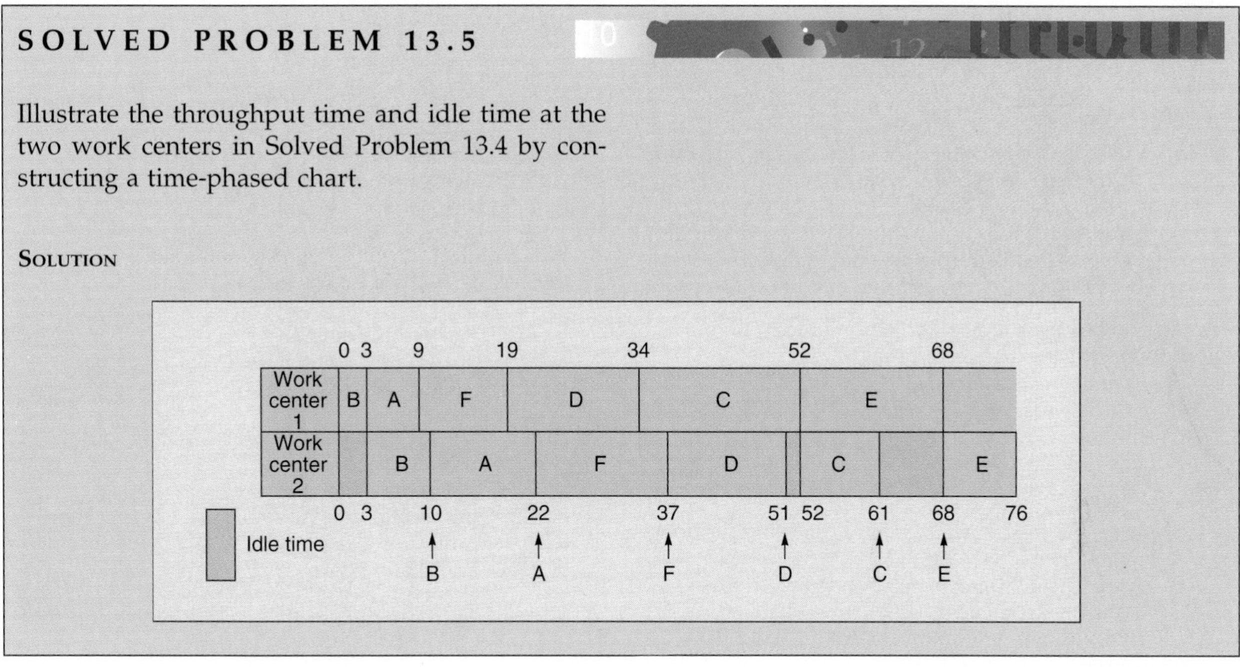

SOLVED PROBLEM 13.5

Illustrate the throughput time and idle time at the two work centers in Solved Problem 13.4 by constructing a time-phased chart.

SOLUTION

DISCUSSION QUESTIONS

1. Name five priority sequencing rules. Explain how each works to assign jobs.
2. When is Johnson's rule best applied in job shop scheduling?
3. What is the difference between a Gantt load chart and a Gantt schedule chart?
4. What are the steps in the theory of constraints?
5. Why is the scheduling of services a difficult problem?
6. What are the criteria by which we evaluate sequencing rules?
7. What are the advantages of level material flow?

OPERATIONS IN PRACTICE EXERCISE

Scheduling people to work the late, or "graveyard," shift is a problem in almost every 24-hour company. An article in *The Wall Street Journal* (July 7, 1988, p. 1), titled "Scheduling Workers Who Fall Asleep on the Job Is Not Easy" describes night-shift dilemmas at an oil refinery and a police department. Scheduling is also difficult for airlines that fly long routes, such as El Al Airline's popular 11-hour nonstop Tel Aviv to New York flight.

Select five companies that require night shifts and discuss how each can deal with its staffing requirements. What are the major issues in each that impact on morale, productivity, alertness, and safety?

SELF-TEST ■ CHAPTER 13

- *Before taking the self-test* refer back to the learning objectives listed at the beginning of the chapter and the key terms listed at the end of the chapter.
- Use the key at the back of the text to *correct* your answers.
- *Restudy* pages that correspond to any questions you answered incorrectly or material you feel uncertain about.

1. A technique used to monitor jobs in process is
   a. a Gantt load chart
   b. the assignment method
   c. Johnson's rule
   d. all of the above
   e. none of the above
2. Shop loading
   a. means the assignment of dates to specific jobs or operations steps
   b. is typically managed using an assembly chart
   c. means the assignment of jobs to work or processing centers
   d. is oriented toward the management of work-in-process inventories
3. Shop loading takes two forms. One is oriented toward shop capacity; the other toward assigning specific jobs to work centers.
   a. True b. False
4. The assignment method cannot be used to sequence a set of jobs through a set of centers.
   a. True b. False
5. The most popular priority rules include
   a. FCFS
   b. EDD
   c. SPT
   d. all of the above
6. Which of the following dispatch rules tends to maximize the number of jobs completed on time?
   a. FCFS: First come, first served
   b. EDD: Earliest due date
   c. SPT: Shortest processing time
   d. LPT: Longest processing time
7. Which of the following dispatch rules tends to minimize the average number of jobs in the system?
   a. FCFS: First come, first served
   b. EDD: Earliest due date
   c. SPT: Shortest processing time
   d. LPT: Longest processing time
8. Of the following dispatching rules, which is considered to be "dynamic"?
   a. FCFS: First come, first served
   b. CR: Critical ratio
   c. SPT: Shortest processing time
   d. EDD: Earliest due date
9. The chief disadvantage of the shortest processing time dispatch rule is that ______________.
10. Popular dispatching rules include
    a. ______, b. ______, c. ______, d. ______, e. ______.
11. The theory of constraints pays special attention to
    a. the nature of the individual in charge of scheduling
    b. the number of part-time employees
    c. bottleneck operations
    d. all of the above
12. When developing a level material-use schedule for a repetitive manufacturing operation, one must consider the process, transportation time, and the containers used for transport.
    a. True b. False
13. When developing a level material-use schedule, one typically determines the setup times for each operation, then uses the EOQ model to determine the necessary lot size.
    a. True b. False

PROBLEMS

: **13.1.** Bob Swan's company has scheduled five jobs. Today, which is day 7, Swan is reviewing the Gantt chart depicting these schedules.

- Job A was scheduled to begin on day 3 and to take six days. As of now, it is one day ahead of schedule.
- Job B was scheduled to begin on day 1 and take four days. It is currently on time.
- Job C was scheduled to start on day 7 and take three days. It actually got started on day 6 and is progressing according to plan.

- Job D was scheduled to begin on day 5, but missing equipment delayed it until day 6. It is progressing as expected and should take three days.
- Job E was scheduled to begin on day 4 and take five days. It got started on time but has since fallen behind two days.

Draw the Gantt chart as it looks to Swan.

13.2. Jenine Duffey's company wishes to assign a set of jobs to a set of machines. The following table provides data as to the productivity of each machine when performing the specific job.

a. Determine the assignment of jobs to machines that will *maximize* total productivity.

b. What is the total productivity of your assignments?

JOB \ MACHINE	A	B	C	D
1	7	9	8	10
2	10	9	7	6
3	11	5	9	6
4	9	11	5	8

13.3. Sarah Mahan's company wishes to assign a set of jobs to a set of machines. The following table provides data as to the cost of each job when performed on a specific machine.

a. Determine the assignment of jobs to machines that will *minimize* Mahan's total cost.

b. What is the total cost of your assignments?

JOB \ MACHINE	A	B	C	D
1	7	9	8	10
2	10	9	7	6
3	11	5	9	6
4	9	11	5	8

13.4. JH Products Corporation has four more jobs to be scheduled, in addition to those shown in Example 2 in the chapter. JH production scheduling personnel are reviewing the Gantt chart at the end of day 4.

- Job D was scheduled to begin early on day 2 and to end on the middle of day 9. As of now (the review point after day 4) it is 2 days ahead of schedule.
- Job E should begin on day 1 and end on day 3. It was on time.
- Job F was to begin on day 3, but maintenance forced a delay of $1\frac{1}{2}$ days. The job should now take 5 full days. It is now on schedule.
- Job G is a day behind schedule. It started at the beginning of day 2 and should require 6 days to complete.

Develop a Gantt schedule chart for JH Corporation.

13.5. The operations manager of King Manufacturing must assign three tasks to three machines. Cost data are presented below.

JOB \ MACHINE	1	2	3
C-3	$800	$1,100	$1,200
C-5	$500	$1,600	$1,300
C-8	$500	$1,000	$2,300

Use the assignment algorithm to solve this problem.

13.6. The scheduler at a small southwestern U.S. plant has six jobs that can be processed on any of six machines, with respective times as shown (in hours) below. Determine the allocation of jobs to machines that will result in minimum time.

	MACHINE					
JOB	*1*	*2*	*3*	*4*	*5*	*6*
A-52	60	22	34	42	30	60
A-53	22	52	16	32	18	48
A-56	29	16	58	28	22	55
A-59	42	32	28	46	15	30
A-60	30	18	25	15	45	42
A-61	50	48	57	30	44	60

13.7. The hospital administrator at St. Charles General must appoint head nurses to four newly established departments: urology, cardiology, orthopedics, and obstetrics. In anticipation of this staffing problem, she had hired four nurses: Hawkins, Condriac, Bardot, and Hoolihan. Believing in the operations analysis approach to problem solving, the administrator has interviewed all the nurses; considered their backgrounds, personalities, and talents; and developed a cost scale ranging from 0 to 100 to be used in the assignment. A 0 for Nurse Hawkins being assigned to the cardiology unit implies that she would be perfectly suited to that task. A value close to 100, on the other hand, would imply that she is not at all suited to head that unit. The accompanying table gives the complete set of cost figures that the hospital administrator felt represented all possible assignments. Which nurse should be assigned to which unit?

	DEPARTMENT			
NURSE	*Urology*	*Cardiology*	*Orthopedics*	*Obstetrics*
Hawkins	28	18	15	75
Condriac	32	48	23	38
Bardot	51	36	24	36
Hoolihan	25	38	55	12

13.8. The Gleaming Company has just developed a new dishwashing liquid and is preparing for a national television promotional campaign. The firm has decided to schedule a series of one-minute commercials during the peak daytime audience viewing hours of 1:00 to 5:00 P.M. To reach the widest possible audience, Gleaming wants to schedule one commercial on each of four networks and have one commercial appear during each of the four one-hour time blocks. The exposure ratings for each hour, representing the number of viewers per $1,000 spent, are presented in the accompanying table. Which network should be scheduled each hour in order to provide the maximum audience exposure?

	NETWORKS			
TIME	*A*	*B*	*C*	*Independent*
1:00–2:00 P.M.	27.1	18.1	11.3	9.5
2:00–3:00 P.M.	18.9	15.5	17.1	10.6
3:00–4:00 P.M.	19.2	18.5	9.9	7.7
4:00–5:00 P.M.	11.5	21.4	16.8	12.8

13.9. The Trang Pham Manufacturing Company is putting out seven new electronic components. Each of Pham's eight plants has the capacity to add one more product to its current line of electronic parts. The unit manufacturing costs for producing the different parts at the eight plants are shown in the accompanying table. How should Pham assign the new products to the plants in order to minimize manufacturing costs?

	PLANTS							
ELECTRONIC COMPONENTS	*1*	*2*	*3*	*4*	*5*	*6*	*7*	*8*
C53	$.10	$.12	$.13	$.11	$.10	$.06	$.16	$.12
C81	.05	.06	.04	.08	.04	.09	.06	.06
D5	.32	.40	.31	.30	.42	.35	.36	.49
D44	.17	.14	.19	.15	.10	.16	.19	.12
E2	.06	.07	.10	.05	.08	.10	.11	.05
E35	.08	.10	.12	.08	.09	.10	.09	.06
G99	.55	.62	.61	.70	.62	.63	.65	.59

13.10. The following jobs are waiting to be processed at the same machine center. Jobs are logged as they arrive:

JOB	DUE DATE	DURATION (days)
A	313	8
B	312	16
C	325	40
D	314	5
E	314	3

In what sequence would the jobs be ranked according to the following decision rules: (1) FCFS, (2) EDD, (3) SPT, (4) LPT? All dates are specified as manufacturing planning calendar days. Assume that all jobs arrive on day 275. Which decision is best and why?

13.11. Suppose that today is day 300 on the planning calendar and that we have not started any of the jobs given in Problem 13.10. Using the critical-ratio technique, in what sequence would you schedule these jobs?

13.12. An Alabama lumber yard has four jobs on order, as shown in the table on the following page. Today is day 205 on the yard's schedule. Establish processing priorities.

JOB	DUE DATE	REMAINING TIME IN DAYS
A	212	6
B	209	3
C	208	3
D	210	8

13.13. The following jobs are waiting to be processed at a small machine center:

JOB	DUE DATE	DURATION (days)
010	260	30
020	258	16
030	260	8
040	270	20
050	275	10

In what sequence would the jobs be ranked according to the following decision rules: (1) FCFS, (2) EDD, (3) SPT, (4) LPT? All dates are specified as manufacturing planning calendar days. Assume that all jobs arrive on day 210. Which is the best decision rule?

13.14. The following jobs are waiting to be processed at Ward Moore's machine center:

JOB	DATE ORDER RECEIVED	PRODUCTION DAYS NEEDED	DATE ORDER DUE
A	110	20	180
B	120	30	200
C	122	10	175
D	125	16	230
E	130	18	210

In what sequence would the jobs be ranked according to the following rules: (1) FCFS, (2) EDD, (3) SPT, (4) LPT? All dates are according to shop calendar days. Today on the planning calendar is day 130. Which rule is best?

13.15. Suppose that today is day 150 on the planning calendar and that we have not yet started any of the jobs in Problem 13.14. Using the critical-ratio technique, in what sequence would you schedule these jobs?

13.16. J. J. Ruppel Automation Company estimates the data entry and verifying times for four jobs as follows:

JOB	DATE ENTRY (hours)	VERIFY (hours)
A	2.5	1.7
B	3.8	2.6
C	1.9	1.0
D	1.8	3.0

In what order should the jobs be done if the company has one operator for each job? Illustrate the time-phased flow of this job sequence graphically.

13.17. Six jobs are to be processed through a two-step operation. The first operation involves sanding, and the second involves painting. Processing times are as follows:

JOB	OPERATION 1 (hours)	OPERATION 2 (hours)
A	10	5
B	7	4
C	5	7
D	3	8
E	2	6
F	4	3

Determine a sequence that will minimize the total completion time for these jobs. Illustrate graphically.

13.18. Bill Penny has a repetitive manufacturing plant producing trailer hitches in Arlington. The plant has an average inventory of only 12 turns per year. He has, therefore, determined that he will reduce his component lot sizes. He has developed the following data for one component, the safety chain clip.

Annual demand = 31,200

Daily demand = 120

Daily production = 960

Desired lot size (1 hour of production) = 120 units

Holding cost per unit per year = $12.

Setup labor cost per hour = $20.

What setup time should he have his plant manager aim for regarding this component?

13.19. The following jobs are waiting to be processed at Nancy Evan's machine center. Today is day 250.

JOB	DATE JOB RECEIVED	PRODUCTION DAYS NEEDED	DATE JOB DUE
1	215	30	260
2	220	20	290
3	225	40	300
4	240	50	320
5	250	20	340

Using the critical-ratio scheduling rule, in what sequence would the jobs be processed?

13.20. Given the following information about a product, what is the appropriate setup time?

Annual demand = 39000

Daily demand = 150

Daily production = 1000

Desired lot size (1 hour of production) = 150

Holding cost per unit per year = $10

Setup labor cost per hour = $40

Internet Data Base Application See our website at http://www.prenhall.com/renderpom for a challenging, computer-based problem.

CASE STUDY

The NASA Space Shuttle

NASA's astronaut crew currently includes eight mission specialists who hold Ph.D.s in either astrophysics or astromedicine. One of these specialists will be assigned to each of the eight flights scheduled for the upcoming nine months. Mission specialists are responsible for carrying out scientific and medical experiments in space or for launching, retrieving, or repairing satellites. The chief of astronaut personnel, himself a former crew member with three missions under his belt, must decide who should be assigned and trained for each of the very different missions. Clearly, astronauts with medical educations are more suited to missions involving biological or medical experiments, while those with engineering or physics degrees are best suited to other types of missions. The chief assigns each astronaut a rating on a scale of 1 to 10 for each possible mission, with a 10 being a perfect match for the task at hand and a 1 being a mismatch. Only one specialist is assigned to each flight, and none is reassigned until all others have flown at least once.

DISCUSSION QUESTIONS

1. Who should be assigned to which flight?
2. We have just been notified that Anderson is getting married in February and he has been granted a highly sought publicity tour in Europe that month. (He intends to take his wife and let the trip double as a honeymoon.) How does this change the final schedule?
3. Certo has complained that he was misrated on his January mission. The rating should be 10, he claims to the chief, who agrees and recomputes the schedule. Do any changes occur over the schedule set in question 2?
4. What are the strengths and weaknesses of this approach to scheduling?

	MISSION							
ASTRONAUT	*Jan. 12*	*Feb. 5*	*Feb. 26*	*Mar. 26*	*Apr. 12*	*May 1*	*Jun. 9*	*Sept. 19*
Vincze	9	2	1	10	9	8	9	6
Veit	8	3	4	7	9	7	7	4
Anderson	2	10	10	1	4	7	6	7
Herbert	4	10	9	9	9	1	2	4
Schatz	10	9	9	8	9	1	1	1
Plane	1	5	7	9	7	10	10	2
Certo	9	8	8	9	1	1	2	9
Moses	3	7	6	4	3	9	7	9

Internet Case Study See our Internet home page at http://www.prenhall.com/renderpom for this additional case study: Oregon Wood Store.

BIBLIOGRAPHY

Akinc, U. "A Practical Approach to Lot and Setup Scheduling at a Textile Firm." *IIE Transactions* 25, no. 2 (March 1993): 54–64.

Ghosh, S., and C. Gaimon. "Production Scheduling in a Flexible Manufacturing System with Setups." *IIE Transactions* 25, no. 5 (September 1993): 21.

Gopalakrishnan, M., S. Gopalakrishnan, and D. M. Miller. "A Decision Support System for Scheduling Personnel in a Newspaper Publishing Environment." *Interfaces* 23, no. 4 (July-August 1993): 104–115.

Heizer, Jay, and Barry Render. *Production and Operations Management,* 4th ed. Upper Saddle River, NJ: Prentice-Hall, 1996.

Jensen, John B., Patrick R. Philipoom, Manoj K. Malhotra. "Evaluation of Scheduling Rules with Commensurate Customer Priorities in Job Shops." *Journal of Operations Management* 13, no. 3 (October 1996): 213–245.

Kim, Y., and C. A. Yano. "Heuristic Approaches for Loading Problems in Flexible Manufacturing Systems." *Industrial Engineering Research & Development* 25, no. 1 (January 1993): 26.

McKaskill, Tom. "There Is a Place for Expert Systems in Finite Scheduling." *APICS* (August 1994): 42–44.

Morton, Thomas E., and David W. Pentico. *Heuristic Scheduling Systems.* New York: John Wiley, 1993.

Render, B., and R. M. Stair. *Quantitative Analysis for Management,* 6th ed. Upper Saddle River, NJ: Prentice-Hall, 1997.

Sivakumar, R. A., R. Batta, and K. Tehrani. "Scheduling Repairs at Texas Instruments." *Interfaces* 23, no. 4 (July-August 1993): 68–74.

Project Scheduling 14

CHAPTER OUTLINE

The Strategic Importance of Project Management

Project Planning

Project Scheduling

Project Controlling

Project Management Techniques: PERT and CPM

The Framework of PERT and CPM ■ Activities, Events, and Networks ■ Dummy Activities and Events ■ PERT and Activity Time Estimates ■ Critical Path Analysis ■ The Probability of Project Completion

Cost-Time Trade-Offs and Project Crashing

Applying Project Scheduling to Service Firms

Installing a New Computer System ■ Relocating St. Vincent's Hospital

A Critique of PERT and CPM

Summary ■ Key Terms ■ Using POM for Windows ■ Using EXCEL Spreadsheets for Project Scheduling ■ Solved Problems ■ Self-Test Chapter 14 ■ Discussion Questions ■ Operations in Practice Exercise ■ Problems ■ Case Study: The Family Planning Research Center of Nigeria ■ Bibliography

LEARNING OBJECTIVES

When you complete this chapter you should be able to:

IDENTIFY OR DEFINE:

Activity
Event
Critical path
Dummy activity

EXPLAIN:

Critical path method (CPM)
Program evaluation and review technique (PERT)
Crashing a project

THE STRATEGIC IMPORTANCE OF PROJECT MANAGEMENT

When Microsoft Corporation set out to develop Windows 95—its biggest, most complex, and most important program to date—time was the only thing that mattered to its project manager. With hundreds of programmers working on millions of lines of code in a program costing hundreds of millions to develop, immense stakes rode on the project being delivered on time.

When Ford management decided to discontinue its fading former star, the Mustang, a group of Mustang loyalists at Ford persuaded the firm to let them take on the redesign. Promising a lower cost than the $1 billion Ford had projected, the 450-member project team brought the new car on-line in 1994 for $700 million, 25% faster and 30% cheaper than any comparable design project at Ford.

Microsoft and Ford are just two examples of firms that face a modern phenomena: Collapsing of product/service life cycles. This change stems from awareness of the strategic value of time-based competition (noted in Chapter 4) and a quality mandate for continuous improvement. Each new product/service introduction is a unique event—a project.

New products, however, are not the only projects firms undertake. Every organization at one point or another will take on a large and complex project. The Bechtel construction company putting up an office building or laying a highway must complete thousands of costly activities. The U.S. State Department, installing and debugging an expensive computer system, spends months preparing the details for smooth conversion to new equipment. Avondale Shipyards in New Orleans requires tens of thousands of steps in constructing an oceangoing tugboat. A Shell Oil refinery about to shut down for a major maintenance project faces astronomical expenses if this difficult task is unduly delayed for any reason. Almost every industry worries about how to manage similar large-scale, complicated projects effectively.

Large, often one-time projects are difficult challenges to operations managers. The stakes are high. Millions of dollars in cost overruns have been wasted due to poor planning on projects. Unnecessary delays have occurred due to poor scheduling. And companies have gone bankrupt due to poor controls.

Special projects that take months or years to complete are usually developed outside the normal production system. Project organizations within the firm are set up to handle such jobs and are often disbanded when the project is complete. The management of large projects involves three phases:

1. *Planning.* This includes goal setting, defining the project, and team organization.
2. *Scheduling.* This relates people, money, and supplies to specific activities and relates activities to each other.
3. *Controlling.* Here the firm monitors resources, costs, quality, and budgets. It also revises or changes plans and shifts resources to meet time and cost demands.

We will begin this chapter with a brief overview of these functions. Three popular techniques to allow managers to plan, schedule, and control—Gantt charts, PERT, and CPM—are also described.

PROJECT PLANNING

Projects can usually be defined as a series of related tasks directed toward a major output. A new organization form, developed to make sure existing programs continue to run smoothly on a day-to-day basis while new projects are successfully completed, is called a **project organization.**

project organization

A project organization is an effective way of pooling the people and physical resources needed for a limited time to complete a specific project or goal. It is basically a temporary organization structure designed to achieve results by using specialists from throughout the firm. For many years, NASA successfully used the project approach to reach its goals.

The project organization works best when:

1. work can be defined with a specific goal and deadline.
2. the job is unique or somewhat unfamiliar to the existing organization.
3. the work contains complex interrelated tasks requiring specialized skills.
4. the project is temporary but critical to the organization.

Project team members are temporarily assigned to a project and report to the project manager. The manager heading the project coordinates its activities with other departments and reports directly to top management, often the president, of the organization. Project managers receive high visibility in a firm and are a key element in the planning and control of project activities.

NOTE
When a project organization takes on a more permanent form, this is usually called a "matrix organization."

The project management team begins its task well in advance of the project so that a plan can be developed. One of its first steps is to set the project's objectives carefully, then define the project and break it down into manageable parts. This **work breakdown structure (WBS)** defines the project by dividing it into its major subcomponents (called modules), which are then subdivided into more detailed components, and finally into a set of activities and their related costs. The division of the project into smaller and smaller tasks can be difficult but is critical to managing the project and scheduling success. Gross requirements for people, supplies, and equipment are also estimated in this planning phase.

work breakdown structure (WBS)

PROJECT SCHEDULING

Project scheduling is determining the project's activities in the time sequence in which they have to be performed. Materials and people needed at each stage of production are computed in this phase, and the time each activity will take is also set. Separate schedules for personnel needs by type of skill (management, engineering, or concrete pouring, for example) are charted. Charts can also be developed for scheduling materials.

One popular project-scheduling approach is the **Gantt chart** (named after Henry Gantt, who was mentioned in Chapter 13). Gantt charts are low-cost means of helping managers make sure that (1) all activities are planned for, (2) their order of performance is accounted for, (3) the activity time estimates are recorded, and (4) the overall project time is developed.

Gantt charts

NOTE
Gantt charts are an example of a widely used, nonmathematical technique that is very popular with managers because it is so simple and visual.

Scheduling charts can be used alone on simple projects. They permit managers to observe the progress of each activity and to spot and tackle problem areas. Gantt charts are not easily updated, though. And more importantly, they don't adequately illustrate the interrelationships between the activities and the resources.

An example of a Gantt chart is shown in Figure 14.1. This illustration of a routine servicing of a commercial jetliner during a 40-minute layover shows that Gantt charts can be used to help point out potential delays.

PERT and CPM, the two widely used network techniques that we shall discuss shortly, *do* have the ability to consider precedence relationships and interdepen-

FIGURE 14.1

SERVICE ACTIVITIES FOR A COMMERCIAL JETLINER DURING A 40-MINUTE LAYOVER

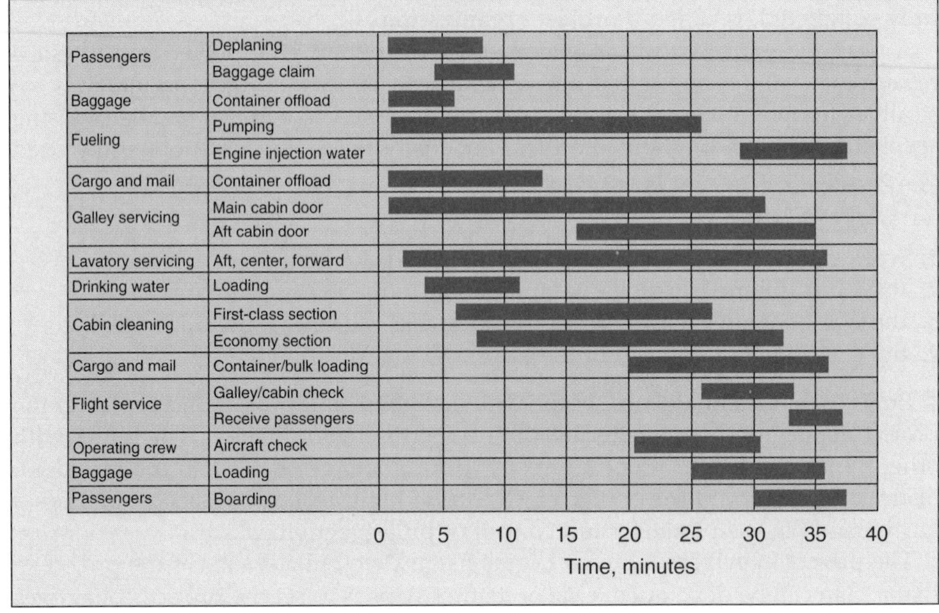

dency of activities. On complex projects, the scheduling of which is almost always computerized, PERT and CPM thus hold an edge on the simpler Gantt charts. Even on huge projects, though, Gantt charts can be used as a summary of project status and may complement the other network approaches.

To summarize, whatever the approach taken by a project manager, project scheduling serves several purposes:

1. It shows the relationship of each activity to others and to the whole project.
2. It identifies the precedence relationships among activities.
3. It encourages the setting of realistic time and cost estimates for each activity.
4. It helps make better use of people, money, and material resources by identifying critical bottlenecks in the project.

PROJECT CONTROLLING

NOTE
Due to the proliferation of microcomputer project management software, PERT/CPM have seen a resurgence of popularity in the 1990s.

The control of large projects, like the control of any management system, involves close monitoring of resources, costs, quality, and budgets. Control also means using a feedback loop to revise the project plan and having the ability to shift resources to where they are needed most. Computerized PERT/CPM reports and charts are widely available today for minicomputers and microcomputers. Some of the more popular of these programs are Harvard Total Project Manager, Primavera, Project, MacProject, Pertmaster, VisiSchedule, and Time Line.

These programs produce a broad variety of reports including: (1) detailed cost breakdowns for each task, (2) total program labor curves, (3) cost distribution tables, (4) functional cost and hour summaries, (5) raw material and expenditure forecasts, (6) variance reports, (7) time analysis reports, and (8) work status reports.

PROJECT MANAGEMENT TECHNIQUES: PERT AND CPM

Program evaluation and review technique (PERT) and the **critical path method (CPM)** were both developed in the 1950s to help managers schedule, monitor, and control large and complex projects. CPM arrived first, in 1957, as a tool developed by J. E. Kelly of Remington Rand and M. R. Walker of DuPont to assist in the building and maintenance of chemical plants at DuPont. Independently, PERT was developed in 1958 by the Navy.

program evaluation and review technique (PERT)

critical path method (CPM)

NOTE
The Navy under the direction of Admiral Rickover successfully used PERT in building the first Polaris submarine ahead of schedule.

The Framework of PERT and CPM

Six steps are common to both PERT and CPM. The procedure is as follows:

1. Define the project and all of its significant activities or tasks.
2. Develop the relationships among the activities. Decide which activities must precede and which must follow others.
3. Draw the network connecting all of the activities.
4. Assign time and/or cost estimates to each activity.
5. Compute the longest time path through the network; this is called the **critical path.**
6. Use the network to help plan, schedule, monitor, and control the project.

critical path

Step 5, finding the critical path, is a major part of controlling a project. The activities on the critical path represent tasks that will delay the entire project if they are delayed. Managers derive flexibility by identifying noncritical activities and replanning, rescheduling, and reallocating resources such as labor and finances.

Although PERT and CPM differ to some extent in terminology and in the construction of the network, their objectives are the same. Furthermore, the analysis used in both techniques is very similar. The major difference is that PERT employs three time estimates for each activity. Each estimate has an associated probability of occurrence, which, in turn, is used in computing expected values and

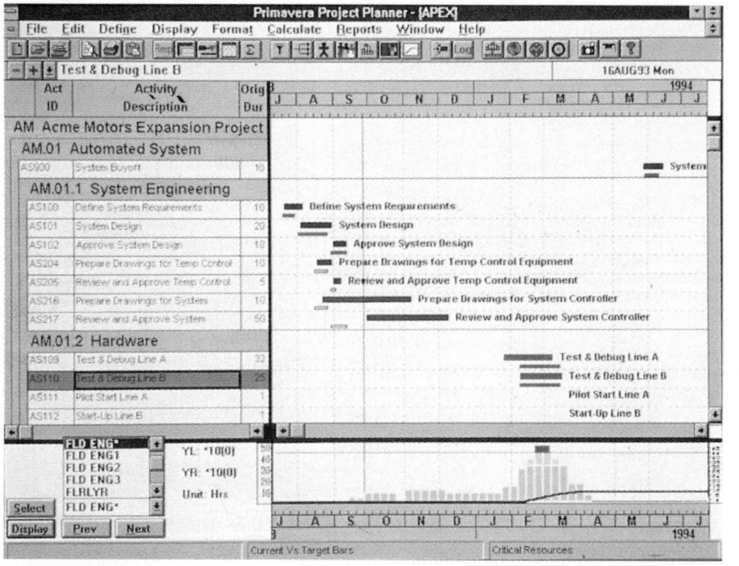

Being able to use powerful project-management software packages such as Primavera (shown here) first requires an understanding of the principles of PERT and CPM. In a competitive job environment, graduates who have experience with one of the popular programs will find themselves valued members of any organization involved in project planning.

standard deviations for the activity times. CPM makes the assumption that activity times are known with certainty, and hence only one time factor is given for each activity.

PERT and CPM are important because they can help answer questions such as the following about projects with thousands of activities:

1. When will the entire project be completed?
2. What are the critical activities or tasks in the project, that is, the ones that will delay the entire project if they are late?
3. Which are the noncritical activities, that is, the ones that can run late without delaying the whole project's completion?
4. What is the probability that the project will be completed by a specific date?
5. At any particular date, is the project on schedule, behind schedule, or ahead of schedule?
6. On any given date, is the money spent equal to, less than, or greater than the budgeted amount?
7. Are there enough resources available to finish the project on time?
8. If the project is to be finished in a shorter amount of time, what is the best way to accomplish this at the least cost?

Activities, Events, and Networks

event

activity

The first step in PERT is to divide the entire project into events and activities. An **event** marks the start or completion of a particular task or activity. An **activity,** on the other hand, is a task or a subproject that occurs between two events. Figure 14.2 restates these definitions and shows the symbols used to represent events and activities.

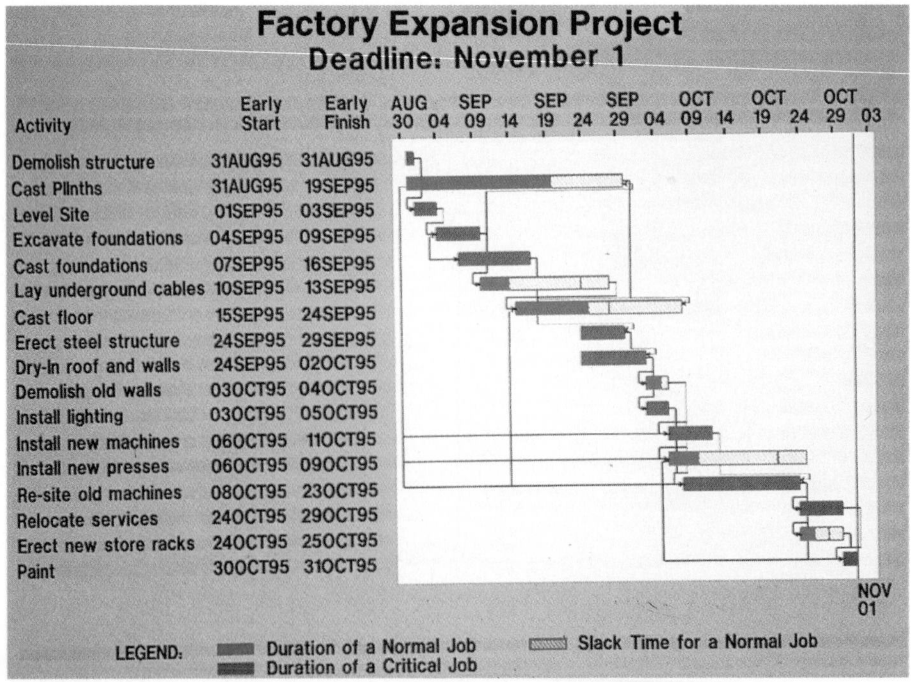

PERT software is also available from SAS Institute, Inc. Here early starts, early finishes, normal tasks, critical tasks, and slack times are indicated for a factory expansion project in Lancaster, Pennsylvania.

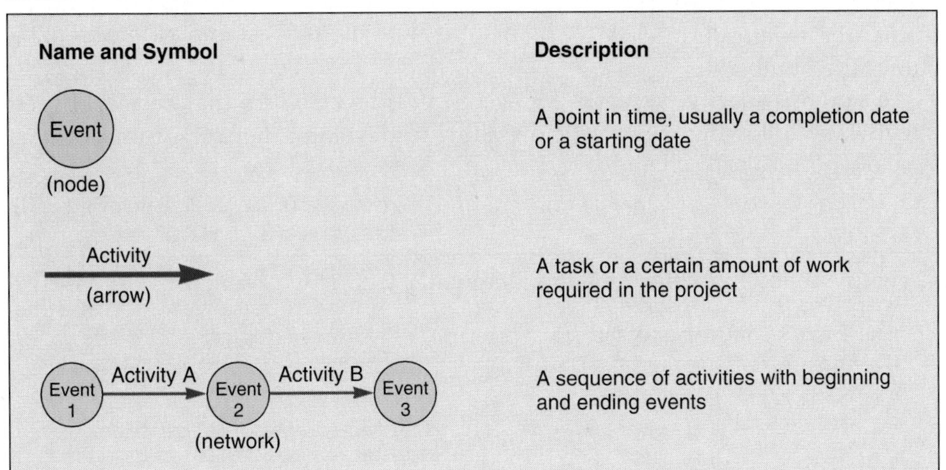

FIGURE 14.2

EVENTS, ACTIVITIES, AND HOW THEY RELATE

This approach is the most common one for drawing networks and is also referred to as the *activity-on-arrow (AOA)* convention. A less popular convention, called *activity-on-node (AON),* places activities on nodes. For simplicity we will focus on AOA.

Any project that can be described by activities and events may be analyzed by a PERT **network.**

network

EXAMPLE 1

Given the following information, develop a network.

ACTIVITY	IMMEDIATE PREDECESSOR(S)
A	—
B	—
C	A
D	B

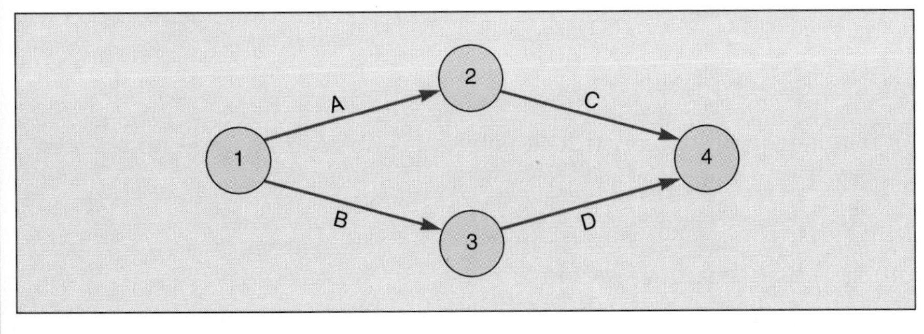

NOTE
To provide a visual example of the AON approach, here is the network analogous to Example 1's AOA approach.

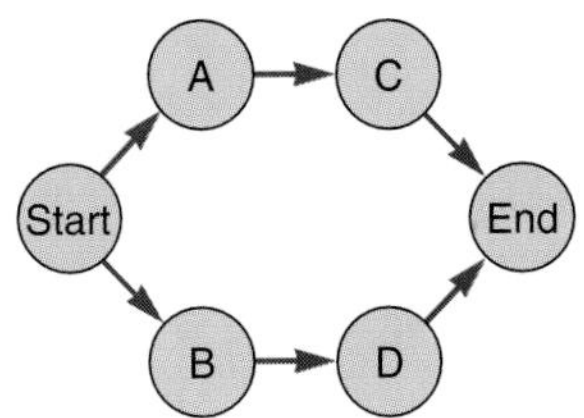

You will note that we assigned each event a number. As you will see later, it is possible to identify each activity with a beginning and an ending event or node. For example, activity A in Example 1 is the activity that starts with event 1 and ends at node, or event, 2. In general, we number nodes from left to right. The beginning node, or event, of the entire project is number 1, while the last node, or event, in the entire project bears the largest number. In Example 1 the last node shows the number 4.

We can also specify networks by events and the activities that occur between events. The following example shows how to develop a network based on this type of specification scheme.

EXAMPLE 2

Given the following table, develop a network.

BEGINNING EVENT	ENDING EVENT	ACTIVITY
1	2	1-2
1	3	1-3
2	4	2-4
3	4	3-4
3	5	3-5
4	6	4-6
5	6	5-6

Instead of using a letter to signify activities and their predecessor activities, we can specify activities by their starting event and their ending event. Beginning with the activity that starts at event 1 and ends at event 2, we can construct the following network:

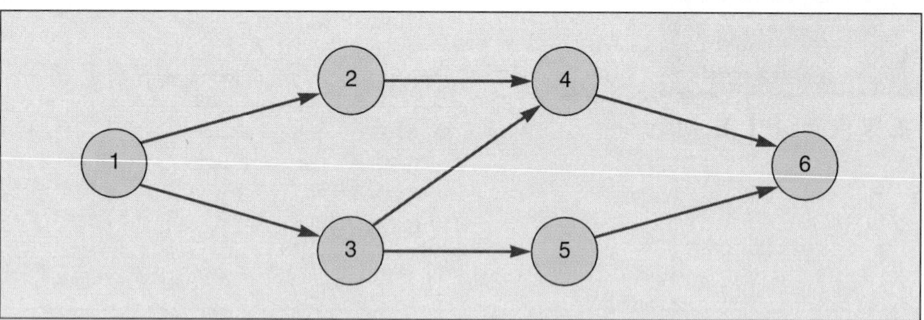

All that is required to construct a network is the starting and ending event for each activity.

Dummy Activities and Events

dummy activities

You may encounter a network that has two activities with identical starting and ending events (see Figure 14.3a). **Dummy activities** and events can be inserted into the network to deal with this problem (see Figure 14.3b). The use of dummy activities and events is especially important when computer programs are to be employed in determining the critical path, project completion time, project variance, and so on. Dummy activities and events can also ensure that the network

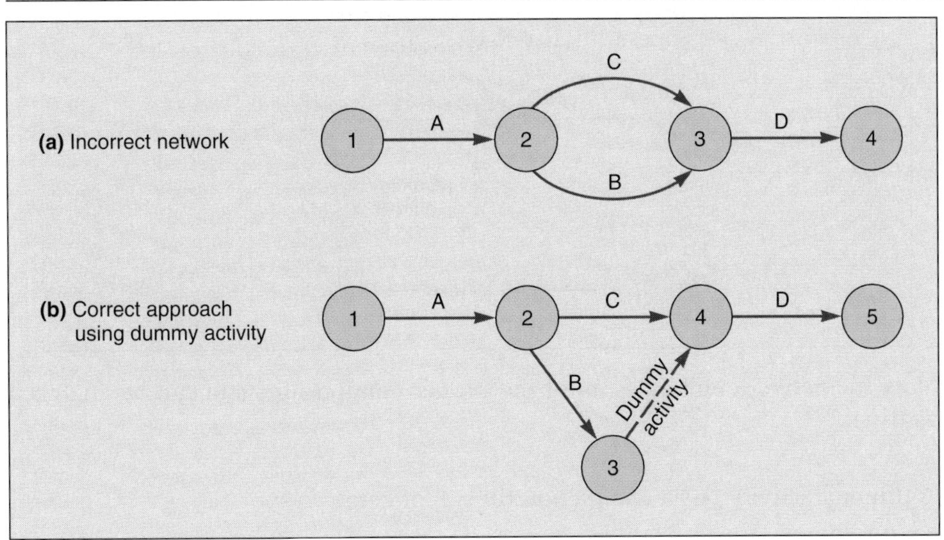

FIGURE 14.3

INCORRECT AND CORRECT NETWORKS WITH FOUR ACTIVITIES

Activities B and C have identical starting and ending events. (a) Incorrect network (b) Correct approach using dummy activity.

properly reflects the project under consideration. The following example illustrates the procedure for a network that has eight activities.

EXAMPLE 3

Develop a network based on the following information:

ACTIVITY	IMMEDIATE PREDECESSOR(S)	ACTIVITY	IMMEDIATE PREDECESSOR(S)
A	—	E	C, D
B	—	F	D
C	A	G	E
D	B	H	F

Given these data, you might develop the following network:

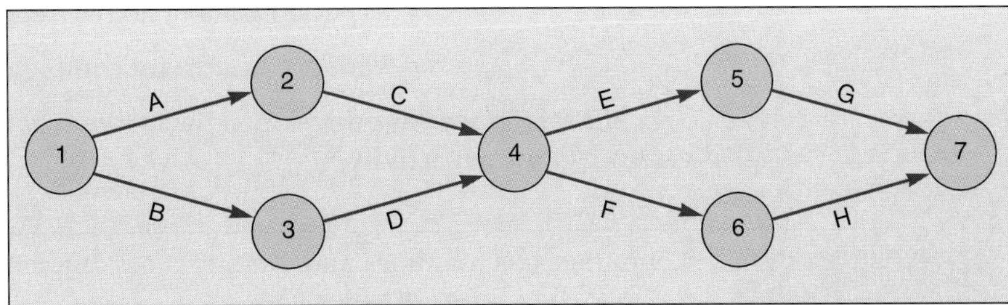

Look at activity F. According to the network, both activities C and D must be completed before we can start F, but in reality only activity D must be completed (see the table). Thus the network is not correct. The addition of a dummy activity and a dummy event can overcome this problem.

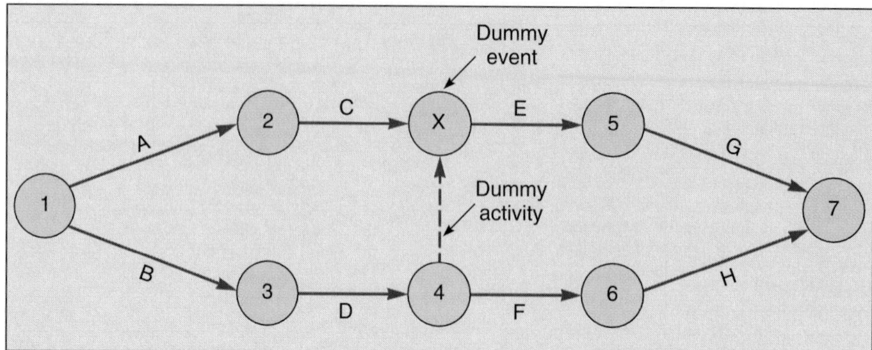

Now the network embodies all of the proper relationships and can be analyzed as usual.

A dummy activity has a completion time, t, of zero.

PERT and Activity Time Estimates

activity time estimates

As mentioned earlier, one distinguishing difference between PERT and CPM is the use of three **activity time estimates** for each activity in the PERT technique. Only one time factor is given for each activity in CPM.

optimistic time

probable time

pessimistic time

beta probability distribution

For each activity in PERT, we must specify an **optimistic time,** a most **probable** (or most likely) **time,** and a **pessimistic time** estimate. We then use these three time estimates to calculate an expected completion time and variance for each activity. If we assume, as many researchers do, that activity times follow a **beta probability distribution,** we can use the formula:

$$t = \frac{a + 4m + b}{6} \quad \text{and} \quad v = \left(\frac{b - a}{6}\right)^2 \tag{14.1}$$

where

a = Optimistic time for activity completion

b = Pessimistic time for activity completion

m = Most likely time for activity completion

t = Expected time of activity completion

v = Variance of activity completion time

In PERT, after we have developed the network, we compute expected times and variances for each activity.

EXAMPLE 4

Compute expected times and variances of completion for each activity based on the following time estimates:

ACTIVITY	a	m	b
1-2	3	4	5
1-3	1	3	5
2-4	5	6	7
3-4	6	7	8

ACTIVITY	$a + 4m + b$	$t = \frac{a + 4m + b}{6}$	$\frac{b - a}{6}$	v
1-2	24	4	2/6	4/36
1-3	18	3	4/6	16/36
2-4	36	6	2/6	4/36
3-4	42	7	2/6	4/36

Critical Path Analysis

critical path analysis

The objective of **critical path analysis** is to determine the following quantities for each activity:

ES—earliest activity start time. *All predecessor activities* must be completed before an activity can be started. This is the earliest time an activity can be started.
LS—latest activity start time. *All following activities* must be completed without delaying the entire project. This is the latest time an activity can be started without delaying the entire project.
EF—earliest activity finish time.
LF—latest activity finish time.
S—activity **slack time,** which is equal to $(LS - ES)$ or $(LF - EF)$.

slack time

For any activity, if we can calculate *ES* and *LS*, we can find the other three quantities as follows:

In the fall of 1990, Iraq invaded Kuwait. In one final, devastating act before Iraq's defeat in "Operation Desert Storm" Saddam Hussein torched the oil wells of Kuwait. When the Bechtel advance team landed in Kuwait, the panorama of destruction was breathtaking. Even for Bechtel, whose competitive advantage is project management, this was a first-of-its-kind logistics problem. Bechtel had to procure, ship, and deploy 125,000 tons of supplies, including some 4,000 pieces of operating equipment, ranging from bulldozers to ambulances. The team also managed a workforce of 9,000 and laid some 90 miles of pipeline, capable of delivering 20-million gallons of water a day to the fire site.

$$EF = ES + t$$

$$LF = LS + t$$

$$S = LS - ES$$

or

$$S = LF - EF$$

Once we know these quantities for every activity we can analyze the overall project. Typically this analysis includes:

1. The critical path—the group of activities in the project that have a slack time of zero. This path is *critical* because a delay in any activity along this path would delay the entire project.
2. *T*—the total project completion time, which is calculated by adding the expected time (t) values of those activities on the critical path.
3. *V*—variance of the critical path, which is computed by adding the variance (v) of those individual activities on the critical path.

NOTE
In making a "forward pass" *all* activities must be completed before any activity can be started.

Critical path analysis normally starts with the determination of *ES* and *EF*. The following example illustrates the procedure.

EXAMPLE 5

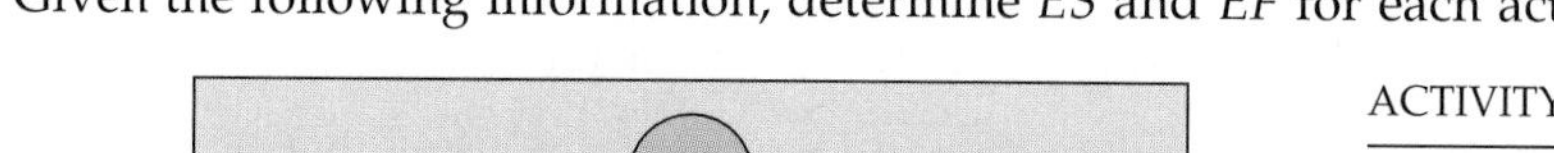

Given the following information, determine *ES* and *EF* for each activity.

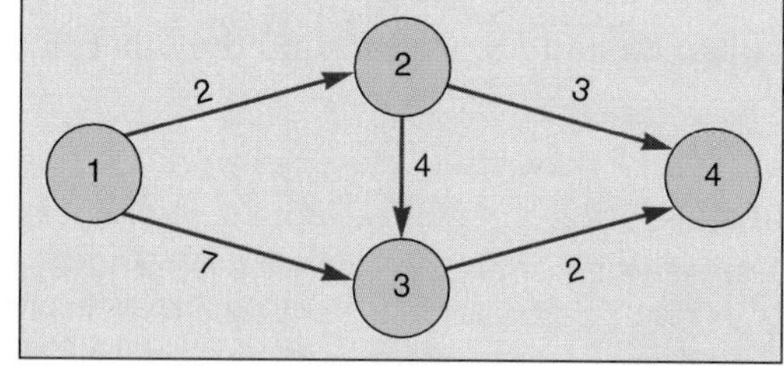

ACTIVITY	t
1-2	2
1-3	7
2-3	4
2-4	3
3-4	2

We find *ES* by moving from starting activities of the project to the ending activities of the project. For the starting activities, ES is either zero or the actual starting date, say, August 1. For activities 1-2 and 1-3, *ES* is zero. (By convention, all projects start at time zero.)

There is one basic rule. Before an activity can be started, *all* of its predecessor activities must be completed. In other words, we search for the *longest* path leading to an activity in determining ES. For activity 2-3, ES is 2. Its only predecessor activity is 1-2, for which $t = 2$. By the same reasoning, *ES* for activity 2-4 also is 2. For activity 3-4, however, *ES* is 7. It has two predecessor paths: activity 1-3 with $t = 7$, and activities 1-2 and 2-3 with a total expected time of 6 (or 2 + 4). Thus, *ES* for activity 3-4 is 7 because activity 1-3 must be completed before activity 3-4 can be started. We compute *EF* next by adding t to *ES* for each activity.

See the following table:

ACTIVITY	ES	EF
1-2	0	2
1-3	0	7
2-3	2	6
2-4	2	5
3-4	7	9

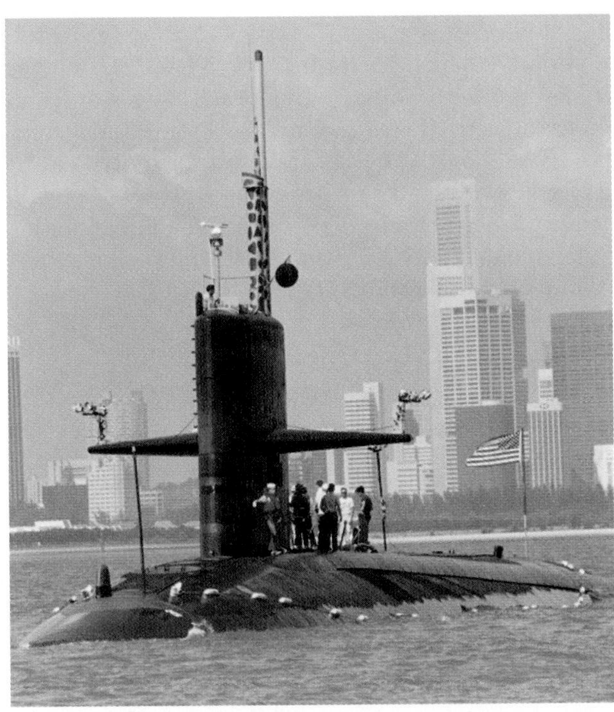

The U.S. Navy, working with Booz, Allen, and Hamilton, devised PERT to help plan and control the Polaris missile program for submarines. That project involved the coordination of thousands of contractors, and PERT was credited with cutting 18 months off the project length.

The next step is to calculate LS, the latest starting time for each activity. We start with the last activities and work backward to the first activities. The procedure is to work backward from the last activities to determine the latest possible starting time (*LS*) without increasing the earliest finishing time (*EF*). This task sounds more difficult than it really is.

NOTE
In making a "backward pass" the latest time is computed by making sure the project would not be delayed for any activities.

EXAMPLE 6

Determine *LS, LF,* and *S* (the slack) for each activity based on the following data:

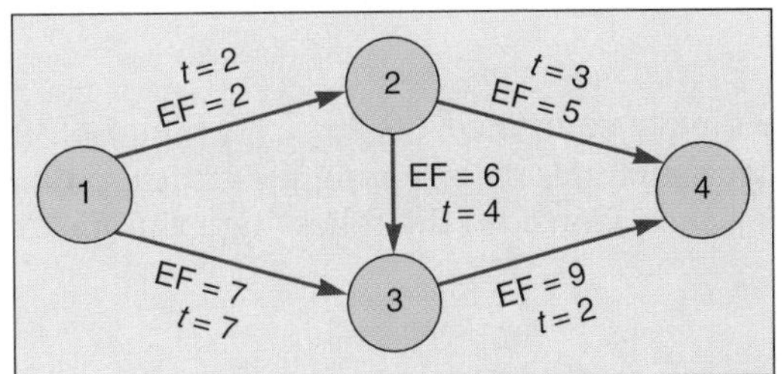

ACTIVITY	*t*	*ES*	*EF*
1-2	2	0	2
1-3	7	0	7
2-3	4	2	6
2-4	3	2	5
3-4	2	7	9

The earliest time by which the entire project can be finished is 9 because activities 2-4 ($EF = 5$) and 3-4 ($EF = 9$) *both* must be completed. Using 9 as a basis, we now will work backward by subtracting the appropriate values of *t* from 9.

The latest time we can start activity 3-4 is at time 7 (or 9 − 2) in order to still complete the project by time period 9. Thus, *LS* for activity 3-4 is 7. Using the same reasoning, *LS* for activity 2-4 is 6 (or 9 − 3). If we start activity 2-4 at 6 and it takes 3 time units to complete the activity, we can still finish in 9 time units. The latest we can start activity 2-3 is 3 (or 9 − 2 − 4). If we start activity 2-3 at 3 and it takes 2 and 4 time units for activities 2-3 and 3-4, respectively, we can still finish on time. Thus, *LS* for activity 2-3 is 3. Using the same reasoning, *LS* for activity 1-3 is 0 (or 9 − 2 − 7). Analyzing activity 1-2 is more difficult because there are two paths. Both must be completed in 9 time units.

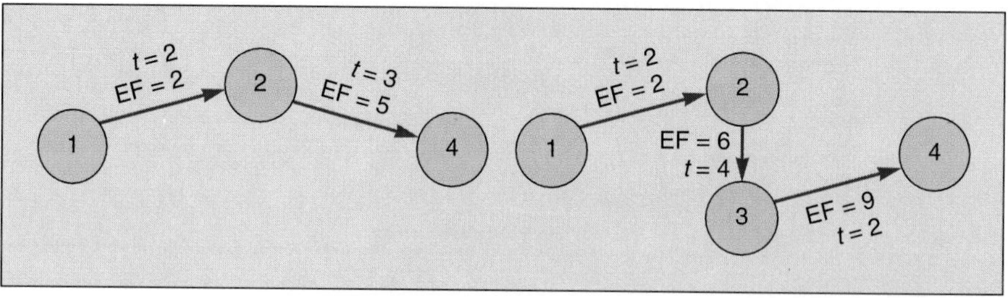

Since both of the above paths must be completed, *LS* for activity 1-2 is computed from the most binding, or slowest, path. Thus, *LS* for activity 1-2 *is* 1 (or 9 − 2 − 4 − 2) and *not* 4 (or 9 − 3 − 2). Noting the following relationships, we can construct a table summarizing the results.

$$LF = LS + t$$

$$S = LF - SF$$

or

$$S = LS - ES$$

ACTIVITY	*ES*	*EF*	*LS*	*LF*	*S*
1-2	0	2	1	3	1
1-3	0	7	0	7	0
2-3	2	6	3	7	1
2-4	2	5	6	9	4
3-4	7	9	7	9	0

Once we have computed *ES, EF, LS, LF,* and *S,* we can analyze the entire project. Analysis includes determining the critical path, project completion time, and project variance. Consider the following example.

EXAMPLE 7

What is the critical path, total completion time T, and project variance V of the following network?

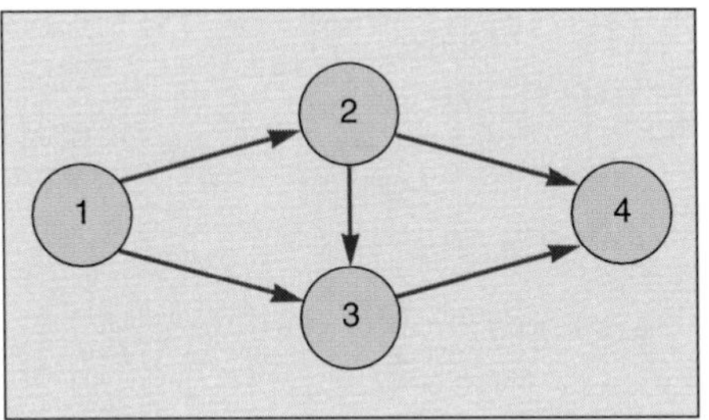

ACTIVITY	t	v	ES	EF	LS	LF	S
1-2	2	2/6	0	2	1	3	1
1-3	7	3/6	0	7	0	7	0
2-3	4	1/6	2	6	3	7	1
2-4	3	2/6	2	5	6	9	4
3-4	2	4/6	7	9	7	9	0

The critical path consists of those activities with zero slack. These are activities 1-3 and 3-4.

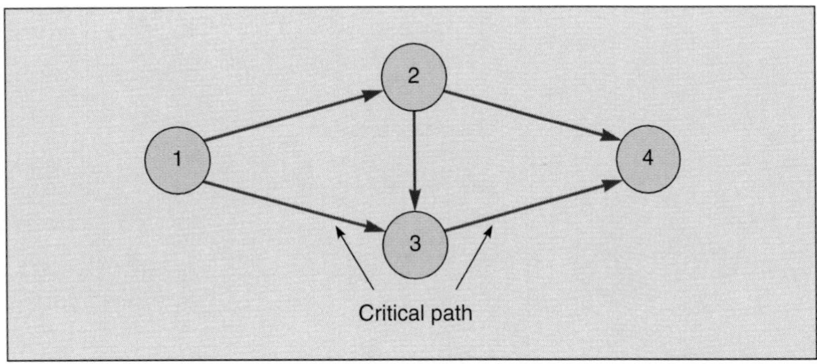

The total project completion time (T) is 9 (or 7 + 2). The project variance (V) is the sum of the *activity variances* along the *critical path*, which is 7/6 (or 3/6 + 4/6).

Knowing a network and values for activity times and variances (t and v) makes it possible to perform a complete critical path analysis, including the determination of ES, EF, LS, LF, and S for each activity as well as the critical path, T, and V for the entire project.

The Probability of Project Completion

Having computed the expected completion time T and completion variance V, we can determine the probability that the project will be completed at a specified date. If we make the assumption that the distribution of completion dates follows a normal curve, we can calculate the probability of completion as in the following example.

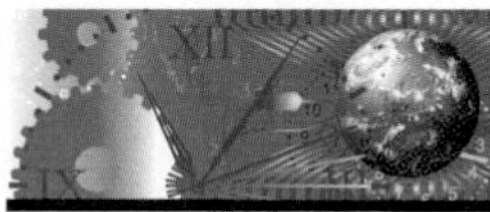

EXAMPLE 8

If the expected project completion time T is 20 weeks and the project variance V is 100, what is the probability that the project will be finished on or before week 25?

$$T = 20$$
$$V = 100$$
$$\sigma = \text{Standard deviation} = \sqrt{\text{Project variance}} = \sqrt{V}$$
$$= \sqrt{100} = 10$$
$$C = \text{Desired completion date}$$
$$= 25 \text{ weeks}$$

The normal curve would appear as follows:

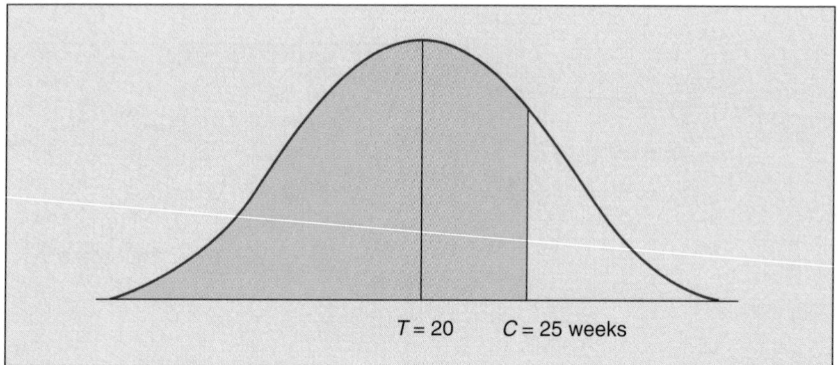

$$Z = \frac{C - T}{\sigma} = \frac{25 - 20}{10} = .5$$

where Z equals the number of standard deviations from the mean. The area under the curve for $Z = .5$ is .6915. (See the normal curve table in Appendix A.) Thus the probability of completing the project in 25 weeks is approximately .69, or 69%.

We must point out that the foregoing analysis should be used with caution. If a noncritical path activity has a large variance, it is possible for it to become a critical path activity. This occurrence would cause the analysis to be in error. Consider the network pictured in Figure 14.4. The critical path is 1-3 and 3-4 with $T = 12$ and $V = 4$. If the desired completion date is 14, the value of Z is 1 [or $(14 - 12)/\sqrt{4}$]. The chance of completion is 84% (from Appendix A). What would happen if activities 1-2 and 2-4 became the critical path? Because of the high variance, this event is not unlikely. With the same values for C and T, Z becomes 0.4 [or $(14 - 12)/\sqrt{25}$]. Looking at the normal distribution, we see that the chance of project completion is 66%. If activities 1-2 and 2-4 became the critical path, the chance of project completion would drop significantly due to the large total variance $(25 = 16 + 9)$ of these activities. A simulation of the project could provide better data.

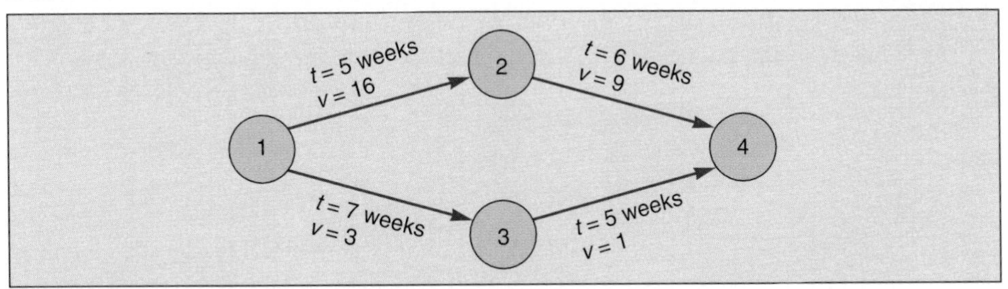

FIGURE 14.4

CRITICAL PATH ANALYSIS

COST-TIME TRADE-OFFS AND PROJECT CRASHING

Until now, we have assumed that it is not possible to reduce activity times. This is usually not the case, however. Perhaps additional resources can reduce activity times for certain activities within the project. These resources might be additional labor, more equipment, and so on. Although shortening can be expensive, referred to as **crashing** activity times,[1] doing so might be worthwhile. If a company faces costly penalties for being late with a project, it might be economical to use additional resources to complete the project on time. There may be fixed costs every day the project is in process. Thus, it might be profitable to use additional resources to crash the project time and save some of the daily fixed costs. But which activities should be shortened? How much will this action cost? Will a reduction in the activity time reduce the time needed to complete the entire project? Ideally, we would like to find the least expensive method of shortening the entire project.

crashing

NOTE
Crashing is especially important when contracts for projects include bonuses or penalties for early or late finishes.

In addition to time, the operations manager is normally concerned with the cost of the project. Usually it is possible to shorten activity times by committing additional resources to the project. Figure 14.5 shows cost-time curves for two ac-

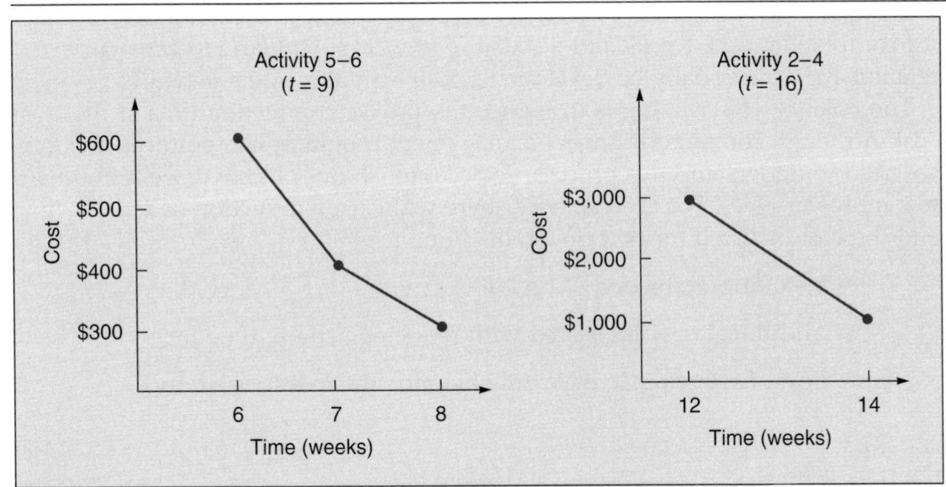

FIGURE 14.5

COST-TIME CURVES USED IN CRASHING ANALYSIS

[1]The term PERT/Cost is also used to describe cost-time trade-offs and crashing.

To transform the corporate image of an international airline is a huge task. Aircraft, check-in desks, lounges, shops, ground vehicles, printed materials—including company stationery, timetables, tickets, baggage tags, and, of course, uniforms—all need to be changed. To help British Airways (BA) plan the changes, a computerized project management package, PertMaster, was used. PertMaster uses the same concepts presented in this chapter. By understanding and using these concepts, British Airways was able to make the project requirements fit together on schedule.

tivities. For activity 5-6, it costs \$300 to complete the activity in 8 weeks, \$400 for 7 weeks, and \$600 for 6 weeks. Activity 2-4 requires \$3,000 of additional resources for completion in 12 weeks and \$1,000 for 14 weeks. Similar cost-time curves or relationships can usually be developed for all activities in the network.

NOTE
Remember that two or more critical paths may exist after performing project crashing.

The objective of crashing is to reduce the project completion time at the least cost. Although commercial project management programs can perform crashing, we need to understand this process. To accomplish this objective, we introduce a few more variables. For each activity, there will exist a reduction in activity time and the cost incurred for that time reduction. Let:

M_i = Maximum reduction of time for activity i

C_i = Additional cost associated with reducing activity time for activity i

K_i = Cost of reducing activity time by one time unit for activity i

$$K_i = \frac{C_i}{M_i} \tag{14.2}$$

With this information it is possible to determine the least cost of reducing the project completion date.

EXAMPLE 9

Given the following information, determine the least cost of reducing the project completion time by one week.

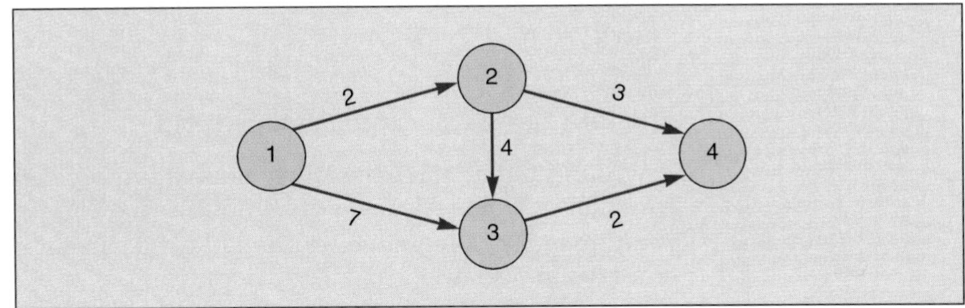

ACTIVITY	t (weeks)	M (weeks)	C
1-2	2	1	$ 300
1-3	7	4	2,000
2-3	4	2	2,000
2-4	3	2	4,000
3-4	2	1	2,000

ACTIVITY	ES	EF	LS	LF	S
1-2	0	2	1	3	1
1-3	0	7	0	7	0
2-3	2	6	3	7	1
2-4	2	5	6	9	4
3-4	7	9	7	9	0

The first step is to compute K for each activity:

ACTIVITY	M	C	K	CRITICAL PATH
1-2	1	$ 300	$ 300	No
1-3	4	2,000	500	Yes
2-3	2	2,000	1,000	No
2-4	2	4,000	2,000	No
3-4	1	2,000	2,000	Yes

The second step is to locate that activity on the critical path with the smallest value of K_i. The critical path consists of activities 1-3 and 3-4. Since activity 1-3 has a lower value of K_i, we can reduce the project completion time by one week, to eight weeks, by incurring an additional cost of $500.

We must be very careful when using this procedure. Any further reduction in activity time along the critical path would cause the critical path also to include activities 1-2, 2-3, and 3-4. In other words, there would be two critical paths, and activities on both would need to be shortened or crashed to reduce project completion time.

NOTE

In large networks there are too many activities to monitor *closely*, but we can *concentrate* on the critical activities.

Applying Project Scheduling to Service Firms

PERT and CPM are certainly not tools that only function in a production scheduling environment. Every firm needs to plan, schedule, and control large projects at one point or another. Here are two examples of how PERT and CPM are used in services.

Installing a New Computer System

Figure 14.6 illustrates the steps involved in replacing one computer system with another at a large Denver consulting firm. The present computer is at capacity and no longer adequate. Additionally, the current software must be modified before it can be run on the new computer.

Relocating St. Vincent's Hospital

When St. Vincent's Hospital moved from a 373-bed facility in Portland, Oregon, to a new 403-bed building in the suburbs approximately five miles away, a large variety of planning considerations had to be taken into account. Army vehicles and private ambulances had to be used to move patients; police escorts were needed; local stores would be affected by the move, among many other concerns. To coordinate all the activities, a project network was developed eight months before the move. A portion of the large network is provided in Figure 14.7.

The Orlando Utilities Commission (OUC) takes one of its steam generating units off-line every three years for a complete overhaul and turbine inspection. These overhauls last from six to eight weeks and are not easy projects to manage—each has 1,800 distinct tasks and requires 72,000 labor-hours. But the value of project management tools are clear. Every day that a power plant is down for maintenance, OUC loses about $55,000 in extra costs.

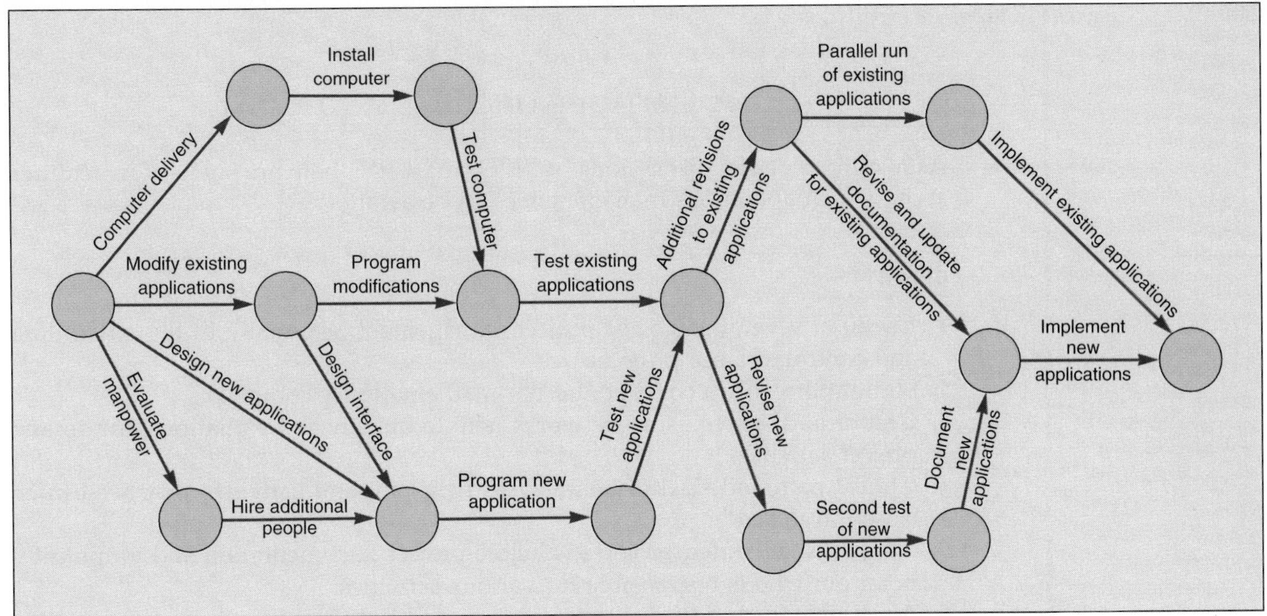

FIGURE 14.6 PERT NETWORK DIAGRAM FOR THE CONSULTING FIRM

SOURCE: S. A. Moscove and M. G. Simkin, *Accounting Information Systems,* 3d ed. (New York: Wiley, 1987), p. 556.

Start
Meet with department heads
Meet with traffic engrs.
Develop preliminary move plan
Develop final move plan
Consult with contractor
Decide move day
Publish plans
Modify plans
Prepare final move tags
Tag equipment
Prepare for patient move
Patient move
Appoint move advisory committee
Establish move admissions policies
Develop paperwork, forms, related to patients
Implement premove admissions policies
Dedication
End
Security at old hospital
Plan public relations activities
Plan dedication
Preliminary meetings with police
Develop police assistance plan

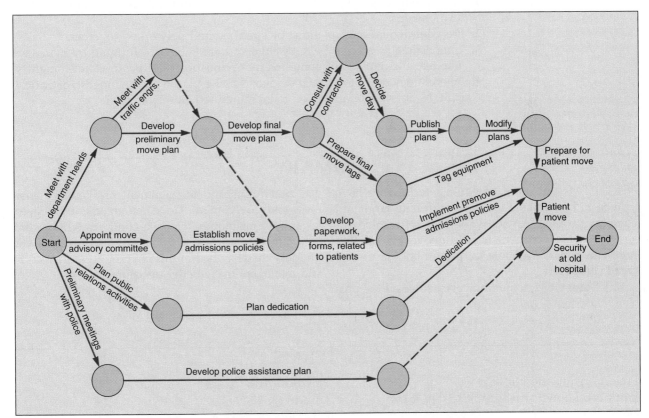

FIGURE 14.7 A PORTION OF ST. VINCENT'S HOSPITAL PROJECT NETWORK

SOURCE: Adapted from R. S. Hanson, "Moving the Hospital to a New Location," *Industrial Engineering* (November 1982).

A CRITIQUE OF PERT AND CPM

As a critique of our discussions of PERT and CPM, here are some of its features about which operations managers need to be aware.

BENEFITS

1. Useful at several stages of project management, especially in the scheduling and control of large projects.
2. Straightforward in concept and not mathematically complex.
3. Graphical displays using networks help to quickly show relationships among project activities.
4. Critical path and slack time analyses help pinpoint activities that need to be closely watched.
5. Networks generated provide valuable project documentation and graphically point out who is responsible for various activities.
6. Applicable to a wide variety of projects and industries.
7. Useful in monitoring not only schedules, but costs as well.

LIMITATIONS

1. Project activities have to be clearly defined, independent, and stable in their relationships.
2. Precedence relationships must be specified and networked together.
3. Time estimates tend to be subjective and are subject to fudging by managers who fear the dangers of being overly optimistic or not pessimistic enough.
4. Inherent danger of too much emphasis being placed on the longest, or critical, path. Near-critical paths need to be monitored closely as well.

SUMMARY

PERT, CPM, and other scheduling techniques have proven to be valuable tools in controlling large and complex projects. A wide variety of software packages to help managers handle network modeling problems is also available for use on both large and small computers.

PERT and CPM do not, however, solve all the project scheduling and management problems of business and government. Good management practices, clear responsibilities for tasks, and straightforward and timely reporting systems are also needed. The models we described in this chapter are only *tools* to aid managers make better decisions.

KEY TERMS

Project organization *(p. 481)*
Work breakdown structure (WBS) *(p. 481)*
Gantt charts *(p. 481)*
Program evaluation and review technique (PERT) *(p. 483)*
Critical path method (CPM) *(p. 483)*
Critical path *(p. 483)*
Event *(p. 484)*
Activity *(p. 484)*
Network *(p. 485)*
Dummy activities *(p. 486)*
Activity time estimates *(p. 488)*

Optimistic time *(p. 488)*
Probable time *(p. 488)*
Pessimistic time *(p. 488)*
Beta probability distribution *(p. 488)*
Critical path analysis *(p. 489)*
Slack time *(p. 489)*
Crashing *(p. 495)*

USING POM FOR WINDOWS

POM for Windows' project scheduling module will find the expected project completion time for a PERT and CPM network with either one or three time estimates. Program 14.1 contains the input *and* output for the data in Example 6.

PROGRAM 14.1

SOLUTION TO EXAMPLE 6 USING POM FOR WINDOWS

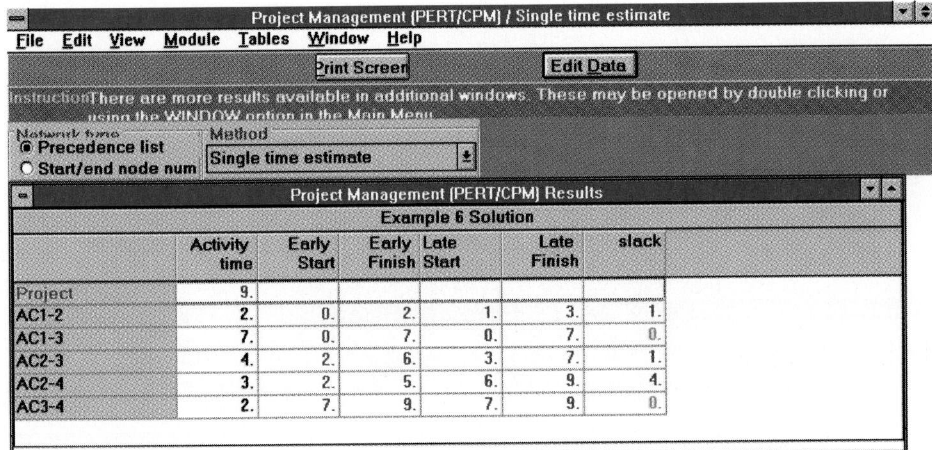

	Activity time	Early Start	Early Finish	Late Start	Late Finish	slack
Project	9.					
AC1-2	2.	0.	2.	1.	3.	1.
AC1-3	7.	0.	7.	0.	7.	0.
AC2-3	4.	2.	6.	3.	7.	1.
AC2-4	3.	2.	5.	6.	9.	4.
AC3-4	2.	7.	9.	7.	9.	0.

The critical path consists of those activities that have zero slack, namely, AC1-3 and AC3-4.

USING EXCEL SPREADSHEETS FOR PROJECT SCHEDULING

Spreadsheets are another tool used for managing projects involving PERT and cost analysis. They allow managers to anticipate difficulties in various stages of the projects and to see the impact of these problems on completing the project on time and on budget.

Understanding the dependency of the activities on each other before putting the information into the spreadsheet is very useful. The process involves 3 steps:

1. The names of the activities are entered on the diagonal of the predecessor array as shown in Program 14.2. It is important to enter those activities with fewest precursors in the top of the array and those with the most precursors in the bottom right of the array.

   The duration of each activity is entered in column A. An "X" below an activity's name indicates that it serves as a predecessor for the activity on whose row the "X" is entered. For instance, AC1-2 is a precursor for both AC2-3 and AC2-4.
2. The Earliest Finish array is calculated from the top left activity to the bottom right activity. The first activity (AC1-2) has no predecessors, so its earliest finish is simply the length of time re-

quired to finish the activity (2). Cells B10-B13 check the predecessor array to see if AC1-2 is a requirement for any of the other activities. If it is a predecessor, the finish time calculated in cell B9 is entered into those cells corresponding to X's. The Earliest Finish of next activity (AC1-3) is calculated by adding its duration to the maximum of the finish time of all its precursors. Obviously, those activities with one or more predecessors cannot begin until the last of their predecessors have finished. The other cells are calculated in a similar fashion, by adding the activity's duration to its latest predecessor (found on the same row), then using the calculated finish time in the column below the variable for those activities that the variable serves as a predecessor.

3. The Latest Start array is calculated from the bottom variable (AC3-4) to the top (AC1-2). AC3-4 is not the predecessor of any other variable, so the latest it can start is the finish time calculated in the earliest finish array minus the duration of the activity (2). This calculated Latest Start time is then placed in those cells on the same row where AC3-4 has predecessors, telling these predecessors that they must be completed before AC3-4 starts at time = 7. Each subsequent activity looks below its cell to see if it is serving as the predecessor of a later activity. The latest start time is computed as the minimum of the last earliest finish time ($F$13) and the latest start times of those activities for which it serves as a precursor. For instance, the latest that AC2-3 can start is the earliest (minimum) of the entire activity $F$13 and start of AC3-4, for which AC2-3 is a predecessor. If an activity serves as the predecessor of several activities, its Latest Start is computed by subtracting its duration from the earliest (minimum) start of its following activities.

The spreadsheet output in Program 14.3 gives important project information for each activity, including ES, EF, LS, and LF.

Enter the activities and durations in the predecessor array (rows 2–6). It is important to enter earlier activities on the left, later activities on the right.

Calculate the Earliest Finish Array from top left to bottom right. The EF time for each element is its duration plus the MAX of all its predecessors.

Calculate the Latest Start Array by moving from bottom right to top left. The LS is the MIN of the earliest finish calculated in $F$13 and all successors.

Make a table with ES, LS, EF, and LF. The two missing variables are calculated using the duration and either the LS or EF.

The assignment of values in the EF and LS arrays can be confusing. Remember, when you determine the value of an cell on the diagonal, you need to use that value: in the EF array you will place it in nonblank cells beneath the element; in the LS array you will place it in nonblank cells to the right of the element.

Microsoft Excel - PAGEE.XLS

	A	B	C	D	E	F	G
1	TIME	**Predecessor array**					
2	2	AC1-2					
3	7		AC1-3				
4	4	X		AC2-3			
5	3	X			AC2-4		
6	2		X	X		AC3-4	
7							
8		**Earliest Finish Array**					
9	=A2	=$A9					
10	=A3	=IF(ISBLANK(B3),"",$B$9)	=$A10+MAX(B10:B10)				=$B$2
11	=A4	=IF(ISBLANK(B4),"",$B$9)	=IF(ISBLANK(C4),"",$C$10)	=$A11+MAX(B11:C11)			=$C$3
12	=A5	=IF(ISBLANK(B5),"",$B$9)	=IF(ISBLANK(C5),"",$C$10)	=IF(ISBLANK(D5),"",$D$11)	=$A12+MAX(B12:D12)		=$D$4
13	=A6	=IF(ISBLANK(B6),"",$B$9)	=IF(ISBLANK(C6),"",$C$10)	=IF(ISBLANK(D6),"",$D$11)	=IF(ISBLANK(E6),"",$E$9)	=$A13+MAX(B13:E13)	=$E$5
14							=$F$6
15		**Latest Start Array**					
16	=A2	=MIN($F$13,B17:B20)-$A16					
17	=A3	=IF(ISBLANK(B3),"",$C$17)	=MIN($F$13,C18:C20)-$A17				=$B$2
18	=A4	=IF(ISBLANK(B4),"",$D$18)	=IF(ISBLANK(C4),"",$D$18)	=MIN($F$13,D19:D20)-$A18			=$C$3
19	=A5	=IF(ISBLANK(B5),"",$E$19)	=IF(ISBLANK(C5),"",$E$19)	=IF(ISBLANK(D5),"",$E$19)	=MIN($F$13,E20:E21)-$A19		=$D$4
20	=A6	=IF(ISBLANK(B6),"",$F$20)	=IF(ISBLANK(C6),"",$F$20)	=IF(ISBLANK(D6),"",$F$20)	=IF(ISBLANK(E6),"",$F$20)	=$F$13-$A2	=$E$5
21							=$F$6
22		**Earliest Start**	**Latest Start**	**Earliest Finish**	**Latest Finish**		
23	=$B$2	=D23-A2	=B16	=B9	=C23+A2		
24	=$C$3	=D24-A3	=C17	=C10	=C24+A3		
25	=$D$4	=D25-A4	=D18	=D11	=C25+A4		
26	=$E$5	=D26-A5	=E19	=E12	=C26+A5		
27	=$F$6	=D27-A6	=F20	=F13	=C27+A6		

Sheet1 / Sheet2 / Sheet3 / Sheet4 / Sheet5 / Sheet6 / Sheet7 / Sheet8 / She

Ready NUM

PROGRAM 14.2 AN EXCEL SPREADSHEET FOR EXAMPLE 6

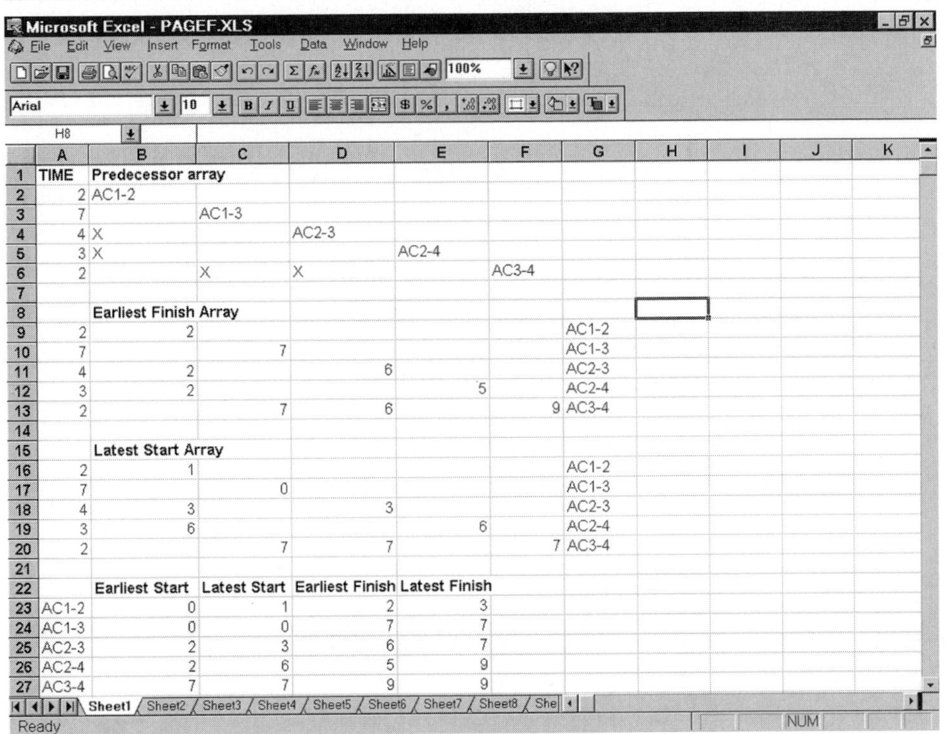

Microsoft Excel - PAGEF.XLS

	A	B	C	D	E	F	G
1	TIME	Predecessor array					
2	2	AC1-2					
3	7		AC1-3				
4	4	X		AC2-3			
5	3	X			AC2-4		
6	2		X	X		AC3-4	
7							
8		Earliest Finish Array					
9	2	2					AC1-2
10	7		7				AC1-3
11	4	2		6			AC2-3
12	3	2			5		AC2-4
13	2		7	6		9	AC3-4
14							
15		Latest Start Array					
16	2	1					AC1-2
17	7		0				AC1-3
18	4	3		3			AC2-3
19	3	6			6		AC2-4
20	2		7	7		7	AC3-4
21							
22		Earliest Start	Latest Start	Earliest Finish	Latest Finish		
23	AC1-2	0	1	2	3		
24	AC1-3	0	0	7	7		
25	AC2-3	2	3	6	7		
26	AC2-4	2	6	5	9		
27	AC3-4	7	7	9	9		

PROGRAM 14.3

Excel Spreadsheet Output from Program 14.2

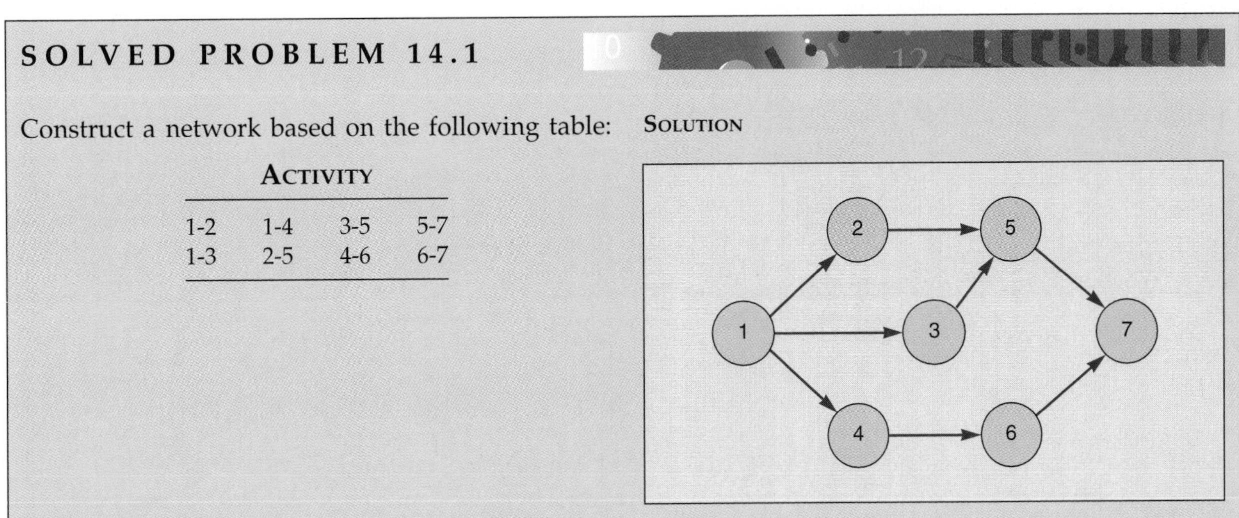

SOLVED PROBLEM 14.1

Construct a network based on the following table:

Activity			
1-2	1-4	3-5	5-7
1-3	2-5	4-6	6-7

Solution

SOLVED PROBLEM 14.2

Insert dummy activities and events to correct the following network:

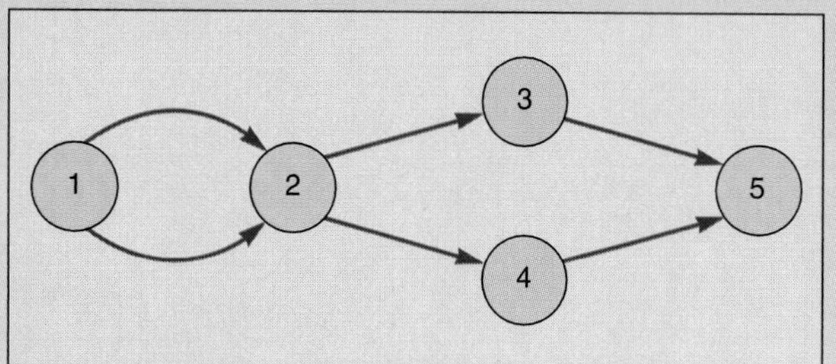

SOLUTION

We can add the following dummy activity and dummy event to obtain the correct network:

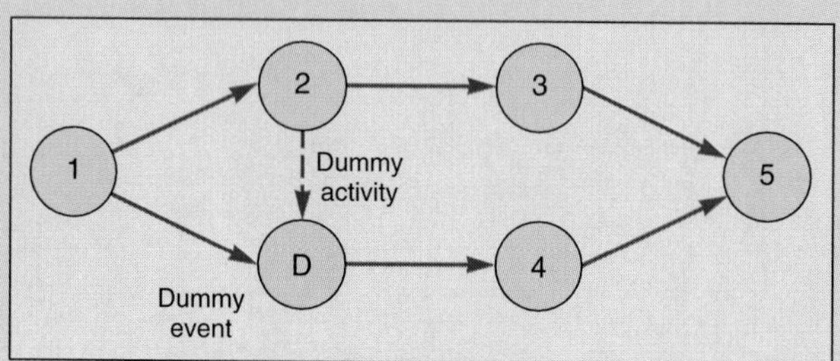

SOLVED PROBLEM 14.3

Calculate the critical path, completion time T, and variance V based on the following information:

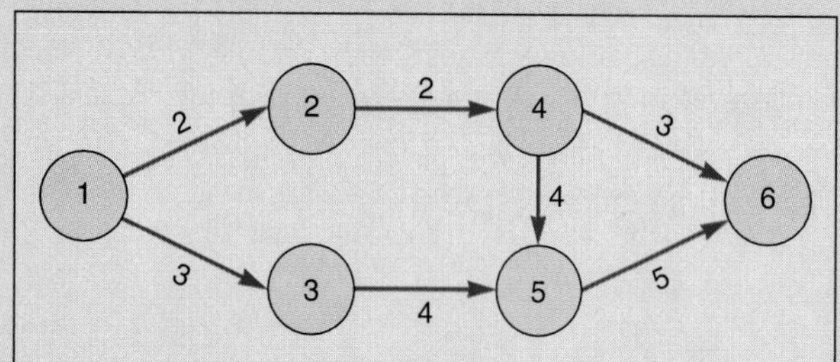

ACTIVITY	t	v	ES	EF	LS	LF	S
1-2	2	2/6	0	2	0	2	0
1-3	3	2/6	0	3	1	4	1
2-4	2	4/6	2	4	2	4	0
3-5	4	4/6	3	7	4	8	1
4-5	4	2/6	4	8	4	8	0
4-6	3	1/6	4	7	10	13	6
5-6	5	1/6	8	13	8	13	0

SOLUTION

We conclude that the critical path is $1 \rightarrow 2 \rightarrow 4 \rightarrow 5 \rightarrow 6$.

$$T = 2 + 2 + 4 + 5 = 13$$

and the variance is:

$$V = \frac{2}{6} + \frac{4}{6} + \frac{2}{6} + \frac{1}{6} = \frac{9}{6} = 1.5$$

SOLVED PROBLEM 14.4

Given the following information, perform a critical path analysis:

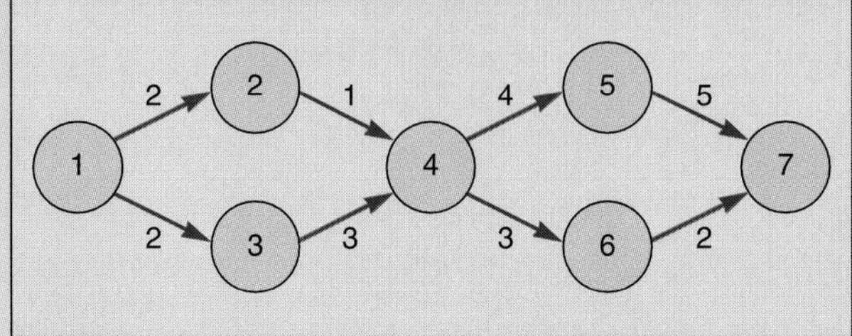

ACTIVITY	t	v	ACTIVITY	t	v
1-2	2	1/6	4-5	4	4/6
1-3	2	1/6	4-6	3	2/6
2-4	1	2/6	5-7	5	1/6
3-4	3	2/6	6-7	2	2/6

SOLUTION

The solution begins with the determination of *ES*, *EF*, *LS*, *LF*, and *S*. We can find these values from the preceding table and then enter them into the following table:

ACTIVITY	t	v	ES	EF	LS	LF	S
1-2	2	1/6	0	2	2	4	2
1-3	2	1/6	0	2	0	2	0
2-4	1	2/6	2	3	4	5	2
3-4	3	2/6	2	5	2	5	0
4-5	4	4/6	5	9	5	9	0
4-6	3	2/6	5	8	9	12	4
5-7	5	1/6	9	14	9	14	0
6-7	2	2/6	8	10	12	14	4

Then we can find the critical path, *T*, and *V*. The critical path is 1-3, 3-4, 4-5, 5-7.

$T = 2 + 3 + 4 + 5 = 14$ and

$$V = \frac{1}{6} + \frac{2}{6} + \frac{4}{6} + \frac{1}{6} = \frac{8}{6}$$

SOLVED PROBLEM 14.5

The following information has been computed from a project:

$$T = 62 \text{ weeks}$$

$$V = 81$$

What is the probability that the project will be completed 18 weeks *before* its expected completion date?

SOLUTION

The desired completion date is 18 weeks before the expected completion date, 62 weeks. The desired completion date is 44 (or 62 − 18) weeks.

$$Z = \frac{C - T}{\sigma} = \frac{44 - 62}{9} = \frac{-18}{9} = -2.0$$

The normal curve appears as follows:

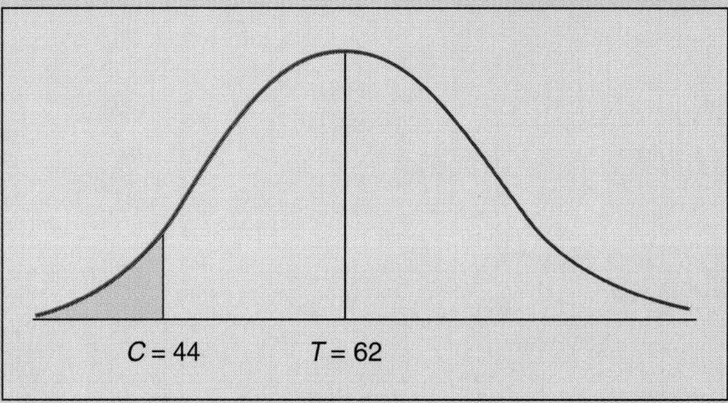

Because the normal curve is symmetrical and table values are calculated for positive values of Z, the area desired is equal to 1 − (table value). For Z = +2.0, the area from the table is .97725. Thus the area, corresponding to a Z value of −2.0, is .02275 (or 1 − 0.97725). Hence the probability of completing the project 18 weeks before the expected completion date is approximately .02, or 2%.

SOLVED PROBLEM 14.6

Determine the least cost of reducing the project completion date by three months based on the following information:

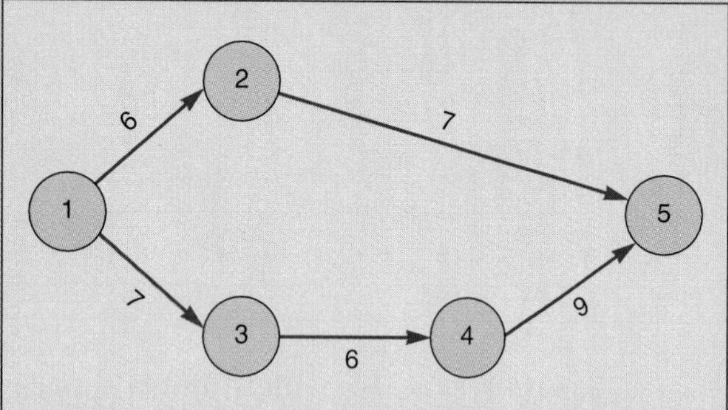

ACTIVITY	*t* (months)	*M* (months)	*C*
1-2	6	2	$400
1-3	7	2	500
2-5	7	1	300
3-4	6	2	600
4-5	9	1	200

SOLUTION

The first step in this problem is to compute *ES*, *EF*, *LS*, *LF*, and *S* for each activity.

ACTIVITY	*ES*	*EF*	*LS*	*LF*	*S*
1-2	0	6	9	15	9
1-3	0	7	0	7	0
2-5	6	13	15	22	9
3-4	7	13	7	13	0
4-5	13	22	13	22	0

The critical path consists of activities 1-3, 3-4, and 4-5.

Next, *K* must be computed for each activity by dividing *C* by *M* for each activity.

ACTIVITY	*M*	*C*	*K*	CRITICAL PATH?
1-2	2	$400	$200 per month	No
1-3	2	500	250 per month	Yes
2-5	1	300	300 per month	No
3-4	2	600	300 per month	Yes
4-5	1	200	200 per month	Yes

Finally, we will select that activity on the critical path with the smallest K_i value. This is activity 4-5. Thus we can reduce the total project completion date by one month (because $M = 1$ month) for an additional cost of $200. We still need to reduce the project completion date by two more months. This reduction can be achieved at least cost along the critical path by reducing activity 1-3 by two months for an additional cost of $500. This solution is summarized in the following table:

ACTIVITY	MONTHS REDUCED	COST
4-5	1	$200
1-3	2	500
	Total:	$700

SELF-TEST ■ CHAPTER 14

- *Before taking the self-test* refer back to the learning objectives listed at the beginning of the chapter and the key terms listed at the end of the chapter.
- Use the key at the back of the text to *correct* your answers.
- *Restudy* pages that correspond to any questions you answered incorrectly or material you feel uncertain about.

1. For each activity, PERT analysis requires
  a. an optimistic time
  b. a most probable time
  c. a pessimistic time
  d. all of the above

2. The three phases involved in the management of large projects are
  a. planning, scheduling, evaluating
  b. scheduling, operating, evaluating
  c. scheduling, designing, operating
  d. planning, scheduling, controlling

3. Popular approaches to project scheduling include
  a. Gantt chart
  b. PERT
  c. CPM
  d. all of the above

4. With respect to PERT and CPM, an event
  a. marks the start or completion of a task
  b. is a task or subproject that must be completed
  c. is the amount of time a task may be delayed without affecting any other task in the network
  d. is the amount of time a task may be delayed without changing the overall project completion time

5. With respect to PERT and CPM, free slack
  a. marks the start or completion of a task
  b. is a task or subproject that must be completed
  c. is the amount of time a task may be delayed without affecting any other task in the network
  d. is the amount of time a task may be delayed without changing the overall project completion time

6. A dummy activity is required when
  a. the network contains two or more activities that have identical starting and ending events
  b. two or more activities have the same starting events
  c. two or more activities have the same ending events
  d. all of the above are true

7. Which of the following is not a basic assumption of PERT?
  a. no activity in the network may be repeated
  b. each activity in the network must be performed
  c. activity completion times are described by Beta probability distributions
  d. all activities have specifiable precedence relationships
  e. none of the above

8. PERT requires three estimates of activity completion time, while CPM requires only a single estimate.
  a. True **b.** False

9. PERT analysis computes the variance of the total project completion time as
  a. the sum of the variances of all activities in the project
  b. the sum of the variances of all activities on the critical path
  c. the sum of the variances of all activities not on the critical path
  d. the variance of the final activity of the project

10. Critical path analysis is used to determine
  a. the earliest activity start time
  b. the latest activity start time
  c. activity slack time
  d. all of the above

11. An event is a point in time that marks the beginning or ending of an activity.
  a. True **b.** False

12. A network is a graphical display of a project that contains both activities and events.
  a. True **b.** False

13. The optimistic time is the greatest amount of time that could be required to complete an activity.
  a. True **b.** False

14. The critical path of a network is the
  a. shortest time path through the network
  b. path with the fewest activities
  c. path with the most activities
  d. longest time path through the network

15. The expected completion time of a PERT project is the sum of the most likely times of the activities on the critical path.
  a. True **b.** False

DISCUSSION QUESTIONS

1. What are some of the questions that can be answered with PERT and CPM?
2. What is an activity? What is an event? What is an immediate predecessor?
3. Describe how expected activity times and variances can be computed in a PERT network.
4. Briefly discuss what is meant by critical path analysis. What are critical path activities and why are they important?
5. What are the earliest activity start time and latest activity start time and how are they computed?
6. Describe the meaning of slack and discuss how it can be determined.
7. How can we determine the probability that a project will be completed by a certain date? What assumptions are made in this computation?
8. What is the difference between an activity-on-arrow (AOA) network and an activity-on-node (AON) network? Which is used in the chapter?
9. What is crashing and how is it done by hand?

OPERATIONS IN PRACTICE EXERCISE

A recent article on Delta Airlines describes ground turnaround procedures of a jumbo jet in one-hour as "well-orchestrated." In fact, turnaround is a serious issue for all airlines "New Airline Fad: Faster Airport Turnarounds," *The Wall Street Journal* (August 4, 1994, pp. B1–B2) article describes scheduling improvements at USAir, Continental, and Southwest. For years, Southwest has turned its planes around in 15 minutes.

Provide detailed suggestions as to how airlines can speed up their turnaround times. What are Southwest's processes? What problems keep other airlines from emulating Southwest? Which is the preferable tool—Gantt charts or PERT and CPM? Why?

PROBLEMS

• **14.1.** Draw the PERT network associated with the following activities for Sarah King's next homework project:

ACTIVITY	IMMEDIATE PREDECESSOR(S)
A	–
B	A
C	A
D	B
E	B
F	C
G	D
H	E, F

• **14.2.** Given the activities whose sequence is described by the following table, draw the appropriate PERT diagram.

ACTIVITY	IMMEDIATE PREDECESSOR(S)
A	–
B	A
C	A
D	B
E	B
F	C
G	E, F
H	D
I	G, H

• **14.3.** The following represent activities in Anne Riddick's Construction Company project. Draw the network to represent this situation.

ACTIVITY	IMMEDIATE PREDECESSOR(S)
A	–
B	–
C	A
D	B
E	B
F	C, E
G	D
H	F, G

• **14.4.** Sarah Mahan is the personnel director of Babson and Willcount, a company that specializes in consulting and research. One of the training programs that Sarah is considering for the middle-level managers of Babson and Willcount is leadership training. Sarah has listed a number of activities that must be completed before a training program of this nature could be conducted. The activities and immediate predecessors appear in the accompanying table.

ACTIVITY	IMMEDIATE PREDECESSOR	ACTIVITY	IMMEDIATE PREDECESSOR(S)
A	–	E	A, D
B	–	F	C
C	–	G	E, F
D	B		

Develop a network for this problem.

• **14.5.** Sarah Mahan was able to determine the activity times for the leadership training program (see Problem 14.4). She would like to determine the total project completion time and the critical path. The activity times appear in the following table:

ACTIVITY	TIME (days)
A	2
B	5
C	1
D	10
E	3
F	6
G	8
Total	35 days

• **14.6.** Gilbert Machinery specializes in developing weed-harvesting equipment that is used to clear small lakes of weeds. Jim Gilbert, president of Gilbert Machinery, is convinced that harvesting weeds is far better than using chemicals to kill weeds. Chemicals cause pollution, and the weeds seem to grow faster after chemicals have been used. Jim is contemplating the construction of a machine that could harvest weeds on narrow rivers and waterways. The activities that are necessary to build one of these experimental weed-harvesting machines are listed in the accompanying table. Construct a network for these activities.

ACTIVITY	IMMEDIATE PREDECESSOR(S)
A	–
B	–
C	A
D	A
E	B
F	B
G	C, E
H	D, F

14.7. After consulting with Tim Collins, Jim Gilbert was able to determine the activity times for constructing the weed-harvesting machine to be used on narrow rivers. Jim would like to determine *ES, EF, LS, LF,* and slack for each activity. The total project completion time and the critical path should also be determined. See Problem 14.6 for details. Here are the activity times:

ACTIVITY	TIME (weeks)
A	6
B	5
C	3
D	2
E	4
F	6
G	10
H	7

14.8. Zuckerman Wiring and Electric is a company that installs wiring and electrical fixtures in residential construction. Jane Zuckerman has been very concerned with the amount of time that it takes to complete wiring jobs. Some of her workers are very unreliable. A list of activities and their optimistic completion time, the pessimistic completion time, and the most likely completion time (all in days) is given in the following table.

Determine the expected completion time and variance for each activity.

ACTIVITY	*a*	*m*	*b*	IMMEDIATE PREDECESSOR(S)
A	3	6	8	–
B	2	4	4	–
C	1	2	3	–
D	6	7	8	C
E	2	4	6	B, D
F	6	10	14	A, E
G	1	2	4	A, E
H	3	6	9	F
I	10	11	12	G
J	14	16	20	C
K	2	8	10	H, I

14.9. Jane Zuckerman would like to determine the total project completion time and the critical path for installing electrical wiring and equipment in residential houses. See Problem 14.8 for details. In addition, determine *ES, EF, LS, LF,* and slack for each activity.

14.10. What is the probability that Zuckerman will finish the project described in Problems 14.8 and 14.9 in 40 days or less?

14.11. Given the activities described by the following table for the Das Corporation:

ACTIVITY	IMMEDIATE PREDECESSOR(S)	TIME
A	–	9
B	A	7
C	A	3
D	B	6
E	B	9
F	C	4
G	E, F	6
H	D	5
I	G, H	3

a. Draw the appropriate PERT diagram for Sidhartha Das' management team.
b. Find the critical path.

14.12. A small software development project at Jim Ruppel's firm has four major activities. The times are estimated and provided in the following table. Find the expected time for completing Ruppel's project.

ACTIVITY	IMMEDIATE PREDECESSOR	a	m	b
A	–	2	5	8
B	–	3	6	9
C	A	4	7	10
D	B	2	5	14
E	C	3	3	3

a. What is the expected completion time for this project?
b. What variance would be used in finding probabilities of finishing by a certain time?

14.13. Given the activities described by the following table:

ACTIVITY	EXPECTED TIME	STANDARD DEVIATION OF TIME ESTIMATE	IMMEDIATE PREDECESSOR(S)
A	7	2	–
B	3	1	A
C	9	3	A
D	4	1	B, C
E	5	1	B, C
F	8	2	E
G	8	1	D, F
H	6	2	G

a. Draw the appropriate PERT diagram.
b. Find the critical path and project completion time.
c. Find the probability that the project will take more than 49 time periods to complete.

14.14. Development of a new deluxe version of a particular software product is being considered by Cynthia Chazen's software house. The activities necessary for the completion of this are listed in the following table:

ACTIVITY	NORMAL TIME	CRASH TIME	NORMAL COST	CRASH COST	IMMEDIATE PREDECESSOR(S)
A	4	3	$2,000	$2,600	–
B	2	1	2,200	2,800	–
C	3	3	500	500	–
D	8	4	2,300	2,600	A
E	6	3	900	1,200	B
F	3	2	3,000	4,200	C
G	4	2	1,400	2,000	D, E

a. What is the project completion date?
b. What is the total cost required for completing this project on normal time?
c. If you wish to reduce the time required to complete this project by one week, which activity should be crashed, and how much will this increase the total cost?

14.15. A project in Harold Allen's company in Tampa has an expected completion time of 40 weeks and a standard deviation of 5 weeks. It is assumed that the project completion time is normally distributed.
a. What is the probability of finishing the project in 50 weeks or less?
b. What is the probability of finishing the project in 38 weeks or less?
c. The due date for the project is set so that there is a 90% chance that the project will be finished by this date. What is the due date?

14.16. B&R Manufacturing produces custom-built pollution-control devices for medium-sized steel mills. The most recent project undertaken by B&R requires 14 different activities. B&R's managers would like to determine the total project completion time and those activities that lie along the critical path. The appropriate data are shown in the following table:

ACTIVITY	IMMEDIATE PREDECESSOR(S)	OPTIMISTIC TIME	MOST LIKELY TIME	PESSIMISTIC TIME
A	–	4	6	7
B	–	1	2	3
C	A	6	6	6
D	A	5	8	11
E	B, C	1	9	18
F	D	2	3	6
G	D	1	7	8
H	E, F	4	4	6
I	G, H	1	6	8
J	I	2	5	7
K	I	8	9	11
L	J	2	4	6
M	K	1	2	3
N	L, M	6	8	10

14.17. Bill Trigiero, director of personnel of Trigiero Resources, Inc., is in the process of designing a program that his customers can use in the job-finding process. Some of the activities include preparing resumes, writing letters, making appointments to see prospective employers, researching companies and industries, and so on. Some of the information on the activities appears in the following table:

ACTIVITY	TIME (days) *a*	*m*	*b*	IMMEDIATE PREDECESSOR(S)
A	8	10	12	–
B	6	7	9	–
C	3	3	4	–
D	10	20	30	A
E	6	7	8	C
F	9	10	11	B, D, E
G	6	7	10	B, D, E
H	14	15	16	F
I	10	11	13	F
J	6	7	8	G, H
K	4	7	8	I, J
L	1	2	4	G, H

a. Construct a network for this problem.
b. Determine the expected times and variances for each activity.
c. Determine *ES, EF, LS, LF,* and slack for each activity.
d. Determine the critical path and project completion time.
e. Determine the probability that the project will be finished in 70 days.
f. Determine the probability that the project will be finished in 80 days.
g. Determine the probability that the project will be finished in 90 days.

14.18. Using PERT, David Brecker was able to determine that the expected project completion time for the construction of a pleasure yacht is 21 months, and the project variance is 4 months.
a. What is the probability that the project will be completed in 17 months?
b. What is the probability that the project will be completed in 20 months?
c. What is the probability that the project will be completed in 23 months?
d. What is the probability that the project will be completed in 25 months?

14.19. Getting a degree from a college or university can be a long and difficult task. Certain courses must be completed before other courses may be taken. Develop a network diagram, where every activity is a particular course that must be taken for a given degree program. The immediate predecessors will be course prerequisites. Don't forget to include all university, college, and departmental course requirements. Then try to group these courses into semesters or quarters for your particular school. How long do you think it will take you to graduate? Which courses, if not taken in the proper sequence, could delay your graduation?

14.20. Stone Builders manufactures steel storage sheds for commercial use. Kevin Stone, president of Stone Builders, is contemplating producing sheds for home use. The activities necessary to build an experimental model and related data are given in the accompanying table. (Note that there is no additional cost in crashing activities A and B by one week each).

ACTIVITY	NORMAL TIME	CRASH TIME	NORMAL COST ($)	CRASH COST ($)	IMMEDIATE PREDECESSOR(S)
A	3	2	1,600	1,600	–
B	2	1	2,700	2,700	–
C	1	0	300	600	–
D	7	3	1,300	1,600	A
E	6	3	850	1,000	B
F	2	1	4,000	5,000	C
G	4	2	1,500	2,000	D, E

a. What is the project completion date?
b. Crash this project to ten weeks at the least cost.

Internet Data Base Application See our website at http://www.prenhall.com/renderpom for a challenging, computer-based problem.

CASE STUDY

The Family Planning Research Center of Nigeria

Dr. Adinombe Watage, deputy director of the Family Planning Research Center in Nigeria's Over-the-River Province was assigned the task of organizing and training five teams of field workers to do education and outreach as part of a large project to demonstrate acceptance of a new method of birth control. These workers had already had training in family planning education but must receive specific training regarding the new method of contraception. Two types of materials must also be prepared: (1) those for use in training the workers, and (2) those for distribution in the field. Training faculty must be brought in and arrangements made for transportation and accommodations for the participants.

Dr. Watage first called a meeting of his office staff. Together they identified the activities that must be carried out, their necessary sequences, and the time that they would require. Their results are displayed in Table 1.

TABLE 1 THE FAMILY PLANNING RESEARCH CENTER

ACTIVITY	MUST FOLLOW	TIME (in days)	STAFFING NEEDED
A. Identify faculty and their schedules	–	5	2
B. Arrange transport to base	–	7	3
C. Identify and collect training materials	–	5	2
D. Arrange accommodations	A	3	1
E. Identify team	A	7	4
F. Bring in team	B, E	2	1
G. Transport faculty to base	A, B	3	2
H. Print program material	C	10	6
I. Have program materials delivered	H	7	3
J. Conduct training program	D, F, G, I	15	0
K. Perform fieldwork training	J	30	0

Louis Odaga, the chief clerk, noted that the project had to be completed in 60 days. Whipping out his solar-powered calculator, he added up the time needed. It came to 94 days. "An impossible task then," he noted. "No," Dr. Watage replied, "some of these tasks can go forward in parallel." "Be careful though," warned Mr. Oglagadu, the chief nurse, "there aren't that many of us to go around. There are only ten of us in this office."

"I can check whether we have enough heads and hands, once I have tentatively scheduled the activities," Dr. Watage responded. "If the schedule is too tight, I have permission from the Pathminder Foundation to spend some funds to speed it up, just so long as I can prove that it can be done at the least cost necessary. Can you help me prove that? Here are the costs for the activities with the elapsed time that we planned and the costs and times, if we shorten them to an absolute minimum."

Those data are in Table 2.

continued on next page

TABLE 2 THE FAMILY PLANNING RESEARCH CENTER

	NORMAL		MINIMUM		
ACTIVITY	*Time*	*Cost ($)*	*Time*	*Cost ($)*	AVERAGE COST PER DAY SAVED ($)
A. Identify faculty	5	400	2	700	100
B. Arrange transport	7	1,000	4	1,450	150
C. Identify materials	5	400	3	500	50
D. Make accommodations	3	2,500	1	3,000	250
E. Identify team	7	400	4	850	150
F. Bring team in	2	1,000	1	2,000	1,000
G. Transport faculty	3	1,500	2	2,000	500
H. Print materials	10	3,000	5	4,000	200
I. Deliver materials	7	200	2	600	80
J. Train team	15	5,000	10	7,000	400
K. Do fieldwork	30	10,000	20	14,000	400

DISCUSSION QUESTIONS

1. Some of the tasks in this project can be done in parallel. Prepare a diagram showing the required network of tasks and define the critical path. What is the length of the project without crashing?
2. At this point, can the project be done given the personnel constraint of ten persons?
3. If the critical path is longer than 60 days, what is the least amount that Dr. Watage can spend and still achieve this schedule objective? How can he prove to Pathminder Foundation that this is the minimum cost alternative?

SOURCE: Professor Curtis P. McLaughlin, Kenan-Flagler Business School, University of North Carolina at Chapel Hill.

Internet Case Studies See our Internet home page at http://www.prenhall.com/renderpom for these additional case studies: Haywood Brothers Construction Company and Shale Oil.

BIBLIOGRAPHY

Cleland, D. I., and W. R. King. *Project Management Handbook.* New York: Van Nostrand Reinhold, 1984.

Dean, B. V. "Getting the Job Done! Managing Project Teams and Task Forces for Success." *The Executive* 6, no. 4 (November 1992): 94.

Dusenberry, W. "CPM for New Product Introductions." *Harvard Business Review* (July-August 1967): 124–139.

Hickman, Anita. "Refining the Process of Project Control." *Production and Inventory Management* (February 1992): 26–27.

Keefer, D. L., and W. A. Verdini. "Better Estimation of PERT Activity Time Parameters." *Management Science* 39, no. 9 (September 1993): 1,086.

Kerzner, H., and H. Thamhain. *Project Management for Small and Medium Size Business.* New York: Van Nostrand Reinhold, 1984.

Kim, S., and R. C. Leachman. "Multi-Project Scheduling with Explicit Lateness Costs." *IIE Transactions* 25, no. 2 (March 1993): 34–44.

Pinto, M. B., J. K. Pinto, and J. E. Prescott. "Antecedents and Consequences of Project Team Cross-Functional Cooperation." *Management Science* 39, no. 10 (October 1993): 1,281.

Render, B., and R. M. Stair. *Introduction to Management Science.* Boston: Allyn & Bacon, 1992.

———. *Quantitative Analysis for Management,* 6th ed. Upper Saddle River NJ: Prentice-Hall, 1997.

Maintenance Management

Supplement 14

SUPPLEMENT OUTLINE

The Strategic Importance of Maintenance

Maintenance Categories

Implementing Preventive Maintenance ■ Simulation Models for a Maintenance Policy

Key Terms ■ *Discussion Questions* ■ *Self-Test Supplement 14* ■ *Problems* ■ *Case Study: Worldwide Chemical Company* ■ *Bibliography*

LEARNING OBJECTIVES

When you complete this supplement you should be able to:

IDENTIFY OR DEFINE:

Maintenance
Preventive maintenance
Breakdown maintenance
Mean time between failures
Infant mortality

EXPLAIN:

How to improve maintenance
How to evaluate maintenance performance

THE STRATEGIC IMPORTANCE OF MAINTENANCE

Managers need to avoid the undesirable results of a system that fails. The results of failure can be disruptive, inconvenient, wasteful, and expensive. Machine and product failures can have far-reaching effects on a firm's operation, reputation, and profitability. In complex, highly mechanized plants, an out-of-tolerance process or a machine breakdown may result in idle employees and facilities, loss of customers and goodwill, and profits turning into losses.[1] Likewise, in an office, the failure of a generator, an air-conditioning system, or a computer may halt operations. A good maintenance strategy protects both a firm's performance and its investment.

The objective of maintenance is to maintain the capability of the system while controlling costs. Systems must be designed and maintained to reach expected performance and quality standards. **Maintenance** includes all activities involved in keeping a system's equipment in working order.

maintenance

Two firms that recognize the strategic importance of dedicated maintenance are Walt Disney Company and United Parcel Service. Disney World, in Florida, is intolerant of failures or breakdowns. Disney's reputation makes it not only one of the most popular vacation destinations in the world, but also a mecca for benchmarking teams that want to study its maintenance practices.

Likewise, UPS's famed maintenance strategy keeps its delivery vehicles operating and looking as good as new for 20 years or more. The UPS program involves dedicated drivers who operate the same truck everyday, and dedicated mechanics, who maintain the same group of vehicles. Drivers and mechanics are both responsible for the performance of a vehicle and stay closely in touch.

The interdependency of operator, machine, and mechanic is a hallmark of successful maintenance strategy. As Figure S14.1 illustrates, it is not only good maintenance procedures that make Disney and UPS successful, but the involvement of their employees as well.

FIGURE S14.1

GOOD MAINTENANCE STRATEGY REQUIRES EMPLOYEE INVOLVEMENT AND GOOD MAINTENANCE PROCEDURES

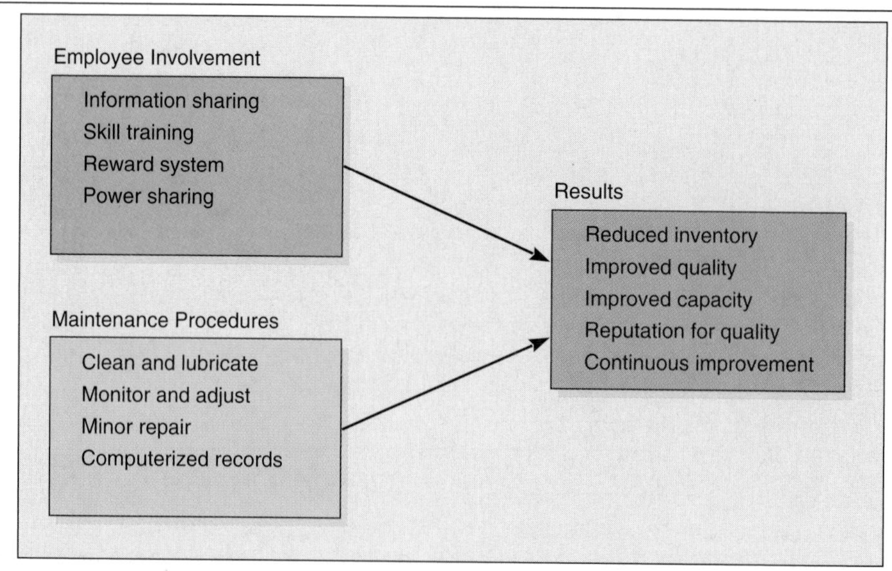

[1]A study noted in *The Economist* (March 9, 1985, pp. 62–63) addressing the weaknesses in British productivity compared British and German firms. The study found that although the machinery in the British plants was no older than that in the German plants, it was poorly maintained. Breakdowns were found to be more frequent and lasted longer. Operators were found less able to do repairs themselves.

MAINTENANCE CATEGORIES

Maintenance falls into two categories: preventive maintenance and breakdown maintenance. **Preventive maintenance** involves performing routine inspections and servicing that keep facilities in good repair. Preventive maintenance activities are intended to build a system that will find potential failures and make changes or repairs that will prevent failure. Preventive maintenance is much more than just keeping machinery and equipment running. It also involves designing technical and human systems that will keep the productive process working within tolerance; it allows the system to perform. The emphasis is on understanding the process and allowing it to work without interruption. **Breakdown maintenance** is remedial; it occurs when equipment fails and then must be repaired on an emergency or priority basis.

preventive maintenance

NOTE
"Prevention is not hard to do—it is just hard to sell." Quality control expert Philip Crosby

breakdown maintenance

Implementing Preventive Maintenance

Preventive maintenance implies that we can determine when a system needs service or will need repair. Therefore, to perform preventive maintenance, we must define when a system requires service or when it is likely to fail. Failure occurs at different rates during the life of a product. A high failure rate, known as **infant mortality,** exists initially for many products. This is the reason many electronic firms "burn in" their products prior to shipment. That is to say, many firms exe-

infant mortality

Preventive maintenance is critical to the Orlando Utilities Commission (OUC), a Central Florida electric utility company. Its coal-fired unit requires that maintenance personnel perform about 12,000 repair and preventive maintenance tasks a year. These are scheduled daily by a computerized maintenance program. An unexpected forced outage can cost OUC from $250,000 to $500,000 per day. The value of preventive maintenance was illustrated by the first overhaul of a new generator. A cracked rotor blade was discovered, which could have destroyed a $27 million piece of equipment.

cute a variety of tests to detect "startup" problems prior to shipment. Other firms provide 90-day warranties. We should note that many infant mortality failures are not product failures per se but failure due to improper use. This fact points up the importance of management building a maintenance system that includes training and personnel selection.

mean time between failure (MTBF)

Once the product, machine, or process "settles in," a study can be made of the **MTBF (mean time between failure)** distribution. When the distributions have a small standard deviation, then we know we have a candidate for preventive maintenance even if the maintenance is expensive.

Once we have a candidate for preventive maintenance, we want to determine when preventive maintenance is economical. Typically, the more expensive the maintenance, the narrower must be the MTBF distribution. Additionally, if the process is no more expensive to repair when it breaks down than the cost of preventive maintenance, perhaps we should let the process break down and then do the repair. However, the consequence of the breakdown must be fully considered; some relatively minor breakdowns have catastrophic consequences. At the other extreme, preventive maintenance costs may be so incidental that preventive maintenance is appropriate even if the distribution is rather flat (that is, it has a large standard deviation). In any event, every individual must be held responsible for inspection of his or her equipment and tools.

NOTE
World-class firms stress the long term. For firms with the long view, expenses from preventive maintenance are not as important as increased capacity from reduced downtime.

Figure S14.2 shows the relationship between preventive maintenance and breakdown maintenance. Operations managers need to consider a balance between the two costs. Allocating inventory, money, and personnel to preventive maintenance will reduce the number of breakdowns. But, at some point, the decrease in breakdown maintenance costs will be less than the increase in preventive maintenance costs, and the total cost curve will begin to rise. Beyond this optimal point, the firm may be better off waiting for breakdowns to occur and repairing them when they do.

The problem with this analysis is that the full costs of breakdown are seldom considered. Many costs are ignored because they are not directly related to the immediate breakdown. That does not make them any less real or their impact any less important. Two costs that are often ignored are: (1) the cost of inventory that is maintained to compensate for downtime, and (2) the devastating effect down-

FIGURE S14.2
MAINTENANCE COSTS

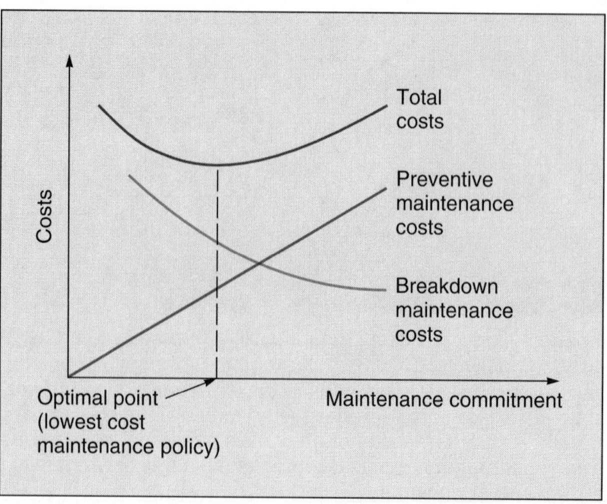

time can have on morale because employees begin to believe that performance to standard and maintaining equipment are not important.

Assuming that all costs associated with downtime have been identified, the operations staff can compute the optimal level of maintenance activity on a theoretical basis. The analysis, of course, also requires accurate historical data on maintenance costs, breakdown probabilities, and repair times. Example S1 illustrates how to compare preventive and breakdown maintenance costs in order to select the least expensive maintenance policy.

EXAMPLE S1

Huntsman and Associates is a CPA firm specializing in payroll preparation. The accountants have been successful in automating much of their work, using a Digimatic II computer for processing and report preparation. The computerized approach has problems, however. Over the past 20 months, the computer system has broken down as indicated in the following table:

NUMBER OF BREAKDOWNS	NUMBER OF MONTHS THAT BREAKDOWNS OCCURRED
0	4
1	8
2	6
3	2
Total:	20

Each time the computer breaks down, the partners estimate that the firm loses an average of $300 in time and service expenses. One alternative is for the firm to accept Digimatic's offer to contract for preventive maintenance. If they accept preventive maintenance, they expect an *average* of only one computer breakdown per month. The price that Digimatic charges for this service is $220 per month. We will follow a four-step approach to answer the question of whether the CPAs should contract with Digimatic for preventive maintenance:

Step 1. Compute the *expected number* of breakdowns (based on past history) if the firm continues as is, without the service contract.

Step 2. Compute the expected breakdown cost per month with no preventive maintenance contract.

Step 3. Compute the cost of preventive maintenance.

Step 4. Compare the two options and select the one that will cost less.

1.

NUMBER OF BREAKDOWNS	FREQUENCY	NUMBER OF BREAKDOWNS	FREQUENCY
0	4/20 = .2	2	6/20 = .3
1	8/20 = .4	3	2/20 = .1

$$\begin{pmatrix}\text{Expected number}\\ \text{of breakdowns}\end{pmatrix} = \sum \begin{pmatrix}\text{Number of}\\ \text{breakdowns}\end{pmatrix} \times \begin{pmatrix}\text{Corresponding}\\ \text{frequency}\end{pmatrix}$$

$$= (0)(.2) + (1)(.4) + (2)(.3) + (3)(.1)$$

$$= 0 + .4 + .6 + .3$$

$$= 1.3 \text{ breakdowns per month}$$

2. $$\text{Expected breakdown cost} = \begin{pmatrix}\text{Expected number}\\ \text{of breakdowns}\end{pmatrix} \times \begin{pmatrix}\text{Cost per}\\ \text{breakdown}\end{pmatrix}$$
$$= (1.3)(\$300)$$
$$= \$390 \text{ per month}$$

3. $$\text{Preventive maintenance cost} = \begin{pmatrix}\text{Cost of expected}\\ \text{breakdowns if service}\\ \text{contract signed}\end{pmatrix} + \begin{pmatrix}\text{Cost of}\\ \text{service contract}\end{pmatrix}$$
$$= (1 \text{ breakdown per month})(\$300)$$
$$+ \$220 \text{ per month}$$
$$= \$520 \text{ per month}$$

4. Since it is less expensive to suffer the breakdowns *without* a maintenance service contract ($390) than with one ($520), the firm should continue its present policy.

Simulation Models for a Maintenance Policy

Simulation techniques can be used to evaluate the impact of various maintenance policies (such as the size of the facility) prior to implementing the policy. Operations personnel can decide whether to add more maintenance staff on the basis of the trade-offs between machine downtime costs and the costs of additional labor. Management can also simulate replacing parts that have not yet failed as a way of preventing future breakdowns. Many companies use computerized simulation models to decide if and when to shut down a whole plant for maintenance activities.

KEY TERMS

Maintenance *(p. 518)*
Preventive maintenance *(p. 519)*
Breakdown maintenance *(p. 519)*
Infant mortality *(p. 519)*
Mean time between failure (MTBF) *(p. 520)*

DISCUSSION QUESTIONS

1. Under what conditions is preventive maintenance likely to be appropriate?
2. Why is simulation often an appropriate technique for maintenance problems?
3. How can the manager evaluate the effectiveness of the maintenance function?
4. Identify some areas where infant mortality appears.
5. How can operations managers overcome infant mortality?

SELF-TEST ■ SUPPLEMENT 14

- *Before taking the self-test* refer back to the learning objectives listed at the beginning of the supplement and the key terms listed at the end of the supplement.
- Use the key at the back of the text to *correct* your answers.
- *Restudy* pages that correspond to any questions you answered incorrectly or material you feel uncertain about.

1. The appropriate maintenance policy is developed by balancing preventive maintenance costs and breakdown maintenance costs. The problem is that
  a. preventive maintenance costs are very difficult to identify
  b. full breakdown costs are seldom considered
  c. preventive maintenance should be performed regardless of the cost
  d. breakdown maintenance must be performed regardless of the cost

2. Periodic maintenance is really a form of preventive maintenance.
  a. True **b.** False

3. Maintenance can be improved by
  a. enlarging repair crews
  b. increasing repair capabilities
  c. providing more inventory of replacement items
  d. all of the above

4. It is always cheaper to implement a preventive maintenance program than to fix the component after it breaks.
  a. True **b.** False

5. The process that is intended to find potential failures and make changes or repairs is known as
  a. breakdown maintenance
  b. failure maintenance
  c. preventive maintenance
  d. all of the above

6. Undesirable results of system failure and downtime include
  a. not producing within quality standards
  b. not producing adequate volume
  c. excessive costs to overcome problems
  d. all of the above

7. Infant mortality
  a. is a very rare phenomenon in the life of products
  b. is generally found from the MTBF (mean time between failure) rate
  c. is often due to improper use
  d. may be eliminated by breakdown maintenance
  e. is none of the above

PROBLEMS

• **S14.1.** Given the probabilities that follow for Marc Cohen's machine shop, find the expected breakdown cost.

NUMBER OF BREAKDOWNS	DAILY FREQUENCY
0	.3
1	.2
2	.2
3	.3
	1.0

The cost per breakdown is $10.

S14.2. Loucks Manufacturing Company operates its 23 large and expensive grinding and lathe machines from 7 A.M. to 11 P.M., seven days a week. For the past year the firm has been under contract with Simkin and Sons for daily preventive maintenance (lubrication, cleaning, inspection, and so on). Simkin's crew works between 11 P.M. and 2 A.M. so as not to interfere with the daily manufacturing crew. Simkin charges $645 per week for this service. Since signing the maintenance contract, Loucks Manufacturing has noted an average of only three breakdowns per week. When a grinding or lathe machine *does* break down during a working shift, it costs Loucks about $250 in lost production and repair costs.

After reviewing past breakdown records (for the period before signing a preventive maintenance contract with Simkin and Sons), Loucks Manufacturing's production manager summarized the patterns shown in the following table.

NUMBER OF BREAKDOWNS PER WEEK	0	1	2	3	4	5	6	7	8
NUMBER OF WEEKS IN WHICH BREAKDOWNS OCCURRED	1	1	3	5	9	11	7	8	5

Total weeks of historical data: 50

The production manager is not certain that the contract for preventive maintenance with Simkin is in the best financial interest of Loucks Manufacturing. He recognizes that much of his breakdown data is old but is fairly certain that it is representative of the present picture.

What is your analysis of this situation, and what recommendations do you think the production manager should make?

CASE STUDY

Worldwide Chemical Company

Jack Smith wiped the perspiration from his face. It was another scorching-hot summer day, and one of the four process refrigeration units was down. The units were critical to the operation of Worldwide Chemical Company's Fibers Plant, which produced synthetic fibers and polymer flake for a global market.

Before long, Al Henson, the day-shift production superintendent, was on the intercom, shouting his familiar proclamation that "heads would roll" if the unit was not back online within the hour. But Jack Smith, the maintenance superintendent, had heard it all before—nothing ever happened as a result of those temper tantrums. "Serves him right," he thought, "Henson is uncooperative when we want to perform scheduled maintenance, so it doesn't get done and the equipment goes down."

At that moment, Henson, furious over the impact the equipment breakdown would have on his process yield figures, was meeting with Beth Conner, the plant manager, charging that all the maintenance department did was to "sit around" and play cards like firemen waiting for an alarm to send them on their way to a three-alarm blaze across town. It was true that the "fix-it" approach to maintenance was costing the plant throughput that was vital to meeting standard costs and avoiding serious variances. Foreign competitors were delivering high-quality fibers in less time, at lower prices. Conner had already been "on the carpet" at corporate headquarters over output levels that were significantly below the budgeted numbers. The business cycle contained seasonal variations that were predictable. That meant building inventories that would be carried for months, tying up scarce capital, a characteristic of most continuous processes. Monthly shipments would look bad. Year-to-date shipments would look even worse because of machine breakdowns and lost output to date.

Conner knew that something had to be done to develop machine reliability. Capacity on demand was needed to respond to the growing foreign competition. Unreliable production equipment was jeopardizing the company's TQM effort by causing process variations that affected first-quality product yields and on-time deliveries, but no one seemed to have the answer to the problem of machine breakdowns.

The maintenance department operated much as a fire department, rushing to a breakdown with a swarm of mechanics, some who disassembled the machine, others who poured over wiring schematics, and others who hunted spare parts in the maintenance warehouse. Eventually, they would have the machine back up, sometimes only after working through the night to get the production line going again. Maintenance had always been done this way. But, with new competitors, machine reliability had suddenly become a major barrier to competing successfully.

Rumors of a plant closing were beginning to circulate, and morale was suffering, making good performance that much more difficult. Conner knew she needed solutions if the plant had any chance of survival.

DISCUSSION QUESTIONS

1. Could Smith and Hensen do anything to improve performance?
2. Is there an alternative to the current operations approach of the maintenance department?
3. How would production make up for lost output resulting from scheduled maintenance?
4. How could maintenance mechanics be better utilized?
5. Is there any way to know when a machine breakdown is probable?

SOURCE: Patrick Owings under the supervision of Professor Marilyn M. Helms, University of Tennessee at Chattanooga.

BIBLIOGRAPHY

Gray, D. "Airworthy—Decision Support for Aircraft Overhaul Maintenance Planning" *OR/MS Today* 19 (December 1992): 24–29.

Hayes, R. H., and K. B. Clark. "Why Some Factories Are More Productive than Others." *Harvard Business Review* 64, (September-October 1986): 66–73.

Linder-Dutton, L., M. Jordan, and M. Karwan. "Beyond Mean Time to Failure." *OR/MS Today* 21, no. 2 (April 1994): 30–33.

Maggard, B. N., and D. M. Rhyne. "Total Productive Maintenance: A Timely Integration of Production and Maintenance." *Production and Inventory Management Journal* 33, no. 4 (Fourth Quarter 1992): 6–10.

Mann, L., Jr. *Maintenance Management*. Lexington, MA: Lexington Books, 1983.

Sherwin, D. J. "Inspect or Monitor." *Engineering Costs and Production Economics* 18 (January 1990): 223–231.

Sivakumar, R. A., R. Batta, and K. Tehrani. "Scheduling Repairs at Texas Instruments." *Interfaces* 23 (July-August 1993): 68–74.

Vaziri, H. K. "Using Competitive Benchmarking to Set Goals." *Quality Progress* 25, no. 10 (October 1992): 81.

Appendices

APPENDIX A
Normal Curve Areas and How to Use the Normal Distribution

APPENDIX B
Using POM for Windows

APPENDIX C
Answers to Self-Tests

APPENDIX D
Answers to Even-Numbered Problems

Appendix A: Normal Curve Areas and How to Use the Normal Distribution

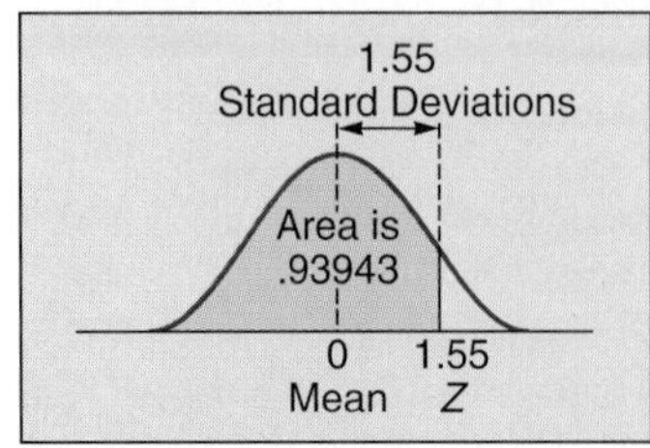

To find the area under the normal curve, you must know how many standard deviations that point is to the right of the mean. Then, the area under the normal curve can be read directly from the normal table. For example, the total area under the normal curve for a point that is 1.55 standard deviations to the right of the mean is .93943.

	.00	.01	.02	.03	.04	.05	.06	.07	.08	.09
.0	.50000	.50399	.50798	.51197	.51595	.51994	.52392	.52790	.53188	.53586
.1	.53983	.54380	.54776	.55172	.55567	.55962	.56356	.56749	.57142	.57535
.2	.57926	.58317	.58706	.59095	.59483	.59871	.60257	.60642	.61026	.61409
.3	.61791	.62172	.62552	.62930	.63307	.63683	.64058	.64431	.64803	.65173
.4	.65542	.65910	.66276	.66640	.67003	.67364	.67724	.68082	.68439	.68793
.5	.69146	.69497	.69847	.70194	.70540	.70884	.71226	.71566	.71904	.72240
.6	.72575	.72907	.73237	.73536	.73891	.74215	.74537	.74857	.75175	.75490
.7	.75804	.76115	.76424	.76730	.77035	.77337	.77637	.77935	.78230	.78524
.8	.78814	.79103	.79389	.79673	.79955	.80234	.80511	.80785	.81057	.81327
.9	.81594	.81859	.82121	.82381	.82639	.82894	.83147	.83398	.83646	.83891
1.0	.84134	.84375	.84614	.84849	.85083	.85314	.85543	.85769	.85993	.86214
1.1	.86433	.86650	.86864	.87076	.87286	.87493	.87698	.87900	.88100	.88298
1.2	.88493	.88686	.88877	.89065	.89251	.89435	.89617	.89796	.89973	.90147
1.3	.90320	.90490	.90658	.90824	.90988	.91149	.91309	.91466	.91621	.91774
1.4	.91924	.92073	.92220	.92364	.92507	.92647	.92785	.92922	.93056	.93189
1.5	.93319	.93448	.93574	.93699	.93822	.93943	.94062	.94179	.94295	.94408
1.6	.94520	.94630	.94738	.94845	.94950	.95053	.95154	.95254	.95352	.95449
1.7	.95543	.95637	.95728	.95818	.95907	.95994	.96080	.96164	.96246	.96327
1.8	.96407	.96485	.96562	.96638	.96712	.96784	.96856	.96926	.96995	.97062
1.9	.97128	.97193	.97257	.97320	.97381	.97441	.97500	.97558	.97615	.97670
2.0	.97725	.97784	.97831	.97882	.97932	.97982	.98030	.98077	.98124	.98169
2.1	.98214	.98257	.98300	.98341	.98382	.98422	.98461	.98500	.98537	.98574
2.2	.98610	.98645	.98679	.98713	.98745	.98778	.98809	.98840	.98870	.98899
2.3	.98928	.98956	.98983	.99010	.99036	.99061	.99086	.99111	.99134	.99158
2.4	.99180	.99202	.99224	.99245	.99266	.99286	.99305	.99324	.99343	.99361
2.5	.99379	.99396	.99413	.99430	.99446	.99461	.99477	.99492	.99506	.99520
2.6	.99534	.99547	.99560	.99573	.99585	.99598	.99609	.99621	.99632	.99643
2.7	.99653	.99664	.99674	.99683	.99693	.99702	.99711	.99720	.99728	.99736
2.8	.99744	.99752	.99760	.99767	.99774	.99781	.99788	.99795	.99801	.99807
2.9	.99813	.99819	.99825	.99831	.99836	.99841	.99846	.99851	.99856	.99861
3.0	.99865	.99869	.99874	.99878	.99882	.99886	.99899	.99893	.99896	.99900
3.1	.99903	.99906	.99910	.99913	.99916	.99918	.99921	.99924	.99926	.99929
3.2	.99931	.99934	.99936	.99938	.99940	.99942	.99944	.99946	.99948	.99950
3.3	.99952	.99953	.99955	.99957	.99958	.99960	.99961	.99962	.99964	.99965
3.4	.99966	.99968	.99969	.99970	.99971	.99972	.99973	.99974	.99975	.99976
3.5	.99977	.99978	.99978	.99979	.99980	.99981	.99981	.99982	.99983	.99983
3.6	.99984	.99985	.99985	.99986	.99986	.99987	.99987	.99988	.99988	.99989
3.7	.99989	.99990	.99990	.99990	.99991	.99991	.99992	.99992	.99992	.99992
3.8	.99993	.99993	.99993	.99994	.99994	.99994	.99994	.99995	.99995	.99995
3.9	.99995	.99995	.99996	.99996	.99996	.99996	.99996	.99996	.99997	.99997

HOW TO USE NORMAL DISTRIBUTION

One of the most popular and useful continuous probability distributions is the normal distribution, which is characterized by a bell-shaped curve. The normal distribution is completely specified when values for the mean, μ, and the standard deviation, σ, are known.

The Area Under the Normal Curve

Because the normal distribution is symmetrical, its midpoint (and highest point) is at the mean. Values of the x-axis are then measured in terms of how many standard deviations they are from the mean.

The area under the curve (in a continuous distribution) describes the probability that a variable has a value in the specified interval. For example, Figure A.1 illustrates three commonly used relationships that have been derived from the accompanying standard normal table. The area from point a to point b in the first drawing represents the probability, 68%, that the variable will be within one standard deviation of the mean. In the middle graph, we see that about 95.4% (more precisely 95.45%) of the area lies within plus or minus 2 standard deviations of the mean. The third figure shows that 99.7% lies between $\pm 3\sigma$.

Translated into an application, Figure A.1 implies that if the expected lifetime of a computer chip is $\mu = 100$ days, and if the standard deviation is $\sigma = 15$ days, we can make the following statements:

1. 68% of the population of computer chips studied have lives between 85 and 115 days (namely, $\pm 1\sigma$).
2. 95.4% of the chips have lives between 70 and 130 days ($\pm 2\sigma$).
3. 99.7% of the computer chips have lives in the range from 55 to 145 days ($\pm 3\sigma$).
4. Only 16% of the chips have lives greater than 115 days (from first graph, the area to the right of $+1\sigma$).

Using the Standard Normal Table

To use a table to find normal probability values, we follow two steps.

STEP 1. Convert the normal distribution to what we call a *standard normal distribution.* A standard normal distribution is one that has a mean of 0 and a standard deviation of 1. All normal tables are designed to handle variables with $\mu = 0$ and $\sigma = 1$. Without a standard normal distribution, a different table would be needed for each pair of μ and σ values. We call the new standard variable z. The value of z for any normal distribution is computed from the equation:

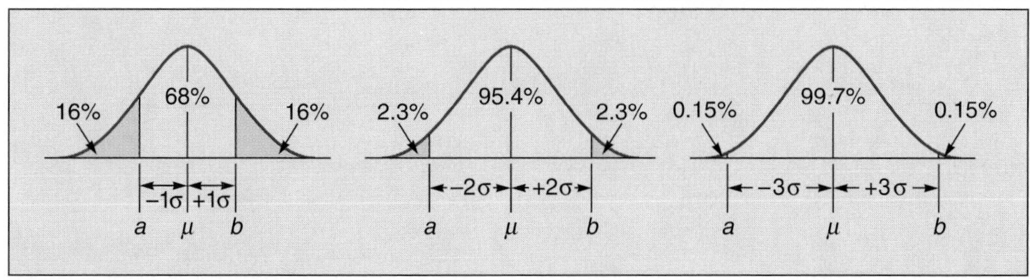

FIGURE A.1

THREE COMMON AREAS UNDER NORMAL CURVES

$$z = \frac{x - \mu}{\sigma}$$

where

x = Value of the variable we want to measure

μ = Mean of the distribution

σ = Standard deviation of the distribution

z = Number of standard deviations from x to the mean, μ

For example, if $\mu = 100$, $\sigma = 15$, and we are interested in finding the probability that the variable x is less than 130, then we want $P(x < 130)$.

$$z = \frac{x - \mu}{\sigma} = \frac{130 - 100}{15} = \frac{30}{15} = 2 \text{ standard deviations}$$

This means that the point x is 2.0 standard deviations to the right of the mean. This is shown in Figure A.2.

STEP 2. Look up the probability from the table of normal curve areas. It is set up to provide the area under the curve to the left of any specified value of z.

Let us see how the table in this appendix can be used. The column on the left lists values of z, with the second decimal place of z appearing in the top row. For example, for a value of $z = 2.00$ as just computed, find 2.0 in the left-hand column and .00 in the top row. In the body of the table, we find that the area sought is .97725, or 97.7%. Thus,

$$P(x < 130) = P(z < 2.00) = 97.7\%$$

This suggests that if the mean lifetime of a computer chip is 100 days with a standard deviation of 15 days, the probability that the life of a randomly selected chip is less than 130 is 97.7%. By referring back to Figure A.1, we see that this probability could also have been derived from the middle graph. (Note that 1.0 − .977 = .023 = 2.3%, which is the area in the right-hand tail of the curve.)

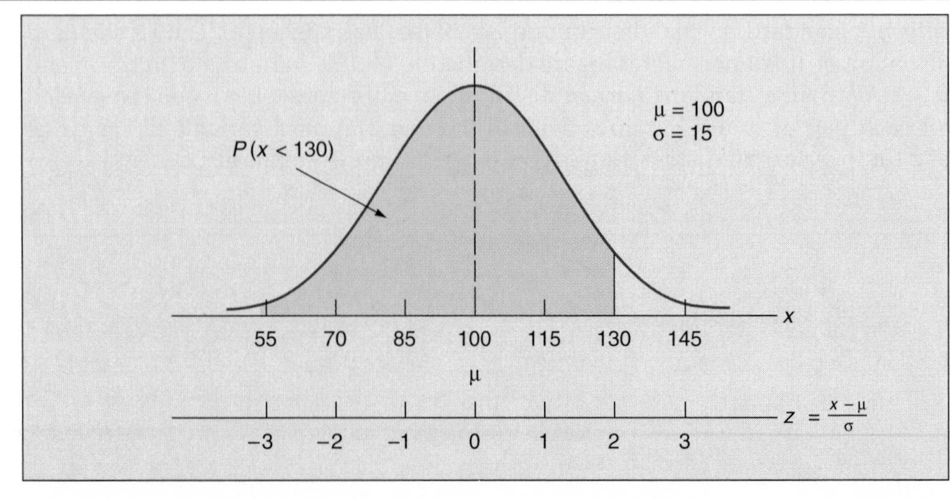

FIGURE A.2

Normal Distribution Showing the Relationship Between z Values and x Values

APPENDIX B: USING POM FOR WINDOWS

INTRODUCTION

Welcome to POM for Windows—the most user-friendly software available for the field of production and operations management (POM). POM for Windows is a package which has been designed to help you learn and understand operations management. The software can be used to either solve problems or to check answers which you have derived by hand. We encourage you to read this appendix while sitting at a personal computer.

The graphical user interface for POM for Windows is a standard Windows interface. Anyone familiar with a standard spreadsheet or word processor in Windows will easily be able to use POM for Windows. All modules have help screens which can be accessed at any time. In addition, the help screens can be displayed at all times (online help).

HARDWARE AND SOFTWARE REQUIREMENTS

Computer

POM for Windows will work on any IBM-PC compatible that is 386 or higher with at least 3 MB RAM and operating Windows 3.1 or better.

Disk Drives

POM for Windows is provided on a single 3.5″ diskette. The 3.5″ diskette version requires a 1.44-MB disk drive (as all are except on very old machines).

Monitor

The software has no special monitor requirements. Different colors or shades are used to portray different items. All messages, output, data, and so on will show up on any monitor, but the display is crispest on a color monitor. Regardless of the type of monitor you are using, POM for Windows has an option that allows you to customize colors or shades in the display to your liking.

Printer

A printer is not required to run POM for Windows, but, of course, if you want a hard copy (printout) then it is necessary to have a printer attached. No special features, characters, or printer are required.

INSTALLING POM FOR WINDOWS

We assume below that the hard drive is named C: and that the 3.5″ disk drive is named A:. POM for Windows installs in the manner that most programs designed for Windows install. That process is:

1. Insert the POM for Windows diskette in drive A:
2. From the Windows Program Manager select FILE, RUN.
3. In the box type **A:SETUP**
4. Follow the setup instructions on the screen.

Default values have been assigned in the setup program, but you may change them if you like. The default values are that the program will be installed to a directory on the C: drive named C:\pomwin and that the program group will be named POM for Windows.

Towards the end of the installation process the installation program will ask you if you want to register. POM for Windows requires some general information in order to operate. The first screen at registration is a software licensing agreement. In the second registration screen you should enter the name under which the Windows version is registered on the computer you are using. This should be your name, which is required. It cannot be left blank. You should also customize the software by selecting Render/Heizer 2nd edition. When you are finished press [OK].

After the registration is complete you will have a program group added to your program manager. The group will be called POM for Windows. To use POM for Windows, double click on the POM for Windows program icon. The screen shown in Program B.1 should appear. Please note that the option named 'Convert AB:POM files' is for instructors who have previously used AB:POM (for DOS) and need to convert files that were stored under this system to be compatible with POM for Windows.

The next screen that appears is the basic screen for the software and contains the assorted components that are part of most of the screens. This screen is displayed in Program B.2. The top of the screen is the standard Windows title bar

PROGRAM B.1

OPENING POM FOR WINDOWS SCREEN

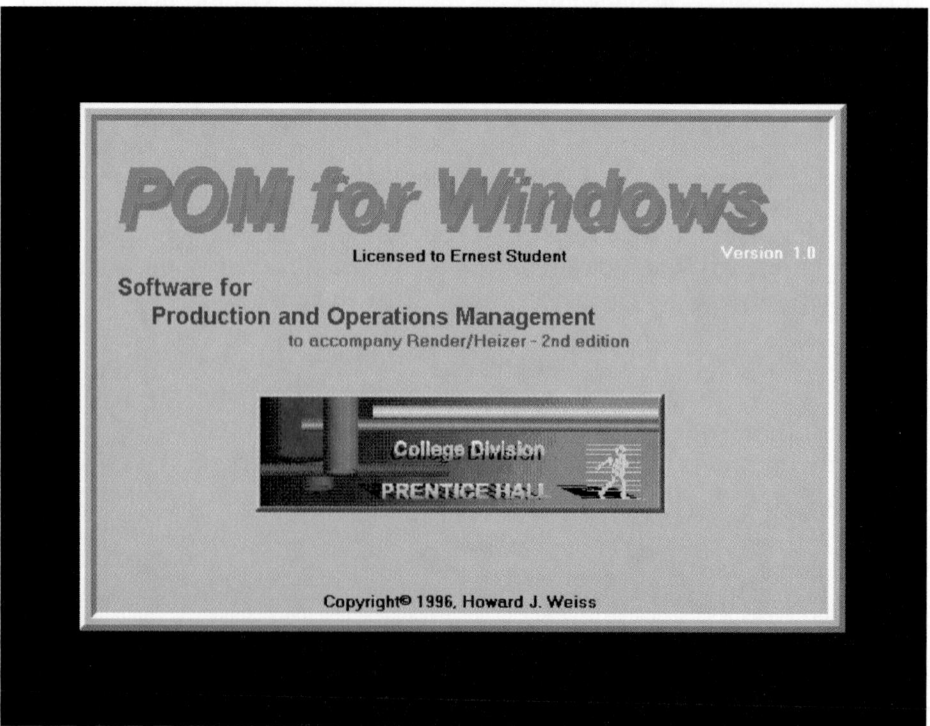

for the window. Below the title bar is a Windows menu bar. The menu bar is very standard and should be easy to use. The details of the seven menu options of FILE, EDIT, VIEW, MODULE, TABLES, WINDOW, and HELP will be explained in this appendix. At the beginning of the program the only enabled menu options are FILE (to open a previously saved file or to exit the program), MODULE (to select the module), and HELP. The other options will become enabled as a module is chosen or as a problem is started.

Below the menu is a toolbar (also called a button bar or ribbon). This button bar contains standard shortcuts for several of the menu commands. If you move the mouse over the button for about two seconds, an explanation of the button will appear on the screen if the button is active.

The bar below the toolbar may be the most important one in the software. It is a command button bar and it contains two (sometimes three) buttons. The button on the left is named **[PRINT SCREEN]** and it is there to emulate the old print screen function in DOS. The other command button is the **[SOLVE]** button. This is what you press after you have entered the data when you are ready to solve the problem.

The next bar is the instruction bar. There is always an instruction here trying to help you to figure out what to do or what to enter. Currently the instruction indicates to select a module or open a file. When data is to be entered into the data table, this instruction will explain what type of data (integer, real, positive, and so on) is to be entered.

In Program B.2 we also show the module list that appears after clicking on MODULE. In some cases after selecting one of these modules a second menu of submodules will appear. The module list has 21 options consisting of 20 POM modules and an EXIT option.

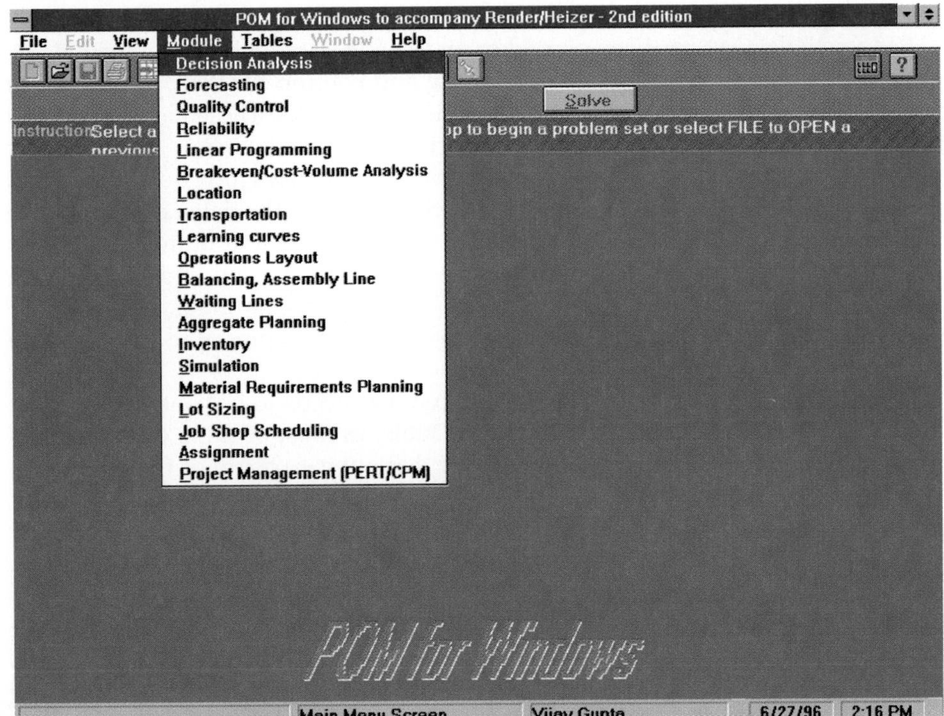

Program B.2

Module List

CREATING A NEW PROBLEM

At this point the first option that will be chosen is FILE followed by either NEW or OPEN to create a new data set or to load a previously saved data set. This is an option which will be chosen very often.

The top line of the creation screen contains a text box in which the title of the problem can be entered. For many modules it is necessary to enter the number of rows in the problem. Rows will have different names depending on the modules. For example, in linear programming rows are constraints while in forecasting rows are past periods. The number of rows can be chosen with either the scroll bar or the text box.

POM for Windows has the capability to allow different options for the default row names. Select one of the radio buttons in order to indicate which style of default naming should be used. In most modules the row names are not used for computations, but you should be careful because in some modules (most notably project management) the names might relate to precedences.

Many modules require the number of columns. This is given in the same way as the number of rows. POM for Windows does not give you a choice of default values for column names. All row and column names can be changed in the data table.

Some modules will have an extra option box, such as for choosing minimize or maximize, or selecting whether distances are symmetric or not. Select one of these options. In most cases this option can be changed later on the data screen.

When you are satisfied with your choices, click on the **[OK]** button or press the **[enter/return]** key. At this point a blank data screen will appear. Screens will differ module by module.

ENTERING AND EDITING DATA

return/enter
This key moves from cell to cell in the order from left to right from top to bottom skipping the first column (which usually contains names). Therefore, when entering a table of data, if you start at the upper left and work your way to the lower right row by row, this key is exceptionally useful!

Formatting
Formatting is handled automatically by the program. For example, in most cases the number 1000 will automatically be formatted as 1,000. Do NOT type the comma. The program will prevent you from doing so!

After a new data set has been created or an existing data set has been loaded, the data can be edited. Every entry is in a row and column position. You navigate through the spreadsheet using the cursor movement keys. These keys function in a regular way with one exception—the **[return/enter]** key.

The instruction bar on the screen will contain a brief instruction describing what is to be done. There are essentially three types of cells in the data table. One type is a regular data cell into which you enter either a name or a number. A second type is a cell which can not be changed. A third type is a cell which contains a drop-down box. For example, the signs in a linear programming constraint are chosen from this type of box. To see all of the options, press the box with the arrow.

There is one more aspect to the data screen that needs to be considered. Some modules need extra data above that in the table. In most of these cases the data is contained in text/scrollbar combinations that appear on top of the data table.

SOLUTION DISPLAYS

At this point you can press the **[SOLVE]** button in order to begin the solution process. A new screen will appear.

An important thing to notice is that there is more solution information available. This can be seen by the icons given at the bottom of the screen. Double click on these to view the information. Alternatively, notice that the WINDOW option in the main menu is now enabled. It is always enabled at solution time. Even if the icons are covered by a window, the WINDOW option will always allow you to view the other solution windows.

Now that we have examined how to create and solve a problem, we explain all of the MENU options that are available.

FILE

File contains the usual options that one finds in most Windows programs, as seen in Program B.3. These options are now described.

New

As demonstrated before, this is chosen to begin a new problem or file.

Open

This is used to open/load a previously saved file. File selection is the standard Windows common dialogue type. The extension for files in the POM for Windows system is given by the first three letters of the module name. For example, all linear programming files have the extension *.lin. When you go to the open dialogue, the default value is for the program to look for files of the type in this module. This can be changed at the bottom left where it says "Click for Module list."

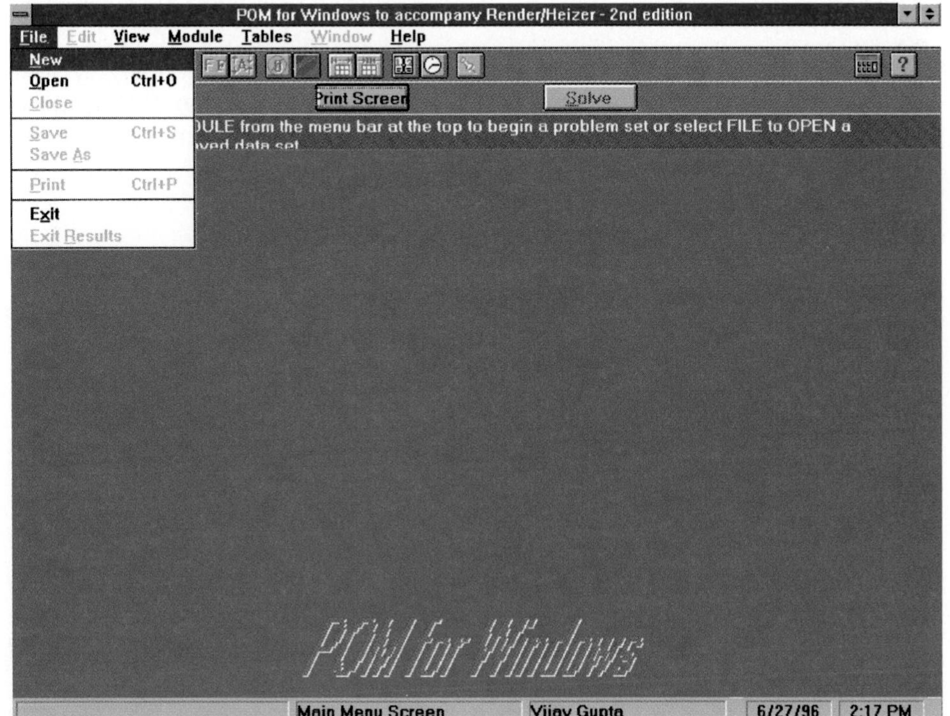

PROGRAM B.3

FILE OPTION

The names which are legal are standard DOS file names *without* extensions. That is, you may type in up to eight characters but the "." (period) is illegal. Case (upper or lower) does not matter. In addition to the file name you may preface the name with a drive letter (with its colon) or path designation. Examples of *legal* file names are

sample
test
b:sample
problem1
c:\bc7\test

You may type them in as uppercase, lowercase or mixed. Examples of *illegal* file names are

sample.lp—The extension must match the first three letters of a module name.
abcdefghij—The name is too long; the program will issue an error message.
lpt1—This is a reserved DOS word.

In the event that there is a problem with the drive or file, then an error message will appear to that effect.

It is not possible, by the way, to delete a file using POM for Windows. Use the Windows file manager to do so.

Save

Save will replace the file without asking you if you care about overwriting the previous version of this file. If you try to save and have not previously named the file, then you will be asked to name this file.

Save As

Save As will prompt you for a file name before saving. This option is very similar to the option to load a data file. When you choose this option, the Windows Common Dialogue Box for Files will appear. It is essentially identical to the one previously shown.

Print

Print will display a Print Menu screen. There are several options on this screen.

Information to Print—The upper left box depends on whether Print was called from the data screen or from the solution screen.
Page Header Information
Print Timing
Answers and Spacing
Print To and Print As
Select Printer

The last option on the FILE menu is Exit. This will exit the program if you are on the data screen or exit the solution screen and return to the data screen if you are on the solution screen. This can also be achieved by pressing the **[EDIT DATA]** command button on the solution screen.

Edit

The commands under Edit have three purposes. The first four commands are used to insert or delete rows or columns. The next command is used to copy an entry from one cell to all cells below it in the column. This is not often useful, but when it is useful, it saves a great deal of work. The last two entries can be used to copy the data table to other Windows programs.

View

View has several options that enable you to customize the appearance of the screen. The toolbar can be displayed or not. The instruction bar can be displayed at its default location above the data, or below the data, or as a floating window or not at all. The status bar can be displayed or not, and if it is, the time and date can be displayed or not.

There is also an area available to annotate problems. If you want to write a note to yourself about the problem, select annotation. The note will be saved with the file if you save the file. A calculator is available for simple calculations including a square root. Colors can be set to monochrome (black and white) or from this state to their original colors.

Module

This was discussed earlier in this appendix.

Tables

Tables also has several options for the display. The colors for the entire screen can be set, and the font type and size for the table can be set. Zeros can be set to display as blanks rather than zeros. The problem title (which appears in the data table and was created at the creation screen) can be changed. The table can be squeezed or expanded. That is, the column widths can be decreased or increased. The input can be checked or not.

Window

This menu option is enabled only at the solution screen.

Help

The first help option, module help, will give a small description of the module, the data required for input, the output results, and the options available in the module. It is worthwhile to look at this screen at least one time in order to be certain that there are no unsuspected differences between your assumptions and the assumptions of the program. If there is a warning needed regarding the option, it will appear on the help screen as well as in the appropriate chapter of this book.

Appendix C: Answers to Self-Tests

Chapter 1

1. c
2. d
3. d
4. b
5. b
6. c
7. a
8. c
9. a
10. d
11. a
12. c
13. d
14. d

15. Production is *creation of goods and services.*
16. The three fundamental functions of any business are *marketing, accounting, and production/operations.*
17. Operations management directs and controls the *transformation process, creating goods and services.*

Chapter 2

1. a
2. d
3. a
4. d
5. d
6. c
7. d
8. a
9. b
10. c
11. d

12. The purpose or rationale for an organization's existence is its *mission.*
13. A plan designed to achieve a mission is a *strategy.*
14. The ten decisions of OM are *quality, goods and service design, process selection, location selection, layout design, people and work systems, supply-chain management, inventory, scheduling, maintenance.*

Chapter 2 Supplement

1. d
2. c
3. d
4. b
5. b
6. b
7. b
8. a
9. d
10. b
11. b
12. a
13. a
14. a
15. a

16. Independent variable is said to cause variations in the dependent variable.
17. (a) moving average, (b) exponential smoothing, (c) trend projection, (d) linear regression
18. trend, seasonality, cycles, random variation
19. **a.** jury of executive opinion
b. sales force composite
c. Delphi method
d. consumer market survey
e. naive approach
20. Alert the user of a forecasting tool to periods in which the forecast was significantly in error.
21. Exponential smoothing is a weighted moving average model where all previous values are weighted with a set of weights that decline exponentially.

Chapter 3

1. e
2. d
3. a
4. f
5. d
6. c
7. d
8. e

9. The six tools of TQM are *quality function deployment's house of quality, Taguchi techniques, Pareto charts, process charts, cause-and-effect diagrams,* and *statistical process control.*
10. In addition to the product per se, quality has major implications for a company. Among these additional implications are *company reputation, cost and market share, product liability,* and *international balance of payments.*
11. The work of Genichi Taguchi is primarily concerned with the development of *robust quality.*
12. Quality cannot be *inspected* into a product.
13. The five basic concepts of TQM are *continuous improvement, employee empowerment, benchmarking, just-in-time,* and *knowledge of TQM tools.*
14. ISO 14000 is an EC standard to address environmental procedures.

Chapter 3 Supplement

1. d
2. b
3. e
4. a
5. a
6. a
7. b
8. e

9. The *producer's* risk is the probability that a lot will be rejected despite the quality level exceeding or meeting the *acceptable quality level, AQL.*
10. If a 95.5% level of confidence is desired, the $\bar{x}$ chart limits will be set at plus or minus *two standard deviations.*
11. The two techniques discussed to find and resolve assignable variations in process control are the *$\bar{x}$ chart* and the *R chart.*
12. *Attribute* inspection is used to determine good parts from defectives, while *variable* inspection actually measures the values of the dimensions of inspected parts.

Chapter 4

1. d
2. d
3. a
4. e
5. a
6. c

7. b
8. b
9. c
10. d
11. c

12. A product-by-value analysis report is *a list of products in descending order of their individual dollar contribution to the firm.*
13. Products must be continually developed because *they all have a finite life.*
14. Products are documented by *engineering drawings and bills-of-material or written specifications.*

Chapter 5

1. b
2. c
3. d
4. b
5. a
6. e
7. e
8. b
9. e
10. c
11. a
12. b
13. e

Chapter 6

1. a
2. c
3. b
4. d
5. a
6. **a.** factor rating method
b. locational breakeven method
c. center of gravity method
d. the transportation method
7. Maximize the benefit of location to the firm.
8. **a.** Determine fixed and variable cost for each location.
b. Plot the costs for each location, with costs on the vertical axis of the graph and annual volume on the horizontal axis.
c. Select the location that has the lowest total cost for the expected production volume.
9. a
10. d
11. b

Chapter 7

1. d
2. c
3. e
4. d
5. a
6. c
7. b
8. b
9. c
10. b
11. c

Chapter 8

1. b
2. a
3. a
4. b
5. a
6. b
7. a
8. b
9. d
10. a
11. b
12. e
13. c
14. b
15. **a.** fixed-position layout: for large bulky products such as ships and buildings
b. process layout: for low-volume, high-variety production
c. product-oriented layout: for high-volume, low-variety
d. retail-service layout: allocates shelf space and responds to customer behavior
e. warehouse layout: addresses tradeoffs between space and material handling
16. **a.** work cells
b. focused work center
c. focused factory
17. **a.** the identification of a large family of like products
b. a stable demand forecast
c. adequate volume
18. **a.** Volume is adequate for high equipment utilization.
b. Product demand is stable enough to justify high investment in specialized equipment.
c. The product is standardized or approaching a phase of its life cycle that justifies investment in specialized equipment.
d. Supplies of raw material and components are adequate and of uniform quality to ensure that they will work with the specialized equipment.

Chapter 9

1. d
2. d
3. c
4. e
5. d
6. b
7. e
8. a
9. a
10. c
11. b
12. d
13. b
14. b

Chapter 10

1. d
2. a
3. e
4. a
5. c
6. c
7. c
8. e
9. b
10. d
11. d
12. The five requirements for an effective dependent inventory model (MRP) are (a) *master production schedule,* (b) *specifications bill or bill of material,* (c) *inventory availability,* (d) *purchase orders outstanding,* (e) *lead times.*

13. A net material-requirements plan differs from a gross requirements plan because it includes (a) *on-hand inventory,* (b) *net requirements,* (c) *planned order receipts,* and (d) *planned order release for each item.*
14. c
15. If it is economical, the best lot-sizing technique to be used for MRP *is lot-for-lot.*

Chapter 11

1. c
2. e
3. e
4. e
5. e
6. c
7. d
8. b
9. storing, queues, inspection, adjusting, delays, and defects
10. 100%
11. a
12. b
13. d

Chapter 11 Supplement

1. d
2. a
3. b
4. c
5. c
6. e
7. b
8. b
9. d
10. c
11. a
12. The objective of the procurement function is *to help in identifying the products and services that can best be obtained externally and to develop, evaluate, and determine the best supplier, price, and delivery for those products or services.*
13. Five purchasing strategies are *many suppliers, few suppliers, vertical integration, keiretsu networks, virtual companies.*
14. Five techniques for improving procurement efficiency are *blanket orders, invoiceless purchasing, electronic ordering and fund transfer, stockless purchasing, and standardization.*

Chapter 12

1. b
2. a
3. b
4. b
5. a
6. b
7. b
8. b
9. a
10. c
11. a
12. d
13. **a.** changing inventory levels
b. varying workforce size by hiring and firing
c. varying production rate through overtime or idle time
d. subcontracting
e. influencing demand
f. backordering during high demand periods
g. counter-seasonal product mixing

Chapter 13

1. e
2. c
3. a
4. a
5. d
6. b
7. c
8. b
9. Jobs of long duration may be continuously pushed back in priority in favor of short-duration jobs.
10. **a.** FCFS: first come, first served
b. EDD: earliest due date
c. SPT: shortest processing time
d. LPT: longest processing time
e. CR: critical ratio
11. c
12. a
13. b

Chapter 14

1. d
2. d
3. d
4. a
5. c
6. a
7. e
8. a
9. b
10. d
11. a
12. a
13. b
14. d
15. b

Chapter 14 Supplement

1. b
2. a
3. d
4. b
5. c
6. d
7. e

APPENDIX D: ANSWERS TO EVEN-NUMBERED PROBLEMS

Chapter 1

2. a. 20 ornaments per hour
b. 26.7 ornaments per hour
c. 33.5%

4. A correlation exists between lower productivity and increased portions of the economy devoted to services. As the data in the problem shows, the more an economy is devoted to services the lower the increases in productivity.

6. The responses will vary depending upon the position in the business cycle. However, it is unlikely that the U.S. productivity (for manufacturing and services combined) will exceed 2% per year until structural changes are made to foster investment and education and/or technological breakthroughs take place. The U.S. service sector's increase in productivity is too low, and the sector is just too large for productivity to exceed 2% for very long.

Chapter 2

2. Answers to this question depend upon the organization considered. However, some general ideas for **a** and **b** follow.

a. For a producer with high energy costs, major oil prices change the cost structure, result in higher selling prices, and, if the company is energy inefficient compared to other producers, result in a change in competitive position.
b. More restrictive quality of water and air legislation increases the cost of production, and may, in some cases, prohibit the use of specific technologies. The high cost of process modification to meet more rigid standards has resulted in the closing of numerous plants including paper mills and steel mills.

4. The missions, or some variation, depending upon source and the changing dynamics of the various environments should look somewhat like the following:

AT&T: *Provide quality long-distance voice and data communication services worldwide. Provide the accompanying PBX and computer switching necessary to support that service.*

However, the 1996 break-up into three companies does violence to this mission statement.

Chapter 2 Supplement

2. 18.67, 16.67, 14, 14.33, 15.33, 17, 18.33, 19.33, 20.33, 21.33

4. a. 337; **b.** 380; **c.** 423

6. 2 year: 5, 5, 4.5, 7.5, 9.0, 7.5, 8.0, 10.5, 13.0
4 year: 4.75, 6.25, 6.75, 7.50, 8.50, 9.00, 10.50

8. Wtd. M.A. MAD = 2,312
Exp. Smooth MAD = 2,581

10. MAD ($\alpha = .3$) = 74.6
MAD ($\alpha = .6$) = 51.8
MAD ($\alpha = .9$) = 38.1 (best)

12. $y = 522 + 33.6x = 623$ if xs are coded as $-2, -1, 0, +1, +2$. Or $y = 421 + 33.6x$ if xs are coded as 1, 2, 3, 4, 5.

14. a. 43.4, 47.4, 50.2, 53.7, 56.3 for $\alpha = .6$, 44.6, 49.5, 51.8, 55.6, 57.8 for $\alpha = .9$
b. 49, 52.7, 55.3
c. 45.8, 49.0, 52.2, 55.4, 58.6, 61.8
d. Trend with MAD = 0.6

16. 5, 5.4, 6.12, 5.90, 6.52, 7.82

18. $y = 5.26 + 1.11x$
Period 7 demand = 13.03

20. a. Moving average forecast for February is 13.6667.
b. Weighted moving average forecast for February is 13.16.
c. MAD for Avg is 2.2.
MAD for Weighted Avg is 2.7.
d. seasonality, causal variables such as advertising budget

22. a. $\hat{y} = 1 + 1x$; $r = .45$
b. $S_{yx} = 3.65$

24. $y = 0.972 + 0.0035x$ using a hand calculator, or $y = 1.03 + .0034x$ by computer; $r^2 = 0.479$; $x = 350$; $y = 2.197$; $x = 800$; $y = 3.77$

26. 131.2 → 72.7 patients; 90.6 → 50.6 patients

28. fall = 270; winter = 390; spring = 189; summer = 351

30. a. 1785; **b.** 1560

32. a. 17.00; 17.80; 18.04; 19.03; 18.83; 18.26; 18.61; 18.49; 19.19; 19.35; 18.48
b. 2.60
c. No, tracking signal exceeds 5 sigma at week 10.

34. a. and **b.**

WEEK	α = 0.1 FORECAST	α = 0.6 FORECAST
1	50	50
2	50	50
3	48.5	41.0
4	46.2	31.4
5	45.5	36.6
6	45.5	41.6
7	44.4	37.6
8	42.0	27.1
9	40.8	28.8
10	40.2	32.5
11	38.2	25.0
12	35.9	19.0
13	36.3	31.6
14	38.2	45.6
15	37.8	39.3
16	36.6	30.7
17	38.4	45.3
18	40.1	51.1
19	40.1	44.4
20	39.5	38.8
21	41.6	51.5
22	44.9	65.6
23	45.4	56.2
24	44.9	46.5
25	46.9	57.6

c. On the basis of forecast and standard error of estimate, $\alpha = .6$ is better. But other α's should be tried.

36. 0.709, 1.037, 1.553, 0.700

Chapter 3

2. Individual answer.

4. a. Changing an automobile tire

8′ ↓ move to trunk
○ open trunk
○ loosen tire and jack
○ remove tire and jack
8′ ↓ move the tire and jack to wheel
○ position jack
□ inspect
○ loosen wheel lugs
○ jack-up car
○ remove wheel lugs
○ remove wheel
○ position good wheel
○ tighten lugs
○ lower car
○ finish tightening lugs
□ inspect
8′ ↓ move tire and jack to trunk
○ position tire and jack
○ close trunk
8′ ↓ move to driver's seat

b. and **c.** Follow a similar style

6. Cause-and-effect diagram (also known as a fish-bone chart or an Ishikawa diagram) for Mismatch of Nut and Bolt.

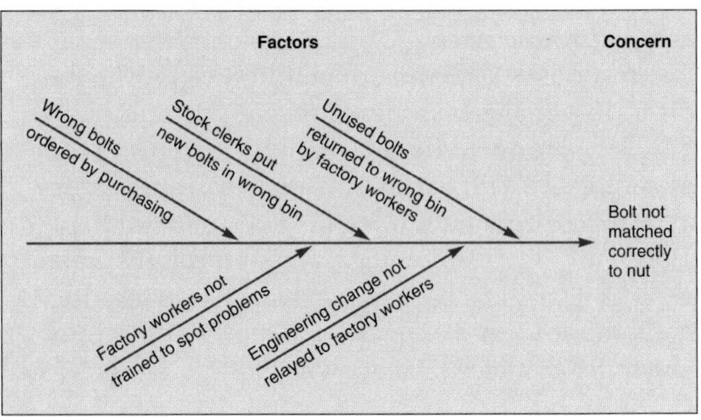

Chapter 3 Supplement

2. $UCL_{\bar{x}} = 52.308$
$LCL_{\bar{x}} = 47.692$
$UCL_R = 8.456$
$LCL_R = 0.0$

4. $UCL_{\bar{x}} = 46.966$
$LCL_{\bar{x}} = 45.034$
$UCL_R = 4.008$
$LCL_R = 0$

6. $UCL_{\bar{x}} = 17.187$
$LCL_{\bar{x}} = 16.814$
$UCL_R = .932$
$LCL_R = .068$

8. $UCL_{\bar{x}} = 3.728$
$LCL_{\bar{x}} = 2.236$
$UCL_R = 2.336$
$LCL_R = 0.0$
The process is in control.

10. $UCL_p = .0596$
$LCL_p = .0104$

12. $UCL_p = .0311$ to $.1636$
$LCL_p = 0.0$ to $.0364$

14. $UCL_{\bar{x}} = 64.6$
$LCL_{\bar{x}} = 62.4$
$UCL_R = 3.41$
$LCL_R = 0$

16. $UCL_p = .0581$
$LCL_p = 0$
18. $UCL_c = 33.4$
$LCL_c = 7$

Chapter 4

2. Assembly chart for ballpoint pen.

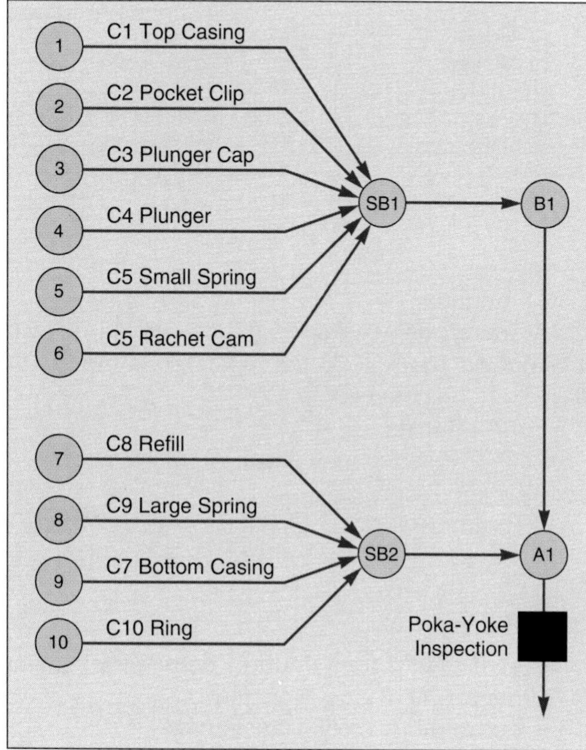

4. (Chart at top of next column.)
6. *Possible strategies:*

Portable computers (growth phase):
Increase capacity and improve balance of production system.
Attempt to make production facilities more efficient.

Lap top computer (introductory phase)
Increase R&D to better define required product characteristics.
Modify and improve production process.
Develop supplier and distribution systems.

Hand calculator (decline phase):
Concentrate on production and distribution cost reduction.

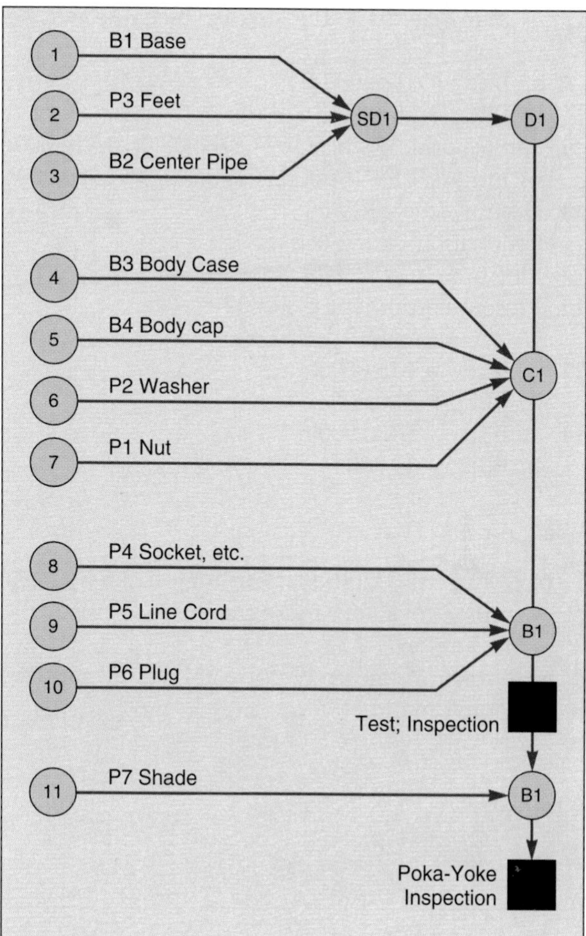

Attempt to develop improved product.
Attempt to develop supplementary product.
Unless product is of special importance to overall competitive strategy, consider terminating production.

8. $R_s = .5814$
10. $R_s = .8379$
12. Reliability increases from .84 to .98.
14. 0.95

Chapter 5

2. In 1997 River Road Medical Clinic has eight machines at 2,500. In 2003 they need capacity of 20,410.

a. Therefore, if they add 5,000 to capacity in 1997, total capacity in 2003 will be 25,000 lenses, more than adequate.

b. If they buy the standard machine in 1997, their capacity in 2003 will be 22,500 lenses; still more than adequate; the smaller machine will suffice.

4. a. $BEP_\$ = \$125{,}000$
b. $BEP_\$ = \$140{,}000$

6. a. Proposal A is best; a = \$18,000; b = \$15,000
b. Proposal B is best; a = \$70,000; b = \$80,000

8. Design = 81,806
Fabrication = 152,646
Finishing = 62,899

10. Present equipment = \$1,000
New equipment = \$2,500

12. a. $BEP_\$ = \$15{,}000$
b. $BEP_u = 300{,}000$

14. a. $BEP_\$ = \$900{,}000$
b. $BEP_u = 30{,}000$

Chapter 6

2. b. Denver, 0–3570 units; Burlington, 3,571–24,999 units; Cleveland, more than 25,000 units.
c. Burlington

4. Suburb B, rating = 197 (or 6.35) but all are close

6. Shopping mall best

8. Hyde Park with 54.5 points

Chapter 7

2.

Time	Operator	Time	Machine	Time
	Prepare Mill			
1	Load Mill	1	Idle	1
2		2		2
3	Idle	3	Mill Operating	3
4		4	(Cutting Material)	4
5	Unload Mill	5	Idle	5
6		6		6

4. The first ten steps are shown in the chart. The remaining ten steps are similar. (Chart at top of next column.)

OPERATIONS CHART	SUMMARY						
PROCESS: CHANGE ERASER	SYMBOL	PRESENT				DIFF.	
ANALYST: ______		LH	RH	LH	RH	LH	RH
DATE: ______	O OPERATIONS	1	8				
SHEET: 1 of 2	⇨ TRANSPORTS	3	8				
METHOD: PRESENT PROPOSED	□ INSPECTIONS	1					
REMARKS:	D DELAYS	15	4				
	▽ STORAGE						
	TOTALS	20	20				

LEFT HAND	DIST.	SYMBOL	SYMBOL	DIST.	RIGHT HAND
1 Reach for pencil		⇨	D		Idle
2 Grasp pencil		O	D		Idle
3 Move to work area		⇨	⇨		Move to pencil top
4 Hold pencil		D	O		Grasp pencil top
5 Hold pencil		D	O		Remove pencil top
6 Hold pencil		D	⇨		Set top aside
7 Hold pencil		D	⇨		Reach for old eraser
8 Hold pencil		D	O		Grasp old eraser
9 Hold pencil		D	O		Remove old eraser
10 Hold pencil		D	⇨		Set aside old eraser

6. Individual solution

8. Sample size of 166 is required.

10. Six observations are required.

12. Normal time = 5.565 minutes
Allowance = 10%
Standard time = 6.183

14. 29.8 minutes

16. 5.4 or 6.67, depending upon observation deleted

18. Standard time: 82.35 seconds; 106 samples for "place bag" on conveyor

20. a. 47.6 minutes
b. 60 observations are required for element 4

22. 336

24. .1092 minutes or 6.55 seconds

Chapter 8

2. Yes, with POM for Windows patient movement = 4,500 feet.

4. Layout number 1, 600 = distance
Layout number 2, 602 = distance

6. Layout number 4, 609 = distance

8. a. throughput of 3.75 people per hour possible
b. medical exam—16 minutes
c. at least 5 per hour now

10. Cycle time = 9.6 minutes; eight workstations with 63.8% efficiency is possible.

12. Station 1, tasks 1, 3; station 2, task 5; station 3, tasks 2, 4; station 4, tasks 6, 8; station 5, tasks 7, 9; efficiency = 78%.

14. Cycle time = .5 minute per bottle; Possible assignments with four workstations yields efficiency = 90%.

16. Minimum (theoretical) = four stations; efficiency = 80% with five stations. Several assignments with five are possible.

18. There are three alternatives each with an efficiency = 86.67%.

Chapter 9

2. A items are G2 and F3; B items are A2, C7, and D1; All others are C.

4. 7,000 units

6. **a.** 78
  b. 200
  c. $3,873
  d. 64
  e. 3.91 days

8. Quantity discount: Cost = $41,436.25

10. Q = 50, C = $1,500; Q = 40, C = $1,230; Q = 50, C = $1,200; Q = 60, C = $1,220; Q = 100, C = $1,500

12. **a.** $1,220
  b. $1,200 with Q = 60
  c. 24 units

14. 1,217 units

16. 51 units; $1,901.22

18. $752.63 (at 100 ordered each time). EOQ = 34 units

20. Safety stock = 30 units

22. Safety stock = 100 units: ROP = 300 units

Chapter 10

2.

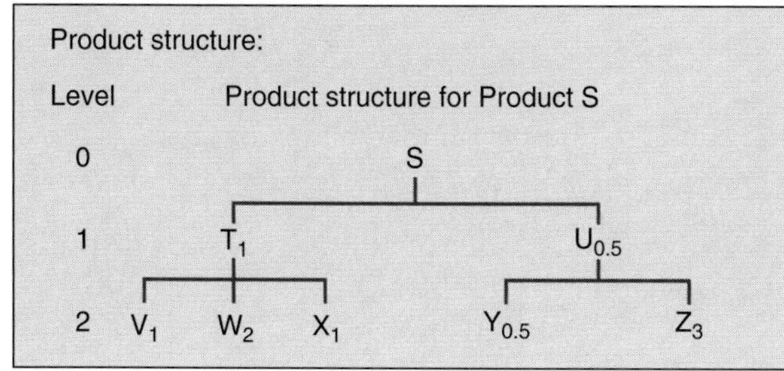

ITEM		WEEK 1	2	3	4	5	6	7	8	LEAD TIME (weeks)
S	Req date							100		
	Ord rel					100				2
T	Req date					100				
	Ord rel				100					1
U	Req date					50				
	Ord rel			50						2
V	Req date				100					
	Ord rel		100							2
W	Req date				200					
	Ord rel	200								3
X	Req date				100					
	Ord rel			100						1
Y	Req date			25						
	Ord rel	25								2
Z	Req date			150						
	Ord rel		150							1

4. Modified product structure:
If an item, in this case C, is used at several points within the product, it should be shown in the product structure at its *lowest* level.

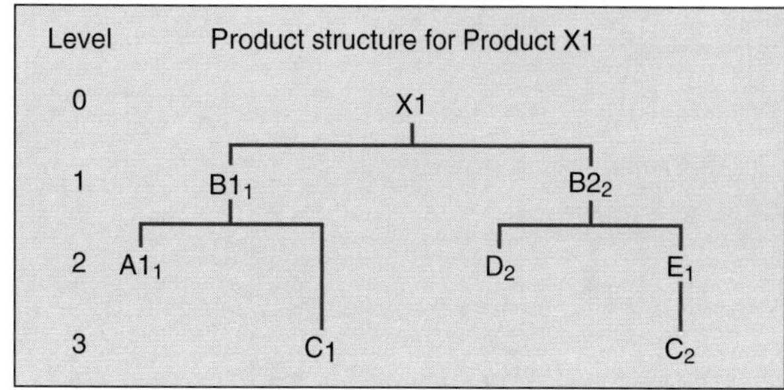

(a) Gross Material Requirements Plan. Note: Elements have been listed in the gross material requirements plan in the order of level, and within a level, from left to right as viewed in the product structure.

		WEEK 1	2	3	4	5	6	7	8	9	10	11	12
X_1	Req date								50		20		100
	Ord rel							50		20		100	
B_1	Req date							50		20		100	
	Ord rel					50		20		100			
B_2	Req date							100		40		200	
	Ord rel					100		40		200			
A_1	Req date					50		20		100			
	Ord rel				50		20		100				

	WEEK											
	1	2	3	4	5	6	7	8	9	10	11	12
D Req date					200		80		400			
Ord rel				200		160		400				
E Req date					100		40		200			
Ord rel				100		40		200				
C Req date				200	50	80	20	500				
Ord rel	200	50	80	20	500							

(b) Net material-requirements (planned order release) plan:

	WEEK											
	1	2	3	4	5	6	7	8	9	10	11	12
X_1 Req date										20		100
Ord rel									20		100	
B_1 Req date											100	
Ord rel									100			
B_2 Req date									20		200	
Ord rel							20		200			
A_1 Req date									95			
Ord rel								95				
D Req date							40		400			
Ord rel						40		400				
E Req date							20		200			
Ord rel						20		200				
C Req date						30		400	100			
Ord rel			30		400	100						

6. Net material requirements plan:

	WEEK											
	1	2	3	4	5	6	7	8	9	10	11	12
A Gr req								100		50		150
On hand								0		0		0
Net req								100		50		150
Ord								100		50		150
Ord rel							100		50		150	
H Gr req									100		50	
On hand									0		0	
Net req									100		50	
Ord									100		50	
Ord rel								100		50		

	WEEK											
	1	2	3	4	5	6	7	8	9	10	11	12
B Gr req							100		50		150	
On hand							100		0		0	
Net req							0		50		150	
Ord							0		50		150	
Ord rel							50		150			
C Gr req							100	100	50	50	150	
On hand							50	0	0	0	0	
Net req							50	100	50	50	150	
Ord							50	100	50	50	150	
Ord rel					50	100	50	50	150			
J Gr req								100		50		
On hand								100		0		
Net req								0		50		
Ord								0		50		
Ord rel								50				
K Gr req								100		50		
On hand								100		0		
Net req								0		50		
Ord rcpt								0		50		
Ord rel								50				
D Gr req							50		150			
On hand							50		0			
Net req							0		150			
Ord							0		150			
Ord rel								150				

E, F, and G follow a similar pattern.

8. a. Solution with lead time = 1 week:
Economic order quantity: = 57.4 or 57 units
Theoretical total cost: = $1,723.42
Actual total cost: = $2,362.50

b. Solution with lead time = 0:
Economic order quantity: = 57.4 or 57 units
Theoretical total cost: = $1,723.42
Actual total cost: = $1,810.00

10. a. Economic order quantity = 104.9 or 105 units
Theoretical cost: = $262.20
Actual cost: = $306.25

b. Lot for lot:
Total cost: = $400.00

12. Master production schedule:

	WEEK										
	0	1	2	3	4	5	6	7	8	9	10
P Gr req		0	0	30	40	10	70	40	10	30	60

Gross material requirements plan:

		WEEK										
		0	*1*	*2*	*3*	*4*	*5*	*6*	*7*	*8*	*9*	*10*
P	Req date				30	40	10	70	40	10	30	60
	Ord rel			30	40	10	70	40	10	30	60	
C	Req date			30	40	10	70	40	10	30	60	
	Ord rel		80			120			90			

Net material requirements plan:

		WEEK										
		0	*1*	*2*	*3*	*4*	*5*	*6*	*7*	*8*	*9*	*10*
P	Gr req	0	0	0	30	40	10	70	40	10	30	60
	On hand	20	20	20	20	0	0	0	0	0	0	0
	Net req				10	40	10	70	40	10	30	60
	Ord				10	40	10	70	40	10	30	60
	Ord rel			10	40	10	70	40	10	30	60	
C	Gr req			10	40	10	70	40	10	30	60	
	On hand	30	30	30	20			0			0	
	Net req	0	0	0	100			80			60	
	Ord				100			80			60	
	Ord rel			100			80			60		

14. Master production schedule:

		WEEK										
		0	*1*	*2*	*3*	*4*	*5*	*6*	*7*	*8*	*9*	*10*
P	Gr req		0	50	30	40	10	70	40	10	30	60

Gross material requirements plan:

		WEEK										
		0	*1*	*2*	*3*	*4*	*5*	*6*	*7*	*8*	*9*	*10*
P	Rec date			50	30	40	10	70	40	10	30	60
	Ord rel		50	30	40	10	70	40	10	30	60	

		WEEK										
		0	*1*	*2*	*3*	*4*	*5*	*6*	*7*	*8*	*9*	*10*
C	Req date		50	30	40	10	70	40	10	30	60	
	Ord rel	120			120			100				

Net material requirements plan:

		WEEK										
		0	*1*	*2*	*3*	*4*	*5*	*6*	*7*	*8*	*9*	*10*
P	Gr req	0	0	50	30	40	10	70	40	10	30	60
	On hand	20	20	20	0	0	0	0	0	0	0	0
	Net req			30	30	40	10	70	40	10	30	60
	Ord			30	30	40	10	70	40	10	30	60
	Ord rel		30	30	40	10	70	40	10	30	60	
C	Gr req	0	100			120			100			
	On hand	30	30			0			0			
	Net req		70			120			100			
	Ord		70			120			100			
	Ord rel	70			120			120				

The lots of 120 in weeks 3 and 6 exceed shop capacity; one solution is to move 45 units of the order earlier by 1 week.

16. a. Ten units of A are required for production plus ten units of B and F for field service repair.

COMPONENTS	QUANTITY
A	20
B	20
C	40
D	20
E	40
F	20
G	20
H	20

b. Net Requirements

COMPONENTS	QUANTITY
A	20
B	18
C	18
D	13
E	30
F	15
G	14
H	10

c. Net requirements by date follow below (for item A) and on the next page (for items B and F)

LOT SIZE	LEAD TIME	ON HAND	SAFETY STOCK	ALLOCATED	LOW LEVEL CODE	ITEM ID		PERIOD (week) 1	2	3	4	5	6	7	8
Lot-for-lot	1	0	-	-	0	A	Gross requirements								10
							Scheduled receipts								
							Projected on hand	0	0	0	0	0	0	0	10
							Net requirements								10
							Planned receipts								10
							Planned releases							10	

LOT SIZE	LEAD TIME	ON HAND	SAFETY STOCK	ALLOCATED	LOW LEVEL CODE	ITEM ID		PERIOD (week) 1	2	3	4	5	6	7	8
Lot-for-lot	1	2	-	-	1	B	Gross requirements						10^A	10^A	
							Scheduled receipts								
							Projected on hand	2	2	2	2	2	2	0	0
							Net requirements						8	10	
							Planned receipts						8	10	
							Planned releases					8	10		
Lot-for-lot	1	5	-	-	1	F	Gross requirements						10^A	10^A	
							Scheduled receipts								
							Projected on hand	5	5	5	5	5	5	0	0
							Net requirements						5	10	
							Planned receipts						5	10	
							Planned releases					5	10		

D, G, H, C, and E follow a similar pattern.

18.

a. Plan for receipt of orders

REQUIREMENTS AT WAREHOUSES

	1	2	3	4	5	6	7	8	9	10	11	12
E.C.W.			40	100	80	70	20	25	70	80	30	50
W.C.W.		20	45	60	70	40	80	70	80	55		
F.W.			30	40	10	70	40	10	30	60		

REQUIREMENTS OFFSET FOR LEAD TIMES

		1	2	3	4	5	6	7	8	9	10	11	12
E.C.W.		40	100	80	70	20	25	70	80	30	50		
W.C.W.	20	45	60	70	40	80	70	80	55				
F.W.			30	40	10	70	40	10	30	60			

RECEIPTS FROM FACTORY AT FACTORY WAREHOUSE

	0	1	2	3	4	5	6	7	8	9	10	11	12
G Req	20	85	190	190	120	170	135	160	165	90	50		
On hand		80	95	5	15	95	25	90	30	65	75	25	
Planned receipt from factory	100	100	100	200	200	100	200	100	200	100			

b. Release all orders two weeks prior to the schedule above (the "planned receipt from factory" date). If the schedule is late, as suggested above, then the initial order for receipt in week 3 should be for all requirements needed prior to that (that is, week 0, 1, 2, and 3, for a total of 500 units). The release schedule would then be:

WEEK	1	2	3	4	5	6	7
Planned order release	500	200	100	200	100	200	100

Chapter 11 Supplement

2. a. Vertically integrated firm includes Ford Motor Company (although less now than 60 years ago).

b. Firms that have reduced vertical integration include Chrysler Corporation and Jaguar Motor Cars.

c. Firms moving toward "virtual" organization include (per the discussion in the text) a number of semiconductor firms (such as S3 Inc. and Visioneer).

Chapter 12

2. Cost = $53,320
No, plan 2 is marginally better
4. Cost = $214,000 for plan B
6. Plan D; $122,000
8. Each answer you develop will differ.
10. Plan C, $92,000; Plan D, $82,300 assuming initial inventory = 0
12. $11,790
14. $1,186,810
16. $100,750
18. $88,150

Chapter 13

2. a. 1-D, 2-A, 3-C, 4-B
b. 40
4.

Job	Day 1	Day 2	Day 3	Day 4	Day 5	Day 6	Day 7	Day 8	Day 9
D									
E									
F									
G									

Now

6. A-61 to 4; A-60 to 1; A-53 to 3; A-56 to 5; A-52 to 2; A-59 to 6; 150 hours

8. 1–2 P.M. on A; 2–3 P.M. on C; 3–4 P.M. on B; 4–5 P.M. on Independent; 75.5 rating
10. a. ABCDE
b. BADEC
c. EDABC
d. CBADE
SPT is best
12. DCAB sequence
14. a. A, B, C, D, E
b. C, A, B, E, D
c. C, D, E, A, B
d. B, A, E, D, C
EDD and FCFS is best on lateness,
SPT on other two measures
16. D, B, A, C
18. 7.26 minutes per setup
20. 3.67 minutes per setup

Chapter 14

2.

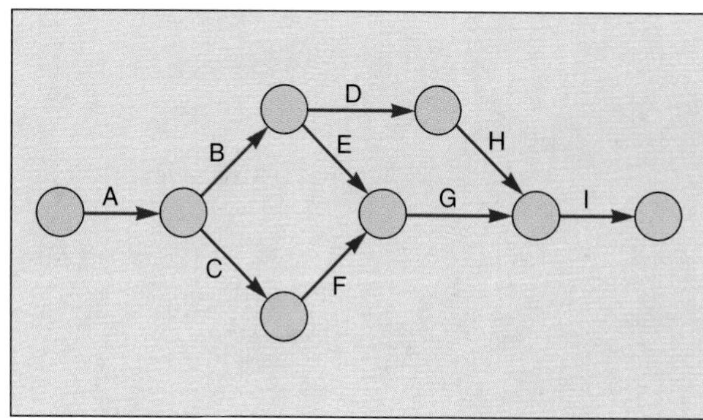

4.

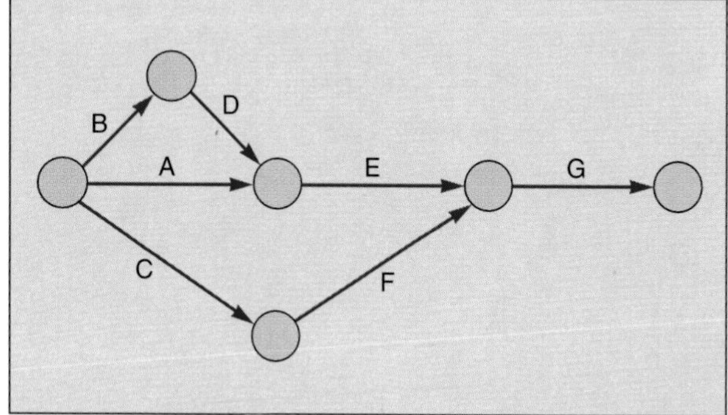

6.

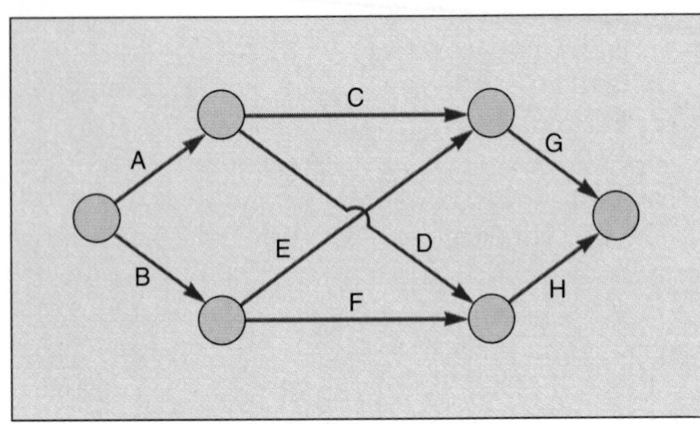

8. A, 5.83, 0.69
B, 3.67, 0.11
C, 2.00, 0.11
D, 7.00, 0.11
E, 4.00, 0.44
F, 10.00, 1.78
G, 2.17, 0.25
H, 6.00, 1.00
I, 11.00, 0.11
J, 16.33, 1.00
K, 7.33, 1.78

10. .9463

12. **a.** 15 (A, C, E)
b. 2

14. **a.** 16 (A, D, G)
b. $12,300
c. D, 1 week for $75

16. A, C, E, H, I, K, M, N; 50 weeks

18. **a.** .0228
b. .3085
c. .8413
d. .9772

20. **a.** 14
b. Crash cost = $275 extra

Chapter 14 Supplement

2. Without contract, $1,255 per week
With contract, $1,395 per week

Glossary*

ABC analysis (p. 307) A method for dividing on-hand inventory into three classifications based on annual dollar volume.

Acceptable quality level (AQL) (p. 128) The quality level of a lot considered good.

Acceptance sampling (p. 127) A method of measuring random samples of lots or batches of products against predetermined standards.

Activity (p. 484) A task or a subproject in CPM or PERT network that occurs between two events; a flow over time.

Activity charts (p. 240) A way of depicting studies and the resultant suggestions for improvement of utilization of an operator and a machine or some combination of operators (a crew) and machines.

Activity time estimate (p. 488) The time it takes to complete an activity in a PERT or CPM network.

Adaptive smoothing (p. 70) An approach to exponential smoothing forecasting in which the smoothing constant is automatically changed to keep errors to a minimum.

Aggregate planning (p. 416) An approach to determine the quantity and timing of production for the intermediate future (usually 3 to 18 months).

Aggregate scheduling See *aggregate planning*.

Assembly chart (p. 154) A means of identifying the points of production where components flow into subassemblies and ultimately into a final product.

Assembly drawing (p. 154) An exploded view of the product, usually through a three-dimensional or isometric drawing.

Assembly line (p. 280) An approach that puts fabricated parts together at a series of work stations; used in repetitive processes.

Assembly line balancing (p. 280) Obtaining output at each workstation on the production line so that it is nearly the same.

Assignable variation (p. 130) Variation in a production process that can be traced to specific causes.

Assignment method (p. 451) A special model that involves assigning tasks or jobs to resources.

Automated guided vehicle (AGV) (p. 177) Electronically guided and controlled carts used to move materials.

*Glossary terms followed by a page number beginning with a "T" refer to those terms found in the Tutorials section of the hardcover version of *Principles of Operations Management*, second edition (*Principles of Operations Management with Tutorials*, second edition).

Average actual cycle time (p. 242) The arithmetic mean of the times for each element measured.

Average outgoing quality (AOQ) (p. 129) The percent defective in an average lot of goods inspected through acceptance sampling.

Back flush (p. 355) A system to reduce inventory balances by deducting everything in the bill-of-material upon completion of the unit.

Backward scheduling (p. 447) Scheduling that begins with the due date and schedules the final operation first and the other job steps in reverse order.

Benchmarking (p. 96) Selecting a demonstrated standard of performance that represents the very best performance for a process or activity.

Beta probability distribution (p. 488) A mathematical distribution that may describe the activity time estimate distributions in a PERT network.

Bill-of-material (BOM) (pp. 149; 346) A listing of the components, their description, and the quantity of each required to make one unit of a product.

Bonus (p. 234) A monetary reward, usually in cash or stock options, given to management or executives in an organization.

Bottleneck (p. 462) An operation that limits output in the production sequence.

Breakdown maintenance (p. 519) Remedial maintenance that occurs when equipment fails and must be repaired on an emergency or priority basis.

Break-even analysis (p. 189) A means of finding the point, in dollars and units, at which costs equal revenues.

Buckets (p. 355) Time units in a material requirements planning (MRP) system.

Buyer (p. 400) In wholesale and retail services, the purchaser who is responsible for the sale and profit margins of merchandise that will be resold.

Capacity (p. 186) The maximum output of a system in a given period.

Cause-and-effect diagram (p. 104) A schematic technique used to discover possible locations of quality problems in manufacturing; also known as an Ishikawa diagram or a fish-bone chart.

c-chart (p. 126) A quality control chart used to control the number of defects per unit of output.

Center of gravity method (p. 209) A mathematical technique used for finding the best location for a single distribution point that services several stores or areas.

Central limit theorem (p. 119) The theoretical foundation for x-charts that states that regardless of the distribution of the population of all parts or services, the distribution of $\overline{x}$'s will tend to follow a normal curve as the number of samples grows large.

Closed-loop MRP system (p. 358) A system that provides feedback to the capacity plan, master production schedule, and production plan.

Coefficient of correlation (r) (p. 66) A number measure, between −1 and +1, of the statistical relationship between variables.

Competitive advantage (p. 31) The creation of a unique advantage over competitors.

Computer-aided design (CAD) (p. 152) Use of a computer to develop the geometry of a design.

Computer-aided manufacturing (CAM) (p. 152) The use of information technology to control machinery.

Computer-integrated manufacturing (CIM) (p. 178) A manufacturing system in which electronically controlled machines are integrated with robots, transfer machines, or automated guided vehicles to create a complete manufacturing system.

Computer numerical control (CNC) (p. 175) The control of machines via their own computer.

Concurrent engineering (p. 147) Use of participating teams in design and engineering activities.

Configuration management (p. 155) A system by which a product's planned and changing components are accurately identified and for which control and accountability of change is maintained.

Consignment inventory (p. 379) An arrangement whereby the supplier maintains title to the inventory until it is used.

Constraints (p. T20) Restrictions that limit the degree to which a manager can pursue an objective.

Consumer market survey (p. 49) A forecasting method that solicits input from customers or potential customers regarding their future purchasing plans.

Consumer's risk (p. 127) The mistake of a customer's acceptance of a bad lot overlooked through sampling (a type II error).

Continuous process (p. 171) A product-oriented, high-volume, low-variety process.

Control chart (pp. 105; 116) A graphic presentation of process data over time.

Control files (p. 449) Files that track each work order's actual progress against the plan.

Corner-point method (p. T26) A method for solving graphical linear programming problems.

Crashing (p. 495) Shortening activity time in a network to reduce time on the critical path so total completion time is reduced.

Critical path (p. 483) The computed longest time path(s) through a network.

Critical path analysis (p. 489) A network model for finding the shortest possible schedule for a series of activities. It usually employs PERT or CPM.

Critical path method (p. 483) A network technique using only one time factor per activity that enables managers to schedule, monitor, and control large and complex projects.

Critical ratio (CR) (p. 458) A sequencing rule that is an index number computed by dividing the time remaining until due date by the work time remaining.

Crossdocking (p. 279) Avoiding the placing of materials or supplies in storage by processing them as they are received for shipment.

Crossover chart (p. 191) A chart depicting more than one process with costs for the possible volumes.

Cumulative probability distribution (p. T110) The accumulation of individual probabilities of a distribution.

Cycle counting (p. 309) A continuing audit of inventory records.

Cycle time (p. 283) The time the product is available at each work station in assembly line balancing.

Decision table (p. T3) A tabular means of analyzing decision alternatives and states of nature.

Decision tree (p. T5) A graphical means of analyzing decision alternatives and states of nature.

Degeneracy (p. T54) An occurrence in transportation models when there are too few squares or shipping routes being used so that tracing a closed path for each unused square becomes impossible. Degeneracy exists when the number of rows plus the number of columns minus one does not equal the number of occupied cells.

Delphi method (p. 49) A forecasting technique using a group process that allows experts to make forecasts.

Demand forecast (p. 48) A projection of a company's sales for each time period in the planning horizon.

Design for manufacturability and value engineering teams (p. 147) Teams charged with improvement of designs and specifications at the research, development, design, and production stages of product development.

Direct numerical control (DNC) (p. 178) A machine that is directly (hard) wired to a control computer that supplies the electronic instructions and controls.

Disaggregation (p. 429) The process of breaking the aggregate plan into greater detail.

Distinctive competencies (p. 38) An organization's unique capabilities which allow it to compete successfully.

Distribution resource planning (DRP) (p. 361) A time-phased stock replenishment plan for all levels of a distribution network.

Drop shipping (p. 399) Shipping directly from the supplier to the end consumer, rather than from the seller, saving both time and reshipping costs.

Dummy activity (p. 486) An activity having no time, inserted into the network to maintain the logic of the network.

Dummy destinations (p. T53) Artificial destination points created in the transportation method when the total supply is greater than the total demand; they serve to equalize the total demand and supply.

Dummy sources (p. T53) Artificial shipping source points created in the transportation method when total demand is greater than total supply in order to affect a supply equal to the excess of demand over supply.

Earliest due date (EDD) (p. 455) A priority scheduling rule that means the earliest due date job is performed next.

Economic forecasts (p. 48) Planning indicators, often provided by forecasting services, valuable in helping organizations prepare medium- to long-range forecasts.

Economic part period (p. 357) That period of time when the ratio of setup cost to holding cost is equal.

Effective capacity or utilization (p. 186) The maximum capacity a firm can expect to achieve given its product mix, methods of scheduling, maintenance, and standards of quality.

Efficiency (p. 186) A measure of actual output over effective capacity.

Electronic data interchange (EDI) (p. 408) A standardized data transmittal format for computerized communications between organizations.

Employee empowerment (p. 96; 231) Enlarging employee jobs so that the added responsibility and authority is moved to the lowest level possible in the organization. Empowerment allows the employee to assume both managerial and staff responsibilities.

Engineering change notice (ECN) (p. 155) A correction or modification of an engineering drawing.

Engineering drawing (p. 149) A drawing that shows the dimensions, tolerances, materials, and finishes of a component.

Ergonomics (p. 236) The study of work; in the United States often called *human factor engineering*.

Event (p. 484) A point in time that marks the start or completion of a task or activity in a network.

Expected monetary value (EMV) (p. T3) The expected payout or value of a variable that has different possible states of nature, each with an associated probability.

Expected value of perfect information (EVPI) (p. T4) The difference between the payoff under certainty and under risk.

Expected value under certainty (p. T5) The expected or average return.

Exponential smoothing (p. 54) A weighted moving average forecasting technique in which data points are weighted by an exponential function.

Fabrication line (p. 280) A machine-paced, product-oriented facility for building components.

Factor-rating method (p. 206) A location method that instills objectivity into the process of identifying hard-to-evaluate costs.

Finished goods inventory (p. 307) An end item ready to be sold, but still an asset on the company's books.

Finite scheduling (p. 461) Computerized short-term scheduling that overcomes the disadvantage of rule-based systems by providing the user with graphical interactive computing.

First come, first served (FCFS) (p. 454) A priority job scheduling rule by which the jobs are completed in the order they arrived.

First in, first out (FIFO) (p. T82) A queuing rule by which the first customers in line receive the first service; or in an inventory system, the first inventory received is the first inventory used.

Fish-bone chart (p. 104) See *cause-and-effect diagram.*

Fixed costs (p. 189) Costs that continue even if no units are produced.

Fixed-period system (p. 326) A system that triggers

inventory ordering on a uniform time frequency.

Fixed-position layout (p. 267) Addresses the layout requirements of stationary projects or large bulky projects (such as ships or buildings).

Flexible manufacturing system (FMS) (p. 177) A system using an automated work cell controlled by electronic signals from a common centralized computer facility.

Flow diagram (p. 252) A drawing used to analyze movement of people or material.

Focused factory (p. 276) A permanent facility to produce a product or component in a product-oriented facility.

Focused work center (p. 276) A permanent product-oriented arrangement of machines and personnel in what is ordinarily a process-oriented facility.

Forecasting (p. 46) The art and science of forecasting future events.

Forward scheduling (p. 447) A schedule that begins as soon as the requirements are known.

Gain sharing (p. 234) A system of financial rewards to employees for improvements made in an organization's performance.

Gantt charts (p. 449; 481) Planning charts used to schedule resources and allocate time; developed by Henry L. Gantt in the late 1800s.

Graphical/charting technique (p. 422) An aggregate planning technique that works with a few variables at a time to allow planners to compare projected capacity with existing capacity.

Gross material requirements plan (p. 351) A schedule that shows the total demand for an item (prior to subtraction of on-hand inventory and scheduled receipts) and when it must be ordered from suppliers, or production must be started in order to meet its demand by a particular date.

Group technology (p. 150) A system that requires that components be identified by a coding system that specifies the type of processing and the parameters of the processing; it allows similar products to be processed together.

Historical experience (p. 241) Estimating the time required to do a task based on the last time it was required.

Holding cost (p. 310) The cost to keep or carry inventory in stock.

House of quality (p. 98) A part of the quality function deployment process that utilizes a planning matrix to relate customer "wants" to "how" the firm is going to meet those "wants."

Incentive system (p. 234) An employee reward system based on individual or group productivity.

Industrial engineering (p. 4) Analytical approaches applied to the improvement of productivity in both manufacturing and service sectors.

Infant mortality (p. 519) The failure rate early in the life of a product or process.

Information sciences (p. 4) The systematic processing of data to yield information.

Inspection (p. 105) A means of ensuring that an operation is producing at the quality level expected.

Intangible costs (p. 205) A category of location costs that can be evaluated through weighting techniques.

Intermittent process (p. 171) A low-volume, high-variety process; also known as a process-oriented process.

Ishikawa diagram (p. 104) See *cause-and-effect diagram.*

ISO 9000 (p. 94) A set of quality standards developed by the European Community.

ISO 14000 (p. 94) A new environmental management standard established by the European Community.

Iso-cost (p. T28) An approach to solving a linear programming minimization problem graphically.

Iso-profit line method (p. T24) An approach to solving a linear programming maximization problem graphically.

JIT partnerships (p. 378) Partnerships of suppliers and purchasers that remove waste and drive down costs for mutual benefits. A critical necessity for a successful JIT system.

Job design (p. 229) An approach that specifies the tasks that constitute a job for an individual or a group.

Job enlargement (p. 230) The grouping of a variety of tasks about the same skill level; horizontal enlargement.

Job enrichment (p. 230) A method of giving an employee more responsibility that includes some of the planning and control necessary for job accomplishment; vertical enlargement.

Job lot (p. 270) A group or batch of parts processed together.

Job rotation (p. 230) A system in which an employee is moved from one specialized job to another.

Job shop (p. 448) A high-variety, low-volume system; intermittent processing.

Johnson's rule (p. 459) An approach that minimizes processing time for sequencing a group of jobs through two facilities minimizing total idle time in the facilities.

Jury of executive opinion (p. 49) A forecasting technique that takes the opinion of a small group of high-level managers, often in combination with statistical models, and results in a group estimate of demand. The most widely used of all qualitative forecasting approaches.

Just-in-time (JIT) (p. 376) A philosophy of continuous and forced problem solving that drives out wastes.

Just-in-time inventory (p. 383) The minimum inventory necessary to keep a perfect system running.

Kaizen (p. 96) The Japanese word for the ongoing process of incremental improvement.

Kanban or kanban system (p. 387) The Japanese word for *card* that has come to mean "signal"; a kanban system moves parts through production via a "pull" from a signal.

Keiretsu (p. 404) A Japanese term to describe suppliers who become part of a company coalition.

Kit number (p. 348) See *planning bill.*

Knowledge society (p. 18) A society in which much of the labor force has migrated from manual work to work based on knowledge.

Labor specialization (p. 230) The division of labor into unique ("special") tasks.

Labor standards (p. 240) The amount of time required to perform a job or part of a job.

Lead time (pp. 316; 349) In purchasing systems, the time between placing an order and receiving it; in production systems, it is the wait, move, queue, setup, and run times for each component produced.

Lean producers (p. 172) Repetitive producers who are world-class.

Lean production/lean manufacturing (p. 233) Using committed employees with ever expanding responsibility in an effort to achieve zero waste, 100% good product, delivered on time every time. The concept implies expanding each employee's job to the maximum and enhancing each employee's responsibility. It is the opposite of some operations that remove responsibility and thinking from jobs to simplify them to the maximum.

Learning curves (p. T66) The premise that people and organizations get better at their tasks as the tasks are repeated; sometimes called experience curves.

Learning organization (p. 234) A constantly improving lean producer where mutual trust and commitment exist.

Level material use (p. 386) The use of frequent, high-quality, small lot sizes that contribute to just-in-time production.

Level material-use schedules (p. 386; 462) Scheduling products so that each day's production meets the demand for that day. (Large or long production runs of the same product for inventory are not allowed.)

Limited, or finite, population (p. T81) A queuing system in which there are only a limited number of potential users of the service.

Linear decision rule (LDR) (p. 429) An aggregate planning model that attempts to specify an optimum production rate and workforce level over a specific period.

Linear programming (LP) (p. T20) A mathematical technique designed to help production and operations managers plan and make decisions relative to the trade-offs necessary to allocate resources.

Linear regression analysis (p. 63) A straight-line mathematical model to describe the functional relationships between independent and dependent variables; a common quantitative causal forecasting model.

Loading (p. 449) The assigning of jobs to work or processing centers.

Locational break-even analysis (p. 207) A cost-volume analysis to make an economic comparison of location alternatives.

Longest processing time (LPT) (p. 455) A priority rule that assigns the highest priority to those jobs with the longest processing time.

Lot-for-lot (p. 355) A lot-sizing technique producing exactly the quantity required.

Lot tolerance percent defective (LTPD) (p. 128) The quality level of a lot considered bad.

Low-level coding (p. 348) A system in a bill-of-material when an item is coded at the lowest level at which it occurs.

Maintenance (p. 518) All activities involved in keeping a system's equipment in working order.

Make-or-buy decision (pp. 149; 401) Choosing between producing a component or a service and purchasing it from an outside source.

Management coefficients model (p. 429) A formal planning model built around a manager's experience and performance; also known as Bowman's coefficient.

Management process (p. 7) The application of planning, organizing, staffing, leading, and controlling to the achievement of objectives.

Management science (p. 4) A systematic approach to problem formulation and solution, typically utilizing interdisciplinary talents and making use of mathematical, behavioral, and computer skills.

Manufacturing cycle time (p. 378) The time between when raw materials are received and when the finished product is shipped.

Master production schedule (MPS) (p. 344, 429) A timetable that specifies what is to be made and when.

Materials management (p. 408) An approach that seeks efficiency of operations through the integration of all material acquisition, movement, and storage activities in the firm.

Material requirements planning (MRP) (p. 344) A dependent demand technique that uses bill-of-material, inventory, expected receipts, and a master production schedule to determine material requirements.

Material requirements planning II (MRP II) (p. 359) A system that allows, with MRP in place, inventory data to be augmented by other resource variables; in this case, MRP becomes *material resource planning*.

Mean absolute deviation (MAD) (p. 56) One measure of the overall forecast error for a model; it is computed by taking the sum of the absolute values of the individual forecast errors and dividing by the number of periods of data (n).

Mean squared error (MSE) (p. 57) The average of the squared differences between the forecasted and observed values.

Mean time between failures (MTBF) (p. 520) The expected time between a repair and the next failure of component, machine, process, or product.

Mission (p. 28) The purpose or rationale for an organization's activity.

Mixed strategy (p. 420) A planning strategy that uses two or more controllable variables to set a feasible production plan.

Modular bills (p. 348) Bills-of-material organized by major subassemblies or by product options.

Modules (p. 172) Parts or components of a product previously prepared, often in a continuous process.

Moment of truth (p. 156) In the service industry that crucial moment between the service provider and the customer that exemplifies, enhances, or detracts from the customer's expectation.

Monte Carlo method (p. T109) A simulation technique that uses random elements when chance exists in their behavior. The basis of this method is experimentation of the chance elements through random sampling.

Moving averages (p. 52) A forecasting method that uses an average of the n most recent periods of data to forecast the next period.

MRO (p. 307) Maintenance, repair, and operating systems.

Multiphase system (p. T83) A system in which the customer receives services from several stations before exiting the system.

Multiple-channel queuing system (p. T83) A service system with one waiting line but with several servers.

Multiple regression (p. 68) A causal forecasting method with more than one independent variable.

Mutual commitment (p. 228) When both management and employees strive to meet common objectives.

Mutual trust (p. 228) An atmosphere in which both management and employees operate with reasonable, documented employment policies that are honestly and equitably implemented.

Naive approach (p. 49) A forecasting technique that assumes demand in the next period is equal to demand in the most recent period.

Natural variations (p. 130) Variabilities that affect almost every production process to some degree and are to be expected; also known as common causes.

Negative exponential probability distribution (p. T83) A continuous probability distribution often used to describe the service time in a queuing system.

Negotiation strategies (p. 407) Approaches taken by purchasing personnel to develop contractual relationships with suppliers.

Network (p. 485) A sequence of activities defined by starting and ending events and the activities that occur between them.

Normal distribution (p. A2) A continuous probability distribution characterized by a bell-shaped curve, the parameters of which are the mean and the standard deviation.

Normal time (p. 243) The time, adjusted for work pace, to complete a task observed during a time study.

Northwest-corner rule (p. T47) A systematic procedure in the transportation model where one starts at the upper left-hand cell of a table (the northwest corner) and systematically allocates units to shipping routes.

Numerical control (NC) (p. 175) The controlling of machines by computer programs on paper or magnetic tape.

Objective function (p. T20) A mathematical expression in linear programming that maximizes or minimizes some quantity (often profit or cost but any goal may be used).

Office layout (p. 267) The grouping of workers, their equipment, and spaces/offices to provide for comfort, safety, and movement of information.

Operating characteristic (OC) curve (p. 127) A graph that describes how well an acceptance plan discriminates between good and bad lots.

Operations chart (p. 240) A chart depicting right- and left-hand motions.

Operations decisions (p. 32) The operations decisions are quality, goods and service design, process and capacity design, location selection, layout design, people and work systems, supply-chain management, inventory, scheduling, and maintenance.

Operations management (OM) (p. 3) Activities that relate to the creation of goods and services through the transformation of inputs to outputs.

Optimistic time (p. 488) The "best" activity completion time that could be obtained in a PERT network plan.

Ordering cost (p. 310) The cost of the ordering process and its supplies and personnel.

Pareto chart (p. 102) Based on a concept of focusing on a few critical items as opposed to many less important ones developed by Vilfredo Pareto, an Italian economist. The concept manifests itself in a chart in descending order from the most frequent occurrence to least frequent occurrence.

Part period balancing (PPB) (p. 356) An inventory ordering technique that balances setup and holding costs by changing the lot size to reflect requirements of the next lot size in the future.

***p*-chart (p. 124)** A quality control chart that is used to control attributes.

Pegging (p. 355) In material requirements planning systems, tracing upward in the bill-of-material (BOM) from the component to parent item.

Pessimistic time (p. 488) The "worst" activity time that could be expected in a PERT network activity.

Phantom-bills-of-material (p. 348) Bills-of-material for components, usually assemblies, that exist only temporarily; they are never inventoried.

Physical sciences (p. 4) The fields of physics, chemistry, biology, and related sciences.

Pilferage (p. 309) A small amount of theft.

PIMS (profit impact of market strategy) (p. 34) A program established in cooperation with General Electric Corporation to identify characteristics of high return-on-investment firms.

Planning bill (p. 348) Paperwork created in order to assign an artificial parent to the bill-of-material. An artificial group of components issued together to facilitate production; not a complete subassembly; also known as a "kit" or "pseudo bill."

Planning files (p. 449) The item master file, routing file, and work-center file in a material requirements planning system.

Poisson distribution (p. T81) An important discrete probability distribution that often describes the arrival rate in queuing theory; derived by Simeon Poisson in 1837.

Poka-yoke (p. 107) Literally translated, "foolproof"; it has come to mean a device or technique that ensures the production of a good unit every time.

Postponement (p. 398) Delaying any modifications or customization to the product as long as possible in the production process.

Predetermined time standards (p. 247) An approach that divides manual work into small basic elements that have established and widely accepted times.

Preventive maintenance (p. 519) A plan that involves routine inspections, servicing, and keeping facilities in good repair to prevent failure.

Priority rules (p. 454) Rules that are used to determine the sequence of jobs in process-oriented facilities.

Probabilistic model (p. 323) A statistical model applicable when product demand or any other variable is not known but can be specified by means of a probability distribution.

Probable time (p. 488) The most likely time to complete an activity in a PERT network.

Process chart (p. 103; 240) A graphic representation that depicts a sequence of steps for a process identifying discrete operations, delay, inspection, storage, travel, and distance of process.

Process control (p. 176) The use of information technology to control a physical process.

Process (or transformation) decision (p. 170) The approach that an organization takes to transform resources into goods and services.

Process focus (p. 171) A low-volume, high-variety process.

Process mapping (p. 180) See *time-function mapping*.

Process-oriented layout (p. 267) A layout that deals with low-volume, high-variety production; intermittent process; like machines and equipment are grouped together.

Producer's risk (p. 127) The mistake of having a producer's good lot rejected through sampling (a type I error).

Product-by-value analysis (p. 148) A listing of products in descending order of their individual dollar contribution to the firm, as well as the total annual dollar contribution of the product.

Product development teams (p. 147) Teams charged with moving from market requirements for a product to achieving product success.

Product focus (p. 171) A product-oriented, high-volume, low-variety process.

Product-oriented layout (p. 268) A production process built around a product and seeking the best personnel and machine utilization via repetitive or continuous production.

Product decision (p. 142) The selection, definition, and design of products.

Production (p. 3) The creation of goods and services.

Production order quantity model (p. 317) An economic order quantity technique applied to production orders.

Productivity (p. 15) The enhancement to the production process that results in a favorable comparison of the quantity of resources employed (inputs) to the quantity of goods and services produced (outputs).

Productivity variables (p. 16) The three factors critical to productivity improvement—labor, capital, and management.

Profit sharing (p. 234) A system providing some portion of any profit for distribution to the employees.

Program evaluation and review technique (PERT) (p. 483) A technique to enable managers to schedule, monitor, and control large and complex projects by employing three time estimates for each activity.

Project organization (p. 481) An organization formed to ensure that programs (projects) receive the proper management and attention.

Pseudo bill (p. 348) See *planning bill.*

Pull system (p. 378) A JIT concept that results in material being moved only when requested and moved to where it is needed just as it is needed.

Purchasing (p. 400) The acquisition of goods and services.

Purchasing agent (p. 400) A person with legal authority to execute purchasing contracts on behalf of the firm.

Purchasing management (p. 405) The management of inventory, plus the transportation, availability of supply and quality of suppliers.

Pure service (p. 11) A service industry that does not include a tangible product.

Push system (p. 378) A system which pushes materials into downstream workstations regardless of their timeliness or availability of resources to perform the work. This system is the antithesis of JIT.

Qualitative forecasts (p. 49) Forecasts that incorporate important factors such as the decision maker's intuition, emotions, personal experiences, and value system.

Quality circle (p. 96) A group of employees meeting regularly with a facilitator to solve work-related problems in their work area; initiated by the Japanese in the 1970s.

Quality function deployment (QFD) (p. 98) A process for determining customer requirements (customer "wants") and translating them into the attributes (the "hows") that each functional area can understand and act upon.

Quality loss function (p. 101) A mathematical function that identifies all costs connected with poor quality and shows how these costs increase as product quality moves from what the customer wants.

Quality of work life (p. 228) Aims toward a job that

is reasonably safe, is equitable in pay, and achieves an appropriate level of both physical and psychological requirements.

Quality robust (p. 100) Products that are consistently built to meet customer needs in spite of adverse conditions in the production process.

Quality robust design (p. 147) A design that yields a good product in spite of small variations in the production process.

Quantitative forecast (p. 49) An approach that employs one or more mathematical models that use historical data and/or causal variables to forecast demand.

Quantity discount (p. 320) A reduced price for items purchased in large quantities.

Queuing theory (p. T80) The body of knowledge about waiting lines.

Random number (p. T111) A series of digits that have been selected by a totally random process; all digits have equal chance of occurring.

Random number intervals (p. T111) A set of numbers to represent each possible value or outcome in a computer simulation.

Rated capacity (p. 187) A measure of the maximum usable capacity of a particular facility.

Raw materials inventory (p. 306) Materials that are usually purchased but have yet to enter the manufacturing process.

***R*-chart (p. 118)** A process control chart that tracks the "range" within a sample; indicates that a gain or loss in uniformity has occurred in a production process.

Reengineering (p. 178) The fundamental rethinking and radical redesign of business processes to bring about dramatic improvements in performance.

Reliability (p. 158) The probability that a machine part or product will function properly for a reasonable length of time.

Reorder point (p. 316) The inventory level (point) at which action is taken to replenish the stocked item.

Repetitive process (p. 172) A product-oriented production process that uses modules.

Retail/service layout (p. 267) An approach (often computerized) that allocates shelf space and responds to customer behavior.

Revenue function (p. 189) An element in break-even analysis that increases by the selling price of each unit.

Robot (p. 176) A flexible machine with the ability to hold, move, or grab items that functions through electronic impulses that activate motors or switches.

Route sheet (p. 154) A listing of the operations necessary to produce the component with the material specified in the bill-of-material.

Sales force composite (p. 49) A forecasting technique based upon salespersons' estimates of expected sales.

Safety stock (p. 316) Extra stock to allow for uneven demand; a buffer.

Scheduling decisions (p. 416) Making plans which match production to changes in demand.

Scheduling by simulation (p. 429) A computer model to find a minimum-cost combination for workforce size and production rate.

Self-directed teams (p. 232) A group of empowered individuals working together to reach a common goal.

Sensitivity analysis (p. T30) An analysis that projects how much a solution might change if there were changes in the variables or input data.

Sequencing (p. 454) Determining the order in which jobs should be done at each work center.

Service level (p. 323) The percentage of demand satisfied through immediate delivery of the service or product. (A 95% service level means 95% of the demand is immediately met.)

Services (p. 11) Those economic activities that typically produce an intangible product (such as, education, entertainment, lodging, government, financial and health services).

Service sector (p. 13) That segment of the economy that includes trade, financial, education, legal, medical, and other professional occupations.

Setup cost (p. 310) The cost to prepare a machine or process for production.

Setup time (p. 310) The time required to prepare a machine or process for production.

Shortest processing time (SPT) (p. 455) A priority job-scheduling rule that assigns the shortest time job first.

Shrinkage (p. 309) Retail inventory that is unaccounted for between receipt and time of sale.

Simplex method (p. T30) An algorithm developed by Dantzig for solving linear programming problems of all sizes.

Simulation (p. T108) The attempt to duplicate the features, appearance, and characteristics of a real system, usually a computerized model.

Single-channel queuing system (p. T83) A service

system with one line and one server; for example, a drive-in bank with one open teller.

Single-phase system (p. T83) A system in which the customer receives service from only one station and then exits the system.

Slack time (p. 489) The amount of time an individual activity in a project management network can be delayed without delaying the entire project.

Smoothing constant (p. 54) The weighting factor used in an exponential smoothing forecast; a number between 0 and 1.

Standard error of the estimate (p. 65) A distribution within which samples of the process under study are expected to fall.

Standard time (p. 243) A time-study adjustment to the total normal time; the adjustment provides allowance for personal needs, unavoidable work delays, and worker fatigue.

Stepping-stone method (p. T48) An iterative technique for moving from an initial feasible solution to an optimal solution in the transportation method; it is used to evaluate the cost effectiveness of shipping goods via transportation routes not currently in the system.

Strategy (p. 28) How an organization expects to achieve its missions and goals.

Supply-chain management (p. 398) Management of activities that procures raw materials, transforms those materials into intermediate goods and final products, and delivers the products through a distribution system.

System nervousness (p. 354) A situation generated by frequent changes in the MRP system.

Taguchi method (p. 100) A quality control technique that focuses on improving the product at the design stage.

Tangible costs (p. 205) Readily identifiable costs that can be measured with some precision.

Target value (p. 102) A philosophy of continuous improvement to produce products that are exactly on target.

Technological forecasts (p. 48) Long-term forecasts concerned with the rates of technological progress; such forecasts are critical in high-technology industries; usually performed by experts in each particular field.

Theory of constraints (p. 461) That body of knowledge that deals with anything that limits an organization's ability to achieve its goals.

Time-based competition (p. 145) Competition based on time; may take the form of rapidly developing products and moving them to market or rapid product or service delivery.

Time fences (p. 355) A way of allowing a segment of the master schedule to be designated as "not to be rescheduled."

Time-function mapping (p. 180) A flow process chart but with time added on the horizontal axis. Nodes indicate the activities and arrows indicate the flow direction. Also known as process mapping.

Time series (p. 50) A forecasting technique that uses a series of past data points to make a forecast.

Time study (p. 242) The timing of a sample of a worker's performance and using it to set a standard.

Total quality management (TQM) (p. 95) Management of an entire organization so that it excels in all aspects of products and services that are important to the customer.

Tracking signal (p. 69) A measurement of how well the forecast is predicting actual values.

Transportation method (p. 211) A heuristic technique for solving a class of linear programming problems.

Trend projection (p. 58) A time series forecasting method that fits a trend line to a series of historical data points and then projects the line into the future for forecasts.

Type I error (p. 129) Statistically, the probability of rejecting a good lot.

Type II error (p. 129) Statistically, the probability of a bad lot being accepted.

Unlimited, or infinite, population (p. T81) A queuing situation in which a virtually unlimited number of people or items that could request the services, or the number of customers or arrivals on hand at any given moment is a very small portion of potential arrivals.

Value analysis (p. 148) A review of products with long life cycles that takes place during the production process.

Variability (p. 376) Any deviation from the optimum process that delivers perfect product on time, every time.

Variable costs (p. 189) Costs that vary with the volume of units produced; also known as direct costs.

Vertical integration (p. 403) Developing the ability to produce goods or services previously purchased by buying a supplier or distributor.

Virtual companies (p. 405) Companies that rely on

a variety of supplier relationships to provide services on demand. Also known as hollow companies.

Wagner-Whitin procedure (p. 357) A programming model for lot size computation that assumes a finite time horizon beyond which there are no additional net requirements.

Waiting lines (p. T80) Queues; items or people in a line awaiting a service.

Warehouse layout (p. 268) A design that attempts to minimize total cost by addressing cost tradeoffs between space and material handling.

Work breakdown structure (p. 481) A structure that defines a project by dividing it into its major subcomponents, which are subdivided into more detailed components, and finally into a set of activities and their related time and costs.

Work cell (p. 274) A temporary product-oriented arrangement of machines and personnel in what is ordinarily a process-oriented facility.

Work-flow analysis (p. 181) A technique to document a network of transactions between customers and performance.

Work-in-process inventory (WIP) (p. 306) Incomplete products or components of products that are no longer considered raw material but have yet to become finished products.

Work order (p. 154) An instruction to make a given quantity of a particular item, usually to a given schedule.

Work sampling (p. 249) An estimate, via sampling, of the percent of the time that a worker spends working on various tasks.

Yield management (p. 431) Capacity decisions which determine the allocation of classes of resources in order to maximize profit or yield (for example, allocation of coach, business, and first-class seats on an airplane to maximize profit or yield).

$\bar{x}$-chart (x-bar) (p. 118) A quality control chart for variables that indicates when changes occur in the central tendency of a production process.

Index

ABC analysis, 307–308
Acceptance sampling, 127–129
  acceptable quality level, 128
  average outgoing quality and, 129
  consumer's risk, 127
  lot tolerance percent defective (LTPD), 128
  operating characteristic curves and, 127
  producer's risk and, 127–128
Accurate records, inventory and, 348–349
Activity, 484
  dummy, 486–488
  in PERT, 484–486
Activity charts, job design and, 240
Activity-on-Arrow (AOA), 485
Activity-on-Node (AON), 485
Activity time estimates, in PERT, 488–489
Adaptive smoothing, 70
Aft, Lawrence S., 240*n*
Agarwal, Anurag, 341*n*
Aggregate planning. *See* Aggregate scheduling
Aggregate scheduling, 415–444
  comparison of methods for, 429
  disaggregation and, 429–430
  in services, 430–431
  mathematical approaches to, 426–429
  methods for, 421–429
  nature of, 417–419
  planning process and, 416
  planning strategies and, 419–421
  strategic importance of, 416
Airfreight, materials management and, 409
Airline industry
  aggregate scheduling and, 431
  scheduling in, 465
Akao, Y., 113*n*
Akinc, V., 414*n*, 478*n*
Alexander, D.C., 246*n*
AM Manufacturing, 175
American National Can Co., 181
Ames, J.M., 414*n*
Anard, Sam, 461*n*
Andon, 389
Ansarl, A., 395*n*
Appendices, A1–A24
  Answers to Even-Numbered Problems, Appendix D, A15–A24
  Answers to Self Tests, Appendix C, A12–A14
  Normal Curve Areas and How to Use the Normal Distribution, Appendix A, A2–A4
  Using POM for Windows, Appendix B, A5–A11
Armacost, R.L., 444*n*
Armor, G.S., 274*n*
Arnold, J.R.T., 414*n*
Assembly chart, 154
Assembly drawing, 154
Assembly line, product-oriented layout and, 280
Assembly line balancing, 281–285
  cycle time, 283
Assignable variations, statistical process control and, 117
Assignment method, loading and, 451–454
ASYBL (Assembly Line Configuration), 286
Atanasoff, John Vincent, 5
AT&T, 50, 147–148
Attribute(s), control charts for, 124
Automated storage and retrieval system (ASRS), 179
Automatically programmed tool (APT), 318
Automatic guided vehicles (AGVs), 177, 179
Average actual cycle time, 242
Average outgoing quality (AOQ), 129
Avery, C., 5

Babbage, Charles, 5, 25*n*, 230, 230*n*, 233*n*
Back flush, MRP and, 355
Backward scheduling, 447–448
Balakrishman, J., 304*n*
Baldrige Quality Awards, 5
Ballow, R.H., 414*n*
Banks, scheduling in, 465
Barnes, Ralph M., 264*n*
Barney, Jay B., 43*n*
Basic economic order quantity (EOQ) model, and inventory management, 312–313
Bassett, Glen, 430*n*, 431*n*
Batta, R., 478*n*, 525*n*
Benchmarking
  supply-chain management and, 410
  TQM and, 95–98
Bennigan's, 31
Berggren, C., 264*n*
Berliner, C., 167*n*
Berry, W.L., 107*n*, 109*n*, 113*n*, 200*n*, 341*n*, 373*n*, 444*n*
Besterfield, D.H., 113*n*, 139*n*
Beta probability distribution, activity time estimates and, 488
Bhote, K., 414*n*
Billington, Corey, 398*n*
Bill of material (BOM), 149–150, 346–348
  low level coding, 348
  modular-bills, 348
  planning and phantom bills, 348
  pseudo bills, 348
Blackburn, Joseph, 145*n*, 403*n*
Blanket orders, 407
Blocher, Douglas, 378*n*
Blumenfield, D.E., 414*n*
Boeing Aircraft, 282

Bonuses, 234
Booz, Allen, and Hamilton, 491
Bottleneck work centers, 462
Bowen, David E., 264*n*
Bowers, Melissa R., 341*n*, 444*n*
Bowman, E.H., 428, 428*n*, 429, 429*n*
Box, G.E.P., 87*n*
Bozarth, C.C., 200*n*
Breakdown maintenance, 519
Breakeven analysis, 189–193
  algebraic approach to, 190–191
  assumptions, 189
  capacity decisions and, 193
  cross-over chart, 191–192
  and fixed costs, 189
  graphic approach to, 190
  locational, 207–209
  objective of, 189
  revenue function of, 189
  variable costs in, 189
Brimson, J.A., 167*n*
Bristol-Myers Squibb Co., 47
British Airways, 496
Brown, Robert G., 87*n*, 148*n*, 341*n*
Buckets, MRP and, 355
Buffa, E.S., 274
Burbridge, J.L., 200*n*
Burger King, 277
Burns, L.D., 414*n*
Burt, D.N., 167*n*, 414*n*
Buxey, G., 431*n*, 444*n*
Buyer, 400
Buzzell, Robert D., 34*n*, 404*n*
Byham, W.C., 231*n*

CAD/CAM approach. *See* Computer-aided design (CAD), Computer-aided manufacturing (CAM)
Campy, James, 180*n*
Canton, I.D., 167*n*
Capacity, 186–200
  break-even analysis of, 189–193
  capacity management and, 186–187
  demand management and, 188–189
  design decisions of operations management and, 32–33
  effective, 186
  efficiency, 186
  forecasting and, 48
  forecasting requirement, 187–188
  making the investment in, 193–194
  options, aggregate scheduling and, 419–420
  rated, 187
  utilization, 186
Capacity planning, material requirements planning and, 358–359
Capital, as productive variable, 16, 17–18
Carbone, J., 408*n*
Carlzon, Jan, 156, 156*n*
Carr, L.P., 113*n*
Carson, R., 264*n*
Carter, P.L., 395*n*
Case studies
  Department of Motor Vehicles, 301
  Des Moines National Bank, 303–304
  Electronic Systems, Inc., 394
  Factory Enterprises, Inc., 413
  Family Planning Research Center for Nigeria, 515–516
  Gazette, 138–139
  General Electric, 166–167
  Johannsen Steel Co., 42
  Lincoln Electric, 263
  Martin-Pullin Bicycle Corp., 340–341
  Michelin, Inc., 43
  Milt and Michael's Cleaning, 112
  Minit-Lube, Inc., 200
  NASA Space Shuttle, 478
  National Air Express, 24
  North-South Airline, 86
  Service, Inc., 372
  Southard Truck Lines, 262–263
  Southern Recreational Vehicle Co., 224
  Southwestern State College, 443
  State Auto License Renewals, 302
  Sturdivant Sound Systems, 340
  Thomas Manufacturing Co., 413
  World Wide Chemical Co., 524–525
Casual forecasting, 50, 62–68
  coefficients for regression lines, 66–68
  linear regression analysis as method for, 50, 63–65
  multiple regression analysis as method for, 68
  standard error of the estimate, 65–66
Cause and effect diagrams,104
c-charts, 126–127
Center of gravity method, location strategies and, 209–211
Central limit theorem, 119
Cerveny, R.P., 373*n*
Chambers, J.C., 87*n*
Chang, T., 113*n*
Chapman, S.N., 395*n*
Cheng, L., 304*n*
Chesbrough, Henry W., 414*n*
Chew, Bruce W., 167*n*
Children, in MRP, 347
Choi, M., 167*n*
Chrysler Corporation, 97
Clark, Kim B., 145*n*, 167*n*, 525*n*
Cleland, D.I., 516*n*
Closed-loop MRP system, 358
Coefficient of correlation, 66–68
Coefficient of determination, 67
Company reputation, product quality and, 93
Comparison of process choices, 174
Competitive advantage, 31–32
Competitive bidding, 407
Components, 347
Computer(s), in forecasting, 71–72
Computer-aided design (CAD), 5, 152–153, 179
  benefits of, 153
Computer-aided manufacturing (CAM), 152–153, 179
  benefits of, 153
Computer-integrated manufacture (CIM), 5, 178
Computer numerical control (CNC) machinery, 175–176
COMSOAL (Computer Method for Sequencing Operations for Assembly Lines), 286
Concurrent engineering, 147
Configuration management, 155
Connors, Mary, 380*n*
Consignment, inventory, 379
Consumer market survey, forecasting and, 49
Consumer's risk, 127, 129
Continuous improvement, TQM and, 96
Continuous processes, 171
Control charts, 105, 118
  for attributes, 124
  for variables, 118–119
  R-chart, 118–119
  steps in using, 123
  x-chart, 118, 121

Control files, 449
Controlling
as management process, 7–9
service inventories, 309
Cook, Laddie, 403*n*
Cooper, Robin, 167*n*
Core job characteristics, 231–232
COSMOS (Computerized Optimization Modeling for Operating Supermarkets), 279
Cost(s)
inventory, economic order quantity model and, 312–315
product quality and, 91
reduction, jobs in operations management and, 10
Cost-based price model, 407
Cost leadership missions and strategies, 28, 31
Cost-time tradeoffs and project crashing, 495–497
Costin, H., 113*n*
Cox, J.F., 462*n*
CPM. *See* Critical path method (CPM)
Craig, C.S., 225*n*
Crashing, 495
Crawford-Mason, C., 113*n*
Critical path method (CPM), 481–482, 483–494
critique of, 500
difference between CPM and PERT, 488
framework of, 483–484
objective of, 489–493
probability of project completion, 493–494
service utilization, 498–499
Critical ratio (CR), sequencing and, 458–459
Crosby, Philip B., 46, 95, 96, 97, 101, 113*n*, 233
Crossdocking, 279–280
Cross functional team, 147
Crossover chart, 191–192
Customer interaction service process strategy and, 183–184
Customer service, jobs in operations management and, 10
Cycle counting, inventory and, 309
Cycles (C) in time series, 51
Cycle time
assembly line balancing and, 283
inventory and, 306
Cyclical scheduling, 465–466
Daganzo, C.F., 414*n*
Darden's Red Lobster, 175
Davies, E.H., 264*n*
Davis, Louis E., 232*n*
Davis, Tom, 399*n*
Dean, B.V., 516*n*
Dean, James, 167*n*, 264*n*
DeForest, M.E., 225
Delphi method, forecasting and, 49
Demand forecasts, 48
Demand management, capacity and, 188–189
Demand options, aggregate scheduling and, 420
De Matta, R., 444*n*
Deming, W. Edwards, 4, 5, 95, 95*n*, 97, 116*n*,
14 points for quality improvement, 95
Demographic change, new product opportunities and, 143
Denton, D.K., 113*n*, 264*n*
Denver's Convention Center's bathrooms, 266
Dependent demand, 600
Dependent demand, inventory and, 309–310, 344–373
benefits of MRP, 350
extensions of MRP, 358–359
lot sizing techniques, 355–358
model requirements, 344–349. *See also* Model requirements for dependent demand inventory
MRP management, 354–355
MRP in services, 359–361
MRP structure, 350–354
Dependent variable, 63
Dertouzos, Michael L., 17*n*
Design of goods and services, 140–168
defining and documenting the product, 149–153
documents for production, 154–155
goods and services selection, 142–147
product-by-value, 148–149
product development, 147–148
product reliability, 158–160
service design, 155–158
transition to production, 16
Design for manufacturability and value engineering teams, 147
Dess, Gregory G., 29*n*
DeVor, R.E., 113*n*
Dickie, H. Ford, 307*n*
Dickson, William J., 231*n*
Differentiation, missions and strategies and, 28–29
Ding, F., 304*n*
Disaggregation, aggregate scheduling and, 429–430
Disney World, 518
Distance reduction, JIT layout and, 382
Distinctive competencies, strategy implementation and, 38
Distribution, materials management and, 409
airfreight, 409
pipe lines, 409
railroads, 409
trucking, 409
waterways, 409
Distribution resource planning (DRP), 361
requirements, 361
structure for, 361
Distributors, new product opportunities and, 143
Division of labor, 230
Dobyns, L., 113*n*
Documents for services, 157–158
Dodge, H.F., 129*n*
Dodge-Romig table, 129
Dolinsky, L.R., 373*n*
Domich, P.D., 225*n*
Draper, A.B., 168*n*
Dreyfuss, Henry, 238*n*
Drezner, Z., 225*n*
Drop shipping, 399
Drucker, Peter, 25*n*, 43*n*
Dummy activities, 486–488
DuPont, 5
Dusenberry, W., 516*n*
Dwyer, F., 414*n*
Dynamics, operations strategy issues and, 35–36

Earliest activity finish time (EF), 489
Earliest activity start time (ES), 489
Earliest due date (EDD), 455
Economic change, new product opportunities and, 143
Economic forecasts, 48
Economic order quantity (EOQ) model, 311–312
inventory costs and, 312–315
lot sizing and, 356–357
Economic part period (EPP), 357

Edmondson, H.E., 43*n*
Effective capacity, 186
Efficiency, 186
Electrolux, 28
Electronic data interchange (EDI), 408
Electronic ordering and funds transfer, 407–408
Ellram, L., 414*n*
Employment empowerment, 95–96, 231, 389–390
Employee impact, JIT layout and, 382
Engelstad, Per H., 232*n*
Engineering chance notice (ECN), 155
Engineering drawing, 149
Eppen, G.D., 168*n*
Ergonomics work methods, 234–240
  controlling input to machine, 238
  method analysis, 238–240
  scientific management, 234–237
  work environment, 237–238
Ettlie, J.E., 200*n*
Europe's ISO 9000 Standard, 94
Europe's ISO 14000 Standard, 94–95
Evaluating location alternatives, 206–211
Evans, James R., 113*n*, 167*n*
Events
  dummy, 486–487
  in PERT, 484–486
Excel spreadsheets
  Factor-rating, 217
  Forecasting, 74–75
  Inventory, 330–332
  Project Scheduling (PERT and Cost Analysis), 501–503
  Quality via Statistical Process Control, 131–132
  Time Study, 253
Exponential smoothing, 50, 54
  smoothing constraints and, 54–56
  with trend, 58
  with trend projections, 58–60
Extensions of MRP, 358–359
  capacity planning, 358–359
  closed loop MRP, 358
  MRP II, 359

Faaland, B.H., 304*n*
Fabricant, Solomon, 25*n*
Fabrication line, 280
Facilities/space utilization, jobs in operations management, 10
Factor-rating method, location alternatives and, 206–211
Federal Express, 212, 419
Feigenbum, A.V., 113*n*
Fein, Michell, 233*n*
Finance/accounting
  option, 7
  organizing for creation of goods and services, 5
Finished goods inventory, 307
Finite scheduling, 461
First-come, first-served (FCFS), 454
Fish-bone chart, 104
Fisher, Bradley, 96*n*
Fitzsimmons, James, 213*n*, 225*n*
Fixed costs, 189
Fixed-period inventory systems, 326–327
Fixed-position layout, 267–269
Flexible manufacturing system (FMS), 5, 177, 179
Flexibility, JIT layout and, 382
Flow diagrams, job design and, 239
Flynn, Barbara B., 389*n*
Focused factory, 276–277
Focused work center, 276–277
Ford, Henry, 4, 5
Ford Motor Company, 2, 3
Forecasting, 45–87
  of capacity requirements, 187–188
  casual methods and, 50, 62–68
  computer's role in, 71–72
  defined, 46
  eight steps in system, 50
  monitoring and controlling forecasts and, 68–70
  product life cycle and, 47
  qualitative approach to, 49
  quantitative approach to, 49–50
  seasonal variations in data and, 61–62
  service sector and, 70–71
  strategic importance of, 48–49
  of time horizons, 46–47
  time series, 50–60
  types of, 48
Forker, L.B., 113*n*
Forward scheduling, 447
Foss, Murray, 14*n*
Foster, S.T., Jr., 113*n*
Francis, R.L., 304*n*
Freeland, J.R., 341*n*, 373*n*, 395*n*
Frick, M.C., 414*n*
Gaimon, C., 478*n*
Gain sharing, 234
Gale, B.T., 34*n*, 43*n*
Gantt, Henry, 3, 5, 481
Gantt charts, 5
  loading and, 449, 450
  project scheduling and, 481
Gardner, E.S., 58*n*, 87*n*
Garvin, David A., 90*n*, 91*n*
Garwood, Dave, 348*n*
General Electric Corporation, 28, 34, 72, 203, 231
General Electric Hawthorne Plant, 231
General Motors Corporation, 3, 203, 408
Geoffrion, Arthur M., 414*n*
Georgoff, D.M., 87*n*
Gershoni, Haim, 243*n*
Ghosh, S., 478*n*
Giant Food Stores, 310
Gilbert, James P., 379*n*
Gilbreth, Frank B., 3, 4, 5, 247
Gilbreth, Lillian M., 3, 4, 5
Gillette, 2
Gilman, Andrew, 461*n*
Glidden Paint, 62
Goldratt, Eliyahu M., 462*n*
Golhar, D.Y., 395*n*
Goods
  decisions of operations management and, 32–33
  different from services, 11–12
Gopalakrishnan, M., 478*n*
Gopalakrishnan, S., 478*n*
Graphical and charting methods, aggregate scheduling and, 422–426
Gray, D., 525*n*
Grimes, Richard, 414*n*
Groenevelt, H., 341*n*
Gross, E.E., Jr., 238*n*
Gross material requirements plan, 351–354
Group technology, 150–151
Grover, V., 43*n*
Gupta, Y.P., 139*n*

Hackman, Jay R., 231, 232*n*
Haddock, J., 373*n*
Hall, Robert W., 341*n*, 395*n*, 414*n*
Hammer, Michael, 178*n*, 180*n*
Handfield, R., 395*n*
Hanson, R.S., 499*n*
Hanson, W.A., 168*n*

Harbison, Frederick, 25*n*
Harley-Davidson, 124
Harris, Ford W., 312*n*
Hart, C., 444*n*
Hart, M.K., 113*n*
Hauser, J.R., 113*n*
Hawthorne studies, 231
Hayes, Robert H., 525*n*
Heizer, J.H., 200*n*, 209, 478*n*
Helms, A.S., 248*n*
Helms, Marilyn M., 25*n*, 525*n*
Helper, S., 414*n*
Henrici, John W., 16*n*
Herzberg, Frederick, 231*n*
Heskett, J., 444*n*
Hewlett-Packard, 392, 398
Hickman, Anita, 516*n*
Hill, Terry, 193*n*, 200*n*
Historical experience, work measurement and, 241
HMMS rule, 429*n*
Hoffman, K.L., 225*n*
Holding costs, 310
Hollow corporations, 405*n*
Holt, Charles C., 429*n*
Horizontal enlargement, 230
Hospitals, aggregate scheduling and, 431
  scheduling for services, 464–466
Hotel chain sites, location strategy and, 213–214
Houck, B.L.W., 304*n*
Hounshell, D.A., 25*n*, 200*n*
House of quality, 98–100
Huang, P.Y., 200*n*, 304*n*
Hubicki, D.E., 373*n*
Human factors, 236
Human resource strategy, forecasting and, 48
Humidity, job design and, 238

Iansiti, M., 168*n*
IBM, 50, 57, 72, 179–180
Illumination, job design and, 237
Improving individual components, product reliability and, 158–159
"Incomplete" orders, 407*n*
Independent demand, inventory and, 309–310, 311–322
  basic economic order quantity (EOQ), 311–312
  minimize costs, 312–316
  production order quantity model, 316–319
  quantity discount models, 319–322
  reorder points, 315–316
Independent variable, 63
Industrial engineering, operations management and, 4
Industrial Standard Z8101–1981, 94
Infant mortality, 519
Information science, operations management and, 4
Inman, R.A., 395*n*
Inspection, TQM and, 105–107
Intangible costs, location and, 205
Intermittent processing, 171
International implications, product quality and, 93
International Paper, 193
International quality standards, 93–95
Internet, 5
Internet Case Studies
  Akron Zoological Park, 86
  AT&T Buys a Printer, 414
  Blue and Gray, Inc., 414
  Haywood Brothers Construction Company, 516
  La Place Power and Light Company, 341
  Oregon Wood Store, 478
  Palm Beach Institute of Sports Medicine, 304
  Professional Video Management, 340
  Rochester Manufacturing, 200
  Shale Oil, 516
  Three Mile Island, Human Factors at, 264
  Westover Electrical, 113
Internet Data Base Applications
  Aggregate scheduling, 442
  Forecasting, 86
  Layout designs, 301
  Location strategy, 223
  MRP, 372
  Project scheduling, 515
  Quality via statistical process control, 138
  Short-term scheduling, 477
Inventory, 305–340
  dependent demand inventory. *See* Dependent demand, inventory and
  economic order quantity model and, 311–312
  fixed-period systems and, 325–326
  functions of, 306–307
  independent demand. *See* Independent demand, inventory and
  just-in-time, 383–384, 390
  Kanban, 387–388
  models, 309–310
  probabilistic models with constant lead time, 322–325
  reduction, jobs in operation management and, 10
  types of, 306–307
Inventory management, 307–309
  ABC analysis and, 307–309
  cycle counting and, 309
  decisions of operations management and, 32–33
  record accuracy and, 308, 348–349
Invoiceless purchasing, 407
Ishikawa diagrams, 104
ISO 14000 Standard, 94–95
ISO 9000 Standard, 94
Israeli, Asher, 96*n*
Item master file, 449

Jackson, H.F., 225*n*
Jackson, Paul, 383*n*
Janaro, R.E., 168*n*
Japan's Industrial Standard Z8101–1981, 94
Jarvis, J.P., 444*n*
"Jelly bean" scheduling, 386
Jenkins, G., 87*n*
Jensen, John B., 478*n*
Jinchiro, H., 341*n*, 395*n*
Job classifications, 229
Job design, 229–240
  core job characteristics, 231–232
  ergonomics and work methods and, 234–240
  expansion, 230–231
  Hawthorne studies, 231
  labor specialization, 230
  lean production, 233–234
  limitations of job expansion, 233
  motivation and incentive systems and, 234
  psychological components of, 231
  self-directed teams, 232–233
Job enlargement, 230
  limitations of, 233
Job enrichment, 230
  limitations of, 233
Job lots, 270

Job shop scheduling, 448*n*
Johnson, Eric, 399*n*
Johnson, Ross, 90*n*
Johnson, R.V., 274*n*
Johnson, S.M., 459*n*
Johnson, T.W., 225*n*
Jones, Daniel T., 44*n*, 145*n*, 173*n*
Jordan, M., 525*n*
Joshi, S., 304*n*
J. R. Simplot, 151
Juran, Joseph M., 97, 102, 113*n*
Jury of executive opinion, 49
Just-in-time (JIT), TQM and, 95, 98
- hidden variability, 383
- Kanban, 387–388
- MRP and, 355
- reduction of, 383
- small lots, 383–384

Just-in-time (JIT) partnerships, 378–380
- characteristics of partnerships, 379
- goals of, 378–380
- supplies, 378–381

Just-in-time systems, 375–395
- attack on waste and variability, 376–378
- contribution to competitive advantage, 377
- employee empowerment, 389–390
- inventory, 383–384
- layout, 381–383
- philosophy of, 376
- quality, 389
- scheduling, 385–388
- services, 390–391
- suppliers, 378–381

Kahu, B.K., 304*n*
Kaizen, 96
Kanban system, 387–388
Kaneko, Masaki, 209
Kanter, Rosabeth Moss, 145*n*
Kaplan, Robert S., 43*n*
Karmarkar, U., 373*n*
Karwan, M., 525*n*
Keefer, D.L., 516*n*
Keiretsu networks, 404
Kelly, J.E., 483
Kerzner, H., 516*n*
Key tasks, strategy implementation and, 38
Kim, S., 516*n*
Kim, Y., 478*n*
Kimes, Sheryl, 213*n*
Kinard, J., 224*n*, 340*n*
King, W.R., 516*n*
Kinnie, N.J., 264*n*
King, W.R., 516*n*
Kit number, 348
Klastorin, T.D., 304*n*
Klompmaker, J.E., 200*n*
Knowledge society, 18
Knoz, S., 264*n*
Krafcik, John, 172*n*
Krogers Supermarkets, 266
Kumar, S., 139*n*

Labbach, Elaine, J., 181*n*
Labor
- content, 204
- as productivity variable, 16–17

Labor specialization, 230
Labor standards
- historical experience, 241–242
- predetermined time studies, 247–249
- time studies, 242–247
- work measurement and, 240–252
- work sampling, 249–252

Lackey, Charles W., 378*n*
Lahtella, J., 233*n*
Landvater, D.V., 341*n*
La Quinta Motor Inns, 213–214
Latest activity finish time (LF), 489
Latest activity start-up time (LS), 489
Law firm, aggregate scheduling and, 431–432
Lawler, Edward E. III, 264*n*
Layout designs, 265–303
- design, operation's management decisions and, 32–33
- fixed position layout and, 267–269
- just-in-time and, 381–383, 390
- objective of, 266
- office layout and, 277–278
- process-oriented layout and, 267, 269–277
- product-oriented layout and, 268, 279–285
- retail store layout and, 278
- service process opportunities and, 185
- strategic importance of, 266
- types of, 267–268
- warehousing and storage layouts and, 279

Leachman, R.C., 516*n*
Leading, as management process, 7–9
Lead time
- dependent inventory model and, 349
- reorder point and, 316–317

Lean producer, 172–174
- advantages held by, 73

Lean production, 172–174, 233–234
Learning organization, 234
Least squares method, trend projections and, 58
Lee, Haw L., 398*n*
Legal change, new product opportunities and, 143
Leone, R.A., 444*n*
Leschke, J.P., 341*n*, 373*n*, 395*n*
Lester, Richard K., 17*n*
Leu, Y., 200*n*
Leung, J., 304*n*
Level material-use schedule, 386–387, 462–464
Level scheduling, 421
Lewis, Jordan D., 414*n*
Linder-Dutton, L., 525*n*
Lindner, C.A., 248*n*
Lindsay, W.M., 113*n*
Linear decision rule (LDR), aggregate scheduling and, 429
Linear regression, casual forecasting and, 50, 63–65
L.L. Bean, Inc., 53, 97, 421
Load reports, 358
Loading, 449–454
- assignment method, 451–454
- Gantt charts, 449–450

Location strategies, 201–225
- attitudes and, 205
- breakeven analysis and, 207–209
- center of gravity method and, 209–211
- costs and, 205
- evaluating location alternatives, 206–211
- exchange rates and, 204–205
- factors affecting decisions, 203–205
- factor rating method, 206–207
- hotel chain sites, 213–214
- labor productivity and, 203–204
- objective of, 202
- selection, operations management decisions and, 32–33
- service strategy, 212–215
- telemarketing industry, 214–215
- transportation model and, 211

Longest processing time (LPT), 455

Long-range forecasting, 46–47
Lot-for-lot, 355–357
Lot sizing techniques, MRP and, 355–358
economic order quantity as technique for, 356–357
lot-for-lot technique for, 355–357
part period balancing technique for, 357
Wagner-Whitin procedure for, 357–358
Lot tolerance percent defective (LTPD), 128
Louis, R.S., 395*n*
Low, James T., 462*n*
Low-level coding, 348
Lubove, Seth, 389*n*
Lukoil, 2

McClain, M.A., 225*n*
McCormick, Ernest J., 238*n*, 243*n*, 264*n*
McCutcheon, D.M., 200*n*
McDonald's Corporation, 2, 3, 38, 149, 151, 156, 171, 174, 202, 277, 390
McDonnell Douglas, 159
McGee, V.E., 87*n*
McGinnis, L.F., 304*n*
McKaskill, Tom, 478*n*
Mabert, Vincent A., 378*n*
Machinery, equipment, technology, process design and, 175–178
automated guided vehicles (AGVs), 177
computer-integrated manufacturing (CIM), 178
computer numerical control (CNC), 175–176
flexible manufacturing system (FMS), 177
numerical control (NC), 175
process control, 176
robots, 176
MAD, 56–57
Magad, B.L., 414*n*
Maggard, M.J., 373*n*
Mahmoud, E., 87*n*
Maine, Jeremy, 135*n*
Maintenance management, 517–525
categories in, 519–522
decisions of operations management and, 32–33
objective of, 518
repair and operating supply (MRO) inventory, 307
simulation model for, 522
strategic importance of, 518
Make-or-buy decision, 149–150
Makens, P.K., 304*n*
Makridakis, S., 87*n*
Malcolm Baldrige National Quality Awards, 92–93
Malhotra, M.K., 43*n*, 478*n*
Management
inventory and, 307–309
process of, 7–9
as productivity variable, 18
Management coefficients model, aggregate scheduling and, 429
Management science, operations management and, 4
Mann, L., Jr., 525*n*
Mansfield, E., 200*n*
Manufacturing based quality, 90
Manufacturing cycle time, 378
Maquiladoras, 203, 205
Make-or-buy decisions, 400–401
Market-based price model, 407
Marketing
option, 6
organizing for creation of goods and services, 5
Market practice, new product opportunities and, 143
Market share, product quality and, 91
Martin, A.H., 373*n*
Martin, R.K., 168*n*
Maslow, Abraham H., 231*n*
Master production schedule (MPS), 344–346, 429–430
Materials management, 408–409
distribution systems, 409
Material requirements planning (MRP), 344–361
benefits of, 350
capacity planning and, 358–359
closed-loop, 358
dependent inventory model requirements and, 344–349
distribution resource planning and, 361
dynamics, 354–355
extensions of, 358–359
lot sizing techniques and, 355–358
management, 354–355
in services, 359–361
structure for, 350–354
Material requirements planning II (MRP II), 359
Mathematical approaches, aggregate scheduling and, 426–429
Mausner, B., 231*n*
Mayo, John, 148*n*
Maytag, 28, 148
Mean absolute deviation (MAD), 56–57, 69
Mean chart limits (x-charts) setting of, 120–121
Mean squared error (MSE), 57–58
Mean time between failure (MTBF), 520
Medium-range forecasting, 46–47
Megeath, J.D., 465
Mehra, S., 395*n*
Meredith, J.R., 200*n*
Merrils, Ray, 378*n*
Methods analysis, job design and, 238–240
Methods time measurement (MTM), 247–248
Methods Time Measurement Association, 247
Meyer, C., 264*n*
Meyer, J.R., 444*n*
Microsoft, 2, 36
Millen, Robert, 388*n*, 409*n*
Miller, Alex, 29*n*
Miller, D.M., 478*n*
Miller, Jeffrey G., 31*n*, 113*n*
Miller, T., 444*n*
Min, Hokey, 414*n*
Minit-Lube, 3
Miscellaneous services, aggregate scheduling and, 431
Mission, 28–32
Mital, A., 200*n*
Mitskevich, Amanda M., 243*n*
Mixed strategy, aggregate scheduling and, 420
Modarress, B., 395*n*
Model requirements for dependent demand inventory, 344–349
accurate inventory records, 348–349
bill-of-material (BOM), 346–348
lead times for each component, 349
master production schedule, 344
purchase orders outstanding, 349
specifications, 346–348
Modigliani, Franco, 429*n*
Modular bills, 348
Modules, repetitive processes and, 172

Moment-of-truth, 156–157
Montgomery, D.C., 139*n*
Montreuil, B., 304*n*
Morris, J.S., 200*n*, 304*n*
Morton, Thomas E., 478*n*
Moscove, S.A., 499
Mosier, C.T., 168*n*
Motorola, 38, 106, 116, 209
Moving averages, 50, 52
  weighted, 52–54
MRO inventories, 307
MRP. *See* Material requirements planning (MRP)
MSE, 57–58
MTM, 247
Mullick, S.K., 87*n*
Muth, John F., 429*n*
Multiple regression analysis, 68
Murdick, R.G., 87*n*, 107*n*, 218*n*, 225*n*, 430*n*, 443*n*, 444*n*, 465*n*
Murray, Susan L., 243*n*
Muther, Richard, 274*n*, 277*n*
Mutual commitment, people and work systems and, 228
Mutual trust, people and work systems and, 228
Myers, Charles A., 25*n*
Mylan Laboratories, 172

Nabisco, 48
Naive approach, forecasting and, 49
National Bicycle, 180
National chains, aggregate scheduling and, 431
Natural variations, statistical process control and, 116–117
NCR Corporation, 149
Negotiation strategies, vendor relations and, 407
Neibel, B.W., 168*n*
Net requirements plan, MRP and, 352, 353
Neter, John, 66*n*
Network(s), PERT, 484–486
Network companies, 405*n*
Ngo, Mike, 385*n*
Noise, job design and, 237–238
Nonaka, I., 168*n*
Northrop Grumman, 447
Norton, David P., 43*n*
Nucor, 170
Numerical control (NC), 175

Office layout, 267, 277–278
Oh, S., 414*n*
Ohmae, K., 44*n*
Oldham, Greg R., 231, 232*n*
Olson, Paul R., 12*n*, 302*n*
"Open" orders, 407*n*
Operating characteristic (OC) curve, 127
Operations chart, 240
Operations decisions, 32–33
Operations environment, 400
Operations management, 1–14
  decisions of, 32–33
  defined, 3
  global economy, 2–3
  heritage of, 3–5
  jobs in, 10
  manager's responsibilities, 7–9
  operations in service sector, 11–14
  option, 7
  organizing for creation of goods and services, 5
  reasons to study, 6
  significant events in, 5
Operations strategy
  goods and services and, 27–44
  mission, 28–32
  strategy, 28–32
Operations strategy issues, 34–36
  dynamics, 34–36
  preconditions, 34–35
  research, 34
Opportunity cost, assignment method and, 451, 451*n*
Optimistic time, PERT and, 488
Ordering cost, 310
Organization, building and staffing, 38–39
Organizing
  for creation of goods and services, 5
  as management process, 7–9
Orlando Utilities Commission, 498, 519
Orlicky, Joseph, 5
Owings, Patrick, 525*n*

Parasuraman, A., 107*n*, 109*n*, 113*n*
Parents in MRP, 347
Pareto, Alfredo, 102, 307
Pareto charts, 102
Pareto principle, 307
Parker, G.C., 87*n*
Parsaei, H.R., 200*n*
Part period balancing (PPB), lot sizing and, 357
p-charts, 124–125
Peace, G.S., 113*n*
Pegging, 355
Penleskey, R.J., 444*n*
Pentico, David W., 344*n*, 478*n*
People, decisions in operations management and, 32–33
People/team development, jobs in operations management and, 10
People and work systems, 227–264
  constraints on, 228–229
  job design, 229–240
  labor standards and work measurement, 240–252
PERT. *See* Program Evaluation and Review Technique (PERT)
PERT/COST, 495*n*
Pessimistic time, PERT and, 488
Peterson, A.P.G., 238*n*
Phantom bills-of-material, 348
Philipoom, Patrick R., 478*n*
Physical sciences, operations management and, 4
Pick lists, 348
Piece rate, 234
Pilferage, inventory and, 309
PIMS (Profit Impact of Market Strategy), 34
Pine, B.J., 200*n*
Pintelon, L., 341*n*
Pipelines, materials management and, 409
Pinto, J.K., 516*n*
Pinto, M.B., 516*n*
Pittsburgh International Airport, 266, 267
Pizza Hut, 31
Planning, as management process, 7–9. *See also* Forecasting
Planning bills, 348
Planning files, 449
Plastic Recycling Corp., 176
Plossl, George W., 69, 70*n*
Poka-yoke, 107
Political change, new product opportunities and, 143
POM for Windows
  aggregate scheduling, 433–436
  facility location, 216
  forecasting, 72–73
  inventory, 329
  layout design, 287–289
  MRP, 362–363
  quality via statistical process control, 130

POM for Windows (*cont.*)
  reliability analysis, 162
  scheduling, 466–467
  use of, A5–A11
Porter, Michael E., 28, 28*n*, 32*n*, 35*n*, 38, 38*n*, 44*n*
Postponement, 398
Preconditions, operations strategy issues and, 34–35
Predetermined time standards, 247–249
Prescott, J.E., 516*n*
Preventive maintenance, 519–522
Price, F., 113*n*
Price, W.L., 225*n*
Primrose, P., 200*n*
Principles of scientific management, 3
Priority rules, 454
Priority rules for dispatching jobs, sequencing and, 454–458
Probabilistic inventory models, with constant lead time, 323–326
Probable time, PERT and, 488
Process charts
  job design and, 240
  TQM and, 103–104
Process choices, 170–174
Process control, process design and, 176
Process mapping, 180
Process options and operations management decisions, 32–33
Process-oriented layout, 267, 269–277
  cellular, 274–276
  focused work center and focused factory and, 276–277
Process design, 171–186, 195–200
  capacity and. *See* Capacity
  comparison of, 174
  lean producer, 172
  lean production, 172–174
  machinery, equipment, and technology and, 175–178
  mapping, 180
  objective of, 170
  process focus, 170–171
  product focus, 170, 171–172
  repetitive focus and, 170, 172
  service sector, 182–186
Process focus, 170–171
Process reengineering, 178–182
  time function mapping, 180–181
  work flow analysis, 181–182
Producer's risk, 127–128
Product-based quality, 90
Product-by-value analysis, 148–149
Product decision, 142
Product development teams, 147
Product focus, 170, 171–172
Product liability, product quality and, 93
Product life, 144–145
Product life cycle, forecasting and, 47
Product opportunities, new generation of, 143
Product options, 142–143
Product-oriented layout, 280–285
  assembly line balancing and, 280–285
Product selection. *See* Design of goods and services
Product strategy. *See* Design of goods and services
Production, defined, 3
Production order quantity model, 317–320
Production/operations, organizing for the creation of goods and services, 5
Productivity, 15–21
  defined, 15
  jobs in operations and management, 10
  measurement of, 15–16
  service sector and, 18–20
  variables, 16–18
Professional standards, new product opportunities and, 143
Profit Impact of Market Strategy (PIMS), 34
Profit sharing, job design and, 234
Program Evaluation and Review Technique (PERT), 481–482, 483–494
  activities, events, and networks and, 484–486
  activity time estimates and, 488–489
  critique of, 500
  difference between PERT and CPM, 488
  dummy activites and events in, 486–488
  framework of, 483–484
  service utilization 498–499
Project controlling, 480, 482
  strategic importance of, 480
Project organization, 481
Project planning, 480–481
Project scheduling, 479–516
  Gantt charts, 481
  with PERT and CPM, 481–482
Pseudo bill, 348
Psychological components, job design and, 231
Pugliese, Phil, 25*n*
Pull system, 378
Purchase orders, outstanding, 349
Purchasing
  objective of, 400
  supply-chain management and, 399–408
Purchasing agent, 400
Purchasing management, 405–408
  purchasing techniques, 407–408
  vendor relations, 405–407
Purchasing strategies, supply-chain management and, 401–405
  few suppliers, 402–403
  many suppliers, 401–402
  Keiretsu networks, 404
  vertical integration, 403–404
  virtual companies, 405
Purchasing techniques, 407–408
  blanket orders, 407
  electronic ordering, 407–408
  funds transfer, 407–408
  invoiceless, 407
  standardization of, 408
  stockless, 408
Pure service, 12
Push system, 378

Qualitative forecasting methods, 49
  consumer marketing survey, 49
  Delphi method, 49
  jury of executive opinion, 49
  naive approach, 49
  sales force composite, 49
Quality. *See* Total quality management
  decisions of operation management and, 32–33
  defined, 90
  function deployment and, 98–100
  importance of, 91–93
  international standards, 93–95
  jobs in operation management and, 10
  just-in-time and, 389
Quality control (QC)
  acceptance sampling and, 127–129. *See* Acceptance sampling

employee empowerment, 95–96
inspection and, 105–107
international standards, 94–95
statistical process control and (SPC), 115–139. *See* Statistical process control
Taguchi method and, 100–102
Quality circle, 96
Quality loss function (QLF), 100–101
Quality of work life, 228
Quality robust design, 147
Quality robustness and Taguchi technique, 100
Quantitative forecasting methods, 50
Quantity discount model, inventory and, 320–323
Quick response, missions and strategies, 28, 31–32

Railroads, materials management and, 409
Random variations (R) in time series, 51
Rated capacity, 187
Ratliff, H.D., 304*n*
Raturi, A.S., 200*n*
Raw material inventory, 306
R-chart, 118–119
setting limits of, 122–123
steps in using, 123
Record accuracy, inventory and, 308
Reduced space and inventory, JIT layout and, 382–383
Redundancy, reliability and, 159–160
Reed, R., 225*n*
Reengineering, process and, 178–182
Reitman, Valevi, 146*n*
Reliability
improving individual components and, 158–159
product and, 158–160
Reinersten, D.G., 168*n*
Render, Barry, 87*n*, 107*n*, 218*n*, 225*n*, 430*n*, 443*n*, 444*n*, 465*n*, 478*n*, 516*n*
Reorder point (ROP) decisions, inventory management, 316–317
Repetitive focus, 172
Repetitive processes, 172
Research, operations strategy issues and, 34
Response time, jobs in operations management and, 10
Restaurants, aggregate scheduling and, 430
Restaurants and MRP, 359–360
Retail store layout, 267
Revenue function, 189
Reza, E.M., 200*n*
Rhyne, D.M., 525*n*
Riggs, W.E., 167*n*
Ritchie, P., 202*n*
Robots, 176, 179
Roethlisberger, F.J., 231*n*
Romig, H.G., 129*n*
Roos, Daniel, 44*n*, 145*n*, 173*n*
Ross, S.C., 444*n*
Rossin, D.F., 304*n*
Roth, Aleda, 31*n*
Route sheet, 154
Routing file, 449
Runger, G.C., 139*n*
Running sum of the forecast errors (RSFE), 69*n*
Russell, R.S., 87*n*, 107*n*, 200*n*, 218*n*, 225*n*, 430*n*, 443*n*, 444*n*, 465*n*
Ryan, T.P., 113*n*

Safety stock, 316
Safford, Robert R., 243*n*
Sakakibara, Sadao, 389*n*
Sales force composite, forecasting and, 49
Sampling, work, 249–252
Sasser, W. Earl Jr., 12*n*, 168*n*, 302*n*, 444*n*
Satinder, E., 87*n*
Scamell, R., 360*n*
Schaaf, Dick, 157*n*
Scheduling
backward, 447–448
by simulation, 429
criteria, 448
decisions, aggregate planning, and, 416
forward, 447
JIT systems and, 385–388, 390
Schmenner, Roger, 183*n*, 225*n*, 444*n*
Schmitt, Tom, 380*n*
Schmitt, T.G. 304*n*
Schniederjans, M., 341*n*, 394*n*, 395*n*
Schonberger, Richard J., 113*n*, 200*n*, 379*n*, 389*n*
Schroeder, Roger G., 389*n*
Schurr, P., 414*n*
Scientific management, 234–237
Scott, L.W., 373*n*
Seal, Kala Chand, 341*n*
Seasonality (S) time series, 51
Seasonal variations, time series, 61–62
Segura, E.L., 87*n*
Seidman, A., 341*n*
Self-directed teams, job design and, 232–233
Sequencing
critical ratio and, 458–459
definition, 454
Johnson's rule and, 459–460
priority rules for dispatching jobs and, 454–458
Service level, probabilistic models and, 323
Service process design, 182–186
customer interaction, process strategy and, 183–184
layout, 185
technology, 185–186
Service sector, 13
aggregate scheduling in, 430–431
decisions of operations management and, 32–33
defined, 11
differences between goods and services, 11–12
environments, supply-chain management and, 400
forecasting and, 70–71
growth of, 12, 13
inventories and, 309, 359–361
just-in-time systems and, 390–391
layout and, 267
location strategies and, 212–215
organizations in each, 14
pay, 13–14
process strategy and, 182–186
productivity and, 18–20
project scheduling, 498–499
scheduling in, 464–466
total quality management in, 107–109
Set-up cost, 310
Set-up time, 310
Shapiro, Roy D., 414*n*
Shaw, B.W., 248*n*
Sherwin, D.R., 525*n*
Shewhart, Walter, 4, 5, 116, 171
Shin, Dooyoung, 414*n*
Shingo, Shigeo, 341*n*
Shortest processing time (SPT), 455
Short-range forecasting, 46–47

Short-term scheduling, 445–478
  finite, 461
  for service, 464–466
  issues in, 446
  loading jobs in work centers, 449–454
  limitations of rule-based systems, 460–461
  process-focused work centers, 448–449
  repetitive manufacturing and, 462–464
  sequencing jobs in work centers, 454–460
  strategic importance of, 446
  theory of constraints, 461–462
Shostack, Lynn G., 12*n*
Shouldice Hospital, 142, 143
Shrinkage, inventory and, 309
Shtub, A., 303*n*
Simison, Robert L., 146*n*
Simkin, M.G., 499
Simon, Herbert, 429*n*
Simulation, for aggregate scheduling and, 429
Sinai, Allen, 20*n*
Sivakumar, R.A., 478*n*, 525*n*
Six sigma, 96, 116
Skinner, Wickham, 44*n*, 276*n*
Slack time, 489
SLIM (Store Labor and Inventory Management), 279
Smith, Adam, 5, 25*n*, 230, 230*n*
Smith, D.D., 87*n*
Smith, P.G., 168*n*
Smith, R.L.C., 264*n*
Smoothing constant, 54–56
  selecting, 56
Snell, S., 264*n*
Snyderman, B.B., 231*n*
Society of Automotive Engineers (SAE), 150
Society for the Advancement of Management, 143
Sociological change, new product opportunities and, 143
Sofianou, Zaharo, 20*n*
Solow, Robert M., 17*n*
Sony, 3
Sorenson, Charles, 4, 5
Souder, W.E., 168*n*
Soukup, W.R., 167*n*, 414*n*
Source inspection, TQM and, 107
Southwest Airlines, 31, 156
SPC. *See* Statistical process control
Specifications, demand inventory and, 346–348
Spendolini, Michael J., 96*n*
Springer, M.C., 304*n*
Square D's Factory, 266
St. John, R., 373*n*
St. Vincent's Hospital, 498–499
Staffing, as management process, 7–9
Stair, R.M., Jr., 87*n*, 225*n*, 478*n*, 516*n*
Stalk, George, Jr., 44*n*, 145*n*
Standard deviation of the regression, 65
Standard error of estimate, 65–66
Standardization, purchasing techniques and, 408
Standard time, 243
Stanton, Steven, 178*n*
Statistical process control (SPC), 104–105
Staughton, R.V.W., 264*n*
Steele, D.C., 43*n*
Stein, Herbert, 14*n*
Steinberg, E., 360*n*
Sterling Software, Inc., 182
Storage layout, 279
Store Labor and Inventory Management (SLIM), 279
Strategic importance of supply-chain management, 398–399
Strategic issues, jobs in operations management and, 10
Strategy
  aggregate planning, 419–421
  human resource, 48
  implementation of, 37–39
  layout. *See* Layout designs
  location, 202–225
  missions and, 28–32
  operations for goods and services, 27–44
  operations issues, 34–36
  service location, 212–215
Strategy development
  mission and, 28–30
  PIMS analysis and, 34
Strategy driven investments, 194
  investment, variable cost, and cash flow and, 194
Statistical Process Control (SPC), quality and, 115–139
  assignable variations, 117
  for attributes, 124
  c-charts, 126–127
  central limit theorem, 119
  control charts, 118
  natural variations, 116–117
  p-charts, 124–125
  setting mean chart limits (*x*-charts), 120–121
  setting Range chart limits (*R*-charts), 122–123
  use of, 116
  variable control chart, 118–119
Stockless purchasing, 408
Sudit, M., 304*n*
Sumanth, David J., 16*n*
Suppliers
  just-in-time systems and, 378–381, 390
  new product opportunites and, 143
Supply-chain management, 397–414
  benchmarking, 410
  defined, 398
  forecasting and, 48–49
  materials management, 408
  operations management decisions and, 32–33
  purchasing, 399–401
  purchasing management, 405–408
  purchasing strategies, 401–405
  strategic importance of, 398–399
Sutherland, J.W., 113*n*
Synchronous manufacturing, 172*n*
System nervousness, MRP and, 354
Szucs, Paul, 385*n*

Taguchi techniques, 100–102
Takeuchi, H., 168*n*
Tangible costs, location and, 205
Tanzer, Andrew, 403*n*
Target specifications, 100
Target value, 102
Taylor, Frederick W., 3, 4, 5, 25*n*, 234*n*, 234, 235, 242
Taylor, James C., 232*n*
Technical change, new products opportunities and, 143
Technological forecasts, 48
Technology
  jobs in operations management, 10
  process opportunities and, 185–186
Teece, David S., 414*n*
Tehrani, K., 478*n*, 525*n*

Telemarketing industry, location strategy and, 214–215
Temperature, job design and, 238
Tersine, R.J., 200*n*, 304*n*, 414*n*
Texas instruments, 29
Thamhain, H., 516*n*
Theory of constraints (TOC) scheduling and, 461–462
Therbligs, 247
Three sigma, 116
Thurow, Roger, 228*n*
Time-based competitions, 145–147
Time fences, 355
Time function mapping, 180–181
Time horizons, forecasting, 46–47
Time series forecasting, 50–60
  decomposition of time series and, 50–51
  exponential smoothing and, 54–56
  moving averages and, 52
  naive approach to, 49
  trend projections and, 50
  weighted moving averages and, 52–54
Time studies, 242–247
Tippet, L., 249
Tompkins Associates, Inc., 10*n*
Tompkins, James A., 280*n*
Tools for TQM, 98–105
  cause and effect diagrams, 104
  Pareto charts, 102
  process charts, 103–104
  quality function deployment, 98–100
  statistical process control (SPC), 104–105
  Taguchi techniques, 100–102
Total quality management (TQM), 89–113. *See also* Quality; Tools for TQM
  benchmarking, 95–98
  continuous improvement, 95–96
  defined, 95
  Deming's 14 points, 95–96
  employee empowerment, 95–96
  in services, 107–109
  just-in-time systems and, 95, 98
  knowledge of tools, 95, 98
Tracking signal, 69–70
Transformation strategy, 170
Transition to production, 160
Transportation method, of linear programming and, 427–429
Transportation model, location strategy and, 211
Trend projections, 50
Trend projections, exponential smoothing with, 58–60
Trend (*t*) time series, 51
Trucking, materials management and, 409
Tsaari, J., 233*n*
Turcotte, M., 225*n*
Type I error, 129
Type II error, 129

Unfilled orders, 407*n*
United Parcel Service, 518
Urban, Timothy L., 303*n*
U.S. Military Standard MIL-STD-105, 129
U.S. Military Standard Q90-Q94, 94
User-based quality, 90
Utilization, capacity and, 186

Vakharia, A.J., 304*n*
Value analysis, 148
Value engineering teams, 147
Vargas, G.A., 225*n*
Variable costs, 189
Variability reduction, just-in-time system and, 376
Vaziri, H.K., 113*n*, 525*n*
Vendor development, 406–407
Vendor evaluation, 406
Vendor relations, 405–407
  development, 406–407
  evaluation, 406
  negotiations, 407
Venkatadri, U., 303*n*
Verdini, W.A., 516*n*
Vergin, R.C., 429*n*
Vertical expansion, 230
Virtual integration, purchasing strategies and, 403–404
Virtual companies, purchasing strategies and, 405
Virtual reality, 144, 153
Vollman, Thomas E., 274*n*, 341*n*, 373*n*, 444*n*
Volkswagen, 213

Wacker, John, 310*n*, 344*n*, 360*n*
Wagner, H.M., 373*n*
Wagner-Whitin algorithm, lot sizing and, 357–358
Walker, M.R., 483
Walleigh, R.C., 395*n*
Wal-Mart, 31, 266, 279
Warehouse layout, 268, 279
Wasserman, William, 66*n*
Waste, just-in-time system and, 376
Waterways, materials management, and, 409
Watmough Plc., 177
Weiss, E.N., 341*n*, 395*n*
Welch, James, 403*n*
Wessel, David, 18*n*
Wheeled Coach Industries, 346
Wheelwright, S.C., 43*n*, 87*n*, 167*n*, 168*n*
Whirlpool, 28
White, J.A., 304*n*
Whitin, T.M., 373*n*
Whitmore, 66*n*
Whitney, Eli, 3,5,171
Whitwam, David, 28
Whybark, D.C., 341*n*, 444*n*
Wight, Oliver W., 69–70, 70*n*, 341*n*
Winchell, William O., 90*n*
Wolf, Richard M., 17*n*
Womack, J.P., 44*n*, 145*n*, 173*n*
Work breakdown structure (WBS), 481
Work cells, layout and, 274–276
  advantages of, 275
Work center master file, 449
Work environment, job design and, 237–240
Work-flow analysis, 181–182
Work-in-process inventory (WIP), 306–307
Work measurement, 240–252
  historical experience and, 241–242
  labor standards and, 240–252
  predetermined time standards and, 247–249
  time studies and, 242–247
  work sampling and, 249–252
Work method, job design and, 234–240
Work order, 154
Work rules, 229
Work sampling, 249–252
Work systems, decisions in operations management and, 32–33
Work systems, people and. *See* People and work systems
Wrege, C.D., 25*n*

Wren, Daniel A., 25*n*
Wyckoff, Daryl D., 12*n*, 302*n*

x-Chart, 118–121, 123
  setting of, 120–121
  steps in using, 123
Xerox, 97

Yano, C.A., 478*n*
"Yellow sheet," 407*n*
Yield management, 431

Zarrillo, M.J., 225*n*
Zeithaml, V., 107*n*, 109*n*, 113*n*
Zemke, Ron, 157*n*
Zenz, Gary J., 407*n*, 413*n*
Zero defects, 96
Zero opportunity costs, assignment method and, 451